The military forces of the crown : their administration and government. Volume 2 of 2

Charles M. Clode

The Making of Modern Law collection of legal archives constitutes a genuine revolution in historical legal research because it opens up a wealth of rare and previously inaccessible sources in legal, constitutional, administrative, political, cultural, intellectual, and social history. This unique collection consists of three extensive archives that provide insight into more than 300 years of American and British history. These collections include:

Legal Treatises, 1800-1926: over 20,000 legal treatises provide a comprehensive collection in legal history, business and economics, politics and government.

Trials, 1600-1926: nearly 10,000 titles reveal the drama of famous, infamous, and obscure courtroom cases in America and the British Empire across three centuries.

Primary Sources, 1620-1926: includes reports, statutes and regulations in American history, including early state codes, municipal ordinances, constitutional conventions and compilations, and law dictionaries.

These archives provide a unique research tool for tracking the development of our modern legal system and how it has affected our culture, government, business – nearly every aspect of our everyday life. For the first time, these high-quality digital scans of original works are available via print-on-demand, making them readily accessible to libraries, students, independent scholars, and readers of all ages.

The BiblioLife Network

This project was made possible in part by the BiblioLife Network (BLN), a project aimed at addressing some of the huge challenges facing book preservationists around the world. The BLN includes libraries, library networks, archives, subject matter experts, online communities and library service providers. We believe every book ever published should be available as a high-quality print reproduction; printed on-demand anywhere in the world. This insures the ongoing accessibility of the content and helps generate sustainable revenue for the libraries and organizations that work to preserve these important materials.

The following book is in the "public domain" and represents an authentic reproduction of the text as printed by the original publisher. While we have attempted to accurately maintain the integrity of the original work, there are sometimes problems with the original work or the micro-film from which the books were digitized. This can result in minor errors in reproduction. Possible imperfections include missing and blurred pages, poor pictures, markings and other reproduction issues beyond our control. Because this work is culturally important, we have made it available as part of our commitment to protecting, preserving, and promoting the world's literature.

GUIDE TO FOLD-OUTS MAPS and OVERSIZED IMAGES

The book you are reading was digitized from microfilm captured over the past thirty to forty years. Years after the creation of the original microfilm, the book was converted to digital files and made available in an online database.

In an online database, page images do not need to conform to the size restrictions found in a printed book. When converting these images back into a printed bound book, the page sizes are standardized in ways that maintain the detail of the original. For large images, such as fold-out maps, the original page image is split into two or more pages

Guidelines used to determine how to split the page image follows:

• Some images are split vertically; large images require vertical and horizontal splits.
• For horizontal splits, the content is split left to right.
• For vertical splits, the content is split from top to bottom.
• For both vertical and horizontal splits, the image is processed from top left to bottom right.

THE

MILITARY FORCES OF THE CROWN;

THEIR ADMINISTRATION AND GOVERNMENT.

By CHARLES M. CLODE.

An armed disciplined body is in its essence dangerous to Liberty·
undisciplined, it is ruinous to Society —BURKE, Vol V. p. 17

IN TWO VOLUMES.—VOL. II

LONDON

JOHN MURRAY, ALBEMARLE STREET.

1869.

Rec Oct. 11, 1882

PRINTED BY WILLIAM CLOWES AND SONS, DUKE STREET, STAMFORD STREET,
AND CHARING CROSS

CONTENTS OF THE SECOND VOLUME.

CHAPTER XV

ON THE RECRUITING, ENLISTMENT, AND DISCHARGE OF MEN INTO AND FROM THE REGULAR ARMY

CHAPTER XVI

ON THE APPOINTMENT AND DISMISSAL OF OFFICERS

CHAPTER XVII.

THE ACTION OF THE MILITARY IN AID OF THE CIVIL POWER

CHAPTER XVIII

THE EMPLOYMENT OF THE MILITARY IN THE RESTORATION OF THE CIVIL POWER

CHAPTER XIX

THE TREASURY AND THE FORMER SUBORDINATE DEPARTMENTS THEREOF

CHAPTER XX

THE LATE BOARD OF ORDNANCE

CHAPTER XXI.

THE OFFICE OF SECRETARY AT WAR

CHAPTER XXII

THE ROYAL COMMISSIONERS OF CHELSEA HOSPITAL

CHAPTER XXIII.

THE OFFICE OF PAYMASTER-GENERAL

CHAPTER XXIV.

THE COMMISSIONERS FOR THE AUDIT OF PUBLIC ACCOUNTS.

CHAPTER XXV

THE OFFICE OF SECRETARY OF STATE.

CHAPTER XXVI

THE OFFICE OF THE COMMANDER-IN-CHIEF

CHAPTER XXVII

THE OFFICE OF JUDGE-ADVOCATE GENERAL

CHAPTER XXVIII

THE CHAPLAIN-GENERAL'S DEPARTMENT.

CHAPTER XXIX

THE CONSOLIDATED WAR OFFICE.

APPENDIX.

NOTES.

ILLUSTRATIONS.

ERRATA.

Vol I, p 386, in lines 6 and 7 from the bottom, *for* "Independence" *read* "Expenditure"

Vol. II, p 277, par. 9, *after* 'placed on pension," *add* 'after twenty years' service, or having become unfit for service." [1]

---

[1] See Regulations of Rewards, &c, for H. M. Land Forces, by James II.—Bk. 795, p. 63.

THE MILITARY FORCES

OF

THE CROWN.

CHAPTER XV.

ON THE RECRUITING, ENLISTMENT, AND DISCHARGE OF MEN INTO AND FROM THE REGULAR ARMY

1. PRIOR to the present century the policy of this country was to fill the ranks of the Army with the cheapest labour, and at the lowest cost to the State. For many years there was little or no inducement for men to enter the Infantry—the principal arm of the Service. The pay was small, the barracks, when they existed, were execrable,[1] the discipline, or rather the punishments, severe, and the service abroad was equal to the late punishment of transportation.[2] In addition to these evils, the National feeling ran as strongly against the Regular Army as it did in favour of the Navy and the Militia.

The ancient Policy of the State was to provide Soldiers at the lowest cost.

2. For the Reader to understand rightly the various questions incident to the Recruiting, Enlistment, and Discharge of soldiers, it is necessary to explain, in the first instance, the financial arrangements under which these duties were carried out.

Financial aspect of the question

3. It has been noticed that the earliest method of obtaining Military forces was for the Crown to contract "with some knight or gentleman expert in war, and of great revenues and livelihood in the country, to serve him

Original method of raising men by contract.

---

[1] Chap XI., par 15   [2] App. LXXIX , and Debate in 1742, 12 Parl Hist , p. 374.

in war with a number of men;"[1] and this principle—though varied in many circumstances—may be said to have prevailed in Army Administration till 1783.

4. It has also been stated, in a previous chapter,[2] that prior to the same year, the incidental expenses of every regiment were included in the item of Pay, and that the Crown held the Colonel responsible[3] for the Finance as well as for the Discipline of his Regiment. Allowances were made to the officers out of this item, more than enough to cover the ordinary charges against them in time of peace, and, after paying these, to leave a balance in their favour. Under this system the Public had the safest guarantee from the Regimental Officers — their self-interest — that the ordinary recruiting expenses of the regiment would not exceed the Estimate, but be kept down to a minimum.[4]

Colonel responsible for finance of the Regiment.

5. These allowances which—so far as they need be here considered—embraced the cost of Recruiting and Clothing, formed part of a common fund, termed the "Stock Purse," or Non-effective Account of the Regiment, out of which fund the men were Recruited and Clothed.[5] The accounts of this fund were made up annually—that of each company being in some instances kept separate—and, after deducting and carrying to the credit of the next year's accounts[6] 5*l.* for each recruit or man wanted to complete the Regimental Establishment, or company, as the case might be, the balance was divided amongst the Captains or handed over to each Captain.

"Stock Purse," or noneffective accounts of the Regiment.

6. When from war, or other casualty, men were rapidly lost, the cost of recruiting exceeded in a considerable degree the allowances, and the fund failed.[7] The Officers were then called on to bear heavy expenses, and application for

Grants to aid recruiting in time of war

---

[1] Appendix, Vol. I, Note A.   [2] Chap VI, par 24

[3] Chap. IV, par 56   The Circular Letter of 10 July, 1760, which is still in force, holds the Colonel responsible not only for the pay of his Regiment and the Regimental funds, "but for the solvency of the Agent" Knowles v Maitland, 4 Bar. and Cr, p 179.   [4] 8 Parl Hist, p 934

[5] Note W. W, on Army Clothing System, in Appendix

[6] See the two Warrants of 19th Feb, 1765, regulating the Stock Purse and Non-effective Accounts of the Dragoon and Infantry Regiments

[7] The question of Recruiting the Regiments in North America in 1767, War Office Letter Bk 209, pp 227 232

relief was not unfrequently made to the Crown, which, if granted, came in times of Peace as an extra allowance[1] by way of respites or vacant pay, or of War, out of "Army Extraordinaries."

7. It is obvious, therefore, that under this system the Officers had a *pecuniary* interest in keeping the men of their Regiments from discharge, desertion or death; and so strong was this motive supposed to be, that, as will be shown hereafter, an argument was founded upon it against the expediency of changing the recruiting system, by providing recruits at the cost of the Crown[2]

Officers had a pecuniary interest in the preservation of their men

8. For established regiments and in ordinary times the recruiting and enlistment of men were strictly regimental. If to gain a second bounty, or for any other motive, a soldier passed, by a fraudulent re-enlistment, from one to another Regiment, or from one to another independent Company in the Army — inflicting thereby a pecuniary loss upon his first Captain—his offence was placed by the framers of the early Mutiny Act,[3] and still continues, in the same category of crimes with that of desertion from the Service, and made punishable with death.

Strictly Regimental and fraudulent re-enlistment punishable with death

9 But though the enlistment *obliged* the soldier to serve in the Regiment or Company into which he had listed, it did not *entitle* him, as against the Crown, to remain there; on the contrary, whenever public convenience required that Regiments should be Reformed or Reduced, either at Home or on Foreign Service, the Crown, as it thought fit, directed some soldiers to be discharged, and others to be " drafted " into other regiments. The misery oftentimes resulting to men from the exercise of this power of drafting is shown from the perusal of the Royal Sign Manual Order of 1718,[4] and of the Lords' Debate and protest on the Minorca Garrison in 1742.[5]

Power of drafting exercised by the Crown.

---

[1] 2 & 3 Anne, c 17, sec 46

[2] Pars. 29 to 31 *post* As to the Stock Purse and Non-effective Accounts and the system of recruiting and recounting, see the Commons' Report of 1746, 2 Com Rep., p 129, and Army and Ordnance Expenditure, 1850, p 15, and two Royal Warrants of 19th Feb, 1766, as to Cavalry and Infantry

[3] See remarks on the severity of this provision 15 Parl Hist, p 254

[4] Appendix LXXIX

[5] 12 Parl Hist pp 374, 402, and 24 Com Journ pp 118, 175-9

10. It is not therefore to be wondered at that Foreign Service soon became a terror to soldiers, and that as such it was resorted to as a punishment. In 1765 the Mutiny Act gave power to a Court-martial to sentence any deserter (whom the Court should not think deserving of *capital* punishment) to serve as a soldier in any corps stationed in foreign parts for life, or for a certain term of years[1] It then became impossible to maintain the power of the Crown to draft soldiers. and—by so doing—to inflict upon them what was in effect a criminal punishment without the sentence of a Court-martial.

Drafting ceased since 1765 except as a voluntary Enlistment or Punishment.

11. It was therefore necessary to change the system of drafting into one of voluntary engagement, and another clause was added to this effect:—That as often as any regiment should be relieved at any Foreign Station, it should be lawful for the officers to enlist soldiers belonging to the regiment as *should be willing* and fit for service, and to incorporate them into any regiment in which they should be appointed to remain; the soldier so enlisted was to be deemed discharged from the former regiment; and a certificate delivered to him as a protection from molestation upon suspicion of having deserted.[2] From the year 1765 drafting ceased, except with the soldier's consent,[3] or as a punishment inflicted by Court-martial.

Clause in the Mutiny Act.

12. When new Regiments were raised, a fixed sum was allowed as Bounty or Levy money for each Recruit, and the Colonel to whom the Letter of Service was given for raising the Regiment in some instances, got the men at so much more or less as his personal influence or good fortune enabled him to do. With regard to the amount of bounty, it is curious to notice the long continuance of 40s. as the sum given by the Crown, to the Recruit on enlistment. In 1597, when Shakspeare[4] wrote the first part of 'Henry IVth,' he puts

Levy Money allowed on augmentation of the Forces.

---

[1] 6 Geo III, c 8 sec 7.   [2] Sec 78.

[3] A 5*l.* bounty appears to have been given to Volunteers in 1768   See War Office Letter Bk., 211, p 94

[4] Act iv, scene 2   It will be remarked that the Falstaff Recruits came from the same social grade in the community that were taken into the Army under Parliamentary sanction in the 17th century. The purchase of the soldiers discharges is also noticeable

it into Falstaff's mouth to say that he had (misused the King's Press, and) "got in exchange of 150 soldiers three hundred and odd pounds." Upon the increase of the Army to meet the Rebellion of 1715, the inducement held out was 40s. "for every man who shall list himself in any of the Regiments of Foot."[1] In later years the same sum will be found mentioned in the Statute Book, and it was not until after Mr. Burke's Act had been in operation for some years, and the cost of recruiting had been transferred to the public, that the amount of Bounty was raised to the excessive prices that in recent Wars were demanded for Military Service.[2]

13. It the allowance made by the Crown proved insufficient to stimulate enlistment, other expedients were resorted to   In the year 1759, several large towns opened subscriptions to be appropriated as "bounty" money to volunteers enlisting into the Army.[3] The London subscription amounted to 7039l. 7s. (procuring 1235 men at 5l. 5s. for each man),[4] and the City, as a further encouragement to voluntary enlistment, passed a By-law to entitle soldiers, upon the expiration of their service, to the freedom of London.

Subscription for increased levy or Bounty Money

14. The expense of raising new corps was frequently provided for in another manner—viz., by an agreement between the Crown and a Nobleman or Gentleman that the latter should raise the Regiment or Corps, receiving —as the consideration for his trouble and expense—the nomination of all or of some proportion of the Officers. This system "of raising men for rank"—as it was afterwards called —has always been in vogue; the proposal of Mr. Appletre in 1704 being the first instance[5] that I can trace since the Revo-

Raising men for Rank

---

[1] Appendix LXXX The Gazette containing a Proclamation of the Rebellion of 1745, also contains an offer of 6l. bounty for the Guards. See No. 8461, 7th Sept 1745

[2] The Warrants of 19th February, 1766, limited the charges for Recruits out of the Stock Purse to 3l 8s for Cavalry, and 3½ guineas for Infantry, out of which levy money the bounty to the Recruit was to be limited to 1 guinea and a crown for Cavalry, and to 1½ guinea for Infantry.* The bounties to the Recruits in 1775-1776 was to be 3l 3s. See 35 Com. Journ , p 111, 36 ib, pp 613, 903

[3] 2 Ann Reg , pp 106, 117, 120   [4] 3 ib , p 111.

[5] 36 Com. Journ , pp 612-622, the various Letters of Service set out

---

* See Lord Barrington's Letters of Reprimand where more had been given to Recruits, 1766, pp. 15, 124

lution.[1] In the American War and in the Revolutionary War with France in 1793-8 most of the new Corps were so raised by noblemen or gentlemen.[2] During the Peninsular War the plan, though censured,[3] was resorted to, and again in the more recent War with Russia.[4]

15. The Colonel of each Regiment whether raising men

Recruiting under Royal Authority   as a new levy or for ordinary waste—carried on the enlistment under the authority of a Beating Order, which was issued—in the time of Chas. I.,[5] under the Great Seal —of Geo. I.[6] under the Royal Sign Manual, countersigned by the Secretary at War,[7]—afterwards (till the abolition of his office) under the hand of the Secretary at War,[8] who held the Royal authority under the countersign of a Secretary of State for the issue,—and now by the Secretary of State. The agents of the Crown, thus authorized, are therefore the only persons capable of making a legal engagement with any person for his enlistment.

16. These arrangements were carried out under the pre-

Action of responsible Ministers   rogative powers of the Crown, and the advice and independent action of Ministers each responsible to Parliament for their due execution. The Secretary of State, before he gave the Secretary at War an annual authority to enlist men, waited for the passing of the Mutiny Act; and the Secretary at War, before he issued his Beating Orders to the different Colonels of Regiments, had to satisfy himself (1) that Parliament had sanctioned their "Establishment," by the Annual votes in supply, and (2) that there were vacancies.

17. Having regard to the Capital consequences[9] that in

Action of Parliament by Legislation   earlier times resulted to the Subject upon the breach of his contract to serve the Crown as a soldier, the action of Parliament was then—and indeed still is—

---

[1] Appendix LXXXI, and War Office Letter Bk, 1765, p 27
[2] 25th Report on Finance, 1798, vol xiii, p 660
[3] 2 H. D. (O. S), pp 190-222, 229, and see Chap XIV, par 73
[4] See 'Report on Military Organization, 1860,' p 610.
[5] 2 Com Journ, pp 368, 548.   [6] Appendix LXXX
[7] The Secretary at War assumed absolute power over *all* Recruiting Parties, and hence by his order no Soldier was allowed to recruit at Bath   War Office Letter Bk 211, p 92 (1768)
[8] Appendix LXXXII (1 and 2)   [9] See par 122, *post*

directed to the protection of the Subject from making a contract of enlistment under *surprise*, or without his *free* assent being given before a Civil magistrate.

18 "That no man might be forced into Foreign Service, or compelled without his free consent to be listed in any Troop or Company of their Majestys' Land Forces," the Mutiny Act of 1694[1] enacted "that no person listed after the 1st March, 1693, should be esteemed a soldier, or be subject to the Mutiny Act, that should not have been brought before a Justice, *not being an Officer of the Army,* or other Civil authority where the person should be listed, and before such Justice or Civil authority declare his free consent to be listed or mustered as a Soldier before he should be listed or mustered as a Soldier." Penalties were inflicted upon any *Military* Officer offending against the enactment, and the Justice or Civil authority was bound to give a certificate of the enlistment to the Officer for the Muster Master, and to lodge a certificate with the Clerk of the Peace

A.D. 1694

That the Enlistment should be attested by the Civil Magistrate

19. This was continued in force until April, 1697,[2] but no similar provision was again placed on the Statute Book until upon the motion of Sir Walter Bagot,[3] in the year 1735, a clause was added to the Mutiny Act (8 Geo. II., c. 2), in substance as follows —The person enlisted was in four days to be taken before the next Justice (not being an Officer in the Army) to assent or dissent to his enlistment. He was to be at liberty to declare his dissent, and to repay the enlisting money with 1*l.* for expenses, and then to be set free in the presence of the Justice. If, however, he did not repay these sums in twenty-four hours, or if he assented to his enlistment, then the Justice was to give a Certificate of the enlistment, setting forth his place of birth, age, and calling, also—though the Act did not require the Justice to read or to administer the oath—that the 7th and 10th Articles of War had been read over to the Recruit, and that he had taken the oath required by the Articles. Further, the clause declared that any one who received enlisting money from any

Omitted from Mutiny Act between 1697 and 1734 Mutiny Act, 1735

---

[1] 5 & 6 William and Mary, c. 15, sec 2   [2] 6 & 7 ib, c 8, 7 & 8 ib, c 23
[3] 9 Parl. Hist, p 819

Officer (knowing it to be such) and absconded or refused to go before the Justice, was to be deemed an enlisted soldier.

20. The *impressment* of Soldiers by the direct orders and

<small>Secretary at War was responsible for the regularity of Enlistments</small>

under the sole authority of the Crown, absolutely ceased after the Revolution of 1688; but an Officer holding a Letter of Service to raise a Regiment, or the Men enlisted by him—not being in pay until their numbers would entitle them to an Establishment—might have stronger inducements than ever influenced the agents of the Crown to press men into the Regiment. Accordingly, in the absence of any legislative provision, the only protection that the Subject had against such an abuse of authority was by appeal through the Parliamentary Officer—the Secretary at War—to the Crown or to the House of Commons. Both the War Office Records[1] and the Journals[2] show that such appeals were not made in vain.

21. In the first instance, when men were raised for a new

<small>As to the mustering of Recruits and Soldiers</small>

Regiment, they had to be produced to two Justices of the Peace, and the Mutiny Act provided that at all subsequent musters two Justices should be present. Notwithstanding these provisions, it soon became apparent that the action of Parliament must be directed to the prevention of frauds in the muster of Regiments or Companies distributed about the country on Billets, and in the issue of pay for men that did not exist, as *effective* soldiers.

22. The agents of the Crown engaged in mustering and pay-

<small>Agents of the Crown</small>

ing the Army were: (1) the Commissary-Generals and their Deputies to take the musters; (2) the Comptrollers of Army accounts to examine them, and, (3) the Colonels or Commanding Officers of Regiments or Companies to receive and distribute the pay of those who were returned in the rolls. The musters were held six times in the year, and it was the duty of the Commissary to have every Officer and Man pass before him, with his horse, armed and accoutred, that the names of effective men only might be entered upon the Muster Roll.

---

[1] Appendix LXXXIII   [2] 10 Com. Journ., pp 836, 837

The integrity of these Commissioners was the sole security that Parliament had that the Regiments were effective up to their Establishments, and that the pay went to *effective* men instead of to the Officers for their own benefit.

23. The early Mutiny Acts contained several clauses framed with the object of securing the integrity of the Muster Rolls, but, notwithstanding these enactments, the Commons' Committee reported to the House in 1746 "that the men granted by Parliament never were effectives, notwithstanding the allowances which had been made at different times to render them so." [1] The reasons why this state of things existed are fully set out in the Report. First, the Muster-Masters received gratuities from the Colonels and Captains, and, instead of discharging their duty as the Mutiny Act directed, passed the Regiment or Company as complete when it was incomplete. Then they obeyed the orders of the General in command by mustering, under his directions, incomplete Regiments as complete ones.[2] And, lastly, the Crown by warrant could give a direct authority to the Commissary to muster any Regiment as complete whatever might be the deficiency of its number.[3]

Frauds and false Musters.

24. The Colonel and Officers had a strong pecuniary interest which was under the nominal check and control of the Commissaries on the Staff of the Army (whose Commissions were purchasable),[4] and hence the gratuities paid these Officers were the sequence to, if not the reward, for their evasion of duty.[5] Either men were alleged to be absent without certificate of existence, and the word of the Regimental Officer was accepted in lieu thereof,[6] or tradesmen or servants were dressed up in regimentals, and passed as soldiers.[7] If the horses or accoutrements were rejected or complained of, "the matter was not taken well by the Officers."[8]

Gain thereby to Colonels and Commanding Officers

---

[1] 2 Com Rep., pp. 112, 114   [2] Ib., p 115.

[3] See the Debate in the Commons, that only 8660 of 29,335 men voted were present at the Battle of Almanza in 1707, 6 Parl Hist p. 611, and 16 Com Journ., pp 411, 447, also Chap VII. par 28, *ante*

[4] When the sale of Staff Appointments was stopped, the Secretary at War (Jenkinson) refused, in June, 1780, to permit these Commissions to be sold.—War Office Letter Bk 238, p 252.

[5] 2 Com Rep, p 117 *b*   [6] Ib   [7] Ib, p 116 *a*   [8] Ib.

25. Against the power of the Crown to muster incomplete
Regiments as complete, the Commons presented an
Action of Parliament Musters abolished
Address in April,[1] 1745; but abuses continued more or
less in the system until the pecuniary interest of the
Officers in the pay of the men ceased, and the Paymaster of
each Regiment was rendered *in some degree* independent of the
Colonel or Commanding Officer.[2] The office of Muster-master
lingered in the Army till the year 1818, when it was abolished
in pursuance of the recommendation of the Commissioners of
Military Inquiry[3] in 1812, and the duties transferred to the
Secretary at War. In the Horse and Foot Guards the old
system of mustering (without the frauds) still continues, and is
regulated by the First Article of War.

26. Having endeavoured to explain the Ordinary method of
Recruiting by impressment
Recruiting the Army, it will be well to examine the
Legislative measures under which Recruits have been
provided in Extraordinary times—as of War with Foreign
Powers,—noting at the outset that the great principle of
supply throughout the last century was that of Conscription
limited to the Criminal and Pauper classes.

27. At an early period after the establishment of a Standing
Difficulty of recruiting the Army in Wm. III.'s reign
Army it became an important consideration how men
should be supplied to carry on the war against France.
The annual waste was said to be 3000 men, and in the
State Tracts of William III.'s reign is found,[4] under date of
the year 1696, 'A Discourse about raising Men,' in which the
author undertakes to show that "it is more for the interest of
the nation that the parishes should be obliged to provide men
for the service of the war than to raise them in the ordinary way."

28 The substance of this writer's recommendations was—
A D 1696 Impressment recommended as applicable to certain classes.
that an Act of Impressment should be passed, with
directions and limitations as to the persons that should
be taken under it,—to this effect .[5]—

"1. That if there be any sturdy Beggar, Fortune-

---

[1] 2 Com Rep, p 120 a   [2] 35th Report on Finance, 1799, vol xiii, p 631,
Chap XXIII, par 9   [3] 19 Rep p 34   [4] Vol ii, p 539   [5] I 541

teller, or the like idle, unknown, suspected fellow in the Parish, that cannot give a good account of himself, he shall be taken *before* anybody else.

"2. That if there be none such, then any one that has been already in a Gaol, or House of Correction, shall be *next* taken.

"3. If there be none such, then any one that has been often complain'd of, and been before a Justice of Peace for his idle disorderly Life, shall be chose *next*.

"4. That no married Person or Widower that is left with a Family of Children shall *ever* be chose, unless it should so happen that they are such *notorious incorrigible Rogues* (as some such there may be) that the Parish had rather maintain their Wives and Children than be troubled any longer with them.

"5. That one or two Justices of the Peace who live in or near the Parish (and for that reason must needs know who are the troublesome disorderly people in it, and fittest to be sent away) shall always be present when the choice is made, to take care that it be made according as the Act of Parliament shall direct; and if it be not, to declare it void, and make 'em chuse again."

29. The various objections that the author supposes would be made to his proposals he answers in detail. The 4th objection,[1] and his answer to it, stand in these words.—

30. "The 4th objection is that this way of raising Recruits will make the Officers careless of their men, the charge and trouble they are put to get men makes 'em look after 'em when they have 'em; but if they are provided ready to their hands they will take no manner of care of them, and lose more men by half, both by desertion and sickness, than they do now."

The principal objection, that the officers would not take care of their men

31. "This objection is grounded upon a plain mistake, for though the Officers will be a little eas'd, as 'tis fit they should, they will still be very far from having all charge and trouble wholly taken off their hands; for if their

Objection answered.

[1] 19 Rep., p 541

Recruits be delivered to them at the county town (and thither is far enough to oblige the parishes to send them), the trouble and charge of marching them from thence into Flanders will be enough to oblige them to take care of them, and look after them as well as they did before."

32. Now it so happens that the Criminal and Pauper classes, from which this author proposed to recruit the Army, have always been resorted to whenever Parliament has sanctioned a conscription for the Regular Army. The Officers were glad to be relieved from expense, and to be furnished with Recruits even from these sources of supply.[1]

Impressment has been applied to the pauper and criminal classes.

33. The persons to whom a conscription in the nature of a duress was first applied were Imprisoned Debtors. In the year 1695-6 occasion was taken to amend the then existing law[2] for the relief of insolvent debtors, and in the amending Act[3] was inserted a clause that no man below the age of forty years should be discharged under the Act, during the war with France, unless he enlisted in the Army or Navy, or found a substitute.[4]

First to imprisoned debtors.

34. In a few years later the Debtor prisons appear to have been relieved of their inmates for the express purpose of recruiting the Army, for the Preamble of the 1 Anne, c. 19,[5] while attributing their miserable impoverishment to war losses, states the ability and readiness of many prisoners to serve Her Majesty by sea or land. This Act was shortly after amended by the 2 & 3 Anne, c. 10,[6] and the general purpose of both Acts is explained to be "the supply of Her Majesty with Recruits both by sea and land during the war, as well as to relieve the poor prisoners." They were limited in operation to prisoners for debt under 100*l.*, and provided that no man under forty years of age could gain relief without enlisting into the Army or Navy—under the first Act for an indefinite period,—or under the second for the period of the war, or without procuring a substitute.

Acts of Anne.

---

[1] Appendix LXXXIV   [2] 22 & 23 Car II, c 20.   [3] 7 & 8 Wm III, c 12
[4] Sec 14, vol vii Stat Realm, p 77   [5] 8 Stat Realm, p 69
[6] Ib, p 271, and Boyer's 'Queen Anne,' p 123.

35 The number of men that joined the Army is not re-corded; but that these Acts furnished Recruits is *Recruits obtained under these Acts.* evidenced by the War Office Books of that period. By a warrant[1] of the 11th June, 1696, from the Lords Justices (under the countersign of the Judge-Advocate General) authority was given for twenty-nine prisoners in York Castle to join Colonel Farrington's Regiment, and again, in Queen Anne's reign, the Warrants were issued, in some instances, for the enlistment of prisoners named,[2] and in others to Colonels of Regiments for the enlistment of *any* insolvent prisoners,[3] including, in one instance, French refugees.

36. The same principle—though limited in its application to those under fifty years of age, and who had pre-viously served by land or sea—is traceable upon the *Same principle recognized until 1760* Statute Book until the year 1760;[4] for by the 1 Geo. III., c. 17, no Insolvent Debtor could take the benefit of that Act unless (if approved) he enlisted for the war

37 The persons to whom the same kind of conscription was next applied were Imprisoned *Criminals*, to whom the *Criminals released on condition of serving in the Army* Crown, acting upon the prerogative,[5] gave a pardon conditional upon their enlisting into the Regular Army. The earliest trace of this system upon the Statute Book is to be found in the Mutiny Act for the year 1702,[6] in these words —

38. "Whereas several persons convicted or attainted of capital felonies and offences are thought fit to be *Reasons for passing this Enactment.* reprieved from execution, in order to obtain their pardon, upon condition of being transported beyond the seas, or as persons fit to serve Her Majesty in her Army or Navy, and oftentimes lay in prison for a long time, in expectation of the passing such pardon under the Great Seal, and the pleading and allowing thereof in the usual form of law, to the great charge and burden of the county where they have been so convicted and afterwards detained in prison:

---

[1] Mis Bk 517, p 194   [2] Mis Bk 517 (Ink), p 9
[3] Mis. Bk 520, Sept., 1704, p 8; Letter Bk 133, p 20
[4] 1 Geo III., c 17, sec 57   [5] Chitty on Prerogative, p 96
[6] See 1 Anne, stat 2, c 20, also the Mutiny Act for 1703, 2 & 3 Anne, c. 17.

39. "For remedy thereof, be it enacted, That during the continuance of this Act, on view and receipt of a Warrant under the *Sign Manual* of Her Majesty *for preparing a Bill* for passing a pardon for such offender or offenders, or for inserting any such convicted person in a pardon after to be passed, upon condition of being transported beyond the seas, *or of listing him or themselves* in the service of Her Majesty in her Army or Navy. it shall and may be lawful for the Judge or Judges before whom any such pardon (if passed) might be pleaded and allowed, and they are hereby required. upon such Warrant under the Sign Manual, to direct his or their Warrant to the Sheriff or Sheriffs, or keeper of the gaol or prison where such prisoner or prisoners are detained in prison (who are hereby required to yield obedience to such Warrant), thereby directing the immediate delivery of such prisoner out of custody to be disposed of according to the condition contained in such Warrant under the Sign Manual, and directed to be inserted in such intended pardon, and the pardon, when passed, shall be entered and enrolled in due form of law, and shall be, to all intents and purposes, of the same force and effect as if the same had been by such prisoner pleaded and allowed after the passing thereof under the Great Seal, any law or usage to the contrary thereof in anywise notwithstanding."

Proviso for delivering of prisoners pardoned upon condition

40. From the date of this enactment to the end of the Peninsular War, a System with Criminals arose— which was analogous to the present Ticket-of-leave System, but with this difference: that formerly the offenders were provided with the means of earning an honest living and a good name under the strict discipline of the Army, whereas in recent years they are turned loose upon the civil community, to get—what is next to impossible under the surveillance of the police—an honest living with a dishonest character. The exact number of this class admitted into the Army during the Peninsular War is not easily traceable. Three Regiments—one of military distinction—were thus formed, and others were recruited. A return of the number of these Recruits was moved for in 1812, but the motion was opposed by the Ministers and negatived by the House of

The ticket-of-leave system in favour of reformed criminals

Commons[1] During the Crimean War a suggestion was made by an experienced Member of the House of Commons,[2] that some of the labour of the siege should be borne by convicts under enlistment; but circumstances had so changed, that it was not entertained

41. Early in the reign of Queen Anne was initiated, and throughout the same reign was continued, the system of recruiting the Army by conscription from the *Pauper* as distinguished from the *Criminal* class; and Statutes, seven in number, were in operation from 1703 to 1712 with this object.

Conscription or impressment from the pauper class

42 Under the 2 & 3 Anne, c. 13[3] (which was the first of the series), the Justices were "to raise and levy such able-bodied men as had not any lawful calling or employment, or visible means for their maintenance and livelihood," to serve as Soldiers, and to hand them over to the Officers of Her Majesty's forces, who were to pay to each Recruit 20s., and to the constable, for bringing, 10s. If any one voluntarily listed he was to have a bounty of 40s.

A D 1703

Impressment Acts of Anne's reign 2 & 3 Anne, c. 13

43. The Mutiny Act and Articles of War were then to be read over to the Recruit in the presence of the Justice, and upon his certificate the man was to be "deemed a listed Soldier" That the proceedings might be deemed *Civil* and not Military, the Statute provided that no Justice of the Peace having any military office or employment (save in the Militia) should execute the Act,[4] and the only exemption[5] contained in it was in favour of any person "who had a vote in the election of any member of Parliament."[6]

44. In 1705 the second Act[7] was passed; and therein appeared for the first time two provisions that are now found in the Annual Mutiny Act, (1) declaring that no Soldier shall be taken out of Her Majesty's

A.D 1705

4 & 5 Anne, c. 21

---

[1] See 21 H. D (O S), p 1254, Return of the 16th by order of 1st May, 1812, Com Journ. (note)   [2] 138 H D (3), p 132
[3] Continued by 6 Anne, c 17   [4] Sec 1   [5] Sec 5
[6] 6 Parl Hist, p 335, and 15 Rap. and Tind, p 615
[7] See 4 & 5 Anne, c 21, 6 Parl Hist, pp 610, 611

service[1] by any process other than for some criminal matter, and (2) that a person suspected to be a deserter shall be taken before the *Civil Magistrate* for *his* adjudication as to the Military or Civil status of the supposed offender.[2]

45. The next Act,[3] that of 1708, may be described as one to stimulate voluntary enlistment under the apprehension of impressment to supply any deficiency in numbers remaining. The Commissioners were first to appoint two General Meetings for volunteers to be received and paid 4*l.* as bounty. After these meetings impressed men were to be brought in and listed, receiving no bounty. For each listed man the reward to the parish officers was increased to 1*l.*, and the churchwardens were to receive 3*l* to the use of the parish, and to aid the poor rates.[4]

A D 1708
———
7 Anne, c. 2.

46. Volunteers might claim their discharge in *three* years, and no man under 5 ft. 5 in. was to be received into Her Majesty's service. This Act contained no prohibition against the enlistment of men by military Officers, and therefore Sir Robert Walpole (then the Secretary at War) was advised that their enlistments were valid.[5]

47. An abuse had sprung up under these Acts, for which Parliament had to apply a remedy. By connivance with the Officers, men were enlisted avoid arrest for debt, and when enlisted, leave of absence or furlough was given to them for the prosecution of their trade or calling. In March, 1705, the Secretary at War (St. John) sent to the Judge-Advocate-General the names and addresses of twenty-two tradesmen in and about London enlisted in the Foot Guards, but absent from duty, for the Board of General Officers to inquire into, so that these men might be sent to the Regiment abroad.[6]

Abuses under these Acts

---

[1] For Sir Simon Harcourt s opinion as to the method of getting this discharge, see Vol I , Appendix LXIII

[2] See Sir W. Erle's judgment in Wotton v Gavin, 16 Q B. Rep , p 71

[3] 7 Anne, c 2, continued by 8 Anne, c 15. Address to put the Act in operation, 6 Parl Hist , p 610

[4] By the 10 Anne, c. 12, this sum was to be paid for the use and benefit of the soldier's poor relations   [5] Appendix LXXXV

[6] Letter Bk. 134, p 185, and see 135 ib., p 179.

48 Accordingly, when the powers of the last Act were continued, its provisions, which exempted a Soldier from Remedied in 1710 by 9 Anne, c 4 arrest, were amended,—by declaring that in case of arrest, for any debt above 20*l.*, and the Judge discharging the Soldier, the latter should go on Foreign Service within two months; or be proceeded against like any other debtor having no privilege from arrest. The last of these recruiting Acts[1] expired on the 12th May, 1712

49. With the exception of two Acts,[2] passed at the time of the Rebellion, in 1745, recourse was not had to Similar Acts of Geo II s reign the expedient of Impressment until 1756-7, in which years two Acts were passed, containing many of the provisions of the previous Acts, and differing little from each other.

50. The 29 Geo II., c. 4, was one of impressment only, not embracing voluntary offers of service, but the 29 Geo II, c. 4, 30 Geo II., c. 9 30 Geo II., c. 8, embraced both methods of raising Recruits These Acts were put in operation "on notice to the Sheriff by the Secretary at War,"[3] and the persons liable to impressment under the first Act were "such able-bodied men who do not follow or exercise any lawful calling or employment, or have not some other lawful and sufficient support and maintenance;"[4] and, under the second, "all such able-bodied, idle, and disorderly persons who cannot upon examination prove themselves to exercise and industriously follow some lawful trade or employment, or to have some substance sufficient for their support and maintenance." The impressed men were to serve for five years, or, under the second Act, till the end of the war,[5] and those to be exempt from service were men ruptured or infirm, or under 17 or above 45 years, or under 5 ft. 4 in. in height, or "known Papists."[6] To secure the Recruits before they joined their Regiments, the keepers of the gaols and houses of correction were bound to receive and subsist them upon the " usual prison

---

[1] 10 Anne, c 12
[2] 17 Geo II, c. 15, see notice in 'London Gazette,' No 8473, 18 Geo II, c. 12. Fictitious arrests were made to avoid the conscription, Bk 721, pp 67-71.
[3] Sec 6   [4] Sec 9
[5] Sec. 23 of first Act, Sec 30 of second Act.   [6] Secs. 11, 15

allowance."[1] The Volunteers enlisted under the second Act were to be at liberty to serve only for three years—if the war were ended, or otherwise until the end thereof,[2] and the same Act gave power to the Crown, acting through the Secretary at War, to suspend or enforce the execution of the Act in any county or place in Great Britain.[3]

51. The powers with which these Acts armed the Commissioners were no doubt arbitrary, and the only protection enjoyed by any Subject against their improper application to him was an appeal to the Secretary at War or to the Common Law Courts. Cases of this kind soon arose, and the Secretary at War, embarrassed by them, consulted the Law Officers whether any steps could be taken for preventing these applications to the Courts of Law. Their answer was, that the interference of the Legislature might be sought to make the judgment of the Commissioners absolutely final; but that great difficulties would be met with in carrying such a Bill through Parliament.[4]

Relief against the Impressment to be obtained in the Common Law Courts.

52. Early in the reign of Geo. III, two Statutes were passed similar in their provisions to those of the last reign. Under these Acts—the 18 Geo. III., c. 53, and 19 Geo III. c. 10—the same class of persons as are described in the 30 Geo. II., c. 8, were liable to impressment, except that Papists were no longer disqualified. By the 19 Geo. III., c. 10, the standard of age was altered from 45 and 17, to 50 and 16 years, and Recruits under 18 years were accepted at 5 feet 3 inches in height.[5]

The like Acts in Geo III.'s reign 18 Geo III., c. 53, 19 Geo III., c. 10

53. The terms of service were three years for volunteers[6] and five years for impressed men,[7] unless the nation should be engaged in war, and then during the continuance of the war. An appeal against the impressment could be made to the Commissioners within 14 days, and the man might be discharged by

---

[1] Secs 16, 23.   [2] Sec 6.   [3] Secs 33, 42.

[4] Appendix LXXXVI ; see Rex v Dawes, 1 Burr. Rep., p 636, Rex v Kessel, p. 637.

[5] See Lord Barrington's Letter of 25 June, 1778, Marshall's ' Military Miscellany,' p. 49. About this time the Ballot was first introduced into the Militia, see Chap III., par 25.   [6] Secs 6, 40   [7] Secs 31, 43

them   If no appeal were made, or on hearing it, the man was
held to serve, he was compelled to do so, for no jurisdiction was
given to the Superior Courts to interfere.

54 Persons convicted of smuggling[1] or of running away
from and leaving their families[2] chargeable to the parish were,
in lieu of the ordinary punishment awarded by the laws, to be
handed over to the Military authorities, and to serve as impressed soldiers.

55. The later Act gave increased encouragement[3] (and was
continued[4] until the 1st May, 1782) to voluntary enlistment,
for, on the expiration of their service, or on previous discharge with wounds, volunteers were exempted from statute
duty, parish offices the Militia service, and future impressment,
with liberty to exercise their trades, &c, under 3 Geo. III., c 8.
As to impressment, the Act expired on the 1st May, 1780, and
since this period all the Soldiers that have served in the Army
have, as a rule, enlisted as Volunteers.

56. The Bounty to Volunteers under both Acts was nearly
the same.   By the first Act,[5] 3*l.*—of which 1*l.* was to   *Cost of men raised under these Acts.*
be paid out of Land Tax, and 2*l.* by the Paymaster-
General.   By the second Act,[6] 3*l* 3*s.*—to be paid by the
Military Officers.   The cost of an impressed man was 1*l* to
the parish officers for their trouble;[7] 2*l* to loss to the parish
for each man having wife and children.   A reward of 10*s.* was
given to any one discovering a fit man for impressment.

57. From these Acts the late Lord Palmerston[8] drew
another cogent argument,—that their provisions   *Office of Secretary at War should be one of Civil control.*
afforded a clear proof that Parliament reposed con-
fidence in the Secretary at War, *as a Civil Minister*
having the control of Army enlistments.   In the first
place, he noticed that they prohibited the holder of any
Military office or employment from acting as a Commissioner;
and, in the next place, that they gave to the Secretary at
War the power of putting the enactments in operation against

---

[1] Secs. 10, 19   [2] Sec 19
[3] See Mr Jenkinson's Speech in 20 Parl Hist , p 112.
[4] By the 20 Geo III , c 37   [5] 18 Sec 5   [6] Sec 39.
[7] Secs. 14, 37.   [8] Appendix CXXIX

the Civil community, and then from time to time of expressing the pleasure of the Crown that the Conscription should
be suspended or revived.

58. A Conscription for the Army was recently adverted to
by a leading Minister of the Crown, as a possible
measure for the adoption of his Cabinet, and the civil
community was said to owe much to the sagacity of
the Statesmen who, by making re-enlistment popular,
with increased pay, had filled the Army with re-engaged men
in time of Peace, and thus rendered a conscription unnecessary. Military service has on other occasions, been held
up as a terror, but seldom for such a purpose. The Duke of
Wellington, though mistaken in saying that "in no instance
had the system of raising men for the service of the Army by
voluntary enlistment been departed from, whatever may have
been the wants of the service for men," yet protested emphatically against the injustice of resorting to Conscription for the
supply of men to the ranks of the Regular Army.[2]

Conscription to recruit the Regular Army—in expedient.

59. In the year 1783 the expense of Recruiting was—under
Mr. Burke's Act—transferred from the Stock Purse
of the Regiment to the Public, by an estimate for the
annual cost of it, being framed and submitted to Parliament by the Secretary at War for a Vote in Supply.[3] The
Act required that an account of the Recruits raised, and of
the expenses incurred should be sent every two months to the
Adjutant-General, and it provided that an allowance should
be made to the officers as a compensation for the loss of the
Stock Purse or Non-effective Allowances. The system of
Recruiting has subsequently become altered, and therefore it
will be convenient, before pursuing the subject in its altered
aspect, to explain the mode of enlisting Soldiers into and discharging them from the Army.

Estimate for cost of re- cruiting the Army

60. Until recently neither the manner of enlistment nor
the conditions of it were prescribed by the Articles of War

---

[1] Mr Disraeli's letter of 1st October, in the 'Times' of the 3rd October, 1858.
[2] See 'Military Punishments,' 1836, p 321 Lord Hardinge's evidence, p 302,
and Debates in House of Lords, 23 April, 1869.   [3] 23 Geo. III., c 50, sec 46

or Mutiny Act, though from the earliest period the Articles have required that the Soldier should take an "oath of fidelity" on enlistment.　From the year 1673 this oath has varied but little in terms, and the present one (for 1869) is in nearly the same words that are to be found in the oath prescribed by the Articles of War for 1717.[1]

Manner and form of enlistment.

Oath of Fidelity

61.　Regarding the oath, the interference of Parliament dates from the year 1799, when the 39 Geo. III, c. 109, imposed one of Fidelity without words of succession ("heirs and successors").　This oath was transferred to the Mutiny Act, and remained without alteration from 1803 to 1810, but in the year 1811 words of succession were added.　It is clear that the oath is not essential to the validity of the enlistment,[2] but is a matter only directory under the Statute—imposed to give a greater sanction to the discharge of the Soldier's duty.[3]

A.D. 1799

Form of it prescribed by Parliament

62.　To avoid any possible question that might arise upon the oath from the omission of the words of succession prior to 1811, the framers of the Mutiny Act from 1815 to 1828 inserted this declaration therein .—

A.D. 1815-28

Declaratory enactment as to the oath.

"And whereas it is highly expedient that no doubt should remain as to the Service of Soldiers by reason of any omission of His Majesty's Heirs and Successors in any Oath of Attestation, be it therefore declared and enacted, that any Oath and Attestation of Service heretofore or hereafter taken and made to His Majesty, is and shall be deemed and construed to be an Oath of Service to His Majesty's Heirs and Successors, as the Sovereign of the Realm for the time being, as fully and effectually, and to all intents and purposes whatsoever, as if the words 'Heirs and Successors' had been inserted in any such Oath or Attestation."

63.　As to the enlistment, the form and substance of it were

---

[1] 19 Tind. Engl., p. 193.　　[2] Appendix LXXXVII
[3] The King v Witnesham, 2 Adol and Ell, p 650, see Report of Royal Commissioners on Oaths, 1867.

first prescribed by Parliament in the same year[1] By the
Statement of Recruits' qualifications. 1 Geo. I. (Stat 2), c. 47, sec. 3,[2] the Recruit was
under the obligation of declaring whether he was or
had been a Papist, but under no other statutory
obligation to disclose any particulars of himself. However,
under the provisions of the several Mutiny Acts passed after
this date, the Recruit has had to pledge his oath that he is
physically capable to act as a Soldier—so far as freedom from
rupture and other defects afford any criterion of ability.[3]

64. Hitherto—that is prior to 1799—the enlistment of every
The Crown recruits for the Army and East India Company's Service Soldier had been strictly Regimental—each Colonel or
Captain in the first instance enlisting men into his
Regiment or Company; but when the Crown, by the
39 Geo. III., c. 109, undertook the duty of raising
Troops for the Army, and also for the East India Company's
Service in India, it became necessary—as no Regiment could
be named to Recruits, whose destination was uncertain—to
enrol men for "General Service;" and to take the right of
attaching them to any Regiment that the Crown or Company
might see fit.

65. Accordingly, with this object in view, new forms of en-
General enlistment necessary listment were framed, and received the sanction of
Parliament, first in the Act under notice, and then
by transfer to the Mutiny Act, 1803; though, by being so
transferred, the enlistment of men for General Service became
dissociated from the original purpose of convenience for which
it was designed.

66. Enlistment for "General Service" soon got into dis-
General Service unpopular favour, and, from a sense of its inexpediency and injustice was discontinued. "I believe," said the late
Lord Palmerston, "there is a great disinclination on the part of
the lower orders to enlist for General Service; they like to
know that they are to be in a certain Regiment, connected,
perhaps, with their own county, and their own friends, and
with officers who have established a connection with that district.

---

[1] 39 Geo. III , c. 20   [2] Repealed by Statute Law Repeal Act 1867
[3] See Schedule A to the Act

There is a preference frequently on the part of the people for one Regiment as compared with another, and I should think there would be found a great disinclination in men to enlist for General Service, and to be liable to be drafted and sent to any corps or station."[1]

67. But there was another potent reason for making enlistment for General Service unpopular—viz., that it was again[2] made a punishment, under the Mutiny Act; thus from 1807 to 1812 inclusive, if a Soldier were convicted of desertion, he might "be transported as a felon for life, or for a certain term of years; and also, if such Court shall think fit, to be, at the expiration of such term of years, *at the disposal of His Majesty for service* as a soldier *in any of His Majesty's forces, at home or abroad,* for life or otherwise, as His Majesty shall think fit;" a power that was freely used, as a return laid before Parliament in 1812 clearly proves.[3] A Colonial Corps was usually appointed to receive these men, until this penal system was put a stop to by a General Order of the 25th January, 1826[4]

[margin: Again made a punishment]

68. Enlistments for General Service were discontinued from the 20th March, 1816, under the authority of the Commander-in-Chief.[5] In probable forgetfulness or possible disregard of previous experience in this matter, the Military witnesses examined before the Recruiting Commissioners[6] 1861 and 1867[7] strongly insisted upon the expediency of having recourse to these enlistments, and they were again sanctioned by Parliament,[8] when a very short trial of the system confirmed Lord Palmerston's views, and they were abandoned in 1869.[9]

[margin: General Service abandoned in 1816 and revived in 1867 till 1869]

69. The period or term of years for which a man should be enlisted into the Army has been a constant subject of controversy between the Crown and Parliament;

[margin: Controversy as to Army Enlistments]

---

[1] Evidence before the Finance Committee, 1828, pp 199, 163
[2] See par 10 *ante*   [3] 67 Com Journ., p 674.   [4] MS Regulations, p 186
[5] Circular 58, and General Order, No. 311, of 15th April, 1816
[6] Questions 354 6, 5791-5   [7] Questions 150-4, 240, 357, 361, *et seq*
[8] 30 & 31 Vic, c 34, sec 10   [9] 14 Parl List, p 428

for while Parliament has declared in favour of short enlistments, it was held against the ordinary rule of Law between
master and servant, where a Life engagement would
be void as against public policy—that an engagement
to serve the Crown—no period of time being named[1]
—was an engagement for life, or until the Crown was pleased
to discharge the Soldier from service. Whenever, therefore,
Parliament has interfered between the Crown and the Recruit
enlisting, it has always been to protect the latter from entering
into an engagement, either incautiously or to serve for the
term of his natural life.

*The engage-
ment to serve
the Crown
was held to
be for life*

70. Of course where the man had been raised at the expense of the Stock Purse, the discharge was a matter
of bargain with the Colonel, who could at any time
discharge a man from his regiment; but, as the cost of supplying his place fell upon himself and his brother officers,
the discharge was only given for an equivalent, varying in the
circumstances of each case, and fixed by the Colonel upon the
application for discharge If the Soldier could find a good and
sufficient substitute, approved by the Commanding Officer, the
money paid for his discharge was proportionably reduced. So
long, therefore, as this mode of providing Recruits was in force,
the officers had a pecuniary interest in continuing the system
of Life Enlistments.

*Discharge by
purchase*

71. The Policy of Parliament, as evidenced by the arrangements made for the Constitutional force—the Militia
—has always been shown in favour of short Enlistments From the time that the Militia was reformed
in 1757 to the last Act relating to the subject, the
engagement of the men has never exceeded a period of five
years—the object of that limitation being to send the men
back to the employments of civil life, and to use the Militia
—rather than the Standing Army—as the school for training
the people to arms.

*Short enlist-
ments the
policy of Par-
liament, as
evidenced by
the Militia
Acts.*

72. Again, it will be seen that, prior to the present century,

---

[1] The Mutiny Act, 1869, last section

short periods of enlistment have always prevailed in the Army whenever Parliament has raised it from a Peace to a War Establishment, and provided the Recruits either under Conscription Acts or by a special vote of Levy Money. In the first place, *impressment* for life would have been intolerable. In the second place, it was the National policy that the Army should always be disbanded at the close of each War; and therefore, had Parliament adopted long enlistments, an excuse would have been given to the Crown for keeping the Army on foot while those enlistments were in force. Lastly, the absence of any Barrack accommodation, sufficient for a large army, rendered it a matter of necessity to disband the troops on the War Establishment upon their return into the Kingdom.[1]

Conscripts or special levies raised for short periods.

73. The men who entered as volunteers under the Recruiting Acts of Anne's Reign were entitled to their discharge in three years from their enlistment,[2] but no limit was put to the service of impressed men. However, after the Peace of Utrecht, the Mutiny Act[3] gave every person who had been three years in the land forces liberty to demand his discharge; and declared that every volunteer who entered the Army should, after three years' service, be at liberty to have a free discharge in writing.

Acts in the reign of Queen Anne

74. It was soon found to be impossible to carry out the regular routine service of the Army with such short-term men; for they demanded their discharges, rather than go into bad quarters or unhealthy climates. The clause, therefore, was omitted from the Mutiny Acts passed after 13 Anne, c 44, s. 8, and the Regiments on the Peace Establishment were recruited upon the ordinary conditions of life enlistments

Short engagements would not enable the troops to be sent on foreign Service

75. Under the two Recruiting Acts[4] of Geo. II., impressed men were entitled to discharges, after short periods of service; under the first Act[5] at the end of five years,

Acts in the reign of Geo II.

---

[1] Chap XI, pars 15-18   [2] 7 Anne, c 2.
[3] 12 Anne, c 13, s. 50, 9 Stat Realm, pp 790, 791; and see the 2nd of the three Mutiny Acts passed in 1715, and the 3rd Mutiny Act which required the Soldier to g've three months' previous notice of claiming his discharge.
[4] 29 Geo II, c. 4, and 30 Geo. II, c. 8   [5] Sec 23.

and under the second Act[1] at that time, if the war was ended, or otherwise at the end of the war. Any volunteer enlisting under the second Act was also entitled to his discharge after three years' service, or at the end of the war[2] The men who voluntarily enlisted between 14th September and 1st January, 1745, were to be entitled to their discharge at the end of two years' service,[3] and by a later proclamation (by order of the Privy Council) those enlisting before the 25th December were to be discharged in six months, or at the end of the Rebellion.[4]

76. The men recruited for the War in 1759 were, as we have seen, paid bounties that had been raised by public subscription ; and, to encourage enlistment, an Order in Council was issued,[5] on 11th July, 1759 "that all persons enlisting as soldiers should not be sent out of Great Britain, and should be entitled to their discharge in three years, or at the end of the war, if they choose it "

A.D 1759
New levies for short period of service

77. The new levies for the American War were also raised for short service; thus on the 16th December, 1775,[6] the Secretary at War "signified His Majesty's pleasure that during the continuance of the rebellion subsisting in North America, every person who should enlist as a foot soldier should be entitled to his discharge at the end of three years, or at the end of the Rebellion, at the option of His Majesty," and under the two Recruiting Acts of Geo. III.'s reign,[7] the soldiers were enlisted for the same periods as were named in the prior Acts of Geo. II.'s reign.

A.D. 1775
The same.

A.D. 1778 80
Acts of Geo. III

78. But, notwithstanding the efforts of two independent Members to introduce short enlistments as the rule of the Service, or clauses into the Mutiny Act to entitle the soldier to his discharge upon fair and open terms the

Ordinary En- listments for life

---

[1] Sec. 30   [2] Sec. 6
[3] 'London Gazette,' No 8472, Oct , 1745, Lord Stair's notice   [4] Ib, 8473, and see 8493   [5] Ib., 9912
[6] Marshall, pp. 28, 58, see order for discharge, of Feb. 4, 1783, in 'London Gazette'   [7] 18 Geo. III , c. 53 , 19 Geo. III , c 10

ordinary enlistments for the established Regiments still continued to be made for life.

79. The first proposal was that of Mr. Thomas Pitt, who in November,[1] 1749, moved for leave to introduce a bill "to limit the period beyond which no man should be compelled to continue in His Majesty's service," but the motion was lost. During the next Session (January,[2] 1750) he so far succeeded as to obtain leave for the introduction of his bill, which (after discussion) met with no better fate than his former motion. His proposal appears to have been to entitle a man after ten years' service to purchase his discharge at a fixed sum (3*l.*)

A.D. 1749
Mr Thomas Pitt's Bill to shorten Enlistments.

80. The other Member who brought the subject before the House of Commons was Colonel Barrè. After the Mutiny Bill had been introduced in 1779, he moved "that it be an instruction to the Committee on the Bill that they should have power to receive a clause or clauses for limiting and ascertaining the time of service of such non-commissioned Officers and Soldiers as are already enlisted, and of such persons as shall hereafter be enlisted in the Army." Mr. Burke spoke in favour of the motion, but it was lost[3]

A.D. 1779
Colonel Barrè s proposal to facilitate discharges

81. After the expense of recruiting had been transferred from the Stock Purse of the Regiment to the Estimates by Mr Burke's Act, the pecuniary interests of the Officer were no longer opposed to the principle of short Enlistments. and therefore the Crown and Parliament were better able to adopt that principle, both as to the new Levies and the old Regiments. Accordingly, in the Revolutionary War with France, Mr. Pitt raised men for the Army, whose Service was limited both as to place—viz., Europe—and as to time, viz., five years from Enlistment, or to the end of the war.[4]

A.D. 1796
Mr Pitt's Acts limited the Enlistment to place and time.

82. The prudence of limiting the service of any part of the

[1] 14 Parl. Hist , p 398   [2] Ib , pp 723, 760
[3] 20 Parl Hist , p 150   [4] Vol I , Chap XIV , pars. 17-20

Army as to *place* or *area* was questioned at the time; but, un
fortunately, in the succeeding War the same scheme
was adopted by Mr. Addington's Ministry,[1] and again
followed up by Mr. Pitt,[2] until the legislation with this object
was repealed at the instance of Lord Grenville's Ministry.[3] The
Force was in fact raised at Army bounty for Militia Service.

Prudence of such limitations.

83. When, therefore, Mr. Wyndham in 1806 proposed to
enlist men for a short term of years, he was—as is
apparent from what has been already written—introducing no novelty into the Army Service. His error
consisted in raising troops for *War* service, but for a
period not limited to the War. Breaking the term
for old Established Regiments into three periods, he
pledged Parliament to give—and encouraged all Soldiers to
enter upon—this total service by offering them a legal and indefeasible right to a pension at the close of it.

Limited Enlistment no novelty in 1806

Mr Wyndham's measures for short Enlistments.

84. That his measures, both as to Enlistment and Pension, added a vast expense to the annual Estimates
cannot be doubted, but whether they secured to the
Crown al arger Army may well be questioned.[4] At the first enlistment, a man, for a small additional bounty, readily enlists
for life instead of for seven years; but at the expiration
of this limited enlistment, a much larger Bounty—than the
small sum originally asked—is needed to induce the Soldier
to re-enlist in War Service. Before the Bill was introduced,
Lord Castlereagh[5] assured the House of Commons that the
difference between twelve guineas for unlimited and ten guineas
for limited service had induced all but 250 out of 9000 men
to enlist for the former service, and at a later period it is
undoubtedly true that the difference of only 16s. given in 1819,
induced Recruits to select unlimited service.[6]

Their effect.

85. The alteration in enlistment made by Mr. Wyndham
was carried out by the Mutiny Act. In the second[7]
of the three Acts passed for the year 1806, the
man was to serve his Majesty without any limita-

A D 1806

Carried out by the Mutiny Act.

---

1 43 Geo. III , c 82.   2 44 Geo. III , c 56   3 46 Geo III., c 51
4 Chap. XXII , par 34, and references in the Note, and Vol I , p 367
5 5 H. D (O S.), p 694   6 39 H D (O S), p 988
7 46 Geo III , c 48, see 6 H D (O S) pp 652, 680

tion of time, but in the Third Act the enlistment was to be —"To serve his Majesty King George III. in the Regiment of   , commanded by   , and to serve for the period of   [This blank to be filled up by the Magistrate with seven years for Infantry, ten years for Cavalry, and twelve years for the Artillery, if the person enlisting is of the age of eighteen years or upwards, but if under eighteen years, then the difference between his age and eighteen to be added to such seven, ten, or twelve years, as the case may be] years, provided his Majesty should for so long require his service; and also for such further period as His Majesty should please to direct,[1] not to exceed, in any case, *three* years, and to determine, whenever six months shall have elapsed of continued peace, subsequent to the expiration of the term of [seven, or ten, or twelve] years."

86 The controversy which this measure gave rise to[2] would be tedious to enter upon here, but as the House of Commons placed upon their Journals various resolutions, at the instance of Mr. Wyndham, and of Lord Castlereagh, these give the facts of the case, and will be found printed in the Appendix.[3]

Controversy on the results of the measure

87. The Duke of Portland's Ministry held, as the Duke himself did,[4] a very decided opinion that Mr. Wyndham's measure was extremely injurious. Their remedy was not its absolute repeal; but when the Mutiny Bill was before the Commons, on 7th March, 1808, Lord Castlereagh moved to insert a clause to enable Soldiers to enlist for life, urging upon the House, that, "He had no objection to limited service, and he had formerly promoted, to a certain extent, engagements limited in space as well as in time. But why should limited service be in a manner enforced, to the total exclusion of unlimited service, even when

The Portland Ministry change the system.

Unlimited Service

---

[1] See Proclamations of 1st July, 1813, for extending this term, and of 24th September, 1814, releasing them 'London Gazette,' 16,758, ib, 16,946, Vol vi. 'Army Regulations,' p. 137.

[2] 8 H D (O S), p 489, 9 ib, pp 862, 866, 902-4, 1064, 1218, 1220-22, 16 ib., pp 981, 985   [3] 62 Com Journ, p 845, et seq, Appendix LXXXVIII.

[4] Vol viii Castlereagh Desp, p 159

the men were perfectly satisfied, and desirous to enter without limitation?"[1]

88. The clause was adopted, and from that year till 1829 the Soldier had the option of enlisting either for life or for a term of years. A small additional Bounty induced the men generally to enlist for life, and limited enlistments were wholly discontinued by order of the Adjutant-General of the 18th April, 1829

A.D. 1808 29

Soldier had the option of limited or unlimited service.

89. This was the aspect in which the matter stood in 1847, when Parliament again interfered with enlistment, and obliged the Crown to enlist *all* men for a limited period. Looking to the *Army* rather than to the *Militia* for training the people to arms, the intention of the framers of that measure as evidenced by its enactments, was to prohibit both long and short engagements—the Act being so drawn as absolutely to prohibit for the Infantry any engagements save for ten years, or any re-engagements save for eleven years.[2] In War the expiration of the Soldier's engagement—where many men are enlisted at and for one period—must cause the Executive Government great embarrassment, and the Act of 1847 did not, as the earlier Acts did, obviate this difficulty by continuing his service over the War period.[3]

A D 1847

Limited Enlistment Act.

90. The only power which the Act gave, was for the Commanding Officer to retain a Soldier "serving on a Foreign Station" for two years; an expression which would be thought to be ambiguous if the Army were engaged in an enemy's country, and not on any "Station," but—however construed—forming a condition not to be found in Mr. Wyndham's Act, where the right of the Crown to extend the service for three years was absolute, unless Peace intervened.

Defects in the Act.

91. Parliament again resorted to short engagements in the Crimean War, and the provisions of 10 & 11 Vic, c. 37, had to be relaxed, to give authority to the Crown to enlist or re-engage men for shorter periods than

A.D. 1855

Short Enlistments sanctioned

---

[1] 10 P D , p 981   [2] 10 & 11 Vic , c 37, Chap XXII , par 38
[3] 91 H. D. (3), pp 300, 650-86, 854, 869, 1317 , 92 ib , pp. 1019, 1288

ten and eleven years. This was done by the 18 Vic., c 4,[1] in the first instance, but the power was continued in force for six years by the 21 & 22 Vic, c. 55.

92. Unless in emergencies, short enlistments must be distasteful to those who are responsible for training and educating the Soldier in military exercises. In time of peace, to have the constant Work of Instruction in hand instead of having the ranks filled with experienced Soldiers, must make no slight difference to the commission and non-commissioned Officers of the Regiment, and this temptation requires to be constantly kept in check, both as regards the Militia and the Regular Army. *Short Enlistments of men must be distasteful to officers*

93. Whatever might have been the success of the Act of 1847, had the policy of taking only ten years' men been rigidly adhered to, it is difficult to opine—but as events happened an alarm arose that the population could not supply the Army with Recruits, and therefore that policy has been interfered with upon the recommendations of the Recruiting Commissioners in 1867,[2] by offering greater inducements—than hitherto had been held out—for men to re-engage. No doubt[3] the expense of an Army constituted of re-engaged men, is vastly in excess of an Army of Recruits, and doubts appear to be entertained whether, as a rule, it is more, if indeed as effective, as an Army of younger men. *The Policy of the Act of 1847 impeached*

94. The 10 & 11 Vic., c. 37, was therefore repealed—save as to Soldiers enlisted under it—by the Army Enlistment Act, 1867,[4] which sanctions re-enlistment for twenty-one years, at any time that two-thirds of the first term of enlistment has been served out, and provides that all future enlistments shall be made for the longer period of twelve years. The number of re-engaged men on the 30th of June, 1867, was 31,205,[5] and from that date to 31st of December, 1868, a further number of 40,988 men re-engaged *Army Enlistment Act, 1867*

---

[1] 136 H. D. (3), pp 1600, 1722, 1734   [2] Report, p xiii
[3] See the Lecture of Colonel Leahy, R E , United Service Institution, April, 1868, pp 18, 19.
[4] 30 & 31 Vic, c 34   [5] Report on Recruiting, 1867, p 222

under the Act of 1867,—making a total of 72,193 long-service men working for future pension.

95. At the present time the enlistment and attestation

The Mutiny Act now provides for the Enlistment of Soldiers. of the Soldier—which contain his engagement to serve the Crown—are to be found in the Annual Mutiny Act. For the protection of the Public,[1] the Recruiter has to ask certain questions to satisfy himself that the Recruit would be eligible for the Service. These, so far as need be mentioned, are whether he is an apprentice—married, and, if so, with children—in the Army or other forces —been rejected as unfit for service—or marked with D or B C. Assuming him to be satisfied with the man's answers to these questions, the enlisting money of 1s. is given, and the Recruit, by the receipt of it, becomes an enlisted Soldier.[2]

96. That no doubt may rest upon the enlistment of a

The attestation of the Soldier's Enlistment. Soldier, the Recruit, by a written notice served upon him within a defined period named by the Act, is warned to attend before the Justice. On the return of the notice, and at the time named in it, the Justice—who *may not* be an officer in the Army—is to adjudicate (if necessary) upon the regularity of the enlistment. If irregular, or the smart money of 1l. be paid, the man is discharged, otherwise the Justice attests the validity of the enlistment by his Certificate.

97. Preceding the attestation, the Justice is to cause the

The Civil Magistrate confirms the engagement. questions prescribed by the Act to be read over and the answers of the Recruit to be recorded Then the Recruit is to declare their truth, and to take the oath of allegiance. Afterwards, and in verification of these facts, the Justice attests them by his Certificate, and the Soldier's attestation is complete.[3]

98. In the enlistment and attestation of Soldiers, the provi-

---

[1] Wotton *v.* Gavin, 16 Q B Rep , p 64   [2] Ib

[3] Mutiny Act, 1868, secs. 42-67

sions of the Mutiny Act—so far as they afford protection to the Recruit—must be strictly adhered to. In the first place the enlistment—though it is not illegal—should not be on a Sunday. Further, it must be made by the agents of the Crown, lawfully appointed;[1] other persons, having no such authority being liable to punishment.[2]

Directions of the Act for the protection of the recruit to be strictly observed.

99. In the next place, the attestation cannot be made either before or after the time named in the Act, and it should be before a Justice residing in the vicinity of the place, or acting for the division, district, or place where the man enlisted. The Recruit has a security in being known to the Magistrate, and hence this qualification of the Justice was inserted[3] in one of the earliest Mutiny Acts in William and Mary's reign. The prohibition against an Officer in the Army acting as a Justice in the attestation of Recruits dates from the 2 & 3 Anne, c. 13; but the Act expressly declares that Officers of Militia are not included in the prohibition.[4]

Time and place of attestation to be followed

100. Lastly, in a doubtful case, the appeal is to be made to Secretary at War as the "proper[5] channel between the Civil and Military part of the community and the Constitutional check interposed for regulating their intercourse, and as specially charged with the protection of the Civil Subject from all improper interference on the part of the Military;" and it is his duty to release any citizen unfairly enlisted. However, as the Mutiny Act has been framed since 1859, no Soldier can raise any question upon the validity of his enlistment[6] after he has been six months on the strength of the Regiment.

Secretary at War the Parliamentary Officer to redress irregularity

101. With regard to the persons legally capable of entering into this engagement, all natural-born Subjects that the Crown is willing to enlist, and Foreigners to the

Who capable of entering into this engagement.

---

[1] Appendix LXXXIX

[2] Mutiny Act, 1816, 54 Geo III , c 10 sec. 99, and Mutiny Act, 1868, 31 Vic , 14, sec. 80.   [3] 5 & 6 W and M , c 15   [4] Sec 4, and 7 Anne, c 2, sec. 18 Appendix CXXVIII —Outline of Secretary at War's Duties Mutiny Act, 1868, sec 59

limit prescribed by Parliament in an Act of the present reign, are included[0].

102. The age at which a Recruit is deemed eligible, is 18

Infancy no impediment

years—though boys of 14 years are often enlisted. No question can be raised as to the legality of such an enlistment. "By the general policy[1] of the Law of England," said Mr Justice Best, "the parental authority continues until the child attains 21; but the same policy also requires that a minor shall be at liberty to contract an engagement to serve the State (as a Soldier). When such an engagement is contracted, it becomes inconsistent with the duty which he owes to the public that the parental authority should continue."[2]

103. The enlistment of apprentices, until specially dealt

A.D. 1758-60

Apprentices.

with by the Mutiny Act in 1805, gave rise to much controversy. When an apprentice made the contract with the Crown, he was not, it was contended, "sui juris," or, in regard to his existing apprenticeship, capable of contracting for service;[3] consequently, in this view of the case, Sir D Ryder and Sir W. Murray, in 1753, and Sir C. Pratt, in 1760, held the enlistment to be void against the master, and advised the Secretary at War that the apprentice should be given up.[4]

104. However, upon a case arising in that country in

A.D. 1773.

The same question raised

1773, the Attorney-General for Ireland, gave a long opinion that the enlistment was valid. In this opinion, the English Attorney-General—Thurlow—agreed "Though I know," he added, "that the current of opinion is the other way, and supported by great authority." The Secretary at War refused, therefore, to alter the practice of his office as established under Lord Camden's opinion, and, when consulted in 1802, the Law Officers thought that the 6 Geo. III.,

---

[1] Rex v Rothersfield, 1 Bar and Cres, p 350, Rex v Walpole, Burr S C, p. 633, Rex v Hardwicke, 5 Bar and Ald, p. 178

[2] See Mr Corry's Speech, 3rd December, 1807, where he explained the law to the House of Commons in a very different sense

[3] Rex v. Norton, 9 East Rep, p. 206, and Rex v Beaulieu, 3 Mau. and Sel, p 239.   [4] Appendix XC Bk 1 (N S), pp 40, 93.

c. 25, gave the master a right to the specific performance of the apprentice's agreement.[1]

105. In course of time, frauds were committed under the apprenticeship system, both by masters and apprentices; and it was necessary for Parliament to interfere. Masters would connive at enlistments, and after three or four years—when the service was irksome—come forward to get the apprentice released. For these evils a remedy was provided in the Mutiny Act, 1805. As to the apprentice, any one denying his apprenticeship on oath was made punishable for perjury; and, as to the master, he was bound within one month from the absence of the apprentice to declare the same before a Justice. The Act further declared, that no one, save such an apprentice, could be taken out of the service for breach of contract or engagement to serve or work for a master and employer.[2] These clauses, as amended in 1807 and 1860, still continue in the Mutiny Act.

Frauds committed, and Parliament interfered

106. By this Legislation, the principle of discharging servants from the Army, by reason of pre-existing engagements, was limited to the claims of masters of apprentices;[3] and some encouragement may be thought to have been given to the enlistment of servants by providing in the Act of 1807, that a servant enlisting should be able to recover wages due for the time that he had actually served his master, notwithstanding by his enlistment he had failed to complete the full term of service agreed for under his hiring.[4]

As to servants.

107. With regard to Foreigners, it has been already noticed that the Act of Settlement relates exclusively to Officers,[5] and there is no Statute which, in terms equally explicit, prohibits their enlistment as soldiers. During the reign of Queen Anne it would appear from the entries in the War Office books that several regiments were raised, without legislative sanction, consisting of French refugees and other foreigners

As to Foreigners.

---

[1] Book 1 (N S.), p 107   [2] 45 Geo III , c 16, secs 67-69.
[3] 47 Geo. III , c. 32, sec 80, and Bk 722, p 199
[4] This clause was withdrawn from the Mutiny Act in 1860
[5] Bk 721, pp 101-106; Bk. 723, p 238

resident in England and elsewhere, who were willing to enlist
into Her Majesty's Army.[1]   However, in 1837, Parliament assumed that the Crown had no power to make such enlistments;
for the 1 Vic., c. 29, enables the Crown, acting through the Secretary at War, to enlist Foreigners, so that the number serving
together shall not exceed one in every fifty native-born Soldiers,
and no Foreigner shall hold any higher rank in Her Majesty's
Army than that of a *Non*-commissioned Officer.[2]

108. The Soldier engages, by enlistment and attestation, "to
What the Soldier engages for serve" for "a stated period," provided Her Majesty
should "so long require his services," and, by his oath,
"to defend Her Majesty, her heirs and successors, Crown and
dignity, against all enemies," and "to observe and obey *all*
orders of Her Majesty, her heirs and successors, and of the
Generals and Officers set over him."

109. Now the terms of the Soldier's engagement are plain and
Only one Rule of Conduct—the Oath of Fidelity explicit—"to defend the Crown against all enemies,"
and "to obey all orders of the Crown and of the
Generals and Officers over him."   "We have not distracted our Army," wrote Mr. Burke, in allusion to the Army
of France that was sworn to obey "the King, the Nation, and
the Law," "by divided principles of obedience—we have put
them under *one single authority* with a *common* oath of fidelity."[3]
The Soldier, according to the theory put forward in Hinton's
Case,[4] knows nothing of the order of either House of Parliament—his allegiance being due to the Crown alone.

110. The end and purpose for which Soldiers are retained
The purpose for which an Army is retained in arms. in arms were thus strongly put by Mr. Wyndham.[5]—
"By an Army," he said, "I mean a class of men set
apart from the general mass of the community, trained
to particular uses, formed to peculiar notions, governed by
peculiar laws, marked by particular distinctions, who live in

---

[1] See Beating Orders to Lord Lifford, April 10, 1706, p 49, and Colonel La
Fabreque, May 27, 1706, p. 65, Mia. Bk 520.

[2] Sec 2, and 88 H D. (3), p 1498, see Note S, Appendix.

[3] Vol v Works, pp 17, 18 ; see th Oath in A D 1579 in Marshall's 'Military
Miscellany' (1846), pp. 13, 29

[4] 74 Com Journ , p 1157. 39 H D. (O S), p. 1265.   [5] 6 H. D (O. S.), p. 654.

bodies by themselves, not fixed to any certain spot, nor bound by any settled employment, who 'neither toil nor spin;' whose home is their Regiment; whose sole profession and duty it is to encounter and destroy the enemies of their country wherever they are to be met with, and who in consideration of their performing that duty, and the better to enable them to perform it, receive a stipend from the State exempting them from the necessity of seeking a provision in any other mode of life."

111. The duties—whatever they may be—that the Soldier has undertaken are such as the Crown and its agents *only* can discharge him from, and until he is so discharged he is under a quasi disability as to his Civil rights and duties. The Crown only can give the Soldier his discharge.

112. In the first place, he is bound to obey and to give his personal service to the Crown under the punishments imposed upon him for disobedience by the Mutiny Act and Articles of War. No other obligation must be put in competition with this; neither parental authority[1] nor religious scruples,[2] nor personal safety,[3] nor pecuniary advantages from other service. All the duties of his life are, according to the theory of Military obedience, absorbed in that one duty of obeying the command of the Officers set over him Implicit obedience to the Crown and his Superior Officers.

113. The orders of the Officer must, no doubt, be within the scope of his Military authority; but a Soldier would refuse at his peril to obey any order because he thought it was illegal. The tribunal for the adjudication of the legality or illegality of the order would be in the first instance a Court-martial, though ultimately—as in the Case of Bailey *v.* Warden—the subject might come before the King's Bench.[4] In the erection of fortifications and works in the reign of Queen Anne, Military labour was used, the work being ordered and the extra pay being fixed at sixpence a day by Orders of the Officer to be within the scope of the Officer's authority

---

[1] Rex *v* Rotherfield, 1 Bar and Cres., p 350.
[2] Capt. Achison's Case, 88 H D (3), p 319, 24 ib (2), p. 299, and 25 ib, pp. 351, 421. [3] Sutton *v* Johnstone, 1 Term Rep, p. 548
[4] Warden *v.* Bailey, 4 Taut Rep, p 67, and 4 Mau and Sel, p. 411.

the Crown.[1] In another aspect of the same question it may be mentioned that Soldiers, as outlyers, were often allowed to exercise their trade or craft on furlough — their pay, or a proportion of it, going to the Stock purse of the regiment.[2]

114. In the next place, it follows that a Soldier is not *sui juris* or capable of making any other legal engagement for service so long as his engagement with the Crown is in continuance;[3] neither can he change his Parish Settlement nor his National Domicile—which remain as they were when he entered into service.[4]

The Enlisted Soldier is not sui juris

115. There is, however, no legal restraint upon his marriage at any period of his enlistment.[5] All that the State does is to give a direct sanction to the marriage of a certain percentage of the Non-commissioned Officers and privates of the Army—by making some provision for their wives, and recognizing their position as such within the barracks or Military quarters of the Army at home. All other wives of the same class are unprovided for, and unrecognized by the State, nor has the Law provided any legal machinery by which a married Soldier can be compelled to make allowance out of his pay for the maintenance of his wife or children.[6]

No legal restraint on marriage.

116. The obligations of the Crown to the Soldier are to pay

---

[1] Mis Bk. 522, 1713, June 18

[2] See Lord Palmerston's Evidence, Finance Committee 1828, p 159: and 6 H D (2), p. 979. Army Expenditure, 1850, pp 843-5   When the profit went to the Stock purse of the officers, there was then no objection, whatever there may be now, to soldiers working at trades

[3] Rex v Norton, 9 East., p 206, Rex v Beardner 3 Man and Sel , p 237.

[4] Horton v Leeds, 5 Ell and Blac , p 596. Hodgson v De Beauchesne, 12 M P C 317, The Pres of U S v Drummond, 33 Bea Rep, p 451, 10 Jur (N S, Formerly an officer or a soldier, whenever he entered the Military service of the East India Company with an Engagement for life, was held to abandon his domicile of origin , but this rule from the various Acts recently passed affecting the Government and the Army of India, and for Limited Service, can no longer have any application 21 & 22 Vic , c 106, 23 & 24 Vic , c 100, and 24 & 25 Vic, c. 74. Forbes v Forbes Kay, p 341

[5] 1685, June 1st, Order for Soldiers not to marry, Mis Order p 42

[6] Circu' r, 9 August, 1867

and to clothe him,[1] to arm him when and as the Responsible Minister sees fit,[2] and (on certain deductions),[3] to feed him, to lodge him, and to preserve him, by all reasonable care, from disease, physical and moral. The agents for the discharge of these obligations, and for the supply of these various wants, have been entirely changed since the date of the Revolution, and the effect has been adverse to economy.

Obligations of the Crown towards the Soldier

117. Prior to the year 1783, the obligations of Parliament were limited to the votes of pay, and of certain defined allowances which were disbursed through the Regimental Officers to the men under their Command. By this arrangement the Officers were bound to the exercise of economy in their administration by the strongest pecuniary interest; if the allowances were more than enough they got the savings, or if not enough, they had to make up the difference or to bear the discontent of the men.

Prior to 1783 the Regimental Officers had a pecuniary interest in Army economy

118. After Mr. Burke's Act had obliged the Crown to bring all these allowances — with their incidents — before Parliament by estimate, the Secretary at War, rather than the Regimental Officers, became the administrator of the moneys so voted by Parliament, and he paid directly through his financial agents many charges that had previously been disbursed by the Regimental Officers out of their allowances. To the extent of the change then made, the argument of the Duke of Wellington[4] against the change in the Clothing system prevailed, viz, that as the Officers no longer *had any pecuniary interest in the economy* of Military Administration, expense would increase.[5]

After 1783 the Secretary at War discharged financial duties,

119. However, prior to 1858, the Agents of the Public for Military Expenditure were the servants of the Civil departments of the Army,—Civilians, owning no other authority save that of the Treasury, or of the Civil departments subordinate thereto, looking up to the responsible Ministers of

and prior to 1858 by Civil servants.

---

[1] As to clothing issued to the Soldier see Sanitary Report 1858, p 433; and Report on Recruiting, 1867, p 297, and Note W W , Appendix.

[2] As to Arms and Ammunition, see Appendix XO.

[3] As to the Soldier's rations, see Sanitary Report, 1858, p xxi , and pp 423 to 433.

[4] Chap VI., par. 99

[5] As to increase of Allowances since 1848, see Parl. Papers (431, of Session 1869.

the Crown for protection and reward in the faithful discharge of their Financial and Administrative duties. Even to Civilians—wholly independent of the General in Command—such security and encouragement were obviously needed, to counteract the bias which might arise in favour or fear of the recipients of the supplies—the Military host surrounding them —and therefore against the unrepresented Public, ignorant of the economy secured by their careful discharge of duty.

120. But these agents have been recently changed from Civil to Military; the Army has got men of their own class or status, under the orders of the General, to supply their wants. All bias in favour of the public is therefore excluded, and there is nothing either in reward or punishment to counterbalance the action of the Military element upon these Officers All rewards or punishments are to be distributed to them through the channel of their Military Superiors, and their success in the Military profession is of course dependent not upon economy, but on providing the best of all things to supply the wants of the General and of the Army serving under his Command.[1]

Since 1853 the status of the Agents of the Crown to discharge these obligations changed

121. But to revert to the Soldier's enlistment, though the engagement is made for a term certain, the Crown is under no obligation to retain the Soldier either in pay or in arms for that period, but may discharge him at any time. It is an essential principle that the Crown should not only have but exercise this power without question or controversy. The safety of the Realm may depend in some measure on the immediate discharge or dismissal of any man or Regiment in arms,[2] and—equally—that the cause of such dismissal should not at the time be disclosed by the responsible Ministers of the Crown. This subject,—which is of more importance to Officers than to Soldiers,—will, however, be more fully discussed in the next chapter.

Power of the Crown to discharge the Soldier at any time.

122. The Soldier, on the contrary, has no power of dissolving his engagement. That has always been enforced

---

[1] Chap XIII. par 51, Chap XIX., pars. 35 and 46, Chap. XXIV, par 22, and Chap XXIX.

[2] The case of 5 Drag. Guards , 2 Gro Military Anti. (p 231), ed. 1801 Vol ix. MS. Army Regulations, p. 254 The Indian Mutiny, 1857

in the same words, though not with the infliction of the same punishment   The Mutiny Act provides that any one "who shall desert Her Majesty's service shall suffer death or penal servitude, or such other punishment as a Court-martial shall award."[1]   No distinction has ever been made on the face of the enactment as to the different circumstances of crime; and "nothing," said a noble peer,[2] "can contribute more to the establishment of slavery than severe punishment with power of mitigation."

But the Soldier has no power to leave the Service Desertion punishable with death

123. The War Office Records prove that the punishment of death for desertion was often inflicted in William III.'s time.[3]   And as during the absence of the King in Holland these sentences came frequently before Queen Mary,[4] Her Majesty asked Colonel Gibson "Whether there had been already made an example sufficient for the deterring and keeping others in their duty?" To which his reply, characteristic of Court-martial Tribunals, was in these words —"My opinion is that the last example ought to have been sufficient for the deterring and keeping others in their duty; but God knows it has taken but little effect, for we have lost several men since, however, at the last Court-martial I did recommend it to the members that they would consider the late example, and not run to the extremity of the law.   *I strove to persuade* them that the running out of an open quarter was *not so ill* as out of a garrison, and that not so ill as running away before the enemy, and that the Act of Parlia-

Old War Office Records as to infliction of death for desertion

<hr>

[1] Mutiny Act, 1868, sec 15   [2] 14 Parl. Hist , p 433
[3] Of this fact one or two illustrations may be given :—

By a Court-martial held 25th May. 1693, one Hugh M'Laughlane, a soldier that deserted on the 16th April previously, was sentenced to be shot to death, and the sentence was confirmed by the Queen.

On the 30th May, 1693, before another Court-martial, three persons "were brought up and examined by the President, and did confess and acknowledge that they did desert, and being found guilty of death, as appeareth by Act of Parliament made in the 4 & 5 W and M., the sentence of the Court was, That one of the three should suffer death by being shot, and that all three shall lott whose chance it shall be to dye"

This sentence was confirmed by the Queen, but, as the execution of M'Laughlane had not taken place, "Her Majesty's pleasure was conveyed to Col. Gibson, C O. at Portsmouth, that one only of the four should dye, and that M'Laughlane should have the liberty of casting lotts with the three above named"—Mis Bk 517, p. 73   [4] Mis Bk 517, p. 87

ment (which is our rule) says 'Death or such other punishment
as the Court-martiall shall think fitt,' and seeing the prisoner
had not been above three months a soldier (and deserted before
the Regiment came hither), a corporal punishment, severely
inflicted, might take place. All this would not help; *all of
them were for death.* This was and is my opinion."

124. When capital punishments for desertion absolutely
ceased in England I have not been able to trace; but
they were inflicted throughout the last and at the
commencement of this century. In the 'Annual
Register' two entries, as of ordinary events, prove this to have
been the case, for there are recorded under dates (1st) of 1758,
May 18,[1] the execution of the sentence of death awarded against
a young Soldier at Plymouth, who had appealed to a General
Court-martial against a sentence of 500 lashes by a Regimental
Court-martial; and (2ndly) of 1803,[2] March 6, the like sentence
against a Soldier, aged 20, at Portsdown, for repeated desertion
from the Army of Reserve, and the receipt of several bounties
from parishes and individuals[3]

Punishment of death inflicted at the beginning of this Century

125. It is the duty of the Soldier to be at all times within
one mile, and between tatoo and reveille in his camp
or quarters,[4] unless he has the pass or leave in writing
of his Commanding Officer[5] for his absence. If absent for
twenty-two days his crime is that of desertion,[6] absence not exceeding five days may be dealt with as a crime of less importance;[7] but the length of the absence is not the only test of
whether a Soldier should or should not be tried for desertion

Desertion— what ?

126. As connected with this crime, it may be observed that
the law awards to others than the Soldier deserting,
severe punishment Any Civilian aiding desertion, or
endeavouring to seduce any person serving in His
Majesty's forces from his duty, shall on conviction be deemed

Punishment to civilians aiding desertion

---

[1] Vol. 1., p 95   [2] Vol xlv , p 464
[3] See Vol. 1 Court-martial Proceedings, as to the execution of a man of the 70th
Regiment at Chatham for desertion from the 26th November, 1802, to the 1st
February, 1803
[4] Queen's Regulations, par 846. Tattoo at 9 p.m from October to April, and
10 p m from May to September Reveille. 5 30 a.m in summer, to 6 30 a m in
winter.   [5] Articles of War, 1868, Art 50   [6] Art. 43.   [7] Art. 50

guilty of Felony, and by the 1 Vic., c. 91, s 1, be liable to transportation.[1]

127. The discharge of a Soldier appears upon the Mutiny Act and in the practice of Army administration, in the contradictory aspect of a reward and a punishment. Looking at the character of the Recruits, and the sources of supply throughout the last century, a discharge was no doubt a substantial reward. The present Mutiny Act grants the Soldier his discharge gratis for information given to the Crown for certain offences committed by others in the Army, as for making unauthorised deductions from his pay (sec. 59), or false musters (sec. 78). In the same spirit, the Royal Warrant permits a Soldier of *good* character to purchase his discharge as an indulgence, allowing his good-conduct service to be reckoned in diminution of the purchase money. *Discharge of the Soldier held out as a reward* *Royal Warrant of 23 July, 1861*

128. The policy on which the Mutiny Act and regulations were founded was strongly upheld by the late Lord Hardinge.[2] "If," said he, "you give the Commanding Officer the power of getting rid of bad men because they are bad, you will offer a premium for misconduct, and would make a great number of men bad for the purpose of gaining their discharges. Even if punishments were to be inflicted, such is frequently the desire to get out of the service that they would take the punishment for the sake of the discharge. I ought to add that, in 1829, the principle upon which I went, and which was adopted by the Commander-in-Chief, was to give men their discharge for good conduct. I know an instance in which I myself applied to a Commanding Officer for the indulgence of purchasing a Soldier's discharge. The man happened to be a very good man, and it was refused ; they did not like to part with the good Soldier. My regulation permitted a man who had conducted himself well to have the indulgence of his discharge by a graduated scale, according to the service performed, and he was entitled to leave the service on very advantageous terms." *Policy of these provisions.*

[1] By the 37 Geo III., c 70 (made perpetual by the 57 Geo III , c 7). 1 Russ 'On Crimes,' p. 141

[2] Military Punishments, 1836, p 305 , Horse Guards Circular, 1st September, 1836, p 82; Chap XXII , para 41-8

129. Formerly the equivalent for a discharge was provid-
Former sys-
tem of ob-
taining a dis-
charge.
ing a Substitute approved by the Colonel of the
Regiment; but in 1810, when much difficulty might
have arisen in complying with this condition, the Regulations offered a Soldier his discharge on providing the levy
money of two Recruits in lieu of a Substitute.[1] In 1817[2]
the sum of 20l. was named in lieu of a Substitute, and in
1819[3] the boon of a discharge was to be given to the good
Soldier. The first Regulations that laid down definite rules
with fixed prices for the Soldier's discharge were those of 1829,
framed by the late Lord Hardinge upon the principles already
explained in his evidence before the Committee on Military
Punishments in 1836. These were altered as to Soldiers enlisting after the 1st March, 1833, by the rules framed and issued
on the 7th Feb., 1833, by the late Sir John Hobhouse.

130. By the Royal Warrant of the 1st July, 1848, a new
Rules of
1848.
schedule was adopted. The maximum prices remained
the same as in the previous Regulations, but a pecuniary value (say 5l.) was given (by way of deduction from the
price of his discharge) to the Soldier for any good-conduct badge
that he might hold. Although Limited enlistments had been
adopted, no break was made in the scale at the periods of
ten or twelve years: thus the Soldier was, and in some cases
still may be, entitled to his discharge on the terms given in
this table :—

	A	B	C
	1829.	1833.	1848
	£	£	£
After 10 years' service	15	15	15[4]
„ 12 „ „	10	10	10
„ 14 „ „	5	5	5
„ 15 „ „	{ Free at home and 3 months pay abroad }	Free	Free.
„ 16 „ „	{ Free, and 3 or 6 months' pay }	Free	
„ { 18 to 21 } „ „	{ Free, and 1 year's or 1½ year's pay abroad }	{ Free, and 10l. to 16l. to settle in a Colony. }	

[1] 22 May, Vol. ii. 'Army Regulations,' p 39, and see 1811, July 10 Vol iii ib
pp 8 , 147   [2] 10 January, 1817.   [3] 25 January, 1819
[4] If in Australia, then the soldier was entitled to his free discharge at any

131. The Royal Warrant of 3rd February, 1866,[1] introduced another scale for purchase,—each branch of the service having a distinct schedule of prices. Thus, the Horse Artillery and Royal Engineers, as distinguished from the Field Artillery, the Field Artillery as distinguished from the Cavalry, and the Cavalry as distinguished from the Infantry of the Line, have special schedules.

Rules of 1866

132. The Royal Commissioners upon Recruiting in 1867, considering the discharge as a boon, recommended that the scale of prices should be considerably raised.[2] "Soldiers are by regulation permitted to purchase their discharges, and this permission is considered to be a boon, and is frequently asked for. We do not recommend its withdrawal; but, considering the high rate of wages to be obtained in civil life,—as compared with those which prevailed at the

Purchase Money for a discharge to be increased.

time after his tenth year of service, and a bonus increasing from his tenth to his fifteenth year of service

[1] It is difficult to discover on what principle the Schedule was framed Take, for illustration, the Royal Artillery—"A" standing for the Horse, and "B" for the Field—the maximum value of the badge in A is 7*l*, and in B is 5*l* The second badge has no value till after the *tenth* year in the first enlistment, when it is placed at its maximum If in the same year the man has re-engaged, it is reduced to 4*l* and 3*l* After re-engagement, the changing value of the first and second badges in A and B are shown by this extract.—

A			B.	
1st Badge.	2nd Badge.		1st Badge	2nd Badge
£	£		£	£
3		After 7 Years . ..	2	
7	4	„ 10 „	4	3
4	3	„ 12 „	3	2
4	2	„ 13 „ . ..	2	1
4	1	„ 14 „	3	1
4	1	„ 15 „ . ..	1	1
1	5	„ 16 „ .. .	1	4

The depreciation of the value of the second-class badge must tend to diminish the efforts of the men to earn it, and there seems less reason in depreciating the value of either badge by the *length* of the man's service.

I have taken the Royal Artillery as an illustration without examining what is the value put on these badges in the case of the soldiers in the Engineers or Infantry. Probably the same arbitrary rules have been adopted in the scale for their use: and, if so, the rule of thumb would appear generally to prevail in assessing the pecuniary value of a badge on a soldier's discharge. [2] P. xii

period when the present piice of discharges was fixed—we are of opinion that the scale should be considerably raised."

133. That some Soldiers are always to be found in the Ranks who desire their discharge so earnestly that they would

Self-Mutila-
tion to gain a
discharge.

resort even to disgraceful conduct to attain it, few, having experience upon the matter, will doubt. If it be not so, why is it necessary to retain those Clauses in the Articles of War inflicting severe punishments on Soldiers for acts obviously against nature, and which nothing but this desire would tempt them to commit—as self-mutilation and destruction of eyesight, rendering the person unfit for Military Service?[1]

134. It has seldom been inflicted as a punishment, except in

Discharge as
a punish-
ment.

Regiments where formerly, as in the Horse Guards, the privates purchased their places from the Colonel.[2] No doubt when the pay and other advantages of the Army have been raised, at the cost of the civil community, to that standard, discharge will, and may be, resorted to as a punishment, without demoralizing the men. The purchase scale must then be withdrawn; but until that time has arrived, and the discharge has ceased to be a reward for good conduct, it is difficult to see how the recommendation of the Commissioners on Military Punishments, 1869, that men guilty of disorderly conduct should be discharged from the Army,[3] can be carried out advantageously to the morâle of the Army. Their Discharge would be, no doubt, a great relief to the Regiment, though a certain expense to the public, and a possible injustice to the Civil Community upon whom they are released. For

---

[1] Articles of War, 1869, No. 81, and Chap. XXII, pars 45-8.

[2] Vol. ii. of Commons' Reports, 1746, pp 75-93. In Freer *v.* Marshall, 4 Fos & Fin, p. 485, the plaintiff claimed damages at Law for his discharge from the Regiment

[3] 1st Report of 1869   Returns of the Recruiting time 1867, p 251, shew that from 1860 to 1865 the Army lost 125,944 men from these causes —

1 Death	22 085	
2 Desertion	22,321	
3 Discharge—as (*a*) Completion of Service	17,585	
(*b*) Purchase	. 11,732	
(*c*) Invalids ..	30,406	
(*d*) Indulgence . ..	. 14,188	
(*e*) Other causes	7,577	

If *e* be increased by the misconduct of Soldiers, *b* and *d* will cease

thus reason the power of discharging men is reserved to a General and not given to Regimental Courts-martial.

135. With regard to the necessity of a Formal discharge, under the Articles of War, the law was laid down by Lord Loughborough, in 1792,[1] to be " that a person in pay as a Soldier is fixed with the character of a Soldier, and if once he becomes subject to the military character he never can be released but by a regular discharge." But in dealing with the question of identity, before the military character is fastened upon a person taken up as a deserter, it is necessary that the Civil power should be appealed to. "The Mutiny Act," said Chief Justice Erle, "has provided that where that question arises in the case of a man who alleges himself to be a civilian being claimed as a deserter, he shall not be consigned to the military authorities until the Civil Magistrate has been applied to, and has given his sanction to the claim." [2] *A Certificate of Discharge essential*

136. As to the form and method of discharges, the Field or Commanding Officer formerly gave them; but in the Articles of War for the year 1817, a provision was inserted, that they should be given according to the General Order for the time being in force. The Articles for 1829[3] then provided that no Soldier should be discharged unless by Court-martial sentence, or order of the Commander-in-Chief or of the Crown, and the Articles of War at present in force further provide that no Soldier shall be discharged unless his services, conduct, character, and cause of his discharge be ascertained before a Regimental Board. *As to form and method of a Soldier's Discharge*

137. As the Guards are not recruited at the cost of the public—being exempted from the operations of Mr. Burke's Act—the Commanding Officers can—save for Pension, when the assent of the War Office is needed,[4]—discharge their men at any time, without the sanction of any higher Military or Civil authority. *Officers of the Guards can discharge men*

138. In recurring to the subject of Recruiting at periods

---

[1] Grant *v* Gould, 2 H Blac., p. 101.
[2] Wotton *v* Gavin, 16 Q. B. Rep, p 71   [3] Article 65
[4] Adjutant General's Order, 8th March, 1836   Freer *v.* Marshall, *sup.*

subsequent to the operation of Mr. Burke's Act, it is open to

Vast increase in the cost of recruiting since 1783. remark that the cost of raising men has very largely increased. Other causes than the direct operation of the Act have contributed to this result. In the first place, though the officers of a Regiment have been relieved from the cost of raising the men, they still hold and continue to exercise through the Colonel the power of approving the Recruits before they join the Regiment. In the next place, from the nature of the danger impending in the French Revolutionary War—the threat of Invasion, and the scene of possible conflict —Foreign Soldiers could not, as in former Continental Wars, be engaged; the strain on the population of Great Britain was therefore greater than at any former period.

139. But the manner of recruiting the Army—by abandon-

Conscription from the vagrant class abandoned. ing conscription against the Vagrant Class—was the principal cause of the great increase of expense. It was not that—by abandoning this limited Conscription, and resorting to a General Ballot—a better class of Recruit was procured : the same class was obtained by the new method in a far more expensive manner, throwing also a grievous, because an unequal, burthen of taxation upon the Industrial Classes, whether rich or poor. Instead of the Crown taking Vagrants, as in earlier times, by a direct process at a Statutory Bounty, the Ballot was applied to a larger circle of the General Community, the members of which,—if drawn in the lottery,—had each for himself to purchase one of the Vagrant Class upon any terms that the Substitute thought fit to impose. This method of re-cruiting, which continued without mitigation till the year 1807, pressed severely upon the selected members of the General Community until the Voluntary principle at high bounties paid by the State partially removed the evil.

140. Upon the renewal of the War with France in 1803,

Raising of an Army of Re-serve. the attention of Parliament was directed to raising Defensive Forces to meet the threat of invasion.[1] The second measure — passed at the instance of Mr. Addington's

---

[1] 36 Parl Hist., pp. 1607-37, and as to the strength and casualties during the War, see Marshall's 'Military Miscellany,' p. 76, and Vol. I., p. 588, Appendix LXXIII

Ministry, with that object—was the 43 Geo. III., c. 82, to establish by ballot under the machinery of the Militia Acts "an Army of Reserve" The service of this force was—like that raised by Mr. Pitt in 1796—to be limited both in Area and in Duration of Service. It was to serve *within* the United Kingdom and the Channel Islands, but *not* elsewhere: the balloted men for five years, and the substitutes and volunteers for an additional period of six months *after* a definitive Treaty of Peace *with France.*[1]

141. This Army was raised upon Bounties and under penalties paid by balloted men or ratepayers. The price to be paid for a substitute, and at which parishes might raise Volunteers out of the rates, was to be fixed by the Deputy Lieutenants of each county.[2] If the Ballot was enforced, each man drawn had to serve—provide a substitute (who might have any number of children)[3]—or pay a penalty of 20*l.*, with a continuing liability to the Ballot;[4] half of which penalty was to be paid to the parish, and half to the Receiver-General.[5] If a balloted man was unfit to serve, and had not 100*l.* in property, the penalty might be wholly remitted; if he was fit, and had only 500*l.* in property, then half the declared value of a substitute was given to him. *{Plan of raising the Force.}*

142. If at any time during the operation of the Act the Parishes failed to supply their quota of men, they were fined 20*l.* for each man deficient,[6] but they were not bound to supply a vacancy caused by the Voluntary Enlistment of any Reserve man into the Regular Forces for General Service.[7] This Army was to consist of 50,000 men, of which 34,000 were to be raised under this Act—6000 for Scotland under c. 83, 10,000 for Ireland under c. 85, and 800 for London under c. 101—of the same Session. *{Ballot and penalties.}*

143. The direct tendency of these measures was either to stop entirely, or to raise enormously the cost of recruiting the Regular Army.[8] As a source of supply to the Regular Forces upon a second Bounty, it was limited to the total of the Army of Reserve, *{One of the results of the measure was to increase the cost of recruiting}*

---

[1] See 19 [2] Secs 20, 25 [3] Sec 14 [4] Sec 15
[5] Sec 17 [6] Sec 35 [7] Secs. 30, 33
[8] See observations at Chapter XIV, par 33, Vol I and Statements A and B in Appendix XCI

while that force on the other hand was reduced or wholly destroyed, because the Parishes were not bound to supply the vacancies created by those enlistments The Act was a mistake of the gravest character,[1] for at the commencement of a long war it introduced—what is very difficult even in time of Peace to terminate—an expensive system of Recruiting. It raised men, no doubt, but they were substitutes provided at the cost of private persons.[2] The Reserve Army gave to the Regular Army[3] 19,553 men as Volunteer Recruits, but to that extent it was destroyed

144. When Mr. Pitt succeeded to office in May, 1804,— after a motion which amounted to a want of confidence in Mr. Addington's Ministry in regard to the Army of Reserve,[4]—it became necessary for his Ministry to reconsider the policy upon which the Regular Army was to be recruited. Instead of repealing the Army of Reserve Acts, Mr. Pitt's proposal[5] was to amend them by what in Parliamentary *conflict* was termed the "Parish Act."[6] His scheme, apart from the reduction and recruiting[7] of the Militia, was, first to raise an "Additional Force," mainly through the agency of Parish Officers, to complete the Reserve Army, and then from it to recruit the Regular Army to the extent of 9000 men per annum. For the year ending 1st February, 1805, 9000 men were to be raised to supply the vacancies in the Additional Force that might arise by reason of men serving therein having enlisted into his Majesty's Regular Forces; and in each subsequent year, men equal in number to those that had enlisted into the Regular Army (but not exceeding 9000 men) were to be raised under the Act.

The parish Act to raise an additional force

145. The Ballot was to be stopped,[8] and men of the Additional Force (as thereafter it was called) were to be raised by a stipulated Bounty, to be laid down by his Majesty's Regulation,[9]) with a penalty of 20*l.* upon any

Plan of raising the Force.

---

[1] See 1 H D (O S), pp 166, 179-81 . 2 ib., pp 194, 209, 222, 229
[2] 60 Com Journ., p 628 ; 61 ib., pp 695, 635   [3] 61 Com Journ , p 628
[4] H D (O S), pp 265, 319.   [5] 2 H D (O S), pp 562, 594
[6] 44 Geo III , c 56   [7] War Office Circular, 12th July, 1805, Vol 1 'Army Regulations,' p 66   [8] Sec 19   [9] Vol 1 ib , pp 59, 60, 66, 67

one giving any higher sum, and it was not to exceed three-fourth parts of the Bounty from time to time allowed for Infantrymen of the Regular Army.

146 Parish Officers producing Recruits from their own or adjoining parishes, were to receive such portion of the Bounty as the Treasury should see fit. If they failed to produce their quota, the Parish was fined 20*l*. for each Recruit deficient, and the Commanding Officers raised the men at the usual Bounty. Parish Officers raising men

147 When raised, the men were to be formed into Additional or Reserved Battalions, to be attached to any regiments or battalions of his Majesty's Regular Forces, bearing the name of the County in which such Additional Force had been raised, or into separate Battalions not attached to any other regiment [1] His Majesty was to appoint officers to command and discipline the men, both officers and men being subject to the Mutiny Act and Articles of War Men formed into 2nd Battalions.

148. The *Area* of Service was to be the same as in the Reserve, but the *Period* was extended; for *every* man raised was to serve for five years, and until six months after the termination of *any* war (by the ratification of a definitive treaty of peace) in which the kingdom might, at the expiration of the five years, be engaged, he was to be enlisted and attested in the same manner as a Soldier Period of service enlarged

149. All the powers of the Militia [2] and Reserve Acts,[3] as varied by the present one, were to be used for raising the Additional Force, and other Acts similar in principle were passed for Scotland (c 66), for Ireland (c. 74), and for London (c. 96), and continued in force till May, 1806, when all of these were repealed by the 46 Geo. III., c 51, s 1. Ballot powers suspended

150. The Army to be raised—as the Additional force—under the provisions of these Acts varied from the Militia mainly in these particulars—1st., it was raised by Parish Officers, instead of the Lord and Deputy Lieutenants, or, on their failing, by Regimental Officers In what respects Militia Reserve differed from the Militia.

---

[1] Instructions of 17th September, 1804, Vol. 1 Army Regulations, p. 59 , Boys enlisted, ib., p 60.   [2] 42 Geo III., c 30.   [3] 43 Geo III, c 82.

of the Regular Army; 2nd, it formed second Battalions to Regiments of the Regular Army, and the Officers held Commissions from the Crown, and therefore passed into or out of the first Battalions[1] as their promotion might lead them; and 3rd, the area of the service though very limited, was not so strictly local, as that of the Militia of that period.

151. The Act was, no doubt, framed (1) to facilitate Recruiting into the Army, and (2) to reduce and regulate the Bounty to be paid to the Recruit; but it may be doubted whether it successfully accomplished either of these purposes. The Opposition failed during Mr. Pitt's life to get the 44 Geo. III., c. 56, repealed,[2] though they pointed out the expense that it entailed upon the country. "For every man raised by the parishes under this Act," said Colonel Crauford,[3] "they receive 14*l.* from Government. for every man of their quota that they fail to raise, they are fined 20*l.* · it is therefore clearly their interest to give any Bounty short of 34*l.*[4] rather than suffer the fine; for if they give 33*l.* bounty, 14*l.* of which is repaid to them by Government, the man costs them only 19*l.*, whereas if they had not procured him, they would have been fined 20*l.* A further Bounty of ten guineas is allowed to such men as shall volunteer from the Limited Service to the Regiments of the Line,[5] and therefore every man who comes into the latter through the medium, of this Parish Army, may be computed to have cost the country 43*l.* in Bounty only. Under these circumstances, it is to be presumed that men, who have determined on going into the Army, will, instead of taking the direct road, have sense and patience enough just to look in upon the Parish Army in their way, and take its bounty along with them."

152. That the plan of raising men for the Regular Army in

Results of this Act (1). Expense of recruiting

---

[1] 2 H. D (O S), p 562   [2] 3 H. D (O S , pp 631-730

[3] 5 H D (O S) p 680

[4] It is difficult to the force of this argument, as sec 22 limited the bounty to be paid under a penalty. However, the Honourable Member's statement was not denied by any subsequent speaker

[5] Volunteering commenced for Scotland in January and for Ireland September, 1805, 62 Com Journ p 899.

these indirect ways pressed unfairly upon one particular class—the landed interest—can scarcely be doubted. "A practice,"[1] said Lord Carnarvon, "has, since the last war, been introduced, which, besides an augmented Militia to the number of 60,000 men, has burthened the Private Purse of the land occupier, and not the Treasury of the Nation, to pay the levy of above 31,000 for the Army of Reserve, and nearly 58,000 *additional force* by the Parish bill, amounting in the whole to 149,000 men not stated by Ministers in the Army Estimates. And let it not be imagined that the expense falls the less on the land-occupier because the Overseer of the Poor may, *if he can*, raise the men by the sum paid to him by the Crown, the Act will show that the Crown cannot give a sum *above* three-fourths of the Bounty that shall be allowed to raise Regular Forces, and it is not easy for the Overseer to obtain a man when Government offers for the same man one-fourth more. But should the Crown give only 6d. to the Overseer, which the King's Minister may do, or any sum much below three-fourths, so as to make it quite impossible to obtain a man, the penalty of 20l. per man attaches on the parishes, to be paid by a rate from the land-occupiers, so that the 58,000 men may be raised at the will of the Crown, at any time, and 20l. per man, viz. 1,160,000l. The whole sum raised, or to be raised, from the land-occupier's purse, since the Peace, amounts to three millions and an half, besides the expenses incurred in keeping up the force of 149,000 men."

(margin: (2). Injustice to the landed interest.)

153 He then pointed out that the scheme had not even the advantage of economy. "40l. and even 50l. has been given for raising the war augmentation of Militia. I put that at the low average of 30l.; less than 12l. I have not yet heard of, as the intended seduction money, making together 42l. for each man so obtained; the present price of Army recruiting is 16l. per man, which deducted from 42l. as before stated, leaves a surplus of 26l., which is the sum given more than the man is worth; so that the land occupier is charged 26l. that the public purse (to which he also pays) may be spared 4l."

(margin: Vast and needless cost of the measure.)

[1] 4 P. D., pp. 202, 203

154. But irrespective of economy—though to waive such a
consideration is a strong argument against any measure
—it was not a great success for obtaining recruits
The Act came into operation on the 5th September,
1804, and was repealed in April, 1806, and up to the
31st January in the l ter year, the results as given in one
Return,[1] were these :—

(3). The efficiency of the measure for gaining Recruits doubtful

	My Parish Officers	Regimental Officers.	Total	Discharged	Dead.	Deserted.	Effective	Volunteered to the Army
Eng and Wales	3042	2740	5782	164	30	873	4726	2200
Scotland	893	290	1183	17	6	130	1034	282
Ireland	3590	488	4078	73	21	1113	2952	1016
	7525	3518	11,043	254	57	2,116	8712	3498[2]

155. At the time of its repeal the strength of our Military
Establishments was a topic of Parliamentary warfare,[3]
and the author of the measure had been removed by
death from the arena of politics.   Hence it is difficult
to glean from the Debates such an admission of facts as may
be cited in proof of its success or failure.   Certainly, though
Lord Castlereagh and Mr. Perceval never sought to re-enact
it,[4] they expressed their belief in its success, and spoke
strongly against the repeal, "for in the fifty weeks ending
the 14th of March, 1806, the Act had produced above 9,000
men.   In the last fifteen weeks it had produced an average of
258 per week, which would give 13,200 in the year; in the last
ten weeks an average of 277, or 14,600 in the year; and in the
last five weeks, an average of 356 per week, being at the rate of
above 18,000 in the year; and this under all the discouragements
which interfered with its operation." [5]

Recruiting the Army a matter of party politics.

156 However, at the instance of Lord Grenville's Ministry,[6]
all these Acts were repealed, and the Counties relieved of the fines for deficiencies then due from

Army of Reserve and Parish Act repealed

[1] 61 Com Journ , p. 618
[2] Another Return gives the final numbers as 4416 men, 62 Com. Journ, p 899
[3] Lord Melville's Letters, 1807, July 16 , 8 Castlereagh's Despatches, pp 79-80
[4] See 9 H D. (O S.), pp 862-65 for Lord Castlereagh's reasons
[5] Mr Perceval, 6 H D (O S.), p. 792   [6] 46 Geo III., c. 51.

them. They were followed by (1) Mr Wyndham's measures for short or limited Enlistments and (2) those substituted by Lord Castlereagh in 1808, which have already been discussed[1] The results of these several plans for recruiting the Army may be seen by examining the Tables in the Appendix,[2] prepared many years since by some official in the War Office, whose name is unrecorded.[3]

157. The general policy to be pursued for recruiting the Army is directed by the Cabinet. It is for the responsible Ministers of the Crown to determine the number and strength of the Military forces to be maintained, at what cost in bounty and levy-money they shall be raised, of what height and age, and for what period the men shall be retained to serve the Crown.[4] The agents to carry out these instructions have hitherto been Military men—Officers and privates either on full or half-pay or on pension—acting under the orders of the Adjutant-General of the Army

General policy as to recruiting with the Cabinet.

158. By the organization for recruiting the Army (as distinguished from the Guards, the Militia, and the Marines), the United Kingdom is divided into districts (7), with a recruiting Staff in each district. The different channels of supply are (1) Regimental depôts, Battalions, and Corps, recruiting at Headquarters, (2) the Recruiting Staff, and parties detached from Regiments; and (3) Pensioners holding Beating Orders. The proportion of Recruits gained by each of these three agencies for the year 1864 is given by one return at (1) 3373, (2) 6988, and (3) 4246, making a total of 14,607 men. The Recruits are sent either direct to the Regiment for final approval, or first to Recruit Barracks for the district in which they have been recruited, and then to the Regiment for final approval. A medical examination precedes the acceptance of men into the ranks of the Army, and a large proportion of men that offer are rejected

Military Officers agents for carrying out method of doing so

---

[1] Chap. XIV, par 32 *et seqq*   [2] Appendix, XCI, Statements D and E
[3] Probably Mr Raper, and, respecting him, see Earl Grey's speech, 137 H D (3), p 1291
[4] See Lord Panmure's Evidence on Military Organisation, 1860, Question 391.

for physical causes   In 1865, 24,884 were medically examined, of whom 9313 were rejected at the primary, and 1319 at the secondary examination.[1]   If an unhealthy or weak man be taken, the pension list has to bear an unnecessary burden.[2]   An examination into the *moral* character of the Recruit has not yet been deemed essential.

159. The Recruits are finally approved at the Regiment or
Final approval at the Regiment. Corps, and are sent there either direct, or first to the Recruit Barrack of the district, and from thence to the Regiment   A large proportion of the Recruits desert before final approval; in the year 1865 as many as 954 before and 375 men after attestation[3]   The cost at which the Recruiting agency is carried on, and the character of the agents to be employed, are both subjects to which the attention of the Royal Commissioners in 1859 and 1867 was given.

160. But though the agents of the Crown for recruiting are
Secretary at War formerly, and Secretary of State now, responsible for recruiting Military men acting under the Commander-in-Chief, the person directly responsible to Parliament for their conduct towards the Civil community is—as the statements in this chapter abundantly prove,—the Civil Minister—formerly the Secretary at War, and now the Secretary of State.   If a man be unfairly recruited, or if the rights of the parent or master be violated in the manner of the enlistment, the appeal for redress is to the War Office in the first instance—if the public have confidence in the Department and in its *personnel*,—and ultimately to Parliament.[4]

161. Recruiting the Army, even in time of peace, is a
General question of recruiting the Army Colonial local forces. matter of National importance.   During the last ten years, two Royal Commissions have been appointed, and have reported on the subject.   The advantage of having Local troops in the various Colonies was discussed before the Finance Committee of 1828, but all the weight of Military experience was against the proposal.   The late

[1] Report on Recruiting, 1867, pp 272-6
[2] See Returns of Temporary Pensions, ib   [3] Ib., p 259
[4] Papers on Army and Ordnance Expenditure, 1850, pp 691-7, and Lord Herbert's Evidence, 'Military Organisation,' p 479

Sir James W. Gordon[1] was strongly opposed to it as utterly prejudicial both to the usefulness of the Corps for Colonial defence or to co-operate with the general Army. "The British Army cannot," said the late Duke of Wellington,[2] " be made a Colonial Corps without destroying its character and strength. Would it not be a most terrible and disgraceful mode of losing the possession of any part of His Majesty's dominions by means of a mutiny of the Officers of a local or Colonial Army, employed to garrison it? Yet that is what we must look to if the Army is to be employed as a mere Colonial Corps, and never to quit the Colonies from the day they enter the service. I should, therefore, entreat the Committee to lay that plan aside." Recent events in India shew the wisdom of this advice.

162. It is frequently suggested that the East Indian—now part of the duty of the Queen's—service, may need a different consideration[3] Such a period of duty forms As to Indian service no inconsiderable portion of a man's life, and the liability to it may lower the inducements which hitherto have brought men of the higher class into the Army. It was not the mere fact of serving the "Company" instead of the Crown that made *the* difference between the two Armies in India, but that *Indian* service attracted to the ranks of the Company's Army a different class of men to that which entered the Regular Army.

163. To secure the Soldier the receipt of his Pay without deduction, — other than such as may be usual, or from time to time be authorized by His Majesty's Soldier to be paid daily Regulations—the Mutiny Act[4] provides that the Officer charged with the payment of it, is liable to be cashiered by Court-martial if he unlawfully detains the same for one month, or refuses to pay it according to His Majesty's Regulations. Prior to the Peninsular War[5] some portion of the Soldier's pay was given to him weekly, and the balance at the end of each month, but the Duke of Wellington, finding that these monthly settle-

---

[1] Memorandum of March 17, 1828
[2] Evidence of 15th April, 1828, and Vol 1 'Supplementary Despatches,' p 127.
[3] See Report of Commons' Committee, 3rd April, 1868, p. 197
[4] Section 60
[5] Memorandum of Horse Guards to Finance Committee, 18th March, 1828

ments introduced disorder and dissipation[1] ordered the infantry Soldiers to be paid daily. This arrangement was first extended to Troops in the West Indies, and ultimately by General Order of 24th December, 1824, to the Infantry throughout the Army. At some time subsequent to the year, 1828, the same principle was extended to the Cavalry, and under existing regulations[2] all non-commissioned Officers and men (save the Royal Engineers who are paid twice in each week) are to be paid daily in the *presence of an Officer.*

164. This latter direction that an Officer should be present when the Soldier is paid, represents almost the only relationship in pecuniary matters now existing between them. Upon the Soldier's death, the Officers have to administer his Estate under the Regimental Debts Act,[3] if he has not left assets sufficient for that purpose, the Captain may have to bury him. On desertion, the Captain has to bear some of the expenses of his desertion out of his contingent[4] allowance; and these possible disbursements represent the only pecuniary interest, such as it is, that the Captain now has in the life and good conduct of the Soldier.

No dependence by the Soldier on the Officer in pecuniary matters

165. That no injustice may be done to a Soldier by his Captain without redress, the Articles of War[5] provide that if he thinks himself wronged, he is to complain to the Colonel, who is bound to summon a Regimental Court of Enquiry for the purpose of determining whether such complaint be just. The Queen's Regulations[6] also provide that the General, upon his tour of Inspection, shall afford Soldiers the opportunity of bringing their grievances before him. So long as Command is intrusted to men whose social condition is such as to remove them from all possible temptation of gaining any advantage in the State or in the Army by this exercise of authority or office of mediation, these appeals may be safely recommen'ed by the State, and be con-

Appeal by the Soldier to the Colonel or General.

---

[1] I fear the recent increase of pay, and the settlement of the arrears have added strong proofs that money still leads the Soldier to the same excesses 181 H D, (?), p. 2003

[2] Royal Warrant of February, 1866, par 524, Queen's Regulations, 1868, par 386

[3] Chap X, par 18.

[4] This originated in 1717, but in 1783 it was recognized by Burke's Act See Army and Ordnance Expenditure (1850), p 845   [5] Art 13   [6] 1868, par 198

fidently accepted by the Soldiers; but alter the Constitutional policy as to the Command of the Army,—by taking the Officers —as the "Adjutators" of the Republican Army were taken —from the ranks; and the provisions in the Articles of War and Queen's Regulations now that the pay and clothing come direct from the Crown—might work to the augmentation of discontent. The strikes of labour against capital so rife in Civil[1] life, have since the Revolution been kept out of the Army, but had the Officers and men in the Indian Mutiny sprung from the same Class, might not the Duke of Wellington's warning[2] have been realized and India lost?

166. Further that the account between the Soldier and the Crown may be clearly settled, and the state of it at all times within his own knowledge, the Articles of War direct that every Soldier shall be provided with a Book (familiarly known to the Service as 'Tommy Atkins') to show his age, date of enlistment. and actual state of his accounts; and every Commanding Officer is bound to see that the same is in the Soldier's possession, and properly attended to each month. This system was introduced by the War Office Regulations of the 25th November, 1829, during the time that Lord Hardinge was the Secretary at War.[3]

Account Book 'Tommy Atkins.'

167. No one can doubt that the advantages held out to the Soldier (contrasted with those offered at the period when this chapter opens) are great; and that the labourer has many inducements offered to him to become a well-conducted Soldier. The pay has been largely increased—since Adam Smith[4] found it so far below that of the labourer as to describe "the romantic hopes of a Soldier as making up the whole price of his life;"—but the pay is but *one* item in the account of money spent on the Soldier for the promotion of his comfort, health, and, if need be, his education. Indeed the expenditure on Barracks,[5] Hospitals,[6]

Present advantages offered to the Soldier

---

[1] Report on Trades Unions, 1869 (by Command).   [2] Par 161, *ante*

[3] War Office Circular (289), vol 5 (MS) Regulations, p 231, and see Lord Hardinge, Evidence on Military Punishment, 1836, p 305.

[4] 'Wealth of Nations,' Bk 10, p 186, and see Vol. I., p. 106, and Appendix XXXI As to Army Schools and Libraries, see Chap XXVIII, and Notes thereto.   [5] See Vol I, pp 222, 223, note

[6] See Note B B, on the Army Medical School, and Parl Return, Sess 1869 (431)

Recreation Rooms and Grounds, Libraries, and Sanitary Measures, since the Crimean War, has been vast, and must create in the mind of the recipient of these bounties a strange idea of the change that has been wrought in the Public mind towards him by his having left his former (industrial) occupation for that of a Soldier. Habits of thrift are encouraged by Military Savings' Banks,[1] and "the effects" left by Soldiers on decease show their emoluments are such that they may accumulate Capital with greater facility than others of the class from which they came into the service.

168. The policy of re-engagement, as a necessity, must

Re-engagements of doubtful expediency

therefore admit of question. The expense—the great evil of Mr Wyndham's scheme—has been repeated— if the break made in the Soldier's service enables him to re-engage with a fresh bounty, with allowances for clothing, with a higher pay, and to secure a pension for life. Up to December, 1868, under the Acts of 1847 and 1867, as many as 72,103 men had re-engaged; and the total cost of these re-engagements, in pensions only, taking the chances of life, may be reckoned at upwards of 12,000,000*l*, if the theory and calculations recently put forward be correct.[2]

169 Some persons are found to advocate the absorption of

As to the absorption of the Militia into the Standing Army

the Militia into the Army; and the late Sir Henry Calvert, viewing the matter as an Officer on the Head Quarters Staff, laid a plan before Lord Castlereagh in February, 1809, for turning the Militia into Second Battalions of Line Regiments. No doubt, if the Civil population could be induced to recruit as readily for the Army as for the Militia, and if it were deemed politically expedient to abolish the Command of the Lords-Lieutenant by converting the Militia into the Army, then the proposal might be safely adopted; but these antecedent conditions should not be too readily accepted as true. Moreover the Military power of the country might be weakened[3] and the counterpoise upon which it rests very greatly disturbed by any further organic change in favour of Generals in Command of the Regular Army.

---

[1] Colonel Lenhy's Lecture *ante*   [2] Note T, Appendix
[3] See the Debate on the Militia in 1852

170 Let those who are disposed to place their sole reliance upon a Standing Army as an instrument of National Defence consider the counsel of Lord Bacon,[1] " Walled towns, stored arsenals and armories, goodly races of horse-chariots of war—elephants, ordnance, artillery, and the like—all this is but ' a sheep in a lion's skin '—except the breed and disposition of the people be stout and warlike—nay, number (itself) in armies importeth not much where the people are of weak courage. Therefore," he continues, " let any Prince or State think soberly of his forces, *except his militia* of natives be of good and valiant soldiers; and let princes, on the other side, that have subjects of martial dispositions, know their own strength, unless they be otherwise wanting in themselves. As for *mercenary* forces (which is the help in this case), *all examples* show that, whatsoever Estate or Prince doth rest upon them, he may spread his feathers for a time, but he will mew them soon after."[2]

The Counsel of Lord Bacon

---

[1] In his Essay ' Of the true Greatness of Kingdoms and States '

[2] EXTRACT from the first part of the Arguments against a Standing Army (Oct 1697), ' State Tracts,' vol ii, p 573

"*Difference between a Standing Army and Militia* —There can be no danger from an Army where the Nobility and Gentry of England are the Commanders, and the body of it made up of the Freeholders, their sons, and servants, unless we can conceive that the Nobility and Gentry will join in an unnatural design to make void their own Titles to their estates and liberties, and if they could entertain so ridiculous a proposition, they would never be obeyed by the Soldiers, who will have a respect to those that send them forth and pay them, and to whom they must return again when their time is expired   For if I send a man, I will as surely chuse one who shall fight for me, as a mercenary Officer will chuse one that shall fight against me, and the late Governments are witnesses to the truth of this, who debauched the Militia more than ever I hope to see it again, and yet durst never rely upon them to assist their arbitrary designs   as we may remember in the Duke of Monmouth's invasion, their Officers durst not bring them near his Army for fear of a revolt   nay, the Pensioners' Parliament themselves turned short upon the Court, when they expected them to give the finishing stroke to our ruin "

CHAPTER XVI.

ON THE APPOINTMENT AND DISMISSAL OF OFFICERS.

1. THE Constitutional Policy pursued by the Crown in officering

The Army under the command of men of high social position

the Army has been invariably shown in the appointment of Gentlemen to command, and that policy has hitherto received confirmation in Parliament. The danger of entrusting an Armed Host to the will and pleasure of one man in time of Peace has hitherto been recognized in Parliament, and this evil can by no better method be averted than that of having the Officers, subordinate to the Commander-in-Chief, drawn from that social class the members of which are more likely to lose than to gain by Military Aggression.[1]

2. Therefore, as a rule, while the rank and file of the Army

Two distinct classes in society have composed the Army

have been recruited from the lower stratum in society, the Command of these men has been intrusted to the higher class, and never—save at the time of the Commonwealth—to any other, or even to that class without that substantial guarantee for their good behaviour which the Purchase-system gives to the Civil Community.

3. The reasons for this marked distinction between the

The reasons for this arrangement

two classes of which the Army is composed are not difficult to assign. Some, however, more readily than others present themselves to notice: one is founded on Economy, and another on Political Expediency; upon the apprehension which the Crown and Parliament would feel, should the Command of the Army—having once been—again be placed in the hands of needy soldiers of fortune.

4. At the time of the Revolution, the Army was in the

---

[1] Sir Robert Walpole, 8 P. H, p. 902, the first Lord Holland (H Fox), 11 ib. p 1287, Charles J Fox, 30 ib, p 172, Lord Folkstone, 32 H. D (O S.), p. 968, Lord Palmerston, 16 ib. (2), p 191.

hands of the Peers of the Realm,[1] and its political *inaction* was mainly attributable to this fact, and to another, viz, that the Commands of the several regiments or companies were held by Noblemen and Gentlemen of great estate and influence, well affected to Constitutional Government then to be inaugurated under the auspices of the Prince of Orange.   An instrument, more or less political,[2] the Army can never fail to be, and nothing more strongly marks the difference with which Parliament has from time to time regarded the political importance of the Army and Navy than the contrast presented by its legislation; on one class of statutes,[3] we find aliens or foreigners *excluded* from the *Army*, on another that they are *encouraged* to enter the *Navy*, by the reward, for a short service therein, of all the rights of English Subjects, save those of serving in the Army or Privy Council. Therefore the persons to hold command, or to enlist in the ranks of the Army, have been scrutinized with far greater jealousy by Parliament than ever fell upon any officer or seaman of the Royal Navy.[4]

[Side note: At the Revolution, Army in the hands of the Peers of the Realm]

5. An Army of some strength was deemed essential by the Government of each monarch succeeding Wm. III., but as the expense of it was stoutly opposed in Parliament, the patriotism of many persons found development by serving in Military command without pay, and in some instances by raising regiments or companies at their own individual cost. The pay of both officers and soldiers was fixed at rates notoriously low for their service, and as, in the case of an officer, a commission had to be purchased—it was clear that few men, but those of independent means, could possibly follow the Military profession on the pay or rather the balance of it over the interest of money paid for the King's commission.[5]

[Side note: The economy of this arrangement.]

---

[1] Chap. V, par 1; Chap. IX, par 1.

[2] In the year 1713 a scheme appears to have been formed by the Duke of Ormond for compelling several Officers, favourable to the Hanoverian Dynasty, to sell their Commissions, and for the Government to advance 10,000*l* to assist persons favourable to the Pretender to become the purchasers   The scheme is said to have failed from the inertness of the Earl of Oxford in not providing the money.—*Lord Mahon's* 'History of England,' vol i., p. 77, and see *post*, Chap XVIII., par 14.

[3] See 1 Geo. I., c. 4, and 13 Geo. II., c 3   [4] Chap. XVIII, par 50 and notes.

[5] Chap VI., par. 27; Chap. VIII, par 98

6. These facts have been within the knowledge of Parliament upon the discussion either of the Army Estimates,
This policy has been known and confirmed by Parliament. or of any proposal to increase the pay of the Army;
but though the *Soldier's* pay has been increased, that
of the Officer remains nearly the same, or nearly so, as
in Wm. III.'s reign—an intimation, by inference, that Parliament has never desired to attract to the Command of the Army,
men dependent upon their pay either to hold their place in
Society as gentlemen or the higher social status assumed by
Military Officers over the Civil community [1]

7. Unquestionably the duties that every officer should be
competent to discharge, call for high mental and
The discharge of the various duties of an Officer require a liberal education physical endowments. "From the moment," [2] said
the late Duke of Wellington, "at which the Officer
enters Her Majesty's Service till he attains the rank
of General Officer he must be prepared to serve in all
climates, in all seasons, in all situations, and under every
possible difficulty and disadvantage. There is no peace or
repose for him; excepting that some powerful party in the
State should think that his services can be dispensed with· in
which case he will be put upon half pay.

8. "While thus serving, he must perform all the duties required of him. He must be, in turn, gaoler, police offi-
As a subaltern and regimental Officer cer, magistrate, judge and jury. Whether in peace or
in war, in the transport in charge of convicts, or acting
as a magistrate, or sitting in judgment, or as a juryman, or
engaged in the more immediate and more active duties of his
profession in the field, either against the internal rebel or the
foreign enemy, he must never make a mistake, *he must never
cease to be the Officer and the Gentleman,*—cheerful, obedient,
subordinate to his superiors, yet maintaining discipline and
securing the affection and attachment of his inferiors and of the
soldiers placed under his command upon his scanty pay and
allowances,—so small in some instances (that of the Lieutenants
and Ensigns of the three Regiments of Foot Guards as one) as not

---

[1] As to increase of pay, 11 Parl Hist , p 1403, 14 ib., p. 901 , 88 H. D (3),
p 866, 139 ib (3), pp. 276, 431

[2] Extract from the Duke of Wellington's 'Memorandum upon Military Governments,' 7th March, 1833 (at p 277 of ' Report on Army and Navy Appointments,
1833 ')

to be sufficient to pay for his lodgings. He has but little hope of promotion unless he can purchase it; nor of rest nor relief from his exertions, if he should obtain it, as long as he has health and strength to serve

9. "When he attains the rank of General Officer he must be qualified to fill the post of a Governor of a Province As a General He must manage a Legislature; he must perform the Officer most difficult and arduous functions of Government which can be entrusted to any Subject, if he means to be a candidate for the situation of Colonel of a Regiment. If stationed in the neighbouring part of the United Kingdom (and even in England), the General Officer must take upon himself, and must be qualified by education, prudence, and other qualities, to perform the duty of the Lord-Lieutenant of a County or of several Counties, to correspond with the Magistrates, to superintend and direct their exertions."

10. Every officer, for the discharge of his duty, holds a Royal Sign Manual commission[1] under the counter- A Commis-sign of a Secretary of State. The form of this strument of instrument has been nearly the same, whether the ment. authority granting the Commission was the Speaker[2] of the House of Commons or the Crown: thus the military Commissions granted by Parliament, and signed by the Speaker at the Commonwealth, upon the nomination of five Commissioners appointed by the House of Commons, ran in substance as follows:—"That the officer was to take the charge and care of the Regiment (or company), duly exercise the inferior officers and soldiers in arms, keep them in good order and discipline, and the officer himself was to observe and follow such orders and directions as he might from time to time receive from Parliament, and obey the superior officers of the Army according to the Discipline of War, in pursuance of the trust reposed in him, and of his duty to the Parliament and Commonwealth." The forms of Commissions at present in use will be seen in the Order of Council of 7th day of June, 1862.[3]

---

[1] Beak v Tyrrell, Carth, p 31, 5 Esp, p. 233, 2 Camp, p. 513, 25 Vic., c. 4.
[2] 7 Com Journ, pp 648, 649, 674   [3] Note U, Appendix

11. Under this retainer from the Crown, the officer, like the
soldier, knows of no other authority to command his
obedience—save the Sovereign and his superior officer
—acting according to the rules and discipline of War.
To compel his obedience to those orders the Mutiny
Act and Articles of War have been sanctioned by Parliament, and
every lawful order—or rather every order not obviously improper or contrary to law[1]—must be obeyed (if possible) under
the penalty of arrest by the Commanding Officer and trial by
Court-martial.[2]

What duties this retainer obliges the Officer to discharge

12. What are the limits of obedience, is a question not removed from the region of doubt; though, according to
the high authority of Lords Mansfield and Loughborough, the duty of a (combative) officer is that of
implicit obedience.[3] This view was adopted by the military
authorities in Captain Atchison's[4] case, which became the subject of much controversy in Parliament.

What are the limits of obedience?

13. There the officer had remonstrated against an order to
fire a salute in honour of a Saint of the Roman Church,
and for this act of disobedience was dismissed the
service by the Duke of Wellington, as the Master-
General of the Ordnance. In the discussion, the Military and
Civilian members took a widely different view of the obligation
resting on Captain Atchison to obey *such an order.* "Every
military man was bound,"[5] according to the theory of one member
of the House and of the Army, "to obey the orders given to
him, let those orders be what they might. It was perfectly
true a man might receive an order which his superior officer
was not justified in giving; but it was the man's duty to obey
that order in the first instance, and afterwards to obtain redress.
Much stress had been laid on this being a *religious ceremony*, but
it was a *Military duty* he had been ordered to perform. Any
military man who was ordered to fire a salute, or to perform
any duty in his military capacity, *whatever the nature of that*

As to a combatant Officer, implicit obedience

---

[1] Reg *v* Trainer, 4 Fost & Fin, p 105. May the Officer require an order to
be authenticated by writing, and, if so, what order?—Warden *v* Bailey, 4 Taunt
Rep, pp. 76, 137; H D (3), pp. 736, 758, 763.   [2] Chap VIII, par 41
[3] Sutton *v* Johnston, 1 Term Rep., p 546   [4] 24 H D (3), p. 815
[5] 19 H D (3), pp 785, 786

duty might be, was bound to perform it; and if he refused, he would be liable, and ought, of course, to be brought before a proper tribunal to judge whether he had acted correctly or incorrectly in so refusing"

14. Obviously this was the view taken by and upon which the Duke of Wellington and Commander-in-Chief *Disputed in* acted; but it was not unanimously accepted even by *Parliament.* the military members of the House. Sir De Lacy Evans protested against the rule so laid down, and deemed the case one of arbitrary and unjustifiable exercise of authority. " He doubted very much the legality of the proceeding, as he did not find that the petitioner had disobeyed any orders that had been given, but had merely stated his religious scruples, which his superior officer bowed to," Sir Robert Inglis, Mr O'Connell, and Mr. Shiel also spoke against the decision [1]

15. Probably the difficulty of finding the true limit of Military authority will not be lessened when due weight *Confirmed in* is given to the evidence laid before the House of *the Harwich* Commons in the Harwich election petition On be- *1866* half of the sitting member—a Major in the Royal Artillery, who was in the receipt of *civil* pay for a duty in the Civil branch of the late Ordnance Department, viz., the superintendence of the Royal Small-Arms Factory—a distinguished member of the House and of the Cabinet, on being asked as a witness, whether a military officer might be required to do *any civil* duty, replied that he was "bound to obey *any* order, even for superintending a *cotton factory*." [2]

16. That an Officer should not be withdrawn from the list of Effective Officers without a previous communication *Consequences* to the Commander-in-Chief that his services are re- *of the doc-* *trine of ab-* quired by the Secretary of State upon Civil duties, *solute obedi-* *ence, when* the rule of courtesy would suggest; but to lay down *extended to* *Civil employ-* the doctrine of implicit obedience to this extent, that *ments* all his subsequent services are rendered *by order* of the Commander-in-Chief may lead to very dangerous consequences. In the employment of Military Officers in financial duties many

---

[1] 19 H D (3), pp 789, 790, 30 ib, p 130; 88 ib, p 318   [2] P. 11

objections suggest themselves; but none so formidable as this, that *by order* of the Commander-in-Chief it would be their duty to superintend the Treasury, or indeed any Civil Department of the State—possibly the conduct of Parliament.[1]

17. When doubt arises, it is a matter of no little moment that the duties of Officers and Soldiers should be limited to those of the Military profession,—viz., to fight the battles of their country; but if these are enlarged or changed, to govern or administer in Civil employments, much confusion may arise. "Our Constitutional liberties will be found to be best maintained by each department of the Government keeping within its own proper limits assigned by law."[2] Not only is it the duty of an Officer to obey a direct command from his superior officer, but in many instances, without any command, to act from a sense of professional duty.[3] If he be thus misled as to the limits of his professional duty, and in error obeys an order which in the opinion of the Superior Courts is plainly not within the scope of the Commanding Officer's authority to give or of his to execute, the officer would be responsible for all the consequences criminal or pecuniary resulting from his acts. "If the Military should injure ordinary Citizens in their persons or in their property, not even the Command of a superior officer would justify a Soldier in what he does unless the Command should turn out to be legal and within the limits of the protection given by the Mutiny Act and Articles of War."[4]

The Officer may be misled and have to answer for consequences.

18. It is from these considerations that the "Regulations and Orders issued with Royal approbation by the Commander-in-Chief, to be strictly observed on all occasions throughout the Army,"[5] become important, for they warn all "General Officers employed on the Staff, and Commanding Officers of regiments and corps, that they will be held responsible that the instructions issued from time to time in local commands, or to brigades or

Royal Orders and Regulations for the Government of the Army

---

[1] See the Debate on the Pay of Staff Officers, 14 P. H, p. 909 *et seqq.*

[2] Willes, Just., in Dawkins *v.* Rokeby, 4 Fos. & Fin., p 831

[3] See the judgments of Sir W. Erle, in Tobin *v.* the Queen, 16 C B., p. 352, James Seddon, Admiralty and Ecclesiastical Cases, p. 62.

[4] Willes, Just., in Dawkins *v.* Rokeby, 4 Fos. & Fin., p 831 [5] Edition 1868

corps, for the general maintainance of discipline and for the details of interior economy, are in strict accordance with these Royal Regulations." So long as these orders and regulations—or even Royal Warrants countersigned by the Secretary of State—are confined in their operation to the Military, as distinguished from the Civil Community, no confusion will arise; but if they order or direct—coercive measures against the Civil Community in times of social or political disturbance, or—any interference in matters of finance, then—in these respects—they might be held to exceed the limits of Military authority, and be considered open to serious Constitutional objections.[1]

19. The issue of these orders is within the cognizance of Parliament, because attention was called to the subject in the House of Commons in 1815.[2] Of course, they are to be upheld under the Constitutional principle, that the Command of the Army entirely belongs to the Crown, other than as that authority is regulated and controled by the Mutiny Act and other statute laws. If cited before a Court of Law, these orders must be proved in the "same manner as any other fact; for the judges are not bound to take any judicial cognizance of them.[3] Where proved—and within the scope of the prerogative powers of the Crown—they are accepted by the Court as conclusive evidence of the rules and orders of the Military Forces.[4]

Authority for their issue—and Orders to be proved.

20. At home, instructions may be sought for from the responsible Ministers of the Crown, but *abroad* each superior Officer is supposed, as against aliens, to carry with him such a portion of Sovereignty as may be necessary to provide for the exigencies of the Service on which he is employed.[5] *There* he must act on what he deems to be the scope of his duty as a Military Officer; and if he ignorantly or wantonly exceeds his authority as defined by the legal tribunals of the Realm, he must bear the penalty. Of course if his acts be adopted by the Crown they become Acts of State, and the Officer indemnified by Parliament.[6]

His authority on Foreign Service.

---

[1] Chap XVII, pars 55 to 64, *post*   [2] 31 P D. (O S.), p 832.
[3] Bradley *v* Askew, 4 Bar and Cr., pp 304, 305, Tobin *v* The Queen. 16 C B (N S), p 320   [4] Laurie *v* Banks, 4 K & John, p 447
[5] The 'Rolla,' 6 Admiralty Cases p 366
[6] Chap XXV., pars 5-13, and Buron *v.* Denman, 2 Exch. Ca, p 189, Rogers *v.*

21. The countersign of the Secretary of State, originally intended as a mere authentication of the Royal Sign Manual has since become a Constitutional guarantee As the Military Establishments are approved by the Secretary of State, he is responsible, in regard to the pay of the Army provided by Parliament, first, that there is an existing vacancy to which the Officer can be appointed without exceeding the supply voted ; secondly, in the case of the first appointment, that the Officer is legally qualified to enter the Military Service of the Crown ; and, thirdly, in the case of promotion, that he is fairly entitled—having regard to his own qualifications, and the claims of others—to the advancement in rank.[2]

The Countersign of the Secretary of State as a responsible Minister

22. Military Commissions[3] have uniformly been prepared and issued out of the department of a Secretary of State :[4] prior to 1855 out of the Home Office for regiments on the Home, and out of the Colonial Office for regiments on the Colonial or Foreign Establishments.[5] But as only regimental Commissions con-

Commissions to regimental Officers and Letter of Service to General Officers.

Rajendro, 13 Moore, P C , p 240 , E A C v the Queen 2 Ell & Blac., p 913 , Keighley v Bell, 4 Fos. & Fin , p 763   The Crown, as represented by the Sec of State for War, defends officers and soldiers in the civil courts only where the act complained of was one sanctioned by competent authority, or clearly within the prescribed course of duty (Circular 799.) See a discussion on defending officers at the public cost, 24 H D (2) pp 1368-95, and Return (608 of 1830), vol xxx Parl Pap , p 211   The Government prosecuted General Picton (Cox's Instit., p 424), and General Wall (Appendix LXIII) The Government defended soldiers for shooting at runaway prisoners of war (Bk 724, pp 19, 63, and 258)   The Sec of State, in 19 How Stat Tri., p 1415, and in Dickson v Peel, 3 Fos. and Fin , p 527   A Lord-Lieutenant in Dickson v Combermere, but not the Colonel of the Militia regiment. The members of a Court of Enquiry appointed, and whose report had been adopted, by the Crown. A General-in-Command, in Dawkins v Rokeby, 4 Fos & Fin , p. 806, and in Keighley v Bell, ib p 768, but not where sued for slander as a witness. A Captain of a man-of-war, in Buron v Denman, 2 Exch Ca , p 159   A Colonel commanding-in-chief, in Bradley v. Arthur, 4 Bar. & Cr , p 293 , and in Nelson s case for the Jamaica command in 1866.

¹ Chap. XXV , par. 1.
² See 14 Parl Hist , p. 909
³ The fees on Military Commissions were abolished in pursuance of the recommendation of the Naval and Military Commissioners' Report, 1840, p. 42, and War Office Circular, 873, of 12th November, 1840, old practice, see B O I (1702), p 870, *et passim*   ⁴ 6 & 7 Wm and Mary, c. 8, sec 5
⁵ Army and Ordnance Expenditure, 1850, p 2

ferred a special duty, the employment of an Officer as a General[1] was always authenticated by a Letter of Service issued to him by the Secretary at War acting on the orders of the Cabinet[2]

23. The office of the Secretary at War was, in regard to Commissions, one only of Registry;[3] that the Pay Lists of

---

[1] *Extract from Report* (1810) *on Naval and Military Inquiry*, p. xxxi. .—

"The Commission Books of the War Office have been examined, to ascertain when the rank of General was first conferred by commission. These books are probably defective, but the first record found therein is in June and July, 1685, when James II made two Major-Generals and five Brigadiers In March and April, 1689, William III made Brigadiers In the same year the Duke of Schomberg, one of those transferred from foreign service, was made General of all the Forces, but this was for special employment. On 18th June, 1689, the Earl of Craven was made Lieutenant-General of all the Forces, and on 4th July, 1689, Count de Solms was made General of Foot Three Lieutenant-Generals were made in 1690 and 1691, six Lieutenant-Generals in 1694, and seven in 1696

"The Peace of Ryswick followed in 1697, and a general reduction of the Army was the consequence

"In March, 1701-2, John Earl of Marlborough was made Captain-General and Commander-in-Chief, and in June, 1702, Prince George of Denmark was made Generalissimo of all the Forces

"The rank of General was then assigned to a particular arm of the service. The Officer was named General of Horse, or General of Foot, or for a Special Service

"As an instance of the latter, the following may be stated :—

"On the 13th of January, 1715, Thomas Whetham was made General and Commander-in Chief in Scotland, in the absence of the Duke of Argyll and Lord Stair, and on the 23rd March in the same year, although holding the rank of General in Scotland by an earlier commission, the same General Whetham was made Major-General, subsequently a Lieutenant-General, and finally a General of Foot ⁺

"In October, 1735, George II introduced the rank of Field-Marshal into the service He created two—the Earl of Orkney and the Duke of Argyll and Greenwich

"This is the first approach to the general promotions of the present time that can be traced, for on the same occasion there were made two Generals—one of horse the other of foot—10 Lieutenant-Generals, 24 Major-Generals, and 39 Brigadier-Generals. In 1739 the two Generals of 1735 were made Field-Marshals

"The appropriation of the Generals to horse or foot continued till the reign of George III. On the 4th March, 1761, the rank of General was given to the eight senior Lieutenant-Generals, without any subjoined distinction of service as had previously been the case "

[2] Bk 723, p 243, 28 H D (O S), pp 251, 664

[3] The fee for the entry was one day's pay, 1689, August 20, Mis. Bk., p 135

⁺ Royal Warrant as to how to be paid, Mis Bk 526, p 37

the various regiments might be properly authenticated, and
the claims arising against the public from an Officer's
service might be known and recorded. In earlier
periods than the present century, the greatest confusion[1] prevailed from Commissions[2] not being entered with
the Secretary of War; and the Articles of War[3] have for many
years imposed a punishment upon any Officer for his omission
of this duty. To facilitate public business, the Annual Army
List was first established and published by authority of the
Secretary at War in 1754;[4] and on the 10th January, 1767,
a notice was issued from the War Office[5] that all the Commissions should for the future be regularly noted in the 'London
Gazette' by the Secretary at War.

Registry of Commissions in Secretary at War's Office

24. The selection of persons to fill vacant Commissions has
been made either by the King or Military Officers
acting under his authority. In raising new levies by
the agency of a nobleman or gentleman (to be Commissioned as Colonel of the newly-raised regiment),
the appointment of some or all of the Officers was
conceded to him as part of the consideration to be
given for his trouble and expense in raising Recruits. In such
instances the Secretary of State satisfied himself, either by
direct inquiries or through the Secretary at War, of the loyalty
and good character of the several nominees, but did not
enquire into the arrangements—either of purchase[6] or of
supply of men to the regiment—which the several nominees
had made with the Colonel[7] before the latter sent in their
names for the various Regimental Commissions.

Selection of Candidates for vacant Commissions; made by the Crown or Military Officers acting by delegation

---

[1] 2 Com Rep. (1747), p. 93, War Office Order, 9 February, 17⅘; Mis Bk., p 5
[2] Commissions were made liable to stamp duty by 5 & 6 Wm III., c. 21, and 55 Geo. III , c 184   [3] Art. 48 of 1673, and Art 27 of 1869
[4] 6th Rep of Military Enquiry (1808), p 507   [5] See Gazette of that date
[6] As to the sale of Commissions by the Colonels of different regiments, see 2 Com Rep (1746), pp. 75, 93, *et seqq*   Lord Palmerston Memorandum, p 40
[7] The Board of General Officers recommended the continuance of the rank of Major, 1772, May 19, Mis Bk , 1768, p. 601. The rank of a Fort-Major was settled in 1720, Mis Bk 523, p 58

25 When the Army went abroad, the General in Chief Command had either authority by his Commission—as in the Case of the Duke of Argyle[1] in 17$\frac{4}{4}$ to appoint Officers—or he had blank Sign Manual Commissions given to him with a less formal authority to fill in the names of persons to act as Officers for the supply of vacancies.[2] The same practice extended even to the Army in Ireland until the Union, after which those appointments came under the control of the Horse Guards. The General's power to fill in vacancies was limited to the Commission of a Lieutenant-Colonel.[3]

[margin: Appointments to vacancies abroad made by Commander-in-Chief]

26. With regard to the Army in Great Britain—and more especially the old regiments making up the 17,000 or 18,000 of which the Establishment usually consisted[4] prior to the appointment of a Commander-in-Chief in 1792,—the selection was made by the King as the Commander-in-Chief.[5] Upon these appointments a controversy not unfrequently arose whether the Crown was bound to act upon the advice of any responsible Minister, or at liberty to exercise this power absolutely according to the will and pleasure of the Sovereign for the time being   "The King," said the first Earl of Chatham,[6] "has at present an absolute power of preferring or cashiering the Officers of the Army. It is a prerogative he may make use of for the benefit or safety of the public; but, like all other prerogatives, it may be made a wrong use of, and when it is, the Minister is responsible to Parliament." When

[margin: Appointments to the Army at home made by the King]

---

[1] Extract from the Duke of Argyll's Commission to Command in Chief in Spain, 21st Feb, 17$\frac{4}{4}$ —

"And that our said Forces may not be unsupplied of Officers to command them whilst they are abroad in the said Service, We do give you power and authority in case of death, removal by Sentence of a Court-martial, or the quitting of any of the present Officers of the said Forces, to supply the said vacancys by such persons as you shall make choice of for that purpose, who are to be acknowledged and command in their respective stations as if they had received Commissions from Us, and to continue in their said employments till Our further pleasure be known   And for executing the several powers and authorities herein expreat this shall be your Warrant "—W. O Com Bk , 1714, p 7

[2] 16 H D (2), p 468. See Report of General Officers, 4 February, 1705-6, as to vacancies unfilled in the West India Regiments, the General in Command having died with 50 blank Commissions in his possession   Mis Bk , 519, (Ink) p 49

[3] Duke of Wellington's Memorandum, p xxxvi , Nav and Mil Promotion, 1840.

[4] Appendix M.   [5] See Chapter XXVI., *post*   [6] 12 Parl. Hist , p 560.

this speech was delivered, in 1743, the principle for which this great Statesman so earnestly contended was disputed—it is now a dogma of Military administration.[1]

27. But purchase of Commissions, adverted to in a previous paragraph as practised in raising new levies, was, in

Purchase System

old established Regiments, carrie l out under the direct sanction of the Crown, given originally in each particular trans- action, and ultimately under general Regulations, with a tariff of prices That the Purchase System should have continued in the Army[2] after the Revolution is not to be wondered at, when the circumstances out of which it arose are taken into considera- tion ; at no period of our History have the Military appointments of the Crown been wholly free from a regular or irregular system of purchase

28. But before entering upon the consideration of the Purchase System in the Army, it may be convenient to state what

The rule of Law applica- ble to the sale of any public office.

is the constitutional rule applicable to the purchase of any Public Employment· and this probably cannot be better done than by using the words of Lord Lough- borough in the leading case of Parsons *v* Thompson.[3]—"The question whether an office is saleable or not is a matter of Public Regulation, and not a question for a Court of Law. If by Public Regulation, right or wrong, certain offices are saleable, the Court cannot set aside the transaction for their sale, the Court is not to make the regulation. Whether by the General Police of the Country an individual office is saleable or not is not a matter of Law." In fact, the Crown (as representing the public interests) is supposed to allow a fair income for the office,[4] taking *all* the conditions attending it—the *purchase* at a fixed price being *one*— into consideration ; when, therefore, a retiring Officer accepts the

---

[1] Bush *v* Harrison, 5 Ell and Blac, p. 351; Dickson *v.* Lord Combermere, 3 Fos & Fin , p 584; and Dawkins *v* Rokeby, 4 ib , p 806. Military Organiza- tion Report, 1860

[2] Before the Standing Army was in existence, the Commons, in 1641, resolved that the buying and selling commands of Forts, Castles, and places of trust, was a great evil , see 2 Com Journ , pp 438, 444   [3] 1 H Blac , p 326

[4] That it actually does so, see par. 37 *post*

regulated price from his successor, no wrong is committed against the latter or against the Crown making the Regulation. If, on the contrary, an office be not saleable, or saleable only at a stated price, the wrong — moral and political — commences when these regulations are evaded by deceit or untruth

29 No doubt when—as in the Army of the late East India Company—a purchase bonus was not—but a pension on Breach of the
Law—a
fraud. retirement was — allowed, a double fraud might be committed by paying an Officer for premature retirement, so as to gain his rank in succession.[1]   " If," said Chief Baron Pollock, " a person is to be remunerated for an office so that he can afford to buy out the holder and create a vacancy (which possibly even by merit he may be entitled to fill), he is paid more than is necessary for the Public Service, and all that he takes beyond that, and by which he is enabled to remunerate the person who retires from the service, is really taken from the Public without adequate consideration.   So also with respect to the person retiring; the Government pays to this man, when he retires, a certain pension or allowance in proportion to his pay. If he would not receive it—except for the premium offered to him to induce him to resign—the consequence would be that he would remain in the Service of the Government ; but if some one gives him a sum of money to retire, then he resigns, not because there is a proper reason for his retirement, but for the pecuniary consideration."

30. When Charles II., for reasons to be afterwards explained, sanctioned the sale of Commissions—and that he did Purchase
System ap-
proved by
Chas II. so his Warrant[2] of 1683-4 is abundant proof—it was entirely within the scope of the Royal Authority to do so, and the sale so sanctioned was legal[3]   The action of Parliament had left the question as to the sale of Military Commissions open to the Regulation of the Crown, for though by the 5 & 6 Edward VI , c. 16, the Sale and Brokerage of various offices had been prohibited, the Act had no application to those held in the Military Service

---

[1] Græme *v.* Wroughton, 11 Exch Ca , p 155.   [2] Appendix XVII
[3] I have recently found this entry, which has hitherto escaped notice —" Whitehall (Xber), 1684   His Majesty was this day pleased to declare that he will not for the future consent to the selling any Military employment" (Mis Bk p 31)

31. The legality of the Purchase System was upheld by the
Lord Chancellor Nottingham in the Court of Chancery,
Legality upheld in 1682 as early as November, 1682, upon a case the facts of
which appear to have been these:[1] In consideration of a bond
for 200*l.* a Captain in bad health resigned his Commission,
and recommended the Lieutenant as his successor. As the
Captain had *freely*[2] received his commission, the Duke of
Ormond refused to sanction the sale or to accept his resignation, whereupon the Lieutenant filed a Bill in the Court
of Chancery to be relieved from the payment of the bond.
His counsel "insisted on the disadvantages that would attend
the countenancing of such bargains, and the discouragement
it would be to Gentlemen that they should not by their continued service raise themselves to preferment; but must either
buy the same, or suffer others to jump over their heads, let
them have never so well merited preferment;" but these arguments were not suffered to prevail, and the bond was upheld.

32. The Policy of William III. was for a limited period
directed against the Purchase System[3] By his War-
From 1693 to 1701 declared against by Parliament. rant of July, 1693,[4] he required each Officer and soldier,
before he was entered on the muster roll, (1) to swear
that he had not been paid either present or gratuity for obtaining
his employment, and (2) that if it ever after came to his knowledge that any friend had given such, then that he would immediately discover the same to His Majesty. The assistance
of Parliament was also obtained by the Mutiny Act of 1695,[5]
"to prevent the great mischief of buying and selling military
employment in His Majesty's Army," and a Clause imposed
the first part of the oath on every officer (omitting[6] soldiers);
but the Act did not otherwise prohibit the Purchase System.

---

[1] Berresford *v* Dove, 1 Vern. Rep., p 98   See also Ive *v* Ash, Prec in Chan.,
p 199
[2] This rule continued to prevail for many years   See *post*, par 47, and note
[3] Vol. ii State Tracts, p 186
[4] Dutch Mis Bk., 1672 to 1695, p 95, and Army Purchase, 1857, p 335
[5] 6 & 7 Wm III., c. 8
[6] So recently as 1790, the places of men in the Regiment of Life Guards were
regular objects of sale, see Flarty *v* Odlum, 3 Term Rep, p. 683.

33. In the year 1701 this Clause[1] was withdrawn from the Statute Book, and the Purchase System re-established under Regulation. Now it should be borne in mind, that at the time and for many years after the Purchase System in the Army originated, there was no other provision either made or sanctioned by the State for the future maintenance of an Officer retiring from age than the sale of his commission. All that he could obtain was a permission from the Crown to retire, and to receive a bonus from his Successor for his retirement.

From 1701 the sale of Commissions re-established as a provision on retirement.

34. The Regulations of Queen Anne were directed—not to the price—but to limit the right of sale for proper objects Thus the Royal Warrant[2] of 11th May, 1711, to correct the irregularities and abuses in the Army —after having prohibited General or other Officers who had sold their commissions from acting as Officers or rising in the service, by the 5th Clause went on to provide, (1) "that no commissions in Our Armies be sold but by Our approbation under Our Royal Sign Manual, (2) that no Officer have leave to sell his commission who has not served *twenty* years, or been *disabled* in the service, (3) unless upon some extraordinary occasion, where We shall think fit for the good of Our service to allow thereof;" plainly shewing that the object of the sale was to make a provision for a deserving Officer on retirement; the test of merit being twenty years'— or being disabled on—service.

The Regulations of Queen Anne as to the Purchase System of May, 1711.

35. In September following, for the reasons set out in the Royal Warrant,[3] this Clause was relaxed; and commissions under the rank of Major were made saleable without special sanction or reference to age or service, that regimental debts might be paid, the widow and family provided

Amended and provisions extended Sept, 1711

---

[1] A sale of a Commission in the Marines, made when this enactment was in force, was held by the Lord Keeper (Sir Nathan Wright) to be legal, and his decision is said to have been affirmed by the House of Lords It should be noticed that the Marines were not liable to the Mutiny Act at the time of the purchase. Ive v Ash, Prec. in Chan , p 199

[2] Army Purchase, 1857, p. 336, and Mis Bk 520, p 50.

[3] Mis Bk. 520, p 52.

for, and promotion in the Regiment accelerated. The reasons for these alterations being thus set out:—

"1st That it will be a very great hardship where subalterns by misfortunes in recruiting have mis-spent the levy money, and outrun themselves so as not to be able to continue in the service; and if they cannot dispose of their Commissions, the debt must fall on the Regiment.

Regimental Debts.

"2ndly. In some cases, Officers die and leave great families in a starving condition, where it would be great charity to permit the Commission to be disposed of, so as that the successors may give some consideration or allowance for the support of the widow and children; and

Provision for Widows, &c.

"3rdly. Where Colonels shall judge it for the good of the service to desire Officers from other Regiments, who are better qualified than those next in rank in their own, the matter might be easily compromised, and the said Officer satisfied with a small acknowledgment, as well as Our service better answered."

Promotion

36. In the following reign, though distasteful to the Sovereign,[1] a more complete system was established. In the first place, by Warrant[2] of February, 1719-20, a tariff of prices for every Commission was fixed by the Crown, and any Officer desiring to retire by sale was required to lodge a declaration at the War Office that he was willing to resign his Commission for the sum named in the Tariff. The appointment of the successor was not to be influenced by the seller, but left wholly with the Crown. Permission was also given to a purchasing Officer to sell in the same manner the Commission which he was relinquishing. A due succession in rank was secured by a provision that a Commission could only be sold to an Officer next in Rank—as a Colonel's Commission to a Lieutenant-Colonel, and so on through all Ranks to the lowest, as that a Lieutenant's could only be sold to an Ensign. To prevent inexperienced Officers rising to Rank too rapidly, the Regulation provided that no officer above a Lieu-

Regulations of Feb, 1719-20

tenant should be admitted to purchase any higher rank, unless he had served ten years as a Commissioned Officer.

37. In the next place, that the Regulation price only should be taken, and that the purchasers should not set up a right against the Crown to sell again, were the objects of the Royal Warrant of the 8th of March, 1721-2, which provided : — that the Colonel[1] in recommending the Officer for a first Commission, or for promotion, should give a certificate in writing, under his hand, to the Secretary at War "that the Officer doth purchase according to the Regulation price, and no higher ; " and further, " that the person so purchasing, or promoted by purchase, should have no pretension or title thereby to sell again hereafter."

Regulations of 8th March, 1721-2

38 The Colonel was the agent for the receipt of the purchase money, over which the Crown, acting upon the advice of the Board of General Officers, and through the Secretary at War, exercised complete control— appropriating the amount in part to the payment of Regimental (and even doubtful debts), and the residue to benefit the wife of the Officer, if deserted by him.[2] Whether a Commission should or should not be sold has always been left to the absolute discretion of the Crown ; and, after a sale permitted, the purchase money has, in many instances, been considered as a donation from one to another servant of the Crown, or directed to be paid into some other channel which the King thought would be more for the honour of the Service.

The Crown exercised an absolute control over the Purchase Money

39. The prices of Commissions have from time to time been altered and re-adjusted by the Crown, as the circumstances of the Service seemed to require. In 1765 a doubt appears to have been raised whether the Commissions in regiments serving in and out of Europe were of the same value, or ought therefore to be sold at the same price. To consider this, and to re-adjust the prices of all Commissions, were matters referred to the Board of General Officers, who, after " duly weighing the pay

A.D 1766

Prices re-adjusted by Board of General Officers and their Report confirmed by the Crown

---

[1] *All* first appointments originated with the Colonel in former times, and this custom still prevails in the Guards   [2] Appendix XCIII

and rank attendant on the several Commissions," declared their opinion " unanimously that the price should be uniform, whether the Regiment was serving in or out of Europe ; but that if any deficiencies should arise on the sale of Commissions of Cornet, Ensign, or Second-Lieutenant, the loss should be borne by the selling officer." This Report was accepted by the King on the 8th February,[1] and confirmed by the Royal Warrant of 10th February, 1766,[2] which ordered, "That in all cases where We shall permit any of the Commissions to be sold, the sum received shall not exceed the prices set down in the said Report."

40. Hitherto the sale of full-pay Commissions only had been sanctioned, but by the Regulation of 14th August, 1783, exchanges from full to half-pay, and *vice versâ*, were provided for by a Schedule showing the value, and the difference in value, between each full and half-pay Commission. If an officer on full exchanged to half-pay, receiving the difference, he made a partial sale of his Commission, and could not return to full-pay; if he exchanged, without receiving the difference, he could return to the Service. The Regulation also provided that on applying for leave to buy or sell, the officer should state, on his honour, that the Regulation price and no more was given ; and that if his word as an officer and gentleman were forfeited he would, according to the rules of the Service, be liable to be dismissed from the Service.[3]

Regulations of 14th Aug., 1783.

41. Upon the appointment of a Commander-in-Chief in 1793, the Purchase System came more immediately under his direction, and by a Circular Letter of 31st November, 1793, to Colonels of Cavalry Regiments from the Adjutant-General (written by direction of Lord Amherst), the price of Cornetcies was reduced to 700 guineas, and remained so reduced by virtue of this order without the official knowledge or sanction of the Secretary at

Establishment of the Reserve Fund by the Commander-in-Chief in 1793

---

[1] See Lord Barrington's Letter set out in extenso at p xxv of 'Report of Naval and Military Promotion,' 1840   [2] Army Purch Rep , 1857, pp 322-335   [3] See 10 H D. (2), p 1040, and par 121, *post.*

War[1]   The Reserve Fund may be held to date from 1795, and consisted of the proceeds of the sales of Commissions made for other purposes than to benefit the retiring officer, and thrown into one common Fund held by the Agents (Greenwood & Co.) under the orders of the Commander-in-Chief These purposes, five in number, were stated to Parliament in 1807 to be as follows :—

1stly. For gentlemen, who, having raised regiments for Rank or Commissions under Letters of Service, had not received Commissions in those regiments because the men had been drafted or disbanded.

Objects of it

2ndly. For the owners of Ensign's Commissions unsaleable in time of war, and therefore filled in by the Commander-in-Chief without purchase.

3rdly. For the owners of Regimental Staff[2] Commissions the sale of which had been prohibited, including Army Chaplaincies valued to the Colonel at 700*l.* in Cavalry and 500*l.* in Infantry.

4thly. For the Half-pay Fund, which needs a separate explanation.

5thly. For the Widows and Relations of Officers and Private Soldiers.

42 The origin[3] of the Half-pay Fund dated from the reduction of the Army in 1802.   At that time the purchase money paid for a Commission appears to have been considered by the Commander-in-Chief as a charge bearing interest upon the Vacancy.[4]   In the case of Cornetcies or Ensigncies, a reducible Lieutenant was put in to the vacant Commission at the lesser pay until a vacancy in the Lieutenant's arose, and the Cornetcy or Ensigncy was sold as a half-pay Commission, viz., by a sale, and by reduction to half-pay on the next day.   During the Peace these sales were readily effected—as the Commission rose in value according to the date of the vacancy, the purchaser obtaining rank and half-pay from the date of reduction; but at the outbreak of the War they be-

Origin of the Half-pay Fund

---

[1] Letter to General Marquis Townshend and endorsement thereon of 1806.

[2] The sale of Staff appointments was not sanctioned by the Crown in Jan 1760   Lord Palmerston's 'Memorandum,' Appendix CXXIX.

[3] 62 Com Journ , p 931

[4] The same principle continued in force till about 1857

came unsaleable, and the owners appealed to the Commander-in-Chief for relief. This was proposed to be given by valuing vacant Commissions at a computation, say twelve years' purchase for Commissions in the Guards, and ten years for the same in Infantry regiments, and charging these amounts on this fund— called the Half-pay Fund—to be raised by sale of full-pay Commissions as they fell vacant to the Crown without purchase.

43. "This measure" was represented by the Commander-in-Chief as "attended with the following good consequences:—

Benefits of the Commander-in-Chief's arrangements

"1st. It retained many meritorious officers in the service who would otherwise have been reduced.

"2nd. It not only lessened the Half-pay Establishment, but prevented many persons from purchasing Half-pay Commissions as *Annuities,* which was a common practice at the end of every war.

"3rd. By paying off the claims, the persons who were entitled to the value can now only receive the interest on the regulated price from the day it became vacant to the period he is paid the value fixed on his Half-pay Commission; whereas, had it been sold, the purchaser must have received *Half-pay* from the date of his appointment.

"This," the memorandum went on to state, "is attended with another advantageous circumstance, as it is understood that all savings from Half-pay are applicable to the Compassionate Fund, on which there are many demands, and from which grants are made from time to time by the Secretary at War, under whose control that fund is placed.

"Besides the Commissions sold to pay off the claims alluded to, His Royal Highness has also directed that sums of money arising from officers repaying the difference they may have received on retiring to Half-pay when they cannot find others to exchange with them, should be applied to this fund; thereby enabling many officers to regain their rank who from temporary distress or other circumstances had been under the necessity of retiring to Half-pay.

"Another addition to this fund arises from Commissions being sold for their full value, although the person retiring receives only the money actually paid for his Commission."

44. That the scheme was designed by the Commander-in-Chief from the most praiseworthy motives, may be admitted. Such arrangements were, however, beyond the province of his office, and therefore it was not long before the House of Commons resolved to address the Crown for information.[1] In answer to their Address, Returns were laid before the House, showing that from 1795 to 1807 the sum of 61,610*l.* 4*s* 8*d.* had been raised by sales, and disbursed by the Commander-in-Chief for the purposes set forth in the previous paragraph.

Such arrangements beyond the province of the Commander-in-Chief, and an account required by the Commons

45 One of the Returns[2] had reference to a supposed saving which was not in any way connected with the other matters, but gave a *result* which in the ordinary course of Army Administration would have occurred upon the breaking out of war, viz., the absorption of half-pay officers into the full-pay Establishment. To assume, as the second paragraph in the Memorandum of the Commander-in-Chief did, that it then or ever was the right of a half-pay officer by reduction to remain for life as a pensioner or annuitant upon the State was then, as it would be now, an assumption against Parliament made without any warrant from the previous history of the question.[3] No doubt, full-pay was provided instead of half-pay on the Army Votes; but the Return, omitting this fact, valued 3019 Commissions against the public at the estimated sum of 2,217,229*l*, and represented this amount as saved to the public by the special and novel arrangements of the Commander-in-Chief.[4]

Return as to Half-pay savings of doubtful value

46. The Establishment of the Reserve Fund, which still exists, and can be traced in various Parliamentary Papers[5] to the present time, has, to some extent, changed the basis on which the Purchase System originally stood. It is a fund created by the purchasing Officers of the Line (for the Guards' Reserve Fund is kept as a distinct fund) for the benefit of non-purchasing officers, limited, as it might be thought to be, to those of the Line.

The Reserve Fund has varied the principle on which the Purchase System was established

[1] 9 H. D (O.S), p 756, 62 Com Journ, p 656   [2] Ib., p 940.
[3] Note G, Vol I, p 369   [4] See also par 83 *post*   [5] Note V, Appendix.

47. The relative positions of these two classes would appear

Contrast between Purchasing and Non purchasing Officers.

to be this :—The Purchasing Officer, if under sixty years of age,[1] and in good health when the application is made, has a *primâ facie* claim upon the Crown to permit him to dispose of his Commission, provided he has not forfeited it by misconduct. The Non-purchasing Officer can only ask, under the same conditions, for permission to sell in respect of services performed (which Queen Anne's Regulations put at twenty years, or disability contracted in service). If the sale be allowed, each officer receives such a sum as the Crown sees fit to allow him, and the residue (if any) is placed to the credit of the Reserve Fund. The selling officer never gets from the fund more than the regulation price of the Commission; a non-purchaser has from it not necessarily its value, but a bonus —after the rate of 100*l* a year for Foreign, and 50*l*. a year for Home service—towards the value.[2] An officer having bought one or more of his steps, may have this bonus added to the purchase money paid by him, until the value of the regulation price of his Commission sold be realised. It is obvious, therefore, that the position of the two classes is widely different. The purchasing class, in the best aspect of their case, receive back their purchase money. The non-purchasing class retire with a bonus provided for them by the other class. In fact, while the one class sink an annuity—in the interest of purchase money—so long as they serve the Crown, the other, in the same period, save the annuity and also gain a bonus from the fund on retirement.

48. The purchasing officers of the Line have, however, done

The purchasing Officers of the Line have provided a bonus on retirement to Officers in other branches of the Service

more than provide a retirement for the non-purchasing officers of their own branch of the service—they have given a retirement to officers of the non-purchase corps, and to others who have never (as a class) been contributors. Their fund has been diminished on

---

[1] Finance Committee, 1828, p 217

[2] It is difficult to say when this bonus system was first adopted The original rule was that no Officer should sell unless he had purchased (Lord Barrington's Letters, 8th April, 1766, and 11th May, 1768, Vol iii 'Junius's Letters,' p 441), but in 1840 some years'service—as twenty for a Field Officer or Captain, fifteen for a Lieutenant, and twelve years for an Ensign—gave a claim to sell (see p 285 of Report, 1840) The present practice is explained in 'Report on Reserve Fund, 1867,' p 2 *et seq*

several occasions since its institution in 1802, by direct payments to the Exchequer, and by indirect payments to the same account, that is, by buying up the Commissions of officers whose half-pay has thus ceased to be a charge upon the Treasury.[1]

49. The value paid or to be received (whichever may be the basis of calculation) by officers for their Commissions, is a guarantee to the State given by them (as a class) for their due obedience to discipline. The possible loss of a pecuniary bonus is a serious consideration to many, and influences, as daily experience proves, the conduct of some whom no other consequence would so strongly control[2] The total pecuniary value of this Guarantee even at regulation price is estimated in millions sterling, but it must never be overlooked that *beyond* this amount many officers have a large capital invested, in prices extra the regulation, which is purely artificial, and therefore *wholly dependent* for its realisation upon the maintenance of the very high social and professional character of those particular regiments to which they belong. Whatever might be the result to the Civil community —as interested in the strict discipline and consequent good conduct of the Army in time of peace—in releasing the officers from this Guarantee it is not possible to predicate, for in England we have no political experience, except a very rueful one, of the consequences that may result to our Constitutional liberties, from the existence within the Realm of a Standing Army, officered by men having, as a class, no property qualification whatever.[3]

The value of Officers' Commissions a guarantee to the State for good discipline

50. It can scarcely be doubted that since the regulations of George I., and the establishment of the Militia[4] on its present basis in 1756, the Officers of both the Regular and Militia[5] Services have in a large proportion possessed a property qualification. For the five years prior to 1787 all the promotion in the Army went by purchase,[6] and the principle of a property qualification was affirmed in 1786 by the express declaration of Parliament.[7] This rule, distasteful to the

Property qualification possessed by Officers.

---

[1] Note V and V*, on the 32 and 33 Vic, c 31.   [2] Chap VIII, par 77.
[3] Chap II, pars. 31 and 32.   [4] Chap III, par 30
[5] The Property Qualification for the Militia was abolished by 32 Vic., c. 13,
sec 3   [6] 26 Parl Hist, p 1283   [7] Chap III, par 41

Crown as limiting its Patronage, has been deemed to be a protection to the people, inasmuch as its existence places it beyond the power of the Crown to select mere mercenaries for Military command.

51 The late Duke of Wellington—whose experience in Military Administration has been deliberately ignored since 1854 — maintained, "that the description of gentlemen of whom the Officers in the Army were composed made, from their education, manners, and habits, the best Officers in the world, and that to compose the Officers of a lower class would cause the Army to deteriorate."[1] That this mainly resulted from the Purchase system he took some pains to explain on several occasions, and the late Lord Palmerston (whose long experience at the War Office gives additional value to his opinion upon this subject) entertained the same views. "He thought it was desirable to connect the higher classes of society with the Army; and he did not know any more effective method of connecting them than by allowing members of high families who held commissions to get on with greater rapidity than they would by mere seniority. Unless the vacant Commissions were given to new Officers, the connection between the Army and the Upper Class of society would be dissolved, and then the Army would assume a very dangerous and unconstitutional appearance It was only when the Army was unconnected with those whose property gave them an interest in the welfare of the country, and was commanded by unprincipled military adventurers, that it could ever become formidable to the liberties of the nation."[2]

The high character of the Officers of the Army

52. It was intended by Queen Anne's Regulations of September, 1711, to accelerate promotion; and though the possession of capital in this,—as in every other profession,—must always give the owner a comparative advantage, yet this advantage is not so exclusively enjoyed by the monied class in the Army as in other professions, for both

Promotion to the Officers accelerated

---

[1] Evidence before Finance Committee, 15th April, 1828, p 3, and Chap VI., par 27.

[2] 16 H. D (2), pp 191-3, and see Lord Dalhousie's Speech (1869), p 195, H D (3), p 1460, quoting Marshal Canrobert's opinion

the purchasing and non-purchasing Officers have the general stream of promotion accelerated by the purchase system.

53. The abolition of the system would entail a vast expenditure upon the Public, and no inconsiderable loss to the purchasing Officers. It was given in evidence before the Army Purchase Commissioners, in 1857,[1] that the total of the regulation prices reaches several millions sterling; but that if this sum were paid to the purchasing Officers, they would lose in prices—extra the regulation—a sum exceeding the total of the Regulation prices.

Cost of abolishing the System of Purchase

54. The loss to the non-purchasing Officers would be the abolition of the provision now made for them on retirement by the purchasing Officers. An equivalent from Parliament would be needed by, but could not be confined to *one* class,—indeed it must be extended to all Officers in the Service equally. Both classes would lose the acceleration of promotion, which the present system procures, unless, to accelerate promotion, the State made rules for a compulsory retirement, or the Officers adopted the purchase system in another form, viz. by the plan of contributions to senior Officers for their retirement which has been held by the Court of Exchequer to be absolutely illegal.[2]

Consequences to the officers.

55. Looking at our experience on this subject, it may fairly be a matter of doubt whether it would be possible by mere legislation—without breaking up the Regimental system, on which the welfare of the Army depends—to eradicate the purchase system from the Army in time of Peace; but before such a measure is adopted, and in considering the expediency of attempting it, it may be well to look at all the surrounding circumstances. In the Army of the East India Company the whole system of purchase was illegal, and in the Army, including (I fear) Staff appointments in the Militia, there has been a fraudulent system,[3] which no provisions of the Legislature have been able to suppress. It is not unreasonable to suppose that the clause in the Mutiny Act of 1701 was withdrawn because it was found to be inexpedient or ineffectual, and in the year 1711, shortly after the issue of

Whether the attempt at abolition would be successful

---

[1] Mr Hammersley's Evidence, p 49   [2] See Note V*, Appendix
[3] Bk 721, pp 135-145, 183

Queen Anne's last Regulations, it was necessary to issue a public notification against illegal agency.[1]

56 To insure only the regulation price being paid, and to

Present Statutory enactments disregarded limit the purchase money to that amount, oaths and declarations of honour have been insisted upon, evaded, and then withdrawn.[2] At the present time, under the enactments of the 49 Geo. III.,[3] it is a misdemeanour—

1. To buy or sell any office, save Commissions in the Army sold at Regulation prices. 2. To receive money or reward for negociating such sales. 3. To open or establish any house or office for the business thereof. 4. To publish or advertise any name or form for such business. 5. To buy or sell any Commission for any sum, save that named as its price by His Majesty's Regulations. The only lawful sales are of Army Commissions at Regulation prices, and all buyers or sellers of Army Commissions at any price *over and above* the Regulation price, or all buyers or sellers of Militia or Volunteer Commissions at ANY price are guilty of a misdemeanour, and are punishable by indictment in the Queen's Bench for every such offence,[4] and yet, if rumour speaks truly, the provisions of this statute are openly evaded.

57. No doubt it is quite possible for the Crown, without the

Scientific Corps or Local Corps no criterion of the Purchase System purchase system intervening, to require, as in the case of the Royal Navy—or of the Scientific Corps, or Local Colonial Corps,[5] such educational qualifications before, and such irksome duties after admission, that one or both of these requirements place a Commission only within the reach of men of high mental culture and capacity, or beyond the desire of ordinary candidates. In the Royal Navy both these restraints—though unequally—exist. "The Great *Admiral*," wrote Adam Smith,[6] "is less the object of Public admiration than the Great *General*, and the same difference runs through

---

[1] Appendix XCIV.

[2] 49 Geo III, c 126, Illegal Sales, 12 H D (O. S), p. 357; 13 ib, p 822.

[3] 10 H.D. (2), p 1040

[4] Reg v Armstrong, November, 1859; Eicke v Jones, 11 C.B (N S), p 633.

[5] As to the twelve non-purchase Corps, see G O, 19 Feb, 1862, in Appendix XCV. [6] Bk. 1, chap. 10, pp 180, 181 (edit 1828)

all the inferior degrees of preferment in both Services. By the rules of precedency a Captain in the Royal Navy ranks with a Colonel in the Army, but he does not rank with him in the common estimation." So long as the Army is held in high estimation, and a Commission confers a social status to wealthy aspirants, to stop the purchase system in time of peace will be found impossible.

58. Before quitting this branch of the subject it may be well to notice that the interest which an Officer has under his Commission has never been deemed "pro- perty" by the Courts of Law.[1] "Apart from the Officer named in it, the Commission is nothing; in the hands of a stranger it is mere waste paper, conferring neither authorities nor rights. The depositary could not go to the War Office, and claim either whole or half-pay, for military pay is not assignable Neither could he give anybody else a right to receive pay. The most alarming consequences might follow," said the late Sir Thomas Plumer, whose words are used, "if it were to be held that an Officer might pledge or mortgage his Commission; and it is of importance that it should be generally understood, that this Court will not entertain the doctrine, that an Officer, while he remains in the Service, can lawfully part with his Commission by way of pledge or mortgage, or that he can, by so doing, give the depositary any rights with respect to it"[2] And this view was concurred in by the late Lord Gifford. "It has," he said, "been settled in various cases, on the ground of public policy, that the pay of an Officer cannot be assigned by him to any other person. It is equally clear that he has no right to alienate his Commission; though, if he wishes to retire from the Army, he may, under special circumstances, and through the medium of the Commander-in-Chief, obtain the leave of the Crown to sell out at the Regulation price.

No property in Commission

[1] In Parliament some have formerly contended for appointments in the Army being deemed Property, but the difficulty of governing the Army under such a theory would be immensely increased, 12 Parl Hist pp 560, 561, 14 ib, p 642. As to actions for damages on this theory, see Freer v Marshall, Dawkins v. Rokeby, Same v Paulett.   [2] Tur. & Rus, 1823, p 468.

Undoubtedly, therefore, the Commission itself was not alienable." [1]

59. After the sale has been sanctioned by the Crown, then *But in the proceeds of sale of the Commission* the proceeds of the sale may (subject to the claim of regimental debts, which have a priority) be paid according to the order and direction of the Officer previously given; and no doubt, in anticipation of the sale being sanctioned on the application of the Officer, the proceeds of it are often made the subject of legal arrangements by mortgage or marriage settlement. [2]

60. The purchase system had the express sanction of Parliament in the year 1809, [3] but no guarantee has ever *No ful' Parliamentary guarantee for the return of the regulation price.* been given by the House of Commons for the return of the Regulation price to any purchasing Officer. In the case of Officers killed in or after the war with Russia qualified guarantee was given, with the sanction of Parliament, for the return of the Regulation price; but in this instance it was rather the exchange of this value paid at once, for the Pension or Allowances that would otherwise be paid to the Officer's widow or children. [4] For all that the Warrants of 15th June, 1855, [5] and 1st March, 1856, provided for, was to give to certain near Relatives the option of receiving the Regulation price (paid by the Officer for his Commission) in lieu of the benefits of Pension, Compassionate, and other Allowances, that under the existing Warrants such relatives might be entitled to from the death of the Officer. Nothing could be received except the money actually paid in conformity with the Regulation, nor could the recipients claim even this without previously showing their title to the Pension or Allowances, in lieu of which a compensation was to be paid in purchase money. Further, it was a condition that the Officer should have been killed in action, or have died within six months of wounds

----

[1] Tur & Rus., 1823, p 474.

[2] Laurie v Banks, 4 Kay and John., p 145, Lestrange v Lestrange, 13 Bea Rep., p 281, Webster v Webster, 31 ib, p 397, Somerset v. Cox, 33 ib, p. 634 Buller v Plunkett, 1 John and Hem, p. 441, Marsh v. Peacocke 9 Jur (N S), p. 788   [3] Par 54 *ante*

[4] See 138 H D (3), pp 2260-2310, 139 ib, pp 536-1280. 142 ib, p 1514.

[5] The arrangement was made in the heat of the Russian War, and is most incongruous

received in the face of the enemy. The money paid under this Warrant was provided for by Parliament, and was not taken out of the Reserve Fund.[1]

61. But in a recent instance, where the Royal Warrant of February, 1860, reduced to future purchasers the prices of Cavalry Commissions, the Crown gave to the existing purchasing Officers, as a class, an express guarantee for the repayment to them of the old Regulation value, out of the Reserve Fund. So also when it was proposed to re-form the Military Train as a non-purchase Corps the retiring Officers who had purchased were held entitled to receive the full Regulation price of their Commissions out of the same Fund, although their Commissions were not sold for the benefit of the fund.

Crown guarantee for return of the regulation price.

62. Whether the Officer shall be appointed or promoted in the Guards or Line with or without purchase, is a matter to be determined under certain regulations— by the Commander-in-Chief,[2] with the sanction, express or implied, of the Secretary of State. But the practice in the present, as distinguished from the last century is, that he must be *qualified* for the duties of the office to which he is appointed or promoted.

The promotion by purchase or non-purchase decided by the Commander in-Chief acting under regulation

63. With regard to first appointments, for many years it was not unusual to appoint the orphan children of deserving Officers to Commissions, and to order the pay to be disbursed for the family or child as a provision from the Crown.[3] That this system was known to, if not approved by, Parliament is evidenced by the 1st and 2nd rules relating to half-pay, enacted in 4 Geo I, c. 5, sec. 18,[4] and it continued in practice until the late Duke of York assumed the command of the Army, when not only did he refuse to make such appointments, but superseded many Officers who were children or boys at school.[5]

Infants were formerly appointed to Commissions as a provision.

64. Since the year 1796 the age of Candidates has varied

[1] Purchase Commission Report, 1857, p 139, and Note V*, Appendix
[2] Organization Report, 1860, pp x, xi   [3] Appendix XCVI
[4] Vol I., p. 373   [5] Naval and Military Promotion Report, 1840, p. xxxii.

from sixteen years upwards, according to the exegencies of
Parentage and qualifications of candidates for first appointments. the Service. But the practice of requiring Educational qualifications in the Candidates was first established by the Duke of Wellington in 1849, and continued by his successors in the office of Commander-in-Chief until the Council of Military Education was appointed in 1857.[1] Under the present arrangements, Commissions are given first to the Queen's and Indian Cadets educated at Sandhurst,[2] then, to stimulate other candidates to a successful career of study, "a certain number without purchase are left open for Competitive Examination, conducted under the direction of the Council,"[3] and the residue of vacant Commissions go by purchase[4] to persons passing a qualifying examination.

65. In each subsequent step, up to and inclusive of the
Qualifications for promotion Rank of Captain, the Officer must pass a qualifying examination;[5] and if he desires to serve on the Staff of the Army or of his Regiment, he must qualify for either appointment by passing through the Staff College, or Schools of Musketry or Gunnery, and obtaining a Certificate of his proficiency.[6] The promotion of Officers in the Guards and in the Line is *not* regulated by seniority—though the principle of selection, when brought to bear against an Officer apparently of equal merit to the one promoted, not unfrequently gives rise to controversy in Parliament, and (recently) in the Courts of Law.

66. But there is one method of obtaining advancement
Political influence to be excluded in the Army—apart from all others—which Statesmen of all shades of Political opinion in previous periods of our history have agreed in reprobating, and to which it would be most dangerous—with the vast comparative increase in the Number of Officers in the present compared with the last century, and yet most easy under our present arrange-

---

[1] 1st Report (1860), p 4   [2] Note W, Appendix.   [3] Note X, Appendix
[4] The extent of this patronage will be seen from these returns —5554 first appointments were filled up between 1853 and June, 1859, of these 1996 by purchase, and 3558 without purchase (Organization Report, 1860, p 603) 4003 between 1st January, 1860, and 30th June, 1867, of these, 3167 with, and the residue without purchase (Report on Reserve Fund, 1867, p 53)
[5] Queen's Regulations, 1868, p 43   [6] Ib, pp 57-60.

ments [1]--to recur, viz., the Political Influence of Military aspirants Such a system would—if the independence of the Commander-in-Chief be destroyed and the influence of the Minister be paramount—make the Army both useless as a National Defence and dangerous as a Domestic Police, destroy its efficiency as a Military Body, but resuscitate it as a great Political Machine to aid, and then destroy, the House of Commons [2]

67 An Increase to the Army—comparatively small—was opposed in the last century—mainly on these grounds, that the Army being political, the Officers were promoted not for their Military efficiency, but for their Parliamentary influence. *Evils of this experienced*

68. "No man," said the Duke of Argyll in the Debate of 1740,[3] "will labour to no purpose, or undergo the fatigue of Military vigilance without an adequate motive. that no man will endeavour to learn superfluous duties, and neglect the easiest road to honour and to wealth, merely for the sake of encountering difficulties, is easily to be imagined. And therefore it cannot be conceived that any man in the Army will very solicitously apply himself to the *duties* of his *profession*, of which, when he has learned them, the most accurate practice will avail him nothing, and on which he must lose that time which might have been employed in gaining an *interest* in *a borough*, or in forming an alliance with some orator in Parliament. To gratify the leaders of the Ministerial party, the most despicable triflers are exalted to an authority, and those whose want of understanding excludes them from any other employment are selected for Military Commissions" *(1) Inefficiency in the officers.*

69. "To obviate those dangers from the Army," said Lord Carteret,[4] "which have been so strongly and justly represented, it is necessary, not only that a legal subordination to the civil authority be firmly established, but that a *personal* dependence on the Ministry be *taken away*. A Minister who distributes preferments at his pleasure may acquire such an influence in the Army as may be employed to secure himself from justice by the destruction of liberty." As to the argument that the country was safe because *(2) The power of the Ministers would be in the Army and Commons united*

---

[1] See Chap XXVI, and Memorandum of the Duke of Wellington in Appendix CXLVII.   [2] Chap. XXVI *passim*   [3] 11 Parl Hist, p 903   [4] Ib, p 925.

the officers were gentlemen, Lord Talbot replied[1] that, "None but gentlemen can injure our liberties, but that *while* the posts of the Army are bestowed as rewards of *Parliamentary* slavery, gentlemen will always be found who will be corrupted themselves, and can corrupt a borough—who will purchase a vote in the House, and sell it for military preferments. By the posts of the Army the *Parliament* may be *corrupted,* and by the corruption of the Parliament, the *Army* be *perpetuated.* Those who are the warmest opponents of the Army, apprehend not any danger from their swords. but from their votes."

70. Throughout the century the same political influence prevailed, and even upon the appointment of Lord Amherst as Commander-in-Chief in 1793, the evil was rampant. "At that time very little was given by Lord Amherst, but the promotions in the Army were given almost entirely for *political influence,* and I know that was extremely against his opinion, and repugnant to his feelings. I can state one very remarkable instance, which is within my own personal knowledge. One of Lord Amherst's Aides-de-Camp asked for his promotion and was refused; he asked a second time, contrary to my advice, and contrary to the advice of his brother Aides-de-Camp, and was again refused; and we wondered Lord Amherst did not speak more harshly to him than he did. He then persisted in asking for it again; and I remember he came out much distressed from Lord Amherst's room, saying he had been again refused, and that he had been reprimanded; and he had pressed it in such a way, that I and my brother Aides-de-Camp told him we wondered Lord Amherst had had not removed him from his Staff. However, he said he would get it, notwithstanding the refusal he had met with, and he did get it through one of the Ministers"[2]

71. These evils were felt when the Government was rather Monarchical than Parliamentary, the influence of the Crown not being always that of the Ministry, but

A.D. 1792

Officers appointed by political influence, not professional merit.

Large increase of the Army led to the separa-

---

[1] 11 Parl Hist, pp 917, 918

[2] Evidence of Sir John Seabright, M P (who was Aide-de-Camp to Lord Amherst on his appointment as Commander-in-Chief) before the Select Committee on Army and Navy Appointments, 1833, p 157.

after the adoption of Popular Institutions to ally the Army so closely with the fortunes of any Political party as to give up to the Ministry all the Military patronage, would be to form an alliance between Parliament and the Army identical in its nature with that existing in Charles I's reign, which destroyed the Public Liberty. Therefore with the progress of Parliamentary Government, and the augmentation of the Army, these evils increasing became apparent, and hence arose the necessity for removing the patronage of the Army *from* the *Parliamentary* Officer—the Secretary at War— to the hands of a *Non-political Officer*—the Commander-in-Chief.[1]

tion of Administration from Command.

72. As to the Scientific Corps of the Army—the Royal Engineers and Artillery — the qualifications being of the highest order (and the same remark applies, in degree, to the Medical Staff) the purchase-system does not exist, and their promotion is by seniority. The Education[2] given by the State after the appointment of these officers ought to—as it does generally—insure professional services of the highest value to the Crown, and whenever the Officers of these Corps break down and fail in health, their claims to half-pay ought probably to stand on a more liberal footing than is applied to the purchase corps. The Scientific Officer has devoted his life exclusively to a technical education for the service of the Crown, and he has not a bonus provided for him out of the Reserve Fund upon retirement[3] His responsibilities are individual, and much higher than those of Officers in the other branches of the Service, and besides the dangers incident to every combatant in the Field, he has the wear and tear of a highly intellectual employment[4]

As to appointment and promotion in the scientific corps.

73. With regard to all Commissions issued by the Crown,

---

[1] See the subject further considered, Chap XXVI., pars 4-10.

[2] See Notes Y and Z, Appendix

[3] Since the above paragraph was written Parliament has provided for their retirement by Statute, Note V*, Appendix

[4] The Administrative Corps, whose duties are civil, have so recently been commissioned, that they are scarcely within the scope of this Chapter. The case of the Army Chaplains will be dealt with in Chap XXVIII, *post.*

the rule of the Common Law is, that they are determined by the death of the Sovereign.[1] To prevent the inconvenience that would result from the operation of this Rule, Statutory provisions have been made at various times: those relating to Military Commissions being found in the 1 Vic. c. 31. Under the provisions of this Act, upon any future demise of the Crown, all the Commissions in the Army and Royal Marines continue in force " until cancelled by direction of the succeeding Sovereign."[2]

By the death of the Sovereign all Commissions expire unless continued by Statute.

74. Subject to this rule, the obligation which a Commission lays upon the recipient is to serve the Sovereign for life, or until it is the pleasure of the Crown to relinquish the services of, or to dismiss the Officer. It is clear that no officer has the right to resign, and therefore, until his resignation is accepted by the Crown, he continues amenable to all the consequences of omitting to discharge the duty of an officer under his Commission.[3]

The officer obliged to serve for life unless the Crown accep's his resignation.

75. So long as he retains his Commission, he is entitled either to full or half-pay, or some other non-effective allowance[4] at the discretion of the Crown. For his efficiency as an officer on full pay, the General in Chief Command of the Army is responsible to the Crown. For his meritorious service to entitle him to half-pay, the Secretary at War formerly was, and the Secretary of State now is, responsible to Parliament. That the Crown has the right at any time, and without any reason assigned, to dispense with the services of any officer, and gazette him out of the Army, will be considered hereafter. At present I propose to deal with the questions relating to the Prerogative of the Crown

The Commission entitles him to full or half-pay at the discretion of the Crown

---

[1] Vane's Case, 6 How State Trials, p 121

On the Demises of Geo III, see 57 Geo. III., c. 45, of Geo IV., see 1 Wm IV, c, 6, and of Wm. IV, 1 Vic, c. 31. As to Colonial Governors, see 1 Wm. IV, c 4, and 9 & 10 Vic., c. 91 As to Irish Commissions, see 1 & 2 Wm IV., c 2 Militia Commissions are saved by the Militia Acts on the Death of the Lord-Lieutenant

[2] The subject discussed in 35 H. D (O. S.), p. 880, 36 ib., p. 3, 87 ib (3), p 122, 88 ib (3), p 288.

[3] Parker v. Clive, 4 Bur Rep. p 3422; Virtue v Clive, ib, p 2472, Attorney-General v Rowe, 1 Hur. and Colt, p. 46

[4] As to these, see Note G, Vol I, p 366

in placing an officer on half-pay, and to the practice of the Secretary at War's office on matters arising upon the administration of half-pay and other non-effective allowances.

76. In the first place it is clear, beyond controversy, that an officer has no absolute right to be placed on the half-pay list, or to remain there. "Every officer distinctly understands, or ought to understand, when he enters the Army, that he has no right whatever to claim to be put on the half-pay list. The public may put a certain number on the half-pay list, if they choose, at the end of the war, to discontinue their services. If the public dispenses with the services of officers, they are bound to provide for them, but no officer entering the Army has a right to claim to be put on the half-pay list, otherwise it will be easily seen how many will enter for the purpose of purchasing an annuity."[1]

An officer has no right to be put on half-pay

77. The transfer from the effective to the non-effective Establishment could only be made by Royal Sign Manual, countersigned by the Secretary at War, and thence arose his responsibility to see (1st) that no officer was improperly placed on the Half-pay List, or (2nd) remained on it when either His Majesty had active employment for him, or the officer had done anything to forfeit the confidence of the Crown.

The transfer to Half pay made on the responsibility of the Secretary at War.

78. A feeling of benevolence would naturally incline the General in Command to send an officer—whose faults arose from simple inefficiency as an effective officer—on to the half-pay List rather than out of the Army. The duty of the Secretary at War commenced where the responsibility of the General ended, namely, on a notification from the latter that, in justice to His Majesty's service, he could no longer retain a particular officer upon the *effective* strength of the Army.

Tendency of the Commander-in-Chief to send inefficient officers on Half pay

79. It was then the duty of the Secretary at War to examine the claim of the officer, either directly or through the recommendation or otherwise[2] of the Commander-in-Chief, to be placed on the non-effective list on

Secretary at War's duty to see that the claims of officers are meritorious.

---

[1] Lord Panmure, Purchase Com., 1857, p. 216   [2] See 139 H D (3), p. 1208

retired full or on half-pay. If the officer could not be employed because of mental or physical incapacity (not contracted on service), or because of his misconduct, he had *no claim* to half-pay; for, to entitle him to come upon the list, his service must have been *meritorious*, the Secretary at War having to satisfy himself that every candidate was a fit object of public *bounty*, either from wounds, length of service, or reduction.[1]

80. To place an officer on half-pay because, from misconduct

To place other than a meritorious officer on Half pay a gross abuse Lord Macaulay's testimony

or other similar cause, the Commander-in-Chief cannot permit him to serve the Crown *on active* service, is an obvious violation of the principle on which the half-pay list was established, and could not, if practised, be too severely censured; " that,' said Lord Macaulay emphatically, "is not the principle on which the half-pay list of this country has been established, nor one to which, while I remain Secretary at War, it shall be perverted. The half-pay is no punishment. It is given as a reward for past services, and partly as a retainer for future services. Why should it be made a reward for *offences*, or should a retainer be given to a man who had proved himself entirely *unfit* for the service of the Crown?"[2]

81. Lord Macaulay was only upholding the established

Other testimony to this effect.

rules of his office when he thus addressed the House of Commons; and another Secretary at War, the present Earl of Dalhousie, stated the rule on which he had acted in this matter in even plainer language. " I held myself accountable to Parliament for every Officer that I put upon half-pay, because I considered that I was burdening the State with a certain fixed annuity which I had no right to do, except upon grounds which I could properly defend. Propositions were occasionally made to me when officers had got into scrapes, and had proved themselves to be unworthy of remaining with their Regiments, to put them on half-pay; but my constant answer was a direct refusal to do so, as I did not think that the half-pay list was a *refuge*

---

[1] Formerly Regiments put Officers on retired allowance by deduction from their own pay 5th April, 1705, see War Office Letter Bks. (133, p 204), and in 1776 (p. 25), vol. 11. of Mack Cold. Guards, p 305

[2] 56 H. D. (3) 1397, see Sir Robert Peel's Concurrence in 57 H D, p. 32, and Earl Grey's, 56 ib., p 1401.

for those who had *misconducted* themselves, but a *boon* to be given to *meritorious* officers, either after long service or under some peculiar circumstances, such as ill-health, produced by long service. I would not open the half-pay list to any but those. I believe Mr. Sidney Herbert always acted upon the same principle, and that was the reason why we had to show to the House of Commons every year a very large reduction in the half-pay list."[1]

82. The Control held by the Secretary at War as the Parliamentary Officer was supreme.   Lord Fitzroy Somerset, as Military Secretary, stated, before the Select Committee on Army and Navy Appointments, 1833,[2] that the practice, being objected to by the Secretary at War in 1830, had been abandoned by the Commander-in-Chief as an unfair proceeding towards the public. Speaking before a Committee of the same House in 1850, on Army Expenditure, the same witness stated that for many years there had been no case of an Officer being placed on half-pay for misconduct   The circumstances suggest the remark that if, in each case of half-pay, the particulars of the Officer's services were laid on the table with the Estimates, as the practice is upon the grant of a good-service pension, all doubt upon the propriety of these grants would be removed. *This control of the Secretary at War had stopped the Commander in-Chief making these recommendations*

83. Although the rules thus laid down are incontrovertible, yet a right to half-pay was formerly admitted to arise upon the *grant* of a Royal Sign Manual Commission, "the service of a single day giving a claim to it as complete as the service of "twenty years."[3] The grant would, however, be only[4] for a short period, or until previous employment, as an officer, upon reduction, has no right to remain on the list. It is the duty of the Secretary at War to urge his employment upon the Commander-in-Chief on any vacancy arising in the *No right to remain thereon*

---

[1] Evidence before Army Purchase Commission, 1857, p 216.

[2] Lord Raglan's Evidence, 1833, 1850, pp 159, 221

[3] 3rd Report of Finance Com., 1828, pp 5, 219

[4] War Office Reg , 1848   As to retirement on half-pay after three years' service, see 42 H D. (3), p. 1407.

effective establishment, and to purge the half-pay list as much as possible.[1] The half-pay officer not obeying the command of the Crown to return to *active* service is liable to be struck off the list, and to forfeit his commission. If he enters into Holy Orders he is required to sell.[2]

84. Formerly,[3] that is from 1698 to 1785,[4] the Commons looked after the half-pay List themselves by having it laid on the Table of the House, with the Estimates. Then this duty was delegated to their officer—the Secretary at War—and, if needed, abundant proof might be offered of this duty resting upon *him*, as distinguished from every other Minister of the Crown. In November, 1765, we find Lord Barrington[5] writing as Secretary at War, to General Leighton in these terms:—"It is *my* duty to take what care I can of the half-pay. I am of opinion that all vacancies at home *shall go* on in this way, but regiments like yours in the West Indies will meet with more indulgence;" and instances may be given where the Secretary at War has felt it to be his duty to reduce the half-pay list (1) by requiring the Officers to serve,[6] or (2) in other cases to sell or commute their half-pay.

The Constitutional function of the Secretary at War to reduce the Half-pay List.

To reduce the Half-pay List

85. As to reduction by service, Lord Hardinge, speaking as a witness before the Commission on the Civil Administration, 1837, said :[7]—I recollect in 1825, when it was necessary to make an addition to the Army abroad, in consequence of insurrections in the West Indies, Lord Bathurst signified to the Commander-in-Chief the orders of the Government, that every Officer, amounting nearly to 250, should be taken from the half-pay list; he notified this order to the Duke of

1 By Service

---

1 Lord Panmure, Purchase Com. 1857, p 216
2 Lord Palmerston's Fin Com, 1828, p 218
3 12 Com Journ., pp 441, 564, 634, and Note G, Vol. I, pp 369-371
4 Compare, for years 1785 and 1786, 40 Com Journ, p 879 with 41 Com Journ
5 Quoted in Lord Palmerston's Memorandum, Appendix CXXIX
6 See Address moved in 1740 for employment of half-pay officers in the new levies, 11 Parl. Hist, p 992 The following are instances in which half-pay officers have been called on to serve —1715, July, Note G, Vol I, p 372, 1729, April 3 (Mis Bk., 1720), 1739, Aug 24 (ib 1785, p 195); 1755, Oct 2 (ib 1751, p 407), 1774 (ib. p 98), 1793 (ib. 189 to 195), 1796, Sept 24 (ib 1795, p 442), 1801, Aug (ib 1799, p 368) As to the rank in which they serve, see 146 H D (3) 250
7 P 24

York, who thought it would be injurious to the efficiency of the Regiments, and unjust to the old Officers on full-pay, if some of great service and merit were not promoted. But the Secretary of State for the War Department and Colonies resisted the remonstrance of, and issued his instructions to the Commander-in-Chief, that every officer should be taken, without exception, from the half-pay list. His Royal Highness obeyed this order with zeal and attention."

86 The same officer took credit[1] to himself, as Secretary at War, for the introduction of the plan of re- 2 By Sale of ducing the List by sale or commutation of the value Commissions. of Officers' Commissions. At the close of the War in 1815, several Regiments were reduced. Some officers retired from the Army by the sale of their Commissions, others—Juniors who in some instances had never served, or done but one year's service—were placed on half-pay.[2] In 1828, Lord Hardinge, thinking it prejudicial to the public interests that these Officers should be continued on half-pay, called upon them either to serve in the Army on vacancies occurring, or to commute their half-pay by receiving the regulation price of their Commission. By this operation 857 half-pay Officers were disposed of by an expenditure of 374,064*l.* out of the Reserve fund, and half-pay to the extent of 58,754*l.* per annum was reduced.

87. It follows, from what has been written, that the Secretary at War was responsible that no person should Responsible remain on the half-pay List after he had been *guilty* person should of conduct inconsistent with the character of an *Officer* remain on and a Gentleman.[3] The necessity for removing a misconduct. Colonel of twenty-three years' service, whose conduct in certain pecuniary transactions attracted notice, arose when Lord Hardinge (for the second time) held the office of Secretary at War in 1843. Lord Hardinge gave the Officer an opportunity of

---

[1] See par 43, *ante*, as to similar claim by the Duke of York, and see Note V, on the Reserve Fund See the Debate on Mr. Hume's motion, in 1827, 16 H D. (2), p 184
[2] See a Comparative Statement from 1851 to 1858, p 365 of Part 2 Army, &c., Expenditure, 11 H D. (3), p. 1285, see Army and Navy Appointments, 1833, pp 227, 228, 140, 141   [3] 17 H. D (3), p. 1349.

explaining what he deemed to be his offence; that explanation not being satisfactory, he obtained, with the concurrence of the Commander-in-Chief, the sanction of the Crown for his removal from the Army.

88. The view taken of the duty of the Secretary at War was plainly stated in an official Memorandum.[1]—

Lord Hardinge's view of the duty of the Secretary at War in this respect

"The rule and custom of the military service has been observed in this case. If this Officer had been on full pay he would have been tried by a Court-martial under the Commander-in Chief. "Being on half-pay this Officer cannot be tried by Court-martial, and it is the duty of the Secretary at War, when such misconduct does come to his knowledge, to investigate all the circumstances of the case, and to submit his opinion for the pleasure of the Crown. It is a leading principle by which the discipline of the Army is maintained, that every officer holding Her Majesty's Commission must not only conduct himself worthily as an Officer, but *honourably as a gentleman*, whether on full pay or half-pay; and in all the Articles of War, which are annually approved by the Crown, it is distinctly laid down that an Officer shall do nothing unbecoming the character of an Officer and a Gentleman."[2]

89. In another instance,[3] where a half-pay Officer had

Another illustration

misconducted himself, and been dismissed from his office (being a public one) the Secretary at War, on the facts being brought to his notice, removed him from the half pay list, and gazetted him out of the Army.[4]

90. The Secretary at War was therefore not unfrequently

Secretary at War often appealed to, that justice and right may be done

appealed to by injured persons to hear complaints against half-pay officers, and to submit to the Crown that the officer's name should be removed from the list. "The King,"[5] said Mr. Justice Best, "has

[1] $\frac{99871}{15, 16, \& 17}$; for cases of officers struck off and suspended, see $\frac{16 \text{ Dragoons}}{149}$.

[2] The Admiralty exercise the same rule over half-pay officers of the navy, 37 H. D (3), pp 907, 1186, Edwards's Case (for non-payment of debt), 35 ib, p 1253, see Return of half-pay officers dismissed, moved for by Mr. Hume, February, 1836, 31 H D (3), p 351, refused, 35 ib, (943) as to Navy

[3] Quoted on $\frac{16 \text{ Dragoons}}{149}$ [4] $\frac{16917}{6\ 9\ 13}$ [5] Fairman v Ives, 5 B. and Ald., p 647

authority to dismiss an officer from his service, and most probably would dismiss any one who hesitated to do what honour and justice required."

91. Other cases—of suspension—arose until the Officer did justice or right to the complaining party, not by the ~Secretary at War's action by suspending his Half-pay~ payment of an ordinary private debt, but where the bounty of the Crown had been pledged as a means of obtaining credit, and the officer had sought to repudiate his engagement. Thus where, having received *an advance* of half-pay from his agent, the officer pledged it to another person,—placing a signed declaration in his hands, with the promise of making it at the proper period before a magistrate,—this conduct was held to be so fraudulent, that the future payment of half-pay was suspended until a satisfactory explanation or arrangement was made.[1]

92. That this power may be *legally* exercised admits of no doubt, having reference to Lord Kenyon's decision in ~That the power may be legally executed is undoubted.~ Macdonald *v.* Steele.[2] There, the plaintiff was largely indebted to the regimental agents, and the Secretary at War signified the King's pleasure to the Paymaster-General that his half-pay should not be continued; the legality of the order was called in question by an action brought against the Paymaster-General, and upheld by Lord Kenyon. "If the public had a demand on the plaintiff, that might be set off against the present action But His Majesty's pleasure supersedes all enquiry, as he has the absolute direction and command of the Army. It is true Parliament has provided a sum of money, but that is to be distributed as the King chooses. The money is under his control until such time as it is paid out. The King cannot take it for his own use, but he may prevent it from being paid to a person who is not entitled to receive it. It is for the honour of Government to see that money due to an officer is applied to the payment of his debts."[3]

---

[1] Approved, $\frac{67183}{45}$, 12th August, 1846, see the same principle enforced by Vice-Chancellor Stuart in Knight *v* Buckley, 4 Jur, p 527, 5 Jur, p 828.

[2] Peake's Cases, p. 175

[3] See Sir W Grant s Judgment in Priddy *v* Rose, 3 Mer, p 102

93. The claims of relatives arise either *on behalf* of the officer when he is lunatic or otherwise enfeebled; or *against* the officer when he refuses to support those legally chargeable upon him. As to the half-pay of lunatic officers, the practice of the Department is regulated by the principles set forth in a correspondence between the War Office and the Treasury, in 1843, which is to be found in the Appendix.[1]

Appeals from the relations of officers in Lunacy Case

94. Where the Court of Chancery has the charge of the estate, the officer is sustained out of his private property, if sufficient, and the half-pay is only brought in aid to make up the sum which the Judge of the Court thinks needful for his maintenance. If the lunatic's person or property is not in charge of the Court, or of any relative, the Secretary at War usually sends him, on medical certificate, to an asylum, under 8 and 9 Vic., c. 100, sec. 45, and pays what is needed for his maintenance, under the authority of the 26 and 27 Vic., chap. 57, sec. 34.

Estate in Lunacy

Officer in an Asylum.

95. Claims for maintenance from a wife and children were occasionally presented against an half-pay officer; and the early records of the War Office[2] show that they were recognised and enforced. Under date of 14th December, 1671, there is a Royal Sign Manual order, for the payment of 10*l.* per annum to Mrs Salway out of the pay of her husband,[3] and in a more recent case an allowance of 25*l.* was made to the wife out of the husband's half-pay.[4]

Claim to maintenance, by wife, &c.

Half-pay so applied.

If these cases were challenged, it is at least doubtful whether the Secretary at War could show that he had any legal justification for making an issue to the wife without the husband's consent expressed or implied.[5] In case of the husband's lunacy, it was the custom of the War Office to apply half of the pay for the maintenance of the wife; and sisters dependent on an unmarried brother have received similar consideration.

Not legal (?)

96. The usual method of protecting the interests of a wife

---

[1] Appendix XCVII   [2] P. 204   [3] See War Office Letter Bk., 1766, p 126
[4] Wakefield, $\frac{112957}{66}$ [5] Note C C, Appendix.

and children was by ordering the payment of the half-pay to be suspended until the officer made such an arrange- Pay stopped till a fair provision is made for the Wife. ment as the Secretary at War considered to be fair and reasonable. Where the status of the wife was disputed by the husband on fair and reasonable grounds, the Secretary at War would not interfere.[1] The Divorce Court has decreed alimony out of the full pay of an officer; but no such order has been left with the Secretary at War to be enforced against the officer's pay.[2]

97. The claims of creditors usually arose under assignment, by deed, or by operation of law. The rule laid Claims of creditors. down in the earlier cases was that half-pay was assignable.[3]

98. It was then held that the uncertain interest that the officer had in half-pay rendered an assignment of it A.D. 1728 void; but in Flarty v. Odlum, the Court of King's Assignments first held valid. Bench held assignments to be void on the ground of public policy, and all future decisions have supported Then void as against public policy. this view.[4] "I am clearly of opinion," said Lord Kenyon, "that this half-pay could not be legally assigned by the defendant, and consequently that the creditors are not entitled to an assignment of it for their benefit Emoluments of this sort are granted for the dignity of the State, and for the decent support of those persons who are engaged in the service of it. It would, therefore be highly impolitic to permit them to be assigned; for persons who are liable to be called out in the service of their country, ought not to be taken from a state of poverty." The same principle extends, and has been applied in later decisions,[5] to assignments of full pay, and to various pensions granted by the State.

---

[1] $\frac{73100}{99}$, $\frac{33573}{106}$, $\frac{32008}{9}$.

[2] Louis v. Louis, 1 Law Rep (Probate), p. 230, but see Dent v. Dent, ib, p 366.

[3] Granger v. Wyvil, quoted in 2 Anstr, p 534

[4] Mouys v Leake, 8 Term Rep, p. 414, 1790, 3 Term Rep, p. 682, Lidderdale v Duke of Montrose, 4 Term Rep, p. 250, Stone v Lidderdale, 2 East, p 533, Wells v Foster, 8 Mee and Wels, p 153, Price v Lovell, 15 Jur p 287.

[5] 2 Bea. Rep, p 549, but query the effect of the Pension Act, 1869? See Appendix, Note V*

99. In addition to the rule thus laid down, a statutory
Void by Statute. prohibition against assignment contained in the 47
Geo. III. (sess. 2), c. 25, remains to be noticed. In
the preamble, the Act refers to "officers who have served
in any of His Majesty's forces, and widows of officers of the
Army entitled to pensions ; and also to persons receiving any sums
of money on the Compassionate List, and also to all other
persons receiving any pension or allowance under the control,
direction, or management of the Secretary at War, by reason of
having served in His Majesty's Army, or in any of his forces, or
in any forces which have been engaged in His Majesty's Service,"
and then the enactment authorizes the Secretary at War "to order
and direct that all such pay, pensions, and allowances to which
any officers or persons who have served in any of His Majesty's
forces, or in any forces which have been heretofore or may hereafter be engaged in His Majesty's Service, or any widows of any
such officers or any person receiving any allowance or pension
on the Compassionate List, or any pension, allowance, or relief,
in respect of any military service, shall be paid such pay, pension allowance, or relief, at or near to the parishes or places of
their residence in any part of His Majesty's dominions, or in
foreign parts." The fourth section then declares "all assignments, bargains, sales, orders, contracts, agreements, or securities whatsoever, which shall be given or made by any person
entitled to any such pay, pension, allowance, or relief as aforesaid, for, upon, or in respect of any such his pay, pension,
allowance, or relief, shall be absolutely null and void to all
intents and purposes."

100. In the case[1] of pension for wounds, Vice-Chancellor
Stuart—his attention not being called to this Act—
Cases on Act gave effect to the assignment; but in a later case,[2] of
an assignment of retired pay to a Captain of Artillery, the Act
being referred to, he refused to make any order. Where an
officer in the Indian military service[3] retired on a pension,
and subsequently assigned it, effect was given to the assign-

---

[1] Knight v. Bulkeley, 4 Jur (N S), p 527.   [2] 5 Jur (N S), p 818
[3] Head v. Hay, 8 Jur. (N. S), p 379, Carew v. Cooper, 10 Jur (N S), pp 11,
429, Dent v Dent, L. R., 1 Pro Ca, p 366

ment, the 47 Geo. III., c. 25, being held not to apply to Indian pensions

101. Independently of the Statute Law, assignments of pay and pension have been held void on these grounds of public policy :— Grounds on which assignments held void

(1.) Every public servant receives enough, and not more than enough remuneration from the Public Treasury to enable him adequately to discharge the duties and to uphold the respectability of his position. Any part of that income which, therefore, is withdrawn from the public servant, tends to diminish his efficiency.[1]

(2.) Half-pay is a retainer paid to enable the officer to come at any moment into the active service of the Crown.[2]

(3.) Half-pay cannot be held with any other employment, civil or military, and therefore the public have an interest in the cessation of half-pay at an earlier period than the death of the holder. "One of the modes," said Lord Justice Bruce,[3] "in which it may cease is by the appointment of the holder to an office of greater value. To be fit to receive such an appointment, he must be a person not deprived of the decencies of life, or of the means of appearing externally respectable The public has an interest in continuing him in such a position as may enable him to receive an appointment on which his pension (the case arose on a civil superannuation) may cease."

102. Even in cases where the Courts have admitted the pension to be assignable, the Judges have felt the difficulty of securing the payment to the assignees, as no execution can be issued against the King's treasure.[4] Lord Eldon said, " The pension being granted to the individual, in what mode can the assignee recover out of funds which are not accessible by the common forms of law? If a Assignment cannot be enforced against Secretary at War.

---

[1] Palmer v Bate, 2 Brod and Bing , p. 677 , Hill v Paul, 8 Cl. and Fin , p 207.

[2] Aston v Gwinnel, 3 Y. and J., p 149 , Græme v Wroughton, 11 Exch Ca., p. 155

[3] See Wells v Foster, 8 Mee and Wels , p 152 , Spooner v Payne, 2 De Grey and Sm , p 450

[4] See Lord Somers' celebrated argument in the Bankers' Case, 14 How. Sta Trials, and Chap XIX , par. 11

subject gives land to A for his life, he gives to A and his assigns; but where property is gained by a Warrant from the Crown, does it follow that the Warrant extends to a person who is in no way described in that instrument?"[1] But in Knight *v.* Bulkeley,[2] the Court, admitting that an order for a receiver could not be recognized by the War Office, granted an injunction to restrain the officer from receiving his pension, or executing any power of attorney authorizing or permitting any person other than the plaintiff to receive it.

103. If a creditor obtained judgment of outlawry, and left
Outlawry of Officer   an office copy of it at the War Office, the issue of pay was suspended; but the only mode of procedure by which the half-pay of an officer can be attached, is by an order made under the provisions of the Bankruptcy Act. This power
Bankruptcy of Officer   originated in Lord Redesdale's Act for the relief of Insolvent Debtors,[3] passed in 1813, and it is still provided by the English Act (and similar provisions are found in the Irish and Scotch Acts),[4] that " the Court may order such portion of the pay, half-pay, salary, emolument, or pension of any bankrupt as, on communication from the Court, the Secretary of State for War may officially sanction to be paid to the assignees, to be applied in payment of the debts of such bankrupt, and such order and sanction being lodged in the office of Her Majesty's Paymaster-General, such portion of the said pay, half-pay, salary, emolument, or pension, as shall be specified in such order and sanction, shall be paid to such assignees until the Court make order to the contrary."

104. Parliament reposes confidence in the Secretary of State that, on behalf of the public interests, he will see that the creditors are not defrauded on the one hand, nor the officer left in the Army with an income wholly inadequate to support the position and duties which his commission entail, on the other; therefore the Secretary of State, if he sees fit, modifies the order as originally proposed, or subsequently withdraws or qualifies his

---

[1] Davis *v* Duke of Marlborough, 1 Swan Rep, p 79.

[2] 4 Jur (N. S), p 529, 5 Jur (N S), p 818   [3] 53 Geo III., c 102, sec 29

[4] England, 24 and 25 Vic, c 134, sec 134, Ireland, 20 and 21 Vic, c 60, sec 319, Scotland, 19 and 20 Vic, c 79, sec 149

present, if the half-pay be altered in amount after the order has been made.[1] The proportion that has been asked for and allowed to creditors is extremely various.[2]

105. Whether an arrear of half-pay, &c., actually due at the time of the bankruptcy, should be entered on the schedule as a debt or asset belonging to the bankrupt, and claimed from the Secretary at War, admits of question.[3] In practice, however, the official assignee does not claim it ; and, the pay or half-pay is given to the bankrupt until the order is made under the Act of Parliament.

106. If an officer neglects to draw this half-pay for two years his name is withdrawn from the list, and not No Statute of Limitations replaced until a satisfactory cause of absence be given; but there is no Statute of Limitations[4] affecting the pay or half-pay of the Army like the 1 Geo. IV., and 1 Wm. IV., c. 20, which prescribes six years as the limit for which the half-pay of Naval Officers can be recovered. In a recent case, where the officer had not earned his half-pay,[5] and a considerable arrear was claimed by his executors, the Treasury sanctioned an issue of two years only, which had probably been voted in the non-effective services before the officer's name was taken from the half-pay list.[6]

107. Half-pay is intended as the sole Emolument which Parliament thinks fit to grant an officer upon the List, Exclusion of Half-pay Officers from other employment Rule of 1718 and, from 1718 to the present time, the rules of Appropriation have remained intact, with the exception of the third rule ("that no person having any other place or employment of profit, civil or military, under His Majesty, shall have or receive any part of the said half-pay"), which was first relaxed, as to military employment, in 1799, and as to civil employment in 1820.

108. The relaxation to enable the recipient to hold other

---

[1] Lyster's Case, $\frac{33573}{58}$ [2] Ib, $\frac{54013}{38}$.

[3] See Mr Justice Buller, p 683, of 3 Term Rep   [4] 103 H. D (3), p. 972.

[5] Treasury Letter, 3rd April, 1861

[6] See General Murray's Case, 103 H D (3), p 972

military pay or employment has been limited, first, to Staff and

Relaxation, first, as to military employment. Garrison employment;[1] secondly, to military employment in any colony;[2] thirdly, to Militia, Yeomany, and Volunteer appointments[3] (by the several Acts under which these forces have been constituted); and, fourthly, to military employment, with the assent of the Crown, under any other Government.[4]

109. The relaxation to enable the recipient to hold a *Civil*

As to civil employment place or employment of profit has been more general, the altered rule being not one of exclusion from any place, but of limitation upon the income to be received from the Civil employment   Upon the discussion of the Estimates in 1817,[5] and again in 1818,[6] it was urged that to prohibit half-pay officers from holding Civil employment with their half-pay was an injustice; but Lord Palmerston upheld the prohibition upon the grounds of expediency and public policy.   "Half-pay[7] was in fact granted merely for the subsistence of officers during the cessation of their services, and as a retaining fee for their future service, when it should become necessary to call them for the defence of the country.   But if officers were allowed to accept civil appointments, it was felt, and justly felt, that it would be difficult to recall them to military duties when occasion should require it.   There was, indeed, reason to believe that if officers were so appointed, they might become so much engaged in civil pursuits as to be disqualified for, or indisposed to, the resumption of military habits."

110. In the circumstances then presenting themselves, there appeared to be so little chance of future *military* employment for the greater number of half-pay officers, and especially those of the lower grade, that the Government, in 1819, decided so to relax the prohibition as to allow an officer to hold civil pay, if it did not exceed three times the amount of his half-pay.[8]   The

A.D.1820. Rule relaxed. Appropriation Act of 1820 was therefore amended so as to enable the officer to hold any "civil place or employment, of which the net emoluments were less than three

---

[1] W. O Circulars, 375-30, Sept., 1817, vol vi, p 149.
[2] By 39 Geo III., c. 144   [3] 57 Geo. III., c 132, sec 32
[4] By 1 Geo. IV., c. 111, sec 20.   [5] 36 H. D. (O S), p 533
[6] 37 H D. (O S), p. 756.   [7] Ib., p 759.   [8] 39 H D. (O. S.), p 898.

times the amount of the highest rate of half-pay attached to his rank;"[1] and further, "with His Majesty's sanction, to hold any such place of which the net emoluments fall short of four times the amount of the half-pay aforesaid, and to receive such a portion of the half-pay as would make up four times the amount thereof."

111. The alterations introduced into the Act of 1820 came under the notice and were wholly disapproved of by the Finance Committee of 1828. In their Third Report it is remarked, "that the abandonment of the restrictions was an ill-advised measure, not more at variance with a due regard to economy than opposed to the very principle upon which half-pay was established."[2] That if half-pay officers adopt the *civil* service, they should receive the same remuneration for it as *civil* servants, and no more; and the Committee recommended, "in the strongest manner, that the payment of all half-pay be forthwith replaced upon the footing on which it stood previously to the year 1820." *A.D. 1828. Finance Committee Report.*

112. This was accordingly done in the Appropiation Act of 1829,[3] which enacted "that no person who, *after* the 28th day of July, 1828, has been appointed to any civil place or employment of profit under His Majesty, or in the Colonies, or in Possessions of His Majesty beyond the seas, or under any other Government, shall have or receive any part of the same half-pay for any time during which he shall hold any such civil place or employment of profit under His Majesty beyond the seas, or under any other Government, other than that of a Barrack-master under the Master-General and Board of Ordnance, who shall, under the restrictions beforementioned, be entitled to receive his half-pay." *A.D. 1829. Rule restored.*

113. In the following year a clause was inserted[4] to enable the Treasury,—in cases where that Board should be of opinion that the employment of half-pay officers in the Colonies or elsewhere, in civil situations of responsibility, *A.D. 1830. Additional Clause*

---

[1] 1 Geo IV , c 111, sec 20.
[2] The Committee stated the increased annual expense thereby occasioned, at 73,053*l.*, including Naval Officers, in the estimate, p. 6
[3] 10 Geo IV , c 60, sec 19.   [4] 1 Wm IV , c 63, sec 22

with small emolument, would be conducive to economy,—to authorise the receipt of half-pay with such employment.

114. In February, 1831, a debate[1] arose upon the exclusion of Officers in the Army from appointments which Naval Officers could hold " in His Majesty's Household " without forfeiting their half-pay, and in consequence of it the Act was altered to enable Military Officers to hold these appointments with their half-pay.

115. The old rule of 1718 and that of 1828 were broken in upon again by the Appropriation Act of the year 1833,[2]

A D 1833

Appropria-
tion Act

containing a clause which authorised half-pay to be issued to any officer appointed to any civil office or employment under His Majesty, or under any other Government, if His Majesty's pleasure thereto should be signified by the Treasury. This permission was to be granted subject to the usual restrictions as to the amount of civil income, and a list of these half-pay officers was to be laid before Parliament. The clause was retrospective, and took in cases of any officers appointed since the 28th July, 1828.

116. It may be useful, before closing the subject, to enumerate

Decisions on
the 3rd Rule.

Offices that
may be
held —(1) By
decision

some of the decisions that have been given by the Secretary at War, and others in authority, as to the places or employments of profit that may, or may not be held with half-pay. (1) as to the offices and emoluments that *may* be so held.—A Parliamentary Commissionership—the person being named in the statute (1807)[3]— A Pension from the King (1812)[4].— Appointments in the Royal Household, including the Corps of Gentlemen at Arms and Yeomen of the Guard.[5]—Superannuation Allowance on Retirement from Civil Employment (1814).[6]— A collectorship of Taxes paid by Poundage thereout[7]—Service in the East India Company's Army.[8]— The Command of a

---

[1] 1 & 2 Wm IV., c 54, sec 21, 8 H D. (3), p 354, Vol iii. of P H (1831) (322), p 445 [2] 2 and 3 Wm IV., c 126, sec 23 [3] Book 1, p 365 [4] Ib 2, p 244 [5] Note E, Vol I p 359. [6] Book 4, p 108 [7] D, p 68, $\frac{130605}{2}$. [8] Army and Navy Appointments, 1833, p 227

Colonial Police Force.[1]—District Registrar in Probate Court —
Superintendent of Windsor Park.[2]—Clerk of the Peace in Scotland.[3]—Poor Knight of Windsor.[4]—Appointment in household
of Lord-Lieutenant of Ireland[5]—Subdistributor of Stamps.[6]—
Sub-Sheriff[7]—Clerk to Poor Law Guardians.[8]—Gazette writer
for Scotland.[9]

117. The following offices and employments may be held with
half-pay under statute:—Any office or employment
in the Irish Constabulary.[10]— Any office or employment under the Dublin Police Act.[11]—Any office or employment in the Metropolitan Police Force[12]—Chief Constable, or
Constable under the County and District Constables Act,[13]—
Inspector of Constabulary under 19 and 20 Vic., c 69.[14]—A
Commission, &c, in the Militia,[15]—A Commission in the Yeomanry.[16]—A Commission in the Volunteers.[17]—A Staff Officer
of Pensioners.[18]

(2) By Statute

118 (2) As to the offices that may *not* be so held.—A Clerkship in the War Office (1805).[19]—A Commissionership
of Bankruptcy.[20]—Clerk of General Meetings.[21]—Distributor of Stamps.[22]—Governorship of Alderney.[23]

That may not be held

119. It should be noticed that the holding a place or employment of profit creates a suspension, not a destruction of
the right to half-pay,[24] and that when the cause of that
suspension ceases, the right to receive half-pay from that period
revives[25]

Half pay not lost, but suspended

---

[1] D, p 68, $\frac{132748}{19}$ [2] Ib, $\frac{23812}{\cdot}$ [3] Ib, $\frac{22057}{8}$

[4] Ib, $\frac{6269}{11}$ See Note D D, in Appendix.   [5] Ib, $\frac{21582}{7}$ [6] Ib, $\frac{39271}{8}$

[7] Ib, $\frac{71145}{5}$ [8] Ib, $\frac{51173}{6}$ [9] Ib, $\frac{108783}{8}$ [10] 6 Wm IV , c 13, sec 30

[11] 1 Vic , c 25, sec 19   [12] 2 and 3 Vic c 47, sec 19

[13] 2 and 3 Vic , c 93, sec. 11   [14] 22 & 23 Vic c 32, sec 27

[15] 42 Geo III., c 90, sec 82   [16] 44 Geo III , c 54, sec 42

[17] Appropriation Act   [18] 5 and 6 Vic., c. 70   [19] Book 1, p 269

[20] Ib, $\frac{22354}{2}$, but see Note E, Vol I , p 360   [21] Ib, $\frac{37838}{\cdot}$ [22] Ib, $\frac{39271}{8}$

[23] Book 4 p 316.   These cases are now met by the amendment inserted in
the Appropriation Act of 1831   [24] Book 4, p 108

[25] In 1719, the opinion of the Law Officers appears to have been given whether,
under Rule 6 of 1718 (par 59), an officer of inferior rank might by His Majesty's
Warrant, be placed on half-pay in the room of an officer of superior rank retiring

120. An officer that has been reduced or put on half-pay
A.D 1814 holds his existing Commission in abeyance,[1] but he
Officers must cannot be brought upon active service without re-
be recommis-
sioned ceiving a new commission in the usual manner.[2] His
commission is saleable, wholly or partially, but the assent
Commission of the Crown will rarely be given where the half-
saleable
pay is charged with payments in favour of his wife
(with his own consent) or of his creditors (by order of the
Bankruptcy Court). In a case where the Commander-in-Chief
Claims on pressed the expediency of permitting the officer to sell
Half pay not his half-pay, the effect of the sale being to defeat the
defeated
thereby wife's claim thereon, the Secretary at War "felt bound
to protect the wife, and refused his consent to the sale unless
the officer placed so much of the purchase money at the Secretary at War's command as should buy an annuity for her life of
the sum then allocated on his half-pay."[3]

121. A partial sale of his Commission is made under Warrant
Receiving the of 14th August, 1783, which permits an officer to retire
difference on half-pay by receiving the sum which the Warrant
specified as the different value between a full and half-pay Commission[4] The object of the Warrant was to enable the officer to
realise part of the value of his Commission on relinquishing a
portion of his advantages as a military officer.[5] While he holds
the difference he is not eligible for advancement or any military
employment, nor, on his death, is his widow entitled to pension,
or her children to the Compassionate Fund; formerly such an
officer could not—but under the present practice he may—
return to the service on repayment of the difference, and then
he is equally eligible with any other officer for promotion.

---

from the service or by exchange They wrote (Book 721, p 85) —"This rule
manifestly supposes a title to half-pay independent of the Royal Warrant, and
there is no other title but what arises from the general appropriation in the Act of
that sum, to the half-pay of reduced officers, the half-pay can mean only half
of that pay which every officer is entitled to according to his rank in the service
when he was reduced We are of opinion that an officer of inferior rank cannot
be put upon the half-pay of a superior one, though that superior officer should be
willing to exchange or retire, since that would be giving him, in reality, more
than the half-pay, and not the same he would be otherwise entitled to"

[1] Note E E, Appendix   [2] Book 721, p 216   [3] Ib, $\frac{38573}{106}$, May 10, 1848
[4] Naval and Military Inquiry Report, 1840, p 41, and par. 40, *ante*
[5] Ib., p 38

122. To recur to the officer's position on the effective strength of the Army. The Crown does not feed the officer or make any contribution—other than by the Regent's Fund,[1] and the Guards' Table at St. James's[2] towards this expense; neither does it clothe the officer—who has to come into the Service with proper clothes, arms, and accoutrements, and to keep them in good and creditable condition for the service of the Crown. Under the present Regulations, if losses in the Service be sustained, which were altogether unavoidable, then an indemnification is granted,—not to make good the full loss sustained, but to such an extent only as will enable the claimant to re-equip himself for Service, according to the Scale laid down in the Regulations.

The Crown does not feed or clothe the officer

123. Prior to Burke's Act, the Regimental allowances covered these charges in ordinary cases; and in 1767 Lord Barrington—in writing upon the claims (referred to him from the Treasury) of officers of the 43rd Regiment, for losses sustained at the blowing up of Fort Augusta—justifies his refusal to make any allowance, as he "found claims of compensation for losses were increasing every day, and was unwilling, without absolute necessity, to introduce a charge upon the *Public*, which might soon grow up to a very considerable amount upon similar pretensions; and knew if he gave way in one instance, how difficult it would be for him to resist in others"[3] In November, 1796, a Code of Regulations appear to have been laid down[4] On the 3rd September, 1825, the Royal Warrant relating thereto required the loss to be put forward within 12 months; and by the Regulations of 1848, it must be made within *one* month, or delay shall be considered a sufficient reason for rejecting the claim.[5]

Indemnification for losses in service

124. The pay of the officer[6]—as it has been before shown—

---

[1] £25 for each Company or Troop at home, for wine, since 1811   Army and Navy Expenditure, 1850, p 216   [2] Note F, Appendix, Vol. I.
[3] Letter Bk, 211, 27th Nov, p 90.   [4] Code of Regulations, 1807, p 490
[5] Ib, p 91. As to losses, see 8th Report of Commissioners on Military Enquiry, pp 130-205
[6] Obviously the Administrative Corps—recently turned into officers—are not

is "not merces, but honorarium."[1] "Honour," as Adam Smith

Pay not merces, but honorarium wrote," makes a great part of the reward of all honourable professions."[2] Admitting this to be so—and that offering pay as an inducement to a lower class of officers to join the Army would be a doubtful expedient —yet it cannot be denied that the present pay, though nominally the same, is far less than the pay of the officer prior to 1783 Pensions for distinguished Service are,[3] no doubt, boons that did not exist at that period, but they are rather substitutes[4] for other advantages that have been taken away, than additional grants to the officers as a class. Pensions for wounds, or loss of limbs, which date from 1812,[5] do not come under that objection.

125. Few of the same questions, therefore, arise upon the Administration of full pay, that have been previously

Few questions on the administration of full-pay arise considered with reference to half-pay. No allocation of any portion of full-pay can be allowed in favour of the Creditors of an officer, and Parliament in legislating for the Militia has laid down the rule that a Bankrupt—and the same would be applicable to an Insolvent—should cease to hold a Lord-Lieutenant's Commission as an officer.[6] The credit of the Army would be seriously damaged by allowing officers to go through the Courts for the Relief of Debtors without an allocation of pay and still to continue to hold Her Majesty's Commission, which is the insignia of an Officer and a Gentleman.[7] Under the Regimental System, the individual character of each officer more or less affects or prejudices that of the Regiment; and therefore, in this as in other instances, the Social question

included in this paragraph. The idea of reaping the *honours of a Soldier* and the *pay of a Civilian* is both modern and unique it began in the Indian Army—where many posts in the Civil Administration were filled with the officers of the East India Company's army, till the discipline and character of the Company's army suffered in proportion as the profits of the officers increased Chap. XXIX , par 79.

¹ Vol. I., p 106, and par 5, *ante*   ² Book 1, chap 10, p 166.

³ As to holding these with retired pay, see 169 H D (3), p 1206.

⁴ Vol I , p. 379, *ante*

⁵ Ib , and, as to wounds equivalent to loss of limb, 145 H D (3), p. 1354.

⁶ 36 Geo. III , c. 100, sec 5, and 1 Geo IV. c 100, s. 5; Rex v. Liverpool, 2 Burr , p 732.   ⁷ Chap X., pars 7-13

is involved with the more general considerations of Military expediency.

126. The character of the Military Service is that in which the Public generally have an interest; and prosecu- *Libel upon the troops.* tions for Libel have been undertaken by the Crown against offenders. In a case happening at Winchester, where a local paper unfairly commented upon a case of flogging in the 90th, of which Colonel Graham was the Colonel, the Secretary at War was advised that the paragraph was an indictable Libel, and that the case was one in which an information at the suit of the Attorney-General was the only proper mode of proceeding, being the most serious and best calculated to bring forward an offence of so patent a nature.[1] In 1810 William Cobbett was indicted for a libel on the German Legion (which had suppressed a mutiny of the Local Militia at Ely) and was fined and imprisoned for his offence.[2] The more important case of the King *v.* Burdett arose in the year 1820, when an information at the suit of the Attorney-General was prosecuted against the defendant for his address to the Electors of Westminster, and he was fined and imprisoned,—the Court holding it to be perfectly clear that slanderous words on any part of the King's Troops might be the subject of Criminal prosecution, although the writer should not define what particular part of the Troops were referred to.[3] In later instances, where the nature of the Military Service has been misrepresented to deter persons from enlistment into the Army, or enrolment into the Militia, the authors of these libels have been proceeded against.[4]

127. But there is another offence, of a totally different character, that may expose those who practise it to *The assumption of army rank by persons not entitled thereto.* punishment, viz., the assumption of Military Rank or status, that does not in fact belong to the person assuming it. "As to officers, the courtesy of the Service is," said Lord Palmerston, "that after a certain rank, when the officer has got the Brevet[5] rank of a Field

[1] Bk 723, pp. 47-49   [2] 52 Ann Reg , p. 342
[3] Rex *v.* Burdett, 3 B. & Ald , p. 717 , [4] ib , pp 95, 314-329
[4] 124 H. D , (3), pp 359 and 649, Book H, p. 87 ; Book G, p 205.
[5] Note F F, Appendix.

Officer, he is allowed to bear the title of the rank, though he has no longer a Commission;[1] and the names are included in the Army List in italics, shewing that they have no Commission, but only the Rank."[2] In a comparatively recent case (1846), where a person assumed the Rank of Captain in a particular Regiment (not being such), it was held by the Court of Queen's Bench to be a false pretence, for which he was punished.[3]

128 If an officer cannot be retained with honour or advantage to the Service, then, if he has no meritorious claim to half-pay, and will not withdraw, he must be dismissed, from the Service by the Crown. Even in the form of notifying the officer's retirement, there are gradations of censure; as by stating the fact of his permission to retire, and also with or without the sale of his Commission; or of his dismissal, either by the sentence of a Court-martial or by the direct order of the Crown.

The dismissal of officers.

129. This prerogative—though questioned in Parliament at various periods of our Constitutional history—has been deemed so essential for the Public Safety, that the leading statesmen of each generation have invariably supported the Crown in the exercise of it. "Persons who entered the Army," said Mr. Villiers, speaking as Judge-Advocate-General in the House of Commons,[4] "did so on the well-understood condition that they might be dismissed without any reason assigned, and without any redress given, at the discretion of the Crown. This power in the Crown was so ancient, and had been so generally recognised, that it was useless to discuss it. In the House of Commons the question had been raised whether such powers should be intrusted to

The powers of the Crown absolute

---

[1] See the Debate in 1745, where a somewhat similar question was raised, 13 P. H , p 1382.

[2] Finance Committee, 1828, p. 217. Mr Collins' Evidence, 1833, before the Committee on Army and Navy Appointments, p 223 , 192 H D , (3), p. 712

[3] Hamilton v The Queen, 9 Q B Rep , p 279 With regard to these, an early Statute (39 Eliz , c 17), was directed against the offence of assuming a false character, but the Act was repealed in 1812—21 H. D (O S), p 791 , and see Vol I , p 354, *ante.*   [4] 137 H D (3), p 1335

the Crown, and there had been attempts to limit the prerogative in this respect, but Parliament had uniformly decided that the Crown was wisely intrusted with this prerogative."

130. For the same reason, the Courts of Law have always upheld the prerogative. "The King's pleasure," said Lord Kenyon, "supersedes all inquiry, as he has the absolute direction and command of the Army." "The King," said Mr. Justice Best, "has authority to dismiss an officer from his service, and most probably would dismiss any one who hesitated to do what honour and justice required."[1] Where a dismissed officer sought to review the sentence that had been adopted by the Crown, how, it was asked, could the King's Bench interfere? "Admitting for a moment," said Lord Denman,[2] "that it were possible to address any writ directly to His Majesty, when it is considered that this power of dismissing any officer is *undoubtedly inherent* in the Crown, and might have been lawfully executed *even without any Court-martial*, it will at once appear manifest that no prohibition can lie in such a case. For what the King had power to do, independently of any inquiry, he plainly may do, though the inquiry should not be satisfactory to a Court of Law, or even though the Court which conducted it had no legal jurisdiction to inquire." Where the Military Status of the Officer—which entirely depends on the Crown, seeing that every one who enters the Military Service engages to be entirely at the will and pleasure of the Sovereign—is the only matter in issue, the Courts will not interfere.[3]

A.D. 1793 Legal decisions support the same view.

A.D. 1833

131. That this, like every other prerogative, is to be exercised under the sanction and advice of a responsible Minister is admitted.[4] But though Parliamentary controversy is now silent, attempts have more recently been made—fortunately without success—to get *pecuniary* damages (1) from the Military Superior[5] tendering his opinion to the responsible Minister, and

Ministerial responsibility, what?

---

[1] Pea, N P C, p 176.
[2] 5 B. and Adol, p 647. In Re Poe., 5 B and Adol, p 688
[3] Re Mansergh, 1 Best and Smith p 407
[4] Chap XXV., par 29, and Bush *v* Harrison, 5 Ell and Bla., p 351, Tobin *v* Reg., 16 C B (N. S), p 353, 30 P H., p 171
[5] Dawkins *v* Lord Rokeby, 4 Fos and Fin, p 806

(2) from the latter tendering his advice to the Sovereign. "This court," said the Chief Justice (Cockburn),[1] in the latter case, "is not a Court of Appeal to determine whether the Minister has discharged his duty wisely, as to which he is responsible[2] to his Sovereign and the country, but not at the suit of a private individual. It is an exercise of the pleasure of the Sovereign through a high officer of State. The Sovereign has the power of dismissing any officer. He receives his commission from his Sovereign, and holds it at his pleasure; and it is in the will of the Sovereign to withdraw it. It is the will of the Sovereign to exercise that power through responsible servants of the Crown, and they are NOT responsible for its exercise before a jury."

132. A Court-martial is the limitation usually suggested
Legislation proposed. by the opponents of the prerogative, and their contention that no officer should be dismissed from the service of the Crown, without its previous sentence or condemnation: in fact, that the Army should be self-governed, and the government of the Crown superseded. Several attempts at legislation have been made with this object;[3] and (if we
A D 1717 may believe Mr. Pulteney), the first measure to limit the prerogative was proposed by Earl Stanhope,[4] and brought in with the assent of George I. However, if the Bill were laid before Parliament, it is not noticed in the Journals or debates.

133. In the year 1734, after the removals of the Duke of
A D 1734
—
Removal of Lords Bolton and Cobham for political reasons.
Bolton and Lord Cobham from their regiments for political motives, the subject was brought forward and warmly discussed in both Houses. In the Commons,
Lord Morpeth[5] moved for leave to introduce a Bill
Bill in the Commons
"to prevent any commissioned officer, not above the rank of a Colonel, from being removed, unless by a Court-martial, or by address of either House of Parliament," a motion which General Wade[6] opposed upon the ground that, should the proposal become law, the discipline of the

---

[1] 3 Fos and Fin , p 584   [2] Bush *v* Harrison, 5 Ell and Bla., p 351
[3] 9 Parl Hist , p 313   Chap XXVII. par 5
[4] See Lord Mahon's 'History of England,' vol iii , p 156
[5] 9 Parl Hist , pp 283, 324   [6] Ib , pp 306, 307.

Army would be so weakened that it would become an "unruly mob," that the Act would take away all dependency upon the Crown, and destroy the subordination so absolutely necessary to be strictly kept up in all armies, of inferior to superior officers. Other speakers pointed out that the effect of the Act would be to create an army *for life,* independent of the King, and Sir Robert Walpole objected, that it would "not be possible to remove any officer from his commission so long as he preserved a character, and an interest in the Army, and that it would afford an encouragement to them in the boldest attempts against the Constitution and Government of their country."[1]

134. In the Lords, a Bill[2] was introduced, printed, and came for second reading on the same day upon which Lord Morpeth's motion was made in the Commons. In opposing the Bill, the Duke of Newcastle pointed out that an officer might be engaged in treasonable practices, which it might be of the highest importance to the Crown not to discover, and yet, unless these were not only discovered to his brother officers, but *they* were convinced that the offender should be punished, he must remain in His Majesty's pay and employ.[3] The Commons refused to allow the Bill to be introduced, and the Lords to give it a second reading.

In the Lords

135 In the year 1738[4] the same subject was referred to in a Lords' debate upon the reduction of the Army. "In my opinion," said Lord Hardwicke, the officers' commissions must always be at the King's *absolute* disposal; that the giving our officers a legal title to their commissions during life, or even establishing it as a rule that no officer should be turned out of his commission but by a Court-martial, would be a cause of great oppression upon the people I am afraid that it would render our Army so mutinous, and would render it so difficult and tedious to get any officer dismissed, that the Army would, in a short time, prescribe laws both to the Crown and to the Parliament."[5]

A.D. 1738.
Subject again adverted to

136 The subject remained in abeyance until in the year

---

[1] 9 Parl. Hist., p 322   [2] See print of it in 9 Parl Hist , p 327, note
[3] Ib , p 334   [4] Ib , p 543   [5] Ib , p 560

1808 Sir Francis Burdett reopened the subject by moving a clause in the Mutiny Act, which was negatived without a division; and in the year 1815 Lord Proby renewed the subject without success.[1] In the year 1823,[2] Colonel Davies failed to induce the House of Commons to accept a clause proposed for the same object,[3] and no legislation has since been proposed in either of the Houses of Parliament. This dangerous expedient has never since been suggested.

137. Hitherto the interference of Parliament, when sought for from either House at the instance of dismissed officers, has rarely been obtained. In the year 1780, after the dismissal of the Lords Carmarthen and Pembroke from the Lieutenancy of their respective counties, the House of Lords negatived a motion for interference.[4] In the year 1789, after the Marquis of Lothian had been dismissed from his regiment, the subject was referred to in the House of Commons; "God forbid," said Mr. Fox, "that I should dispute the King's prerogative of appointing or dismissing an officer of the Army without assigning any reason whatever; I had hoped that undoubted branch of the prerogative would never be disputed;" and the subject dropped.

138. In February, 1822, Sir Robert Wilson brought his own case before the Commons,[5] but after a long debate, the House refused to interfere. "If there were any prerogative of the Crown," said Lord Palmerston, speaking as Secretary at War,[6] "undisputable and undisputed, it had been always held, and was now held, to be that of the right of dismissing any officer without trial, without assigning reasons, and without reference to whether his Commission had been purchased or not purchased. It rested on the most ancient and undoubted usage. If that prerogative were relinquished—if an officer could not be divested of his commission but by the

---

[1] 10 H D. (O. S), p 1082 .
[2] The Returns laid before Parliament showed that, between 1795 and 1822, 989 Officers had been dismissed from the service
[3] 30 H. D. (O. S), p. 46, 31 ib, p. 831, 8 H D (2), p 569
[4] 21 Parl. Hist., p. 226.   [5] 6 H. D (2), p 325   [6] P 309.

decision of members of his own body—a fourth estate would be created in the Realm, most prejudicial to the Constitution. Let Parliament once make the Army independent of the Crown, and it would not be long ere the Army would make itself independent of Parliament."

139. "I hold in my hand," said Lord Londonderry, "a paper containing the names of 210 officers who in the last ten years have been removed without a trial. . . . There were instances after instances in which, after acquittal by Court-martial, the parties had been dismissed, because there were many cases in which legal guilt could not be proved, but in which, notwithstanding, there were circumstances to affect the character of a gentleman or the harmony of a regiment, or in some way or other the good of the service." *Instances of dismissals by the Crown.*

140. It would be tedious to go through all the subsequent instances[1] in which Parliament has refused to interfere, but the two recent cases[2] attended with very different results in their subsequent issue, confirm the wisdom of the old Constitutional rule of non-interference. *Two cases of interference and non interference, in 1865 and 1867*

141. The Non-Commissioned Officers—upon whose conduct and instruction the efficiency of a Regiment so much depends—are by long custom in the Service appointed by the Colonel in command of the Regiment,[3] indeed, the same reason for giving to the Commander-in-Chief the promotion of Commissioned Officers in the Army extends to the appointment of Non-Commissioned Officers in the Regiment by the officer in command of it. Originally—or at least in 1746—they could only be reduced by the sentence of a Regimental Court-martial,[4] but in that year authority was given by the Mutiny Act to the Colonel to reduce Non-Com- *Non commissioned officers. Appointment and removal*

---

[1] The House of Commons refused repeatedly to interfere in Colonel Bradley's case (see 15 H. D. (2), p 1099, 16 ib, pp 321, 466, 38 ib, p 1155; 50 ib, p. 483, 30 ib (3), p. 54) It is perhaps scarcely too much to say that the interference of the House, when known in its ultimate results, inflicts great injury to both public and private interests

[2] Colonel Crawley's case, 173 H D, p 1161, and 174 ib, Colonel Dawkins's case, 179 ib, p 744   [3] Barwis v Keppel, 2 Wils Rep, p 315.

[4] Mutiny Act, 1746, sec 30

missioned Officers.[1] In 1750,[2] a long debate was taken on this power, but the enactment continued without amendment, until in the year 1830 (it having been previously transferred to the Articles of War) authority was given to the Sovereign, through the Commander-in-Chief, to reduce these officers;[3] and ultimately, in 1860, to the Commander-in-Chief without the express sanction of the Crown.[4] The power is to be exercised, not by the Colonel having the Honorary, but the actual Command of the Regiment; for in Barwis *v.* Keppel, the defendant contended the officer for the time being in command had this power.[5] In other respects the status and rights of the Non-Commissioned Officers are the same as those of Private Soldiers, not of Commissioned Officers.[6]

---

[1] Mutiny Act, 1746, sec 16   [2] 14 Parl. Hist., pp 642-668.
[3] Articles of War, 1830, Art 74, compared with 1829, Art. 66.
[4] Articles of War, 1860, p. 140.
[5] Wils. Rep , p. 317, Circular 442, 27 Dec , 1826, p 107; and see Vol iii , of the Wellington Supplementary Dispatches, p. 619
[6] Re Douglass, 3 Q. B. Rep , p 828, Lloyd *v.* Woodall, 1 Black Rep , p 30

CHAPTER XVII.

THE ACTION OF THE MILITARY IN AID OF THE CIVIL POWER.

AFTER the establishment of Guards and Garrisons[1] in the reign of Charles II., the immediate sequence was their employment under the orders of the Crown in the discharge of Police duties.[2] The introduction into our Civil polity of such an instrument of coercion was calculated to create—as it failed not to do—a spirit of aversion towards the Army, and of suspicion towards the Dynasty resting its authority upon such support. *(margin: Interference of the Military in Civil affairs before the Revolution)*

2. Obviously, until Charles II.'s reign,[3] the aid of Soldiers to maintain the public peace was unknown; and though the Lord-Lieutenant might have acted in aid of the Civil Power, under the 3 & 4 Edward VI.,[4] if the Act had not expired before the commencement *(margin: Until Charles II.'s reign interference of the Military unknown)* of the reign, yet the existence of Rebellion or other commotion, or unlawful assembly beyond the power of the Peace Officers alone to cope with, was to be the occasion of such interference —the law of England, as will be shown, having by other methods made ample provision for preventing riotous and disorderly meetings of the people, and for their prompt and effectual suppression whenever they arose.

3. By the Common Law, every private person may lawfully endeavour, of his own authority, and without any warrant or sanction of the magistrate, to suppress a riot by every means in his power. He may disperse, or assist in dispersing, those who are assembled; he may *(margin: Provisions (1) of the Common Law for the suppression of riots.)*

---

[1] Chap II, par 22, Chap V, par 4   [2] Chap IV, pars 5-7
[3] 14 Car II, c 11, sec. 30, Appendices XI-XIII, *ante*; 22 Car II, c 1. Chap IV, par 6, *ante*   [4] Chap III, par 4, *ante*

stay those who are engaged in it from executing their purpose; he may stop and prevent others whom he shall see coming up from joining the rest: and not only has he the authority, but it is his bounden duty, as a good Subject of the Crown, to perform this to the utmost of his ability.   Still further, not only is each private Subject bound to exert himself to the utmost, but every Sheriff, Constable, and other Peace Officer, is called upon to do all that in him lies for the suppression of riot, and each has authority to command all other Subjects to assist him in that undertaking.   It must not be overlooked that it was also the interest of the inhabitants of the Hundred to prevent the destruction of property, for which they were liable to make compensation.[1]

4. And lastly, by a resolution[2] of all the Judges, any Justices of the Peace, Sheriff, or other Magistrates, or any other Subjects, may arm themselves to suppress riots, rebellions, or resist enemies, endeavouring themselves to suppress such disturbers of the Peace.   But the resolution suggested that "the most discreet way was for every one to attend and assist the Justices in such case, or other Ministers of the King" in doing their duty.[3]

The use of arms.

5. By the Statute Law the duty of maintaining the Public Peace was, and still is, thrown on the Civil Power, By 34 Edward III., c. 1, Justices may restrain and arrest rioters, and the Statute—having been liberally construed—empowers[4] a single Justice to arrest, or authorize others to arrest, persons riotously assembled.   By another early Statute, still in force,[5] any two Justices, together with the Sheriff or Under Sheriff of the county, shall, if need be, come with the power of the county, to arrest any rioters, and shall arrest them; and they have power to record that which they see done in their presence against the law; by which record the offenders shall be convicted, and may be afterwards brought to punishment.

(2) of the Early Statute Law

---

[1] 7 & 8 Geo. IV , c. 31, secs 2, 3
[2] Kelyng Rep , p 76 , Popham Rep , p 121   [3] 1 Rus on Crimes (1865) p 403
[4] Chap I , pars 6 and 7, *ante*   [5] 13 Hen IV , c 7

6. "It is not," said the late Chief Justice Tindal,[1] "left to the choice or will of the Subject—as some have erroneously supposed—to attend or not to the call of the Magistrate, as he may think proper; but every man is bound, when called upon, under pain of fine and imprisonment, to yield a ready and implicit obedience to the call of the Magistrate, and to do his utmost to assist him to suppress any tumultuous assembly: for, in the succeeding reign, another Statute was passed, which enacts, "That the King's liege people being sufficient to travel, shall be assistant to the Justices, Sheriffs and other Officers, upon reasonable warning, to ride with them in aid to resist such riots, routs, and assemblies, on pain of imprisonment and to make fine and ransom to the King."[2] In explanation of which Statute, Dalton, an early writer of considerable authority, declares, " that the Justices and Sheriff may command and ought to have the aid and attendance of all Knights, Gentlemen, Yeomen, Husbandmen, Labourers, Tradesmen, Servants, and Apprentices, and all other persons being above the age of fifteen years and able to travel."

Comment of Tindal, Chief Justice, on the Statute Law

7. This being the Common and Statute Law of the Realm in force—contrast with it the Legislation, and the Civil Administration of Charles II.'s reign.

These provisions contrasted with the Acts of Charles II's reign.

8. In the first place, by the Militia Act, a Military Officer[3] —the Lord-Lieutenant—was made directly responsible for the Public Peace. having the power of searching for, and—without the intervention of any Civil authority —of ordering the Militia under arms and into service for the suppression of what this officer deemed to be insurrection[4] or rebellion. Then the Soldiers of the Regular Army could be called on, under the 14 Car. II., c. 11, sec. 30,[5] to collect Customs, and, under the 22 Car. II., c. 1, to suppress conventicles.[6]

As to Legislation

---

[1] Bristol rioters, 5 Cav and Pay , p 261, *note* I have (as the legal reader will observe) availed myself of the language of this judgment in several paragraphs
[2] 2 Henry V., c 8.   [3] Chap III par 16; Chap XIV, pars. 7, 10
[4] 14 Car II , c 3, secs. 1, 6   [5] Appendix C, Vol I   [6] Chap IV , par 6

9. With regard to the Civil administration, the preface to the Articles of War, 1668,[1] shows that the King maintained the Army for "*the Peace* of the Kingdom till the *minds of the people* should be composed to unity and *due obedience;*" and its employment was that of armed Police, acting under the direct orders of the Crown. In being placed in billets throughout the Kingdom,[2] the maintenance of the Army added to the oppression of the people.

As to Administration

10. Throughout the reign of Charles II. the action of Parliament was therefore incessantly directed to the disbandment of the Forces, and when the Houses failed to secure this object, and James II. elected to govern by a Standing Army, the Nation did—what any Free People would do under the same circumstances—namely, they got rid both of the Dynasty and of the Army—established a free Government under a Constitutional Monarch, with proper limitations upon the Power of the Crown to maintain a Standing Army.[3]

Action of Parliament against a Standing Army

11. To trace the subject of the present Chapter from the epoch of the Revolution it is sufficient to commence with the time of George I.; for Parliament had shown a determination, in the reigns of William and Anne, to restrain the Crown from using Military Force to coerce the people, by limiting the Army in number barely sufficient to maintain the Garrisons of the Kingdom.[4] And in the reign of George I. it will be seen with what deliberation the responsible Ministers of the Crown first sanctioned the use of the Military in aid of the Civil Power; and, moreover, that, prior to the Crimean War, the Constitutional rule was that this use was controlled by one Responsible, and expressly sanctioned by another Parliamentary, Minister before the Troops moved from their quarters at the call of the Magistrate.

Subject traced from the reign of Geo. I

12. At the close of Queen Anne's life there were plain indications of Political disturbance, and that on her decease, the friends of the Pretender would endeavour to

The Riot Act passed

---

[1] Appendix X., Vol I., p 446   [2] Chap. IV., pars 9, 10 15, 18
[3] Chap V.   [4] Chap XI., par. 4, Chap XIII., pars 3 6

recover his throne; therefore one of the earliest Statutes of George I.'s reign gave the *Civil* Magistrate additional power for the suppression of Tumult or Political disorder. This Act,[1] known as the Riot Act, varies little—save in omitting all reference to the Lord-Lieutenant and mentioning *only* Civil Officers—from the Statute of Edward VI.

13. It provides, in substance, as follows.—

That if twelve or more persons unlawfully and riotously assemble together to the disturbance of the public peace, and—after being required by any Justice, by proclamation to be made in the King's[2] name, to disperse, and peaceably to depart to their habitations— shall remain or continue together *for one hour* after the proclamation, then such continuing together shall be adjudged felony, and the offenders felons.

Provisions of it.

(1) Proclamation for rioters to disperse

(2). After the hour, every Justice and such other persons as he shall command to assist him (such Justice being thereby authorized to command all Her Majesty's subjects of age and ability to assist therein), shall seize and apprehend such persons as aforesaid, in order to their being proceeded against for such their offences according to law; and if the persons so unlawfully and riotously assembled, or any of them, shall happen to be killed, maimed, or hurt, in the dispersing, seizing, or apprehending, by reason of their resisting the persons so acting, that then every such Justice, and all and singular persons aiding and assisting, shall be free discharged, and indemnified of, for or concerning the killing maiming, or hurting of any such person as shall happen to be so killed, maimed, or hurt as aforesaid.

(2) Power of Justices to Act after an hour

14. The object of the Act is to give all Her Majesty's subjects due notice that unless they disperse and separate from a meeting deemed by the Justices to be unlawful, they must—happen what may in dispersing it—take the consequences. "By the Act," said Lord Mansfield,[3] "a parti-

Object of the Act

---

[1] 1 Geo. I, sess 2, c 5, Chap III., par 4, and see Chief Baron Parker's remarks in Rex *v* Gillan, Appendix CII. (13), *post*

[2] Or the Queen's name, as the Cabinet on the 9th April, 1848, decided.

[3] Rex *v* Kennet, 5 Car and Pay., p 295, *note*

cular direction is given to every Justice for his conduct; he is required to read the Act, and the consequences are explained. It is a step *in terrorem* and of gentleness; not made a necessary step, as he may *instantly* repel force by force. If the insurgents are not doing any act, the reading of the proclamation operates as notice. There never was a riot without bystanders, who go off on reading the Act."

15. Though plainly the intention of the Act, this view was not understood at the time of Lord George Gordon's Riots, for an impression then prevailed that no effectual measures could be taken by the Justices, or others, until *the hour* spoken of in the Act had expired. "It has been imagined," said Lord Loughborough,[1] in charging the Grand Jury on that occasion, "that because the Law allows an hour for the dispersion of a mob to whom the Riot Act has been read by the Magistrate, the better to support the Civil authority, that, during that time, the Civil Power and the Magistracy are disarmed, and the King's subjects, whose duty it is at all times to suppress riots, are to remain quiet and passive. No such meaning was within view of the Legislature, nor does the operation of the Act warrant any such effect. The Civil Magistrates are left in possession of those powers which the Law had given them before. If the mob collectively, or a part of it, or any individual within or before the expiration of that hour, attempts or begins to perpetrate an outrage amounting to felony, to pull down a house, or by any other act to violate the law, it is the duty of all present, of whatever description they may be, to endeavour to stop the mischief, and to apprehend the offender." "A mistake," as Sir James Mansfield[2] thought, "the more extraordinary because formerly the the *posse comitatus*, which was the strength to prevent felonies, must, in a great proportion, have consisted of Military tenants who held lands by the tenure of Military Service. If it is necessary for the purpose of the preventing mischief, or for the execution of the Law, it is not only the right of Soldiers, but it is their duty to exert themselves in assisting the execution of a legal process, or to prevent any crime or mischief being com-

[1] 21 Howell, State Trials, p 493   [2] Burdett *v* Abbot, 4 Taunt. Rep., p 449

In the left margin beside paragraph 15: *Misunderstood in 1780.*

mitted. It is, therefore, highly important that the mistake should be corrected, which supposes that an Englishman, by taking upon him the additional character of a Soldier, puts off any of the rights and duties of an Englishman."

16. Now, passing to the more immediate subject of this Chapter, it may be observed that the earliest evidences that the War Office Records afford of the use of Troops in suppressing riots (so far as the Records have come under notice) bear date in Jan., 1716-17, and June, 1717. Some Subjects in Scotland and Ireland appear to have acted upon Lord Holt's suggestion,[1] and indicted the Soldiers for manslaughter or homicide. In each case the Law Officers of the Crown were directed to enter a *Nolle prosequi.*[2]

In 1716-17 Law Officers of Scotland and Ireland instructed to enter a *Nolle prosequi*

17. In August of the same year the Government was called upon to give specific directions for the Military to act under the 14 Car. II., c. 11, sec. 30, in aid of the Civil Power and Customs Collectors, as the Commanding Officers had—on application from these authorities—refused to give them aid. Accordingly the authority of the Privy Council was invoked; and a Council Order issued, sanctioning the employment of the Army, and directing the Secretary at War to carry the same into effect.[3]

A.D. 1717
Order in Council for the use of the troops in aid of Customs Officers.

---

[1] 33 H. D (S), p 1159 ; Life of Lord Holt (1846) (Sweet, London), p. 125.

[2] Appendices XCVIII, XCIX , *post.*

[3] Appendix C

Memorandum from the Custom House, 23rd April, 1869 —The last Act I can trace which distinctly authorized the employment of Soldiers for the purpose of preventing illicit practices on the Revenue, is the 47 Geo III , c 66, s. 30, which enacts, " That is shall be lawful for any Warrant or other Non-commissioned Officer not being below the rank of a Sergeant in the Army, who shall be approved of by the Officer for the time being commanding the Regiment in which he serves, as proper and qualified for the service to patrol with any number of Soldiers under his command, for the purpose of preventing illicit practices on the Revenue, and to seize, *without having any deputation from the Commissioners of Customs or Excise for that purpose,*" &c , &c

This Act, as well as the 13 & 14 Car II , c 11, continued in force until the year 1826, when they, and all other Acts for the prevention of smuggling, were repealed by the 6 Geo IV , c. 105 The Smuggling Acts repealed were con-

18. This order (so far as the War Office Records show)
This Order in Council the original authority for the employment of the Military is clearly the foundation of the existing practice of calling out the Military in aid of the Civil Power. The subsequent issue of orders by the Secretary at War is attributed to Mr. Pulteney [1] (who was in office at the time, and only for a few weeks after the date of the Privy Council Order), and they are easily traced from that period.

19. The next order to the Military to aid the Magistrates
1st Order by the Deputy-Secretary at War. was a measure of preservation from plague, and appears to have been issued without consulting the Law Officers of the Crown. It is dated 3rd December, 1720,[2] under the Sign Manual of the *Deputy* Secretary at War to the Commanding Officer of the Troops at Lancaster, "to aid and assist the Civil Magistrates in preventing boats with persons coming over from the Isle of Man to land upon any part of the coast of Lancashire, in regard there is advice that the plague is in that island, and to follow such orders and directions as you shall receive from the Civil Magistrates for the purposes above mentioned, and *to repel force with force in case* the Civil Magistrates shall at any time think it necessary.".

20. In 1721-2 the legality of using Troops in aid of the
A.D. 1721. Legality of employing the troops considered by the Responsible Ministers. Civil Power to put down riots, irrespective of the Statute Law, appears for the first time to have been deliberately considered by the Responsible advisers of the Crown. In the case dealt with by the Privy Council that Law sanctioned the employment of Troops, but in the present instance the question rested solely upon the Common Law. Lord Raymond's Report—obviously written with great care—specifies the circumstances under which the Army

---

solidated into one "Act for the prevention of Smuggling" (6 Geo. IV., c. 108), which authorized only *Officers of the Army*, navy, or marines, *duly authorized and on full pay*, to seize Vessels, Boats, and Goods, and to search and detain Persons, &c. (Sections 34 to 36 and others)

These powers to Officers have been continued through all subsequent Smuggling Acts, and were finally embodied in the Customs Consolidation Act, 1853, which is still in force. (See 16 & 17 Vic. c. 107, secs. 228, 229, 249, 251, 253, 254 and 259.)

[1] Appendix CII. (4).   [2] Mis. Bk. 523, p. 91.

could be lawfully used to aid the Magistrates, but adds a caution—which Lord Carteret also enforced—that the Army "should not at all interpose in any of these things but at such times as they shall be desired by the Civil Magistrate."[1]

21. The orders then issued were plain and explicit, they left no room for doubt, so far as the acts of the Government were concerned. The Warrants of the King or of the Secretary at War, from 1716 to 1723, directed the Troops " to repel force with force in case the Civil Magistrate should find it necessary," or "to repel force with force in case it should be found necessary;" and the orders from 1724 to 1732 sometimes ran in the affirmative, but generally in the negative—viz., "not to repel force with force unless the Civil Magistrate (or the Civil Magistrates and Officers of the Customs) should find it necessary." Indeed, in one instance, the order was still more restrictive, viz., "to repel force with force if it shall be found absolutely necessary *and not otherwise.*'"

The Orders issued were definite and plain.

22. In this aspect of the question the Secretary at War in 1732 appeared to be in doubt as to the form in which his Warrant should run, and, with regard to the repelling force by force, to think that it might be further extended; Sir P. Yorke, however, considered it to be advisable to express the order in general terms agreeably to some of the precedents—viz., "*Not* to repel force with force unless it shall be found absolutely necessary."[2]

A.D. 1732

Sir P Yorke's Report on the form of the Orders

23. The form in which the Warrant continued to stand is shown in the Appendix,[3] until, in May, 1735, an alteration was made at the instance of the Treasury, acting at the request of the Commissioners of Customs. The Warrant which stood thus:—"But not to repel force with force unless [thereunto required by the Civil Magistrates];[4] was altered by omitting the words placed in brackets and by inserting the words, "it shall be found absolutely necessary." In the old Warrant the Military were to act strictly under orders, and in the other to exercise a discretion as to the absolute necessity for repelling force by force.

A.D. 1735

Report of the Law Officers.

---

[1] Appendix CII (2).   [2] Appendix CII (3).   [3] Appendix CII (6).
[4] Appendix CII (7)

24. From the entries in the War Office Letter Books, the
General Order to act in aid. Bread Riots in the West of England in 1766 appear
to have been the first occasion upon which the Secre-
tary at War issued anything like a General Order for the
Troops to act in aid of the Civil Power, without a previous
reference to him. The terms in which these instructions were
framed show that the course adopted by the Secretary at War
was novel;[1] but certainly, from the debates, first, on Mr.
Burke's motion in 1769 for an inquiry "as to the employment
of the Military in St. George's Fields," and then on Mr.
Pownall's motion in 1770 "to introduce a clause into the
Mutiny Bill that the Justice should make his requisition *in
writing*," it is evident that the authority of the Justice was
then fully recognized as a *sufficient* justification to a Military
Officer for using his men in aid of the Civil Power.

25. Now the first occasion on which the action of the Mili-
A.D. 1737
Murder of Cap ain Porteous. tary in aid of the Civil Power was challenged in
Parliament was after the murder of Captain Porteous
at Edinburgh in 1737,[2] when the whole subject came
before both Houses. The order to fire having been obeyed by
the Soldiers, the Officer, by his conviction at law, was held not
justified in having given the order. The Guard was not under
the Crown; nor was the prosecution stopped by the Lord
Advocate as in 1716-17,[3] though a reprieve was ultimately sent.

26. In the period which intervened before the employment
A.D 1758-63.
The Crown restrained from using the Militia in aid of the Civil Power except on terms. of the Military in aid of the Civil Magistrate again
came under discussion, the Legislature had restrained
the Crown from employing the Militia[4] as a Military
force except in case of rebellion, and then only upon a *previous* communication to Parliament, if sitting,
or by Order in Council. Moreover, the power of the

---

[1] Appendix CII (9, 10) The Secretary at War apprised the two Secretaries
of State of these orders

[2] 9 Parl. Hist., p. 1274, *note*, 10 ib, pp 187, 206-209, 280, 292-318, 22 Com
Journ, Proceedings on "Wilson's Bill," and "Porteous," and vol ii. of Lord
Hervey's 'Memoirs of George II,' p. 139   [3] Par. 16, *ante.*
[4] Chap. III., par 33, Chap XIII, par. 9

Lord-Lieutenant to search for arms to secure the Public Peace was withdrawn. The restriction still remains, and there is at the present time no statutory authority for the *disembodied* Militia to act in aid of the Civil Power, while, on the other hand, an opinion of some weight has been expressed in Parliament that the force should never be used in that service.[1]

27. In April 1768, in anticipation of a Riot that ultimately took place, Lord Weymouth suggested to the Lord-Lieutenant and the Magistrates of Surrey, in terms that were censured by Mr. Burke,[2] the employment of the Military *in case of need*, and further that, if called upon to act, the Military should do so effectually. The Secretary at War, Lord Barrington, appears to have acted with more caution, inasmuch as he refused to sanction the movement of Troops to the probable scene of disorder until necessity required their aid.[3] The Troops were placed under general orders[4] to attend the call of the Civil Magistrates, but no trace is to be found on the War Office Books of that care which was manifested on previous occasions when the Military had been used with the direct sanction of the Crown or its responsible Ministers.

28. Although Lord Barrington[5] thanked the Guards on this occasion in the name of the King, yet their behaviour became the subject of investigation in the Criminal Courts. The prosecution of the most importance was that directed against the Magistrate who gave the orders: but the Soldiers who obeyed them were also placed upon their trial for murder. In the first case, that of the Queen *v.* Gillam, Esquire, the defendant was held justified in having sent for the Military and in having ordered them to fire. The Evidence in the Case is to be found printed in the Annual Register,[6] but the decisions of the Judges who sat with the Recorder have not (that I am cognizant of) been published until inserted in the Appendix.[7] In the second case against the Soldiers, the Crown, having abandoned the practice of a *Nolle*

Marginal notes: A.D. 1768. Riots in St George's Fields. Criminal proceedings against the Civil Magistrate and the Military

---

[1] Chap III, par 46.
[2] See Appendix CII (11), and 'Junius's Letters,' vol i p 126, ib, vol iii, p 57.
[3] This was his rule   See War Office Letter Book, 1766, p 301
[4] Appendix CII (13).   [5] Appendix CII (14)
[7] Appendix CII (15)   [6] Vol ii, pp 227-233

prosequi, defended them.   The Report of the case was not allowed to be published by authority, but the men were acquitted, and afterwards received a pecuniary reward from the Crown for their imprisonment.[1]

29. In Parliament the subject was brought to notice upon several occasions.   In the first instance, before the Trials had been prosecuted, the Houses voted addresses of thanks to the King and to the Lord Mayor for their conduct in the suppression of the disturbances;[2] but after these votes had been disposed of, Mr. Burke, on the 8th of March, 1769, moved in the Commons for a Committee to "inquire into the conduct of the Magistrates and the employment of the Military power in suppressing the riots in the St. George's Fields on the 10th of May last, and into the orders and directions given relative thereto, by any of His Majesty's Secretaries of State, or by His Majesty's Secretary at War, together with the course that has been held concerning the public prosecutions on that occasion."   The motion failed of success; but in urging it he suggested that the inquiry, if granted, might show the necessity for a Bill to regulate the use of the Military by the Civil power,—a suggestion which Mr. Grenville answered by saying that the relation between the Civil and Military authorities stood on as good a ground as it could do, for the Civil Magistrate might call out the Military to his assistance when he wanted it, but if he used them improperly he did so at his own peril.[3]

A.D. 1769

Subsequent discussions in Parliament.

Mr Burke's motion

30. The subject was not, however, permitted to rest upon this discussion; for in 1770, when the Mutiny Bill was introduced, Mr. Pownall carried a motion "that it be an instruction to the Committee to receive a clause for regulating the manner in which the Civil Magistrate requiring the aid and assistance of Officers and Soldiers of His Majesty's Forces, shall call for that aid and assistance," and introduced a clause framed in these words:— "That whenever the Civil Magistrate called for the Officers *or* Soldiers of the Army to aid him he should make his

A.D. 1770

Mr Pownall's motion to amend the Mutiny Bill

---

[1] See Lord Barrington's justification of this, and of his view, 17 Parl Hist, p 175.   [2] 16 Parl. Hist., p. 462.   [3] Ib., p. 603.

requisition in writing, and give the reason of it and sign his name; or if he was so circumstanced that he could not do so, then the Officer called upon should take down the message in writing before witnesses" There appeared every disposition to adopt this or some other amendment until Lord Clare puzzled the House with the suggestion that as neither the Magistrate nor Officer might be able to *write*, what then was to be done?[1] No one was prepared to meet this difficulty, and the Clause was negatived with an understanding—never realized—that the subject should be resumed in the next Session.

31. The father of one of the persons killed—and that rather by accident than design—William Allen, addressed a petition first to the King and then to the House of Commons for inquiry and redress of wrongs. The latter petition, which is to be found printed in the Annual Register,[2] was brought before the House on the 25th April, 1771, by Mr. Serjeant Glynn; but, as Lord North and Lord Barrington strongly opposed the motion for receiving it, the House refused to have the petition read,[3] and nothing more was heard of these riots or of the acts of the Executive for their suppression.

A.D. 1771
Petition from the father of William Allen for inquiry

32. From this period the legality of employing the Military[4] in aid of the Civil Power has never been seriously questioned.[5] Indeed, one of the charges imputed to Kennett,[6] upon his trial for neglect of duty as Lord Mayor, was that he had *not* used the Military in aid, and therefore all the subsequent controversies that have arisen have turned upon the relative responsibility imposed upon the Ministers of the Crown on the one hand, and the subordinate Officers (Civil and Military) on the other, in the suppression of riots by the Military.

Legality of employing the Military admitted.

---

[1] 16 Parl Hist, p. 1333. [2] Vol. x.

[3] 33 Com Journ., p 353, 17 Parl Hist, p. 175

[4] 21 Parl Hist, p. 592, 28 ib. p 872, but the appearance of the Military, except under the order of the Civil Magistrate, was strongly objected to, 10 H D. (3), p 968.

[5] Rex v Kennett, 5 Car and Pay, p 282, and Appendix CII (16 and 17)

[6] As to riots at Clitheroe in 1832, see 14 H D (3), p. 1257

33. As matter preliminary to the consideration of these questions, it may be well to ascertain what direct sanction, since the Revolution, Parliament has given to this employment of the Regular and auxiliary forces in this service.

What sanction Parliament has given to the employment of the Military

34. With regard to the Regular Troops, there are no statutory provisions whatever; but Parliament has indirectly sanctioned their employment by granting on former occasions—in the case of the Guards—an extra allowance when they were on duty for the preservation of the public peace.[1]

1st. As to the Regular Troops

35. The Pensioners were enrolled expressly for the purpose of aiding the Civil Power,[2] and the Act under which the Army Reserve Force is established gives the Officers and Men authority to act, and the Mutiny Act to march without payment of tolls.[3]

2nd Army Reserve

36. In recent years the Legislation for the establishment of the auxiliary Forces has altered the characteristic of the Statutes of Charles II's. reign, Parliament having evinced a desire to withdraw these Forces entirely from Police duties. The *dis*embodied Militia, as previously shown, cannot be brought out except under certain eventualities, not under present consideration, but the Permanent Staff is serving under a different arrangement.

3rd The disembodied Militia.

37. The General Militia Act[4] of 1802 provides "that the Staff may be billeted when employed on any duty upon which they may be commanded by any legal authority," but fails to define the term "legal authority." The Act then directs[5] that the Serjeants are to act under the command of the Adjutant, who again is to act under the orders of the Colonel, the Chief Command being vested in the Lord-Lieutenant."[6]

4th Permanent Staff of the Militia.

38. When the Local Militia was raised in 1808 the 48 Geo. III., c. 111,[7] establishing the force, directed that by order of the Lord or Vice-Lieutenant, or of the Sheriff, and in their absence of any two Justices and one

Rule of the Local Militia.

---

[1] 1 H. D (2), p. 1188, 11 Sess. Pap. (1820) [214, 215], pp 173-5
[2] Chap XIV, par 161.   [3] Sec 73.   [4] 42 Geo III, c 90, sec. 108
[5] Sec 107.   [6] Sec. 5   [7] See also 52 Geo III., c 38, s 92

Deputy Lieutenant, it might be brought out,[1] for the suppression of riot or tumults in such county, or in any adjoining county, and that every one enrolled was bound to attend, under the same penalties that attached for absence from training and exercise.

39. The Annual Pay and Clothing Act,[2] 1809, provided that "the Regular and Local Militia should have pay and allowances for such period or periods for which they should be called out for suppressing riots or tumults;" and the same clause stood in the several Annual Acts passed from that period until the year 1815 inclusive. The Militia being disembodied, this Clause was withdrawn, and the direct statutory authority for calling out the Militia ceased. However, the practice of calling out the Permanent Staff for the aid of the Civil Power continued with the knowledge and sanction of the Secretary at War.[3] Pay and Clothing Act, 1809 to 1815

40. No alteration in the Law was made until the enrolled Pensioners had been established as a Local Force, when Lord Hardinge deemed it expedient to transfer the allegiance of the Militia Permanent Staff *from* the Lord-Lieutenant *to* the Staff Officer of Pensioners   Accordingly, in the Militia Pay and Clothing Act of 1843, a clause[4] was inserted that the Permanent Staff should "be liable to be employed within the county under the Staff Officers of Pensioners in such manner as one of Her Majesty's Principal Secretaries of State may determine." This has been continued in each subsequent Annual Act, and contains the only statutory authority (such as it is) for employing the Militia Permanent Staff in aid of the Civil Power. A.D. 1843. Permanent Staff transferred to the command of the Staff Officer of Pensioners.

41. The use of the Yeomanry in aid of the Civil Power has been shown in treating of the Reserve Forces.[5] The wording of Section 23 of the Yeomanry Act— which section appears to have been proposed by Mr. Pitt, and introduced when the Bill was in Committee[6]—is not clear; the construction put upon it is that a Yeoman cannot be punished as a deserter if he does not, in answer to the summons of the 5th The Yeomanry

---

[1] Under Sect. 41.   [2] 49 Geo III , c. 38, s. 4

[3] Appendix CIII , and $\frac{155221}{1}$, A, Dumfries, 125   [4] Sec 3.

[5] Chap XIV , par. 103   [6] 1 P D , pp 721, 722.

Lord-Lieutenant, come out in case of riot.[1] Certainly he should, if he does come out, be liable to the Mutiny Act and Articles of War, though the view taken of the Act in 1821 may tend to throw some doubt upon his liability.[2]

42. The Bill on which the Volunteer Act, 1863, was passed, when introduced into the Commons contained a Clause (19)—not enabling a Volunteer Corps, with the approval of the Secretary of State to aid the Civil Power, because in times of riots that may be an obligation, and not an option, but—declaring such an assembling to be *actual service*, and—as a consequence—rendering the Corps liable to the Mutiny Act and Articles of War. The House, however, manifested so strong a disposition to dissociate the Volunteers, *as such*, from all Police duties, that the Clause was struck out when the Bill was passing through Committee.[3] Thus the Statute Law is entirely silent as to the duty of a Volunteer to aid the Civil Power.[4]

6th The Volunteers.

The Volunteer Bill and Act, 1863.

43. Upon the appearance of strangers in Chester, the Volunteers, like the loyal Train Bands of old, obeyed the call of the Constituted Authorities, and protected the Castle and town from intrusion.[5] That and other events[6] made it essential that specific directions should be given by the Government to the Volunteers as to their duty under similar circumstances. A Circular Memorandum was therefore issued on the 3rd June, 1867. After a debate in the House of Commons[7] it was withdrawn, and another of the 13th June issued. Both circulars will be found in the Appendix.[8]

A.D. 1867

Circulars to the Volunteers.

44. The measures adopted by the late Sir Robert Peel in 1829,[9] on the advice of the Duke of Wellington, for establishing, as a counterpoise to the Guards, the

Police Establishment.

---

[1] Reg *v* Witneshaw, 2 Adol. and Ell., p. 648

[2] Chap XIV., pars 116, 117, and Appendix LXXVII.

[3] Compare Prints (108), 5th May, with (152), 4th June, 1863

[4] The Commons' Debates on the Bill are to be found in 170 H D (3), pp 1247, 1693; 171 ib, pp. 332-367, 958, the Lords' Debates, ib, pp 966, 1244, 1427, 1718, 172 ib., pp 45, 725, 1141.

[5] Chap. I., par. 16   [6] Lords' Debate, 185 H. D (3), pp 371, 919

[7] Ib, pp. 1550, 1575.   [8] Appendix CIV

[9] 10 Geo IV., c 44, and see the Mem of the Duke of Wellington to Lord Liverpool's Cabinet, 1820, vol. 1 Supplementary Despatches, p 127

(Metropolitan) Police Force—the principle of which in more recent years has been extended throughout the United Kingdom—convey in a practical manner the intentions of Parliament that the Peace of the kingdom shall be entrusted to a Police acting under the Home Secretary, rather than to a Military Force acting under an indefinite responsibility. The present Police in the United Kingdom capable of bearing arms (in some instances almost with, as much efficiency as Soldiers) exceed in number the Army of Great Britain before the year 1793.

45. From the Judicial Statistics for 1867 (laid before Parliament by Command in 1868) the Returns of the Police for England only, made pursuant to the 19 & 20 Vic., c. 69, shew the following as the numbers, composing the different forces in each of the years 1866-7, and 1865-6:—

A.D. 1866-7
Strength of that Establishment in Great Britain

	1866-7.	1865-6.
Constables of Boroughs appointed under the Municipal Corporation Act of 1835	6946 ..	6777
County Constables appointed under the Constabulary Acts of 1839 and 1840	8746 ..	8674
Metropolitan Police Constables appointed under the Police Act of 1829	7114 ..	6839
Her Majesty's Dockyard, &c., Police	568 ..	739
Constables for the City of London appointed under the City Local Act of 1839	699 ..	699
Total Police and Constabulary	24,073 ..	23,728

and the Metropolitan Police (if I mistake not) has been increased by 1000 men since these Returns were prepared; when to these numbers are added the Irish Constabulary of 12,572 men,[1] and the Police Force in Scotland, the total Force will be found far to exceed the strength of the Regular Army in and prior to the year 1793.[2]

46. However, assuming that these "ordinary officers are not sufficient for the preservation of the peace," Parliament has made provision under the 1 & 2 Wm. IV., c. 41, for the nomination of householders as Special

Power of appointing Special Constables

---

[1] Return pursuant to 6 Wm. IV., c. 13, sec 57 (476), 27th July, 1868.

[2] See Appendix, Note M

Constables, having all such powers and immunities, and liable to all the duties and responsibilities of any Constable duly appointed by virtue of the Common Law of the Realm or of any Statute. If a duly appointed person should not act when called upon to do so, then the Justices have power to fine him in any sum not exceeding 5*l*. The poor have no reasonable excuse for neglect, as the Constables may be paid; and in the case of the Chelsea Pensioners[1] (until the 5 & 6 Vic., c. 70 was passed) the usual course was for the Home Office to authorise their enrolment and payment out of the County rates.[2] Volunteers are not, but Yeomen are, exempt from the offices of Constable and Special Constable.[3]

47. With regard to the employment of Military in lieu of the Police, there is this apparent defect in the present Law, viz., that the Military are sent to and remain in a particular Town (where their services are needed by the inhabitants as armed Police for the protection of property[4] or the preservation of peace) not at the expense of the Local but of the General Community, giving thereby a premium, instead of inflicting a pecuniary mulct upon the inhabitants of the town or place for their insufficient ordinary Police arrangements. Where Soldiers are used as Police, the rule of that service should be followed, and the inhabitants should bear their expenses at, and their removal to their town or city for their service as Police. This principle has been adopted in other Police matters by the 1 & 2 Vic., c. 80, and in Ireland by the 11 and 12 Vic., c. 2, secs. 5 to 8.[5]

As to the cost of Police and Military acting in aid, and by whom borne.

---

[1] Chap XIV, par 164   [2] 1831, Nov 30, War Office Regulations, p 104.
[3] 57 Geo III, c 44, sec 3, and 5 & 6 Vic, c 109, secs 3, 5
[4] 7 & 8 Geo IV, c. 31
[5] For example, if the Manchester Magistrates request 500 men of the Metropolitan Police to be sent down to aid in maintaining the peace and order of the town, the Magistrates provide for the men and the Ratepayers of Manchester bear their expenses, but if the same Magistrates request 500 Soldiers to be sent for the same purposes, the *Taxpayers* of the kingdom have to bear all the expenses of the 500 Soldiers, and the *Ratepayers* of Manchester nothing   The Magistrates requisition for the Military should be held as an engagement to pay for their expenses out of the County or Borough rates   Again, if litigation arises from their obedience to the Civil Magistrates, why should the Imperial funds be made to bear 300*l* or 400*l* for the legal expenses of their defence?

48. In considering the legal and constitutional questions resulting from the employment of the Regular Troops in aid of the Civil power, no confusion must be permitted to arise upon the doctrine laid down by the late Lord Chief Justice Tindal, as to the duty of every soldier—because he is also a citizen—to suppress Riot. In the debate[1] of 1843 upon the 6 & 7 Vic., c. 95, it was plainly understood that no Military Body should act *as such* in aid of the Civil Power, unless the officers and men were under the Mutiny Act. What, I apprehend, that learned Judge intended to point out was, that, if need be, the action and presence of a Soldier in aid of the Civil power *might* be justified on this ground, viz., that a Citizen, by becoming a Soldier, has not put off any or assumed less responsibility in matters purely Civil and not Military, than pertains to a Citizen. "The soldier is still a citizen, lying under the same obligation and invested with the same authority to preserve the peace of the King as any other subject. If the one is bound to attend the call of the Civil Magistrate, so also is the other; if the one may interfere for that purpose when the occasion demands it, without the requisition of the Magistrate, so may the other too; if the one may employ arms for that purpose, when arms are necessary, the soldier may do the same. Undoubtedly the same exercise of discretion which requires the Private Subject to act in subordination to and in aid of the Magistrate, rather than upon his own authority, before recourse is had to arms, ought to operate in a still stronger degree with a Military force."[2]

The duty of a soldier equal to that of a citizen in riots.

49. In extreme cases where the danger is pressing and immediate—where a felony has actually been committed, or cannot otherwise be prevented, and from the circumstances of the case no opportunity is offered of obtaining a requisition from the proper authorities —the Military, like the Civil subjects of the King, not only may, but are bound to do their utmost, of their own authority, to prevent the perpetration of outrage, to put down riot and tumult, and to preserve the lives and property of the people.[3]

In extreme cases independent action of the military justified

---

[1] Sir James Graham, 71 H D. (3), pp 642 83   [2] 5 Car. and Pay.   [3] Ib.

50. But although the law *might*—if that aspect of the case arose—justify the action of a Soldier upon the theory of his duties as a citizen—for the Magistrates have no power to call for the assistance of the Military in cases in which they cannot call for the assistance of others of His Majesty's subjects—yet it must not be assumed that when the Officer or Soldier goes to aid the Civil Power, he does so to fulfil any other obligation than that of an officer or soldier acting under a lawful order given within the terms of the Mutiny Act, or that he could refuse either to go or to act in obedience to orders, except under the penalty of forfeiting his life—upon trial by Court-Martial — for mutiny and insubordination. "We conceive," wrote Lords Eldon and Redesdale, "His Majesty may, by orders given to the Troops, make assistance to the Civil Magistrate in the execution of his Civil duty a part of their Military duty, that the Troops acting at the requisition of the Civil Magistrate in obedience to such orders, would still be subject to Military discipline, and would therefore act as a Military Body, commanded by Military officers, and that the orders of the Civil Magistrate would not warrant them in disobedience to the orders of their Military Commanders, acting in discharge of their Military duty." [1]

The action of the Military to be justified on the grounds of Military duty

51. "This being so, it follows that the Magistrates cannot require from the Military any assistance repugnant to the obligations of their military duty, such as to march from that part of the country in which they are stationed by their military orders, to another part of the country to which their military orders do not direct or authorize them; neither can they detach soldiers from their officers, by requiring them to assist in executing a warrant without asking the permission of their Commanding Officer The soldiers thus absent from their military duty without leave would be guilty of a military offence, for which the requisition of the constable would afford them no lawful excuse, although the circumstances might be such as to induce their Commanding Officer to consider their fault as not meriting very severe reprehension."

The requirements of the Civil Power must be consistent with this duty

[1] Extracts from Report of Lords Eldon and Redesdale in Appendix CII (18 to 21).

52. "It also follows that the military duty of a Soldier remains whilst he acts under the orders of a Civil Their military obedience is not interfered with. magistrate; that he is still necessarily subservient to, and that the command of the Magistrate cannot exempt him from, military discipline. On the contrary, when His Majesty, and officers by his command, authorize any Military corps to act in the assistance of the Civil magistrate, they do not authorize the individuals composing that corps to leave their Military duty, but require them to afford assistance to the Civil magistrate in obedience to and exercise of their Military duty"

53. This view of the law, so stated in 1796, was confirmed by the learned Judge (Mr. Justice Perrin) A.D 1853 in the Six-mile Bridge case tried at Ennis, in Feb. Six-mile Bridge case 1853.[1] He laid down to the Grand Jury this pro- Presence of armed soldiers justified by their Military Orders position in plain terms, viz, that Soldiers aiding the Civil Power owe obedience to their Officers:— "With respect to the requisition, its terms, grounds, or sufficiency, the soldiers could have no knowledge. The orders of the General, which they are bound to obey, and not permitted to canvass, were obligatory on them; and for its sufficiency they are not responsible, and you are happily relieved from any inquiry into that matter. Under that order, and the command of Captain Eager, and the conduct of Mr. Delmege, they assembled. They proceeded to Six-mile Bridge, and were there with their arms in their hands in obedience to orders. Those orders will not justify any unlawful conduct or violence in them, but it accounts for their presence there in arms: for *ordinary* persons going on such an occasion as that to the hustings would act very indiscreetly and very dangerously if, perhaps not very illegally, to arm themselves with deadly weapons, in order to meet obstruction or opposition if it were expected." He then pointed out that as the soldiers were bound by—and were there under—orders, "that which in other persons might denote a previous evil or deadly intention, plainly suggested none in them, for they must obey their orders *as soldiers*."

---

[1] I am indebted for the Report of this to Mr Prendergast's 'Law of Officers,' pp 178-82.

54. But this, instead of giving them licence,—obliged them to obey their officers—in the use of arms; having failed to do so, and fired without command, they were prosecuted for homicide, and their conduct could be justified only under the law applicable to " ordinary persons." In this aspect of the case " there was nothing illegal in their proceeding through the crowd with the freeholders, possibly like any other body of free-holders and their companions, but doing or offering no un-necessary violence, nor were they to be subject to any violence beyond others. They had no right to force a way through the crowd by violence, nor to remove any obstruction by arms, still less by discharging deadly fire-arms. They had no right to repel a trespass on themselves, or on the escort, by firing or in-flicting mortal wounds. In considering the matter," continued the learned Judge, " you will recollect that there were of the party forty soldiers fully armed, with fixed bayonets, under the command of two officers and two sergeants; and further, that it is at least doubtful whether there was any legal command upon them to fire. No command was given by their officers,—I think that is admitted on all hands. And, further, you must recollect that the firing cannot be justified upon the ground merely that otherwise the freeholders might either have escaped or been withdrawn. That would afford no justification for slay-ing the assailants." [1]

[margin note:] They were therefore bound to act under orders, and falling in obedience, tried for murder.

55. The primary Law for the guidance of the Military acting in aid of the Civil Power is therefore to be found in the General Orders and Regulations issued for the strict observance of the Army, and referred to in the previous Chapter.[2] These orders define the relationship towards the Civil Magistrate under which the Com-manding Officer shall discharge his duty; and certainly by obedience or disobedience thereto would he be justified or con-demned in case his conduct was arraigned before a Military tribunal. It becomes therefore important to examine upon what

[margin note:] The Primary Law for the guidance of the Military is Her Majesty's Orders and Regula-tion.

---

[1] See the Discussion on this case in Parliament, 124 H D (3), pp 28, 335, 740, 125, ib, pp 316-396, 883, 128 ib, p 699, 129 ib, p. 292

[2] Pars 18, 19, and Appendix CV, and see Note G G., Appendix.

authority in Constitutional Law these orders rest; for though a Court-martial might be appealed to by the Crown to justify or punish the Officer, it is far from probable that any other Court than that of Queen's Bench or of Parliament would be appealed to by the Subject for redress against a cruel or unlawful Military Act.

56. Now Royal Authority, though enough for some theorists in Military Administration, is not plenal in a Court of Law, or sufficient to justify an act done in obedience to the Royal Command. "If," said Lord Hale,[1] "the King command an unlawful thing to be done, the offence of the instrument is not thereby indemnified; for though the King is not under the coercive power of the law, yet in many cases his commands are under the directive power of the law, which consequently makes the act itself invalid if unlawful, and so renders the instrument of the execution thereof obnoxious to the punishment of the law;[2] yet," he goes on to say, "in the time of peace, if two men combat together at barriers, or for trial of skill, if one kill the other it is homicide; but if it be by the command of the King, it is said it is no felony."

Authority upon which these Orders rest is that of the Sovereign.

57 Now, as the Law contemplates the possibility of an unlawful thing being ordered by the Sovereign, how is the Officer—who knows no other authority—to be assured that in carrying out an order from the Sovereign he is not thereby breaking the Law and exposing his own life and liberty to hazard?

But not necessarily legal.

58. The distinctive feature of our Military allegiance is that of implicit obedience. "We have not," to quote the words of Mr. Burke, already used, "distracted our Army by divided principles of obedience, we have put them under one single authority."[3] In acting, therefore, against the Civil community under Military orders, what intervening sanction between the Sovereign and the Military officer does the Law require, to make the order as between the officer and the Civil community a lawful order, and one to be implicitly obeyed by him?

---

[1] 1 Hale, P. C., pp 43, 44   [2] *Vide* Stamf P C., 102 b (o)
[3] Chap XV, par 111.

59. The answer to this question is suggested by the words
of a great Soldier. "Soldiers," wrote the late General
Sir Charles Napier, "must obey the King, and the King
acts by the advice of his Ministers. If in his name they
order the soldiers to do wrong, let the Minister's head pay the
forfeit,—with that the soldiers have nothing to do beyond taking
care, when guarding the scaffold, that no man impedes the
executioner in the functions of his calling."[1]   Unquestionably,
therefore, the authority of a responsible Minister *is* needed to
give Constitutional validity to orders for the action of the
Military in matters affecting the Civil Community   When the
command of the Sovereign is communicated to the Military
officer through the channel of his responsible Minister, the
remedy, when sought by legal proceedings, civil or criminal,
must (it is submitted), be rather against the Minister giving
than against the Officer honestly obeying the command[2]

60. If the Crown, through its responsible Ministers, ratifies
an act the character of the act becomes altered,
Their adop-
tion by the
Minister of
the Crown
transfers the
remedy
the ratification does not give the party injured the
double option of bringing his action against the agent
who committed the trespass, or the principal who
ratified it, but gives a remedy against the Crown only (such
as it is), and exempts from liability the agent who commits
the trespass.   Whether the remedy against the Crown is to
be pursued by petition of right, or whether the injury is an
act of State without remedy, except by appeal to the justice
of the State which inflicts it, in either view the wrong is no
longer actionable against the agent.[3]

61. This case—of Captain Denman—appeared to leave
the Subject without any definite or precise remedy
Which is to
be had against
the Minis-
ter?
for possible injustice at the hands of the Crown
agents.   Therefore, in Feathers v. the Queen, the
Lord Chief Justice Cockburn sought to remove this impression.
"It must not be supposed," said the Lord Chief Justice,[4] " that

---

[1] 'Remarks on Military Law,' 1837, p 23   [2] See Chap XVIII , pars 46, 47
[3] Buron v Denman, 2 Exch. Cases, p 167 , see Secretary of State for India v.
Kamachee, 13 P & C , c 86 , the " Rolla,' 6 Admiralty Cases, p 24
[4] Feathers v the Queen, 6 B & S , p 257.

a Subject sustaining a legal wrong at the hands of the Minister of the Crown is without a remedy.   As a Sovereign cannot authorise wrong to be done, the authority of a Crown would afford no defence to an action brought for an illegal act committed by an Officer of the Crown." He then points out that the decision in Captain Denman's case "leaves the question as to the right of action between Subject and Subject wholly untouched.   The case of the General Warrants, Money *v* Leach, 3 Burrow, 1742, and the case of Sutton *v.* Johnson, 1 Term Rep , 493, and Sutherland *v.* Murray, *ibid.* 538 N., are direct authorities that an action will lie for a tortuous act, notwithstanding it may have had the sanction of the highest authority in the State.   But in our opinion, no authority is needed to establish that a servant of the Crown is responsible in law for a tortuous act done to a fellow-subject, though done by the authority of the Crown; a position which appears to us to rest upon principles which are too well settled to admit of question, and which are alike essential to uphold the dignity of the Crown on the one hand, and the rights and liberties of the Subject on the other."

62. But the Constitutional Law not only required the sanction of a Civil Minister to the orders to be obeyed by the Troops at—but, as the early part of this Chapter shows, the like sanction from a Financial Minister for their movement to—the scene of any riot or disorder. *Sanction of Responsible Ministers needed for for the presence of Troops*
It was the intervention of the Responsible Ministers that gave the Civil sanction to the employment of Troops in putting down civil *émeute*, and shielded the Military from the character of oppressors.   Once remove or alter the character of this agency—as by turning (as some Politicians suggest) Civil into Military Departments, so that Commands will be endorsed only by Military men—and a great Constitutional Safeguard has been lost; the Troops obeying such orders would stand in a different aspect, both in regard and confidence, to that which they now enjoy from Parliament and their fellow countrymen.

63 Under the constitutional arrangements existing prior to 1854, this *one* fact was held up by the late Duke of Wellington as an evidence of the *complete control of the Civil over the Military power,*—viz., that the Com- *Prior to 1854 all movements of troops under the absolute*

control of Civil Minister

mander-in-Chief could not remove a Corporal's guard from Windsor to Hounslow without the intervention of the Secretary at War, directly responsible to Parliament (for finance). This security has been released,[1] and hence the Minister at the War Office cannot be called on to defend the movement of Troops if the same should be impeached.

Totally distinct functions of the Civil Minister and Military Officer in these matters

64. In no Act of State ought the duties of the Responsible Minister and of the Executive Military Officer to be kept so entirely distinct from each other as in the use of the Military as armed Police. In the administration of justice, the Judge and the Sheriff have each totally distinct functions. It is not enough that the criminal is executed by their joint agency, for the criminal would be murdered and not executed unless each acted strictly within the limits of his duty. Not less important is it that the Responsible Minister should decide upon his own independent judgment, without a scintilla of influence from the Military Officer whether or not the Troops shall be employed against the Civil community. The responsibility of the act cannot be diluted between them; but if the Minister and the Military Officer were formed into a Board, individual personal responsibility, in a matter of vital importance to the Public Liberty, would soon be lost.[2]

Rule of criminal responsibility as to Officers

65. Now as the Military enjoy no immunity from punishment[3] if they exceed their powers, but, on the contrary, may be tried both by Court-martial at the suit of the Sovereign, or by the Civil Court at the instance of any Fellow Subject, it is a matter of some moment to ascertain what the law has laid down to be their duty under the circumstances of Riot or disorder.

Magistrate must be present with the Military

66 In the first place, the primary responsibility rests upon the Civil Magistrate. The Report[4] previously quoted advised the Secretary of State that a Magistrate "cannot of his own authority order the Military or any other person to assist in the preservation of the public

---

[1] Chap X, par 1, and Mis Book, 1802, p 68, and Evidence before the Finance Committee, 1828, p 5   [2] Chap XXIX, pars 31, 32
[3] Lord Mansfield, 21 Parl Hist, p 695   [4] Appendix CII (19)

peace, unless he is *personally* present, except as he may command the attendance upon him of all persons in such cases in which he has a right to call out the power of the county; and so far we consider the presence of the Magistrate as indispensably necessary." From the Reports made to Lord Stormont in 1780, it is clear that the Officers refused to act as the Magistrates were not present when the Troops were called out, and the other Reports show that this refusal was justified by the War Office Orders then extant.[1]

67. In the next place, if the Magistrate be present, the Military Officer must act under his orders, and not intentionally exceed them. In Kennett's case the Magistrate refused to order the Troops to act, and that was alleged as one of his omissions of duty; but in Pinney's case the dissuasion of the Military Officer from that course was held to justify the Magistrate[2] in withholding his orders. An Officer having received the orders of the Magistrate to fire, or otherwise to disperse the mob, would delay doing so at his peril. If, from his want of decision, the mob were to gain the ascendency, the Officer would be liable to be charged with neglect of duty.

<small>He must also give orders for the military officer to Act.</small>

68. Such are the grounds upon which the Officer would be justified in giving the order; and the justification of the Soldier in obeying it would be, first, under the rule of the Common Law, that an Inferior, in an ordinary criminal case, must be held justified in obeying the directions—not obviously improper or contrary to law—of a Superior Officer, that is, if the Inferior acted honestly upon what he might not unreasonably deem to be the effect of the orders of his Superior;[3] and, secondly, under the Mutiny Act and Articles of War.

<small>Rule as to the criminal responsibility of the men</small>

69. Unfortunately, Chief Justice Bushe is said to have thrown some doubt upon the question whether a Soldier is so bound to obey his officer, as to be free from criminal responsibility for the act of obedience. At

<small>A.D 1831</small>

<small>As to the Newtonbarry affair</small>

---

[1] Appendix CLXII (19)   [2] Car and Pay, p 273
[3] Reg v Trainer, 4 Fos and Fin., p 105, Ilott v Wilkin, 3 B. and Ald, p 315, Cobbett r Grey, 4 Exch Cases, p. 735

the trial arising out of a Riot at Newtonbarry, Wexford, in July, 831,[1] in reply to inquiry by the jury, whether, "if a Military body be called out, and if the commander gave the order to fire, are those acting under his orders exempt from the consequences?" he is reported to have said, "My opinion is that no Subject of the King is bound to obey an illegal order, and if an Officer gives an illegal order, those who obey him are not exempt." A ruling which, however, assumes the whole question.[2]

70. "If this be true," said Sir Charles Napier, "such a
Law
disputed principle dissolves the Army at once; it reduces the Soldier to a choice between the hanging—awarded to him by the Local Law—for obeying his Officer, and the shooting—awarded him by the Military Law—for disobeying his Officer. In such law there is neither sense nor justice, and (being one of those unlucky red-coated gents thus agreeably placed between shooting and hanging) I beg to enter my protest against this choice of deaths. If such is Law, the Army must become a deliberative body, and ought to be composed of attorneys, and the Lord Chancellor should be made Commander-in-chief."

71. It is presumed that such is *not* the Law, but so long as
Obedience to
to the com-
mand justi-
fied by the
Mutiny Act. the Military are acting in the *bonâ fide* discharge of their duty, obedience to a Military command is a justification. "*How far*," said Mr. Justice Willes, "the orders of a superior Officer are a justification to his inferior who acts on them, I do not undertake to decide Of course in actual war with reference to foreigners, there is an *absolute* justification. With regard to Englishmen in England, questions have been raised. I believe the better opinion to be that an Officer or Soldier acting upon the orders of his superior not being plainly illegal, is justified; but if they be plainly illegal, he is not justified as to Her Majesty's subjects, though he is as to foreigners; for as to them, it would be an act of war if Her Majesty chooses to ratify it."[3] The Legislative Council of India in framing their Criminal Code in 1860, put forward this case of absolute obedience and consequent immunity as an illustra-

---

[1] Napier, p 23   [2] See the question discussed, Chap VIII , par 35 *et seq*
[3] Keighley ₹ Bell, 4 Fos and Fin , p. 763

tion. "A," a Soldier, fires on the mob by the order of his superior Officer in conformity with the commands of the Law. "A" has committed no offence.

72. Probably the indictment preferred at the Summer Assizes for 1864 at Exeter,[1] against Major-General Hutchinson (in Command of the Western District, for the death of a man resulting from the Artillery practice at Plymouth, negligence being imputed to the accused), is the most recent instance of criminal proceedings being taken against a Military Officer. "Manslaughter," Justice Byles charged the Jury, "is where one man is killed by the culpable negligence of another. If in using the place for firing, although it might be too low (for safety), he was simply obeying the Military orders of his Superior, in my opinion he would not be guilty of manslaughter,"—transferring, I presume, the criminal responsibility to such Superior giving the order.

A.D. 1864
Case of General Hutchinson

73. It is clear that there is no *exact* definition of what are the relative duties of the Civil and Military authorities when acting together in the suppression of Riot.[2] Of this the late General Sir Charles Napier, made serious complaint. His contention[3] was that, in Riots, the whole responsibility of calling out the Military should rest with the Civil Magistrate; but that when the Military were called out, they should have a separate and distinct action and responsibility, that the Civil Magistrate should act with his constabulary under his own Code till he can act no longer; and that then the Military Officer should act with his force and under his Code. For his action the latter should be responsible under his Code to his Military superior, or to Parliament, but that he should not be liable (as to a trial by Jury) for anything he may have done in executing the duty imposed upon him by the Civil Magistrate, viz., of quelling the riot or insurrection. After the Bristol Riots, two Officers, Colonel Brereton, and Captain Warrington,[4] were tried by Courts-

No definite rule of responsibility between Civil and military authority

---

[1] 9 Cox, Cr Ca , p 555, and MS Report   [2] 26 H. D (3), p 51.
[3] See 'Remarks on Military Law' (1837), p 38   [4] Note H H, Appendix

martial, and the Magistrate (Charles Pinney, Esq.) by the Court of King's Bench.

74. Both Civil and Military authorities have hitherto re-ceived a fair consideration from the Country when, in times of admitted difficulty, their conduct—which may alternate between fear and cruelty—has come under review. "Where anything is in my discretion," said Lord Mansfield,[1] "I will never punish where the intent is good, and the Magistrate has only mistaken the Law, but that is only where it is in my discretion. In such a case I always leave the party complaining to go before a Grand Jury. In Law to say, 'I was afraid,' is not an excuse for a Magistrate, it must be a fear arising from danger, which is reduced to a maxim in Law to be such danger as would affect a firm man. The defendant used none of the authorities vested in him by Law; he did not read the proclamation, nor restrain or appre-hend the Rioters, or give orders to fire, or make any use of the Military under his direction. But this does not exclude a de-fence, and the defence relied on is—' 'Tis true, I did not restrain or apprehend any rioters nor use the Military; but, under all the circumstances, this was not a neglect' It is *primâ facie* the duty of a Magistrate to read the Act, but this duty depends on circumstances; he might be alone and not be able to do it. If he did what a firm and constant man would have done, he must be acquitted. If, rather than apprehend the Rioters, his sole care was for himself, this is neglect" And again, "every person acting in support of the Law is justifiable respecting such acts as may arise in consequence of a faithful and proper discharge of the duties annexed to his office, if he does not abuse the power legally vested in him, which may in that case, according to the circumstances accompanying the transaction, degenerate into an illegal act, though professedly committed under the colour or pretext of law."[2]

As to the rule of judging the con-duct of the Civil Magis-trates

75. The rule for judging of the conduct of Military Officers was laid down by the same Judge[3] in these words:— "In trying the legality of acts done by Military Officers

The like as to the Military Officer

---

[1] Rex *v.* Kennett, *sup*   [2] 21 Parl. Hist, p 695
[3] Wall *v* M'Namara, 1 Term Rep

in the exercise of their duty, particularly beyond the seas, where cases may occur without the possibility of application for proper advice, great latitude ought to be allowed, and they ought not to suffer for a slip of form, if their intention appears by the evidence to have been upright; it is the same as when complaints are brought against inferior Civil Magistrates, such as Justices of the Peace, for acts done by them in the exercise of their Civil duty. There the principal inquiry to be made by a Court of Justice is *how the heart stood;*[1] and if there appears to be nothing wrong there, latitude will be allowed for misapprehension or mistake. But, on the other hand, if the heart is wrong, if cruelty, malice, and oppression appear to have occasioned or aggravated the imprisonment, or other injury complained of, they shall not cover themselves with the thin veil of legal forms, nor escape under the cover of justification, the most technically regular from that punishment, which is the province and the duty to inflict on so scandalous an abuse of public trust."

76. The policy of the Secretary at War was that of non-intervention in any disputes arising from the aid of the Military to the Civil Power. Acting under the Magistrate, their conduct has been justified by the Civil Authorities; and for the Crown, in any legal investigation, to interfere on behalf of the Military and against the Civil Community would give rise to feelings of hostility towards the Army, that in Great Britain have been allayed for many years. Occasionally legal expenses were necessarily incurred by the Regiment, which were admitted by the Secretary at War into the Regimental accounts if the circumstances appeared to him to justify the employment of legal agents, to explain their conduct. It seldom arises that a Commanding Officer fails to satisfy a jury, on appearing before them, that his conduct, and that of his men, have been forbearing and humane towards their Fellow Countrymen.

Policy of the Secretary at War that of Non intervention

---

[1] Unfortunately, his remark does not apply to Ireland. In the 1869 Elections, a man was killed at Drogheda —whereupon the Irish Treasury prosecuted, and the War Department defended, the Soldier this legal tournament costing several hundred pounds. A woman was killed at Newport, and, on the Officer's explanation, the Jury returned "Accidental Death."

CHAPTER XVIII.

The Employment of the Military in the Restoration of the Civil Power.

1. In the previous Chapter I have endeavoured to show the use that, according to the Constitutional Law, may be made of the Military in aid of the Civil power when the duty of suppressing Riots arises for the Magistrate to discharge. I propose in the present Chapter to follow Riot to its possible sequence,—viz., the destruction of the authority of the Magistrate, and to show how the Military may be used by the Executive Government of the country under a proclamation of Martial Law, such a proclamation being (of course) issued by the Crown, on the advice and with the sanction of its responsible Ministers, and declaring—in effect, if not in express terms—that the Civil Institutions are for a time destroyed or in abeyance; that the Military have been called in to extinguish Rebellion, and thus to restore the authority of the Magistrate.

Introduction.

2. Martial Law—as understood at the period immediately preceding the era of the Petition of Right,[1] and as distinguished from [...] [...] he Revolu-tion[2] and the enactmen[...] [...]ly been explained in earlier Cha[...] [...]eeping in view what has bee[...] [...]ill be considered in reference [...] [...]ppened within the United Kingdom and the Colonies since the Revolution.

Martial Law

3. Now the words of the Petition of Right—and of the Mutiny Act since the Reign of Anne—are plain in this respect—that *they* restrain the Crown from issuing these commissions *only* in time of Peace[3]—therefore if

Restraint on the Crown— what?

---

[1] Chap. II., par. 6 *et seq*, Chap. IV., par. 63 *et seq*, Appendix XXIV
[2] Chap. VIII, par 4 *et seq*   [3] Chap. VIII, par 5

the Crown possessed : right of issuing them at other times—as in War, or Rebellion, before those Statutes passed—the words used in them do not restrain the exercise of that right by the Crown at the present time.

4. In the argument upon the Petition of Right preserved in Rushworth the power of the Crown to use Martial Law on some occasions was not disputed—but the difficulty arose upon the definition of the just occasions and objects for and to which such a rule of Law could be applied. "In this disputation," said Mr. Rolls,[1] "I will not trench on Power, but the abuse of it. 37 H. 6, 20, the Law of the Marshall is the King's Law, and the common law takes notice of it; *we acknowledge it so to be,* but now the question is, *when* it is to be used?

Margin note: Arguments on the Petition of Right by Mr Rolls.

"*Potestas vitæ et mortis* belongs to the Common Law, or to the Martial. The question is now *when* this *Martial Law* is to be used, and *upon whom?* The common law is the highest for the subject, 7 H. 8, *Kellway* 176, every liege man inherits the law, 19 H. 6, 63, it is the inheritance of the King, this great inheritance is not to be taken from him, and Martial Law is merely for *necessity,* where the Common Law *cannot* take place. Now for the time when that necessity falls out, in time of peace it cannot, so we must consider when is time of peace or war?

"If the *Chancery* and Courts of *Westminster* be shut up that are *Officina Justitiæ,* it is time of war, but if the Courts be open it is otherwise; yet if war be in any part of the kingdom, that the sheriff cannot execute the King's writ, *there* is *tempus belli.*

"If an enemy come into any part where the Common Law cannot be executed, there may the Martial Law be executed. If a Subject be taken in rebellion, if he be not slain in the time of his rebellion, he is to be tried after by the Common Law. 2 H. 5, Parliament Roll, 2 *Pars,* John Montague, Earl of Salisbury, was in rebellion against H. 4.; was taken and put to death, 2 H. 4."

5. For these Limitations Sir Edward Coke[2] contended:—"I shall maintain *Jus belli.* But God send me never to live under the law of conveniency *or discretion.* Shall

Margin note: By Sir E. Coke

---

[1] 3 Rush. Col., p 79   [2] P. 80.

the soldier and justice sit on one bench? The trumpet will not let the crier speak in Westminster Hall. *Non bene conveniunt.*

"The time of peace is when the Courts of Westminster are open. For when they are open, then you may have a commission of *oyer* and *terminer;* and where the Common Law can determine a thing, the Martial Law ought not.

"Drake slew Doughty beyond sea. Doughty's brother desired an appeal in the Constable and Marshal's Court, and Wray and the other Judges resolved he might there sue. We make no law, we must not mediate *ubi lex non distinguit.* To hang a man *tempore pacis* is dangerous · I speak not of prosecution against a rebel, he may be slain in rebellion; but if he be taken, he cannot be put to death by the Martial Law. 28 E. 2 M. 13. When the courts are open, Martial Law cannot be executed."

6. Now, as instead of restoring the Civil, the Military may

Danger of Military usurpation when the Civil Government is destroyed. establish their own, Power—or only restore the Civil Power *sub modo*, making the Military ultimately supreme—by placing, as at the Commonwealth, all Governing authority in the hands of Major-Generals (an event always the more or less likely to happen as the Army is drawn from the lowest or lower stratum in the Body Politic), and gaining by the aggression—the vigilance of Parliament and of great Constitutional statesmen has always been directed to the limitation of Martial Law both in duration and in the exercise of Military authority under the Proclamation.

7. The terrible certainty of conviction by Courts-Martial summoned under Military authority,[1] made Par-

Courts martial destructive of human life. liament hesitate long, even in time of great social disorder, before it gave any sanction (and for 4 months only[2]) to such tribunals acting under Martial Law, and certainly our larger and more recent experience,[3]—ending

---

[1] Chap VIII, par 55 *et seq.*   [2] 5 Rush Col, part iii, pp. 723-7

[3] Colonel Gibson complained on the convictions at Portsmouth in 1693 (Chap. XV par 123) The Court-martial at Preston, 1715, without hesitation, convicted the half-pay officers, not liable to Martial Law (Chap. VIII, pars 100, 101, *ante*) The Governor at Ceylon represented the great facility he had in gaining convictions from Courts-martial (Note I I (5), Appendix, and the Morant Bay case, the

with the trial at Morant Bay, in Oct, 1865,—has not removed the apprehension felt by the Civil Community at entrusting Judicial or Administrative powers to Courts-martial, or to the Officers convening them. It may not therefore be deemed a superfluous task to place on these pages some information upon a Subject—great and important as—affecting the Lives and Liberties of many Colonial Subjects of the British Crown

8. That the law *of necessity* is admitted to arise, and may lawfully be used—against persons liable to *the* Mutiny Act, but without resorting to the forms of it,—cannot be doubted "If," said Lord Ellenborough, then Attorney-General, in conducting the prosecution in Governor Wall's case,[1] "there did exist, in point of fact, a mutiny within His Majesty's garrison which it required the strong arm of power to suppress; if it was a mutiny so enormous in its size, so dangerous in its probable and immediate consequences, as to supersede the ordinary forms of trial for that or such like offences, I do not stand here to require of you—God forbid I should—that you should conceive this or any other man similarly circumstanced, as being other than not only an innocent, but even a meritorious man, who uses the effective powers with which his situation arms him, or which he has it within his reach to command and use, for the discharge of the trust, and the protection of the interests committed to him."

Rule of necessity

9. And Lord Loughborough,[2] in leaving the case to the jury, expressed the same view. "As the Attorney-General stated at the outset, undoubtedly the principal fact is the fact of mutiny, aye or no; whether any such mutiny did take place as would put a good Officer, as I said before, a man of common firmness, into such a state of alarm,

Ruling of Lord Loughborough

---

words of the Lord Chief Justice were—" A man has been condemned—sentenced to death—and executed upon evidence which would not have been admitted before any properly constituted tribunal, and upon evidence which, if admitted, fell *altogether short* of establishing the crime with which he was charged.'—P. 153 of Charge (Ridgway, 1867)

[1] 28 State Trials, p. 56, as to necessity justifying a breach of the law, **Rex v.** Stratton, 21 How Sta Tri, p 1223 and par 45 *post*   [2] Ib, p 175

as would make extraordinary means necessary instantly to quench the fire by overlaying it in the speediest way that he possibly could." " If it shall appear to you that there was a mutiny,—if it shall appear to you that there was such a Court-martial as could be had, and that there was reasonable notice to the deceased that he was so and so charged, and was called upon to say how he came to be one of those mutineers, I have the Attorney-General's liberal authority for saying, in this case before us, that if you are satisfied of that, and do not derive from the degree of punishment and the mode in which it was inflicted by the instrument used, a malicious intent to destroy this man, or a wilful disregard of human life, in case you see all the circumstances in that light, you will give the benefit of such a view of them to the prisoner, and acquit him." [1]

---

[1] 28 State Trials, p 176   The following is an Extract from Sir D Dundas's Evidence before the Ceylon Committee :—

" 5475 Does not martial law supersede both military and civil law ?—I think it over-rides, in respect of the persons upon whom it is to operate, all other law For instance, if five or six regiments were to mutiny in the field, would any one tell me you must apply to Parliament before you could reduce those persons to subjection ? There must be somewhere, for public safety, a right to exercise such power in time of need   I have heard it stated that such a thing has happened in our own times   Four or five regiments in open mutiny in the field, and no time to take the opinion of any executive authority, and the officer in command did that which a soldier in command is bound to do, namely, he took measures for the purpose of suppressing such disorder, and he was prepared to put those people to death, if it were necessary   There have been instances, again, in our own times, where martial law has been proclaimed in several of the Colonies   It has been proclaimed in Jamaica, it has been proclaimed at the Cape of Good Hope, it was proclaimed at Ceylon in the time of General Brownrigg   Those are cases where I understand there was no appeal to any Parliament, properly so called, unless it was in Jamaica, as to which island I believe there was an Act of Parliament to govern the question   In the other instances, the Executive, acting for the public safety, did the best they could

" 5476. (*Sir R Peel*) A wise and courageous man, responsible for the safety of a colony, would take the law into his own hands, and make a law for the occasion, rather than submit to anarchy ?—I think that a wise and courageous man would, if it were necessary, make a law to his own hands, but he would much rather take a law which is already made, and, I believe, the law of England is, that a Governor, like the Crown, has inherent in him the right, when the necessity arises, of judging of it, and, being responsible for his work afterwards, so to deal with the laws as to supersede them all, and to proclaim martial law for the safety of the colony   I think a good man will do it with very great care, and a prudent man too, but a wise and courageous man, I think ought not to be shy of doing it.

" 5477. (*Mr Gladstone*) You spoke of his being responsible for that which

10. Limit Martial Law to the rules of extreme necessity, and few people will probably be found to controvert it. "Suppose," said Lord Brougham, in arguing the Demerara case,[1] "I were ready to admit that on the pressure of a great emergency, such as invasion or rebellion. when there is no time for the slow and cumbrous proceedings of the Civil Law, a Proclamation may justifiably be issued for excluding the ordinary tribunals, and directing that offences should be tried by a Military Court, such a proceeding might be justified by necessity; but it could rest on that alone. Created by necessity, necessity must limit its continuance. It would be the worst of all conceivable grievances—it would be a calamity unspeakable—if the whole law and constitution of England were suspended one hour longer than the most imperious necessity demanded. I know that the Proclamation of Martial Law renders every man liable to be treated as a Soldier. But the instant the *necessity* ceases, that *instant* the state of soldiership ought to cease, and the rights, with the relations, of civil life, to be restored."[2]

11. The late Sir James Mackintosh[3] made the same admission of a justifying necessity. "The only principle on which the law of England tolerates what is called Martial Law is necessity; its introduction can be justified only by necessity; its continuance requires precisely the same justification of necessity; and if it survives the necessity on which alone it rests for a single minute, it becomes instantly a mere exercise of lawless violence. When foreign invasion or Civil

[margin: Necessity the justification and limit of Martial Law]

[margin: Lord Brougham.]

[margin: Sir James Mackintosh]

---

he has done; if he is responsible for that which he has done, does not it seem to follow that what he has done has not been done under the law so to be called, but under a necessity which is above the law?—I say he is responsible for what he has done, just as I am responsible for shooting a man on the King's highway who comes to rob me. If I mistake my man, and have not, in the opinion of the judge and jury who try me, an answer to give, I am responsible

"5478 (*Mr Adderley*) Under martial law, would there be any difference in the treatment of a soldier and a civilian?—I should say none, but that is a matter upon which, of course, I can have no knowledge, my notion is, that an offender ought to be subjected to the punishment of death if it be necessary, so other punishments which are fit, and that there is not any difference between a soldier offending and a common man, he is an offender against the peace '

[1] 11 H D (N S), pp 968, 976

[2] Note I I (2), Appendix [3] Ib, pp 1046-9, and vol iii of Works, p 407.

War renders it impossible for Courts of Law to sit, or to enforce the execution of their judgments, it becomes necessary to find some rude substitute for them, and to employ for that purpose the Military, which is the only remaining Force in the community. While the laws are silenced by the noise of arms the rulers of the Armed Force must punish, as equitably as they can, those crimes which threaten their own safety and that of society; but no longer. every moment beyond is usurpation· as soon as the law can act every other mode of punishing supposed crimes is itself an enormous crime. But Martial Law exercised against enemies or rebels is only a more regular and convenient mode of exercising the right to kill in war: a right originating in self-defence, and limited to those cases where such killing is necessary, as the means of insuring that end. Martial Law put in force against rebels can only be excused as a mode of more deliberately and equitably selecting the persons from whom quarter ought to be withheld, in a case where all have forfeited their claim to it. It is nothing more than a sort of better regulated decimation, founded upon choice, instead of chance, in order to provide for the safety of the conquerors without the horrors of undistinguished slaughter. It is justifiable only where it is an act of mercy. Thus the matter stands by the law of nations."

Martial Law against enemies and rebels

12. As it must be limited in Duration of time, so also in the extent of Country to which it is applied. Offences committed before the Proclamation issued,[1] or out of the district, cannot rightly be tried by the Court constituted under Martial Law; and though the Court is bound by no rule of procedure, yet an Officer would do well to follow the oath, and the analogy which proceedings under the Mutiny Act suggest.[2]

Limit in duration of time and in area.

---

[1] Sir N Tindal, Note II (2), Appendix.

[2] *Extract from Sir D. Dundas's Evidence.*

"5490 (*Mr Villiers*) Your apprehension of the proceedings which take place in such an extreme exercise of the power of the Crown in any district, is that they are subject to no rule whatever?—I did not say that

"5491 You do not know of any?—I know of no rule, except the rule of common sense and humanity A man executing the law under a Court-martial must go by something, he must go by the evidence He goes by a shorter mode of taking evidence, very likely, than he would do in a Court in Westminster Hall.

"5492 Are there any rules laid down for the conduct of proceedings where they take place under martial law?—I think it is altogether *lex non scripta*."

13. Fortunately, in England—though in three instances, viz., in 1715, 1745, and 1780, the authority of the Civil Power was for a time partially suspended—we have had but little experience, since the Revolution, of the effect of Martial Law. Upon the threat of invasion, followed by Rebellion in 1715,[1] the first action of the Government was to issue a Proclamation on the 25th July, authorising all Officers Civil and Military, by force of arms (if necessary) to suppress the Rebellion.[2]

Instances since the Revolution (1715)

"5493 I understood you to say, that where martial law is proclaimed, the civil tribunals are suspended, and military tribunals are established?—Yes

"5493*. Am I to understand that wherever martial law is proclaimed, the judges are soldiers?—I did not say that

"5494 Will you inform the Committee what is the meaning of a military tribunal?—Three officers are, I think, the minimum of any military tribunal under the Mutiny Act

"5495 Are not military tribunals presided over by soldiers?—All tribunals under the Mutiny Act consist of soldiers only.

"5496 Where military tribunals are substituted for civil tribunals, after the proclamation of martial law, are not those tribunals also presided over by soldiers?—I cannot answer the question, because I know nothing of the practice, but, in my opinion, they need not be. I am clearly of opinion that all good citizens are called on to take part with the power, which we will suppose a righteous power, in case of necessity, and whether they wear a red coat or a blue coat, they are each called on to come in and aid the common welfare.

"5531. (*Mr. Hume.*) It appears by the latter part of the oath which is taken by officers sitting on Courts-martial assembled under the Mutiny Act, that they are bound, if any doubt shall arise which is not explained by the said Articles or Act, to act according to their conscience, the best of their understanding, and the customs of war. Is it your opinion that in Courts-martial assembled under martial law, where all other law is supposed to be set aside, officers placed on such Courts-martial are bound by such considerations as have been now set forth?—In point of fact, I know nothing of the practice in such cases, but my own opinion is that an officer cannot go very wrong who adheres, as closely as the circumstances will permit him, to the mode of administering the law under the Mutiny Act, and if he will take the latter part of the oath taken under the Mutiny Act, it appears to me to afford him a very safe and honest guide in such a critical case

"5532 Are you aware whether any oath is taken in cases of Courts-martial under martial law?—I am not aware of the practice.

"5533 (*Mr. Adderley.*) Is not such an officer bound, in your opinion, as far as circumstances will admit, to be governed by the forms prescribed by the Mutiny Act and the Articles of War?—I do not know whether he is bound; I consider that martial law might be proclaimed, and orders given by the Executive to carry it into execution in a given manner, and then he would be bound to carry it out in that manner, in my humble judgment"

[1] See the Address of 18th July, 1715, 7 Parl. Hist., p 108
[2] Appendix CVI, and 7 Parl. Hist., p 114

M 2

14. Upon the opening of Parliament, in the January following the speech from the Throne referred to the "brave and faithful discharge of duty by the Army as having *disappointed* our enemies, and contributed to the safety of the nation."[1] Each House mentioned the same fact as a matter of special congratulation. There was no attempt to bring persons before Courts-martial who ought to be tried by the Common Law (save in the instance of the half-pay Officers at Preston) and all the extraordinary acts of the Crown were sanctioned by Parliament.

Action of Parliament.

15. In the first place, authority was taken by the 1 Geo I, sec. 2, c. 8, to suspend the Habeas Corpus Act, and, strange as it may appear, to seize the horses of suspected persons.[2] Then authority was taken to try the rebels —distributed for safe custody in the various prisons throughout the country,—in any county including that where the offences had been committed.[3] After the Rebellion had been suppressed two Statutes were passed, one for indemnity and the other for pardon.

Various measures that were passed.

16. The first Act,[4] to indemnify from vexatious suits and prosecutions, described the persons and acts to which the Statute was intended to apply, thus.—"As divers Lords-Lieutenant, Deputy Lieutenants, Justices of the Peace, Mayors, Bailiffs of Corporations, Constables and other Officers and persons well affected to His Majesty and His Government, who, in order to preserve our present happy establishment, and the peace of the kingdom, and to suppress and put an end to the said Rebellion, had apprehended and put into custody and imprisoned several criminals. and several persons who they suspected might disturb the public peace and foment or promote riots, tumults, rebellions, or evil designs against the Government, and also had seized and used several horses, arms, and other things, and also pressed divers horses, carts, and carriages, for the service of the public, and did, for the purposes assigned, enter into the houses and possessions of

Indemnity Act and terms of it.

---

[1] 7 Parl Hist., pp. 223, 225, 244. [2] Ib., p 275
[3] 1 Geo I, 2, c., 33 [4] Ib., c 39

several persons, and did quarter and cause to be quartered divers Soldiers and others in the houses of divers persons, and did divers acts which could not be justified by the strict forms of law, and yet were necessary, and so much for the service of the public that they ought to be justified by Act of Parliament, and the persons by whom they were transacted ought to be indemnified;" and then made void all actions, suits, and prosecutions for or by reason of the premises, or of any other matter or thing advised, commended, or appointed to be done in 1715, in order to suppress the Rebellion, and every person sued might plead the general issue, and give the Act and the special matter in evidence.

17. The second Statute granted a general and free pardon for all offences committed prior to the 6th May, 1717, with certain exceptions and reservations set forth in the Act. General pardon

18. Upon the Rebellion of 1745 [1] Parliament was in recess, but on the 5th September the King, by the advice of the Privy Council, issued a Proclamation against Papists, and charged all Civil Magistrates to do their utmost to prevent and suppress all riots, and to put in execution all laws made for the preventing the same. Both Houses, on their reassembling in October, voted addresses pledging themselves to support the authority of the Crown.[2] A.D 1745

19. The action of Parliament was much the same as on the occasion of the former Rebellion. Authority was obtained for the suspension of the Habeas Corpus, by 19 Geo. II., c. 1; for the speedy trial of offenders by the Common Law Courts, by c. 9; and for indemnity, by c. 20, the same terms being used as in the Act of Geo I., c. 39, except that the present Act went beyond that Act in indemnifying gaolers from whose custody prisoners had been discharged by the Rebels.[3] Action of Parliament the same as in 1715

[1] Appendix CVII
[2] 13 Parl. Hist, pp 1309-1382, vol ii of Harris's 'Life of Lord Chancellor Hardwicke,' p 143 *et seq*, vol iii. Lord Mahon's 'England,' p 334 *et seq*.
[3] Report of Sir D. Ryder on its operation, see Appendix CVIII.

20. The outbreak in 1780[1] became serious in its results from the neglect or apathy of the Civil Magistrates on the first appearance of riot and disorder. The Official Documents in the Appendix show that they refused to attend with the Troops, and therefore the Secretary at War put forward a request that some authority or instructions should be issued how the Troops were to act in such an emergency. A Council was then hastily summoned, and authority given to the Military to put down the riot without the intervention of the Civil Power. This was an extreme measure, partaking in some degree of the character of Martial Law.[2]

A.D 1786

Causes of the disorder

21. Upon this ground it was justified by the Lord Chancellor (Thurlow).[3] "In all cases of high treason, insurrection, and rebellion within the Realm, it was the peculiar office of the Crown to use the most effectual means of resisting and quashing such insurrection and rebellion, and punishing the instruments of it. But the King, any more than the private person, could not supersede the law, nor any act contrary to it, and therefore he was bound to take care that the means he used for putting an end to the Rebellion and Insurrection were legal and constitutional, and the Military employed for that purpose were every one of them amenable to the law, because no word of command from their particular Officer, no direction from the War Office, or Order of Council, could warrant or sanction their acting illegally. In the Rebellions of 1715 and 1745 it was in their Lordships' recollection what were the measures then pursued, not but he saw he was verging towards the discussion of a situation very different from that in which the late disturbances put the metropolis, but yet their cases were alike in their respective degrees, and the late insurrection was similar to the Rebellions of 1715 and 1745, as far as it went."

Extreme measures of the Government.

22. Lord Thurlow then proceeded to show the analogy between the two cases:—"The rioters having lifted the axe of outrage and violence against several of the great branches of the King's Government, were

Analogy between this and the two previous rebellions

---

[1] See Vol. vii. of Lord Mahon's 'England,' p 25 *et seq*, 23 Ann Reg, pp 191, 254 *et seq*

[2] Appendices CII. (16 and 17), and CIX   [3] 21 Parl Hist, p. 736.

aiming it at the root of the tree itself, and having burnt the Public Prisons and attacked the Bank of England, had already begun their endeavours to destroy the Government, it was high time, therefore, for the Executive Power to interfere in that manner which was most likely to prove effectual in order immediately to quell the outrages, and to bring those offenders to condign punishment who had busied themselves in the perpetration of the various felonies and treasons that had fixed a National disgrace on the country. Under these circumstances it was, and after it had been in vain endeavoured to quell the riots *by the intervention and authority of the Civil Power*, that the Military were employed; and therefore, the case being so far similar to the Rebellion in 1715 and 1745, that there was an actual insurrection, that the laws of the land were trampled under foot, and the King's Government opposed "

23 "No doubt Measures were taken for the suppression of the riot beyond what the ordinary rule of law would be found to justify, some things which, under a cool legal investigation, would appear to be contrary to law, and punishable either by the Common or Statute Law of the Realm; for, undoubtedly, in opposing, repressing, and quelling such daring outrages as had been perpetrated, the Military, as well as individuals, must necessarily have been forced into excesses; but when the occasion was duly considered, and the extreme hurry and violent confusion in which all men who joined in restoring the public peace were obliged to act, those excesses would be seen to have been unavoidable, and to be the proper objects of an Act of Indemnity, but not an Act more necessary for the Military than for other persons who had done as the Military had done, and been instrumental in effecting that good purpose which the Military had effected."

Excesses in the exercise of authority

24. The total of killed and wounded was returned at 458, and a fear arose in the minds of the Public that the prisoners taken were to be tried by Martial Law. To allay this apprehension the Government put forth this notice :—"Whereas some ill-designing and malicious persons have published, for the purpose of disquieting the minds of His Majesty's faithful subjects, that it is

Public notification that the prisoners would not be tried by Martial Law

intended to try the prisoners now in custody by Martial Law; notice is given, by authority, that no such purpose or intention has ever been in the contemplation of Government, but that the said prisoners will be tried by the due course of law, as expeditiously as may be."

25. After the outbreak had been quelled, a correspondence arose between the citizens of London and Lord Amherst upon the constitutional question of the right of all free citizens to carry arms. Probably at this time (12th June) the Civil Government had not returned to the acknowledged channels or it never would have been permitted that a Military Officer should dispute such a question with a great Municipality. The Constitutional doctrine enunciated by Lord Amherst[1] was " that no person can bear arms but under Officers having the King's Commission;" and the Adjutant-General's order of the 7th June required all arms to be given up. It was modified after the Corporation had called attention to the Bill of Rights, and ultimately withdrawn.

Correspondence with the Citizens as to arming the Citizens.

26. All our future experience of the operation and effect of Martial Law is to be gleaned from the events that have from time to time arisen in Ireland, and in the several Colonial possessions or settlements, to which, in the order of date, some reference will be made.

Martial Law in Ireland and the Colonies.

27. With regard to Ireland, the recent instances in which Martial Law has been declared and the ordinary course of Criminal Justice interfered with occurred in 1798, 1803, and 1833.

I As to Ireland.

28. In the first case, the facts, so far as they are affirmed on public documents, appear to be that a traitorous conspiracy for the subversion of all lawful authority having broken out in open Rebellion, Lord

The case of 1798 Proclamation of 30th March

---

[1] Correspondence with the London Magistrates, 23 Ann. Reg , p 266.

Camden (Lord-Lieutenant) issued an Order in Council[1] on the 30th March, 1798,[2] to the officers commanding Her Majesty's forces to employ them with the utmost vigour and decision for the immediate suppression of the Rebellion.

29. Unfortunately the Rebellion considerably extended itself, and a second Order in Council was issued on the 24th May,[3] 1798, to all General officers commanding Her Majesty's Forces to punish all persons acting, aiding, or in any manner assisting the Rebellion according to Martial Law, either by death or otherwise, as to them should seem expedient for the suppression and punishment of all Rebels.

Proclamation of the 24th May

30. Earl Camden communicated these orders and Proclamations by message to both Houses, and by their addresses to his Excellency they expressed their cordial acknowledgments and entire approbation of the decisive measures taken, by the advice of the Privy Council,—however deeply they lamented the necessity by which they were dictated,—and they pledged their full engagement of support to every measure of firmness and vigour which might be necessary for the speedy and effectual suppression of the rebellion.

Both Proclamations laid before, and the addresses of, Parliament

31. It was during the period that the second Order in Council was in operation, that Wolfe Tone's case arose[4] Having been captured at sea on board a French man-of-war, he was brought, on the 10th November, 1798, before a Court-martial sitting at Dublin Barracks, for trial on charges— "implicating him as a natural-born subject of our lord the King, having traitorously entered into the service of the French Republic, at open war with His Majesty, and being taken in

Mr Wolfe Tone's case in November

---

[1] Before this Order in Council was passed (viz, in 1796 and 1798), statutes for the suppression of disturbances had been passed by the Irish Parliament

In 1796, the 36 Geo III , cap 20, which was amended by 37 Geo. III , cap 38, and continued by 38 Geo III , cap. 21 It was again amended by 38 Geo III, cap 82

In 1797 the 37 Geo III , cap 1, an Act for detaining persons in custody, which is similar in terms to the 29 Vic , cap. 1

These statutes gave no authority, and contained no reference to the subject of Martial Law

[2] Appendix CX   [3] Appendix CXI

[4] 27 How Sta Tri , p 613, see the discussion of this case before the Ceylon Committee, Questions 5457-72

the fact, bearing arms against his King and country, and assuming a command in an enemy's army approaching the shore of his native land for the purpose of invasion, and acting in open resistance to His Majesty's forces, with several other charges of a treasonable nature"

The Court-martial found the prisoner guilty, and, pending the execution of the sentence of death, Mr. Curran made an application for a *Habeas Corpus* to the Queen's Bench, then sitting in Dublin. "I do not pretend to say," said Mr. Curran, "that Mr. Tone is not guilty of the charges of which he was accused—I presume the officers were honourable men; but it is stated in the affidavit, as a solemn fact, that Mr. Tone had no commission under His Majesty, and, therefore, no Court-martial could have cognizance of any crime imputed to him, while the Court of King's Bench sat in the capacity of the great Criminal Court of the land. In times when war was raging, when man was opposed to man in the field, Courts-martial might be endured; but every law authority is with me, while I stand upon this sacred and immutable principle of the Constitution—that Martial Law and Civil Law are incompatible, and that the former must cease with the existence of the latter. This is not the time for arguing this momentous question. My client must appear in this Court. He is cast for death this day. He may be ordered for execution while I address you. I call on the Court to support the law. I move for a *Habeas Corpus* to be directed to the Provost-Marshal of the barracks of Dublin, and Major Sandys to bring up the body of Mr. Tone." That Court granted the application, and the Sheriff was ordered to take Mr. W. Tone out of military custody, but as the state of his health prevented this being done, an order for suspending the execution was made. He died on the 19th November, 1798 (from the effect of self-inflicted wounds), and therefore no ultimate decision was ever given in the case

32 It became, therefore, necessary,—or at least it was *Application to Parliament for express sanction to Martial Law* deemed expedient,—to apply to the Irish Parliament for further powers. An Act was passed on the 25th March, 1799.[1] Setting forth on the Preamble the two

---

[1] 39 Geo. III , c 11.

Orders of the Privy Council, and then declaring, (1), "That by the wise and salutary exercise of His Majesty's *undoubted prerogative in executing Martial Law*, for defeating and dispersing the armed and rebellious force, and in bringing divers rebels and traitors to punishment in the *most speedy and summary manner*, the peace of the kingdom had been so far restored as to permit the course of the common law partially to take place; but that the rebellion still continued to rage in very considerable parts of the kingdom, and to desolate and lay waste the country, by the most savage and wanton violence, excess and outrage, and has utterly set at defiance the Civil Power, and stopped the ordinary course of Justice and of the Common Law therein; and (2),—to meet Mr. Curran's argument in Mr. W. Tone's case,—that " many persons who had been guilty of the most daring and horrid acts of cruelty and outrage, in furtherance and prosecution of the rebellion, and who had been taken by His Majesty's Forces employed for the suppression of the same, had availed themselves of such partial restoration of the ordinary course of the Common Law to evade the punishment of their crimes, whereby it had become necessary for Parliament to interpose."

Preamble.

33. The Enactment declared that Martial Law should prevail, and be put in force whether the ordinary Courts of Common or Criminal Law were or were not open. Thus, it was declared lawful for the Lord-Lieutenant, during the continuance of the rebellion, whether the ordinary Courts of Justice should or should not at such time be open, to issue his orders to all Officers commanding His Majesty's Forces, and to all others whom he should think fit to authorise in that behalf, to take the most vigorous and effectual measures for suppressing the rebellion which should appear to be necessary for the public safety, and for the safety and protection of the persons and properties of His Majesty's peaceable and loyal Subjects, and to punish all persons acting, aiding, or in any manner assisting in the rebellion, or maliciously attacking or injuring the persons or properties of His Majesty's loyal Subjects, in furtherance of the same, according to Martial Law, either by death or otherwise, as to them should seem expedient, for the punishment and suppression of all

Substance of the Enactment.

rebels in their several districts, and to arrest and detain in custody all persons engaged in such rebellion, or suspected thereof, and to cause all persons so arrested and detained in custody to be brought to trial in a summary manner, by Courts-martial, to be assembled under such authority, and to be constituted in such manner, and of such description of persons as the said Lord-Lieutenant should direct, for all offences committed in furtherance of the rebellion, whether such persons should have been taken in open arms against His Majesty, or should have been otherwise concerned in the rebellion, or in aiding, or in any manner assisting the same; and to execute the sentences of all such Courts-martial, whether of death or otherwise, and to do all other acts necessary for such several purposes."

34. The Statute then went on to declare, that "No act which should be done in pursuance of any order which should

Clause to declare the prerogative of the Crown unabridged by the Statute.

be so issued, should be questioned in His Majesty's Court of King's Bench, or in any other Court of the Common Law." And, that the Prerogative of the Crown might not be prejudiced by this interference from Parliament, this saving Clause was inserted:—"That nothing in this Act contained shall be construed to take away, abridge, or diminish, the acknowledged Prerogative of His Majesty, for the public safety, to resort to the exercise of Martial Law against open enemies or traitors, or any powers by Law vested in the Lord-Lieutenant, with or without the advice of His Majesty's Privy Council, or of any other person or persons whomsoever, to suppress treason and rebellion, and to do any act warranted by Law for that purpose, in the same manner as if this Act had never been made; or in any manner to call in question any acts theretofore done for the like purposes."[1]

35. After the suppression of the Rebellion, an Act of Indemnity[2] was passed, setting forth in the Preamble

A.D. 1801
Indemnity Act in favour of Officers (Civil and Military) engaged in the suppression of the rebellion

that several Officers, Civil and Military, and other persons, to suppress the Rebellion, had apprehended persons without due authority, and had done divers other acts in suppressing the Rebellion not justified by

---

[1] As to readiness of these Courts-martial to convict the accused, see Lord Cornwallis's Correspondence, vol. iii. (1859), by C. Ross   [2] 11 Geo. III., c 104

Law, which acts were so necessary for the suppression of the Rebellion that the persons ought to be indemnified. It then enacted, That all personal actions and suits, all Indictments, Informations, Attachments, Prosecutions, and Proceedings whatsoever, Judgments and Orders, if any be, against such Officers, Civil or Military, or other persons as aforesaid, for or by reason of any matter or thing commanded, ordered, directed, or done since the 25th day of March, 1799, in order to suppress the said insurrections and Rebellion, and for the preservation of the Public Peace in Ireland, should be discharged and made void; and that every person by whom any such act, matter, or thing should have been advised, commanded, ordered, directed, or done for the purposes aforesaid, since the 25th day of March, 1799, should be freed, acquitted, and indemnified, as well against the King's Most Excellent Majesty, his Heirs and Successors, as against all and every other Person and Persons whomsoever.

36. Unfortunately, in 1803 coercive measures became again necessary towards Ireland, and as upon this occasion the action of Parliament was that of the United Kingdom, the terms in which the 43 Geo. III., c. 117, was framed, and passed at the instance of Mr. Pitt, became important. The Bill was introduced in July, and passed in precisely the same words as the Irish Statute, except that it declared that the Courts-martial should be constituted of *Commissioned Officers*, not less in number than seven, nor more than thirteen, and that no sentence of death should be given unless two thirds of those present concurred therein. A difference between the two measures sufficient to show that the latter received the consideration of His Majesty's Ministers, if not of the Houses of Parliament.[1]

A.D 1803

Similar Act passed by the Parliament of the United Kingdom.

37. In introducing the Bill Mr. Pitt plainly stated the view he entertained of the Power of the Crown to declare Martial Law:—" The Bill[2] which I have to propose is not one *to enable* the Government, in Ireland, to

Mr Pitt's speech in introducing the Bill.

---

[1] 36 Parl. Hist, p 1675

[2] The Act was renewed in December following, after debate, 1 H. D (O. S), p 79.

declare Martial Law in districts where insurrection exists, for that is *a power* which His Majesty *already possesses,* but a Bill purporting to be for the protection of the lives and properties of His Majesty's loyal Subjects, and for the better suppression of insurrection and rebellion, and the object of which will be to enable the Lord-Lieutenant, when any persons shall be taken in rebellion, to order them to be tried immediately by a Court-martial. I do not mean even to give the Lord-Lieutenant of Ireland the power of superseding, by Martial Law, the operation of the Civil Code, nor to deprive the Subject in Civil cases of the advantages derived from the ordinary course of the Law of the land. Should the House adopt the present motion, I should follow it up with another, for leave to bring in a Bill to suspend, for a time to be limited, the Habeas Corpus Act in Ireland. This Bill is calculated to effect, if possible, by more lenient means, the suppression of those crimes which, without this suspension, must force the Government to the necessity of bringing to trial, by Court-martial, persons against whom suspicions of high-treason are entertained; but by detaining such persons in custody, we prevent them from engaging in treasonable machinations; and persons so arrested may be tried in the ordinary process of the Law without any Military interference."

38. The remaining instance—that of 1833—is worth notice in regard to the establishment of Courts-martial for the trial of ordinary Criminal offences, in modern times. The 3 and 4 Wm. IV., c. 4,[1] which sanctioned this system for a limited period, contained the same proviso or reservation as to the Prerogative of the Crown that the two earlier Statutes contained; and, looking at this fact, it cannot be doubted that the Crown, by the *admission of Parliament,* has the *undoubted right* of executing Martial Law for the defeat and dispersion of armed rebels, though the manner in which this Prerogative should be exercised, and what may be the legal effect of the Proclamation, are points upon which information may be gleaned (when sought

A.D 1833
The 3 & 4 Wm IV, c 4, and the reservation thereunder

---

[1] 15 & 16 H. D (3), *passim.*

for) in tracing the application of Martial Law in the Colonial Dependencies of the Empire.

39. In entering into the wider field of Inquiry — Martial Law in the Colonies—it is necessary, in the first instance to notice the distinction between the two classes of (1) Crown and (2) Settled Colonies, the Law with regard to each class being essentially different.   " A Crown Colony," said Lord Chief Justice Cockburn, in the Jamaica Case,[1] "is one which has been acquired by conquest, or, what is considered equivalent to conquest, by cession from some other State or Power.   A Settled Colony is a Colony which is established where land has been taken possession of in the name of the Crown of England, and, being unoccupied, has afterwards been colonized and settled upon by British Subjects." *As to the (1) Crown, or (2) Settled Colonies*

40. With regard to such Crown Colonies as are acquired by conquest,—except so far as rights may have been secured by any terms of capitulation,—the power of the Sovereign is absolute.   The conquered are at the mercy of the conqueror.   Such possessions keep, it is true, their own laws for the time; but subject to this, they are under the absolute power of the Sovereign of these Realms to alter those laws in any way that to the Sovereign in Council may seem proper: in short, they may be dealt with, Legislatively and as the Sovereign may please. *Power of the Sovereign in Crown Colonies.*

41. In a Settled Colony the inhabitants have all the rights of Englishmen.   They take with them, in the first place, that which no Englishman can by expatriation put off, namely, allegiance to the Crown, the duty of obedience to the lawful commands of the Sovereign, and obedience to the Laws which Parliament may think proper to make with reference to such a Colony.   But, on the other hand, they take with them all the rights and liberties of British Subjects; all the rights and liberties as against the Prerogative of the Crown, which they would enjoy in this country. *The like in Settled Colonies.*

42. The importance of the distinction is obvious.   In Crown Colonies—as the power of the Crown is absolute— Martial Law may be declared at any time.   In Settled *Importance of the distinction*

---

[1] Charge, pp 10, 11.   Ridgway, 1867.

Colonies, as the inhabitants are entitled, as against the Crown, to all the rights and liberties of British Subjects which they would enjoy here, Martial Law can only be declared under the conditions existing by the Law of England, as altered or varied by Local Legislation.

43. But whether all Settled Colonies are entitled to the benefit of the Petition of Right was one of the questions raised and discussed in the Jamaica case. According to the opinion of some, the Petition of Right was not made applicable to Jamaica or to any other Colony, either by express words or necessary intendment of any Act of Parliament; while, in the opinion of others, the attempt to limit its application to the shores of this country arose from an entire misconception of the character and effect of the Statute. "It is not," said the Lord Chief Justice, "an enacting Statute at all. It is not a Statute by which any new limitation was put upon the Prerogative of the Crown, or by which the Subject acquired any rights or immunities against the Prerogative. It is a Statute declaring where, according to the Law and Constitution of this country, the Prerogative of the Crown ends and the rights and liberties of the Subject begin. Therefore, if the Common Law of this country is, as I have already shown it to be, applicable to a Settled Colony, it follows that if the Petition of Right would prevent the exercise of Martial Law by virtue of the Prerogative in England, it must of necessity do so in Jamaica."[1]

How far the Petition of Right extends to Settled Colonies.

44. No doubt when *the Army* is beyond the Realm of England and the Mutiny Act has not been made specially applicable,[2] then Martial Law—as it existed prior to the Petition of Right—prevails. In Barwis v. Keppel, the Court held that when the Army is out of the National Dominions, the Crown acts by virtue of its Prerogative and not under the Mutiny Act and Articles of War. *Flagrante bello,* the Common Law has never interfered with the Army: indeed the maxim "Inter Arma silent leges" forbids such interference.

Does not extend to the Army in foreign countries.

---

[1] See the argument of Lord Mansfield (when Solicitor-General) that the Crown had the absolute power to declare Martial Law in the Colonies, 15 Parl. Hist., p. 262   [2] 2 & 3 Anne, c. 20.

In comparatively modern times the extreme penalties of transgression have been enforced against Soldiers without trial of any kind,[1] and the correspondence between the Duke of Wellington and Lord Castlereagh shows the opinion entertained in 1809, of this exercise of power.[2]

45 Not deeming it necessary to place on the text a detail of the circumstances, or to dwell upon the legal bearings of each case where Martial Law has been declared in the Colonies, I have given in the Appendix[3] some recent instances that have come under Parliamentary notice, where the Crown, acting through the Local Governor,[4] has adopted the extreme measure of proclaiming Martial Law for the suppression of Rebellion

Instances of Martial Law in the Colonies

46. The Jamaica Case of 1865 raised constitutional questions of great importance, that were discussed before Parliament and the Courts of Law. The action of the Jamaica Committee opened up a novel subject of controversy. No doubt, the policy that suggested the enactment of the 11 & 12 Wm. III., c. 12, and of the 42 Geo. III., c 85, assumed that upon the trial of a Colonial Governor the Crown would not—by defending him through the agency of the Home Treasury—interfere in his behalf, but probably its authors did *not* assume that an organised association would be raised for the prosecution of the Governor. However, the successive Ministries of Earls Russell and Derby and Mr. Disraeli pursued the same course—viz., that of giving the Governor access to all official documents needed for his defence, and a promise of pecuniary indemnity in the event of his defence being successful.

Jamaica Case, 1865

The Defence of the Civil Governor

47. The Ministry of Earl Derby pursued a different course towards the Executive Officer (Colonel Nelson), who had been engaged in carrying out Martial Law. His defence from the commencement was, with the sanction of the

The defence of the Military Officer

---

[1] Barwis *v* Keppel, 2 Wills, p. 314, Bradley *v* Arthur, 4 B and Cr, p 306

[2] Appendix CXII.; as to Drum-head Courts-martial, see 8 P. D (2), p. 492, and 41 ib (3), p 1275   Military Punishments, 1836, p 326

[3] Note I I, Appendix.

[4] As to the power of the Local Governor, and how far he represents the Crown, see Hill *v* Bigge, 3 Moore P C C, 1 166

Cabinet, taken charge of by the War Department—a distinction, founded upon that which it is obvious enough to trace between the responsibility of an Administrative Officer—giving commands as the Governor—and an executive Military Officer, obeying them[1] rather than acting wholly on the sense of his professional responsibility.[2]

48. Upon the Local Act of Indemnity the question arose whether it could be pleaded as a bar or estoppel to any action or prosecution instituted in the Courts of Westminster   In Lord North's time all Acts of Indemnity ought, in the opinion of his Colleagues, to be limited to actions at Law, and never extended to any criminal matter.[3] The duty of the responsible advisers of the Crown to consider these Statutory Indemnities, arises upon each occasion that any such Colonial Act is sent home for the Royal Assent.[4]   In 1836 Lord Glenelg refused to sanction a Local Ordinance,[5] which included the Governor in its provisions, because such an enactment appeared necessarily to imply that Her Majesty's representative was amenable to the Local Tribunals, which the Home Government were unwilling to countenance. "As Governor," the despatch proceeded, "you are responsible for acts done by you in that capacity, to the King, to Parliament, and in certain cases to the Court of King's Bench at Westminster, but not to the Colonial Tribunals." In the Jamaica Case it was argued against the Governor, that the Act could not be pleaded as a bar to Legal proceedings in the Supreme Courts—a contention which, if successful, would have deprived the Governor of all Statutory Indemnity.[6]

As to the operation of the Act of Indemnity

---

[1] See Question in House of Commons by Major Jervis, and Mr Disraeli's reply, 14th February, 1867   [2] Tobin *v* the Queen, 16 C B (N S), p 353
[3] 18 Parl Hist , p 817.   [4] Philips *v* Eyre, 4 L Rep (Q B), p 243.
[5] Appendix, Note II (7), *post*

[6] *Extract from Sir D Dundas's Evidence before the Ceylon Committee*

"5,480 The Governor of a colony, representing the Crown, can exercise the self-same power as the Crown itself, if the urgency and the necessity of the case justify it ?—I think so

"5,481 And I presume parties so acting would, in the event of their having

49 It is perhaps a matter of regret that no deliberate decision after argument was obtained from the Court of Queen's Bench upon the grave questions raised in the prosecutions instituted against the Governor and the Military Officer. In the latter case it was earnestly desired that some certain and definite rule might be laid down for the guidance of officers (civil and military) acting in regions too far removed from the Supreme Government to enable them to get instructions upon any great emergency. The Home Government, however, issued the General Circular that is printed in the Appendix [1] *Results of the Case*

50 The duties that devolve upon the Army under the circumstances mentioned in this and the preceding Chapter, would of themselves destroy all the analogy that some persons endeavour to present between the political influence of the Army and of the Navy. The Army, spread over the United Kingdom, is the offspring of the Great Rebellion. The Navy, afloat, is the emblem of our National strength, and no Political crisis has yet arisen when the Navy has been called upon to aid or to restore Civil authority. At the Mutiny of the Nore, and during the Blockade of the Texel, our supremacy at sea was no doubt seriously imperilled. The mutineers being (as a punishment) cut off from all communications with the shore, there was little fear — except that the Army might join the mutiny [2] — of any great *The duties of the Army and Navy in these matters and their political consequences.*

---

to defend their conduct, have entirely to rely upon the necessity and urgency of the occasion which called for the proclamation of Martial Law ?—I do not admit the word 'proclamation' They would have to justify themselves by the law under which they acted, the law under which they acted being Martial Law Whether the authorities who set it going had a right to do so, is another question

"5,482 Which question the Constitution provides a power of by settling an Act of Indemnity?—An Act of Indemnity is, of course, a prudent measure at all times Whenever you overstep the law, I recommend you to obtain an Act of Indemnity, if you can get one, but I am not sure that an Act of Indemnity is necessary I think it would be wise for a Governor who has proclaimed and executed Martial Law, to have the sanction of his Sovereign for his act, and it would be prudent for all persons who have acted under such a law to have an Act of Indemnity It is a short answer to any person who asks you questions about your conduct during the time Martial Law existed " [1] Appendix CXIII

[2] 39 Ann Reg, p 223, and Mr Pitt's Speech, introducing the Bill for 37 Geo III, c 70, 33 Parl Hist, p 806

social or political disorder. The Constitutional History of the two Services is essentially dissimilar. The Debates on the Army are redolent with Political Strife;[1] and, though every increase to the Army has been resolutely opposed, there has been no Annual contest as to the number of Seamen to be maintained A reference to the Journals of either House of Parliament will readily prove that the entries relating to the Navy number a very small proportion to those relating to Army affairs—though the Navy for many years was the larger force. Again, in another aspect of the case, it must be noticed that the obligations created by a great Military engagement are kept alive by visiting the scenes of conflict, while the same influences cannot arise in connection with the Navy Every person may visit the Field of Waterloo, but no one can discover the arena of Trafalgar

51. Looking, therefore, at the two Services in regard to their political influence, it is a matter of far greater moment that the Command of the Army than of the Navy should be entrusted to Subjects "assured and well reported of," or the assistance of the Military to the Civil Magistrates may work greater evils than those which the Army is brought to allay. "Let Princes," said Lord Bacon, "against all events, not be without some *great* person—one or rather *more* of military valour—near unto them for the repressing of seditions in their beginnings, ... but let such military persons be 'assured' (which Archbishop Whately explains as 'not to be doubted, trustworthy') and well reported of, rather than factious and popular, holding also good correspondence with the *other great* men in the State, or *else* the *remedy* is worse than *the disease.*"[2]

The Counsel of Lord Bacon

---

[1] Par. 14 *ante,* and Chap XVI , par 4, *note* 2, Chap XXVI , pars 28 and 50 *note,* Chap XXVIII , par 2 Further, contrast the conduct of Parliament towards the antithetical force—the Police—since 1828, with its conduct towards the Military Force during the last century Although the Police outnumbers the Army of the last century, yet no trace of this fact is to be found in the Debates or Journals of either House [2] Essay xv , pp 131, 132

CHAPTER XIX.

The Treasury and the former subordinate Departments thereof.

1. Having endeavoured to show, in the earlier part of this Work, the Constitutional Arrangements under which the Standing Army has become established within the Realm in time of Peace, and in the two preceding Chapters the secondary use to which the Military Forces of the Crown may be applied, either in Aid or in the Restoration of the Civil Power, it only remains for me to describe those Departments of the State that are, under the authority of the Crown, charged, firstly, with the Civil Administration, and, secondly, with the Government and Command, of the Army. *As to the Departments of the State that are charged with the Administration and Government of the Army*

2 With regard to the Civil Administration—a function totally distinct from, and therefore not to be associated with, the Command and Government of the Army [1]—the responsibility, prior to the Crimean War, mainly rested with the Treasury and its subordinate Departments. It has been already shown,[2] and will be hereafter more fully explained, that for the *payment* of the Army the offices of the Secretary at War and Paymaster-General were created, and that each of these Ministers had a direct Parliamentary responsibility.[3] For the *supply* of the Navy and Army—the Board of Ordnance, with an independent Parliamentary responsibility, and the Commissariat, in subordination to the Treasury, were originated. These were the expending Departments of the State. *The Civil Departments of Administration The Treasury*

3. That all the issues of Public Money might be duly accounted for to *independent* officers wholly unconnected with the Administration, the Auditors of Imprests, under the authority of the Crown, in the first instance, and the Audit Commissioners, with the authority of Parliament, afterwards—were appointed, and lastly, as—between *Comptrollers of Army accounts and Commissariat.*

---

[1] Chap XXVI   [2] Chap IV, pars 51-55   [3] Chap VII, pars 16, 61, 72

the original issue and the time for final audit—frauds might arise, the Comptrollers of Army Accounts were appointed by the Crown in the year 1704, to aid the Treasury with such information as might be required upon Army expenditure.

4. The policy of thus protecting the Public Treasure from too close a proximity to the Standing Army, had been taught by the experience of the Commonwealth,[1] and as it is difficult always to get a fair argument accepted by an armed opponent, these intervening offices—if not for the purpose created, at least—acted as safeguards or outworks to the Treasury. Upon notice, and before any concession was made—to a host of men[2] they gave information of the probable total increase of expense, and—their authority being limited—a reason for delay was afforded until a matter, apparently trifling. but often in fact great, could be carefully considered by the Treasury or submitted to the deliberation of the Cabinet   A country ceases to be free when its Treasure is under the influence of the Army.

Policy of interposing subordinate Departments between the Treasury and the Army

5. Now nothing is more incontrovertible than that this Kingdom has been raised to its present Wealth under the principle of exercising great thrift and care of the Public Treasure.   The maxims of the Constitution are clear and emphatic.   Lord Bacon deemed the Public Treasure one of the four Pillars of the State.   According to Lord Coke, " it is the Ligament of Peace, the Sinews of War, and the Preserver of the Honour and Safety of the Realm" Lord Somers described it to be " of the highest estimation in the consideration of the Law ; " and indeed the remedies against the Debtors to the Crown for Money due, or the punishment inflicted for theft of it, can only be reconciled with justice or expediency upon the theory of the vast importance of the Public Treasure.[3]

Care and frugality of the Public Treasure a political axiom

6. Nor is the vigilant guardianship designed by the law for the safe issue of Public Treasure less remarkable " No officer," wrote Lord Coke,[4] "that the King has, nor all of them together, can *ex officio* issue or dispose of the

Issue of the Public Treasure by the Sovereign

---

[1] Chap II , par 25, Chap XXVI , par 27 *et seq*   [2] Chap XX , pars 110, 111
[3] As to these, 1 Madox, 'Exch ,' chap xxiii , pp 128-261.   [4] 11 Rep , p 91c

King's Treasure, although it be for the honour or profit of the King himself, but it ought to be by Warrant from the King himself, for it is true that it is for the honour and profit of the King that good service done to the King should be rewarded; but it ought to be rewarded by the King himself, or by his Warrant and by no other; for," he adds, "the King's treasure is of so high estimate in law in respect of the necessity of it, that the embezzling of Treasure Trove, although it was not in the King's coffers, was *treason*."

7. But to guard the Sovereign and the Realm against improvidence or surprise, the Warrant of the King needed authentication from the highest officers of the State. *Issue to be made only on the Great or Privy Seal* If it came by word of mouth, or even under the signet or countersign of a Secretary of State, it was not sufficient—the authority for the issue of the Public Treasure being nothing less than the Great or Privy Seal, *founded upon the signet*. The use of the Great Seal involved the Lord Chancellor in responsibility, and the use of the Privy Seal an officer of State little inferior in degree to the Lord Chancellor;[1] "for which reason," adds Lord Somers, "as no part of the King's treasure could be issued but by such Warrant, the law put such a guard upon these Seals that it was high treason to counterfeit them."[2]

8. The officer of State holding the Public Treasure was the Lord Treasurer (Dominus Thesaurarius Angliæ); *The Lord Treasurer was the Custodian and dispenser of the Public Treasure* to which office he was appointed in former times by the delivery of the golden keys of the Treasury, but when Lord Coke wrote,[3] by the delivery of a White Staff, at the King's will and pleasure. "When Treasure failed, the White Staff served to rest him upon it, or to drive away importunate suitors."[4]

9. By his oath of office the duty of the Lord Treasurer stands upon eight articles, thus [5]— *Oath of Office*

"1 That well and truly he shall serve the King and his people in the office of Treasurer.

[1] Bankers' case, 14 How Stat Tri , p. 68.
[2] Ib., p 67, and Chap XXV, par 4   [3] Chap xi , p 104
[4] See Lord Somers' Remarks on these reasons for the White Staff, 14 How Stat Tri , p 103   [5] 4 Coke Inst , p 104

"2. That he shall do right to all manner of people, poor and rich, of such things as concern his office.

"3 The King's treasure he shall truly keep and dispend

"4. He shall truly counsel the King.

"5. The King's counsel he shall layn and keep.

"6. That he shall neither know nor suffer the King's hurt, nor his disheriting, nor that the rights of the Crown be decreased by any mean, as far forth as he may let it

"7. And if he may not let it, he shall make knowledge thereof clearly and expressly to the King, with his true advice and counsel.

"8. And he shall do and purchase the King's profit in all that he may reasonably do; which in effect agreeth with the oath of the Lord Chancellor, as you may read *ubi supra.*" [1]

10. Before passing to other subjects, it may be noticed, that even against so high an officer of State, with power all but supreme, the characteristic feature of the English Constitutional Government, which is everywhere so apparent, viz, that of check and control, is not wanting; for, according to the high authority of Madox and the traditions of the Treasury, the Chancellor of the Exchequer, by the constitution and function of his office, was appointed to be, and still is, a check upon the Lord Treasurer.[2]

The Chancellor of the Exchequer a controlling officer

11. The issue and disposal of the Public Treasure, according to the judgment of Lord Somers, rest solely with the Crown and the responsible Ministers—no Court of Law having any power or authority whatever over it.[3] "If the King's Treasure be so far subject to the administration of an ordinary Court of Justice as that it must be regularly issued upon the application of the Subject who has a demand thereupon for an annuity or any other debt, this may turn to the weakening of the Public Safety to a very high degree The Judges cannot, as such, be conversant of the necessities of the State; and

The Courts of Law have no power over the Public Treasure.

---

[1] This oath still continues to be administered, and under the sanction of it the business of the Treasury is conducted. See Appendix to 'Report on Oaths,' 1867

[2] Vol ii, p 113, and the late Lord Monteagle's Memorandum at p. 539 of 'Report on Public Moneys, 1856,' and at p 62 of Report, 1857.

[3] 14 How. Stat Tri, p. 103.

if they were, and knew them to be ever so pressing, they must act according to one rule, and must order a pension granted upon no consideration, or perhaps upon a very ill one, and for a pernicious end, to be paid with the very money which ought to be employed, and possibly was provided by Parliament for suppressing a rebellion, or resisting an invasion, or setting out a fleet."[1]

12. Such being the Constitutional theory under which the Public Treasure is held for the Crown and Realm, the practical working of the Department to provide for and control Military Expenditure and the Appropriation of Supplies, since the Revolution, remains to be explained, —at least so far as the previous portions of this Work render further explanation necessary[2]

The Treasury Authorities at the present time

13. In expenditure, the two great motive powers in the State are the House of Commons and the Army. The latter, in the early history of Parliamentary Government, was under the control of the Crown, and, as the stability of the Throne was dependent, amongst other circumstances, upon reconciling the people to a Standing Army by a very frugal Military expenditure,[3] the Commons, cognizant of this truth, resolved to receive no petition for money, except upon the recommendation of the Crown;[4] and—to impose a definite Ministerial responsibility upon some Department of the State—they recognised the distinct functions of the Treasury in questions relating to Public moneys, and repudiated that of any Military Officer.[5]

The National Expenditure as operated on by the Army was controlled by the Crown

14. The House of Commons could only be controlled in expenditure by the wisdom and influence of its own Leading Members, and hence these resolutions were made at their instance. When—by drawing a *fixed* income from the Exchequer—the Sovereign ceased to have any direct pecuniary interest in National Economy, the duty of pro-

The Commons influenced by their own Leaders.

---

[1] See the Provisions of the Petition of Right Act, 23 & 24 Vic., c. 34, sec 14

[2] Chap IV , par 50 *et seq* , Chap VI , par 6, and Chap VII

[3] See 7 Parl Hist , p 538 , 8 ib , p 887 , 13 ib , p 1434   The adherents of the Stuarts desired a small Army for the success of the Pretender See 11 ib , p 942 , 14 ib , pp. 452–60 , 30 ib , p 191   [4] Chap VI , par 7   [5] Chap VII , par 24

moting it devolved upon Parliament, and was fulfilled with more or less success, according to the strength of the political power or honesty of the Ministry. It always has been the case, that the further any Member is removed from the sense of Official or Parliamentary responsibility, the more readily he proposes an increase of expenditure.[1]

15. As, in matters of policy and expenditure, the Commons

The Commons to be kept free from the Influence of the Army

might be influenced by the great coercive power in the State—the Army—the Constitution, as we have seen, removed it from the scene of the Parliamentary Elections,[2] and, with extreme jealousy,[3] guarded the House from any encroachment upon its freedom on the part of the Military. "This country is free, because this House is so, which this House can never be, but from the freedom of Elections to it," and of the many ways for violating that freedom, none can be more pernicious than Military interference.

16. The Army being—in this aspect unlike the Church or

Civil Departments in the State created to guard the Public Expenditure.

most other professions—maintained by Supply taken on Annual Vote, its action on the House of Commons is constant and continuous; having more tongues than Fame, its wants are heard in a voice loud and potent in time of Peace, and all but omnipotent in time of War. A strong Civil Administration is needed to stem this current; and hence, soon after the establishment of a Standing Army, Departments, ranging in different degrees of authority, but charged with the disbursement of Military Expenditure, were formed in the State. Each Minister is responsible to Parliament by his employment, and may be said to receive a retaining fee on behalf of the tax payer to advocate economy, and so to watch the disbursement of the public money that it may not be wasted by extravagance

17. All supplies being granted to the Crown, Royal Orders

The Treasury responsible for all supplies and expenditure

to the Treasury (under the countersign of the Commissioners) and Treasury Warrants to the Exchequer and Paymaster-General, were adopted in lieu of the

---

[1] As to the increased expenditure of the 'Reform Parliament," see General Peel's speech, 182 H D. (3), pp 1207, 1210

[2] Chap. IX, pars 15, 16　　　[3] Ib par 23

more solemn Acts of Great and Privy Seals,[1] as the methods of obtaining the issue of moneys for the public service   The Treasury therefore continued to be primarily responsible, (1), for all Estimates submitted to Parliament, and, (2), for all moneys voted to the Crown; but in framing the one, and in disbursing the other, the Ministers in charge of the Ordnance and the War Offices, each in degree, were responsible to Parliament for these financial services

18 The expenditure of the Ordnance and War Offices was regulated by fixed Establishments sanctioned by the Crown on the advice of the Treasury, and other responsible Ministers;[2] and by Royal Warrants or Regulations issued under similar authority, which defined the annual expense, or in some instances the pay and allowances, of all persons who from time to time might be placed on the Establishments; out of or beyond these Establishments, or Royal Warrants, the subordinate departments had no authority to act, and therefore, of necessity, all cases of extra expenditure went to the Treasury. *Subordinate Powers of the Ordnance and War Offices.*

19. "The control," said Lord Palmerston,[3] "the Treasury exercises over the office of the Commander-in-Chief and War Office is this. that no new Regulation can be established, involving additional expense, and no addition made to the Official Establishment, without the special authority of the Treasury, on written representation, which they consider and determine upon.   When a Regulation is established with their sanction they are not consulted upon its detailed application; it is left to the Secretary at War and the Commander-in-Chief, as the case may be, to decide on the instances as they arise, whether they fall within the limits of the rule; but if any case occurs which is not provided for by the rule, then it must specially be submitted to the Treasury."[4] *As to War Office*

---

[1] As to the mode of issuing supplies for the payment of the Army, see Papers laid before the Finance Committee, 1828, and Reports on Public Moneys in 1856 and 1857

[2] Chap IV , par 50, and Appendix XIX , *ante*, and see the Remarks of the Commissioners of Military Inquiry, 17th Report, p 147, as to the Field Train Department   [3] Evidence before the Finance Committee, 1828, p 216

[4] Chap XXIV , par 21 *et seq*

20 The Master-General of the Ordnance, on the other
hand, was one of those Officers who (according to the
late Duke of Wellington[1]) was enabled to expend
money on unexpected services which had not been considered,
and for which money had not been granted by Parliament.
The reason was obvious. Suppose that any accident destroyed
works at Gibraltar or elsewhere, a power must exist to apply a
remedy immediately, and it was understood that the Master-
General of the Ordnance had the power of expending money for
such a purpose directly. Under modern directions from the
Treasury, that power was restricted to the sum of 500*l*. Without
the permission of the Treasury the Master-General could not
expend more than that amount; but, before those directions
from the Treasury, it was understood that he had the power
of directing the supply in case of the occurrence of such a
misfortune.

As to the Ordnance Department.

21. An annual Act limits[2] the appropriation of the supply
to the specific services described in the Votes, and
— in regard to the Naval and Military services—
enjoins that the respective Departments charged with
the detailed application of the sums granted, shall confine
their expenditure within the particular amounts apportioned
to each separate service comprised in the aggregate amount
appropriated to each department.[3] But Parliament, recog-
nising the impossibility of providing specially in the Estimate for every exigency which may arise in carrying on
those great services in all parts of the world, has granted
to the Crown,[4] in cases of indispensable necessity, authority
to provide temporarily for payments in excess of particular
grants out of surpluses on other grants in the same department, provided the aggregate sum voted for each department
be not exceeded

A.D. 1868

The appro-
priation of
supplies.

22. Prior to the year 1846 these were allowed as absolute
payments; but since 1866 they must be submitted to
Parliament and voted as supplemental Estimates. The

Limited
powers of the
Treasury

---

[1] Civil Administration, 1857, p 36   [2] Report on Public Moneys, 1857, p 27
[3] 31 & 32 Vic, c 85, sec 27   [4] Ib., sec 29

duty of the Treasury is therefore limited by the Appropriation Act,[1] but the power of issuing money "with" or "without account"[2]—in effect to supersede the provisions of the Audit Act—still remains with the Board.

23. But, within these limits, the functions of the Treasury, as a controlling Department in Naval and Military expenditure, may be so exercised as to be of the highest importance. In administration, both Services give rise to many questions of detail, and no fallacy is so great—or ruinous to the public—as to deem these *unimportant*. "A fraction a-day saved in any allowance on 100,000 men, would amount," said the late Lord Hardinge, "to a large annual sum, and therefore," he argued, and his arguments have proved unfortunately to be too true, that "expense would enormously increase when these financial duties were delegated to persons of inferior intelligence, and the Minister had so many other matters on his hands as to be prevented from *personally investigating* important details"[3]

Importance of the Treasury for Control

24 Two subordinate Departments formerly gave direct assistance to the Treasury, which was withdrawn from the Department—as to the Comptrollers of Army Accounts in 1836, and as to the Commissariat in 1854. By other changes subsequently made,[4] there now remains only ONE official source from which information as to Military Expenditure can be derived by the Cabinet, viz, the War Minister who is wholly dependent on Military Officers acting under the Commander-in-Chief for Information. Of this great change the *importance* will be seen in tracing the history of the Subordinate departments, and the probable future *effect* in contrasting the present with past Military Expenditure.[5]

Aids to the Treasury that have ceased to exist

25. Firstly, as to the Comptrollers of Army Accounts.—

---

[1] Indemnity Act to Mr Pitt, 45 Geo III, c 78, Impeachment of Lord Melville, 29 How Stat. Tri, pp 550-1482, 4 & 5 H D (O S), *passim*

[2] As to this, see Appendix to the 19th Report of the Finance Committee, 1797, and Report on Public Moneys, pp 561-3, 838   [3] Civil Administration, 1837, p 26

[4] Paras 33, 36 *post*, Chap. XX, par 21, and as to the Control Scheme, Chap XXIX., pars 61, 62

[5] See the able Memorandum of the Assistant Under-Secretary of State for the War Department printed in the Appendix, Note J J

To assist the Treasury in controlling Military Expenditure, Lord Godolphin, by letters patent, erected an office of "Comptroller of all Accounts relating to the Forces," with directions that the Comptrollers (two in number), should observe such instructions as might be given them under Royal Sign Manual. The substance of their original instructions of the 26th June, 1703, will be found in the Appendix,[1] and these, or others nearly similar, continued in force for many years.[2]

A.D. 1703

Comptrollers of Army Accounts instituted

26. At the close of the American War, in 1783, new instructions were issued, directing the Comptrollers[3] to examine the accounts of the Paymaster-General and his Deputies, charging upon sub-accountants all sums issued to them by the Pay Department, and to examine the accounts of Military stoppages, to ascertain that the items which composed the voluntary charge upon the Paymaster-General were correct. Provision and store accounts of Commissaries at home and abroad were likewise to be examined and certified by the Comptrollers. All contracts for supplying money, provisions, and stores for the Army, and all Army accounts, *whether ordinary or extraordinary* (when the latter should be referred to them by the Treasury) were to be examined by the Comptrollers. They were to inspect the muster-rolls, superintend the provision of clothing for the invalids, and lastly, to report all frauds, neglects, abuses, and defaults, to the Treasury, to which Department *alone* they were to be responsible.

A.D. 1783

New Instructions and duties given them

27. The expenses of Army Extraordinaries at home were incurred under the direct authority of the Treasury by contracts for supplies issued by the Commissariat Officers, examined by the Comptrollers, and paid for by the Treasury on their Certificate. The expenses of Army Extraordinaries abroad, incurred by the Governors or Military Officers, were first examined and reported on to the Treasury by the Comptrollers, and then submitted to the general independent Audit of the Commissioners for Public Accounts[4] The ex-

The Army Extraordinaries under their control.

---

[1] Appendix CXIV   [2] See Report of 1746, Appendix, pp. 198, 200

[3] Statement laid before the Finance Committee, 1828

[4] 19th Report of Finance Committee, 1797, p 350

penses incurred by the Army on active service were contracted for by the same financial agents of the Treasury, and then subjected to the examinations by the Comptrollers and Auditors

28. In 1806 the accounts unaudited and in arrear were so considerable in number that Parliament[1] was applied to for the grant of further powers, enabling the Crown to appoint additional Auditors, and to confer on the Comptrollers Statutory powers for the examination of Army Accounts. These powers were conceded, and the Act exempted Military Accountants—who had rendered a satisfactory statement to the Comptroller—from liability to account to the Auditor of Public Accounts.[2] *A.D. 1806. Proceedings in Parliament 46 Geo. III c. 80 & 141*

29. A third Comptroller was appointed, and a new patent issued, vesting in the Comptrollers the most extensive jurisdiction over the Military expenditure of the Country (the Ordnance excepted), and directing that in all practicable cases their examination should precede payment. It also placed the Commissariat (Home and Foreign) under the Comptrollers, and empowered them to examine finally all provision and store accounts, including in the latter Military stores, such as tents and camp equipage, &c. Their patent required them to examine, when necessary, all persons upon oath on matters touching expenditure of money, provisions, and stores, and they were enjoined to report to the Treasury all *frauds, neglects,* or *abuses,* and to render their department a depository, or record office, for every species of information relating to these various matters. *A.D. 1806. New Patent and Instructions.*

30 The savings effected by the Comptrollers in Military expenditure, the regularity and correctness which they had partially succeeded in introducing into the proceedings of Departments abroad, suggested to the Government[3] the idea of appointing a fourth Comptroller, with a separate *A.D 1814. Local control in Spain and Portugal*

---

[1] See 7 H D (O S) for the Debate on this, and the West India Audit Act, pp 332, 354, 614, 662, 791, 876, 1022
[2] 16 Geo III, c 141, sec. 20   [3] Statement (1828), par 2, *ante*

establishment, to act with the Army abroad, and to exercise powers still more extensive than those which were entrusted to his colleagues at home. Accordingly,[1] the 53 Geo. III., c. 150, was passed for the Local audit of the Military expenditure in Spain and Portugal.

31. The main feature of the arrangement was the appoint-
Powers of the Comptroller under 53 Geo. III c 150[1] ment of an Auditor-General by the Crown to proceed at once to Spain or Portugal, there to execute his office under the direction and control of the Treasury, with authority to require all persons receiving money or public stores for which they were accountable, to render an account of the same on oath, and to exhibit all papers and vouchers necessary to substantiate the account.

32. Although the Auditor-General had powers as ample as
Local Audit not to supersede General Audit. those conceded to the Comptrollers by the 46 Geo. III, c. 141, Parliament did not see fit to pledge the Treasury to accept his audit—made in the presence of the Army—as final: on the contrary, the preamble stated it might be necessary and expedient that the accounts should be *again* examined by the Commissioners of Audit, and the Act left the option of allowing or disallowing the accounts, without further investigation, to the judgment of the Audit Commissioners at home. As the Army passed into France, the powers of the Auditor-General were transferred to that country by the 54 Geo. III., c. 98.

33. When the Select Committee on Finance in 1828 called
A.D. 1828 Enquiries of the Finance Committee for information as to the duties of the Comptrollers, the Statement printed in the Appendix[2] was laid before them, together with a Register of papers received by them from the Treasury between the 1st and the 15th of March. No one can reasonably doubt that the investigation of claims by an Independent Board under the Treasury, most effectually controlled—by objecting to—expense before it was incurred. However in 1835, with the view of saving Depart-

---

[1] 26 H. D (O. S.), p 886   [2] Appendix CXV

mental expenses—not of losing the advantages (which have been lost) of independent advice—the office of the Comptroller was merged in the Audit Board.

34. "It appears to their Lordships," were the words of the Treasury Minute,[1] "that from the Board of Audit thus constituted the Treasury may receive the same preliminary advice, on the first view of the Commissariat Accounts, as at present, that they may resort to the same authority as at present for reports on all proposals for special cases of Military Expenditure, and on the general regulations involving expense, which emanate from time to time from the Secretary at War, on which the Comptrollers are at present a check; and as two of the Commissioners of Audit may be appointed Members of the College at Chelsea, and of other Military Boards, where their services might be considered useful, they would thereby be enabled to render that assistance by their attendance there which has hitherto been given by the Comptrollers." *A D 1835 — Merged in the Audit Board*

35. Secondly, as to the Commissariat.—

This subordinate department, formerly attached to the Treasury, consisted of a Financial Staff not less important to the public service than the Comptrollers *The Commissariat Department of the Treasury*

36. In the interval elapsing between the dates of the Report of the Commissioners on Public Acts in 1782,[2] and of the 19th Report of the Finance Committee in July, 1797, the recommendations of the Commissioners appear to have been adopted; for the Committee reported to the House that all the Financial business of the Army abroad was then conducted by Commissaries of Moneys and of Stores, appointed by the King's Sign Manual Warrant, directing them to obey all instructions (which had had been prepared by the Comptrollers) given by the Treasury   Through the agency of these Civil servants present with the Army at the seat of operations, the Treasury was furnished with direct independent com- *Between 1782 and 1797 the Commissariat staff enlarged*

---

[1] Civil Administration, 1837, p 17 a   [2] Chap VII, par 62 *et seq*

munications; and the Government—with the full knowledge of all circumstances—was able to exercise an efficient control over Military expenditure.[1]

37. The numbers and allowances of the Commissariat Establishment were fixed by the Crown, the appointments and promotions therein being made by the Treasury under the Regulations of the 19th March, 1810.[2] No one was eligible for appointment under sixteen years of age. Upon admission he had to serve for one year as a clerk, then he became Deputy-Assistant Commissary General, and rose, after due service in each rank, to the rank of Commissary General.[3]

A D 1810

Establishment fixed for the Commissariat.

38. The Department, in 1812, came under the notice of the Commissioners of Military Inquiry, who reported that they found the Commissaries holding *double* appointments for the *same* duty, one from the Treasury and one from the War Office. Questioning the propriety of adhering to a *Military* form of appointment—a circumstance not remarkable when the particular reason for their employment as Civilians is taken into consideration,—or to the Military usages of daily pay and forage allowance, the Commissioners suggested—as the Service must be considered as *purely Civil*—that the Military commission and pay should be abandoned.[4]

A D 1812

Report of the Commissioners of Military Enquiry

39. So stood the matter when the duties of the Commissariat, with reference to the Treasury and Army, were thus described in a work of official authority, published in 1846 [5]—

Duties of the Commissariat.

40. "The Commissariat raises, keeps, and disburses, according to fixed regulations, the whole of the funds required to carry on the foreign expenditure of this country Certain classes of payments are made under specific directions from the Treasury; other payments are made under warrants from the Officers Commanding, or (as in the case of the Convict expenditure) of the Governor of the

Holder of the Public Treasure, and check on Military expenditure

---

[1] Vol. 12 of House of Commons Reports, pp 350 (*a*, *b*), 373

[2] Chap. XIII, par 51   [3] Civil Administration, 1837, p 8*a*

[4] 18th Report of March, 1812, pp 253, 256   As to the evils of such a doubtful allegiance, see Chap XXI, par 2, Chap XXIII., par 10, and Chap XXIX

[5] Thomas's 'History of Public Departments,' p 177

Colony. It is the duty of the Commissariat Officer to call the attention of the Officer Commanding, or of the Governor, as the case may be, to every instance in which a payment may be authorised, at variance with the established regulations, or with any particular direction of the Treasury Board, as well as to report on the subject to the Treasury.

41. "An account is constantly kept open, by means of the Commissariat chests, between Great Britain and all its foreign dependencies: so that if a sum has to be received or paid in Canada, Australia, or China, for any branch of the Public Service, it may be done by a transfer in the Commissariat Chest Account, without any remittance The Commissariat Officers act, in effect, as Sub-Treasurers to the Lords Commissioners of the Treasury in the Foreign Possessions of the Crown *Under the Treasury*

42 "The financial functions performed by the Commissariat render it indispensable that the officers of the department should act under the immediate orders of the Treasury *which cannot transfer to others the responsibility of the various operations connected with the provision, the custody, and the due appropriation of the funds which are required for carrying on the public service.* *Financial Officers*

43 "The Commissariat also provides, keeps in store, and issues the provisions, forage, fuel, and light, for the use of all the different branches of the Service abroad; furnishes the Troops with the necessary supplies of water; provides all land and inland water transport, and, in the absence of a properly authorised naval agent, takes up all the freight required for the conveyance of Troops and Stores by sea. Salt meat, coals, candles, and some other articles, are procured by the Commissariat through the medium of the Admiralty and the Ordnance, while the fresh provisions are purchased on the spot. The materials of various kinds required by the Ordnance, and supplied for the service of the Navy, in the absence of a naval agent, are also provided by the Commissariat. *Supplies of provisions*

44. "The Commissariat purchases are all made under written contracts, entered into after open competition, according to certain prescribed rules. Copies of every *Made all contracts for Supplies*

advertisement, tender, contract, &c., are immediately sent to the Treasury, where the whole of the proceedings are carefully scrutinised, and proper notice is taken of any irregularity that may have been committed.

45. "It is the duty of the Commissariat Officers to take care
To examine quality that the provisions and other supplies, are of proper quality according to contract; and if any difference of opinion should arise on this point, it is usual for the Officer Commanding to appoint a Board of Officers, who survey the articles complained of; and if the articles are condemned, others of proper quality are immediately obtained from the contractor, or are purchased by the Commissariat at his expense. Copies of the Reports of all such boards of Survey are sent to the Treasury. All the Accounts of the Commissariat, both cash and store, are sent home at the termination of each month to the Commissioners of Audit, by whom they are examined and audited."

46. Obviously, for any Employer to permit those Employed
Their functions were discharged for the Treasury and not for the Army to provide at his expense, and without control, their supplies of food and provisions would be a concession tending to extravagance. Economy and efficiency are always principles of antagonism—the views of one who has to bear the expense, and of others who enjoy the benefit, are not certain to be identical. A margin—and possibly a large one—of economy may be found to lie between the two extremes, and for this saving of public money the Treasury was held responsible to Parliament.[1]

47. Therefore when the Army Extraordinaries were abo-
A.D 1835. lished,[2] the Treasury refused on good grounds[3] to give
The Treasury refused to part with the Commissariat Staff up the direction and control of the Commissariat, but resolved to retain that Staff under its own immediate superintendence, and to administer the Extraordinary expenditure through their agency. That this should

---

[1] Chap.XV, par 120, and Note J J. Take an illustration 12,000 lbs of meat at Aldershot are said to be bad, having changed in 12 hours Now, dare a Commissariat Officer risk the issue of any part of it? All must be given to the pigs, and another 12,000 lbs provided by the public Between the General and his Military subordinate, how are the public protected?

[2] Chap VII, par 70, *et seq*

[3] Mr Herries' Letter, 27th Feb, 1835, p 15 a, and Treasury Minute, p 17 a

have been the Treasury view was not surprising; and as the Commissariat, rather than the War Office, were retained to aid the Treasury, the intention of the Government—that the decision on extra expenditure was to be that of the Supreme Civil authority, free from all Military bias—was clear.

48. That the Commissariat should be maintained as an independent Department, responsible to the Treasury *alone*, was the view of the late Duke of Wellington, not less as a Statesman than as a Soldier; for his opinion was recorded after he had filled the office of the First Lord of the Treasury:—"I think that the Commissariat should be, both in peace and war, under the Treasury and responsible to the Treasury *alone*. The authority over the Commissariat Officer should be direct, he could not be put under any other Board without inconvenience;"[1] and when writing on the same subject to Earl Russell in 1849, he again *earnestly* recommended *the Treasury* to keep the Commissariat in their own hands, *wholly* and *exclusively* under their *immediate* control.[2] However, when the Ministry decided upon abolishing the Established Departments, and creating a new department out of the old materials under one Cabinet Minister, so minimizing Civil control over Military expenditure, these counsels were disregarded. The Commissariat was transferred to the War Office, and, after a few years of decadency of Civil control, placed under the Mutiny Act—with either a divided allegiance to the Civil Minister and Military Chief, or a sole allegiance to the latter, possibly with enough of uncertainty to evade the commands of either.[3]

The Duke of Wellington counselled the Treasury never to do so in peace or war

49. The transfer was made under a Treasury Minute of the 22nd of December, 1854, which, after alluding to the origin of the staff, proceeds to describe its efficiency in these words.[4]—"The custody of large sums of public money has always been found to be full of temptation, and in this case the danger is enhanced by the remoteness of the scene, and the emergent circumstances under which the service often has to be conducted. No money security is

A.D. 1854

Transfer of the Commissariat to the "War Minister"

[1] Civil Administration, 1857, p 39   [2] Appendix CXLVIII *post*
[3] Chap XXIII, par. 10, and Chap XXIX, par 65 *et seq*
[4] Military Organisation, 1860, p 535.

taken from Commissariat Officers, because it has been considered that no amount that would be required would cover their pecuniary responsibility.[1] Nevertheless, many years have elapsed since a *trained officer of the department* has been guilty of malversation, and the whole body of officers is animated by a spirit of *fidelity and economy* which is of the greatest public value. This result has been attained by a *well arranged system of checks,* which has been gradually adapted to all the contingencies of the case by a careful selection of tried men for the more responsible situations, and by making every Commissariat Officer feel that his prospects in reference to the annual promotion, and to his appointment to the charge of the department at the different stations, depend entirely on his vigilance and activity in the discharge of *his trust.*"

50. To the Treasury no change of system appeared to be needed:—"The existing regulations have been proved by experience to be sufficient to secure correctness in all the transactions connected with the Commissariat chests, provided they are strictly enforced; and a careful observation of the conduct of the clerks and junior officers, and a system of promotion based upon merit, have formed a body of officers of approved integrity, from whom fit persons may be selected for every situation of *trust.*"

No change of system thought necessary by the Treasury

51. The transfer having been provided for, the Minute refers—as the last point to which it is necessary to call attention—to the control of Extraordinary Expenditure by the Commissariat, under the directions of the Treasury.

Cautions to be observed

52. "The Commissariat chest is under the guardianship of the Officer Commanding; and, except for Commissariat services, or services in respect to which special instructions have been given by the Treasury, no issue can be made from the chest which is not directed by Warrant under his hand. If, however, the Officer Commanding should direct any payment to be made which is not authorised by any established regulation, it is the duty of the Commissariat Officer to make a representation on the subject to him; and if, not-

The sole check on the Commanding Officer on a Foreign Station

---

[1] As to security to be given by Public Officers see 52 Geo III, c 66, 6 & 7 Wm IV, c. 28, 1 & 2 Vic, c. 61, and Note T T in Appendix

withstanding this, the Officer Commanding maintains his decision, the Commissariat Officer obeys the order, and reports all
the circumstances, for the information of the Treasury. This is
not a complete check, but it is the best of which the nature of
the case admits, and it has sufficed to put a stop to practices
which formerly prevailed, whereby the funds of the Commissariat
chests were made available to a great extent for various Colonial
purposes, and for carrying on unauthorised Ordnance works.

53. "In time of war this subject immediately assumes
greatly increased public importance. Parliament
places at the disposal of the Treasury a grant of the *Expenditure in war under the control of the Commissariat*
nature of a vote of credit for defraying the extraor-
dinary expenses of the war. All the expenditure connected with every department of an army in the field, except
that which is provided for in the ordinary Estimates, comes
under this head, and the whole of that portion of it which has
to be carried on abroad is at present conducted by the Officers
of the Commissariat on behalf of the Treasury. The stern
exigencies of war do not allow of much discretion as to the
objects of this expenditure, but there is greater freedom of
action as to the mode in which it is carried on. The public
have every *practicable* guarantee, in the *fact* that the agency
employed is that of *trained* officers acting *under a Commissary-
General*, who is responsible to the authorities at home for the
regularity *and economy*, as he is to the Military Officer
Commanding for the efficiency of his arrangements."

54. For a few years only, the Commissariat Staff remained
as the Civil employés of the " War Minister." Assum- *Was the public security the same?*
ing his control to have carried with it the same
authority, and to have been as purely *Civil* as that of
the Treasury Board, then—the status of the Commissariat remaining the same—the Public *might* have felt assured " that
one of the most essential of the functions of a financial department "—that of control over extraordinary expenditure—would
certainly continue to be discharged " in the spirit of fidelity
and economy," which the Minute described " as of the greatest
public value."

55. But the change of 1851 did not suffice for the Army,

and therefore with the "War Minister" the advice of "Military Officers" prevailed. Hence in 1858, under the plea of increasing their efficiency, and to render them subordinate as Military Officers to the General in Command, the Civil status of the Commissariat was abolished.[1] The circle of events since 1782 revolved; for the Military, as represented by the Commissariat Staff, under the nominal control of the War Office were restored to the expenditure of the Public Treasure, *not only abroad or in War, but also at home, and in time of Peace.*

A.D. 1858

The civil status of the Commissariat abolished

56. That the control of the Treasury over Military Expenditure has been very greatly weakened by taking away from the Board—what might be regarded as analogous to—its organs of sight and action, and by creating a War Minister surrounded by Military Officers, cannot, I think, be reasonably questioned. For the same organs are not now to be found in the Administrative Body, nor the same constitutional safeguards existing, as will be seen when the other subordinate departments—the Ordnance, War Office, and the Audit Offices —are treated of in later Chapters.

Results as affecting the efficiency of the Treasury

57. Now, to summarise for the purposes of the present, what will be found in those Chapters, it will be seen that, as to the Ordnance Department, the abolition of the Principal Officers has led to these results —(1). The loss of efficient Parliamentary and responsible control over Ordnance expenditure, which consequently has very largely increased in all its branches,—the Ordnance Corps, Fortifications, Armament, Barracks, Hospitals, and Arsenals. (2). The transfer to the Commander-in-Chief of the most important part of the Civil, viz, the Store Officers as custodians of the Public Treasure,[2] as well as the whole of the Military branch of the Ordnance. The Government, therefore, has lost both Parliamentary and Civil control over a vast amount of Military expenditure by the abolition of Offices formerly held by Colleagues fairly sharing their Parliamentary responsibility.

As to the Ordnance Expenditure and Control.

58. As to the War Office it will be seen that it has

---

[1] Chap XIII, par 51. Are the provisions of the 1 & 2 Geo IV., cap 121, secs 27-9, any longer applicable to Military expenditure abroad? [2] Ib., par 52

cca ed to be regarded as formerly—an office exclusively Civil—raised up as Statesmen [1] asserted, to protect the people from the Army, because the principal and many subordinate appointments are held by Military Officers, receiving Military pay, subject to the orders of, and looking for promotion from, their Military Superior, against whom the Constitutional functions of the office are to be exercised The office so worked is the only check that the Public has upon the pay and allowances to the Army, or against extravagance in Military expenditure.[2]

As to the War Office Expenditure and Control

59. As to the Audit Office, this check is only in appropriation—and not in expenditure, for the latter is left solely with the War Office, either to allow or disallow doubtful items, as the Chief, acting on the advice of his officials, sees fit [3]

As to the audit by the Audit Board.

60 Certainly, prior to the Crimean War, the policy of Parliament had been to have the authority of the Treasury not only supreme, but exclusive in all matters of Finance. After the establishment of the Commander-in-Chief's office, some embarrassment arose from the interference of the Military authorities with the Secretary at War in the discharge of his financial duties; but that controversy was terminated by a renunciation on the part of the Commander-in-Chief of all power or authority whatever in any matter of finance,[4] and by cancelling the Secretary at War's Military Commission [5] Therefore the system, re-inaugurated in 1858, is directly opposed to these principles, and to build up a system of Military Finance, to be conducted by Commissioned Officers under the General of each district, is entirely inconsistent with the relative positions that these officers ought to hold towards the Commander-in-Chief, and which the latter officer has hitherto held towards Parliament. Either the Commander-in-Chief must have authority in matters of finance—and so raise again all the Constitutional jealousies that it was to be hoped were for ever set at rest, or his subordinates must

The policy of 1858 was opposed to the principles of Finance

---

[1] Chap IX , par 29, and Appendix CXXIX , *post*, Chap XXI
[2] Chap XXIX , par 32   [3] Chap. XXIV , par 20 *et seq*
[4] Chap XXVI , par 34   [5] Chap XXI , par 3.

return to their Civil Status and to an exclusive allegiance to the Finance Minister.

61. Parliament is standing at the threshold of this new Military organisation for the Finance of the Army
The bulk of the Commissariat and store officers at present in Commission received their early training as clerks in the Treasury and Ordnance,[1] and not as Officers and Soldiers in the Army. They have therefore had some official experience, and in the discharge of their Financial duties their allegiance has been given rather to Parliament than to the Crown. In both these respects their successors drawn from the Army will differ essentially from them. In abandoning the front for the rear of the Army, they will bring with them no official experience for the discharge of their *new* duties, but the *old* principle of allegiance to the General (whose favour is to be conciliated), and some leaven of the doctrine that the Army knows *only* the authority of the Crown, and ignores that of Parliament[2]

Parliament is standing at the threshold of this new system

62 "The principle of our Constitutional Army," said the late Mr. James Mackintosh, "is that command, preferment, and honour, come to it from the Crown, but that for all pecuniary remuneration it is made to depend on Parliament."[3] This, however, is far from being an accepted doctrine by Military men. According to their views —as expressed by the late Lord Hardinge—"it is of the utmost importance that the Army should look up to *no* authority but that *of the King.*"[4] It is not easy to reconcile principles so contradictory, but if those of Sir James Mackintosh be accepted by Parliament it is a matter of some importance that the House of Commons should be quite sure that the Military Expenditure is entrusted exclusively to a class of officials who honestly adhere to that theory and do not intend to justify themselves in making a lavish expenditure of public money upon Lord Hardinge's axiom, that the Army ought not to look

Two contradictory principles in Army finance

---

[1] From 1860 to 1864 eleven Soldiers had been admitted against thirty-five Civilians, 2nd General Report of Council of Military Education, p 84
[2] Chap XXV, pars 10-19, and Chap XXVI, pars 36-40
[3] Chap VI, par 23   [4] Ib., par 9

to any authority but the King.[1] Both the Duke of Wellington and Lord Hardinge assured Parliament that Military officers of their era had an utter repugnance to have anything to do with money, but in a few years a change—difficult to account for— *may* have occurred in the Army in this matter

63 "When any of the four pillars of Government"—the Public Treasure being one—"are mainly shaken or weakened, men," said Lord Bacon, "had need to pray for fair weather" Can any one doubt that the security for the expenditure of the Public Treasure has been and will be mainly shaken or weakened by the transfer of power from the responsible Departments of the State to Generals in command of the Army by their action on the War Minister?[2]

Counsel of Lord Bacon

64. One other suggestion remains to be carried out, in order to reverse completely the plan of Army Administration, upheld by the Duke of Wellington, that is, for one officer or class of officers at each place or station to discharge both Store and Commissariat duties "I do not think it possible," said the Duke,[3] "to intrust the establishments of the Ordnance abroad and in the country with the transaction of the business of the Commissariat; I am now adverting to a time of peace. In, time of war I consider it *absolutely* impracticable—quite out of the question, it could not be done. the persons charged with the care of the Ordnance and Stores in the field, could not take charge of all those branches of business which are performed by the officers of the Commissary-General, which go to feed the Troops and their horses and animals, and to supply them with the means of transport, and all that is necessary." In this view he was confirmed by Lord Hardinge "There might by the proposed consolidation be some saving in time of peace, but a great deal of danger in time of war My opinion decidedly is, that everything that is consumed by man or by horse had better be left to the Commissariat; it would be imprudent to place it under the Ordnance."[4]

One other suggestion remains to be disregarded

---

[1] Chap. XXI, par 48, and again see Mr Fox's Speech, 29 Parl Hist, p 245—"The Constitution knows no such thing as confidence"

[2] Chap XXIX, pars 56-63   [3] Civil Administration 1837, pp 37, 38

[4] P. 28, see Chap XX, par 114, and Chap XXIX, as to the Control Scheme, and the various duties of those Officers

CHAPTER XX

THE LATE BOARD OF ORDNANCE.[1]

1. THE Department of the first importance in Army Expenditure
Financial importance of the Ordnance Department. after the Treasury was the Ordnance. It was of great antiquity, and constituted before the existence of the Standing Army for the service of the Navy. When the Ordnance Department was reorganised in Charles II.'s reign, it was charged with the duty of " providing armament for all the Ships and Forts, and bound to obey equally the Lord Admiral and the Lord Treasurer." The Navy has never been held by Parliament to be a Service of secondary importance to the State; but, during the century, the Army has so rapidly increased in numbers and in political importance, that its possession of the Ordnance as a department of Military Administration is only thus to be accounted for.

2. Without Ordnance the Navy and Army are useless, and
Political importance of the Ordnance. therefore at the time of the Great Rebellion the possession of the Department was—as between the King and Parliament—of the greatest possible importance The officers in charge, appointed by the King, recognised no other authority, nor would they part with either arms, or gunpowder, or tents, except upon Royal order. To meet this difficulty, in the case of the Irish war, Parliament prevailed on the King to place the Ordnance Office under orders to obey both Houses,[2] and when in later troubles the King failed to satisfy their requirements, the office was seized by Parliament.[3]

3. The Master-General and Principal Officers, to whom the

---

[1] See Vol I , Chap. I., par. 11 *et seq.*, Chap IV., par 59 *et seq* , and Appendix XVI , p 456   [2] 2 Com Journ., pp 372 75, 457, 578, 590

[3] Ib , p 730, 5 ib, pp. 182-6, see also 2 State Tracts, p. 226, where it is alleged that on the expedition to Ireland the stores and arms were placed in the custody of King James II 's friends, and that Wm III had to seize them Chap. XXV , par. 24

possession of so vast an amount of Public Treasure was thus necessarily entrusted, were therefore persons of high Political importance; subordinate only to the Treasury and auditors of Imprest in matters of account, and to the Secretary of State for the issue of military equipment.

The Master-General and Board Officers persons of high station

4. After the Revolution,[1] the Department became divided into two distinct branches—traces of which were to be found at the time when the Board was dissolved. The "Military branch" was ultimately developed in the Ordnance Corps (the Royal Artillery and Royal Engineers), under the command of the Master-General (or, in his absence, of the Lieutenant-General), and the "Civil branch" remained to administer the Military branch, and to discharge those important functions that may be roughly classified as (1) of custodians of Public Treasure in Lands and Stores; (2) of contractors or manufacturers—to supply the Navy and Army with warlike munitions and equipments.

After the Revolution divided into 2 branches— (1) Military, and (2) Civil

5. The constitution and action of the Department evidence the same care and thrift of the Public Treasure that I have already noticed in the Treasury The Principal Officers were placed in charge of separate duties, and were to be a check upon each other on behalf of their Common master, the King. They were only to part with property upon proper warrant When they handed over a building it was to some person or persons—as the Governor for a Fortress, or a Barrack-master for Barracks [2]—responsible for dilapidations and repair. When stores were to be given out, it was on an indenture with a schedule, that a "Remain" might readily be taken, and the recipient made responsible for deficiencies [3]

The great care manifested for the security of the public property entrusted to the Department

6 From the Revolution to the death of the first Lord Raglan,[4] the office of Master-General had generally been held by an illustrious Soldier [5] After the office of Commander-in-Chief had been created, and the Army largely

Master-General an illustrious soldier

---

[1] See Return of 1704, 14 Com Journ, p 420

[2] Appendix I., p. 413, *ante.* [3] See Vol I, pp 457-461

[4] In the Memorandum of the Duke of Wellington it is stated that up to 1828 the Master-General had always been in the Cabinet (See Appendix CXLVIII)

[5] For instance —Schomberg, Marlborough, Cadogan, Argyll, Ligonier, Cornwallis, Hastings, Wellington, Anglesey, and Hardinge Military honours were paid to him by Royal Order of 13 May, 1686 (Bk 795, p 107)

increased, the Master-General became the adviser of the Cabinet on Military affairs.[1] Obviously such advice was needed, nor could there be found any one better qualified to discharge that office. The Constitutional objections that present themselves against the admission of the Commander-in-Chief into the Cabinet did not prevail, in the same degree, against the Master-General; for his Command in the Army was limited to the Scientific Corps—numerically small, and serving in detached quarters. The office, therefore, was one of the prizes—both in regard to acknowledged position and emolument—which the Country had provided for the Military profession, and, as such, it was from time to time conferred on a General Officer, who by great Military attainments and distinguished service in the Field had established himself in the foremost rank of his profession. The Master-General was therefore a representative man in the Cabinet, and in the Army his decisions deservedly carried an authority with them that has been unknown since his office has been abolished.[2]

7. The Board Officers were Naval, Military, or Civilian,

The Board Officers— Naval, Military, or Civil —as deemed expedient. according to convenience, their ability for public business, and influence in the House of Commons Having regard to the official responsibility that rested upon them, and to their accountability to Parliament, three members, two of whom sat in the Commons, did not entail an improvident bestowal of Public salaries. At any rate, the Commons had *their* interests represented in the Board, and by this arrangement gained some security against the wasteful expenditure of Public money.

8. The relative positions filled by the Principal Officers

Relative positions of the Master General and Board Officers towards each other are shown upon their original Instructions in 1683,[3] and were described to Parliament by the Report of the Commissioners on Public

---

[1] As to the Military adviser of the Cabinet, see Lord Herbert's Evidence, Organization Rep, 1860 (Questions 6615-30), 193 H D (3) p 1241, and 194 *ib*, p 858

[2] It was a position to which men of small means might rise, for instance, the late Lord Vivian—who held office as Sir Hussey Vivian—began his life in the office of Mr. Foot, an attorney in Devonport (see Mr. Foot's Memorial of 5 January, 1842, to the Board of Ordnance) The continuance of the office might have been justified on Sydney Smith's argument in favour of Church prizes, in his 'Second Letter to Archdeacon Singleton'　　　[3] Vol I, p 456.

accounts in 1784[1] In the first place, the Master-General held the sole command over the Military branch, the Ordnance Corps, and also an absolute power—when he was pleased to exercise it —over the whole Civil business of the Board; but in the absence of the Master-General, or of his instructions, the members of the Board acted in all matters at their discretion—each having an individual responsibility for his own department, as well as a joint responsibility for his acts as a Board Officer. This several and joint responsibility was fully recognised in Parliament, and acted upon.[2]

9. The Ordnance, like all other expending departments charged with Parliamentary responsibility, prepared its own estimates, and after their approval at the Treasury, laid them before the House of Commons. These were founded on Establishments settled at the commencement of each reign, and sanctioned by Royal Sign Manual, or from time to time by Royal Warrants issued for particular services. All the expenditure was primarily made subject to certain Rules; but as in the course of events the Ordnance Establishments became scattered over our Colonial possessions, defensive works were erected and maintained abroad, and contingent expenses arose that created a Departmental debt, until the whole system was reformed by Parliament[4]

The Estimates and Expenditure controlled—(1) by the Ordnance, and (2) by the Treasury

10. Starting from this outline, I shall endeavour to show more in detail what were the duties of the Civil branch of the Ordnance Department at the time it was deemed expedient to abolish the Principal Officers, and to transfer their duties, with many others, to one Parliamentary Officer, acting as a fourth Secretary of State—dividing the matter under these principal heads :—

The subject to be considered

(1) As to Stores
(2). As Landowners.
(3) As to the Survey of the United Kingdom.
(4). As to Defensive Works.

---

[1] See Appendix CXVI
[2] Resignation of Captain Boldero, 82 H D (3), p 800
[3] See Estimates for 1688, 10 Com Journ , Ordnance Estimates signed by four Board Officers, pp 60-2, War Office Estimates unsigned, pp 57-9
[4] 12th Report of Commissioners on Public Accounts, 1784

(5). As to Contracts

(6). As to Manufacturing Establishments.

I shall then review the Evidence laid before Parliament as to the *efficiency* of the Ordnance Department anterior to the period at which the Principal Officers were abolished

I. As to the Store Department.

11. It was as custodians of a vast amount of Public Treasure,

The Store branch of the Ordnance
which it was of the highest importance to the State —both in reference to its Domestic Police and Foreign Policy—should be held in the hands of responsible officers, that the functions of the Civil Branch of the Ordnance Department were important

12. The earliest Remain (or account) of Stores that is extant

The Store Remain of 1559
in the Ordnance Department dates from April, 1559, and is of all Her Majesty's Stores in the Tower of London, the Minories, Woolwich, the Artillery Garden, and other places. It was taken under Commission, addressed to the Lieutenant of the Tower, and others,—John Conyers, the Auditor of Imprest, being one of the quorum,—and contains a Schedule of all the Naval and Military Stores then belonging to the Crown.[1]

13. The Remain of 1683 appears to have followed upon

The like of 1683
the re-organization of the Department in July of the same year, and purports to be a General Statement of all Her Majesty's Ordnance Stores, and other provisions of War, within the Tower of London, lately under the charge of Edward Conyers, and now transferred (by a Remain taken by virtue of Her Majesty's Commission, dated 11 August, beginning 15 March, 1683, and ending 17 November following, taken in the presence of the Principal Officers of Ordnance, and Auditors of Her Majesty's Imprest[2]) into the charge of William Bridges, Esq., the Principal Storekeeper.

---

[1] Appendix CXVII The records of the Ordnance would well repay a careful examination, and are of National interest.

[2] The Auditors originally appeared to have authority over Stores (Madox, vol. ii , p. 293)

14. The liability of the Principal Storekeeper being thus certified, he could only clear his account, if impeached in Parliament, by issues duly sanctioned under Royal Sign Manual, and made to persons responsible to the Crown for the future care of the Stores issued. All the Storekeepers at the out-stations were Bonded Accountants, and the Board had representatives,—as Clerks of the Survey, and of the Cheque—holding appointments for life, at the particular place or station to which they were appointed.

Liability of the Principal Storekeeper

15. Issues being made by the Principal to the Local Storekeeper, the latter was charged on the Ledger Account with their receipt, and from this responsibility he could only relieve himself by lawful issues or a just Remain The issue having been sanctioned by the Crown,—in the reign of George II.,[1] under the authority of a Royal Sign Manual Order, and in later periods by a letter from the Secretary of State,[2]—the Board made an order to their Storekeeper for delivering out the Stores.

Of the Local Storekeepers

16. The person to whom the Stores were handed over, then became responsible to the Crown for their safe custody or fair usage; and, that no doubt whatever might rest upon this liability, he was required to give to the Storekeeper originally an Indenture,[3] and afterwards a receipt, covenanting or agreeing that, if in the case of arms, they should be lost by negligence or other defaults of the regiment, he would buy a re-supply of as many good arms as those lost As the recipients were usually in the employ of the Crown, either in the Army or Navy, Regulations directed them to send in to the Ordnance periodical accounts of the state of the Arms, and a system of stoppages was originated, to make good out of their pay any damage that would be otherwise sustained by the Crown in repairing or replacing them.[4]

Of the persons to whom the Stores were issued

17. To avoid all confusion in the Store accounts, or any implied acquittance of claims for damage by acceptance, the Storekeepers were not permitted to receive

No Stores to be received without a Board Order

---

[1] Appendix CXVIII   [2] Report of 1837, p 12, and Chap XXV, par 24
[3] Appendices CXIX and CXX See Royal Order of 4th August, 1686, making Captains liable for the Arms of their Companies—Bk 795, p 88
[4] See proposed Report of 1834, p 7, Civil Administration, 1837

either new stores from contractors, or old stores from Naval or Military Officers, except upon the previous orders of the Board.[1] When, however, Stores were received, the Storekeeper entered them in his ledger, and became responsible for them to the Crown.

18. As the business of each out-station became in a degree
Board of respective Officers. assimilated to that of the principal office, each Board Officer had his representative there to discharge the duty for which he was specially responsible to Parliament And the Local expenditure was controlled through the agency of a Board of Civilians, called the "Respective Officers," consisting originally of the Storekeeper and of the Clerks of Survey and Cheque, or only of the Storekeeper where the other officers were not at the station.[2]

19. As the Administration of the Master-General and Principal Officers became more Military, the Civil element
Change in the status of its members. was first made subordinate, and then all but eliminated; for the Board of Respective Officers, at the time of its abolition, in 1857, was formed of two Military Officers (the Commanding Officers of Artillery and Engineers), and of one Civilian—the Storekeeper.[3]

20. The number of out-stations, of course, increased with
The out-stations increase in number with the Army. the growth and service-area of the Army In Charles II.'s reign they were eleven or twelve in number, and confined to England;[4] at the Union with Scotland they were established in that kingdom, and as the Colonial System of Defence extended, Stations were needed for the supply of the Troops sent to the various Colonies to protect Imperial interests. When the Army went into a foreign country, a Field Train and a Store Department were improvised; the instructions for the guidance of the officers being prepared by the Civil and Military Authorities, and issued under Royal Sign Manual to the persons selected for the Chief Control.

21. With regard to the Ordnance Store System, there never

[1] Appendix CXXI
[2] 13th Report of Committee on Military Inquiry, pp 22, 146
[3] Dec 10, 1824   [4] See List at p 469, Vol I

was (that I am aware of) any doubt as to its efficiency or security. The Master-General and Principal Officers *(Store system of the Ordnance efficient, and secure for the public interests.)* were accountable to Parliament, but all their subordinate Civil Officers were responsible (under bond with securities to the Crown), as the custodians of the Public Treasure, for the faithful discharge of their duties. By their *appointments* they were not under the General of the district, but under the higher authority of the Principal Officers, who could at any time direct them to act under the General. They were therefore capable of being independent, and of exercising some financial control over the Army Expenditure. Their Reports of military extravagance went direct to the Master-General [1] (as a Member of the Cabinet), and not through the General Officer to the Commander-in-Chief. The Ordnance, therefore, as well as the Treasury, had open and free communication with their Financial officers serving with the Army; and thus the Government could learn the merits of any question by hearing all that could be said upon it by its Civil as well as Military servants.

22. Now although the Ordnance Establishments existed under these departmental arrangements, yet the Secretary at War, in the American and earlier wars, originated another Service for the supply of the Army, and established independent Store depôts in Great Britain and the Channel Islands. *(A.D. 1775. Store Department set up by the Secretary at War)* Fortunately, both the Supply and the Store arrangements were made by merchants of incorruptible integrity, Messrs Trotter, or the plunder would have been enormous. The Secretary at War neither checked price by open contract, nor examined into the quality of the supply,[2] and, until Mr. Trotter asked permission to place the articles in Store, they were sold, at the end of each war, at any sacrifice.

23 These rival Store Establishments were commenced at Portsmouth, by order of the Secretary at War in 1794, and then extended by Messrs Trotter to various places (109 in number), for the Military Service. *(Extension of the system, and entire absence of any financial control)* To provide against emergency, and thus prevent a high rise in

[1] See Duke of Wellington's Letters, Vol. II of Supplementary Despatches, pp 239-257, and Chap XXIX, pars 42, 43   [2] P 228, Question 17

prices upon a demand for the Public Service being made, Messrs. Trotter, with more forethought than the War Office, accumulated a Store of Army Equipments, and fixed a fair average price for each article. The Military authorities were supreme; and any financial check on the issue of Stores was altogether lost sight of in these Establishments.[1] "In London," said Mr. Trotter, "the Camp necessaries were issued by authority of the Quarter-Master-General, and the Hospital Stores by that of the Surgeon-General. Occasionally they were issued by order of the Commander-in-Chief, the Secretary at War, the Inspector-General of Hospitals, or those deputed by them. In the country they were issued by order of the General of the District, the Assistant Quarter-Master-General, the principal Medical Officers, and those deputed by them."

24. In 1807 the union of so many duties in Messrs. Trotter without control, appeared to the War Office to be faulty in principle; but the remedy was not to be found by the *Secretary at War* in placing these duties under the *Board of Ordnance*, but under a new Officer: therefore, by a Treasury Warrant[2] of the 8th March, 1808, the Office of Storekeeper-General was created, and Mr. John Trotter placed in charge of Army Stores.

A.D 1807

A new office of Army Storekeeper created.

25. Under his appointment he was "to be Storekeeper-General of all Military Stores in the departments of the Quartermaster-General, the Commissary-General, the Commissioners for the Affairs of Barracks, and the Surgeon-General, and of all such stores as had theretofore been provided under the direction of the Secretary at War, and also of all such other Military Stores, of whatever description, as he might be required from time to time to take into his charge by the Commissioners of Our Treasury, or the Commander-in-Chief, or the Quartermaster-General for the time being. And, further, he was to observe, follow, and obey all such instructions as he should from time to time receive from Us, or the Commissioners of Our Treasury for the time being."[3]

Treasury Warrant.

26 From the Instructions accompanying the Warrant,[4] it

[1] P 228, Question 19
[3] Ib, p 252

[2] 8th Report on Military Inquiry, p 253
[4] Ib, p 160

will be seen ' that his duties related to the receipt and safe custody of Stores committed to his care by the several departments of the Quartermaster-General, Barrack-master-General, and Surgeon-General, in storehouses to be provided by the Storekeeper-General; to the inspection of all stores received, except barrack stores; to ascertaining their quantity and quality, and their conformity to pattern, to transmitting, every six months, to the different departments concerned, a statement of the articles in store at each depôt, and to the Comptrollers of Army Accounts a complete store account, with vouchers; to a constant control over the expense of the establishment.

(margin: Treasury Instructions.)

" 1st. By the transmitting annually to the Treasury a list of persons in the Department, with the salary and allowances of each.

" 2nd. By the delivery of a monthly estimate of money wanted for the ensuing month, and

" 3rd. By a statement, every three months, of the contingencies of the Department.

" The Storekeeper-General was further enjoined not to have any concern in the provision of Stores, or to receive any fee; to report any waste or embezzlement, and to submit to the consideration of the Treasury such retrenchments or amendments as, in his opinion, might be made in the Department."

27. After the close of the Peninsular War, these separate Army Stores were transferred, first to the Treasury, acting through the Commissariat, and then, in May, 1822, to the Board of Ordnance.[1] The Treasury Minute provided that the duties, both of providing, and also of inspecting, packing, and forwarding, stores for the Military service in Great Britain and in the Colonies, should in future be executed by the Ordnance Department. The transfer of the stores commenced in June, and was completed in December: the Store premises in Tooley Street were then relinquished

(margin: Storekeeper's duties transferred, first to Commissariat, and secondly to Ordnance Board)

28. This, however, was not all that was then added to the

---

[1] 2nd Report of the Finance Committee, 1828 p 237, and Appendix CXLVIII, and p 418 note *post*

Ordnance.[1] The Store Branch of the Commissariat was transferred, and the warehouses and Storekeepers placed
under the Department; those in Ireland in September, and those at the foreign stations in December,
1822.

Irish and Foreign Stations transferred to the Board of Ordnance

29. After these transfers had been made, it became necessary to revise the Establishment of the Civil Branch
of the Ordnance, and a Royal Warrant of 19th
December,[2] 1825, sanctioned a new Establishment,
including the Storekeepers. The result was, as might
have been anticipated, a consolidation of Outpost Stations,
which in 1832 and 1849 numbered only 34 in Great Britain, in
Ireland 7, and abroad 35 and 49.[3]

A.D. 1825 — Ordnance Establishment revised

30. The Commissioners appointed to take the earlier
Remains were instructed to assess the value of each
article, but their instructions were not uniformly
carried out. In more modern times—probably without political motive — valuations have been attempted; thus
in the year 1831, the stores amounted in value to 7,243,510*l.*;
in the year 1858 (March 31st), to 9,529,629*l.*; and in the year
1867 to 11,026,229*l.*; therefore the total value of the real and
personal property of the Ordnance was immense.[4]

Value of Stores in custody of the Storekeeper

31. The variety of articles is beyond accurate assertion
Before the modern improvements in Ordnance and
small arms were introduced, the tradition of the office
was that the ledger headings at the Tower exceeded 18,000,
and at Woolwich 12,000 in number, but these changes have
considerably increased the variety of Store articles. It is not,
therefore, a service of which the Administration can be prudently
entrusted to persons untrained to such employment. In each
station a large number of labouring men are kept in pay under
the Storekeeper, and obviously he should rather be capable of
instructing them in the Store arrangements, than obliged to
learn *his* business from them

The variety of Store Articles.

---

[1] 2nd Report of the Finance Committee, 1828, p 239
[2] Ib, p 235   [3] Ordnance Expenditure, 1849
[4] Army and Ordnance Expenditure, p 980

32. There is scarcely anything connected with Military Administration in which Parliament must so entirely rely upon the Ministers of the Crown, and *experienced* persons serving under the Crown, as in the matter of Ordnance Stores   To place before the House of Commons the monied value of the Stores in Reserve, or to establish a reputation for economy based on that valuation, would be the most easy or the most difficult thing to do, according to the flexibility of principle in the person by whom the account was stated.   Stores, as assets, are like the good, bad, or doubtful debts of a Joint-Stock Company, which the managers may place at a high or low percentage of value, and base their profit or loss upon a calculation which is not found to be erroneous until disaster has arisen

[margin: Fallacy in the Statement of Store Valuations]

33 Patterns become obsolete by invention, but whether the existing supply is to be used up or abandoned may render a saving just or unjust, according to the wisdom and experience with which the decision is made.[1]   Again, the stores to be held in Reserve not being a fixed or agreed quantity,[2] each Ministry—if Army affairs become a matter of party politics—may present widely different estimates from very different motives.   The vote of Stores, as contrasted with the vote of Men, presents, therefore, a very uncertain test of the disposition of any Ministry towards an honest saving in Public Expenditure.   And hence the Parliamentary contest against Military Expenditure was always taken in the early history of the Army on the vote for "numbers," and that for "Stores" passed with little comment.

[margin: The Store vote an uncertain test of Ministerial Economy]

34. But, as noticed elsewhere,[3] a change of no inconsiderable importance has already been made in the Store Department by abandoning the old system, of Civil employés, and commissioning them as Officers in the *Army*[4] (though the *Navy* is served by these officers).   As custodians of the Public Treasure, they were formerly localised

[margin: The security for the Public Stores lessened]

---

[1] Sir H Vivian's Evidence, 'Civil Administration,' 1837, p. 35.
[2] See the subject discussed by the Committee on Ordnance Expenditure, 1849
[3] Chap. XIII , par. 52.   [4] Ib.

bonded accountants; the Public therefore had a substantial guarantee that the Real and Personal property of the Department—which from William III's reign has been protected by special legislation [1]—was in safe custody. These arrangements have been abandoned; no bond is given to the Crown, and the Store Officer is moved from station to station at short intervals. Having conceded Military Rank to the Civil employés of the Treasury, it was deemed unfair to withhold it from the same class of officials in the Ordnance Service; and hence, since the Crimean War, this Public Treasure has passed into the custody of Military officers serving under the Commander-in-Chief.

35. One other suggestion, which the experienced Military witnesses examined in 1837 strongly condemned, remains to be carried out, viz., the attempt to get Commissariat duties discharged by Store officers.[2] Indeed the union of the Administration of Treasure both in the Store and Commissariat Departments was held by them to be impossible, with any regard to efficiency in time of War. Of course, anything may be done in Peace, if the experience of such men be disregarded

Consolidation of Store and Commissariat duties.

II. As Landowners.

36. From the reign of Anne, Parliament, as occasion required, conferred Statutory Powers on the Department for the acquisition of land at, and for the defence of, particular stations—as Portsmouth, Chatham, and Harwich [3]—but in the year 1821, a general power was given—which, in late years, has been extended—to acquire real Estate for the Ordnance or Public Service whenever the same is needed. The nature and extent of these powers—formerly possessed by the Ordnance Board, and now by the Secretary of State—are fully stated in the Appendix.[4] To entrust the execu-

As Purchasers of Lands.

---

[1] 9 & 10 Wm III, c 41, 9 Geo I, c 8, 39 & 40 Geo III, c 89, 54 Geo III, c 60, 55 Geo III, c 127, 30 & 31 Vic, c 128 As to security by Public servants, see Appendix, Note T T

[2] Lord Hardinge, p 28, Duke of Wellington, p. 35.

[3] 7 Anne, c 26, 8 Anne, c 21, and Appendix, Note N N　　　[4] Note K K

tion of such powers to a Board of *quasi* Military Officers, for the purpose—strictly limited—of Defending the Realm, was one thing, but to clothe *one* Minister—open to Parliamentary influence—with such power is another.

37. The value of the possessions in Land and Works held by the Board in and beyond the United Kingdom must be reckoned—including the Defence Works of 1860— in several millions sterling. Of the *real* estate—most of it purchased for use or occupation—the annual rents of " surplus " lands in the year 1848[1] amounted to a sum of 20,000*l.* 8*s.* (12,841*l.* at home, and 7167*l.* in the Colonies); and in the year 1867 (including canteens), they amounted to 26,860*l.*[2] The Canteen Rents having been abandoned in favour of the Soldier, 28,592*l.* per annum is realized as the rent of the Ordnance unoccupied Lands in the United Kingdom, consisting of 4160 acres. Each tenancy—whether one of the 1024 holders of the nominal, or of the 431 holders at a rack rent under a political officer open to solicitation from partizans—is subject to comment, and the grant of such extensive powers for sale and disposition of land, as are held by the same Minister, is objectionable

The extent of the Ordnance Lands

III As to the Survey of the United Kingdom.

38. As a measure of defence, the Survey of the United Kingdom was entrusted to the Ordnance Department. It is said to have originated in Scotland after the Rebellion of 1745, when General Wade was the Lieutenant-General of the Ordnance, and to have commenced under the direction of General Roy, who was quartered with a body of infantry at Fort Augustus. The design of making the Survey general over the whole island was brought under the notice of the Government at the conclusion of the peace of 1763, but little was done during the next twelve years, and the American War put a stop to the work altogether.

39. On the return of peace,[3] in 1783, General Roy re-

A.D. 1715

Ordnance Survey commenced—(1) in Scotland.

---

[1] ' Army and Ordnance Expenditure, 1849,' p 873

[2] Annual Estimate 1868-9, p 127

[3] 17th Report of Military Inquiry, 1811 p 166

commenced operations, for his own amusement; they were

A D 1763
——
Then (2) In
England

confined to ascertaining the relative positions which the most remarkable Public Buildings in and about the Metropolis held to the Royal Observatory at Greenwich. Whilst the General was thus engaged, the French Government made an application to the British Ministry, for their co-operation in carrying on a series of triangles from London to Dover, in connection with similar operations in France, that the relative positions of the Royal Observatories of Greenwich and Paris might be accurately fixed

40. This application was forwarded, by command of George

A.D 1783
——
Renewed in
conc. it with
France

III., to the Royal Society, and Sir Joseph Banks, K.B , then President, committed the work to General Roy, the funds for defraying the expense of it being furnished by the King. In the spring of 1784 the operations commenced by measuring a base line on Hounslow Heath, and, as the season and weather permitted, were continued through the three following years. General Roy, however, died before the difference of longitude between the two Observatories was completely ascertained; but as in the Survey the inaccuracy of the best County Maps was so frequently shown, the Duke of Richmond (as Master-General) gave directions for resuming the design of a General Survey of England, which commenced in 1791, with a re-measurement of the base line at Hounslow.

41. The Survey of Ireland appears to have been determined

A D 1801 24
——
(3.) In Ire-
land

upon in 1801, and General Vallancy was employed, but made little progress in the work. The Report on Local Burdens being presented to Parliament in 1824, a Survey was immediately determined upon and commenced.[1] No Parliamentary authority (other than the appropriation of supplies)[2] was ever given to the Survey until, in the year 1825, the 6 Geo. IV., c. 99, was passed for Ireland, and in 1841, the 4 & 5 Vic., c. 30, received the Royal Assent to authorise and facilitate the completion of

---

[1] 'McLennan's Life of Drummond,' 1867, 'Ordnance Memoir of Ireland,' 1844,
80 Sess Papers   [2] Fin Rep., 1828, p 94.

the Survey of Great Britain, Berwick-upon-Tweed, and the Isle of Man[1]

IV As to Works of Defence.

42. The Ordnance Department had always been charged with the care of all buildings[2] connected with the Defence of the Realm, as Forts, or needed for the use of the Army, as Barracks, or Hospitals. *All forts and Military buildings in charge of the Ordnance*

43. For the construction of Works of Fortification, the Engineers were employed under the direction of the Board, as scientific officers, without reference to the Military authority of any General in the district,[3] and when the Works were completed, they were held in charge by the Board, under Royal Sign Manual Regulations, similar in terms to the existing Warrant of the 1st September, 1778, printed in the Appendix.[4] *The Engineers were the constructors of forts and Military buildings*

44 The erection and charge of Barracks, for the same reason, devolved upon the Ordnance, and in 1717 the Board originated the system of stoppages for Barrack damages[5] which, though it is now strongly objected to,[6] has effected a large annual saving of Public money. The office of Barrackmaster dates from as early a period—first as a Military appointment,[7] but since 1808 as a Civil office — though the Engineer Officers have taken the charge of the Department[8] since the abolition of the Board of Ordnance. *Barracks under the Ordnance*

45 As the whole Work or Supply had reference to the plan or pattern selected by the Crown, it was a matter of the highest importance to have these approved on *Design and Pattern to be selected by the Ordnance*

---

[1] Note as to the Statutory Powers for the Ordnance Survey, Appendix L L.

[2] Ordnance Letter Bk , 8th Feb , 1711, p 155

[3] Mr Skinner designed the Scotch Forts, and the General complained to the Board of Ordnance that *he* had no authority, Feb , 1746 , Ordnance Bk , p 552

[4] Appendix CXXII

[5] Chap XI , pars 35, 36, *ante* , Mis. Bk (523), p. 61 , St John to Harley, 1st March, 170⅔, Letter Bk 134, p 184

[6] See Report and Evidence given before Transport and Supply (War Office) Committee, 1867, and Chap. XXIX , par. 66 *et seq*

[7] Commission to the Barrackmaster of the Savoy, 1st Feb , 174⅘, War Office Bk , p 38

[8] Chap XI , pars 11 36, and Chap. XII.

the advice of men Responsible to Parliament, and also of such competent, technical, and professional experience, that their Approval would give an assurance to the Army that the Work or Arm would be efficient, and to the Country that a vast expenditure would not be wasted.

46 Now, in the instance of the Master-General, these qualifications existed.[1] His experience bore no analogy to that gained by a Civilian Minister, in being led about to look at guns or fortresses, under the inspiration of a guide, possibly pledged to instil one view of the requirements of the Service, on which his *personal* reputation is wholly dependent. The Master-General had a vast experience in actual Service, and no fear.[2] He had a reputation to sustain, rather than to make, by a prudent expenditure in these special matters—when any was *really* needed. From his position, Officers would not venture to impose on him, and men in the highest rank in any branch of the Service would readily lend him their assistance There was, therefore, no chance of the largest experience being lost to the country in Fortification or Armament, because the executive officer held a comparatively low rank in the Army.

Competency of the Master-General and a Civil Minister contrasted.

47. It was not only for efficiency but for due economy that the Master-General held himself responsible to his colleagues in the Government. "The public also, I conceive," said Sir James Kempt,[3] "derive great advantage from the Ordnance Department being *an office of account*, responsible to Parliament for the due and faithful application of all moneys voted for Ordnance services. The Master-General has a twofold duty to perform one, to uphold the character and efficiency of the two military corps under his command; the other, to reduce the expense of the department, in conjunction with the Board, by every practicable means, in order that the Estimates submitted to Parliament may be as low as the nature and extent of the services to be performed will possibly admit of"

Master General responsible for finance to his colleagues.

Sir James Kempt's view

48. This view of the Master-General's duty was concurred in

[1] Statement of the Master-General's Duties, 2nd Report of Finance Committee. 1828, p 142   [2] Chap XXIX, par 45   [3] Civil Administration 1837, p 10

by Lord Hardinge :[1]—"I consider that the Master-General has a professional and military reputation to sustain, and that he will always take care, for his own sake, to preserve the efficiency of his department. He is generally a distinguished Military Officer, being most frequently in the Cabinet, and a high Officer of State. He must attend to the economy of the Department, for the *credit* of the *Government* of which he is a *member*, and because he knows that all his acts—military and civil, executive and economical—will be brought annually in review before a very searching tribunal, namely, the House of Commons, where he or one of his Board Officers, the Clerk, or the Surveyor-General, must defend his measures before the Public; if there is any appearance of undue waste of Public money, it must be explained. thus he has a very strong stimulus to do his duty to the King, to the Government, and to the Public, by taking care that efficiency and economy shall be combined." *Lord Hardinge's.*

49. Nothing was adopted as a Design or Pattern but under Royal approval and Seal. Before the Ordnance Office was abolished these were given under the advice of Military Officers, not standing behind the chair, and only employed by the Civil Minister, but before the Country, and directly responsible to Parliament for the advice given. The plan or pattern once so approved could not be altered, except by the same authoritative act; and if failure arose, the loss or shame could immediately be brought home to the Master-General and Board in Parliament *Design or Pattern then approved by the Crown*

50. What has been lost to the country from withdrawing this action of a highly qualified and responsible Military Officer from the Expenditure of the Country in fortresses, barracks, hospitals, and armaments (four items[2] which for the ten years *after*—by contrast with the ten years *before*—1855, have enormously increased), it has not yet become the Policy of any great party in the State to discover.[3] But some experience of the increase of expenditure *What loss has been sustained by the absence of the Master-General's control?*

---

[1] P 23   [2] See Mr Galton's note, Appendix J J
[3] See Major Anson's Motion on 6th July, 1868, as to Warlike Stores

may be gleaned, in periods antecedent to the abolition of the Board, when any novice in Ordnance duties undertook to supersede the Board, and to act without its intervention.

51. No person was more ready to usurp these functions than
Secretary at War usually aggressive on the Ordnance Department, and with what result.
that ambiguous official the Secretary at War.[1] In the early institution of his office he would have made the Ordnance subordinate to him[2] Later,[3] he raised a rival Store Establishment; then he undertook to build Barracks through the agency of the Barrack-master-General's Department;[4] and, lastly, to defend the country with the Martello towers,[5] scattered about the coast, and with the Military Canal[6] at Hythe. In each of these three undertakings the Constitutional functions of the Ordnance were set aside in favour of the Commander-in-Chief (who has no duties whatever to discharge as to the construction of Defensive Works), and a vast amount of Public treasure was wasted.

V. As to the Contract Department.

52. After the plan was approved, the work was carried out
Power and method of contracting.
under the Engineers; or, in the case of a pattern for an Arm, the supply was made by Contract or Manufacture. For these works—and for supplies—the Board were authorised to contract, on behalf of the Crown. These contracts were made under the sanction of the Clerk of the Ordnance,[7] as the Financial Officer directly responsible to Parliament for estimates and expenditure. The Instructions to the Board were clear — not to suffer any monopoly,[8] but to call before them such persons as they should know able to supply them, and to deal fairly with the ablest artificers or merchants. The receipt and examination of the supplies rested with the other Parliamentary Officer, the Surveyor. It was his duty to make proof of them,[9] if good and serviceable, to mark them with the Crown mark, probably the same as that described in

---

[1] See Earl Grey's evidence before the Organization Committee, 1860
[2] Chap. XXI, pars. 21-7   [3] See par. 22, *ante*   [4] Chap. XII, *ante*
[5] 15th Report of Military Inquiry, pp. 320, 321.
[6] 30 & 31 Vic, c 110, 11th Report of Military Inquiry, pp. 23, 24
[7] Vol I, p 459   [8] Ib p 462   [9] Ib, p 458.

Rymer,[1] and now known as the Broad Arrow. The Storekeeper, the custodian of the Board, was prohibited from receiving anything into Store except upon the Surveyor's certificate; so that the Ordnance System secured the Public against frauds in Public Contracts, by making the Clerk responsible for price, the Surveyor for quality, and the Storekeeper for record of service.

53. With regard to the Contract business, it may be observed that nothing is probably more important to the Public—who are served by deputies, having no pecuniary interests in the success or failure of the supply—than a sound system of Public Contract. In the first place. whether the several Departments of the Crown should have separate operations in the same market, conducted by independent agents (either Military Officers or trained Civilians), who may thereby raise prices against their common employer, may be open for consideration. If the wants of each department would be as zealously attended to by one agent for all, as by separate agents for each, then the purchases would be made at a minimum profit to the merchant, for undue competition would cease.

Contract system of the Ordnance Importance of a sound system of contract for public supplies.

54 But, until a common agency can be accepted for all Public supplies, some rules should be laid down by the Treasury as to the general principles—if not as to the terms and conditions of contract—by which each Department of the Government should be guided in their purchases. Given, that the best market is always to be adopted, are no general instructions to rule the Departments as to *the* best market?—whether it should be Local, as the town or village of Aldershot, for the supply of the Army there; or special, as at the place of production; or general, as in London? In a large annual expenditure, a very considerable sum may be either lost or saved by a right decision of such questions.

Principles of public contracts to be laid down by the Treasury

55. Now the Instructions to the Board of Ordnance were plain in this matter. There was to be no general delegation of duty to Military Officers The Clerk and Surveyor were responsible to Parliament, and they

As to the Ordnance system of contract

---

[1] Appendix CXXIII

were required to have the merchants and contractors before them.[1] When the supply was made, it was to be placed in Store for future issue. The wants of the Department were drawn from a Reserve, and not from the Market; that the necessity for supply to a large consumer might not create the price of a monopoly against the Crown

56. The separate function of each Board Officer gave an additional security to the Public. The Consuming Department—as the Navy, or the Army—were represented on the Board, but no *one* Officer had either a direct temptation to extravagance or the opportunity to indulge it without immediate control. The Clerk of the Ordnance was answerable to Parliament for expenditure, but would not alter the quality. The Surveyor was responsible for efficiency and quality, but was unable to alter price. The Storekeeper, as the recipient of the goods, had no control over either price or quality; but he kept an independent record of the use and service that the Public ultimately received from the supply. The Ordnance System of contracts was made the subject of frequent inquiry, but no objection was ever raised to the fundamental principles on which it was conducted.[2]

Separate responsibility of each Principal Officer

VI. As to the Manufacturing Departments

57. Probably so much cannot be said with regard to the Manufacturing Departments of the Ordnance. "Princes," wrote Adam Smith,[3] "have frequently engaged in many mercantile projects, but they have scarcely ever succeeded. The profusion with which the affairs of princes are always managed, renders it almost impossible that they should The agents of a Prince

Manufacturing Departments of the Ordnance

Objection to Crown factories

[1] The Ordnance Regulations of 1823 (p 120) directed the Local Officer to quote the price of production on the *spot*, that the Board might decide on purchase *there* or issue from the Tower, see also 5th Report of Military Inquiry, p 64

[2] 12th Report of the Commissioners on Public Accounts, 1784, 21st Report of the Finance Committee, 1797, and 16th Report of Military Inquiry, 1811, 2nd Report of Finance Committee, 1828, p 266, and Ordnance Expenditure Report, 1849   [3] Bk V, Chap ii, p 356

regard the wealth of their master as inexhaustible, are careless at what price they buy, are careless at what price they sell, are careless at what expense they transport his goods from one place to another." He then remarks that no two characters seem more inconsistent than those of a trader and a Sovereign (or a Soldier, might he not have added?); and he instances the fact that so soon as the East India Company assumed the Government of India, their servants no longer looked upon themselves as the clerks of merchants, but as Ministers of Sovereigns

58. In the instances of Ordnance Factories, *necessity* was the justification of their original establishment, and, while so *limited*, their existence may be reconciled with the principles of sound Financial Administration   Limited to the necessity of the State.

59. The principal site of these Factories, since 1695, has been Woolwich Arsenal Upon the King's Warren were thrown up Works and Batteries, in 1667, as a protection against the Dutch Fleet invading the Thames In 1681, Butts, for the proof of Ordnance were erected there; and, in 1695, the "Barn," standing in the Tilt Yard at Greenwich was taken down, and a similar one placed at Woolwich—then the place of disposal for ships, carriages, and saltpetre. The Laboratory also underwent a similar removal, and, as the place was being used for the same purposes as the Tower, it began to be known as "Tower Place, Woolwich."[1]   A.D 1695 Woolwich Arsenal

60. The establishment of manufactories dates from an early period in George I.'s reign, and the accident at Moorfields—which happened on the 16th May, 1716, at the re-casting of the guns taken by Marlborough from the French—is said to have originated the Woolwich Foundry for brass guns, under the following Board order —   A.D 1716 Brass Gun Factory established

"Martis, 19 die Junii, 1716 It having for many years been the opinion of the most experienced Officers that the Government should have a Brass Foundry of their own, and whereas Mr. Bagley's Foundry is the *only one* for casting *brass*

---

[1] The name was changed to that of "Royal Arsenal" on the occasion of George III's visit on the 9th April, 1805

ordnance, and liable to dangerous accidents which cannot be prevented. It is therefore ordered that a proposal and estimate be made for building a Royal Brass Foundry at His Majesty's Tower Place at Woolwich, and the charge thereof defrayed out of the 5000*l* given this year by Parliament for re-casting brass ordnance, and that no time be lost herein, inasmuch as there are but two 12-pounders and not one 18 or 24-pounder for Land Service. A letter to Mr. Henry Lidybird to attend the Surveyor-General the 20th, about providing bricks for the Royal Brass Foundry at Woolwich."

61. Acting, as the rules of their department instructed them

<small>Public Advertisement for a Master founder</small>

to do, in the spirit of free and open competition, and with the honest desire to procure the ablest and fittest artificers, the Board issued the following advertisement in the 'London Gazette' of the 10th July, 1716.—

"Whereas a Brass Foundry is now building at Woolwich for His Majesty's Service, all founders as are desirous to cast brass ordnance are to give in their proposals forthwith, upon such terms as are regulated by the Principal Officers of His Majesty's Ordnance, which may be seen at their Office in the Tower."

62. Not discouraged by his foreign extraction, one of the

<small>Mr Andrew Schalch appointed</small>

applicants was Mr. Andrew Schalch, and the results of the application were—first a provisional engagement "in building the furnaces and providing the necessary utensils at 5*l* a day, until everything was provided and his performances approved;" and then—a final one under the following Board order :—"Veneris, 5° die Octobris, 1716. The Board having received a letter from Mr. Leathes, His Majesty's Minister at Brussels, giving an account that Mr. Andrew Schalk (*sic*) bears a good character at Douay, and was an able founder. Ordered that the said Mr. Schalk be employed in the Royal Foundry at Woolwich at 5*l*. per diem from the 29th of September last." [1] Under which appointment he served as the Master-Founder of brass guns at Woolwich for sixty years.

63. Until recent years the Royal *Gun* Factories produced

---

[1] I am indebted to 'Historical Notes of Royal Arsenal at Woolwich,' by Lieutenant Grover, R E , 1869, for these extracts and other facts

brass guns only, all the iron ordnance being supplied by contract[1]   The private foundries holding Government Iron Ord-
nance sup-
contracts were under the surveillance of a Superin- plied by con-
tendent appointed by the Crown—a civilian until com- tract, but
paratively recent years   The proof of all guns was Arsenal
always conducted at the Arsenal ; and by Royal Warrant of 24th
January, 1783, this duty was placed under the Officers of the
Royal Artillery.[2]   "That the superintendence of casting brass
and iron ordnance, and of making gun-carriages or mortar-beds,
and the preparing drafts for the same, shall (under the direction
of the Master-General or Board of Ordnance) be committed to
the care of the Inspector of our Artillery , and that all proofs
of ordnance shall be made in the presence of our said Inspector,
with his Assistant and the Proof-Master, or any two of them "[1]

64. The Laboratory appears to have been put upon a
Peace Establishment, under the care of a Bomba- A.D. 1746
dier, about the time that the Gun Foundry was Laboratory
established   It so continued till the year 1746, when remodelled
the offices of Comptroller, Fire-Master, and Mate were restored,
and a Clerk to the Comptroller appointed ; "By which means
(as the Warrant expresses it) the art of making fireworks for
real use, as well as for triumph, may be again recovered."[4]

65. Such an establishment was not to be set on foot again,
except under well-digested rules, and these were issued A.D. 1747
by the Board, under date of the 1st August,[5] 1747 ; Rules and
the Comptroller, responsible for the government of the Regulations.
Laboratory, was to follow the directions of the Board, and the
Fire-Masters those of the Comptroller. The keys of such rooms
as the Board appropriated for the service, were to be kept by
the Comptroller ; but the rest of the buildings within or belonging

---

[1] See 'Ordnance Expenditure, 1849 '—Index, " Iron Ordnance "

[2] It may be noticed, as illustrating the contest between economy and efficiency,
that such was the Military Officer's anxiety to get the best Ordnance for the
Service that in the first year of his appointment he condemned **490** Guns in
proof (Lord Hardinge, 'Second Report Finance Committee, 1828,' p. 43)

[3] 12th Report on P A , 1784, pp 165, 663, and see 16th Report of Military
Inquiry, p 31   [4] 27 MS Warrants, p 344

[5] 16th Report of Military Inquiry, p. 67   These rules were in force when the
Commissioners of Military Enquiry reported in 1811 (p 21).

to the Laboratory to be continued in the possession of the Store-keeper, for the safe keeping of all Stores that were made up in the Laboratory. In other instances the relative duties of the Comptroller and Storekeeper towards each other were set forth, and the latter, as the financial officer, was to pay all the wages

66. The artificers were to be men in civil life,—"There be
Artificers to be civilians fixed for the service of the Laboratory, one turner, at 3s.; one carpenter at 2s. 6d.; one smith at 2s. 6d; and two labourers at 1s. 6d. per day; no one of which shall belong to the Royal Regiment of Artillery; the said artificers are to be sober, able, and skilful workmen, to do no kind of work for private use, or any but what tends immediately to the service of the Laboratory." It was to be a school for the instruction of the Royal Artillery,[1] to which the inmates of the Military Academy were to be permitted access[2]

67. A Gun Wharf and Laboratory were erected at Ports-
At Plymouth and Ports-mouth mouth under a Board order of the 7th September, 1761,[3] but the Laboratory at Plymouth was established by Lord Chatham in 1804, on the recommendation of the Comptroller. The object of forming these establishments was to aid the Woolwich Laboratory, in getting up unappropriated Small-Arm Ammunition for the Depôts throughout the country, and to be in readiness to provide Laboratory articles, should the Woolwich establishment be destroyed either by accident or design.[4]

68. The other Factory at the Arsenal consists of the Royal
Royal Car-riage Depart-ment Carriage Department, which prior to the year 1803, was under the immediate superintendence and control of a civil officer (Mr. Butler), with the title of "Constructor of Carriages;" but on the 21st April of that year it was placed under the superintendence of an Artillery Officer, with the title of "Inspector of the Royal Carriage Department at Woolwich."[5]

---

[1] 16th Report of Military Inquiry, p. 68   [2] Note A A, Appendix.
[3] Warrant, p 31   [4] 16th Rep., p 25
[5] 16th Report on Military Inquiry, pp 35, 117, Report of the Committee on Ordnance Expenditure, 1849, p 32.

At that date there were dependent establishments at Rother-hithe and Chatham, with branches at the different dockyards; but the whole were to be under the Inspector and his subordinate officers.

69 A Field Train Department appears to have been constituted, but under no Warrant of Establishment,[1] during the Peninsular War, and to have consisted (in 1811) of a Commandant and two other Military officers, with a large Civil Staff of Commissaries, Clerks, and Conductors of Stores under them.

Field Train.

70 " The Inspector-General of Artillery " (whose appointment and establishment were authorised by a Royal Warrant of the 10th June, 1805) acted as the Commandant of the Train, and also as the President of the Select Committee

A.D 1805

71. The Ordnance did not become manufacturers of gunpowder until the year 1759.[2] In Wm. III.'s reign, the Crown obliged, first the "General Society," and afterwards the East India Company, to furnish His Majesty's stores annually with 500 tons of saltpetre, at a statutable price.[3] This saltpetre was manufactured into gunpowder by contractors with the Ordnance, residing in Great Britain. During the war under Marlborough all the powder-makers could barely supply the Service yet in time of peace there was not employment for above one mill, the makers having been obliged to convert most of them to other uses.

A.D. 1759

Powder Factories

72. In 1717, the Parliament of Ireland[4] was desirous of encouraging the manufacture of gunpowder in that country, but the Board of Ordnance strongly opposed it. "As it may be supposed that they will be able to make it cheaper in Ireland, the merchants will naturally go there for it; the consequences of both which will be to disen-

Establishment of Factories in Ireland opposed by Board of Ordnance

---

[1] Ordnance Report, 1849, pp 12, 13, 17th Report on Military Inquiry, p 148.
[2] Chap I, par. 27.
[3] 1 Anne, c 13, sec 113, 12th Rep P A, 1784, p 164, Debate on Saltpetre Contracts, 2? Parl Hist., p 946   [4] Earl of Sunderland, MS Letter Bk. (20), p 365.

courage and destroy that manufacture here, which now furnishes the best powder of any State in Europe, and may oblige the Government either to fetch it from abroad, *or otherwise to be at the extraordinary charge of erecting works of their own.'*

73. The Ordnance established powder works at Faversham [1]

Faversham in the year 1759, and upon memorial to the Treasury, settled an establishment under Royal Warrant,[2] 17th November, 1759, at the total annual cost of 398*l.*; a Store-keeper, at 100*l.*; a Master Worker. at 90*l.*; a Clerk of the Cheque, at 54*l* 15*s*, with other subordinates.

74. In the same year, an Act[3] was passed, at the instance of the inhabitants,[4] for taking down and removing Purfleet the Greenwich Gunpowder Magazine, and for erecting another at Purfleet. These works were entrusted to the Board of Ordnance to carry out.

75. That the quality of the powder might be proved by Proof of powder by independent officers officers wholly independent of the Master Workers, and with a distinct responsibility to the Master-General, the Royal Warrant of the 24th January, 1783, provided, " With respect to the proofs of powder and ordnance, it is Our further will and pleasure that the superintendence of saltpetre and making of powder shall, under the directions of the Master-General or Board of Ordnance, be committed to the care and inspection of the Controller of Our Laboratory at Woolwich, and that all proofs of powder shall be made in presence of Our said Controller, the Fire-Master, and Assistant Fire-Master, or any two of them, with one of the respective officers of Our Magazine at Purfleet."

76. The works at Waltham appear to have been established Waltham Works. about the year 1788. The lands were acquired and vested in the Board of Ordnance in the year 1795, and later years; both Faversham and Waltham were under the control of an officer of the Royal Artillery, "as Inspector of the Manufactory,"[5] in the year 1811.

77 A powder factory was established in Ireland in the year

---

[1] They were sold in 1854   [2] King's Warrants, p. 159.
[3] 33 Geo II , c 11   [4] 28 Com Journ , p 640
[5] Fin Rep., 1828, p 47, 16th Report on Military Inquiry , 43 Com. Journ, pp. 178, 222.

1805, under a lease granted to the (five [1]) " respective officers for conducting the Civil and Military Department of the Ordnance in Ireland," of the powder mills situate at Ballincollig, for a period of 999 years. These premises were used during the Peninsular War, but were disposed of in 1834 and 1857.[2]

Ballincollig, Ireland

78. The connection of the Ordnance with the small arms trade dates from June, 1631. In that month a Commission was issued by Charles I. to certain armourers, gunmakers, and bandaliers of the City of London, appointing them Commissioners for certain purposes in connection with their trade, and the small arms of the country. They agreed to supply the Tower stores, on seven days' notice, with 1500 armours and as many muskets every month, and to train up apprentices to their trade so that the Realm might be supplied by their means, and not be dependent on Foreign Princes and States.

A.D 1631
Connection with the Small Arms Trade

79. A Standard Arm of one uniform pattern was established at the Ordnance Office; and all the arms of the Train Bands were to be made conformable with it. A fixed tariff of prices was also added for the supply and repair of arms, a monopoly being thus given to these Commissioners.[3]

Standard pattern, and tariff of prices.

80. In March, 1637, the present Gunmakers' Company was established under Charter, with powers for searching, viewing, proving, and marking all manner of hand-guns, daggs, and pistols, whether made in or within ten miles of London, or imported or brought there for sale. A scale of proof was established, and a proof stamp was to be placed on the arm. They were and still are to be subject and obedient to all orders and directions of the Privy Council, touching and concerning all manner of hand-guns.[4]

A.D. 1637.
Gunmakers' Charter

---

[1] C O. R A., C O R. E, Store keeper, Clerk of Survey, Clerk of Cheque

[2] The Acts to regulate the manufacture of gunpowder are 23 & 24 Vic., c , 139, 24 & 25 Vic , c 130, ib. 97, sec 54; ib 100, secs 28, 64.

[3] 19 Rym. Fœd , p 310.

[4] This Company is still in existence, and doing useful service to the Public, see " Gun-barrel Proof Act, 1868 "

81. The trade at Birmingham originated in the last century, and a Proof House[1] was established there by the Ordnance to facilitate supplies from that town. The business of the Small-Arms Department at the Tower was carried on by civilians deputed by the Surveyor-General, and the principal Storekeeper, assisted by the Master Furbisher. They received their orders either directly from the Master-General and Board, or through the principal Storekeeper; but by Royal Warrant of the 1st of April, 1804, the Small Arms Department,—as to the provision, inspection, and care of small-arms,—was committed to a new officer called "the Inspector of Small-Arms," with an establishment consisting of an Inspector (400*l*), an Assistant-Inspector (300*l*), and other subordinate officers, to be defrayed at the total annual cost of 1170*l*. A Military Officer was appointed the first Inspector, and resided at Birmingham; and a civilian the Assistant Inspector.[2]

The Small-Arms Factory

82. The Government commenced the manufacture of small-arms in 1804, under the Assistant-Inspector, in the Tower. The business was first confined to rough-stocking, and setting up arms with the materials supplied from Birmingham, but in 1807 their operations were extended, and a factory erected at Lewisham for the supply of gun barrels and locks. In 1811, the Ordnance acquired the Royal Factory at Enfield, and that at Lewisham was closed. The former Establishment then bore no comparison with the size or importance that it has since assumed; but after the Minie Rifle was introduced, a Select Committee of the House of Commons appointed to consider the whole subject of small-arms, recommended that the Enfield Factory should be re-organized, and that policy was carried out.[3]

A.D. 1804
Ordnance commence Small-Arms Factory

83. It was in manufacturing operations that the Ordnance Board had to deal with the claims of Inventors; and to aid the Master-General in this respect the Ordnance

Ordnance Select Committee

---

[1] Acts relating to Proof of Small Arms, 53 Geo. III, c 115, 55 Geo. III, c 59 but repealed by 18 & 19 Vic., c 148 (Local and Personal), see now 31 & 32 Vic., c 113 (Local and Personal)   [2] 15th Report on Military Inquiry, p 329
[3] Report on Small Arms of 1854, p 236, and Appendix CXXIV, on the Enfield Factory

Select Committee was appointed in 1805 [1] In the affairs of the Army it was usual (as will be shown hereafter [2]) for the Crown to summon a Board of General Officers to take any particular matter into consideration, and to report their opinion thereon , in analogy to this practice, the Ordnance Select Committee was formed.

84. The Warrant of the 10th June, 1805, [3] addressed to the Master-General, stated the intention thus — *A.D. 1805* "Whereas you have represented to us, that in many *Warrant of Appointment* cases it may be essentially useful to the general objects of our service, and more particularly with a view to the important purpose of considering and methodising the several establishments of our Artillery in its various branches, to afford to the Inspector-General the assistance of other officers of our Royal Regiment of Artillery, whose local knowledge or professional information and experience may best qualify them for this duty, it is our royal will and pleasure that Committees of such officers do assemble from time to time, under your special authority, or that of our Master-General for the time being, as often as it shall be judged necessary to require their opinions, either at Woolwich or elsewhere;" but the first President of the Committee (Colonel Farrington [4]) described his duty to be, "To assemble Committees of Officers of the Royal Artillery, to assist in forming opinions upon *any inventions and suggestions of individuals*, as likewise all improvements that may be proposed for the advantage of the Artillery service, under the authority of the Master-General, and to make Reports upon the same "

85. Probably no duty is more difficult to discharge with satisfaction to the Public than that of rewarding In- *Claims of Inventors to* ventors   In the first place, it is a rare thing to *gain* *patent rights* any originality, and more so to find that *the* com- *or remuneration.* pensation due is claimed by the real Inventor or even by the originator of any useful combination.   In many instances the claimant's views are so extravagant, both as to merit and reward, that he is unapproachable in reason; while so long

---

[1] Ordnance Expenditure, 1849, pp 111, 112   [2] Chap XXI , par 13.
[3] MS. Warrant, p. 79.   [4] 17th Report on Military Inquiry, p 205

as he is dealing with the Government he insists in his argument that he is looking exclusively to this Country for reward, though immediately that the Inventor is paid he usually goes off to Foreign Governments to reap a further personal benefit by placing his invention at their service.

86. In too many instances, an invention becomes identified
Names asso-
ciated with
Inventions
not really be-
longing to
them
with the name of a person who, on subsequent inquiry, is shown to have little or no right to it. This arises, on the official correspondence, from his assumption of being the Inventor: which assumption it is no one's duty, in the first instance, to challenge or investigate. The same fallacy is often strengthened—if not perpetuated—by the Debates in Parliament; and where a Minister attributes, as he is naturally inclined to do, great advantages to the public from his adoption of the invention, the difficulties, first, of fairly adjusting the reward, and then of displacing a factitious title—duties which may fall to the lot of the legal advisers to discharge—are greatly increased; indeed, in such a negotiation, the agents of the Government may be placed in an invidious position, which no subsequent explanation of the truth may effectually efface.[1]

87. The Ordnance Select Committee consisted, for many
Ordnance
Select Com
mittee
abolished
years, as it was originally appointed; but it was dissolved and reconstituted, in the year 1859,[2] of purely Military Members, Civilians being excluded. In December, 1868, it was abolished altogether,[3] and the claims of Inventors are now dealt with under a Circular that will be found in the Appendix.[4] The Treasury has also laid down the wholesome rule that Public servants employed in the National Arsenals and Factories shall not be permitted to acquire, against the public, the monopoly of Patent rights.

88. The extent to which Government Factories may be
The extent
to which
Government
Factories
may be
carried
advantageously carried on, both in regard to monopoly and to the variety of supply, is a frequent subject of controversy. It can scarcely be denied that, in regard to Invention, the Public derive greater advantages

---

[1] See Appendix, Note MM, on Mr. Snider's Case.　[2] Military Organisation, 1860
[3] Circular Memorandum, No 13　　　　　　　　[4] Appendix CXXV.

from private than from their own factories. If those of Sir W. Armstrong and Mr. Whitworth had not existed, it may be questioned whether the Artillery Service would have been raised to its present condition of efficiency. Therefore, in time of peace, to extinguish private enterprise in the manufacture of warlike inventions, by a monopoly of supply to the Royal Arsenals, may be found a policy disastrous in the time of war. In that emergency the reserve power for supply should surely be held in the hands of the Government, for to depend upon raising up *new* contractors for such a service at that time would be to chance the success of the war upon a very hazardous experiment. Extra supplies from Established Contractors, and from the Royal Arsenals, are not attended with this risk.

89. Given, therefore, that the principle of Monopoly must be abandoned, for what objects are Government Factories to be maintained? These may be limited to two in number: first, as a means of instructing the Ordnance Corps for the discharge of their duties in the field; secondly, as a source of information to the Government as to the actual cost at which special articles needed *only* for the public service can be made, and therefore at which they should be purchased by the Crown. *The purposes for which Government Factories are maintained*

90. The first object may no doubt be readily obtained by these establishments; but the second—a comparison of cost between Government and private work —opens up a large question. In the first instance, does the Crown ever know accurately *the* cost at which any article is produced in its own Factories?[1] The manufacturer's profit ought to be the only difference, in the most favourable view of the comparison; but is not this difference more than consumed by one item only—the greater cost at which a public Factory is supplied with labour? It is not so much Wage as Work that causes this difference of cost between the two establishments. What interest have any—from the highest to the lowest—classes of the employés in a public *Comparison between a private and public factory*

---

[1] See 193 H D (3), p. 761 Report of Commons' Committee, 24th July, 1868, on the Woolwich Gun.

factory in the pecuniary success of the undertaking? and yet *such* an interest—always in operation—is the mainspring of success in private enterprise.

91. As financial operations, their management should be
Factories, as financial operations, should be superintended by Civil employés. held by Civilians—trained as manufacturers—and hol ling permanent appointments. To turn a Military officer of average age into a manufacturer for five or seven years is scarcely a fair experiment either to the Public at whose cost he is to learn how to conduct the factory, or to the officer who has received the education and training of, and therefore hitherto has passed his time as a gentleman. To look for the profitable employment of capital under such arrangements is scarcely reasonable, and to carry on Public Factories under such conditions involves a wider departure from Commercial Principles than Adam Smith ever could have anticipated when he held out a warning against the Crown entering upon the pursuit of trade or manufacture.[1]

92. These duties were no doubt unsuited to the office of
Factory duties unsuited to the office of Master-General Master-General, and the employment of a large number of artisans and factory hands by a distinguished General Officer reduced his responsibility in this department to a merely nominal supervision.

93. The System of Army Agency or Clothing was never
Clothing and Pay of Ordnance Corps adopted by the Ordnance Board; but, from the date of the original establishment of the Royal Artillery and Royal Engineers, the Ordnance Office provided their clothing and accoutrements. The clothing operations were subsequently enlarged by having to supply great coats for the Army and clothing to the Colonial Corps, Enrolled Pensioners ,the Constabulary and Revenue Corps,[2] Officers in Ireland, and the Militia in the Colonies; the Ordnance also provided for convict and other Colonial Services. The Board estimated for, and disbursed the pay of, the Ordnance, through the Agents acting as Paymasters

---

[1] The Artillery Officers may now be trained in the Arsenal for these objects, Appendix, Note A A

[2] Army and Ordnance Expenditure, 1849, pp 659, 729

94 Such being the outline of the various duties discharged by the Ordnance, was the constitution of the Board such as to entitle the Department to the confidence of Parliament on the one hand, and of the Army on the other?

Did the Ordnance Board hold or deserve the confidence of (1) Parliament, (2) the Army?

95. To answer only the first enquiry—for the second needs none—it may be remarked that the Ordnance Department was under Public investigation upon several occasions. 1st, in the year 1784,[1] when the Commissioners on Public Accounts reported upon the Constitution of the Board. 2nd, in the year 1797,[2] when the Select Committee on Finance entered upon a similar enquiry. 3rd, in the year 1811, when the Commissioners on Military Enquiry reported fully[3] on the subject. 4th, in the years 1817 and 1818, when the Finance Committees reported to the House of Commons. 5th, in the year 1828, when the Finance Committee again reported.[4] 6th, in the year 1833, by a Royal Commission, under the Presidency of the Duke of Richmond, who prepared a draft, but never issued[5] a Final Report. 7th, in the year 1837, when the Royal Commission on the Civil Administration of the Army reported to the Crown. And lastly, in 1849, when a Select Committee of the House of Commons reported on Ordnance Expenditure.

Reports and evidence before Parliament on the Ordnance Office from 1784 to 1849

96. The Commissioners on Public Accounts did not report in adverse terms of the Ordnance Department, indeed in one instance they reported highly in its favour, inasmuch as they were so satisfied with the examination of the Accounts of Imprest Accountants[6] by the Departmental Officers of the Ordnance, that they advised Parliament that any other audit was an unnecessary expense, and should be discontinued. In 1780, before their Report appeared, Mr. Burke had proposed,[7] to abolish the "Artillery

*A D 1784

Report in favour, and no organic change made*

---

[1] 12th Report, and see Appendix CXVI.   [2] 21st Report
[3] 12th to 17th Reports   [4] 2nd Report
[5] See Civil Administration, 1837, 21 H D (3), p. 968
[6] In June, 1784   [7] 21 Parl Hist., p 38

as a Military concern not well suited to its Martial, though exceedingly well calculated for its Parliamentary, purposes." He proposed to render the Civil subordinate to the Military—to send the Military Branch to the Army, and the Naval to the Admiralty, and to arrange the detail of the arrangements by a Commission. To execute by contract all that could be so executed; and, lastly, to have all estimates approved, and all moneys expended under the Treasury. Nothing of the kind was done;[1] but in the Appendix will be found what (I presume) was put forward by the Officers of the Ordnance Board at that time for their Defence.[2]

97. The earliest suggestion of an alteration in the constitution of the Board is contained in the Report of
1811. Those Commissioners suggested[3] the abolition
of the office of "Lieutenant-General," and, further,
in analogy to the Treasury, that the business of the Department should be entrusted to "Commissioners" of the Board of Ordnance, two of these being Officers of the Royal Artillery and Royal Engineers, and only two sitting in Parliament.

A D 1811
Suggestions for change.

98. The Report[4] of the Committee of 1828 (their *declared*
object *being retrenchment*, "in consequence of the
great permanent burdens which the vast amount of
the National Debt had imposed on the people"),
made after a lengthened examination of the Duke of Wellington and Lord Hardinge, was strongly in favour of the Department.[5] "In reporting upon the estimates, the Committee have been induced to give the precedence to those of the Ordnance, because they have found, in the course of their inquiries, many circumstances to lead them to the opinion that the principles on which the Ordnance Department is constituted, *are better for securing an efficient and economical dispatch of business than those on which the other two* (the War Office and the

A.D 1828
In favour of Ordnance Office

---

[1] 23 Parl Hist., p 122, and 25 ib , p. 302   [2] Appendix CXXVI
[3] 12th Report, 1811, p 44
[4] Subsequently to this Report, and before that of 1837 was made, the Board was reduced to three members, by the abolition of the offices of Lieutenant General and Clerk of Deliveries.   [5] P. 4

Admiralty) *Departments are founded*   They are disposed to think that they may have occasion to recommend to the House to examine whether the mode of conducting business and controlling the expenditure in the Ordnance Department may not *be usefully introduced into* the other Departments"

99. This suggestion did not pass unnoticed by Earl Grey's Cabinet in 1831   The different departments of the Admiralty needing re-arrangement and consolidation, the late Sir James Graham, then the First Lord, was satisfied that no better model could be found for a Public Department than the constitution of the Ordnance.[1]   Far from disregarding, as it is the fashion of Military reformers of the present day to do, the opinions of the Duke of Wellington—"no bad judge and no bad administrator"[2]—Sir James Graham paid great attention to the proceedings of this Committee, and came to the conclusion that, in describing the Ordnance Department, the Duke had laid down a principle for the management of a Department worthy of imitation.[3]   The scheme, therefore, introduced to Parliament by Sir James Graham, as a member of Lord Grey's Cabinet, and sanctioned by 2 Wm. IV., c. 40, was identical in principle with the Constitution of the Ordnance Board.

A.D. 1831-2
Admiralty Departments remodelled on the Ordnance system by Earl Grey's Ministry

100 It was during the same Administration that the Commission of December, 1833, issued to the late Duke of Richmond and others to inquire into the practicability and expediency of consolidating the different departments connected with the Civil administration of the Army. The object of this Commission was not therefore to abolish but to *extend the Ordnance system* by consolidating the War, the Paymaster-General's, the Commissariat, and other smaller departments into a Board under a Civil Commissioner (being a member of the Cabinet), transferring the command of the Ordnance Corps to the Commander-

A D 1833
Duke of Richmond's Commission issued by the same Ministry

---

[1] See his Evidence before the Commissioners as to the Control and Management of Her Majesty's Naval Yards, 1861, p 417
[2] The like, Select Committee on the Admiralty, 1861, p 104, Question 807
[3] Ib, p 133

in-Chief; for the success that had attended Sir James Graham's reorganization of the Admiralty was the inducement presented to Earl Grey's Cabinet to prosecute this enquiry.

101. Possibly the enquiry was not completed, but—as representing a very long official experience in the War Office as Deputy Secretary—the evidence of the late Right Hon. L Sullivan, before the Commissioners,[1] is worthy of notice. He said,[2] "I should view *with much alarm* such a consolidation of departments as would too much *divide the attention of the chief authority*, or interpose those delays which are inseparable from the operations of a Board. The only interest which the public can take in such a measure as that which is proposed, must arise from an expectation of increased *efficiency*, or of greater *economy* in conducting the service. Now I believe that these objects have already been more successfully pursued under the War Office arrangements, than they would have been under any system less dependent on the valuable principle of *individual responsibility.*" . . . . "The head of too large a Department *cannot* or will not *bestow* upon it the *requisite* attention together with that which is demanded by general questions of Government, and by the harassing duties of Parliament "[2]

A.D. 1834.

Mr Sullivan's evidence

102. In effect he predicted[3] a result identical with that foretold by Lord Hardinge and the Duke of Wellington, at a later period (in 1837), which has come to pass in the present time, viz., the existence of a Parliamentary control virtually inefficient in proportion to its nominal extent:—"The consolidation proposed by the Commissioners would cause persons to consult together, whose habitual occupations vary extremely; and would give the supreme control to a chief, combining the functions of Master-General of the Ordnance, Secretary at War, and Paymaster-General. Decisions would, I think, be greatly impeded; the supposed control would be *virtually inefficient* in proportion to its *nominal* extent; and the *real* management would get very much into the hands of the *subordinate officers.*"

Consolidation would destroy all efficient control

---

[1] As to this and the Commission of 1837, see the present Earl Grey's Evidence in the Organisation Report, 1860, pp 377-399   [2] P 59   [3] P 60

103. It is clear that the Commissioners of 1833 were alive to what may be deemed *the* danger of consolidation —viz., that of creating an unwieldly department, without any efficient Parliamentary check or control. They stated in their draft Report that, "The limit to consolidation appears to be either where it trenches upon efficiency, incorporates to such an extent as to render incorporation *unwieldy*, or where *amalgamation destroys any of those checks which one department* now holds *over another, or within itself*; checks which it has *cost so much to bring to that state* of perfection which, generally speaking, all our establishments may now very fairly lay claim to," and looking at the sequel to all the enquiries made by Commissioners and Committees, it would have been well had this counsel been heeded.[1]

Evils of consolidation shown by the Commissioners.

104. The two great objects which the authors of the Report of 1837 had in view were (1) the concentration of the Civil Administration, and (2) an absolute Parliamentary control over Military Expenditure The subject of Consolidation was considered, having before them the evidence and the draft Report of the Duke of Richmond's Commission; and as the scheme of those Commissioners suggested the abolition of the office of Master-General, these Commissioners, as a preliminary question, had to decide whether such a measure would be politically expedient? The Duke of Wellington very clearly answered this question in the negative, and the unhappy experience of the Crimean War—during the whole of which emergency the Government were, for the first time in modern history, without the advice of the Master-General—amply justifies the wisdom of his counsel, and the view adopted by the Commissioners to retain the office

Report of 1837 Was the abolition of the Master-General's office expedient?

105 "I should think," said the late Duke,[2] "that an officer in the high situation of Master-General would be very useful to the Government at all times they can refer to him on all Military questions. If he has not experience himself on a particular point on which reference might be made, he would be able to collect

The evidence of the Duke of Wellington, and the Report of the Commissioners against abolition

---

[1] 21 H D (3), 968, 27 ib, p 330, 37 ib, p 791, 42 ib, p 628
[2] P 40. See Lord Herbert's Evidence (Questions 6611-17), Organ. Report, 1860.

information, and give Government the most exact information
on every subject upon which it might become necessary. I
have always been of opinion that the Commander-in-Chief ought
not to be a member of the Cabinet; my reason for thinking so
is, that he ought not to be supposed to have any political influence as a bias upon his mind—most particularly upon the
subject of the promotions in the Army; and, therefore, that
the military resource for the Government is the Master-General
of the Ordnance; and under these circumstances I certainly
should be very sorry, for the sake of Government, to see that
office abolished. I saw with great regret the abolition of the
office of Lieutenant-General, because that imposed upon the
Master-General the performance of the military details of the
Engineers and Artillery. The Masters-General have been able,
I understand, to carry on those details without inconvenience;
but I am certain that at some time or other the Government
will find it necessary to have an officer in that situation who
can assist them with military opinions and military information
on points on which they may require it;" and this view was
adopted by the Commissioners.

106. But assuming the office to be abolished, could not the
As to the command and employment of the Ordnance Corps Ordnance Corps be put under the Commander-in-
Chief as Military men, and yet be retained to serve the
Secretary of State as Civilians—or in civil duties?
In effect, what is the objection to the arrangement made and
in operation since 1855? Let the answer be given in the words
of another great soldier:—"To separate them," said Lord
Hardinge,[1] "would produce great confusion—the unprofessional
chief would command the professional officers of the Ordnance,
who would have two chiefs to obey; whereas, at present, every
Military Ordnance officer for every duty has only one chief to
obey, and to whom alone he looks for approbation and reward
. . . . . If separated, the authority would be weakened, conflicting orders might be sent, the Commander-in-Chief might
order the Military officer abroad, who was usefully employed
under the civil Board at home—he would have to obey two

---

[1] Pp 23, 25 These opinions of Lord Hardinge were shared by the Duke of
Wellington, as will be seen on referring to his own evidence at p 36 of the same
Report

masters in the transaction of daily duties. This risk of a conflict of authority over a Military officer is now avoided by having a department, such as the Ordnance is, with a Master-General at its head, who has the supreme control over the Military and Civil branches of his Consolidated department. . . . . There would then be a divided authority, which no interference of the Secretary of State could obviate, for it would be required at every step; the Engineer officers would have to look to the Commander-in-Chief in some respects, and to the Civil chief, in a much greater degree than to their Military chief." [1]

107. Other Military officers of great, if not of equal experience, assured the Commissioners that the inevitable result would be increase of expense, the Military Officer would hold himself responsible to his Military chief (to whom he looks for promotion) for *efficiency* only, and would *totally disregard expense.* For instance, "The Artillery officers," Sir A. Dickson pointed out, "would become indifferent about their stores, except on account of the credit they were to gain in using them; their endeavour would be to have as large a supply as possible, and, as no ready check would exist to curtail their demands, profusion would lead to waste; and the only object at length would be, how to afford plausible reasons for such expenditure."

Increase of expense the consequence

108. Knowing what the professional training of an English Officer is—does it surprise any reader to learn that he, of all men, is least able to serve two masters, that an undivided allegiance is the essence of all—not less of Military—honour, and that as the conflict between efficiency and economy did not cease in 1855, these anticipated results are in daily progress of realization? [2]

Natural result of the principle of Military obedience

109. On the principal matter—that of Consolidation—the weight of experience was directed to this consequence, that the Consolidation of the War and Ordnance Officers under a Board (of four officers) would—with-

Consolidated Office too large for management.

---

[1] See Chap XVI, par 12 *et seq*   [2] Appendix, Note J J.

out the transfer of Commissariat duties from the Treasury—create a Department so unwieldly in size as to be unmanageable by the responsible Ministers in administration, and by the executive officers of the Army in the field.

110. "Consolidation," said Lord Hardinge,[1] "is *bad* when it prevents the *head* of a department from personally investigating all the *important* details, and this applies more particularly to a military department, because the Army is a great mass of *small* details. A fraction a-day saved in any allowance on 100,000 men would amount to a large annual sum; therefore I infer that, in this department of great detail, consolidation should stop when the officer in charge has as much upon his hands as *he can well get through.*"

111. Then, referring to the duties that would fall on the Chief of the Department, as member of the Cabinet, and their consequences upon his Departmental Superintendence, he continues:—"If the Chief is to be a Cabinet Minister, and is to attend to his duties as a Minister in the Cabinet and in the House of Commons, considering the very arduous nature of a Parliamentary Session, I consider that he could not *in reality* perform the duty of Chief; he *must* delegate it to other officers: he would be a *nominal* Chief, incapable of dealing with many professional subjects, which would be decided by *irresponsible* persons under him; *he would be of no authority with the Army;* and, in my judgment, the proposed arrangement would neither be *effective nor economical*, and no improvement, but the reverse."

Other claims on the time of a Cabinet Minister in Parliament

112. Sir James Kempt had filled the office of Master-General, and his view of the question was not less decided.[2]— "I fear that the business of so many departments, if merged in one Board, would be of so extensive and multifarious a nature, that the Cabinet Minister at its head, and the responsible person, would have but *an indifferent knowledge of what was going on;* it would be too unwieldly. A department, in my opinion, should not be so extensive as to prevent the responsible person at its head from taking upon

Sir James Kempt's view that the Minister would be imperfectly informed

---

[1] P 26   [2] P 11.

himself the general direction of the business, and deciding *personally every* important point."

113. The objections on financial or constitutional grounds entertained by the Duke, against separating the Commissariat from the Treasury have already been noticed.[1] on this inquiry he dealt with the same question in another aspect—viz., the *efficiency* of the Commissariat service—if it was handed over to a Minister, or rather to a Board of several Ministers—for the idea of loading *one* Minister with such a responsibility never originated before it was adopted in 1855 "I do not think that that consolidation is practicable; my reason is, that I think that the Board of Ordnance have as much to do at present as they can *well* manage. But when you come to throw upon a great public department, such as the Ordnance, the feeding of His Majesty's troops, and all the various duties performed by the Commissariat in England and all parts of the world, and the duties done by the office under the Secretary at War, I conceive that a great deal *more* would be thrown upon the Board than they could undertake. I confess I do *not think any* money would be saved by this arrangement I doubt that the Board could give any efficient assistance in the performance of those duties, or could *exercise any efficient control over them.*"[2]

114. The union of Commissariat and Store duties in the same officer, the Duke, as before shown, held to be impracticable,[3] and he then went on to show that the same Department could not safely—having regard to the efficiency of the public service—be made responsible for such a mass of detail. "The Board would be overloaded by details, with those of the War Office and those of the Commissariat in addition to the details it has at present to attend to. If the Commissioners will be so kind as to look at this return of the Stores of the Ordnance, though I can name some articles which are not included, they will find the articles are very numerous: the return includes everything which can be wanted

Marginal notes:
Objections of the Duke of Wellington to hand over the Commissariat to the Ordnance Board

That evil consequences would result therefrom

---

[1] Chap XIX, par 48　　　[2] P 35　　　[3] Chap XIX, par. 64

by men or ships, and in all parts of the world; there is a journal kept of the receipts and issues of all these articles, and these journals and returns require to *be very closely looked into* to ascertain that *there is no malversation,* and nothing wanting in the magazines at home or abroad. I do not say that the performance of the duty of such a Board would be absolutely impossible; but I do not see the advantage of such an arrangement. The duties are entirely different. *I am certain* that in time of war the union of these departments in the field or elsewhere would be *absolutely* out of the question."

115. Now, of the several important recommendations made by these Commissioners, this is the outline:—

Commissioners' Proposals:—

(1) Secretary of State. I. The authority of the Secretary of State as the channel or medium of conveying the orders of the Crown to the Army was to be preserved; but all formal duties relating to the affairs of the Army, as for instance, preparing commissions, and signing for the delivery of arms, were to be transferred to the Secretary at War.

II. The duties of the Board of Ordnance were to be more completely divided into Civil and Military, the latter

(2) Ordnance. to be held by the Master-General, retaining the command and discipline of the Artillery and Engineers, with the charge of Fortifications and Works; and the former were to be increased by part of the Commissariat business, and to be conducted by the *three* Board officers, in subordination to the Secretary at War as the supreme Civil Minister.

III. The Secretary at War was to be in the Cabinet, his duties were to be increased in manner before men-

(3.) War Office tioned, and he was to be responsible for the whole Military Expenditure of the country.

116. Had these recommendations been carried out, the Work of the Departments would have been redis-

Redistribution of work, but not the destruction of any Parliamentary Departments and safeguards tributed, but the Departments themselves would have been preserved, and none of the Parliamentary safeguards destroyed. The Commissioners threw out that, ' *Ultimately, perhaps,* it might not be found impossible to dispense with *one* of the three Parliamentary situations now held by the members of the Board of Ordnance. This, however, should not be *too hastily* attempted ; it would be better, as we have already observed, to begin by maintaining, *undisturbed*, the existing internal arrangements of the *three* subordinate offices of the Clerk of the Ordnance, the Surveyor-General, and the Principal Storekeeper, only converting them into so many branches of the War Office. This postponement of any diminution of establishment would be the more expedient, as we should propose adding to the duties of the department the charge of the Commissariat business, *exclusive* of the pecuniary transactions committed to the Treasury, the transfer of which we recommend upon grounds precisely similar to those which we have stated in support of the suggestions we have already made."

117. No action was taken upon this Report, though Orders in Council were drafted to carry some of the recommendations into effect,[1] but in the year 1842 Parliament evinced the most unbounded confidence in the Master-General and Principal Officers. The Defence Act passed, giving them the most *absolute* power for the *sale* and exchange of *all the fortresses and military buildings of the United Kingdom*, having the purchase-money paid to any persons they should direct.[2] The ordinary scheme for such a measure might have authorised the Master-General and Board under an Order in Council to demolish the Military Works, and then to dispose of the sites, vesting the legal estate in the purchaser upon the payment of the purchase-money into the Bank of England to the credit of the Paymaster-General; but the whole matter was left to the *sole* discretion of the Principal Officers, to whom was given by Parliament the power to dispose of the fortifications and works of defence, as such, to any person—at any time and at such price (paid to their own nominees) as they might see fit. The Act was passed under the administration of the late Sir Robert Peel. The Bill

A.D 1842
—
No action taken by the Crown on this Report, but unlimited power given by Parliament to the Ordnance Board

---

[1] 27 H D , 1835 (3), p 330, 37 ib, 1837, p 791, 42 ib, 1838, p 628, Appendix CXLVII [2] See Appendix, Note K K

on which it was passed came before the Parliament several times by adjournment,[1] and Clauses introduced at the instance of the Treasury and Office of Woods. It was also settled by the Law Officers of the Crown.

118 How far the Department after this period, and before its abolition, had deservedly lost the confidence of Parliament, must be judged by a perusal of the Report of the Select Committee on Ordnance Expenditure, 1849, and the Treasury Minute of 1854. The Committee, towards the end of their Report, make this observation :[2]— " Your Committee have already observed that additional business has been of late years imposed on the Ordnance, and that new duties have been performed by the several departments without a *corresponding increase of* the establishment ; having noticed the large increase of establishment which has been made *in other public departments,* willingly bear testimony to the more economical administration of the Ordnance Office in this particular;" and close their Report in these words :— " Your Committee desire to direct the attention of the House to the practical working of the Department according to its present constitution. Upon this subject they must refer to the evidence, but they are of opinion that the construction of the Office, the division of the subordinate departments, and the mode of transacting business, are capable of considerable improvement. The various duties which the Ordnance is required to perform render it necessary, according to the present arrangements, that the Master-General should be an officer of high military rank, and it is expedient that among the members of the Board there should be a person conversant with *naval armament and stores.* The large grants annually placed at the disposal of the Ordnance, require for the economical administration the superintendence of persons who can give their attention to a variety of complicated details, while the Master-General must be qualified to offer advice to the Executive Government in regard to the outlay requisite for the defence of British

A.D. 1849.

Report on Ordnance Expenditure

---

[1] 97 Com Journ It was introduced into the House of Commons on 25th June, and received the Royal Assent on 10th August, 1842 [2] P. xxii

territory and British interests in every quarter of the world. The proper constitution of this Office is therefore a subject of great importance and of great difficulty, and requires the attentive consideration of the Government."

119. After this Report had been submitted to Parliament,[1] the Principal Officers made some, and a Special Committee appointed by the Treasury suggested other, improvements in the conduct of Departmental business, which received the entire sanction of the Treasury, as expressed in their Minute of the 17th January, 1854. "Request the Secretary to state to the Master-General and the Board that my Lords have observed with much satisfaction the many useful reforms that have already been made in the Ordnance Office, and great Public benefit cannot fail to be derived from a more full development of these improvements, as well as from an extension of the same careful revision to the other Establishments under their superintendence "[2] A.D 1854
The Treasury Minute

120. Each succeeding sovereign had confirmed Charles II's instructions with trifling amendments, and the last Royal Warrant of Confirmation, dated 18th June, 1839,[3] was countersigned by Earl Russell   No one, therefore, could allege that the Ordnance was one of those Establishments that escaped notice either from Parliament or the Constitutional advisers of the Crown, or that—if defective for the purposes of military administration—the Army, as represented by the Master-General and Principal Officers, were not responsible for its defects Ordnance Rules confirmed by each Sovereign down to Her present Majesty

121. But on what premises did the opponents of the Ordnance Establishment proceed, when they resolved to abolish the Principal Officers?   As contrasted with the Secretary at War's office, even in matters of Army administration, the Ordnance had little to fear in the comparison.   The corps raised by the Ordnance were free from what some may term the abuses of the Army System.   The On what premises was the Ordnance abolished?

---

[1] See the Duke of Wellington's Memorandum of Nov , 1849, Appendix CXLVIII
[2] 129 H D (3), 233 , 130 ib , pp 817-1264 , 132 ib , pp 606
[3] Ordnance Expenditure, 1849, p 728

Master-General employed Regimental Agents as Paymasters—but neither used Clothing Colonels nor recognised Purchase On the contrary, the Civil branch clothed the men, and the Master-General, in lieu of Purchase money, insisted upon Educational qualifications in those who bore Military employment under the Crown.

122. No doubt the Ordnance Administration was that of the Military as a class; indeed, the Civil branch had become so largely infused with the professional spirit, that it almost ceased to be recognised as a Civil branch.[1] With every professional chief, whether in the Army, Law, or Church, his preference is obviously and naturally shown towards those trained in his own pursuits, who look up to him as holding the highest claim to their respectful obedience. In the case of the Master-General this feeling extended so far that many Civil duties had been placed in the hands of Military Officers to discharge.

Ordnance was a military department

123. But this being so, no great Constitutional rule was violated, nor any control over the Military authority —vested in the Master-General for the protection of the liberties of the Civil community—lost, for the Ordnance differed essentially from the War Office in this respect. If, therefore, it was wrong to entrust Civil duties—as of manufacture—to Military Officers, it was only a violation—which still continues unheeded—of the principles of the division of labour, or of making the best selection of agents. "It is certain," said Lord Bacon,[2] "that sedentary and within-door arts have in their nature

No constitutional rule infringed by employing military officers in the Ordnance

disposition, and generally all i

and love danger better than t

124. But the Department, c

General presented the o⌐l⌐ employing Military Officers with advantage to themselves when, from the Constitutional duties entrusted to the Secretaries at War and of State, their offices were scrupulously closed against them. No political question, as to the power

Therefore it might be expedient so to employ them

[1] Lord Hardinge, 2nd Report of Finance Committee, 1828, p 13

[2] 29th Essay, p 291

of the Crown, was rais   by their employment under the Master-General, against which Constitutional statesmen might warn the House of Commons; for, though the abolition asserted the supremacy of—it was not provoked by any antagonism to—Parliament.

125. Of course an antagonism against the Ordnance Department existed on the part of the Secretary at War, which he inherited in the traditions of his office.[1] This found expression on many occasions, and never more effectually than during the absence of the Master-General in the Crimea, when the administration of the Army was brought under the notice of the House of Lords on the 29th January, 1855.[2] Following upon that debate Lord Palmerston became Premier, and the counsel of the Secretary at War to abolish the Ordnance Board[3] readily prevailed. From the first Cabinet at which Lord Palmerston ever sat as Premier, the Secretary at War brought home half a sheet of paper, containing a memorandum that the Ordnance, one of the oldest Constitutional Departments of the Monarchy, originated by Lord Burghley,[4] and upheld by Wellington—the antidote to the Horse Guards—was to be abolished, and its duties undertaken by the War Minister.[5]

[margin: Antagonism against the Ordnance Department.]

126. The work of destruction commenced, and has never ceased. The principles embodied in the Draft Report of the Committees of 1833[6] were utterly disregarded. The consolidation was unwieldy: it destroyed those checks which the Ordnance Department had within itself (under three Parliamentary officers each with separate duty), and which had cost so much time to bring to perfection. One—and *only* one—Parliamentary Minister was substituted for several, who, either as Soldiers or Civilians, had administered the Ordnance and War Offices separately, when the Regular Forces were small in number and the Auxiliary Forces did not exist.

[margin: 1855-1857. Ordnance abolished.]

127. What followed might have been anticipated: the Consolidated Office has deteriorated in official experience. The Ord-

---

[1] Par 51, *ante*, and Chap XXI, pars 21, 23   [2] 136 H D, 131, p. 1066.

[3] Lord Panmure's and Earl Grey's Evidence, 2114, and 5255-7, on Military Organization, 1860   [4] This was the tradition of the Ordnance Office.

[5] Chap XXIX, pars 42, *et seq*

[6] Contrast the speeches in the Lords' Debate with Lord Palmerston's speech, 16th Feb, 1855, 136 H D (3), p 1425   [6] Par. 103, *ante*

nance duties, so widely differing from the War Office duties. were
Consolidation
has injured
each office. strange to the latter Minister, and the Public, as a consequence, lost all competent Parliamentary supervision
over a large Department. The experienced men in their special
business were then—by a strange contrariety of official arrangements—placed in charge of important functions respecting which
their knowledge had to be learnt ; and thus, as the Department
became consolidated, the experience which really existed in it
was lost, and expenditure largely increased.

128 It needs little insight into human nature to trace out
Inexperience
in official
duty how the principle of *inexperience* finds development in
a Public Department. The Political Chief is obliged
either to cast off responsibility, or to gain knowledge to satisfy
the wants of Parliament. Now, in the first place, he cannot cast
off responsibility upon his Civil employés, because they hold no
delegation recognised by Parliament ; but he can at least endeavour to do so with regard to Military Officers commissioned by
the Crown, and known to have more technical knowledge than
himself. Therefore the natural tendency of every Civilian Minister in matters of *Professional* importance is to shield himself behind some Officer of more or less fame, and direct responsibility,
as it existed in the Ordnance Department, is lost.

129. To gain knowledge from others, it is essential that they
As to the
competency
of the Per-
manent Staff should have Official experience ; but as any member
of the Permanent Staff fails in this, his first object is
not so much to gain knowledge as to prevent his ignorance from being detected by the Parliamentary Chief—in effect,
to remove more experienced men from open competition with him.
This system was inaugurated at the Chaos—following upon the
breaking up of the traditions and the wasting of the experience
of two old-established departments. As it is practically impossible for the Parliamentary Chief to have a thorough knowledge
of the Consolidated Department, the competency of his several
permanent officers to discharge their functions is also a matter
of conjecture. Since 1855 the changes have been frequent, and
each has developed in some new phase the want of efficient
Parliamentary control.[1]

---

[1] See Memorandum, shewing the changes, &c , Appendix CXLIX.

CHAPTER XXI.

The Office[1] of Secretary at War

1 There was perhaps no office ever created the powers of which were, at its establishment, so undefined, as that of the Secretary at War. In the course of time, and in the progress of events, certain duties became definitely assigned to the office; but even in the discharge of these the Secretary at War held an ambiguous place of responsibility: neither a Military Officer—though the Commander-in-Chief claimed his allegiance as such, nor a responsible Minister—though the House of Commons strove to fix upon him that character.

On the establishment of the Secretary at War's office, duties wholly undefined.

2. The main cause of this ambiguity—which has recently been so largely extended to other persons discharging Civil duties towards the Army, and financial operations for Parliament,—was that of holding an appointment under Military Commission, and it would seem that no sooner had Parliament freed the Military Administration of the country from this evil, as applied to one Minister, than the same evil is thrown broadcast over subordinate agents, so that the conflict of authority,[2] when it arises, will not, as heretofore, be confined to two high officials—the Commander-in-Chief and Secretary at War, both under the authority of the Premier—but be extended to every Military Command throughout the Empire

Cause of the Ambiguity

3. The form of the Secretary at War's appointment is given in the Appendix,[3] and though it never could have been intended, in later years, when this commission was issued, to make the Secretary at War obedient to the orders of the Commander-in-Chief, or General of the Forces (which cannot be said of the motive for appointing Commissariat

Form of the Secretary at War's appointment

---

[1] As to this office, see Vol I, Chap IV, pars 51-3, Chap VII., pars 61-72, Chap VIII, par 7, Chap IX, pars. 16, 20, 26, Chap XI, pars 5, 6, 49, 140 It D (3), p 1023   [2] 188 H D (3), p 600, par 32 *post*, and Chap XXIII, par. 10, Chap XXIX, par 60 *et seq*   [3] Appendix CXXVII

and Store Officers by Commission), yet to within a few years of the extinction of the Secretary at War's office, the Commander-in-Chief used the words of the Commission to show his superiority over the Secretary at War, and to supersede the Financial and Parliamentary functions of the latter in controlling Military Expenditure.

4. A memorandum of what the Secretary-at-War deemed to be his duties was laid before Parliament on various occasions; and, therefore, those so set forth may be said to have received Parliamentary sanction. In later years, each Secretary at War on coming into office had this Memorandum placed before him by his Deputy,[1] and thus had a charter to govern himself by, which, since the abolition of his office, has been lost sight of Another document exists, of perhaps greater value, a Memon prepared by the late Lord Palmerston, in the year 1811, after a very careful perusal of many of the MS. volumes that were then (and I hope still are) preserved in the War Office Both of these papers will be found in the Appendix,[2] and will render less elaborate description of his duties upon the text acceptable.[3]

Summary of duties in later years

5. As preliminary to the subject, it may be well to remind the reader, that the Horse Guards is a Modern Establishment. and that, for many years after the office of Secretary at War was instituted, there was no such officer (as now existing) as Commander-in-Chief. In the year 1789, when General Burgoyne made the suggestion in the House of Commons that such an appointment was needed for the better discipline of the Army,

Outline of the Constitutional functions of the Secretary at War, prior to appointment of Commander-in-Chief

---

[1] A description of the duties of the Secretary at War was laid before Parliament in 1808 (see 6th Report of the Committee of Military Inquiry, p 397), Army and Navy Appointments, 1833, and again in the Report on Army Expenditure, 1850, p 1, and Appendix CXXVIII   [2] Appendix CXXIX

[3] Probably, to some persons, Lord Palmerston's Memorandum may have additional value from the recommendation which is found in his own handwriting upon an official paper, containing "a rough outline of some of the chief duties of the Secretary at War," prepared by the late Mr Sullivan —" This seems to me to be a very correct and concise description of the duties of the Secretary at War, but I should advise any new Secretary at War (perhaps from a feeling of authorship) to read over, whenever he has time for it, the controversy between Sir David Dundas and myself, as I think a great deal of useful information as to the duties and authorities of the Secretary at War is brought together in that correspondence — P 11/6/28 "

the Government replied by the Secretary at War, that "whenever the country needed the services of such an Officer, he should be appointed; but that in a time of profound peace they were not prepared to admit that a Commander-in-Chief was necessary."[1] Therefore, in the War Office are to be found the Records both of the Government and of the Administration of the Army prior to the year 1792.

6 Now, the Secretary at War's office, when created, bore a double aspect. First, it had some analogy to that of Military Secretary[2] to the (King as) Commander-in-Chief; and, secondly, as no other Minister accompanied William III. abroad to the War,[3] it had an analogy to the office of Secretary of State (Mr. Blathwayte's countersign to the Royal Sign Manual on State papers being accepted). As Military Secretary he is referred to as "the Secretary" in 48 of Articles of War, 1673, and as the "Secretary to the Commander-in-Chief," in 6 & 7 Wm. and Mary, c. 8, sec. 5. His pay was 1*l.* a-day at home, and 3*l.* a-day when in the field with the King.[4] As a Minister, he countersigned the grant of the Alford Peerage (1698), and the King's assent to the Archbishop of Canterbury's nomination to the See of Bangor.[5]

Double aspect.—1st, as Military Secretary, 2nd, as Secretary of State.

7. In fact, he held neither of these offices, but was originally a Financial and Ministerial agent, of subordinate importance, and was referred to as such in the statutes of Anne's reign; for finance, by 3 & 4 Anne, c 5, whereby the Army agents, in matters of small importance, were to follow the directions "of the Secretary at War—Royal Sign Manual —or the Treasury,"[6] and for recruiting and desertion by c. 10, 4 & 5 Anne, c. 21, and 7 Anne, c 2, sec. 20

Only a financial Officer

---

[1] 27 Parl Hist, p 1310, and see 14 ib., p 907

[2] "For and in consideration of the good service, &c, of George Clarke, son of Sir William Clarke, *our late Secretary at War, who was slain in our service*, and in memory of the many faithful services of us"—Extract from the patent of 13th March, 1 Jas II, appointing George Clarke Judge-Advocate-General

[3] See the entries in the 'Dutch Misc. Book, 1692 to 1695'

[4] It was reduced to 1*l.* a-day by the Commons, 14 Rap and Tin. History of England, p 51 In 1700, his extra pay was 1000*l.*, and 455*l.* for his clerks (Pay Bk., p 72), and in 1714 the allowance was increased to 1000*l.* for clerks, and 200*l.* for rent—total, 2365*l.* (Pay Bk, pp 117, 129 275), and, deducting Poundage and Hospital Fees, it was fixed at 2180*l.* in 1784 (Pay Bk).

[5] Mil Bk, 518, p 8   [6] Ib, p 151

8. When the business of the Command of the Army was

Command of the Army exercised by the King

carried on in the office of the Secretary at War, it must be borne in mind that the King, in *fact*, exercised the Command in Person. Even George III., until illness prevented it, continued the Government and Command of the Army in his own hands "From the expiation of the American War," said Mr. Wynn, speaking in the House of Commons, in 1812, "to the commencement of the present one, George III. has acted not only as a King, but as Commander-in-Chief."[1] The readers of Junius and of Lord North's Correspondence will not probably dispute the fact.

9. The two principal Officers that the King had to assist him

Adjutant-General and Quarter-Master on the Staff

on the Staff of the Army, were (as now) the Adjutant- and Quartermaster-Generals. They were persons not necessarily high in rank, for the Warrant of Queen Anne, in 1711, gave them the brevet rank of "Colonel,"[2] and there is an order extant in the War Office books,[3] under date of 23rd December, 1673, commanding the Adjutant-General to receive 264 Soldiers at Harwich, and to take them to the Earl of Peterboro's Regiment in France, and then to return "to your employment here." That *he* went is certain, for, his account for this service on the 2nd January, 1674, under date of 1st April following, amounting to 150*l.* 10*s.*, and an order for payment, are found entered.

10 Whenever the *Sovereign did not command in person*, a

General Officers acting in aid of the Sovereign (1). On particular service

General Officer was selected for the particular Service, and appointed thereto by a Letter under Royal Sign Manual, countersigned by the Secretary at War. Instances may be given in Queen Anne's Reign, when, in August, the Duke of Marlborough, and in November, 1703, the Duke of Schomberg, were appointed to serve in Portugal, by Letters of Service countersigned by Will. Blathwayte.[4]

11. In certain parts of the kingdom, far removed from

(2) In certain home districts.

head-quarters, General Officers were in like manner appointed to serve. In 1711, Major-General Earle

---

[1] 22 Cob Parl Deb, p 334, and see Lord Sidmouth's Life, vol ii, p 416, Ann Reg. for 1806, 20 H D (O. S), p 1130

[2] Mis Bk 520, p 54　　　[3] Ib, pp 42, 242　　　[4] Ib, pp 56, 62.

was appointed Commander-in-Chief of South Britain, in the absence of the Captain-General,[1] and in 1719 Lieutenant-General Carpenter was appointed in North Britain, acting under the King's, or a Secretary of State's, or the Secretary at War's instructions, " with the latter of whom he was constantly to correspond."[2]

12. Where no such Commander-in-Chief was appointed, —which was then generally the case, as the present Military Districts and Commands were created since 1793, and it was necessary that the Troops (then scattered throughout the country on billet) should be reviewed; a similar Letter of Service was given to a General Officer, requiring him to proceed to a particular place to muster and review certain Regiments named in his Letter, and to report to Her Majesty as to their condition in discipline, clothing, &c.[3] Thus, on 20th July, 1720, a full Letter of Instructions was given to Lieutenant-General Macartney, to review the three Regiments named at the margin of the Letter and in the note.[4]

(3) To review regiments.

13. In Military matters of general importance to the Army, it was usual to appoint by Royal Sign Manual Warrant a Board of General Officers, to whom the Judge-Advocate-General for the time being acted as Secretary One of the earliest instances of these Boards was that appointed by Queen Anne,[5] 22nd May, 1710, to inquire into irregularities and misbehaviour of any Officers and men that might be brought before it.[6] George I. appears to have appointed a Standing Board of 21 General Officers chosen by the Army, and to have issued a Warrant of 29th November, 1714 (on the submission of the Secretary at War) of which the substance will be found in the Appendix.[7]

(4) As a Board to advise

14. This Board was continued on foot for three months from the 25th March then next, by a later Warrant of 25th February, 1714-15,[8] and upon its recommendation

(5) Board to settle Accounts.

---

[1] Mis Bk 519 (ink), p 25

[2] Ib 523, p 9, and see the debate on the Pay of Staff Officers (1751), 14 Parl. Hist , p 909   [3] Ib. 520, p. 50 , ib 521, pp 81-113 ; ib 523, p 148.

[4] Brigadier Grove's, Colonel Cadogan's, and Colonel Fielding's

[5] Mis. Bk 519 (ink), pp 11, 13 , and see Appendix CII

[6] Ib 521, pp 38 67 , Letter Bk 134, p 161.

[7] Court-martial Bk., pp 7-9, and Appendix CXXXII   [8] Mis Bk 522, p. 22.

originated a "Board of Brigadiers," chosen by lot, to settle all financial disputes between the Colonels, Officers, and Soldiers of each Regiment; for at that time—viz., 4th April, 1745—the pay of a Regiment was issued in one sum to the Colonel, and the Public left him to distribute it to the Regiment, rendering an account to the Secretary at War.[1]

Reports presented to the King through the Secretary at War

15. The Reports from the Board of General Officers came up through the Judge-Advocate-General to the Secretary at War, to be laid before the King for his commands and directions thereon; and in this manner the Government and Command of the Army were—until the Commander-in-Chief's office was established in 1793—carried on, and the Secretary at War and the Judge-Advocate-General made responsible in Parliament.

This method of Command not satisfactory

16. That this was a satisfactory method of Governing the Army—either in the opinion of Parliament or of the Army—few people were found to admit. There was no definite responsibility. The King could do no wrong, and the Secretary at War was *not* (as that official contended) a Responsible Minister. He was both everything and nothing—he was everything to the King, as the Army knew no one but the Secretary at War,[2] and he was nothing towards Parliament, as that Assembly could not fix upon him the responsibility of a Secretary of State.

Responsibility repudiated by Secretary at War

17. The security that was lost to the Public by this arrangement, even in matters of life and death, will be seen from one incident. In the debate of 1749, the Earl of Bath, who held the office of Secretary at War in 1717, justified the orders he had issued for the illegal trial and execution of the half-pay officers taken at Preston,[3] upon the plea that "the Secretary at War is but a Ministerial, not a Constitutional Officer, and is obliged to issue orders according to the King's direction, when properly authenticated to him," then adding, "that a man will (it is true) refuse to sign or transmit orders which he knows to be unjust and illegal, and

---

[1] Mis Bk 522, p 22   [2] 11 Parl Hist, p 904
[3] 14 Par. Hist., p 479, see also, Vol. I., p 373, Chap VIII, par. 100, and Appendix XLIX

will rather resign than comply; but when it is only a matter of doubt, I think he is obliged to obey, because a delay in the execution may be attended with danger to the State"

18. The Secretary at War's primary duties were those of finance The Estimates, "by order" in 1702, and ' by address" in subsequent years, were presented by the Secretary at War and Paymaster-General. From the time of Mr. Blathwayte until the year 1855 (when Lord Panmure held office), the Secretary at War had *always* been a Member of the House of Commons, and usually a Civilian To the latter rule the only exceptions were Colonel Fitzpatrick (1783-4 and 1806-7), General Pulteney (1807-9), and Sir Henry Hardinge (1828-30 and 1841-4) The measures of principal importance during Colonel Fitzpatrick's tenure of office were carried through Parliament by Civilians; for the Act to regulate Military Expenditure, known as Mr. Burke's, was framed by him, and the scheme for limited enlistment in 1806 was passed by Mr. Wyndham.[1]

Primary duties, those of finance, and the Secretary at War, until 1855, a Member of the House of Commons and usually a civilian

19. In matters of Finance, the Secretary at War claimed, as acting under the immediate directions of the Treasury, to be supreme over the Commander-in-Chief. The sphere of his duty was properly confined to the Regimental Establishments of the Army, in regard to numbers, pay, and allowances These items of expenditure being settled by the Crown, on the advice of the Treasury and other Responsible Ministers the decision[2] was sent to the Secretary at War, that the Estimates might be prepared in his office upon the usual scale and submitted by him to Parliament[3]

Had the charge of the Establishments when fixed

20 Such, for many years, was the limit of his responsibility regarding the Estimates, for when (they were under notice, in Dec. 1779), Mr. Fox challenged the Government for an explanation as to the number of men to be voted, the Secretary at War, Mr. Jenkinson—the Secretary

Such was the limit of his r ponsi .bility

---

[1] Lord Hardinge, Civil Administration, 1837,' p 24

[2] War Office Letter Bk 132, p 70, ib 134 p 299, ib 136, pp 16-30, 101, and Report on Civil Administration, 1837, p 6

[3] But see Memorial from Dragoon Regiments to the Secretary at War, to move His Majesty for increase of pay, and represent it in Parliament, M's Bk 523 p 75 As to the Regulations made, see ib, p 145

of State being present—refused to give any other answer than that of saying he was no Minister, and therefore could not be supposed to "have a competent knowledge of the destination of the Army, and how the war was to be carried on."[1]

21. But though irresponsible to Parliament, the Secretary at War was not unwilling to assume the *power* of a responsible Minister towards other Departments, and especially so towards the Ordnance Board. In 1715 the Secretary at War assumed to exercise a financial control by requiring that Board to send *him* their Estimates; and, having in this instance succeeded in procuring them, he subsequently communicated the King's commands to the Principal Officers, that one of them should lay the same before the House of Commons.[2]

But the Secretary at War originally assumed to Control the Ordnance Department.

22. But authority in matters of prerogative was not originally conceded, though it was too frequently assumed by the Secretary at War; for instance, the established rule of the Ordnance was to issue Arms *only* on the orders of the Crown, and to require the countersign or letter of a Secretary of State; but the Secretary at War, in 1702, put forward a claim—which the Ordnance refused to recognise[3]—that Arms should be issued upon *his* order. In a few years later (1714) it was necessary for the Board to remind the same Officer[4] that the charge of all the Fortifications was entrusted by the Crown to the Principal Officers of the Ordnance, and not to the Secretary at War.[5]

As to a similar assumption against the Transport Board.

23. Between the War and Ordnance Offices a feeling of antagonism always existed; and it is curious to notice these early indications of an aggressive spirit which was mani-

Antagonism between the Ordnance and War Offices.

---

[1] 20 Parl Hist , p 1254. 27 ib , p 1312.

[2] Ordnance Letters in 1715, pp 69-161, in 1716, p 232, and in 1717, p 320

[3] War Office Letter Bk (132), pp 22-24, 24th Mar , 1702-3, Mis Bk (524 , p 210

[4] Ordnance Letter Bk., p 155, 8th Feb , 1714, and see War Office Letter Bk. (134), p 184, 1st Mar , 1705-6

[5] He assumed the same authority over the Victualling Board, but without success, 1707, War Office Letter Book 136, pp 8, 14, 61, 85 and see Letters to Lord Sunderland, pp 8 and 67 In July (14), 1705, St. John complained to Colonel Jones that he had written to the Prince and not to himself about the misconduct of officers, Letter Bk. 133, p. 277

fested by the Secretary at War upon—until it overthrew—the Ordnance Department. Though ever ready to assert his own authority *against* the General in command, the Secretary at War was at all times willing to unite and make common cause *with him* in any matters that would supersede the Ordnance. In Parliament, or in the Councils of the State, none were more ready to condemn that Department than those Statesmen knowing least about it, who had served in the less important Office of Secretary at War; while it will be found that, *whenever* the Ordnance *has* been superseded (as in 1855, by the Cabinet under the Secretary at War's influence), a vast increase of expenditure has resulted.

24. As the Ordnance Department had its own Treasurer, power was given to the Secretary at War at an early period in the reign of George I. to issue Royal Orders for the payment of the Army This authority, in 1715-6, was by the Treasury Letter printed in the Appendix.[1] At that time—and until Mr. Burke's Act came into operation—the greater part of the present War Office work was done by the agents of the several Regiments (as they were raised); and hence the Secretary at War's Establishment in 1720, and for many years after, consisted of nine persons only.[2]

A D 1715

Authority given to the Secretary at War by the Treasury to issue orders for the Army Pay

25. The agents of Regiments were then, as now, appointed by the Colonels in Chief, but approved by the Secretary at War. The agents to Independent Companies were appointed by the Secretary at War, who claimed their appointment against the Crown. Their duties (set out in an appointment of 1720, as Agents and Paymasters) were to take care of the affairs, and to keep the accounts, of the Company; to receive their pay from the Paymaster-General: to disburse it to the Officers and Men, and to do all such other necessary things relating to the Company as to His Majesty's Service should appertain; finally, they were duly to account to the Auditors of Imprest for all moneys issued to them.[3]

Agents' appointment and duty before 1783

26. No doubt, prior to Mr. Burke's Act, Regimental Agency

---

[1] Appendix CXXXIII   [2] Appendix CXXXIV   [3] Appendix CXXXV

provided official labour equivalent to the wants of the Army,
for as created, so it also ceased. with the Regiments

Altered posi-
tion of the
Agent at the
present time raised or disbanded   Further, the War Office had
not then (as now) a staff of Military accountants
spread as a network over the United Kingdom, and indeed over
the Colonies, holding daily communication with the War Office
in regard to matters of Finance. Hence the aspect of the
Agency question has totally changed.[1]   To insure then implicit
obedience to the Secretary at War, a Clause was inserted, and
still remains, in the Mutiny Act, imposing penalties upon them
for disobedience.[2]

27. These and other duties unconnected with Finance—
which the earlier Chapters in this work show to have

The great
object was to
fix the Sec-
retary at
War with
Parliamen-
tary Respon-
sibility been discharged by the Secretary at War—were too
important to be left in the hands of a Minister dis-
claiming Parliamentary responsibility. He was neither
of the Cabinet[3] nor of the Privy Council and yet it
was admitted by his official opponent, the Commander-in-Chief,
that he was rightly allowed to enter the King's closet to transact
the business of his Office. The great object, therefore, which
the House of Commons sought to gain, with regard to Military
Administration, was to fix the Secretary at War with a plain
and definite Parliamentary responsibility; and this was done by
various Statutes, some of which are, as we have seen, of Constitutional importance[4]

28. The Statute that had the most important bearing upon
the financial duty of the Secretary at War was Mr.

A.D 1783

Mr Burke's
Act fixed
Financial
Responsi-
bility on the
Secretary at
War Burke's Act, so often referred to in the previous pages.[5]
In effect it transferred all the financial and adminis-
trative business of the Regiments *from* the Colonel's
Agent *to* the War Office. It placed the Secretary

[1] The Agency system has come under consideration in the following Reports and Papers —1747, Vol ii Common Reports, p 95, 35th Report of the Finance Committee, 1798, 6th Report of Military Inquiry, 1808, p 333, Lord Palmerston's Evidence, 14th March, p, 129, Mr Merry's Evidence, 31st March, 1828, Finance Committee; Army Expenditure, 1850, *passim*, 'Audit of Naval and Military Accounts, 1856,' p 34 (160); 23 H D (O.S), p 1288.

[2] Mutiny Act, 1869, sec, 77.

[3] The Secretary at War that first sat in the Cabinet was Mr Wyndham

[4] Chap IX, par 16, Chap XV., par 57   [5] Chap. VII, par 61.

at War[1] in a highly responsible position,[2] and from 1783 to 1792 the whole direction of the Army was in his hands. From the operation of this Act, and the subsequent appointment of Paymasters[3] to supersede the Agents at the Regiments, the War Office continued to increase, for, in fact, the expenses of Army Administration were duplicated.[4]

29. It was, therefore, impossible for the Secretary at War any longer to repudiate responsibility, and when General Burgoyne in the debate before referred to,[5] insisted that "there ought to be some person who should be considered the Military Minister,—some ostensible person responsible for every step taken in the Military Department, — and that person ought to be the Commander-in-Chief,"[6] the Secretary at War (Sir W. Yonge) replied that though not professionally bred, "he did not hesitate to stand up in his official situation, and say that he conceived it was the notion of our Government that he was in some sort officially responsible for every measure taken in the Military Department, and he assured the House that he never would shrink from that responsibility." This direct admission of Ministerial responsibility for the affairs of the Army was probably the first ever made to Parliament; for Mr. Fox, in addressing the House, said, "that he was glad to hear, and that they had for the *first* time learnt, that they actually had such a person as a responsible *Military* Minister."

A.D. 1789.
Secretary at War admits his responsibility to Parliament.

30. In 1793 that portion of the Secretary at War's duty that arose in connection with the Board of General Officers was detached from the War Office, and the nucleus of the present Horse Guards Establishment arose. Lord Amherst[7] was placed on the Staff, acting as a General Commanding-in-Chief, taking with him a principal

A.D. 1793.
Portion of the Secretary at War's official work transferred to the Horse Guards.

---

[1] Chap IV, par 57; Chap XV, pars 4, 117, 118

[2] Army and Navy Appointments, 1833, p 205

[3] 6th Report of Military Inquiry, pp 305-308, 10th Report on Public Expenditure, 26th July, 1811, Finance Committee, 1828, p 228

[4] Chap XXIII, par 8   [5] 27 Parl Hist., p 1310.

[6] It appears from Mr Fox's reply (p 1318), to have been suggested that one of the King's sons should hold this office, and see 14 Parl Hist, p 909

[7] 8th Report of Military Inquiry, pp 139, 207

clerk from the War Office, Mr. Leonard Morse, as his Military Secretary. The Adjutant and Quartermaster-Generals were placed under Lord Amherst; the office of the Secretary at War was therefore relieved from the business resulting from the discipline and government of the Army.[1] Notwithstanding these arrangements, the Finance Committee, in 1797, reported that the War Office Establishment had increased[2] from a Deputy, 8 established, and 12 other Clerks, in 1782, to a Deputy, 12 established, and 21 other Clerks in 1796.[3]

31. The *immediate* effect of this appointment was an in-

The immediate effect of the appointment of a Commander-in-Chief was increase of Military Expenditure

crease in Military Expenditure. The powers of the Commander-in-Chief were totally undefined, and it was not an unreasonable conclusion for him to come to, that as the Secretary at War held a Military Commission, directing "him to follow all orders and directions received from the General of the Forces, according to the discipline of War," he was bound to obey and not to control the Commander-in-Chief's authority. Their joint action in 1793, and at later periods, was directed to the Defence of the country, and to the erection of Barracks, at a grievous cost to the people[4] —the work of responsible Ministers which should more properly have been given into abler hands to execute.

32 The Constitutional relationship that should exist between

Constitutional relationship between the Secretary at War and Commander-in-Chief

the Secretary at War and Commander-in-Chief was not recognised, or at any rate acted upon, until Lord Palmerston entered upon the former office in 1809, and continued in it until 1828. Therefore, so soon as the Secretary at War took an independent course, which his Parliamentary responsibility obliged him to, a controversy between the two departments arose[5] that was ultimately

---

[1] See Sir H Torrens' Memorandum to Finance Committee, 1828, p 185

[2] 19th Report, pp 358, 399

[3] See the increase of War Office and Horse Guards Establishments, traced out in the 6th Report of Military Inquiry, 1808, and referred to 7 H D (O S), p. 305, and Lord Palmerston's evidence before Finance Committee, 1828, pp 226, 227, 33 H D (O S), p 998, 6 ib (2), pp 85, 214, 6 ib, p 1216; 32 ib (3), 211, 10th Report on Public Expenditure, June, 1880, p 24

[4] See Chap XII, *ante* The total of the sums voted for Barracks from 1793 to 1809 was 13,008,759*l* (see 7th Report on Public Expenditure, 20 June, 1810)

[5] Civil Administration, 1837, p 9

settled by the Warrant of the 12th May, 1812.[1] The memoranda from several members of Mr Perceval's cabinet, printed in the Appendix,[2] show that the difficulty of determining the true official position of the Secretary at War towards the Commander-in-Chief resulted mainly from the form of his appointment, and from having to reconcile an officer's duty to the Crown under a Military Commission with a full recognition of his responsibility to Parliament

33. The Constitutional doctrine—that all Army Expenditure should rest upon the decision of the Civil Minister responsible to Parliament—was ultimately established ; for, to allow the Army to determine the amount of its own Expenditure would be to terminate all Civil government. Therefore, until 1858 and 1867, no one in recent years has contended that the Commander-in-Chief, or his subordinate officers, have or should have *any* control in financial matters.

Pay and allowances rest with the Secretary at War

34. As against the Army, this is put beyond doubt by the testimony of two Military men of the highest authority, who had held respectively the offices of Secretary at War and Commander-in-Chief. "The *exclusive* control over public money voted for Military purposes rests," said Lord Hardinge,[3] "with the Secretary at War." "The Commander-in-Chief," said the Duke of Wellington,[4] "has and can have nothing *whatever* to say to finance. The Secretary at War has a clear simple duty to perform,—he has to take care that the Votes of Parliament are not exceeded, and that no expense is incurred by the Commander-in-Chief which is not necessary ; in short, that no expense can be incurred *without his consent.*" "The Commander-in-Chief," said the Duke, upon another occasion,[5] "has no power of giving an allowance to anybody, or of incurring any expense whatever. It is much better that the Secretary at War should be the person to regulate that matter than that *it should be in the hands of Officers connected* with the Army."

Put beyond doubt by the testimony of Lord Hardinge and the Duke of Wellington

35. The other position taken up by Lord Palmerston, that the Secretary at War was "in point of law a sort of barrier

---

[1] Appendix CXXXI. [2] Appendix CXXX. [3] Civil Administration, 1837, p. 24.
[4] Civil Administration, 1837, p. 37.
[5] Finance Committee, 1828, pp 8, 9, and see Chap XXVI., par. 34, *post*

between the Military authority of the Officer in command of
Civil Authority to control the Military Authority the Army, and the Civil rights of the people," was also conceded. Having shown that it was his duty to frame the Military Code, Lord Hardinge explained that the Secretary at War was a check on the Commander-in-Chief "When the liberty of the subject and Civil rights are involved, this duty is left to the Civil Officer — the Secretary at War — who has to discuss and pass the Act through the House of Commons"[1] And again, — when Sir John Hobhouse, recently appointed to the office of Secretary at War, thought that framing the Mutiny Bill did not rest with him, but with the Commander-in-Chief as the authority to decide upon Military punishments, Lord Hardinge at once corrected him — "I regret to differ from the Right Hon. gentleman with respect to the principle on which he has placed the formation of the Mutiny Act I must confess that I take a very different view of that subject; for I think that the Secretary at War is, in a Constitutional point of view. the proper person to draw up the Mutiny Bill and the Articles of War. He is bound to stand between the Civil subject and the Military, and it is his duty to take care that the Civil part of the community are properly protected, and that those who enter the Army are not treated in an unnecessarily strict manner. If the Right Hon. gentleman meant to say that he ought not to make any alteration in the Mutiny Act or the Articles of War without the concurrence of the Commander-in-Chief, I entirely concur with him, but having held that office of Secretary at War, I must maintain that it is, in a Constitutional point of view, the duty of a Secretary at War to be responsible for all Military transactions to this House and to the country."[2]

36. No sufficiently good result would be attained by going
Secretary at War acts as Commander-in Chief when latter office vacant into further detail of the special duties of the "Secretary at War;" but, fully to appreciate the importance of the office, it must be stated that when the Commander-in-Chief's office is vacant the duties of it devolve—not upon the Adjutant or Quartermaster-General,

---

[1] Evidence before the Royal Commissioners on Civil Administration, 1837 p. 26. and Vol. I, par. 7, *ante*　　[2] 11 H D (3rd), 1832, p 1223.

as the Officers highest in authority under the Commander-in-Chief, or His Majesty's Staff, but—upon the Secretary at War. This is clear, not only from Official records, but from the Statute Law of the Realm.

37. Upon the death of the Duke of York, in January, 1827, the Adjutant-General, having issued a circular to the Army, in His Majesty's name, Lord Palmerston, in Official Correspondence asserted,[1] and the Adjutant-General conceded to him, that when there was no Commander-in-Chief it was the duty of the Secretary at War to promulgate the Orders of the Crown to the Army.[2] Shortly afterwards, the Adjutant-General submitted to the King the draft of an Order which he proposed to issue by His Majesty's command; but George IV., though approving the Order, underwrote these words upon it:—"It should be submitted previous to its being given out in Orders to the Secretary at War, as he is *now* responsible for those duties attached to the Commander-in-Chief,—19th January, 1827." When it came to the Secretary at War he amended and re-submitted the Circular for His Majesty's approval. Upon the resignation of the Duke of Wellington, in May of the same year, Lord Palmerston resumed the duties of the Commander-in-Chief's Office, and acted therein until the Duke resumed the command of the Army in August. During this period, Lord Palmerston prepared an official memorandum of the duties of the Commander-in-Chief for the approval of George IV,[3] which is printed in the Appendix,[4] and Sir Herbert Taylor (Military Secretary) was appointed a Deputy-Secretary at War.

(1) Shown by the Official Records, 1827

38. Parliament affirmed the principle on which Lord Palmerston had acted. The Mutiny Act[5] then in force having provided that certain sentences should

(2) By the Statute Law

---

[1] Official Records, p 156

[2] As to the intention of George IV to resume the command of the Army, see Vol III. Supplementary Wellington Despatches, pp. 531, 631, 645

[3] Upon the vacancy in the office by the death of the Duke of Wellington, the Secretary of State for the Home Department took the pleasure of the Crown on the circular to be issued to the Army (September, 1852), and the same was communicated by the Secretary at War to the Adjutant-General, and promulgated by that Officer   [4] Appendix CXLII.   [5] 7 & 8 Geo IV., c. 4.

be certificated by the Commander-in-Chief, or *in the absence of the Commander-in-Chief*, then by the Adjutant-General,—the *then vacancy* was thought to be unprovided for. Parliament was therefore applied to, and a Bill[1] passed—stating that doubts had been suggested whether the Adjutant-General or the Secretary at War was authorised to give such certificate and to remove them, by enacting that when there should not be *any* person appointed Commander-in-Chief, the certificate of the *Secretary at War*, or his Deputy, should be deemed and taken as effectual

39. All antagonism ever existing between the Civil and

Antagonism between Civil and Military authority Military authorities, resulting from Constitutional or Departmental arrangements, rightly found expression in the Offices of the Secretary at War and the Commander-in-Chief; and, therefore, as the late Lord Hardinge told the House of Commons (and as the fact is proved by daily experience), no Minister, doing his duty faithfully to the Civil Community, was so certain to be unpopular with the Army as the Secretary at War. How could it be otherwise? Restraint, surely, is irksome to most people, and the interference of any official, especially one of comparative insignificance, who restrains pecuniary advantages, and controls power, must be essentially distasteful to any person, and not the less so to the members of the Military profession.

40. Of course it would have been in the power of the Secre-

Might have been removed by appointing Military Officers to act for the Secretary at War tary at War to do as the Secretary of State has done since the Crimean War, viz., take Officers from the Commander-in-Chief's Staff, and work his Financial and Constitutional functions through their agency. No doubt all fuction would have been removed by changing the employés. Moreover the character of the office would gradually, if not entirely, have been altered by the Military education and experience of such (five years) appointees. Possibly Parliament, finding the War Office and Horse Guards both garrisoned by Military Officers, might have shared Mr. Fox's belief[2] that the people held not the *same* security for the due administration of Finance and Constitutional law under

---

[1] 7 & 8 Geo IV., c. 63   [2] Par. 46, *post*

such an arrangement as when Civilians, though called clerks, acted after special training for these duties, and owned neither allegiance nor favour to any Military superior.

41. However, it is not to be denied that the functions both of the Secretary of State and of the late Secretary at War were formerly carried out in their several departments by the *exclusive* agency of the *Civil* servants of the Crown, not only wholly independent of the Commander-in-Chief, but trained in the *rules and traditions of their several offices*, viz., as the guardians of the Public Purse and of the Civil liberty of the community. Neither can it be denied that these functions were conferred upon these Ministers, or at least represented to Parliament—*as great constitutional safeguards* against the encroachments of the Standing Army upon the finances and liberties of the people.

Personnel of the War Office, Civil.

42 It was therefore thought to be a matter of the first importance to uphold, in perfect integrity, the Civil authority of the Secretary at War, and to continue the office as one of independent control over Military Expenditure. "The theory of our Constitution," said Mr. Fox, "consists in checks—in oppositions—one part bearing up and controlling another."[1] "The principle, I take it," said Lord Palmerston,[2] "upon which the Public Service has been constructed has been to make one Department a check and a control on another, and not to leave it in the power of *any* one Department to make an unlimited issue of public money, making one Department the judge of the amount to be issued, and the giver of the authority to make the issue, and make another Department the depositary of the money, and charged with the duty of issuing according to the documents which it may receive."

The War Office was maintained as an Office of Check and Control

43 The discharge of the executive duties of the Commander-in-Chief, and of the administrative duties of the Secretary at War, could not therefore be blended in one Department without endangering this great principle of independent action and control by a Civil Minister

Union of the War Office and Horse Guards would violate this principle.

---

[1] 24 Parl Hist., p 287.   [2] Finance Committee, 1828, p 221

over an executive Military Officer. Besides there is an Army view of the question, thus stated by the Duke of Wellington, which cannot be overlooked.—"Let Her Majesty's Government try the experiment whether they can find an Officer *whom the Army would respect, and to whose control and command the Officers and soldiers will cheerfully submit,* who will consent to be placed in this subordinate situation, under the superior military direction of a political officer, the business of whose department in relation with the predecessors of such military officer has been solely matters of account, and to be an assistant to the military officer."

44. The Finance Committee of 1828 directed their en-
Sir Herbert Taylor's Evidence quiries to this object, viz, whether the Horse Guards and the War Office might not be united in one Office under a Civilian or a Military Chief. Referring to the period when Lord Palmerston held both offices, Sir Herbert Taylor reminded the Committee that a Civil Minister of great experience thus had the means of judging whether the mode of doing the business of the two Offices could be simplified. Sir Herbert[1] was then asked whether the two Offices could not be thrown together with advantage to the Public Service, and his answer is well worthy of attention:—"I do not think it could be done with advantage to the *Army;* and I should say not to the advantage of the *Public* Service. No man was more sensible of that, I believe, than Lord Palmerston himself during the time he tried it The War Office is a check on the Commander-in-Chief, and if the Offices were united that check would be lost. Whatever affects finance, that is done in the Commander-in-Chief's Office, must go through the Secretary at War; if there is anything incorrect or irregular, it is immediately checked there, and therefore I do not see how the Public Service could be advantaged by doing away that Office which checks the other, or by combining the two Offices, of which the one is a check upon the other."

45 The language of the Duke of Wellington[2] before the same Committee was even more emphatic. "I should

---

[1] Finance Committee, 1828, p. 254.　　[2] Ib, pp 8, 9, Chap XXIX, par 40

earnestly recommend that it should *not* be adopted; the Commander-in-Chief's Office is entirely disconnected with money, the Commander-in-Chief has no power of giving an allowance to anybody, or of incurring any expense whatever. . . . . Considering who the persons are who are likely to be Commanders-in-Chief of the Troops in this country, I do not think it would be an economical arrangement to put the power of incurring expense in their hands, instead of keeping that power in the hands of the Secretary at War, who must answer to Parliament for every expense incurred. It is much better the Secretary at War should be the person to regulate that matter, than that it should be in the hands of the Officers connected with the Army. In former times the Secretary at War was, in fact, the Secretary of the Commander-in-Chief, and of course he was obliged to obey the commands of the Commander-in-Chief. Owing to different circumstances, he is no longer in that situation; he is an Officer responsible himself for certain duties, and, in fact, he is a check on the Commander-in-Chief for the object of economy." *The Duke of Wellington's Evidence.*

46. The modern theory of maintaining the War Office under the nominal control of a Civil Chief, with Military subordinates to regulate Army Expenditure, was not then in vogue. When it was first attempted in the Barrack Department, Mr. Fox[1] exposed the danger of trusting Parliamentary control to such instruments :— *The theory of employing Military Officers in the War Office not then in vogue*
"I have as high an opinion of the integrity, the honour, and principles of the Officers of the British Army as any man, but I will not pay them a compliment at the expense of the *Constitution.* I will not sacrifice to them that jealousy which it is the duty of the House of Commons to entertain of *every set of men* so immediately connected with the Crown. To the Crown they must look for promotion; by the Crown they may be dismissed from their profession without any cause assigned, and to the Crown they must be attached in different degrees from men on whom similar motives do not operate. This attachment arises from the situation in which they are placed; it applies to them collec-

---

[1] 30 Parl. Hist., p. 488, and Chap. XXIX, par 32, *post*

tively as a body, and is no disparagement whatever to any of them as individuals. . . . . Such being the situation of all Military Officers, they are fit and necessary objects of the jealousy and vigilance of the House of Commons, as are indeed, in a greater or less degree, all persons whatever employed by the Crown."

47. The office of Secretary at War offered to young statesmen an introduction to official life, an advantage that

Secretary at War's Office afforded an introduction to Political life

was of the first importance to the Public Service of the country. Surrounded by experienced officials of more than five years' growth, they were able to learn the details of Army Administration without exposing the country to any great loss from their want of experience. Each Member of the Lower House so instructed was able to give in debate a plain explanation of every item in the Estimate,—of its first introduction, and of its gradual development.[1] Information was not monopolized by a vast number of irresponsible *employés* in one vast department of the State, the Chief of which, from necessity, has a less perfect knowledge of any one subject of Army Administration than the subordinate persons around him.

48. The Secretary at War's Office afforded ample employment for St. John, Walpole, and Pulteney, in earlier,

Offered sufficient employment for a Parliamentary Officer

and for Lords Palmerston, Macaulay, Panmure, and Herbert, in later times. With official aid, they could and—what is more—*did* master the details of the Secretary at War's business;[2] but there is not to be found an iota of evidence, from any Statesman who had ever served in the Cabinet as Secretary of State or Master-General, that the office of Secretary at War could be abolished, or its duties transferred—with any degree of safety—to a single Cabinet Minister overwhelmed with the whole Board work of the Ordnance, the Commissariat work of the Treasury, and the responsibility of office as a Secretary of State. On the contrary, *all* experience was against such destruction, and a warning voice

---

[1] See Papers by the late Mr John Croomes in the Appendix to the 'Army Expenditure, 1850,' and the Evidence of Mr George Collin, 'Army and Navy Appointments, 1833,' and the 'Report of Naval and Military Promotions, 1840'

[2] See the eight days' Evidence of Lord Panmure, at pp. 1-172, 'Army Expenditure, 1850'

was raised that the Parliamentary control would be "nominal; neither effective nor economical," and "the decisions of such a Minister of no authority with the Army"[1]

49. This Act, which may be said to have commenced in February, 1855, was consummated on the 4th May, 1863, when the 26th Vic, c. 12, received the Royal Assent, abolishing the office of Secretary at War and his Deputy and transferring the statutory duties,[2] with the execution 'of all Powers and Authorities," to the Secretary of State for the War Department and his Under Secretary.

Abolished 1854 to 1863

50. The abolition of the office of Secretary at War left duties of no inconsiderable importance without Parliamentary supervision, for the Minister standing between the Crown and Parliament in the affairs of the Army being removed, the administration of his office fell into irresponsible hands, either Military or Civil. How much security to the Civil community had been derived from the independent action of the Secretary at War in restraint of the Military power, some of the preceding pages of this work testify. That authority had been respected by the Army as emanating from a Minister acting on the *personal* instructions of the Sovereign, and enjoying the confidence of Parliament.

Secretary at War's duties unprovided for

51. Looking at the class in society from which the Officers were drawn, it was—to say the least of it—expedient that their individual pecuniary interests should be brought under the *personal* consideration of this Minister and be disposed of by him. Many of his decisions settled the future of as many persons' lives, and left them with time and opportunity to brood over their real or imaginary wrongs. If the votes for non-effective allowances increased, Parliament had the assurance, from the personal supervision of an experienced member of their own Assembly, that the increase was just or inevitable; and if these allowances were refused to any applicants, it was by the Minister himself, not by persons in a rival or a subordinate position to the claimant. The administration of these grants alone—irrespective of other business—brought upon the Secretary at War a

The claims of Officers to be dealt with by the Minister, and not by his subordinates.

---

[1] Lord Hardinge, 'Civil Administration,' 1837, p 26 [2] Appendix CXXXVI.

large amount of responsibility, both towards the Army and Parlment, a duty which he could only fulfil by a very careful consideration of every case that came before him.[1]

52 But the office of the Secretary at War was—as Lord Palmerston again and again repeats—one of " Law and Finance." The official channel by which—at all former periods of our history—great Constitutional functions[2] had been exercised for the Civil community against the Military power of the Crown. Possibly some may think that a Political Millenium has arrived, and hence that all safeguards against a Standing Army may be abandoned ; Law and Finance may be disregarded ; a Civil Minister be no longer needed, because his Civil functions may, with perfect safety, be entrusted to, and are better discharged by, Military Officers, than by Civilians Against such a view of this Political question, no arguments would avail with the believers in it , but if the Millenium exists here, the armed condition of Europe affords strong presumption that it does not exist elsewhere,—a fact which, if undisputed, may lead some readers to admit the expediency of governing the Army at home upon those principles of Law and Finance established at the Revolution and so firmly advocated by Lord Palmerston[3] in 1811.

(margin note: Secretary at War's office one of " Law and Finance")

---

[1] Chap IX , *ante*   [2] Chap XVI , par 71 *et seq*

[3] The Deputy Secretary at War was for many years a Barrister, and the Secretary at War had a legal adviser attached to the office, the late M· William Harrison (See Preface)

In reference to the War Office, it is curious to notice how Junius charges Lord Barrington with making appointments that would now be thought to be meritorious Of Bradshaw he writes, "Though an infant in the War Office, he is too old to learn a new trade" (Letter 109) vol iii , p 444 "For what signifies ability, or integrity, or practice, or experience in business, as he (Lord Barrington) feels himself uneasy while men with such qualifications are about him"—Letter 110, p 446

CHAPTER XXII.

THE ROYAL COMMISSIONERS OF CHELSEA HOSPITAL.

1. THE Establishment of Chelsea Hospital in the Reign of Charles II. has already been referred to,[1] but no mention has been made of a kindred Institution, the Hospital of Kilmainham, founded in Ireland at an earlier date in the same reign, and which afforded to the Soldiers on the Irish Establishment[2] the same refuge that Chelsea gave to the British Soldiers.

Hospitals—
(1) At Chelsea

2. The first endowment of this Hospital was by Royal Warrant of the 27th October, 1679, whereby " SIXpence in the pound was to be deducted from all pay, to be applied in building and settling an Hospital for such aged and maimed Officers and Soldiers as shall be dismissed out of Our Army as unserviceable men, and for making provision for their future maintenance." The lands of Kilmainham,—formerly belonging to the Knights Templars, but at that time enclosed by the walls of Phœnix Park,[3]—were thought to be the fittest place for the Hospital, and by another Royal Warrant, 9th April, 1681, were ordered to be so appropriated   This was carried into effect under an order of the Lord-Lieutenant, dated 23rd December, 1681, whereby part of the estate, not exceeding 64 acres, plantation measure. was to be applied to the use of the Hospital.   On the 25th March, 1684, as many soldiers as were qualified were appointed to lodge in it; and by letters patent of 19th February, 1686 (36 Car. II.), a charter was granted to the Governors, and the "Hospital of King Charles II, for ancient and maimed

(2) At Kilmainham

---

[1] Chap IV, par 49   [2] War Office Letter Bk, 1766, p 177
[3] As to proposal in 1834 to abolish this Hospital, see vol xlii. Parl Papers, p 127, 21 H D (3), p 1384

officers and soldiers of the Army of Ireland," established. A supplementary charter was granted by Geo. II. on 24th April, 1757.

3 Premising that the Pensions of Chelsea and Kilmainham now stand upon a similar footing,—the business of the two Boards being consolidated at Chelsea,[1]—I propose to give an outline of the duties of the Royal Commissioners of Chelsea Hospital, under the Prerogative and Statutory Powers conferred upon them in regard, first, to Soldiers' Pensions, and then to the distribution of Prize.

Annihilated, and pensions under the Chelsea Board

4. The Commissioners are appointed by the Crown under Letters Patent. At their original institution they were Civilians, and down to the end of the reign of Geo. III.[2] two Military Officers only were members of the Board, which consisted of the President of the Council, the First Lord of the Treasury, the Secretary of State, the Paymaster-General, the Secretary at War, the Comptrollers of Army Accounts, and of two Military Officers, viz, the Governor and Lieutenant-Governor of the Hospital. At the present time the Military element prevails at the Board meetings; the places of the Secretary at War and Comptrollers of Army Accounts are filled by the Adjutant-General—and his Deputy, the Quartermaster-General, and the Under-Secretaries of State for War have been added.

Chelsea Commissioners appointed by Patent.

5. The Instructions under which they act emanate from the Crown, and vary little in their outline from those in force in the reign of Geo. I.[3] In carrying them out, the Commissioners are guided by the Statute Law and Royal Warrants from time to time in force with reference to the special duties they have to perform.

Act under Instructions.

6. The Commissioners are not a corporation other than by Legal intendment; but by 7 Geo. IV., c. 16, sec. 44, the Crown has a Statutory Power to convey the fee simple of the Royal Hospital and premises to the Royal Commissioners, and they have power under the same Statute[4] to purchase lands for the improvement of the Hos-

Chelsea Hospital may be vested in the Royal Commissioners

---

[1] 7 Geo IV , c 16   [2] 19th Report of Military Enquiry, 1812, p. 404
Vol I , p. 366   [4] See 44

pital or the neighbourhood. They have also powers of leasing and of management under a later Act;[1] but the last sale or exchange made by the Commissioners appears to have been confirmed by Parliament.[2]

7. The Establishment for Chelsea Hospital is settled from time to time by Royal Warrant, the duties, emoluments, and qualifications of the Officers being prescribed by it. It is issued by the Treasury upon the advice and under the countersign of the Secretary of State for War.[3] The Royal Warrant, now in force, is dated 23rd June, 1862.[4]

Establishment for Chelsea Hospital settled by the Treasury

8. The sources from which the Royal Hospital was maintained prior to 1847 were threefold. First, the poundage from Pay, which was finally discontinued under the 10 & 11 Vic., c. 4.;[5] second, the residue of unclaimed Prize Money granted for the use of the Hospital, under 2 Wm. IV., c. 53, sec. 42; and, lastly, the Votes in supply made for the support of the Hospital and for the In and Out Pensioners. At the present time only the two latter sources exist, and the last will be the subject of the following observations

Sources of supply for its maintenance

9 No doubt, when established by Charles II., and until Queen Anne's reign, Chelsea Hospital was intended to contain all the Soldiers placed on pension, and to be maintained by the Poundage levied on the Pay of the Army. From a statement prepared and laid before the King on the 5th of March, 1689, it appeared that a muster had been taken "Of the men disabled by wounds in fight or other accident, or who having served the Crown twenty years, had been judged unfit for service," and that 579 men had been admitted on the Pension List "by the Commissary-General of Musters or his Deputy, upon the certificate of the Commanding Officers," at varying rates of Pension (from 1s. 8d. to 5d.), at the total cost of 6087l. 17s. 11d.

Original Intention as to the Poundage

---

[1] 6 & 7 Vic, c 31.   [2] 21 Vic, c. 18

[3] There is also a fund given by Colonel Drouly, and referred to in 1 and 2 Vic, c 89, and 6 and 7 Vic, c 31.   [4] Army Pensions (128) 14th March, 1865

[5] Chap IV, par. 49, and Appendices XVII and XVIII, 88 H D (3), p 560, 89 ib p. 485

10. The revenue was then given at 12,084*l*. 16s. 4*d*—
which, deducting the 6087*l*.17s 11*d*. and 1289*l* 11s 3*d*

Revenue
and charges
on it in
1689
as the cost of the Establishment, left 4734*l*. 7s. 1¼*d*
in favour of the Hospital, which was to be annually
applied to answer the charge of the new buildings. However,
when the Hospital was completed, only 472 men could be
accommodated, and 107 had to remain in out-quarters, unless—
as it was suggested—the 579 men, some of which were then in
eight invalid companies, were "reviewed," and sent back to
the Army,[1] or to serve in the forts or garrisons.

11. From a note on this Report, by Lord Ranelagh, under
A D 1703

State of the
Out-pen-
sioners
date of 1703, it would appear that this annual
balance and something more, had been appropriated
by Royal Order verbally given. A Report presented
on the 6th May, 1703, stated that the out-pensioners (only 98
in number) had not been settled with since the 1st July, 1696,
and that nothing could be paid to them out of the Hospital
Revenues.[2] This led to a reduction of four of the Invalid
Companies to 75 men in each company,[3] and when Marlborough, as Captain-General, sent seven men for pension, two
only could be taken into the house, and five were placed on
out-pension at 5*d* a day, until vacancies arose.[4]

12. I do not trace any Estimate for Chelsea Out-pension,
First Esti-
mate for
Chelsea Out-
pensioners
until the year 1712, when a Clerk from Mr How
(the Paymaster) presented to the House of Commons
—(1.) An Estimate up to the 21st December, 1713;
(2.) A Report as to the reduction of the Out-pensioners; (3.)
A draft of a new Establishment; (4.) Another Report from the
Paymaster-General, of February, 1712, as to the methods of
reduction.[5] In the Committee of Supply for that year,
61,464*l*. 5s. 7*d*. was voted for the Out-pensioners.[6] On the
6th April, 1713, the Commissioners addressed a letter to the
Treasury, recommending the reduction of all pensions to an

---

[1] Book of Instructions at Chelsea, pp 51, 57
[2] Chelsea Journal, p. 12, 2 and 3 Ann, c 10, sec 21
[3] Book of Instructions, p 72   [4] Chelsea Journal, pp 18, 19
[5] 17 Com Journ, pp 186, 391   1882 men of 20 years' service were dismissed
from Pension, as "not being visibly disabled by wounds and infirmities"
[6] Ib, p 141

uniform rate of 5*d.* per day. which was acted upon towards every Pensioner except letter-men. of whom 200 were in pension up to 1783, and 402 after that year[1] These letter-men were Sergeants from the Army appointed—as the Secretary at War contended, on his nomination—by the Commissioners.[2]

13. The charge for Chelsea is now included in the Non-effective Vote, and made up by the Secretary on the representation of the Commissioners acting through their Parliamentary Officer, the Paymaster-General.[3] It is, however, submitted to Parliament by the Secretary of State, and he would (I apprehend) have to answer for the expenditure (if challenged) as being made according to the Regulations in force for the Establishment of Chelsea, and for pensioning Soldiers[4]

[sidenote: Estimate for Chelsea.]

14. The power of giving any man a provision for life, however small in amount, is one that needs the vigilance of Parliament; and the increase of the Pension List since 1783 has raised an Army of *non-effective*—as well as of effective—soldiers.[5] In the early history of Parliamentary Grants, the number of Pensioners did not exceed 2000; in 1713, when reduction was suggested, the Commissioners ordered "that such men as had served thirty years in the Army, though not disabled by wounds, should be continued on the Out-pension," and then signed the List for 4102 men.[6] A fraudulent increase to 9109 by the Duke of Ormond was detected in 1714 by a Privy Council Enquiry,[7] which led in its result to the issue of the Regulations put forth at the commencement of the reign of George I.[8]

[sidenote: Importance that the power of pensioning men should be prudently exercised]

15. For many years Parliament had a security against the discharge of men for Pension which ceased in 1783.[9] It is

---

[1] Compare 39 Com Journ , p 245 with p 985

[2] Letters to Commissioners of Chelsea, as to the increase from 200 to 400 men in 1784 (254 Bk), pp 50, 52   In 1779 and 1785 (255), pp 591, 592

[3] 19th Report on Military Enquiry, p 387.

[4] Evidence before Committee on Army Expenditure, 1850, *passim*, Report 1851, pp 42-4, and Chap XXIII., par 2

[5] See Lord Hardinge's Evidence on Military Punishments, 1836, pp 305 to 508

[6] Chelsea Journal, p 20   [7] 'London Gazette,' 15 Jan , 1714 (No 5295)

[8] 8 Parl Hist , pp 929 934, and Vol I p 366, *ante*   [9] Chap XV par 7

not unlikely that every Colonel was proud of having hale and strong men in his Regiment, but as the Place of each Discharged man had to be supplied by a Recruit, raised at the cost of the Officers, their personal interests were promoted by keeping the men in the ranks —and therefore out of Pension—as long as possible And this fact may probably account for another, viz, that prior to 1783 there was no regulation in force shewing the exact amount of service to be performed by a soldier to entitle him to Discharge and Pension [1]

Security against the discharge of men for pension prior to 1783

16 It is gathered, by way of information, from the debate of 1717, that a service of 20 years *might*—with other circumstances—be held to entitle a soldier to a Pension,[2] but that such service alone was not a qualification. Prior to Mr. Wyndham's Act,[3] his claim rested solely upon the selection of the Crown[4] and the bounty of Parliament, it being held that the soldier had *no right* whatever to Pension. The selection was made by the Commissioners, but they were guided in their choice by the discharge documents and the good-conduct certificates given by the Commanding officers.[5]

What service entitled a man to pension

17. From the Pension system now existing,—which has been brought about by the operation of Mr. Burke's and Mr. Wyndham's Acts combined,—the Army occupies a very different position towards Parliament to that which it assumed throughout the last century. In that period the members of the *effective* and non-effective soldiers combined were less in total than the present number of Pensioners. Neither was Parliament under any positive pledge to maintain a vast Army of Pensioners for life—so soon as each man under enlistment had completed a certain number of years, and whether that service was given—in the Mess Room, or as an Officer's servant, or in the Field before the enemy.

The pension system under Mr Burke's and Mr Wyndham's Acts.

---

[1] In going over the Chelsea Register for the early part of the last century, the great age of the Candidates is a noticeable feature

[2] 8 Parl. Hist., p 943

[3] As to this, see Lord Palmerston's Evidence before the Finance Committee, 1828, and Lord Hardinge's Evidence, vol 1, p 367

[4] Military Punishments Committee, 1836, p 365 *et seq*   [5] 19th Report, p 107.

18. The number of Out-pensioners in the year 1782[1] was 11,907—and in 1795 16,955—(men all liable to serve in the Invalid or Garrison Battalions, at the call of the country), and their total cost 85,586*l.* and 114,136*l.* Increase of the Pension List. The number of Out-pensioners prior to the operation of Mr. Wyndham's Act in 1806, and after a war of nearly 13 years (which included the campaign of 1794 on the continent, the campaign in the Leeward Islands, and St. Domingo, Egypt, and India),

Amounted to 21,689 men, and the cost to .. £181,402
but which was immediately increased by the
King's Warrant, of Oct., 1806, under the
Act, to ..   ..   379,642[2]
In 1816 to 39,217 men, and the cost   .   ..   707,575
In 1826 to 82,734 men, and the cost   1,372,330
In 1828 to 85,515 men, and the cost   ..   ..   1,437,756[3]

And when the Government called out the Pensioners in 1819, some members of the House of Commons argued that the Proclamation was an infringement of Mr. Wyndham's Act, which —though it gave the soldier an absolute right to pension— did not give the Crown any right to future service from the Pensioner.[4]

19. The Statutory Powers of the Commissioners, so far as they need be here referred to, commence with the 7 George IV., c. 16, which repealed Mr Wyndham's Act, consolidated the Law, and placed the payment of Pensions, allowances, and relief granted to disabled, invalid, and discharged soldiers—including the Out-pensions of Kilmainham —under the management, control, and authority of the *Chelsea* Commissioners, and empowered them to make rules and regulations in relation thereto.[5] A.D 1826
Acts repealed and consolidated

---

[1] 34th Report of Finance Committee, 1798, p 595.
[2] Compare 60 Com Journ , p 609, with 62 ib , p 422
[3] So that the increase of this charge was nearly in the ratio of an arithmetical progression or inversity to that of the effective Army, for while the latter decreased the former proportionably augmented Sir W Gordon's Evidence before the Finance Committee, 17th March, 1828, p 7, and Lord Hardinge's Evidence, *ut sup*
[4] 41 H. D (O S), p. 1402   [5] Chap XIV , pars 161-170, *ante*

20. As introductory to the provisions of this Act, it may be remarked that the Commissioners had been recognised by Parliament as the Paymasters of the Pension Force—first, in the year 1754 by the 28 Geo II., c. 1,[1] and then in 1817 by the 57 George III., c 77, which latter Act authorised them, on proof of fraud with respect to the receipt of Pension, or of other gross misconduct by a Pensioner, to suspend or entirely take away the pension of the offender.

Commissioners of Chelsea Hospital formerly the paymasters of the Pensioners.

21. Under the Consolidated Statute the Kilmainham Commissioners are to act as a branch Board to Chelsea, they are required to sit once a month, and to transmit to the Chelsea Commissioners the particulars of any claims of Pensions submitted to them The admission of In-pensioners to their own Hospital is, however, left to the Kilmainham Commissioners.

As to Kilmainham Commissioners.

22. The Act lays down this main principle for the protection of the Soldier:—that every pension shall be granted according to the orders and regulations in force at the time of his enlistment; and that (subject to any existing rights) he is to receive his Pension under the provisions of the Act, or of any rules or regulations made by the Commissioners in pursuance thereof.[2]

Pension granted according to the Regulations in force on enlistment.

23. That no person guilty of misconduct may be found on the Pension List, the Commissioners—upon complaint and proof of any fraud with respect to the claiming, obtaining, or receiving any Pension, or of other gross misconduct attempted or practised by any Pensioner, or person claiming as such—are empowered to suspend or take away the Pensions, or altogether reject, or refuse, the title or claim to Pension of the person so offending. So, also, if any In-pensioner be convicted of felony or misdemeanour, or so misconduct himself as to be undeserving, in the judgment of the Commissioners, of continuing a Pensioner, he may be removed and expelled from the Hospital [3]

Commissioners power to strike off the Pension List.

---

[1] 15 Parl Hist, p 374   [2] Secs 10 and 12

[3] The 11 Geo I, and 1 Wm IV, c 41, sec 4, authorises the restoration of such person by the Commissioners

24. An assignment of a Soldier's pension, with certain exceptions[1] that are provided for by this and subsequent Statutes, is declared void. The first assignment permitted by Parliament was to the Crown, in consideration of a certain sum paid to the Pensioner by way of commutation for all future claim to pension. The principle was an old one—introduced into the Commissioners' patent, granted in Anne's reign, and exercised at their first sitting under it[2]   In 1812 it was revived as applicable to Foreign Soldiers, and the 52 Geo III., c. 109, passed to enable the Commissioners to pay those pensioners, a capital sum in liquidation of all future payments. and the same power,—limited to foreigners,—was continued in the Act now under notice.[3] *Assignments void, with certain exceptions*

25. In 1830 the principle of commutation was extended to any Out-pensioner who was recommended to the Commissioners by a Royal Order (under the hand of the Secretary at War) as desirous of living abroad; and the 11 Geo. IV, and 1 Wm. IV., c 41, sec. 2, authorised the Commissioners to pay him a sum not exceeding the amount of four years' pension, as a commutation, or gross equivalent for his pension, and in entire satisfaction of all future claim on the Crown. The object was to promote emigration, and to enable Pensioners to settle in the Colonies with the money thus realised. The provisions of the Act were abused,[4] and the manner in which the power had been exercised was so generally condemned in several debates in Parliament, that it was found to be both expedient and just to place again upon the Pension List[5] some persons who had commuted their pensions *Commuting pensions for a gross sum*

26. The other instances of assignment arise out of the 19 Vic., c. 15, which provides for two cases,—payment (1) to wives or children, (2) to parishes for maintaining pauperism or lunacy. *Assignments for special purposes sanctioned by Parliament*

[1] 28 Geo II , c 1, and 7 Geo IV , c 16, s 26
[2] "26 Feb , 1705, 2l paid Arthur Miles for all claims on the Hospital for the loss of his leg" (Chelsea Journal, p 2), see also a similar payment to Robert Preston, p 5   [3] Secs 17 to 19.
[4] Lord Hardinge's Evidence before Military Punishment Committee, 1836, p 307
[5] War Office Memorandum (36,546), 1st March, 1831, 11 H D (3) p 1190, 14 ib (3), p 1092, 91 ib (3), pp 709-19, 93 ib p 1692, 1817

27. For the first object, the Act authorizes[1] the Secretary at War "with the consent of any Pensioner residing temporarily out of the United Kingdom, to pay to or for the benefit of his wife, or, if he have no wife, to or for the benefit of his child or children, such portion of his Pension as may be agreed upon; and the receipt or acknowledgment of the person or persons to whom the same shall be paid shall be a full and sufficient discharge to the said Secretary at War for the amount so issued by him."

(1) Assignments to wives

28. For the second object, as to parishes[2]—for general relief,—the Act provides[3] that if any Pensioner be relieved, or become chargeable in Great Britain or Ireland (in respect of relief afforded to himself, or to any person whom he is liable to maintain), or if in any case the Secretary at War and the Guardians, or the Heritors, think it desirable that the whole or any part of the pension of such Pensioner should be advanced out of the poor's rate or funds applicable to the relief of the poor, it shall be lawful for the Secretary at War, by any writing under his hand, to agree with such Guardians or Heritors for the repayment to them out of the pension of the amount of relief so advanced to or expended on his account, not exceeding in any case where relief has been administered to his wife or one child only, whom he is bound to maintain, the amount of one-half, or where such relief has been administered to two or more such children, or to his wife and one or more such child or children, the amount of two-thirds of his pension so advanced.

(2) To Parishes for general relief.

29. For relief in lunacy, the Act further provides,[4]—In case any Pensioner shall become insane, the Secretary at War may order the pension, or so much thereof as shall appear to be necessary for his care and maintenance, to be paid to the Guardians, or Heritors, or to the wife, child, or any other person to whom the care of such insane Pensioner may be entrusted, or who may be chargeable for or liable to

In case of lunacy

---

[1] Sec 7.

[2] Application is sometimes made to the Secretary at War, under 12 & 13 Vic , c. 103, for sums of money due as pension, to be applied in the Pensioner's maintenance or burial, but the Act stated in the text is the expressed intention of the Legislature on the subject   [3] Sec 8   [4] Sec. 9.

the expense of his care and maintenance; but that where no claim or demand shall be made for the support of the insane Pensioner, or where the charge for his care and maintenance does not amount to the full rate of his pension, then the Secretary at War, at his discretion, may order his pension, or part of it to be paid to his wife or child or children, if he have any.

30. This Act assumes (as the fact is) that prior to its enactment the payment of Pensions had been transferred from the Chelsea Commissioners into the hands of Officers acting under the Secretary at War. The transfer was made by the 5 & 6 Vic., c. 70, and the manner in which it was effected has been already shown in an earlier part of the work.[1] The discipline of the enrolled men was also transferred to the Secretary at War by the 6 & 7 Vic., c. 95, and subsequent Statutes; but, notwithstanding these Acts, the Chelsea Commissioners still have the sole responsibility of admitting and continuing Pensioners upon the Pension List.

Payment of pensions transferred to Secretary at War and Staff Officers.

31. This, if before doubtful, is clear by the last Statute (19 Vic., c 15), which—though it authorizes the Secretary at War to make such rules and regulations[2] for the management and payment of the Outpensioners as appear best calculated for their and the public advantage—expressly declares[3] that nothing in it contained "shall be held to interfere with the powers of the Chelsea Commissioners in regard to granting, increasing, reducing, suspending, taking away or restoring of pension, or to abridge, take away, or interfere with any power, authority, or duty of the said Commissioners other than by the Act is expressly provided;" intending obviously to preserve the Pension system free from political purposes[4]

Other powers of the Commissioners not infringed upon

32. Before quitting the subject of the Statute Law relating to Chelsea Pensioners, it may be well to notice, though not administered by the Commissioners, the 5 & 6 Vic., c. 70, sec. 2, which, on the death of the Pensioner, authorizes the Secretary at War to pay any arrear of pension due at his death, 1st for the funeral, and then to such person as the Pensioner shall have appointed to receive it; and

On death, distribution of pensioners' estate.

---

[1] Chap XIV, paras 161-168   [2] Sec 2   [3] Sec 4   [4] But see Chap. XIV, par 164.

that the 10th sec. of the 19th Vic , c. 15, authorizes him to pay, without probate, to any person or persons who shall prove him, her, or themselves, to be the next of kin or legal representative of, or otherwise legally entitled thereto, the amount of the pension money, not exceeding fifty pounds.

33. With reference to the Warrants and Regulations relating to Pensions, it has been noticed that the Statute Law gives every Soldier the advantage of any Regulation as to pension that was in force at the time of his original enlistment   Of these Regulations there may be several, but none (I apprehend) in practical operation of an earlier date than Mr. Wyndham's Warrant of the 7th October, 1806.[1]   The arrangements made by it were greatly to the prejudice of the Public, or to the advantage of the Soldier, according to the point of view from which the subject is considered.[2]   It cannot be disputed but that he largely increased both the amount and the number of the Pensions.   Further—which few people would complain of—he laid down definite rules for the guidance of the Commissioners, in lieu of an indefinite instruction to pension " worn-out Soldiers "

A.D 1806
The Pension Regulations of Mr Wyndham

34. To improve the condition of the Non-commissioned Officers and Soldiers, he divided the enlistment into three periods, with an encouragement to every Soldier —by increase of pay, and by acquiring a pension right—to enter into the successive periods of enlistment until twenty-one years in infantry or twenty-four years in cavalry service had been completed.[3]   The whole tendency of his measure was towards *long* service, but obtained from the Soldier at a higher rate of pay and pension than had before been granted by Parliament for the same service.

The outline of his system.

35 The first period was .	7	10 and	12	years
The second .	7	7	5	„
The third . .	7	7	5	„
Making these totals of .	21	24	22	

Three periods of enlistment to complete 21 or 24 years

Pension after 2nd period

[1] See Vol I , p 368, *ante*

[2] See the Remarks of the Finance Committee, 1817 (2nd Report, p 53)

[3] See Chap. XV , pars 83-7, 151

for Infantry, Cavalry, and Artillery. The Warrant gave the Soldier a pension, after the second or last period, for *service* only, without wounds or disability, and, indeed, in some instances *without* actual service.[1]   Thus, if discharged *during* the second period, the Soldier, subsequent to such discharge, might reckon, for two years' absence, one year for pay and pension, to make up the second period, and be entitled to a pension at the close of it.   Of course this assumed that the Soldier was discharged for the convenience of the State,—that he registered his name and address with the Commissioners (which, it must be noticed, very few cared to do),[2]—and that, on a Proclamation desiring his service, he came forward to serve, or, on being required to do so, joined a Garrison or Veteran Battalion.

36. The same rules were applicable to men—not receiving a pension as invalid, wounded, or disabled Soldiers— discharged during the third period, with this further advantage, that they at once enjoyed their pension accruing on the second term.   After discharge on the completion of the three full periods, they were not liable to serve upon the call of the Crown or of the Commissioners; but they were at liberty to continue their service in the ranks, and had an extra pension for each year's service beyond the full periods   In the East or West Indies two were reckoned for three years' service towards pay and pension, but not for discharge. {.sidenote: Pension after 3rd period}

37. Soldiers discharged as disabled or unfit for Service had special rates of pension, graduated according to their inability to earn a livelihood, or their ability to earn something towards it, or materially to assist themselves or to earn a livelihood.   If the disability arose during the third period of Service, an increase was granted to disability rates; but no man was to be allowed to claim of right any such pension whose disability or unfitness arose from vice or misconduct.   No Pension for Service was to be forfeited *except* by sentence of Court-martial:—though the Commissioners could move the {.sidenote: Special pension for disability}

---

[1] If a soldier be taken prisoner in war, both his pay and pension cease during the period of his imprisonment, unless it be proved to a Court-martial that the event happened without any neglect of duty on his part   31 H D (O S), 831, 30 & 31 Vic, c 24, sec 6   [2] 20th Report of Finance Committee, 1817

Pensioner from one to another rate of pension, or oblige him to serve for the completion of the period of his Enlistment

38 The immediate effect of the Warrant was—as already
The Warrant caused a great increase of expense
shown—to add a large increase of charge to the Effective and Non-effective Vote; and the total cost, in a year or two after it came into full operation, has been variously estimated as ranging between 1,300,000*l* and 500,000*l* per annum. Whether any fair equivalent was ever received for the vast increase in Military expenditure may be questioned. Certainly two or more enlistments for *long* service conduce to extravagance, and if the operation of the Act of 1847 be traced in its financial results it will probably be found to have added to the cost of raising and of retaining men in the Service.

39 At the conclusion of the War, the whole subject of
A.D 1817
Results of Warrant reviewed by the Finance Committee.
Pension and the vast increase of expense came under the notice of the Finance Committee in 1817, and in their second Report they suggested some modification of Mr Wyndham's arrangements. The Royal Warrant of February 1818, as applicable to Soldiers enlisting after the 14th March then next ensuing, may be considered as based on their recommendations. The limitations imposed were these: the Pension was not to exceed the rate of full pay enjoyed by the Soldier on his discharge; Service in the East and West Indies was to reckon as ordinary Service; years of absence were not to reckon, but only years of *actual* service. As the reduction of the Army was the Policy of Parliament, small pensions were offered to men leaving the Service before their full period of twenty-one or twenty-four years were completed.[1] And, lastly, the disability to entitle to Pension must have been contracted *on Service.*[2]

40. By the Warrant of August, 1823, the principle appears

---

[1] This boon was revoked by the Warrant of March, 1822.
[2] See 7th Report of Finance Committee, 1818, p. 17

to have been established that after twenty-one or twenty-four years' full Service had been completed, the Soldier might be discharged, as of course, by his Commanding Officer, and a Pension awarded to him without appearing before the Chelsea Board.[1]

A D 1823
Warrant of August dispensing with appearance at Chelsea.

41. After the consolidation of the Statute Law in 1826, Lord Hardinge consolidated the Pension Regulations in November, 1829. He dealt with Discharge as well as Pension, and enabled a good Soldier to work out his discharge, either with or without a gratuity; but he refused to discharge a bad Soldier, except with disgrace. Thus he raised the tone and morâle of each Regiment.[2] The Regulations were framed with the desire to diminish the Pension List, and "to take service and character as the principal ingredients for Pension, and not disability." A Regimental Record of each Soldier was to be kept by the Colonel (in like manner as a similar Record is kept of each officer by the General), from which his discharge papers were to be made up and signed by the Commanding Officer.[3]

A.D 1829
Pension Regulations of Lord Hardinge.

42. In February, 1833, the Ministry of Earl Grey revised the Pension Regulations — reducing the amount of Pension and increasing the term of Service to twenty-five and twenty eight years, unless at twenty-one or twenty-four years the Soldier could be shown to be incapable of further Service. No doubt the tendency of this Warrant was materially to reduce the Pension Vote, but Lord Hardinge opposed it as prejudicial to recruiting.[4] However, the warrant remained in force until 1847, and no want of Recruits was experienced.

A D. 1833
The Pension Regulations of Earl Grey's Ministry

43. The Warrant of 23rd July, 1863,—which contains the Pension Regulations at present in force,—was laid before Parliament in March, 1865, and, therefore, is so readily accessible that it would be useless to place

A.D. 1863.
Warrant of July

---

[1] See Lord Hardinge's Evidence on Military Punishments, 1836, p. 305
[2] 11 H D (3, pp 1188-1227   [3] Military Punishments, 1836, p 305-7
[4] Ib., pp 306, 307, and Chap XV par 127 *et seq*

the detail of it in these pages. The Discharge of the Soldier is dealt with by the Warrant, and the offences or misconduct by the commission of which he forfeits his claim to Pension— or forfeits it when granted—are fully set out.

44. It will have been noticed that Mr. Wyndham introduced a system of giving Pension for *years of absence* upon certain conditions: one of such being that the Pensioner should enter his name at Chelsea Hospital as a man ready and willing to rejoin the Army for Service. That system was repudiated by the Finance Committee of 1817, but revived in the year 1847 with no practical result. When a man seeks his discharge from the Army, his motive may reasonably be assumed to be his distaste, either in peace or war, for the occupation of a soldier (in which he has been trained, and in which he has become a proficient), or he would never leave a certain for an uncertain future subsistence.

Pension without actual service revised

45. How *earnestly* a Discharge from the Service is sought for by some men is evidenced by facts.[1] "When men maim themselves, or commit crimes," said Lord Hardinge, "as they have done in some instances, to obtain their discharge, and even to become convicts, as was the case in New South Wales a few years ago, the men were ordered to remain to perform the duties of scavengers to the rest of the Regiment, according to the old custom of the Service, formally authorized by the Articles of War in 1829. A Commanding Officer lately complained that he had six or seven of these maimed men, who were a dead weight and disgrace; but the example is so important, that the Commander-in-Chief has, I understand, not given way, but has directed the Commanding Officer to keep them as long as they live in the sight of the Regiment as a warning to others to avoid the same fate."

Men earnestly desire their discharge

46 The Pension Regulations of 1863, by providing against, shew that the same offences exist: they declare that— "A soldier found guilty by Court-martial of either of the following offences, forfeits all claim to reckon his Service anterior to such conviction for Pension or Discharge[2]   .   ."

Self mutilation punished.

[1] 'Military Punishments,' 1856, p 396
[2] See also the Articles of War, 1869 (par. 81)

"(2). Of wilfully maiming or injuring himself, or any other soldier, whether at the instance of such other soldier or not, or of causing himself to be maimed or injured by any other person with intent to render himself, or such other soldier, unfit for Service.

"(3). Of tampering with his eyes, with intent thereby to render himself unfit for Service."

47. Notwithstanding these facts, after Wyndham's attempt failed, another was made in 1847, to form a "Reserve Force" by granting discharges after 14 years' service, with the condition that the man should register his name at Chelsea for a defined Pension of 4*d.* a day upon attaining 50 years of age; and the 10 & 11 Vic., c. 54, sec. 2, gave the Crown a right to enrol these men as a Reserve Force. As an additional bait to enter a "Reserve," and to become Pensioners, the 22 and 23 Vic., c. 42, was passed; and although the terms offered by the Warrant of the 9th December, 1859,[1] for this service were extremely liberal to the men, and expensive to the Public, this attempt to establish such a Reserve was a "complete failure."[2]

Reserve to be formed out of discharged men.

48. That men of bad character are ready aspirants to join the Reserve, experience proves; but whether men deliberately leaving the Army will, on settling in Civil life, place their lives at the service of the State for Foreign Service in time of war is chimerical. It does not at all follow, with the temptations offered, that men may not enrol in the Reserve as they do in the Militia, but where embodied Service is called for, many may be unable or unwilling to serve the State. To have a dormant Army of Pensioners, under the belief that on Proclamation they will come forward for Service abroad, amounts (I venture to think) almost to credulity.

Expediency doubtful.

49. In writing of the duties undertaken by the Chelsea Commissioners in the distribution of Prize,[3] a few sentences may be needed to explain the General Law under which Grants of Prize are made.

Duties of the Commissioners in matters of prize.

---

[1] Return (308) 19th May, 1864, and Vol. I, p 341.
[2] Report of Recruiting Commissioners, 1867, p xv, Chap XIV., par 171 *et seq*
[3] Report of General Officers, July, 1863   See Mis Book, 1862 pp 108-115

50. When the expenses of the War were borne by the Crown —which might have been the case before the appropriation of the Supplies in William III's reign—the spoils of War belonged to the Crown, as part of the Personal rather than of the Public Revenue. In that aspect of the case, the disposition of the Prize was made by the Articles of War,[1] and Parliament was not called upon to interfere.

Prize the sole property of the Crown prior to the appropriation of supplies.

51 But after the Appropriation Acts were recognised as separating the Public from the Private Revenue of the Crown, and the expenses of the War were provided by Parliament, then the Crown dealt with Prize as a Trustee for the Public. The House of Commons appointed Commissioners of Prize,[2] and by aiding them with Statutory Powers,[3] the sanction of Parliament was given to this distribution. However, subject to this change of circumstances, the Constitutional rule remains as it was before the Revolution, viz., that the Crown has the absolute disposition of all Prize of War.

After this appropriation the Crown only a Trustee

52. Now this right of the Crown is a Public right, conferred by the Constitution, "not for private purposes or for personal splendour, but for the Public Service: to answer the great exigencies of Public interest, and the claims of Public Justice."[4] Neither is this attribute of Sovereignty conferred without reason; it is given—as will afterwards be shown—as supplementary to the higher attributes of Peace and War.[5]

Prize to be used for the public advantage

53. The rule upon this subject cannot be better stated than in the words of the late Lord Stowell, in a case where the plenary rights of the Crown were brought under controversy—"Prize is altogether a creature of the Crown. No man has, or can have, any interest but what he takes as the mere gift of the Crown; beyond the extent of that gift he has nothing. This is the principle of law on the subject, and founded on the

Rule stated by Lord Stowell

---

[1] Section 25 of Articles of War, 1672 —"In what place soever it shall please God that the Enemy shall be subdued and overcome, all the Ordnance, Amunition and Victuals that shall be there found shall be secured for Our use, and for the better relief of the Army, and one-tenth part of the spoil shall be laid apart towards the relief of the sick and maimed Soldiers."

[2] 14 Com Journ, pp 387, 388, 410, 411   [3] 4 & 5 Wm III, c. 25, 6 Anne, c. 64.   [4] The Elsebe, Sir W Scott 5 Rob Rep, p 177   [5] Ib., p 181

wisest reasons. The right of making War and Peace is exclusively in the Crown. The acquisitions of War belong to the Crown, and the disposal of these acquisitions may be of the utmost importance for the purposes both of War and Peace. This is no peculiar doctrine of our Constitution; it is universally received as a necessary principle of public jurisprudence by all writers on the subject. *Bello parta cedunt reipublica.*"

54. It was then contended that the Crown could not recal or revoke a general grant of Prize made in favour of cap- tors; but—having once made the grant—that the power of the Crown was exhausted. After shewing that this Sovereignty was vested in the Crown—as an inherent Prerogative incident to the right of deciding on Peace or War, and therefore to be used in the most beneficial manner for the purposes of both—Lord Stowell laid down that all principles and all forms of law, together with all considerations of Public Policy, support the right of the Crown to interfere until the Prize is actually disbursed.[1]

Right of the Crown not extinguished till the prize be paid.

55. The same Propositions were stated with great force by Lord Brougham, in the year 1831:[2]—"That Prize is clearly and distinctly the property of the Crown, that the Sovereign in this Country, the executive Government in all countries, in whom is vested the power of levying the Forces of the State, and of making War and Peace, is alone possessed of all property in Prize, is a principle not to be disputed. It is equally incontestable that the Crown possesses this property *pleno vire*, absolutely and without control; that it may deal with it entirely at its pleasure; may keep it for its own use, may abandon it or restore it to the enemy, or, finally, may distribute it in whole, or in part, among the persons instrumental in its capture, making that distribution according to whatever scheme, and under whatever regulations and conditions, it sees fit."

Rule stated by Lord Brougham.

56. Upon the second question which had been raised in that case, whether the grant having once been made, the Crown could either vary or revoke it, Lord Brougham

The 2nd Rule also stated.

---

[1] P 192

[2] Alexander *v* Duke of Wellington, 2 Russ and Mylne, p 49, the Deccan, 2 Knapp, P C C, p 35.

continued —" Whether, where that act has once been completed, and it distinctly appears that the Crown was minded to depart with the property finally and irrevocably; whether, even in that case, the same paramount and transcendant power of the Crown might not enure to the effect of preserving to His Majesty the right of modifying or altogether revoking the grant, is a question which has never yet arisen, and which, when it does arise, will be found to have been determined in the negative. But this, at all events, is clear; that when the Crown, by an act of grace and bounty, departs, for certain purposes, and subject to certain modifications, with the property in prize, it by that act plainly signifies its intention that the Prize shall continue subject to the power of the Crown, as it was before the act was done"

57. The title of the party claiming Prize must therefore
No claim can be set up against the Crown for prize in all cases be the act of the Crown, by which the Royal pleasure to grant the Prize shall have been signified. *Against* the Crown no rights can be obtained :—" Is there," continued Lord Brougham, " a shadow of pretence for asserting that, as against the Crown, or against trustees standing in the place of the Crown, prize is a matter of right and not of bounty? Such a decision will be sought for in vain The only question—and I doubt whether in a matter so purely the creature of the Crown it be a question—is, whether, inasmuch as the arrangement is revocable up to the last moment, the Crown could Constitutionally render it irrevocable."

58. The grant is made by Royal Warrant to the Army in
Grant made by Royal Warrant, and the terms of it. certain definite shares and proportions; but, as many difficulties may arise in the course of the distribution, an authority is generally given by the Warrant to the Secretary of State or some other officer of the Crown, to decide such questions. The clause in the recent grants of Indian Prize, was as follows[1] :—

" And we are graciously pleased to order and direct, that in case any doubt shall arise in respect of the distribution of

---

[1] Prize Report, 1864, p xxi

the booty, the same shall be determined by the Secretary of State for India in Council, or by such person or persons to whom he shall refer the same, which determination thereupon made shall be notified in writing to the Commissioners of our Treasury, and the same shall be final and conclusive, unless within three months after the receipt thereof we shall be pleased otherwise to order."

59. Independently of this tribunal, there is power, under a comparatively recent statute, to send the adjudication on matters of Prize to the Court of Admiralty. A course that was taken with so much advantage in the Banda and Kirwee booty.[1] The jurisdiction is conferred on the Admiralty Court by the 3 and 4 Vic., c. 65, in these words :— *Statutory Jurisdiction of the Judge of the Court of Admiralty.*

"The High Court of Admiralty shall have jurisdiction to decide all matters and questions concerning booty of war, or the distribution thereof, which it shall please Her Majesty, her heirs and successors, by the advice of her and their Privy Council, to refer to the judgment of the said Court; and in all matters so referred, the Court shall proceed as in cases of Prize of War; and the judgment of the Court shall be binding upon all parties concerned."

60. The Statute[2] under which Prize is distributed is based on these recognised principles, and declares—that in all future captures the Officers and men shall have such right and interest therein as shall be established by the Crown. But before any such grant is made, the Officer in Chief Command is to appoint agents for the collection and realization of the booty by sale, and, within one month after receiving the money realized, these agents are to transmit the amount to Chelsea Hospital *Statute law consolidated.*

61 From the money so received, the Chelsea Commissioners are authorized to deduct 5*l* per cent for their expenses in distribution and to aid the general purposes of the Hospital. The residue is to be distributed at the end *Distribution by the Chelsea Commissioners*

---

[1] 1 L L (Admiralty Cases), p 109, 12 Jur (N S), p 819, 35 Law Journ (A C), p 17

[2] 2 Wm IV, c 53, sec 2, see 'Report of Royal Commissioners on Army Prize, 1861'

of three months, or as soon after as the distribution is practicable.[1] After the receipt of the whole Prize money, the Commissioners are to keep open an office daily from 10 till 4 o'clock, free of all charge to the recipients of Prize.

62. The Act then lays down the manner in which Prize is

Manner of distribution to be paid to the claimant, or to his assignees or administrators while alive—the Regimental Agent being here recognised as the proper person to act for the Soldier in regard to the remuneration paid for Agency by the Public.[2] Upon the death of the claimant, all Regimental or Public debts due from the deceased may be deducted by the Commissioners[3] on the Secretary at War's certificate of the amount. The residue may be paid to a creditor, holding administration to the extent of his debt;[4] and the balance (if any) under 50*l.* may be distributed to the next of kin, without probate or letters of Administration.[5]

63. Prize that is not legally demanded within six years after

Prize forfeited to be applied to the use of Chelsea Hospital the same shall have been paid to the Chelsea Commissioners (but how it is to be demanded at all before the Commissioners have taken action by public advertisement, for distribution is not apparent) and Prize that would be payable to Deserters is forfeited[6] to the use of the Chelsea Commissioners for the general service and expenses of the Royal Hospital.

64. The Act contains Clauses applicable to Prize taken in con-

As to prize, conj int as to the Army and Navy, and the Royal Army and Indian Forces joint expeditions of the Navy and Army,[7] and to secure the Share or proportion awarded to the Army being paid to the Treasurer of the Commissioners. But, with regard to Prize taken conjointly by the Troops of the East India Company and of the Crown in India, no such Statutory provisions were made. If the Army of the Crown in India made the capture, or was acting, even by one soldier only, with the army of the East India Company, all Prize taken became the property of the Crown, but if the capture was made by the Company's troops alone, then, under the Letters

---

[1] Sec. 27   [2] Secs 19, 20, 22, 'Army Expenditure,' 1850, p 373.
[3] Sec 27, and Chap X, par. 19   [4] Sec 28   [5] 27 & 28 Vic c. 36, sec. 3.
[6] Secs. 8, 42   [7] Secs, 29, 33

Patent of George II. (1758), the Prize belonged to the Company. In either case, the Prize was granted by the Crown or the Company to the captors, in fair and equitable proportions, through the Company or Government in India.[1]

65. In such cases where the Grants had been originally made through the agency of the East India Company, *Distribution of Indian Prize by the Chelsea Commissioners* or of the Secretary of India, and the distribution in England had been entrusted to the Chelsea Commissioners, the Statutory Provisions of the 2 William IV, c. 53, did not apply. In 1866, when this view of the matter came under notice, it was thought desirable to apply for an extension of the Act to Indian Prize, and for a Parliamentary Indemnity to the Chelsea Commissioners for their distribution of Indian Prize, made upon an analogy of the Statute Law as contained in the 2 Wm. IV., c. 53. The result of the application is embodied in the 29 and 30 Vic., c. 47.

66. Before closing this Chapter, I cannot do better than call the reader's attention to a Note on the subject of this Chapter, which is printed in the Appendix, and for *Conclusion* which I am indebted to the Secretary of the Chelsea Commissioners.[2] I have besides added an account of the Royal Military Asylum at Chelsea,[3] and of the Hibernian School,[4] Dublin—and also—as germane to the provision for disabled Officers and Soldiers—of the Royal Patriotic Fund.[5]

---

[1] 'Report of the Royal Commissioners on Army Prize,' 1864, Questions 167, 168
[2] Appendix, Note P P.   [3] Note R R   [4] Note S S   [5] Note Q Q

CHAPTER XXIII.

THE OFFICE OF PAYMASTER-GENERAL.

1. THIS office is coeval with the Army, for the holder of it was
the custodian of such moneys as Parliament raised for
carrying on the War, in respect whereof he was appointed the Paymaster.[1] His office was therefore originally looked upon as Parliamentary, and the Paymaster-General became associated with the Secretary at War in preparing and bringing in the Army Estimates : first by order, and then upon address from the House of Commons.[2] In this aspect of his relationship towards Parliament, those proceedings were taken against him by the House of Commons which have been already referred to in an earlier portion of this Work.[3]

Office of Paymaster-General coeval with the Army

2. This Parliamentary responsibility was soon, however, abandoned. In the Debate of 1743, his Office was described as purely Ministerial, and it was admitted that he was bound to obey the orders and directions of the Treasury.[4] The Finance Committee of 1797 took the same view, and reported to Parliament that the Paymaster-General had no active control over the Public Expenditure, it being his duty to make payments ministerially and without discretion, in pursuance of Warrants directed to him by the Secretary at War or the Treasury,[5] and lastly, the Committee on Public Moneys, 1857, went so far as to recommend that the Paymaster-General should cease to be a Political Officer acting

Office purely Ministerial.

---

[1] See the complaints of the Earl of Leicester against the Treasurer of the Wars in the Low Countries, Cottonian Library, Galba, D 1, p 54   As to the Treasurer of the Wars in the Rebellion, see 2 Com. Journ , pp 338, 355, 582, 695, 711 , 4 Com Journ., pp. 38, 42, 85, 149, 161, 166

[2] 10 Com Journ , pp 278, 288, 431

[3] Chap. VII , par 16 *et seq*

[4] 13 Parl. Hist., p 14

[5] 19th Report, p 356

by deputy, but become the Head of the Pay Office, performing his duties in person.[1]

3. It has been already noticed, that the Paymaster-General was originally the Banker of the Crown and Parliament, in regard to the moneys voted for Army Services.[2] After the Revolution it became his duty, on the orders of the Treasury, to disburse these moneys through his Deputies on Foreign Stations, and through the Regimental Agents at home. The Books and Papers of the Office were his own private property; but he was an Accountant to the Crown, and in that character held in his hands large balances, till his accounts were delivered to and passed by the Auditors of Imprest. *Originally the Banker for Army supplies.*

4. The scandal that resulted from this system, and the loss of interest and of security that the public sustained by large sums of public money being withdrawn from the Exchequer and retained by the Paymaster-General for his own advantage, were reasons that induced Mr. Burke to frame a Bill for the better regulation of the office. Under this Act,[3] when it became law, the custody of public money was given to the Bank of England, and the Paymaster-General had only the power of drawing on the Bank for any services that were thereby specified.[4] Local payments and Paymasters, except for Soldiers' pay, had—as a rule—been abandoned prior to the Crimean War. *A.D. 1783. Office reformed by Mr Burke*

5 The issues of the Paymaster-General were made to the Agents of the Regiments holding the power of attorney of the Colonel. Those of the Agents were made to the Paymaster of each Regiment (who prior to the year 1797 was one of the Regimental Officers selected by the Colonel to discharge this in addition to his ordinary duties) and those of the Paymaster were made to the Captains of Companies, to pay their own men. Notwithstanding these arrangements, the only person recognised, as between the Public and the Regiment, was the agent; and for all moneys issued *Issues made to the Regimental Agent.*

---

[1] No 279, sess 2, p 3; but see Chap XXII, par 13
[2] See Chap IV, pars 54,58, and 4th and 5th Reports of Committee on Public Accounts, 1781, 23 Parl Hist., pp 130, 900
[3] 23 Geo III, c 50   [4] See 19th Report of Finance Committee, 1797

to him he was responsible to the Colonel, upon whom any loss fell if the agent failed in his pecuniary engagements.[1]

6. The method of accounting for the Issues, was as follows.

Manner of accounting for Issues. —The Captains accounted to the Regimental Paymaster; the Regimental Paymaster accounted with the Agent, and the Agent with the Secretary at War, on whose certificate the final account between the Paymaster-General and the Agent was closed. The "arrears" of pay were withheld from the Captains until this account was closed, for each of these Officers was held responsible to the Colonel for the accuracy of the Regimental accounts.[2]

7. It was found impossible to work Mr Burke's Act according to the scheme which he had framed, and the hardship of withholding the arrears of the Officers' pay was felt to be so great that, in the year 1797,[3] to facilitate financial affairs, an additional Officer was appointed to each Regiment as Paymaster, and the combatant Officers were relieved from that duty, except that each Captain continued to act as Paymaster to his own Company.

A D 1797.

Paymasters for each regiment.

8. These Regimental Paymasters were, like the former ones, appointed by the Colonels, upon the theory of their pecuniary responsibility. If they had acted as clerks or subordinates to the Colonel or to his Agent, this would have been only right; but the course taken by the Secretary at War upon their appointment, placed them in a different position Passing over the Colonel and his Agent, the Secretary opened a direct communication with the Paymaster; thereby creating Establishment charges without lessening those of Agency, and at the same time depriving the Public of the Agents' service. The evils of this course of action were strongly adverted to by the Commons' Committee on Public Expenditure,[4] in 1811, but it has never been altered. Though the Agent continued, for some purposes, as a channel of communication between the

Originally appointed by the Colonel.

---

[1] Lord Palmerston before Finance Committee, 1828, p. 226, so early as 7 & 8 Wm. and Mary c. 23, sec 5, he was required to give bond to the Colonel, Knowles v Maitland, 4 Bar and Cres., p 174, 23 P D. (O S), p. 1283

[2] See the Remarks of Committee on Public Expenditure, 1811, 10th Report, p 19   [3] Circulars of 18th November and 6th December, 1797   [4] P 21.

Colonel and the Secretary at War, his financial position and that of the Colonel were reduced to a fiction towards the Regiment or the Treasury.[1]

9. Accepting the Paymaster as a Financial Officer on behalf of the Public, he should have been subordinate to the War Office and Treasury, but independent of the Colonel. His right position as a Local Treasurer would then have been tenable and consistent with his responsibilities as a Bonded Accountant to the Crown. As it is, he is liable under the Mutiny Act to obey the Colonel as a commissioned Officer, and to account before any Court of Equitable Jurisdiction as a Civil Servant. Therefore, to use the words of Mr. Harrison's Opinion[2] laid before the Treasury in 1811, the whole system of account may be destroyed by the Commands of his Superior Officer.[3]

Ambiguous position of the Paymaster.

10 The evils of this divided allegiance were forcibly pointed out by the Commons' Committee of 1811.[4]—" If a Sub-Accountant has *any* authority to which he can directly refer, and under whose orders he can act in opposition to the instructions he may receive from his Principal, he has the power to resist, to misconstrue, and to evade the directions of that Principal, and to protract, by various modes of reference and controversial correspondence, a satisfactory and final explanation upon any point of *doubtful* expenditure. It is, therefore, exceedingly detrimental to the public service, and very dangerous to an individual, to pay money to any person whatever upon account, unless that individual has the absolute control over the public financial conduct of the person to whom he pays it." And these remarks apply with equal force to all other Military Accountants standing between the Finance Minister on the one hand and the Military Superior on the other.

Evils pointed out in 1811

11. The office is held as a retirement from more active

---

[1] See Mr Anderson's Report on the War Office Accounts, 1841, in Papers laid before the Commons, 9th May, 1856 (160) on "Naval and Military Accounts"

[2] Vol I, p 527

[3] As to Paymasters, see 6th Report of Military Inquiry, pp. 304, 511.

[4] 10th Report of Commons' Committee on Public Expenditure, 1811 (Audit of Accounts), p 21, and see Chap XXI., pars 2-32, and Chap XXIX, par. 77.

service, and the Colonels, when they had the appointment of
Paymasters, were recommended to select Officers
from the Half-pay List[1] However, as any loss resulting from failure of duty on the part of the Paymaster usually falls upon the Public and not upon the Agent or
Colonel,[2] the Secretary of State in August, 1856, took these
appointments into his own hands, furnishing—if such be needed
—an additional reason why Paymasters, as originally designed,
should be purely Civil servants subordinate only to the Finance
Department, and not to the Commander-in-Chief through the
Colonel.[3]

A D. 1856

Appointed by the Secretary of State

12 Within a certain period of his appointment, the law
requires that the Paymaster should give security for the
due performance of his duty and the safe custody of
all Public moneys intrusted to him by the Crown. The rule that
Public Accountants should give bond was in force at the time[4]
when the 50 Geo. III., c. 85, was enacted; but that there
might be no excuse for evading it, this and later statutes have
made the appointment of accounting parties *void* unless the
security required by Parliament be given. The particulars of
these enactments, which are still in force but sometimes disregarded, will be found in the Appendix.[5]

Required to give security to the Crown

13. The Pay List represents the financial account between
the Secretary at War and every Officer and man in the
Regiment. It is made up from the Adjutant's Muster
Roll and the Pay Account of each Company. The
size of it is (say) 170 foolscap sheets, and each sheet
contains many entries Each name is given upon it, and therefore after Regimental Paymasters were instituted, the office of
Muster-Master and his duties were abolished[6] If the thorough
Independence of the Paymaster could be secured, his entries
might be accepted on behalf of the Treasury, but, as he is the
representative of the Colonel, the Audit and examination of

Pay List, that of the Colonel and not of the Secretary at War.

---

[1] War Office Circulars, 18th November, 1797, 5th December, 1815, and 10th
August, 1831.

[2] List of defaulters in 1808, see 6th Report on Military Inquiry, p 475

[3] $\frac{120931}{14}$, 91 H. D. (3), p 699, and see Circular 641, 27th September, 1860
Chap XXVI, par 34.   [4] 16 H. D. (O S) pp 650, 657.

[5] See Note T T   [6] Chap. VII, par. 31, and Chap XV, pars 21-5.

his accounts have to be exact. For the statistics needed by Parliament, the number of separate items is increased, and hence the Audit Staff for this speciality is considerable.

14. As a sub-accountant to the War Office, each Paymaster holds public money, and not—as in the case of the Paymaster-General—only the power of ordering payments. All issues for Regimental Pay continue to be nominally made to the Colonel through the Agent, but are in fact made to the Paymaster. These are obtained on Estimate (of the probable expenses of the Regiment for the month next ensuing) sent to the War Office with the approval of the Colonel, and an abstract for the Agent. The issues to the Paymaster are disbursed through the Captains of Companies, each of whom keeps a sub-account with his own men. From these sub-accounts, sent in to the Paymaster at the end of each month, he compiles his quarterly account for the War Office. The pay of each Regiment, therefore, still involves a large amount of official labour, and of nominal responsibility, when all that is really required is to prevent fraud in a very simple transaction of paying wages.

[margin: Pay system of each Regiment]

15. There are other than public moneys which the Paymaster receives for tradesmen or for Regimental purposes under the Queen's or War Office Regulations; the Secretary of State does not hold himself responsible to make repayment of these if the Paymaster should happen to fail. In the first cases, the tradesmen make their supplies on the faith of the Regulations, so that, if the Paymaster fails, any loss falls on the tradesmen,[1] and not upon the Public. In the other instances, as the deposits are not made for the public advantage, it is held that the Public should not bear the loss.[2]

[margin: The Crown not responsible for funds trusted to the Paymaster]

---

[1] Prosser *v* Allen, Gow Cases, p 117: Macheath *v* Haldemand, 1 Term Rep., p. 172   [2] Circular 1130, 25 Sept., 1852, $\frac{151551}{2}$

CHAPTER XXIV.

THE COMMISSIONERS FOR THE AUDIT OF PUBLIC ACCOUNTS.

1. FROM the feeble action of the Auditors of Imprest,[1] who
were not members of either House of Parliament or
Audit of
Expenditure
by the
Commons of the Ministry, when Parliamentary Government was
inaugurated in the year 1688, the Commons were led
to place their reliance—as a financial check—upon Committees
of their own members,[2] who framed or re-modelled the Estimates, and subsequently—whenever any increase demanded their
attention—investigated the expenditure. In course of time,
however, the Secretary at War, as a Parliamentary Officer,
assumed both these functions, and the direct interference of the
House was limited to special occasions, when the Commons
appointed the Audit Commissioners, who for a limited time held
Statutory Powers.[3]

2. In the affairs of the Army far less trust was originally
placed in the Executive Government than is shown in
Originally
very vigilant. the present day. Until the middle of the last century,
the Commons insisted upon Returns as to the strength and
disposition of the Forces that would now be withheld;[4] the half-
pay list was laid upon their table with the yearly Estimates,[5]

---

[1] As to the ancient functions of these Officers, see Vol II of Madox's 'History
of the Exchequer,' p 290   As to their functions in modern times, see Reports 8 to
13 of Committee on Public Accounts, 1783-4

[2] Chap VII, par 8, and see entries, War of 1694   State of it ordered, 11 Com.
Journ, p. 17, and laid before the Committee, p. 18.   Treaties ordered (p 20), and
laid before the House, p 24   Supplies voted pp. 36, 37   The Army was to be disbanded, and a Committee appointed, 12 Com Journ, pp 5, 8, 22, 28, and 37
Supply voted p 44   Disbanding resolved, p 51   List of half-pay officers
ordered, pp 52, 77   On breaking out of the War in 1702, the same course adopted
by the House in requiring information, Com Journ, p 20, and when the Army
was dis' anded, see 17 Com Journ, pp 305 500, 524 530, 590, 655

[2] As to their right of appointment, see Chap VII, pars 10 and 22

[4] Chap XXV, pars 33-9   [5] Vol I., Note G, p 370

until 1785, and the non-effective allowances were vigilantly watched by Independent Members.

3. Having in previous Chapters shown what the *direct* action of Parliament has been in controlling Military expenditure,[1] and what departmental arrangements at one time existed under the Crown,[2] for the same object, I propose to explain the nature and extent of the control which at present is exercised over Military expenditure by the Audit Commissioners, premising that, though an independent audit of all expenditure is a desideratum which every Statesman strives to secure, we are further removed from it—as affecting Military expenditure—than ever.

Audit by Commissioners.

4. The History of the Audit Office, as at present constituted, dates from the year 1785. The Reports of the Commissioners on Public Accounts, and more especially their 8th, 9th, 10th, 11th, 12th, and 13th Reports, presented to Parliament between January, 1783, and March, 1785,[3] on which the Act was framed,[4] led to the abolition of the Auditors of Imprest, and the substitution of other Auditors—viz., Commissioners appointed by *the Crown* under the authority of Parliament. The Bill passed without opposition, or any claim from the Commons to appoint the Commissioners by ballot.[5]

*A.D. 1785
Audit Act
Appointment of Commissioners by the Crown*

5. The independence of the Auditors was supposed to be secured by the Statutory declaration that they should be appointed for life in the same manner as the Common Law Judges, whose tenure of office is during good behaviour (*quamdiu se bene gesserint*).[6] It is, therefore, only by a joint address from both Houses of Parliament to the Crown that they can be removed from office. Their salaries are paid in the same manner as those of the Judges, out of the Consolidated Fund, and do not come annually under the consideration of Parliament for Supply.

Independence of the Audit Board

6. The Commissioners—from analogy to the Auditors of

[1] Chap VII   [2] Chap XIX., par 24 *et seq*   [3] 25 Parl Hist , p 299.
[4] 25 Geo. III., c 52.   [5] 40 Com Journ , pp 967, 1047, 1055
[6] See 'Report of Select Committee on Public Moneys, 1856,' p 835

Imprest—were placed under the Treasury, and in some sense

But subordinate to the Treasury subject to their orders. By oath of office they were sworn faithfully, impartially, and truly, "to try and examine the several accounts and vouchers which should be transmitted to them from time to time, and upon trial and examination thereof to make full, just, and perfect accounts. To allow such articles of expenditure only as the accountants should have been duly authorized to incur, *unless* upon a special statement of the matter to the Lords of the Treasury, they should be *directed* to make further or other allowances to the accountants by warrant under the hands of the Lords of the Treasury." The Act also made them "subject to the same control to which the Auditors of the Imprest were then subject or liable by law, usage. or custom;" and the letters (patent) of appointment, authorized and directed them to "audit and determine accounts by and with the advice, authority, and consent of the Lords of the Treasury and Chancellor of the Exchequer" [1]

7. Still they have refused, either to alter "the general rules

The mode of Audit left to the Commissioners of accounting in their office, or to authorize a relaxation of those rules in favour of a particular accountant," [2] at the instance of the Treasury. With respect to the sums to be *allowed* to the accountant's credit, the decision of the auditors is final,—they are to decide whether the payments are duly authorized and vouched. If of opinion that they are so, the Treasury cannot direct their disallowance. But as to sums *disallowed* by the Auditors, the case is different: here, according to long practice, an appeal lies to the Lords of the Treasury, who are empowered, if they think fit, to direct, by Warrant, that all such sums be allowed, these allowances appearing on the face of the account as the act of the Treasury, and not of the Auditors [3]

8. But the Statute left to the Ministers of the Crown a

Power to issue money without account continued discretion for the issue of public money, either with or without account, trusting to their Parliamentary responsibility for an honest decision whether the

---

[1] 'Report of Select Committee on Public Moneys, 1856,' pp 839, 840
[2] Ib., p 841.   [3] Ib, p 835

recipient should or should not account to the Audit Board for the money issued by them.[1]

9. The necessity for some more effectual Control over Public expenditure has often been admitted, and in the Session of 1807, a Commons' Committee was appointed to "examine and consider what regulations and checks have been established in order to control the several branches of Public Expenditure."[2] The Committee presented several Reports to Parliament, and in reporting on the Audit Office, laid down these general principles upon the efficiency of *any* audit as a control over expenditure.

Necessity for more efficient control.

10. "An account[3] of public expenditure, with the view to all the purposes of audit and control, should be made, subject to strict examination upon the following points:—

Recommendations of Commons' Committee as to efficient Audit

1st. To ascertain whether the Accountant has been properly charged with the whole of the money for which he is accountable.

2nd. Whether the account is arithmetically correct as to the casting and computations, and double credits guarded against.

3rd. To see that the disbursements are vouched by proper receipts and acquittances, or other sufficient evidence of payment.

4th. Whether the expenditure has been duly authorized before it was incurred, or has been subsequently sanctioned by a competent authority.

5th. To see that the articles of expenditure are proper and reasonable in their nature and amount.

6th. That the prices of stores or other articles purchased for the public service, appear to be fair and reasonable.

7th. That the balances of public money suffered to remain in the hands of the principal Accountant or his Sub-Accountant may not have been greater than the nature of the service required.

---

[1] 1st Report of Military Inquiry, p 73 *et passim*, and 'Report on Public Moneys, 1856,' p 840

[2] 1st Report, 22 July, 1807, and 11th Report, 1st July, 1811

[3] 5th Report, 2nd part, Committee on Public Expenditure (1810, p 20

And, lastly, whether any irregularity appears in the mode of conducting the service, to which the attention of Government ought to be directed."

11. The Committee accepted the first four points, as fairly dealt with, but called the attention of Parliament to the fact that there was no Independent audit of the *Expenditure* made in Departments, for "there is an essential difference between the examination of a mere cash account, and that of the actual expenditure—the latter being the real and substantive audit of the account."[1] "It remains to be considered," continued their Report, "how far a Department of Accounts, which as to most of the great Public Accounts is confined systematically to the former mode of examination, is fully entitled to the appellation it has received from the Legislature of ‘An Office for Examining and Auditing the Public Accounts of the Kingdom,’ and whether the accounts of the public expenditure are examined and audited with the precision and correctness to which they ought properly to be made subject."

[margin: Appropriation and Expenditure Audit]

12. Dividing the subject of Audit into the two branches— (1) of Appropriation, and (2) Expenditure—it may be well to examine—so far as the Military Expenditure of the country is brought under notice—what security Parliament and the Crown have provided for this service being faithfully carried out by independent and impartial Auditors.

[margin: What has been provided for in each branch.]

I. As to the Appropriation Audit.—

13. In the year 1846 an Act was passed to provide that an account—of the receipt and expenditure of the sums granted, and classed under the several heads of service as expressed in the Appropriation Act—shall be sent by the War Office to the Audit Board for a certificate of the correctness of the sums charged therein, *as compared with the books and vouchers of the department.*[2] No sum, in the nature of

[margin: A.D. 1846 — The Appropriation Audit]

---

[1] 5th Report, 2nd part, Committee on Public Expenditure (1810), p 22
[2] 9 and 10 Vic, c 92, sec 2 As to papers leading up to the passing of this Statute, see ‘Naval and Military Accounts,’ 9 May, 1836 (160), 38 Parl Rep, p 203.

an imprest or advance, is to be allowed in the account; and to enable the Commissioners to give their certificate, all the office books and vouchers are to be open to them. The Audit is not intended to limit the discretion of the responsible departments of the Executive Government in which it is established, but to secure a revision of their accounts by an independent authority, invested with sufficient powers of investigation to detect any misapplication of the votes, or any deviation from the appropriation sanctioned by Parliament.[1]

14. That this is an *Appropriation* audit in the strictest sense, and nothing else, will be proved beyond controversy by an extract from an Official Memorandum put in by the Audit Commissioners ·—"Every voucher[2] is accessible to the Auditors; but, provided they bear evidence of the expenditure having been duly authorized and *passed* by the proper authorities, no objection could be raised by the Commissioners to any item of that expenditure, except for the purpose of questioning the *head* of service to which such item has been placed *as expressed* in the Appropriation Act. The vouchers, therefore, are examined with that view *only.* . . . . If the Auditor saw that payment had been ordered *contrary to the express provisions of a Royal Warrant, to an Order in Council, a Treasury direction, or even the provision of an Act of Parliament;* or if he had reason to know that a sum taken credit for as paid had *not been paid,* or that there had been *a double* payment, or a wrong computation affecting the total; provided the accounts in which these irregularities had occurred had *duly* passed the constituted authorities of the Army or Navy departments, he would be exceeding his duty if he remarked upon them His province is to see that the items which have passed the departmental ordeal are *posted* to the proper *heads.*"

Only an Appropriation Audit

15. It must not be assumed that the voucher here referred to is the receipt—for it is only the authority —for making the expenditure.[3] The auditors are not responsible for the correctness of one single payment made in the account.[4] This depends upon the good

Accounts on which the Audit to be based accepted on the faith of the War Office

---

[1] 'Report on Public Moneys, 1857, p 6.   [2] Ib, 1856, p 142.
[3] Ib, pp 424, 437.   [4] Ib, p 440.

faith of the Department, the accounts being taken entirely upon the authority of the War Office.[1]

16. But limited as are the functions of the Audit Commissioners in this respect, and protected as the Commissioners are from influence or coercion by publicity, the "Committee on Public Moneys, 1857," deemed it essential that they should be raised to greater independence, and hold a direct responsibility towards Parliament. "Your Committee suggest that the Audit Board should no longer transmit through the Treasury those accounts which they are bound to lay before Parliament, but should communicate them *direct,* and that in the appropriation and inspection of Army and Navy Accounts, the *selection* of officers for the respective duties, their removal or *dismissal,* should rest *entirely* with the Audit Board. The Board of Audit is responsible to Parliament alone, and the station and emoluments of the person at the head of it should be equal to the importance of the duties to be performed, and not second in rank to any of the permanent officers presiding over other principal departments."[2]

Independence of the Audit Board upheld

17. Accordingly when the Exchequer and Audit Departments Act, 1866,[3] was passed, these improvements were effected The Auditors present their reports to the House of Commons direct; and, although the Crown appoints the Auditors (upon a tenure of office equally independent as the Judges), the Commons have regained something of their former privileges—in having a direct relationship with these officers.

Their Reports made to the House of Commons direct.

II. As to the Expenditure Audit.—

18. "The real and substantial audit of any account is that of the actual expenditure," and no one, looking at the annual amount of the Army Votes, can question the vital importance of the subject. From the earliest period of a Standing Army the Independent audit of Military Expenditure

The Expenditure Audit.

---

[1] 'Report on Public Moneys,' p 426, but see secs 28, 29 of 29 and 30 Vic, c. 39.
[2] Mr. Romilly's Evidence, Question 1599, on Public Moneys
[3] 29 and 30 Vic, c 39, sec 3

has been *the* subject to which the Commons have directed their attention.[1] Not only as an essential part of their duty to the people, but as being the only check that the House has against corruption or extravagance.[2]

19. Recipients of public money, either for their own advantage or to disburse it to others, are not always ready to submit to financial control ;[3] therefore the Independence of the Audit is open to impeachment from that quarter.[4] How sensitive honourable men are of any possibility of influence—or the imputation of it—being justly raised against them may be seen by the evidence of one of the Audit Commissioners taken before the Public Moneys Committee. When it was proposed that the Commissioners should audit the accounts of the Treasury, they pointed out that it was *essential* that the accounts should be sent *from* the Treasury to the Auditors, that the audit should be carried on under their own roof,[5] and not at the Treasury.

20. In checking the accounts of any Department by Audit officers placed there, the risk is that the latter officers are more influenced by the views and feelings of the Department than of the Audit Office ; a risk which is increased if the Department has a large amount of patronage at its disposal   "It must be borne in mind,[6] that the officers by whom the duty of Appropriation Audit is at present conducted are subordinate officers of a subordinate department, and that they have more to hope for in their advancement in life from the chief officers of the Executive, than from their own official superiors, the Commissioners of Audit. Nothing is further from my intention than to throw the smallest doubt upon the high integrity of those gentlemen who are now employed upon the responsible duty in question, or to suggest that,—if, indeed, the occasion presented itself, —they would not be ready to act with independence, but no system can be permanently sound and useful which requires an *unusual* amount of judgment *and moral courage* to carry it satisfactorily into effect, and is not based upon the *ordinary* principles known

Audit objected to by recipients.

Risk of audit and expending officers being associated together

---

[1] Chap VII , *ante*
[2] Ib , pars 10, 23, 24, 28,
[3] Ib , 25 , Chap XII , pars 17, 21 29
[4] Chap XXIX , par 63
[5] Report, 1856, Question 4399.
[6] Public Moneys, 1857, p 58

commonly to actuate human conduct. To place, therefore, at the Treasury,—officers of a department subordinate to the Treasury, in order to maintain an efficient Parliamentary check over the Treasury, would, as it appears to me, be a delusion " Admitting the force of these observations, the Treasury, as I have shown, placed the Audit Commissioners in a more independent position towards that Department.

21. In the position formerly held by the War Office towards the Horse Guards, the apprehension of Parliament

Relative position of the War Office and the Horse Guards.

might have arisen, having reference to the Chiefs of these departments, that the higher social position of the one might induce the other to subserviency. As a guard against this derangement, each office was served by a different class of public servants—the War Office (prior to the Crimean War) held only Civilians, though the Staff at the Horse Guards was composed of Military officers. The War Office employé owed nothing to and could gain nothing from *any* military officer, and hence had no temptation whatever to deviate, as an auditor, in any degree from the prescribed line of his duty. It was, therefore,—as it has been so frequently described, and ought to be still,—a check upon the expenditure of Military Officers under the Commander-in-Chief.[1]

22. Upon the faith of its entire independence,[2] as a Civil

Parliament has hitherto trusted to the entire independence of the War Office

Department of Account, the audit of Military expenditure has been exclusively intrusted to the War Office.[3] Assuming the office to have remained, with regard to its *personnel*, as it was constituted prior to

---

[1] Chap XXI, pars 45 to 46

[2] 1856, Questions 4524, 4527, and the Evidence generally of Messrs Romilly and Macaulay, 5th Report (2nd part) Committee on Public Expenditure, June 1810, and Naval and Military Accounts, 1856—Chap XV, pars 119, 120

[3] Extracts from Evidence taken before the Public Moneys Committee, 1856, p. 435 —"4504 *(Sir Henry Willoughby)*—With regard to the detailed account in the Army, Navy, and Ordnance Departments, is that made by the clerks of the departments over whom you have any control, or no control?—It is made entirely by clerks over whom we have no control, the detailed examination we have nothing to do with 4505 Therefore you know nothing about the detailed audit?—No, except that we see that it has been subjected to the proper audit. 4506. Then does it come to this, that that detailed audit is conducted by the department itself?—Yes 4507 Then, in point of fact, do they not audit their own accounts ?—The audit is done in the department itself, no doubt 4508 Is that audit

1854, the only objection would have been this,—that the same department authorized through one, and audited through another class of Civil servants, the same expenditure; neither of the two classes being the same as the third or Military class on whom, or by whom the expenditure was actually made; in truth, that the latter class was *wholly* unconnected with, and of a different status, to the *personnel* of the War Office.[1]

23. Such as it was, this objection was thought to have some weight with the Commissioners, and to raise a *doubt* upon the *security* that the Audit gave to the Public. Putting aside motive, nor suggesting any wrong one, it appeared scarcely right—as to that portion of expenditure which depended upon Treasury Regulation Statute, or any higher Authority than the office itself,—that no independent officer should be interposed to see that these rules had been duly observed by the expending Department,[2] for it is admitted to be within the power of those superior in office to the Accountant-General, to order him to make *any* payments, taking upon themselves the responsibility of infringing rules.[3]

Audit of expenditure still desired (1) as to authorised payments.

24. But this expenditure is not the *only* one upon which the

any check on the expenditure?—It is a check upon the sub-accountant of that department 4500. Suppose anything goes wrong, who is to detect it?—The head of the check branch of the department; it would be his duty. (*Mr. Macaulay*)—The Accountant-General 4510. What check is there on the Accountant-General himself?—(*Mr. Romilly*)—The Heads of the Department, I suppose 4511 It is quite clear that of that audit you are in no way cognizant at all?—We are not responsible for it in any way 4512. Do you understand the details—are the details in any way brought before you?—No, not of that detailed audit. 4513 Can you state roughly to what extent the expenditure goes?—It depends upon the Votes (*Mr Macaulay*)—While it is true that the Audit Office enters, in no sense, into the detailed audit of that expenditure, as I understand it, the inspector who is charged with the duty of the appropriation audit, examines the vouchers, with the view of seeing that they have been previously examined, that they bear about them the evidence of previous examination, and also that the orders for payment are drawn in conformity with the Regulations of the Service 4514 Assuming that the Army, Navy, and Ordnance Votes were 35,000,000*l*, would the detailed audit by the clerks of those departments extend to that amount?— (*Mr Romilly*)—Yes, it would extend to the whole of the amount of the Votes taken by those several departments 4515 The detailed audit of the whole of that 35,000 000*l* would be by the clerks of the departments?—Yes 4516 And the officers of the audit office would in no way be concerned in that audit?—No ''

[1] 1856, Question 4146, Chap. XXIX, par 32.   - Ib., Question 4388

[3] Ib, 4391 Reg t Russell, 16 L J. (N S), p. 478.

influence of an Audit ultra the Department Audit would be felt
The contingent expenses of any office or class of officers
are always liable to increase,[1] and in the War Office there
are "expenses" which—to use the words of the Treasury Minute
—are "not warranted by Regulations, or of a questionable nature,
and that are within the discretion of the War Office authorities,
either to refuse or allow as they may see fit."[2] The expediency
of an Audit independent of the War Office has therefore never
been lost sight of, though it has been postponed on the grounds
of extra expense and trouble, without equivalent advantages.

(2) As to the questionable expenditure

25. As, however, all Military expenditure is now audited exclusively in the War Office, and by its employés, the internal
Organization of that Department,—as free of or subject
to the Military element,—is a question that obviously
assumes an aspect of great Constitutional importance.
The late Duke of Wellington represented the original function
of the office as a check on expenditure incurred by the Army;
and hence he stoutly and wisely opposed the Amalgamation of
the Expending and Controlling Elements of the Civil and
Military Staff in one department, because the Financial and
Civil Control would be at once lost and gone.[3]

The only audit is by the War Office—the constitution of the office important

26. But a worse evil than an open avowal to Parliament
of this Organic change in the Constitutional functions of the War Office, may happen by an act of
benevolence to highly deserving men, changing thereby the
class or status of the Auditors, by taking commissioned or non-
commissioned officers into the War Office for the audit[4] and
control of military expenditure, and by sending away civilians
whose abilities have been trained, and their lives spent in the
discharge of those duties. No doubt in India, and other conquered countries, all the expenditure (Military or Civil) is often
in the hands of Military—but this analogy does not exist until,
for the same reasons, our other Civil Institutions are changed
into Military ones.[5]

Military officers as auditors

[1] 5th Report of 1810, p 22.   [2] Chap VII, pars 72, 73
[3] See *ante, passim,* and Appendix CXLVII   [4] See Note H, vol I, p 384
[5] Mr Burke thus sketches the rise and progress of Military Finance in India
"The Military do not behold without a virtuous emulation the moderate gains
of the Civil Department They feel that, in a country driven to habitual

27. This change in the *personnel* of the War Office may render an Independent Audit absolutely necessary, unless, indeed, Parliament is prepared to hand over the *audit* of *all* accounts, as well as all expenditure (as Military Expenditure is obviously *the last* that should be entrusted)— to the officers of the Army, and to withdraw all Civil agency and control which has hitherto been exercised under the supreme authority of the Treasury over all Public Expenditure.

An independent audit then needful.

28. To render an audit anything but "a delusion," it is of the very essence of security to preserve the Auditors free from all possibility of being tempted to serve two masters, or to flinch from honestly serving one—the absent Public Apart from questions affecting their ability or experience, they must look to the Civil Minister, and to him alone. Further, Parliament must be assured, as was recently pointed out,[1] that his inspirations—when the Audit Officers appeal to him for protection or support—are wholly free from the Military element, whose allowances, as a Class, are the subject of controversy; for unless he acts on Independent advice (and where is it to be obtained by the Minister surrounded by Military men?), the Auditors will soon forsake him, and serve the Advisers to whom he is trusting.

Audit useless until wholly free from influence

29. One other point remains to be observed upon with reference to the Treasury Minute of 1835. Do the Audit Board and War Office give the same assistance to the Treasury, which it gained from the Comptrollers of Army Accounts before they were abolished?[2] The Report on Public Moneys, 1856-7, would lead the reader to give a decided negative to that inquiry.

Audit Board not of equal use to the Treasury as to the Army Comptrollers.

---

rebellion by the Civil Government, the Military are necessary, and they will not permit their services to go unrewarded Tracts of country are delivered over to their discretion. Then it is found proper to convert their Commanding Officers into Farmers of Revenue Wherever the collectors of Revenue and the farming Colonels and Majors move, ruin is about them The people in crowds fly out of the country, and the frontier is guarded by lines of troops—not to exclude an enemy, but to prevent the escape of the inhabitants "—Vol vi, pp 50, 51

[1] Chap XXIX, par 32. [2] Chap XIX., par 34

CHAPTER XXV.

THE OFFICE OF SECRETARY OF STATE.

1. IN treating of the prerogative of the Crown in the "Government, command and disposition" of the Army, the office of primary importance is that of the Secretary of State.[1] From the time of the establishment of a Standing Army, that Minister has been held responsible for three essentials:—1st, the number of the military forces to be maintained; 2ndly, the appointment of officers duly qualified; and 3rdly, the employment of the Army. The 1st was secured by the Warrant[2] of 1668-9, which Lord Palmerston states to have been annually renewed for many years.[3] The 2nd by his countersign of the Royal Sign Manual upon every commission granted, for which Parliament held him responsible;[4] and the 3rd, by the Constitutional rule that every Command of the Crown needs authentication by a Secretary of State.[5]

Prerogative for the government and command of the Army

2. It will be convenient to divide the consideration of the subject into separate Chapters. In the present one to consider the office of Secretary of State, as it is constituted, under the Common Law, and as applicable to any Department of the Secretariat, and in the last Chapter to describe the arrangements made at the time of and after the Crimean War, upon the appointment of a "War Minister," and the Statutory Authority conferred upon him.

Secretary of state's office at common law

3. For the practical purposes of this Work, it is not essential

---

[1] Chap III., par. 9; Chap IV, pars 45, 50
[2] Vol I, Appendix XIX, p. 472   [3] Appendix CXXIX
[4] Chap IV., pars 43 and 46, Chap XVI., par 21, 14 Parl Hist, p. 909 *et seq*
[5] Par, 11, *post*

to go into the Constitutional history of the Office at any great
length ;[1] but I shall deem it sufficient first to refer Description
the reader to the Patent of Appointment and Oath of the Office
of Office of the Secretary of State printed in the Appendix,[2]
to give then the substance of Lord Coke's description, and,
finally, an extract from a modern Parliamentary authority.

4. In commenting on the Statute of 28 Edward I.,[3] c. 6
(which provided that no writ touching the Common Office of
Law should thereafter go forth under any of the Secretary of State in Edward I's
Petty Seals), Lord Coke says,[4] "at the time of the reign
making of this statute (A D. 1300) it is to be understood that the
King had three Seals :—(1) The Great Seal, in the custody of
the Chancellor.   (2) The Little or Privy Seal, in the custody
of the Lord Privy Seal.   (3) The Signet—which Seal is ever
in the custody of the Principal Secretary."

5. He then goes on to describe the Establishment and Office
of the Principal Secretary in his own time, thus,— A.D. 1628
"And there be four Clerks attending on the Principal Establish-
Secretary.   The reason wherefore the Signet is in office duties.
the Secretary's custody is for that the King's private letters
are signed therewith ; also the duty of the Clerk of the Signet
is to write out such Grants or Letters Patent as pass by Bill
signed—that is a Bill superscribed with the signature or Sign
Manual or Royal hand of the King—to the 'Privy Seal,' which
Bill, being transcribed and sealed with the 'Signet,' is a warrant to the Privy Seal ; and the Privy Seal is a warrant to the
Great Seal.   Such," he continues, " was the wisdom of prudent
antiquity, that whatever should pass the Great Seal should come
through so many hands, that nothing should pass by undue or
surreptitious means.   And of the 'Signet' the Law on some cases
taketh notice for a 'ne exeat regno' may be, by the King's Writ,
under the Great Seal, or by commandment under the Privy Seal,

---

[1] The history of the office of Secretary of State is to be found in Lord Camden's Judgment in Entick v Carrington, 19 How Stat Trials, p 1050 , in Thomas's History of Public Departments (p 846), pp 23 to 36, and in Sir W Nicholas s observations in the preface to the 1st Vol of the Proceedings and Ordinances of the Privy Councils of England (1837) , and Lord Campbell's Judgment of Harrison v Bush, 5 Ell. and Blac , p. 351   These cases may also be referred to :— Felkin v Herbert, 8 Jur. (N S), 90 Foster v Dodd, 6 B & S , 169 Ex parte Bird, 1 Ell and Ell , p 982   [2] Appendices CXXXVI , CXXXVII
[3] 1 Stat of Realm, p 139   [4] 2 Inst., p 556

or under the 'Signet;' for in this case the public ought to take notice as well of the 'Privy Seal and Signet' as of the Great Seal, for this is but a signification of the King's commandment, and nothing passeth from him, but a Warrant under the Signet to issue any treasure is not sufficient, but there it ought to be either under the Great or Privy Seal."

6. This description shows that the Secretary of State was

In Charles II's reign the medium of conveying the Commands of the Sovereign, and that these Commands, when so authenticated, ought to be obeyed However, when it was written the Secretary of State was not a member of the Privy Council; but a subordinate Minister, with a salary of 100*l.* a year, for so late as Charles II.'s reign Lord Clarendon[1] describes the Secretary as employed *only* to make up the despatches at the conclusion of the Council.

7. The Office appears to have been originally conferred

Mode of appointment. by the delivery of the Signet, and the same method of appointment—taking place at the Council Board where the Minister is sworn into office—is recognized at the present time.[2] Since the year 1558,[3] a more formal grant has been made by patent under the Great Seal; but whether such a grant be really needed, is a question that has frequently been raised in recent years, but not decided.

8 In the reign of Charles I., and at an early period in that

Not a Finance Minister of Charles II., the Secretary of State had been appointed one of the Lords of the Treasury; but from the Report of the Audit Commissioners in Queen Anne's reign, it is clear that he was not then considered to be a Finance Minister.[4]

9. In fact, his office in reference to Army affairs became

A D. 1688
His office increased in importance after the Revolution important after the Revolution, when, as Sir James Mackintosh declared, the Parliament bent the neck of Military power under the yoke of Law. "The Revolution found Standing Armies kept up without the sanction of Parliament, and in defiance of Law; the Revolution found the King claiming and exercising the power

---

[1] 5 Parl Hist, p 890　　　　[2] Appendix CXXXVII
[3] Thomas 27. See 141 H D (3), pp 1105 and 1247, 142 ib., p. 620, 143 ib,
p 1226, 'Report on Military Organisation,' p 6　　　[4] Chap VII., par 24.

of keeping up as large an Army as he could find means (abroad or at home) to pay; the Revolution branded the usurpation, and expelled the usurping King; the Revolution bent the neck of Military power under the yoke of Law, and rendered armies the creatures of Parliament, made and destroyed by its breath; it permitted, indeed, the annual vote of an Army with an annual grant of money for its support; and an Annual Mutiny Bill for its government, rendering that Army every year a new establishment to be proposed on particular grounds, and adopted only on the same principle, as if each year were the first of its proposition. The Revolution tolerated such annual Standing Armies, or rather did not attempt to limit the power of Parliament to provide for the public safety by such an expedient as often and as much as it became necessary. But it was on such principles, and under this triple control, as well as for this limited term, that the Revolution allowed an Army. The principle of the Revolution on this subject, I conceive to be, that an Army without the consent of Parliament is destructive of liberty, and that an Army with the consent of Parliament is dangerous to liberty, though policy may compel us to suffer it, and though these multiplied securities may abate its mischievous tendency." [1]

10. The Army, and the means of maintaining and disciplining it, being given by Parliament, the Crown has, by the Constitution, authority for "the Government and Command" of it. For the contentment of the people, these powers are to be executed under the advice of a responsible Minister, and that Minister, from the necessity of the case, is the Secretary of State.

Prerogatives of the Crown exercised under the advice of the Secretary of State.

11. The number of Principal Secretaries, acting at the same period, has varied from two to five during the last century. It is said that all these Ministers constitute but one office, that each may act interchangeably in their several departments, and all change without vacating [2] their seats in Parliament; but how far this rule may be applicable to the execution of Statutory powers delegated to any one specifically named as holding the seals of a particular

Number of Secretaries of State.

---

[1] See 32 H. D. (O. S.), p. 986

[2] Harrison *v.* Bush, 5 Ell. and Bl., p. 352; May, Parl. Practice, p. 551

Department, may deserve some further consideration.[1] From an early period, until the year 1767, the office was divided into two departments, denominated Northern and Southern, according to the States in Europe with which each Secretary corresponded On the 20th January, 1768, a third Secretary "for the Colonies" was appointed, and continued in office until abolished by Mr. Burke's Act.[2] The business of the Secretariat was then re-arranged under the present titles of Home and Foreign, and so continued until (on the 1st July, 1794,[3]) a third Secretary was again appointed—the Department of War and Colonies being given into his care.

12. Under these arrangements the affairs of the Army were divided between the Home and Colonial Secretaries. Each of these Ministers countersigned Military commissions, and in their respective Departments communicated with the Commander-in-Chief and Master-General of the Ordnance upon all points connected with the internal defence of the country and the protection of the Colonial possessions. The Secretary for the Colonies, as Secretary for the War Department, had a general authority in all matters relating to the Army; further he submitted to the King from the Cabinet the amount of force to be kept up each year, and communicated with all the General Officers commanding in time of war on Foreign Service.[4]

Responsibility as to the Army

13. The Home Secretary had the responsibility of all the forces upon the Home Establishment including the Reserve Forces; the Colonial Secretary had the responsibility attaching to troops upon Colonial and Foreign Service, including Local Corps raised abroad; but, subject to these Departmental arrangements, their responsibility was the same. "The Secretaries of State," wrote Sir James Graham,[5] "are the channels which convey the Royal pleasure throughout the body

In Queen Victoria's reign.

---

[1] A third secretary was appointed for Scotland 3rd February, 1708, and acted till 1746, when the Marquis of Tweedale resigned the seals

[2] 22 Geo. III , c. 82 , 21 Parl Hist , p 190 , and 22 ib., p 1412.

[3] 33 Parl Hist , p 971 (Mr Pitt's speech), and motion to suppress it in 1816 , 33 H. D. (O S.) 892 in 1817 , 36 ib., p 51.

[4] 'Report on Civil Administration, 1837,' p. 5

[5] 'Military Organisation Report, 1860,' p vi

politic, both at home and abroad.[1] The counter-signature of one of these is necessary to give effect to the Royal Sign Manual. The patronage of the Crown, both in Church and State, is administered under this safeguard To every public document, signed by the Sovereign, the signature of a Secretary of State is appended; and the Minister must answer for what the Crown has done."

14. The official Establishment of each Secretary is settled by Order in Council, but Under-secretaries or clerks are appointments made by him, and not by the Crown.[2] To prevent the House of Commons from being filled with placemen, limitations have been imposed from time to time upon the number of Principal and Under-Secretaries of State that may sit therein. The limitation first imposed was two of each,[3] then three were allowed to sit,[4] and ultimately, when the 5th Secretary of State (for India) was created,[5] it was extended to four In the year 1864 a suggestion was made in the House of Commons, that the provisions of these Statutes were infringed, and the subject was submitted for inquiry, to a Select Committee,[6] who reported that the Seat was not vacated, though a Bill of Indemnity was passed.

[margin: Secretary of State's Establishment and seat in the House of Commons.]

15. Seeing that Parliament determined, in 1863, that " all the duties, powers, and authorities of the Secretary at War should thereafter be exercised by the Secretary of State," it is not necessary to trace out the distinction between the powers which the Secretary of State and the Secretary at War respectively exercised; but it is important to ascertain what, by Constitutional Law or official custom, are the powers which properly belong to the Secretary of State as a Civil Minister, against the Commander-in-Chief, as the supreme Military authority, in respect to the other officers and soldiers of Her Majesty's Army. Hitherto in this, as distinguished from other European States, the Civil power

[margin: Civil control in Secretary of State for War]

[1] Sir W Scott's Judgment in 'The Elsebe,' 5 Rob. Admiralty Cases, p 177 Buron v. Denman, 2 Exch Cas , p. 189.   [2] 2 Hats, Prec , p 63, note
[3] 15 Geo II , c 22, s 3, 22 Geo III., c 82, 20 Parl. Hist , p. 250
[4] 18 Vic., c 10   [5] 21 & 22 Vic , c 106, s 4
[6] 174 H D (3) pp 1218-1250 , Parl Papers, No 226, 27 & 28 Vic., c 21.

has been acknowledged to be supreme; and hence whenever the Civil control over the Army has been controverted by the Commander-in-Chief, it was exercised not by the Secretary of State, but by the Secretary at War.

16. Now,[1] in entering upon this enquiry, it may be re-

Constitutional importance of— 1 supremacy of Civil Minister

marked in the first place, that if the rules of military obedience be such as were contended for in the instances of Captain Atchison—the Harwich Election Committee—and Stinton—(and there can be little doubt entertained but that a Court-martial would hold them to be so), then the Public Safety demands from the Commander-in-Chief a most explicit recognition at all times of the supreme authority of the Secretary of State over him and the subordinate officers of the Army.' Nor is it scarcely less important that this Civil should be sustained in complete Independence of the Military authority, that to the full conviction of every member of the civil community the Secretary of State's office may afford that Constitutional security which it was designed to fulfil against a Standing Army.

17. How this vital purpose may be best secured must de-

2 The *Personnel* of his official staff

pend in no inconsiderable degree upon the *personnel* by whom—when called upon to act in his higher constitutional functions—the Civil Minister is assisted and by whom the ordinary daily duties of his office are carried out. Obviously, if the Civil Minister seeks to restrain or sanction the acts of the Commander-in-Chief, upon the advice or through the agency of Military Officers (looking to the latter for promotion hereafter, and serving on Staff or Full pay), the Secretary of State's office in the degree to which this agency is used must cease to be—or at least, in public estimation, to be esteemed as—that of a Civil Minister, wholly independent of the Commander-in-Chief. In either view, the Secretary of State's Constitutional authority and functions, if not destroyed, are materially impaired.

---

[1] Chap. VIII., par 35; Chap IX., par 14, Chap XV. par 109, Chap XVI., pars 12-15

[2] See the Duke of Wellington's advice to Lord Combermere as Commander in-Chief in India, vol iii of Supplementary Despatches, p 502

18. This aspect of the case is not imaginary; on the contrary, one that presented itself strongly to the minds of the late Duke of Wellington and Lord Hardinge, as expressed in their evidence before the Commissioners on the Civil Administration of the Army. *They* thought it to be impossible—even in the less important matters of supply—for an officer to serve two masters—a Civil Minister and a Military superior, and therefore they forewarned the Government against inaugurating a system of duty for military officers that would be incompatible with that true and perfect allegiance that can be given only to one master.

Conflict of duty in Military officers holding civil appointments in War Office

19. The relative position and power of the Commander-in-Chief and Secretary of State may be thus definitely described.[1] In delegation from the Crown with the sanction of the Cabinet, the Commander-in-Chief acts in the command and discipline of the Army under the Secretary of State, just as—to compare great things to small—the Chief Commissioner of the Metropolitan Police acts in the command and discipline of that Force under the Home Office. Both the Army and Police would be useless, and become demoralized, if they were appointed for the sinister purposes of personal or political patronage. "If," said Lord Dalhousie, "there were anything in the conduct of the Commander-in-Chief which required the interference of the Secretary of State, the Secretary of State has not only the right but it is his bounden duty to interfere. It was his business to trust to the Commander-in-Chief the administration of the discipline of the Army, and, except under very peculiar circumstances, not to interfere with that at all." And again, "the Secretary for War, and through him the Executive Government of the day, is responsible for all the acts of the Commander-in-Chief, but that the Government and the Secretary of State putting confidence in the Commander-in-Chief trust to him entirely, and without interference with the discipline of the Army."

Relative position of the Secretary of State and Commander-in-Chief

20. There is, therefore, nothing more involved in the arrangement than a complete division of labour. The Commander-in-Chief's Office and the Secretary of State's Office, when properly constituted, have little in

The arrangement is one of division of labour

---

[1] Report of the Organisation Committee, 1860, p ix.

common, most of their functions are totally distinct. The expediency of placing the patronage of the Army beyond the immediate control of a Parliamentary officer, renders this division of labour and responsibility essential. The position of the Secretary of State towards the Army is this,—as a Parliamentary Minister, representing the civil community, he stands between it and the Crown; and as a Minister of the Crown upholding these prerogatives, he stands between it and Parliament.[1]

21. "Dual Government" never ought to exist; the Constitution has provided—and the Ministry are supposed to maintain in its integrity—a Civil Department, independent, and supreme over, the Military employed in the government and command of the Army. Once constitute the War Office and Horse Guards of the same *personnel*, destroying the distinctive character of each office, and a dual government is created; the line between Civil Administration and Military Command—of essential importance to maintain—is destroyed, and indefinite responsibilities arise against the Minister, on the one hand, and the Military Officer on the other, leading, in their natural development, to Constitutional derangement.[2]

Dual government of the Army

22 It is essential that the Secretary of State, as the responsible Minister exercising the Prerogatives of the Crown, should enjoy the confidence of Parliament   Unless that confidence exists towards the Minister, and the Department over which he presides, the Commons will be apt to take the functions of the executive Government into their own hands—to assume towards the Army the discharge of duties vested in the Crown. The evils' that would inevitably result from this encroachment upon the prerogative of the Crown are proved by the evils that did result at that period of our history when the Speaker of the House of Commons was appointed to the Chief command, and the House itself appointed all officers in the land and sea forces. "The Army trampled on all Law, compelled a remnant of this House to become the instrument of its Generals, and when their services were no longer needed, they expelled even that remnant with outrage, and drove your predecessor, Sir, from the chair

Balance of power between the Crown and Parliament.

[1] Chap XVII, par 56 *et seq*   [2] Chap XVII, pars 56-62

which you now fill." [1]   It has, therefore, been the endeavour of great Statesmen in the subsequent period of our History to define, and, if possible, to maintain the boundary that lies between, and limits the powers of the Crown on the one hand, and those of Parliament on the other, that each may act strictly within the scope of its own authority.

23. Many illustrations have been given, in the previous pages of this Work, of the duties that devolve upon the Secretary of State as the Minister of the Crown with regard to the Army; and therefore what appears to me necessary here to shew is, that the three essential Prerogatives of Government, Command, and Disposition, rest with the Crown, and not with Parliament: first explaining how, so far as the Secretary of State was involved in responsibility, Arms were formerly issued to the Forces under the authority of the Crown.

The three essential prerogatives of the Crown

24. As already shown, the functions of raising men were discharged through the Secretary at War, and of arming them through the agency of the Board of Ordnance. All that the Commander-in-Chief could do, with regard to the issue of Arms, was to make the requisition to the Secretary at War. If he objected to the expense, no issue was made, but if made, a Royal Sign Manual Warrant, countersigned by the Secretary of State, authorized the issue upon the demand of the Secretary at War. [2] "The issue of arms," said Lieutenant-General Sir John Macdonald, "will always be regarded with great jealousy, and the more departments it goes through in that sort of way the more secure the public are in the issue of arms. The concurrence of those various authorities, according to my experience, act not only as a check on abuse, but it makes the issue of arms an issue of the gravest character, which can only be done through the highest departments of the Government." [3]

Raising and arming men

I. As to the Government and Command of the Army :—

25. As incident to these functions, the power of reward and

[1] Sir James Mackintosh, 32 H D (O S), p 986
[2] Civil Administration, 1837, p. 12, Ordnance Expen, 1850, pp 214, 215.
[3] See Order of 1728, Mis Book 521, p 240, Chap XX, par 2, Chap XXI, par 21

punishment rests wholly with the Crown, subject to a limit incident to the nature of our Parliamentary Govern-ment, viz, that all pecuniary recompense needs the express sanction of Parliament. The Secretary of State, not being a Finance Minister, could only act in the grant of pecuniary rewards by way of recommendation to the Treasury, but for the bestowal of honours by the Sovereign—the greater part of the reward to every honourable profession—he was alone responsible. In the Orders of the Bath and Victoria Cross,[1] the Letters Patent and Warrant provide that the Secretary of State shall be the channel for representing the claims of candidates, and he discharges this duty as a Minister of the Crown and not as a Parliamentary officer [2]

26. "If ever the day came," said Lord Palmerston,[3] "when the power of rewarding military services should be transferred from the Crown to the House of Commons, those who saw it might say that they had witnessed the deathblow to the Constitution." "To dispute the old legal maxim that the Crown was the fountain of honour could not be maintained; and," continued Mr. Wynn,[4] "History should show the danger of transferring to any other power than that of the Crown, the grant of military rewards and distinctions. Upon such a transfer the country must become an absolute republic; for he was persuaded that they who began by petitioning would very soon end with demands. Let the House consider how short a time elapsed before the Parliamentary Army, in the

The bestowal of rewards

Lord Palmerston's and Mr Wynn's views

---

[1] Notes U U and V V, Appendix, and 136 H D (3), p 1244

[2] Medals for the Army date (I think), from the Egyptian campaign under Sir R. Abercrombie, but for the Navy, from William III's reign   The 4 Wm and Mary, c 25, sec. 10 (1692), declared that "one-tenth part of the prize taken by any private man-of-war, should be paid to the Treasurer of the Navy for medals and other reward for officers, mariners, and seamen in Her Majesty's ships at sea, who shall be found to have done any signal or extraordinary service ' And see 14 Com Journ, p. 411. As to Soldiers medals, see H G. (Gen Order), p 582, 1 June, 1847, and p 597, 12 Feb, 1850, 167 H. D. (3), p 825, and Lords' Papers 1850, Vol xx, p 461

It may be here noticed that no one in the Military Service can, without criminal offence, accept any pension or honour from any foreign Sovereign, save with the consent of his own Sovereign   3 Coke Inst., p. 144, and 4 Rep, p. 268 1 Russ. on Crimes, pp 136, 140

[3] Debate of 22nd March 1822.   [4] 6 H D (2), p 1244

reign of Charles I., insisted upon their claims being attended to. This would always be the case when a popular assembly attempted to distribute military rewards, and to keep in its own hands the command of the Army. It had always been found that that House was disposed to go beyond the measure of reward recommended by the Crown in cases of extraordinary merits."

27. For Parliament to be indifferent as to the manner in which honours are bestowed by the Crown upon Public servants, would be inconsistent with the interest that the people take in their advancement; therefore, returns [1] have been granted of the appointments made, and discussions raised upon the merits of the recipients.[2] But the late Lord Palmerston again warned the House against the evils that would result to the service from any such interference. "He thought [3] the Commons were not the most competent judges of the relative merits of officers, with reference to the grant of honours to be conferred by the Crown. If the House should be pleased to take into their hands to pick out the officers who were fitted to receive the different degrees of Orders of the Bath, those honours would become the subjects of canvass in Parliament, instead of being awarded according to the judgment of the authorities at the head of the Army, who must be the most competent judges of the relative merits of officers who might be candidates for honours of this kind. He thought such a course, instead of improving the feeling of the Army, would lead officers to believe that the way to acquire honours was to get some friend to come down to the House, and to complain that distinctions had been conferred upon certain officers, while others had been passed over. A feeling would thus be created in the Army that they must look to the House of Commons for these rewards instead of to the Crown."

Bestowal of rewards criticised in Parliament.

28. In the general question of Military Punishments the Secretary of State is responsible. One of the earliest entries in the War Office books is a Royal Sign Manual Order,[4] countersigned by the Secretary of State, and

As to military punishments.

---

[1] 144 H. D. (3), p 495.   [2] 2 Mai. 1856, Admiral Sir Charles Napier
[3] 110 H D (3), pp 1740, 1741
1676, 17th May, Mis Bk 513, p 160 ; and see Bk 721, p. 29

addressed to Prince Rupert, for the punishment of drunkenness in the Army, and the Articles of War have been uniformly framed by the Crown. In the year 1866, after they had been altered in a manner prejudicial to the liberty of persons subject to them, a motion in the Commons was threatened, to deprive the Crown of the power of making Articles, except with the previous sanction of Parliament;[1] but, the Judge-Advocate-General explained to the House that the prerogative of the Crown was exercised in the instance under notice by a Minister responsible to the House, and the motion was withdrawn.

29. The power of appointing and dismissing officers and soldiers is, vested solely in the Crown;[2] but though this Constitutional rule is incontrovertible, none, in its exercise, is more imprudently canvassed in Parliament The Secretary of State is plainly responsible, while the interference of Parliament, except by vote of censure against the Minister, relaxes the discipline of the Army, and tends to weaken the authority of the Crown. "Of all the royal prerogatives, this was unquestionably the one which a well-informed and well-intentioned House of Commons would be the least inclined unnecessarily to meddle with; for he was sure the House would see that the gradation between a frequent interference with the exercise of that prerogative, and taking the prerogative entirely into their own hands, was so easy, that if they indulged in the former they would soon virtually do what, substantially, they would never be disposed to agree to Before the House could be induced to enter into any investigation of the exercise of the prerogative connected with the command of the Army, there must be a strong presumption of abuse in that exercise."[3]

As to appointment and dismissal of officers.

30. In all matters of discipline, the Royal authority is supreme, and the decisions of the Crown final; but, after the sentence of a Court-martial has been confirmed, Parliament is often invited to review and constitute itself a Court of Appeal from the decisions of the Court

In matters of discipline Court-martial sentences

---

[1] 187 H D (3), p 1671.　　[2] Chap XV, par 111. XVI, pars. 129-111
[3] Lord Palmerston, 6 H D. (2), p 311

and of the Crown. In Captain Robeson's case, Earl Russell prevailed upon the House of Commons to refuse such an inquiry.[1]— "I do not think that were the House convinced of the existence of such circumstances in this case, it would proceed in the manner proposed,—viz., the appointment of a Select Committee; but that it would rather proceed by asking for the Minutes of a Court-martial, and then addressing His Majesty to take such steps as might be necessary in case of injustice, partiality, or illegality of sentence. There can be no doubt that, under that kind of superintendence and supervision which this House ought to exercise, there might arise cases which would require such a proceeding as I have hinted at, but I can hardly believe it possible that any case whatever should induce this House to say, 'We think the proceedings before this Court-martial were not justifiable, that the conduct of the officers composing it were not according to Military Law, and therefore we will appoint a Committee of our own number to whom these proceedings shall be referred, and before whom this case shall be tried over again.'"

31. In other cases—the House of Commons has sought to punish officers that have not been brought to Court-martial. A motion for inquiry into the conduct of an officer, which was alleged to render him unfit to serve Her Majesty, was resisted by Lord Macaulay on these grounds:[2]—"His first objection was a very obvious one. It was a Constitutional objection. While there was no prerogative of the Crown which that House was not entitled to offer its advice upon, yet in offering advice on such points, it should be guided by a very sound discretion. Indeed, none but the most imperious reasons, in the most extreme cases, could warrant such interference with the royal prerogative; and he believed that, above all other prerogatives, in all well-organized States, the control of the Army, and the awarding of rewards and punishments to military men, were considered most exclusively to belong to the Supreme Executive authority, and that such matters ought not to be submitted to large popular assemblies of men, who are too apt to be influenced by party and factious

[marginal note:] For enquiry into conduct of officers

---

[1] 30 H D (3), p 117, Chap VIII, par 90   [2] 58 H D (3), pp 339-41

impulse. . . . . . Into the merits and demerits of the officer's
conduct he would not go; but, viewing that conduct in whatever light it might deserve, he still said that the present motion
was highly objectionable, because, in all matters of this kind,
they should be guided by general rules; they should beware
how they hastened to take advantage of the unpopularity of an
individual, to introduce a precedent which, if once established,
would lead to the most fatal effects to the whole of our military
system, and work a great injustice to all officers in Her Majesty's
service. . . . . . As to the proposition for erecting that
House into a penal Court of Inquiry, he must protest against it
as a species of tribunal dangerous and revolutionary. It would
make that House, which had not the power to administer an
oath to witnesses, or punish them if they prevaricated, a Court
for passing a sentence which might ruin a poor man, in the
shape of a pecuniary fine, or in attaching a stigma to his name
almost worse than death itself." By the division, the House
adopted this view.

32. All regulations are framed by the responsible Minister,
Regulations and not by Parliament. Therefore, when the late
made by the
Crown Lord Herbert was requested to lay the draft resolutions for altering the Purchase System upon the table of the
House of Commons, that they might be discussed, and the
opinion of the House expressed upon them, he plainly refused
to do so. After their issue they might be moved for, and
presented, for "the Army was governed not by the votes of the
House of Commons, but by the Queen's Regulations; and he
should not be doing his duty if he produced any Regulation for
discussion in that House before it had been decided upon by
the Queen."[1]

II. As to the Distribution of the Army:—

33. Where or how the Army shall be disposed of and
Disposition employed rests solely with the Cabinet;[2] for the
and employ-
ment of the movement of troops, formerly by a Royal Sign
Army Manual Warrant countersigned by the Secretary

---

[1] 157 H. D. (3), p. 342.   [2] 'Army and Navy Appointments,' 1833, p 151

of State, was authorised in later years by a letter from the Secretary of State to the Secretary at War, directing him to issue "a route" for the Army to march from one place to another in the United Kingdom. This arrangement rendered the *Military* wholly subordinate to the *Civil* power; for "the Commander-in-Chief," said the late Duke of Wellington, in 1837,[1] "cannot at this moment move a corporal's guard from hence to Windsor without going to a civil department for authority. He must get a route."[2]

34. Members of the Commons have occasionally sought for information as to the distribution of troops, which the Ministers of the Crown have thought it to be their duty to withhold, and the House has supported them in their refusal. *Information as to the distribution of the Army given or withheld.*

35. The responsibility of defending the empire rests upon the Executive Government, and that object might be wholly defeated if the policy of the Cabinet were disclosed to Parliament, and through that assembly to the whole world. In ordinary times, and to justify the votes in supply, the Commons have insisted upon having a distribution of the forces laid before them,[3] but on a recent occasion a member of great experience and authority in the House, Mr. C. W. Wynn, declared "that he never knew any member insist on such returns, after it had been declared by Ministers, on their own responsibility, that the returns would be injurious. It was interfering with the undisputed rights of the executive power."[4] *At the discretion of the Ministers of the Crown.*

36. Where troops are to be employed abroad, Parliament has protested against their being sent away;[5] but then the reasons for secrecy are more readily accepted than upon the removal of troops from one to another part of Great Britain. The disposition of the Winter Guard having been made known to the enemy in 1689, the Commons in- *Withheld as to troops employed abroad.*

[1] 'Civil Administration, 1837,' p 37, and see Appendix CXLVII

[2] Lord Panmure's Evidence, Questions 404-417, General Peel's,—Questions 3716-3723, Lord Herbert's,—Questions 6360-6368, in Committee on Military Organisation, 1860, and Memorandum of 1802, in Mis Book, p 68.

[3] Chap VI., par. 4, and distributions granted, 17 Com Journ, p 294, 37 ib, p 36, 41 ib., p 255, 9 Parl Hist., pp 870-83, 74 Com Journ, pp 573, 747, 87 ib, pp 76, 646   [4] 16 H D (3), p 381   [5] 19 Parl Hist., p 650

stituted an inquiry with a view to bring the offender to punishment;[1] and the House readily supported the Ministers in refusing a return of the number, state, and disposition of the troops in America, which Colonel Barré desired, in the year 1775 before the Estimates were taken into consideration, on the ground that such a return would form a most dangerous precedent

37. The Ministry of Earl Grey refused in 1833 to lay the distribution of the forces upon the table of the House of Commons with the Estimates, and they were supported by the House upon a division. "No House of Commons," Sir John Hobhouse said,[2] "at the commencement of every session, could fairly call upon the Government to state the manner in which the Army of the country was disposed of—at home or abroad. That was certainly a matter which should be left to the discretion of the Crown, and the existing Government, according to the emergencies of the times; for there might be circumstances, with which the Government alone could be acquainted, to render it of the utmost importance that the mode in which the military force was disposed of should be concealed. With the vast interests of our great empire—with colonies spread over the whole surface of the globe—it was apparent, looking to England, Ireland, and the West Indies, and, indeed, to all parts of the world, that no man could have a right to call upon the Government to proclaim how many troops were stationed in this place, and how many regiments in that. It would not only be the grossest imprudence,[3] it would be usurping the power delegated to the Government; and it would be exposing to those who might take advantage of such exposition, what force was to be stationed, in disciplined array, in different parts of the empire."

38. Lord Palmerston objected on Constitutional grounds.

Margin notes: A.D 1833 As to troops at home, refused by Lord Grey's Ministry

---

[1] 10 Com Journ, p 278, 17 Parl Hist, p 568, and 18 Parl Hist, p 838, and in 1840 a Clerk in the War Office was dismissed on suspicion of having given a distribution of the Army to the Press [2] 16 H D (3), p 381

[3] In June, 1865, arrangements were made by the War Office for the supply of authentic information as to the disposition of the Forces to every purchaser of the Monthly Army List.

The tendency of the motion went to invest that House with the command of the Army   If he had no other objection   Lord Palmerston s concurrence to it, that with him would be sufficient.   On one day the hon. member held that the House would be the best judge of rewards to meritorious officers, on another, he considered that the House was to judge the propriety of continuing small or large forces in particular stations, garrisons, or colonies   The fact was, that the object of hon. gentlemen opposite was to vest the command of the Army and Navy in that House.   This he resisted as most dangerous and unconstitutional "

39 Sir Robert Peel's Ministry were equally firm ; and when a man, experienced in public affairs—especially in   A D 1842 the office of Secretary at War,—sought for informa-   Sir Robert Peel s Ministry tion in Parliament as to the movement of Troops in Scotland, Sir James Graham, the Home Secretary, expressed himself as " somewhat surprised that such a question should be put by the gentleman, considering his official experience.   His answer was, that the fact was true ; certain troops had been removed   But as to the object and purpose which induced Her Majesty's Government to direct it, he must positively decline giving any answer whatever.   The only answer he could give was that Her Majesty's Government were responsible for the maintenance of the peace in Scotland." [1]

40. The duties of the Secretary of State, as I have endeavoured to describe them in this Chapter, are not   Miscellaneous Duties such that the office can be—though the Department   of the Secretary of State may be worked by able assistants—safely bestowed   as a Member of the upon any novice in politics.   It follows, therefore,   Cabinet that the Statesman charged with the Secretariat must be a man to share largely in the general affairs of the Cabinet, and to defend, in a fair proportion with his colleagues, the general policy of the Government.   These duties are scarcely less imperative upon him than those of his own Department. When, therefore, due allowance is made for the official time thus absorbed, little—it is not an exaggeration to say, that,

[1] Coll D (3, i 1350

in the Session, but *very* little—time remains, for the speciality of the Department. In the latter service, his intercourse with the outer world and with the Commander-in-Chief consumes much of his attention, and the residue—such as it is—is left to rule with diligence the Civil affairs of a large Army, and to control the expenditure of some millions sterling of the Public Treasure.

41. What is there of "prudent antiquity," or of prudence of any kind, in overwhelming such a Minister with a vast variety of employments? Unless existing, who would be found to justify an organization that trusted the highest powers of Government, and, maybe, the policy of the Cabinet,[1] to the care of the conflicting elements found in the heterogeneous staff of which the Department is composed? And, again, is it not trifling with the authority of the Crown to dwarf down the highest Constitutional Officer, whose legitimate acts are "those of State,"[2] to the level of such small and insignificant functions as many of his official staff now have to discharge?[3] If the Board of Trade or of Works were so overweighted, where would be the political danger which is apparent when the "Pleasure of the Crown may at any time be conveyed," or a "Control Scheme approved," in a letter for which a responsible Minister can—in theory only—be held responsible? But this is anticipating the subject of the concluding Chapter of this work.[4]

[margin note: Imprudence of these arrangements.]

---

[1] As to the Political Unity of the Cabinet, see 'Cox's Institutions,' p 252.

[2] Chap XVI, par 20, Chap XVII, pars 56-64

[3] The late Sir George Lewis was twitted by Mr B Osborne with being a monster "Moses and Son" 165 H D. (3), p 1091. Again, in any trifling prosecution instituted (of necessity, in the absence of any Public Prosecutor, by the Secretary of State), to consider it as a "State Prosecution," to be conducted by the Attorney and Solicitor-General and other counsel for the Crown, would be a monstrous injustice to the Prisoner and to the Public

[4] Chap XXIX In reference to the Secretariat, it may be noticed that the office of Private Secretary to the Sovereign was, when established in 1812, looked upon with great jealousy. (See 22 H D. (O S.), p 335) It was suggested, at a later period, that he should be sworn to the Privy Council, but it was not done (Vol II of Wellington 'Supplementary Despatches,' pp. 103-105) As to Private Secretary to a Minister, see Harrington v Kloprogge, 2 Bro & Bing, p 678

CHAPTER XXVI.

The Office of the Commander-in-Chief.

1. It has been already noticed that in the year 1793 the office of Commander-in-Chief was established,[1]—and it may here be added, for many years continued,—without the express sanction of Parliament; for the contingent expenses of the office were paid out of Army Extraordinaries[2] until 1812,—when an estimate for the Establishment was formed, and voted by Parliament in that year.

A.D. 1793.

Office established.

2. Lord Bacon, in enumerating the causes of danger in an Empire, unless care and circumspection be used, includes Military Force. "It is a dangerous thing," he observes, "when the men of war live and remain in a body, and are used to donatives." Of such evils we had abundant evidence at the time of the Commonwealth, when largess was given by Parliament in the first instance to the General,[3] and ultimately to his troops. "But training of men," he continues, "and arming them in several places and under several Commanders, and without donatives, are things of defence and of no danger."[4] Upon this theory our national Militia has been formed, and upon the same theory William III. acted, at the Revolution, when he dispersed the Army in small detachments all over the kingdom,[5] and committed the management of it to *several* Commanders, probably that, as Lord Bacon suggests, of counsellors, one should keep sentinel over another.[6]

The ancient policy of England was to keep the Army in small detachments.

---

[1] Chap XII, par 1, and Chap XXI, pars 5 to 16

[2] 'Army and Navy Appointments,' 1833, p 207.

[3] See the present of 5000*l* to the Lord General (Essex), 2 Com Journ, pp 833 8, 944, Grants to Cromwell and Fairfax, 5 C J, pp 162-7, Grants to the Soldiers, 2 C J, pp 842, 4 C J, p 162, 5 C J, pp 231-4   [4] Essay 19, p 189

[5] Chap II, par 4, *ante*   [6] Par. 50 and note (*post*)

3. For a century after the Revolution, our National Policy
towards the Army remained the same   The troops,
This policy
followed at
and for a cen
tury after the
Revolution
few in number, were scattered over the country in
Independent Companies or small Regimental Detachments acting, where needed, under the sanction of the
Reponsible Ministers in aid of the Civil Power.   To entrust
the command of the Army or Navy—the coercive power in the
State—to one person other than the Sovereign is a danger
at any time,[1] and this feeling of insecurity often found expression in Parliament.   Even the King's presence in this Country
was thought to give security against Military aggression, and,
in the Lords' Debate upon the Mutiny Bill of 1724, Lord
Wharton went so far as to aver that if, during the King's
absence in Hanover, the Command of the Army should be
delegated to *one* person, the liberty and property of the people
would be endangered.[2]

4. The appointment of a Commander-in-Chief had often
been mooted in Parliament by those interested in the
The Ap-
pointment
suggested in
Parliament
as a remedy
against a
greater evil
Army; for as the King assumed the duties of Command,
and—as occasion required—acted upon the suggestions of a Parliamentary Minister, the Army became
essentially Political.   Therefore, in the course of experience, all Statesmen were ready to admit that the solution
of the difficulty was to be found in this appointment.

5. The first suggestion of it came in the year 1740, and—as
A.D. 1740
might be supposed—from the Military Officers in
Political in-
fluence to be
remedied by
appointment
of Com-
mander-in
Chief
Parliament.   Upon the proposal to augment the Army,
an effort was made by the Opposition, first to defeat the
measure, or, failing in this, to get a Commander-in-
Chief appointed,—that professional merit, and not
political influence, should guide the Sovereign in the selection
and promotion of Officers   The Duke of Argyll,[3] who, notwithstanding his great Military services, had been recently dismissed from Political motives, raised an important debate upon

---

[1] Sir James Graham s Evidence before the Select Committee on the Admiralty,
1861 Question 1012, *et passim*.   [2] 8 Parl Hist, p 388
[3] Debate in the House of Lords 11 Parl Hist, p 902, and Chap XVI, pars.
66-71

the condition of the Army, and the Opposition objected to the *political* patronage which the augmention of the Army in the method proposed would throw into the hands of the Ministry.

6. It was suggested, in the course of the debate, that the Duke's observations reflected on the King.[1] "I know not," said Lord Cholmondeley, "how the general regulation of our Forces, and the distribution of Military honours, can be condemned without extending some degree of censure to a person who ought not to be mentioned, as concurring in any measures injurious to the public. Our Army, my Lords, is maintained by the Parliament, but commanded by the King, who has not either done or directed anything of which his people may justly complain." But the Duke at once interposed, by saying that "he imputed no part of the errors committed in the regulation of the Army, to His Majesty; but to the Ministers whose duty it was to advise him, and whom the Law condemns to answer for the consequences of their counsels." The Commons were equally in earnest in deprecating the Political Patronage in the Army; for upon the Estimates the augmentation was opposed on similar grounds, but without success.[2]

7. In the year 1751, upon the Estimate for the Staff of the Army being brought up on Report, the reception of it was opposed by Lord Egmont, and an important Debate ensued.[3] At that time the Duke of Cumberland was the Captain-General, and the Political danger of entrusting the *small army* then existing to the authority of any one man was fully discussed.[4] If his allegiance were given loyally to the person of the Sovereign, his power might be used against the Ministers and People. If an open breach arose between them, then the Captain-General would influence the Army to make *him* the master of the Country and of the Sovereign;[5] therefore—it was argued—such an appointment in the time of Peace was of most dangerous consequence both to the People and to the Sovereign. The answer to these objections was given by Mr. Pelham. The commission of Captain-General having been originally granted for the command of the

[Margin note: Minister and not the king responsible]

[Margin note: A.D. 1751. As to Captain-General's appointment.]

---

[1] Pp. 913, 914.   [2] Debate in 1742, 12 Parl Hist., p 611-23   [3] 26 Com. Journ., pp. 16, 38, and 14 Parl. Hist., pp 902-29.   [4] P 903.   [5] P. 906.

Army in War continued, as was usual, in the time of Peace. That the post was one only of dignity and not of power, for all commissions were granted and orders issued by the King under the countersign of his Responsible Ministers, and, lastly, that the Commons might *expose* themselves to *danger* by acting ungratefully to a brave and beloved *General*, because that would attach to *his* interest not only the Army but a great part of the people. These or other arguments prevailed, for the vote was carried by a majority of 205 to 88.

8. The expediency of appointing a Commander-in-Chief came again under discussion in the year 1789,[1] after the Marquis of Lothian (upon the eve of the King's recovery from illness), had been removed from his command of the Life Guards with the offer of another regiment. In the debate upon the Estimates, the conduct and management of the Army came under notice ; the Ministers justified Lord Lothian's removal on the ground that he acted in a double capacity as Military Officer and as—Gold Stick—a State attendant, personally employed about His Majesty.[2] This idea Mr. Fox ridiculed, declaring that His Majesty had been made the instrument of party views, inspired with sentiments of political vengeance ; obviously used as the engine of Ministerial revenge and punishment.[3] He then went on to advocate the appointment of a Commander-in-Chief, who might bring merit to the foot of the throne, and draw it forth from places where *Ministers* never looked for it,—viz., from the field of *actual* service ; that there could be no Minister for the Military so fit as a Commander-in-Chief, and none more so than a member of the Royal Family.[4]

9. That the government of the Army, even so lately as the reign of George III., was regulated by the political conduct of its members, cannot be questioned, when the dismissals of General Conway for his vote on General Warrants, and of other Officers, for discharging their Parliamentary duties, are remembered. Military *governments*, according to the theory of that Sovereign, were to be given to the political supporters of his Ministry, and

A.D. 1789.

Appointment of a Commander in Chief again urged.

Political government of the Army in Geo III's reign

---

[1] 27 Parl Hist., p. 1310.   [2] Ib , p 1314   [3] Ib , p 1316   [4] Ib , p. 1318

therefore forfeited when their adverse votes were recorded to be in the Division Lists.[1] It became highly expedient, for the efficiency of the Army, if not for the safety of the State, that the promotion of Officers should be removed from the arena of Politics, and entrusted—as the best method of effecting this object—to an *executive* Officer not directly responsible to Parliament.

10 Mr. Fox having, in the discussion upon the Estimates of 1792, called attention to the dismissal of Officers—and especially of three[2] whom he named — for Political reasons, occasion was soon taken—upon the augmentation of the Forces on the outbreak of the War with France in 1793,—to appoint Lord Amherst to act as Commander-in-Chief. With an Invasion threatening and the official duties of the Commander-in-Chief totally undefined, it need not excite surprise to find that the Duke of York, who succeeded to office in 1795,[3] should fall into the mistake of supposing, as Lord Palmerston expresses it, " that the whole and absolute control over every part of the Military Service was vested in the Commander-in-Chief."[4] Few persons can read the Reports of the Commissioners of Military Enquiry (made in pursuance of the 45 Geo. III., c. 47), without coming to that conclusion ; for certainly the Master-General and Board of Ordnance were superseded by the appointment of officers under the Secretary at War to take instructions from the Commander-in-Chief, not only in the instance of the Barrackmaster-General, but in matters relating to Works erected for the Defence of the Realm, with which the office of the Commander-in-Chief has nothing whatever to do.

A.D. 1793.

On the appointment of Lord Amherst, duties of his office wholly undefined.

11. The authority which a General Officer exercising the Chief Command of the Army holds is either a Patent under the Great Seal, or a Letter of Service, under the countersign or signature of a responsible Minister.

Authority on appointment held by Commander-in Chief

---

[1] See Chap IX , pars 6 to 11, *ante*   [2] 30 Parl Hist., p 171

[3] The office of Commander-in-Chief was transferred to the present rooms in the Horse Guards, and Mr Dundas, the Colonial Minister, transferred to Parliament Street in 1794-5 , the Secretary at War, until 1857, occupying the other rooms A passage running over the archway divided the two departments then and until 1857   [4] Lord Palmerston's Memorandum (Appendix CXXIX)

12. The Patent may appoint the holder to be Captain-General and Commander-in-Chief (which was the case when the late Duke of York held the Command in 1808), or Commander-in-Chief only, which was done when Sir D. Dundas [1] succeeded to the Command in 1809. The last Patent granted to the late Duke of Wellington,[2] appointed him ‚‘to be Commander-in-Chief, during pleasure, of all and singular the Land Forces employed or to be employed within our United Kingdom of Great Britain and Ireland." He was carefully to discharge the trust of Commander-in-Chief (by doing and performing all things thereunto belonging), and the Patent "commanded all officers and soldiers who were or should be employed in the land Service, to acknowledge and obey him as their Commander-in-Chief, and enjoined the Duke to observe and follow such instructions, orders, and directions, from time to time, as he shall receive from the Queen, in pursuance of the trust thereby reposed in him."

A Patent of Appointment.

13. The Letter of Service appoints the holder—as in the instances of the late Lord Hardinge and the present Commander-in-Chief—under the hand of the Secretary at War, " to serve as a General,[3] with four paid Aides-de-Camp, upon the Staff of the Army," and signifies Her Majesty's pleasure that the holder should obey orders received from Her Majesty, the Commander-in-Chief, or any other his superior officer."

On a letter of service

14. In describing the duties of the Commander-in-Chief's official Staff, it is necessary to observe that, at the time of Lord Amherst's appointment, the Adjutant-General occupied two rooms in Crown Street, Westminster, and the Quartermaster-General occupied one room in the War Office—both officers acting under the Secretary at War. From the year 1793 they have been attached to the Staff of—

Official Staff of the Commander-in-Chief

---

[1] Appendix CXXXVIII   [2] Organization Report, 1860, p. 730.

[3] November 30, 1852. Appendix CXXXIX The pay of a Commander in-Chief is 16*l* 8*s* 9*d*., and of a General commanding, 5*l* 13*s* 9*d* per day —Sir H. Taylor before the Finance Committee, 1828, p 268.

and report on all matters of military detail to—the Commander-in-Chief.[1]

15. The office of Adjutant-General was one of great antiquity. It is said that he had the charge of all matters relating to the discipline, arming, and clothing of the Troops,[2] and was responsible for the Regulations and Orders to the Army, issued from time to time with the King's sanction. Before the appointment of a Commander-in-Chief, the Adjutant-General's correspondence was confined to the Army in Great Britain and the discipline of the Troops in the Field,[3] other matters being sent to the Secretary at War. But from the System inaugurated in 1795, " his department assumed a new and more important character. The Army was re-modelled—special and confidential Reports of the conduct of each Regiment and Officer in it were made to him. General regulations were issued to all the Forces, laying down one uniform system of discipline. The Returns of the Army, formerly few in number and inaccurately made, were largely increased and carefully prepared by Civil assistants, then introduced; that the information required by Parliament might be supplied through the Adjutant-General's department wit accuracy."[4]

Adjutant-General of the Forces

16. In the year 1807 an addition was made to his duties by the abolition of the office of Inspector-General of Recruiting, and the transfer of the work to the Adjutant-General's Department. He thus had the arrangement and regulation of the Recruiting Service of the Army. Therefore from 520*l*, which was allowed for contingent expenses in 1792, the expenses of the Establishment rose to 1537*l*. 1*s*. 1*d*. in 1808.[5]

A D 1807

Recruiting of the Army transferred to the Adjutant-General

---

[1] 'Army and Navy Appointments,' 1833, pp 203, 206, Chap XXI par 9

[2] I cannot confirm this description, for I find no traces in the War Office Records that the Adjutant-General exercised these functions

[3] 11th Report of Military Inquiry, pp 48-59, 'Army and Navy Appointments, 1833,' Sir John Macdonald's Evidence   [4] Vol. I., p 387

[5] In 1827 the expense was 6806*l* 6*s* 2*d*. See further, as to increase of the office, Evidence before Finance Committee, 1828, p 192, and before Army Expenditure, 1850, *passim*. In 1853 and 1868 the expenses were 7,347*l*. and 21,468*l* respectively

17. The Quartermaster-General, acting under the Commander-in-Chief, filled a more ambiguous position. Under him was raised—as rivals to the Royal Engineers —a Staff Corps for the erection of Field and other works of defence that properly devolved on the Master-General of the Ordnance to execute.

The Quarter-master-General of the Forces.

18. To educate Line Officers for these duties, a Military College had to be raised;[1] and in 1799, a Staff Corps (of one Company) was formed for Service with the Expedition to the Helder[2] It was augmented in 1802 to four Companies, and, during the succeeding years prior to 1808, undertook the formation of Field and other works in the United Kingdom, approved by the Commander-in-Chief, and executed under the Generals of the Districts. In this manner—without any definite responsibility attaching to any Established Department of the State—was Public money expended in Military works,—as the formation of the Canal at Hythe, the Martello Towers, and the Intrenched Camp at Colchester.[3]

Staff Corps and College.

19. The more legitimate functions of the Quartermaster-General were said to be giving orders, and making arrangements for the movement of Troops; a business which was first taken into his Department in 1803, and a Military Staff created to carry out.[4] Information and Survey branches were formed, with a depôt for Military Plans and Papers. Prior to 1803 no return of the Quartermaster-General's Establishment can be traced,[5] but the salaries and contingent expenses for the year 1807 amounted to upwards of 7000*l.*[6]

Other duties of the Department.

20. The Office of Military Secretary dates from 1795 Upon Lord Amherst's appointment, he took, as his Secretary, Mr. Morse, one of the principal Clerks of the War Office,[7] who had the usual allowance of 10*s.* per day besides his salary, but on the appointment of the late

Office of Military Secretary to the Commander-in-Chief

---

[1] See Note W, *post*   [2] 11th Report on Military Inquiry, pp. 50, 119.
[3] List of these, p. 101   [4] Ib , p 13, and Mis. Book (1802), p 68
[5] Ib , p 87
[6] In 1827, it amounted to 5531*l* 18*s* 8*d* See Evidence before Finance Committee, 1828, p 291 In 1853 and 1868, to 5708*l* and 8736*l*
[7] Establishment for 1793-5 of H G Clerks, 8th Report of Military Expenditure, p 207

Duke of York as Commander-in-Chief, in the year 1795, he brought with him Colonel Brownrigg as " Public Secretary " to succeed Mr. Morse.[1] In 1794 Lord Amherst left the expenses of his office at 846*l*. 8*s*, but when the Commissioners of Military Enquiry reported in 1809,[2] they found the salaries and expenses amounted to 7638*l*. 15*s*. 6*d*.[3]

21. The Staff Officers of the Commander-in-Chief are appointed by the Crown on his recommendation, and as he is responsible for the discipline of the Army, they would be removed upon his representation. The first two Officers are appointed for a term of five years only ; but the Military Secretary,[4]—as on the Personal Staff of the Commander-in-Chief—during his pleasure or tenure of office[5] *Appointment of these three officers by the Commander-in-Chief*

22. All the appointments are strictly professional, and not political. "I know," said Lord Hardinge,[6] speaking of these Officers, "that the late Duke of York was extremely anxious that his Military Secretary, or some other of his official officers, should be in the House of Commons, to assist the Secretary at War in the explanations of his military Administration of the Army ; but the Government of that day, particularly my Lord Liverpool and Lord Castlereagh, objected to any such interference on the part of the Horse Guards ; and I recollect when Sir Herbert Taylor, the Military Secretary to the Duke of York, was returned for the borough of Windsor, in 1820, that Lord Liverpool or Lord Castlereagh sent to him, and told him that he ought not to interfere in the Military discussions of the Estimates, that by ancient custom and usage that duty had been delegated to the Secretary at War, who, aided by the Judge-Advocate-General in the House of Commons, was the mouth-piece of the Government to sustain any attacks that might be made *upon the Commander-in-Chief or his office.* *Strictly professional and non political.*

---

[1] 8th Report, 1809, p 139   [2] Ib , p 140.
[3] In 1821 the expenses were 6831*l* See the Evidence before Finance Committee, 1828 p 277 In 1853 and 1868, 13,252*l* and 18,331*l* respectively.
[4] 8th Report of Military Inquiry, *passim*, and Lord Dalhousie's Evidence before Committee on Army Expenditure, pp 78, 79
[5] ' Civil Administration, 1837,' p. 27

Lord Liverpool objected to Major-General Sir Henry Torrens accepting a seat in Parliament for the purpose of preventing the Commander-in-Chief from interfering in the House of Commons; Sir Henry Torrens therefore declined the offered seat, as he was to be mute on Military discussions; and Sir Herbert Taylor never interfered in the discussion of the Estimates."

23. It was some time before the position assigned to the Commander-in-Chief in relation to the Civil Administration and Military Government of the Army was either accurately defined by the responsible Ministers of the Crown or accepted by the Officers from time to time holding the command of the Army. The controversy between the Secretary at War's Office (as represented by Lord Palmerston), and the Commander-in-Chief's Office (as represented by Sir D. Dundas) has been already referred to. The Statement of the Commander-in-Chief's duties that was laid before Parliament in January, 1809, is printed in the Appendix,[1] and it must be accepted with the qualifications that subsequent Constitutional Usage has since attached to the office.

Position of the Commander-in-Chief in the Military Administration for some time undefined.

24 The Office of Commander-in-Chief is *strictly* Executive, and for the discharge of his duties he is directly responsible to the Constitutional Ministers of the Crown, but not responsible in any other manner to *Parliament*. Exercised within the limits of the Constitution, his duties are those of "Government ~~~~ ~~~~nd" over the Army. "The late Lord ~~~~~~~~~~~~ considered the Commander-in-Ch ~~~~~~~~~~ cer, and that it was unconstitu~~~~~~~~~~~~~ give him any direct official con~~~~~~~ Commons which might lead to encroachm~~~~ ~~e Royal Prerogative, the command of the Army being one of the King's most peculiar and important functions."[2]

Strictly an Executive Officer under the Crown.

---

[1] Appendix CXL

[2] 'Civil Administration, 1837,' p 27   The first communication opened between the House of Commons and the Army was on the 4th May, 1641 (2 Com Journ, p 133)   On the 5th, the House declared itself perpetual (Ib, pp. 136, 140).   On the 5th July, it gave direct orders for the payment of a particular Regiment (Ib,

25. The Commander-in-Chief represents the inherent prerogative of the Crown[1] in the *Command*, as the Ministers represent the Constitutional power of the Crown in the *Administration* of the Army.[2] If the Commander-in-Chief is to exercise his duties without interference from *Parliament*, it is essential to the preservation of this immunity that he should not interfere with the duties of Parliament or of the Finance Minister. As the Executive Officer of the Crown, he should preserve a scrupulous neutrality towards Parliament and the Army in all matters of pay, and avoid any interference in those duties which the Constitution—for the protection of the Civil community—has entrusted to Ministers and not to Soldiers. Whenever the Commander-in-Chief, either directly or indirectly (as through officers subordinate to him), exceeds his authority for Command, and assumes any for Administration, Parliament will justly complain of his encroachment upon the functions of the Constitutional Ministers. In the relationship of the Army to the Crown and to Parliament—wise Statesmen have hitherto kept the Ministers—as representing the interests of Parliament,—and the Commander-in-Chief—as representing the executive duties of the Crown,—scrupulously within those limits which Constitutional usage has marked out for each of them; the best guarantee for the loyal discharge of their relative duties to Parliament and the Crown.

[margin: Not to encroach on duties of Constitutional Minister]

26. The functions of the Commander-in-Chief depend upon Departmental arrangements rather than Statutory authority.[3] The powers conceded to him are granted solely with the view to promote the efficiency and discipline of the Army. In its efficiency all members of the Civil community are interested as a measure of protection from foreign aggression; in its discipline (apart from efficiency), as a means of protection against Military encroach-

[margin: Duties of the Commander-in-Chief dependent on Departmental arrangement.]

---

pp 212, 472) On the 18th August, Hollis asked them for orders, indeed, they sought authority from the King to give such (Ib , pp. 262, 263), and it soon followed that the Commons raised an Army by their own authority and for their own purposes (Ib., pp 302, 306, 401, 710, 729).

[1] Chap I , par 5, Chap VI , par 23   [2] Chaps V , VI., and VIII.
[3] As to signing Commissions under Statute, see Appendix, Note U

ment upon their civil rights. For both efficiency and discipline they hold the Government—acting through the Civil Minister at the War Office—responsible to them in Parliament.

27. The powers that are essential for the Commander-in-Chief to hold for the government and command of the Army will be found in the Mutiny Act and Articles of War, but a negative view of his duties will be seen by reference to what already has been or may hereafter be ascribed to the responsible Ministers of the Crown.

Powers of Commander-in-Chief

28 There are, however, two rules of conduct — at least so far as Constitutional Law and the opinion of distinguished Soldiers who held the office are entitled to respect — to be observed on the part of the Commander in-Chief absolutely, and admit of no controversy. These are, that his official duties (and inferentially those of General Officers serving under him) are not either political or financial.

Two absolute Rules to be observed.

I.—*First*—that his duties are not Political :—

29. Since the Revolution, and especially in modern times, the fundamental rule of the Army has been, and is, that "Officers non-commissioned, and soldiers, are forbidden to institute or take part in *any* meetings, demonstrations or processions for party or political purposes in barracks, quarters, camps, or elsewhere;"[1] and, therefore, having regard to this regulation. and to the special reasons that led up to the appointment of a Commander-in-Chief in modern times, it is plain that his office is essentially *non* political. Although General Conway[2] sat in the Commons in 1783, and the Duke of Wellington in the Lords in 1843,[3] and each as a Member of the Cabinet while he held the Command of the Army; yet the Constitutional usage is one of absolute exclusion on the part of the Commander-in-Chief from all political action, and from all political party in the State.[4]

First Commander in-Chief non-political.

---

[1] Queen's Regulations, 1868, par. 362, and Chap. VIII., par 50, *ante.* As soon as the Army became Political, the People petitioned it (and not the Commons) for a redress of grievances See 5 Com Journ., pp. 629, 634; and the Commons had to enter into treaty with the Army (Ib , pp 230, 232, 662)

[2] 24 Parl. Hist., pp. 114, 116.   [3] 66 H. D. (3), p 1350.   [4] 70 ib , p. 611.

30. To make the office Political would be the greatest possible evil, and it was so felt when, in the year 1837, Mr. Hume urged Lord Hill's retirement from the command of the Army because he did not happen to agree with the Whig Ministers. In the discussion on the Estimates, he moved a reduction by the amount of the Commander-in-Chief's pay; but the late Mr. Wynn objected to it "as an improper interference with the prerogative of the Crown, and an attempt to dictate to the Crown whom it should *not* employ, and that the House would thus arrogate to itself the management of the Army, than which nothing could be more dangerous to the Constitution." The motion was negatived.[1]

A.D. 1837

Mr. Hume's Motion as to Lord Hill's retirement.

31. In the same year, the Duke of Wellington expressed a very decided opinion that though the Master-General of the Ordnance should,—the Commander-in-Chief certainly should *not*—be in the Cabinet. "I have always been of opinion that the Commander-in-Chief ought not to be a member of the Cabinet: my reason for thinking so is that he ought not to be supposed to have any political influence as a bias on his mind; most particularly upon the subject of the promotions in the Army."[2]

Duke of Wellington's opinion.

32. Lord Hardinge expressed the same view. "More stability would be secured for maintaining the organization and discipline of the Army by not requiring the Commander-in-Chief to follow the particular fortunes of any party. All the directing policy of the Government can be altered according to the views of a new Cabinet by the exercise of that control which exists over the Commander-in-Chief through His Majesty's Secretaries of State; but, in order to preserve stability in matters of discipline, in order that the Commander-in-Chief should not be a political partisan, thereby discouraging the Officers of the Army from being political partisans for the advancement of their professional expectations (which would more or less be the case if the Commander-in-Chief was of necessity and *ex-officio* a political character,

The opinion of Lord Hardinge

---

[1] 37 H. D., pp. 814, 822.

[2] 'Civil Administration,' p. 40, and see 'Supplementary Despatches,' vol. iii., p. 636.

changeable under every varying circumstance of politics), it was, in my judgment, a wise object to release the Commander-in-Chief and the King from political partialities, which would hurt the service and disgust the officers." He had before remarked to the same Committee that the separation between finance and discipline brought the expenditure of the Army *into* the House of Commons, and kept the discipline and management of the Army *out* of it, and in the King's hands.[1]

33. When the Duke sat as a member of Sir Robert Peel's Cabinet, the arrangement was justified by the analogy of the Master-General of the Ordnance and of the First Lord of the Admiralty, and by urging—there being no absolute *rule* of exclusion,—that the Duke's great experience in *civil* as well as in Military affairs ought not to be lost in the civil counsels of Her Majesty.[2] The Duke himself disclaimed political responsibility, and declined to receive a deputation as a Minister: "He begs the deputation to observe that he is *not* in the Queen's *political* service, that he does not fill any *political* office, and exercises no power or authority."[3]

A.D. 1842.
Sir Robert Peel's explanation.

II. That his duties are not financial is equally certain:—

34. The reasons are, if possible, more cogent that the Commander-in-Chief should exercise no control whatever over the finance of the Army.[4] In such a position it would soon be practically impossible for him to govern the Army. "A Commanding Officer," said Lord Hardinge, "had better exercise *any other* authority than that of touching the pecuniary rights of the Soldier." If the authority for command to the performance of a hard duty, and for the payment of it, rested in the same hands, either disobedience or extortion would be the inevitable result.

2nd. The Commander-in-Chief not to interfere in Finance.

35. "Under our Constitution it would be very undesirable to have the Commander-in Chief of the Army transacting the finance of the Army. He has always been

As prejudicial to his Military Authority

---

[1] 'Civil Administration,' p. 27.   [2] 66 H D (3), p 1350

[3] 70 ib, p 613   [4] Chap. VII, pars 5, 25-8, 64, Chap XXI., par. 33.

held to be simply an Executive, and not a Ministerial Officer, and the *Officers* of the Army are extremely *anxious* to have *nothing to say to the handling* of *money*. This is even provided for in every Regiment, by having a Paymaster, who is not appointed by nor under the control of the Commander-in-Chief, but is under the immediate control of the Secretary at War: for purposes of discipline he is liable to be tried by a Court-martial, as any other Officer would be; but that Officer, as the regimental accountant, acts under the Secretary at War's regulations and control."

36 But, as affecting the Civil Community, there is another and infinitely more important view of this question The Army of the Commonwealth laid its iron grasp upon the Public Treasure,[1] and extorted pay at the rate of its own assessment out of the Commons. That experience has hitherto been sufficient to arouse Parliament to the danger of bringing the Military element into too close proximity[2] to the Public Treasure, or associating the Officers of the Army with Finance. In this matter principles of no mean import are at stake; for since the Commonwealth the authority of a Military officer, *as such* over the Public Treasure has been resolutely ignored

As a violation of Constitutional rule.

37. This point was pressed home with great earnestness by Lord Palmerston, in writing to the Cabinet of Mr. Perceval: — "The Commander-in-Chief cannot," he goes on to explain, "by his own authority order the issue of money to *any* individual. His Warrant would *not* be noticed by the Paymaster-General, and no officer who should pay money by his order would be reimbursed, unless he obtained also the authority of the Secretary at War. Independently, therefore, of its being inconsistent with the *Spirit* of the Constitution, and the Undeviating practice of office from the *Revolution* downwards that the Commander-in-Chief should issue orders *affecting* the Public Expenditure, there is an inconsistency inherent in the thing itself; because his order is by itself of no authority, and if the arrangement which he proposes and orders is afterwards approved by the Secretary at War, or through him by the

Lord Palmerston's Memorandum.

---

[1] 2 Com Journ., pp 776, 778 , 4 Com. Journ., pp 26, 47, 92, 117.
[2] Chap. XIX , par. 4.

Treasury, and the Secretary at War issues his order in support of that of the Commander-in-Chief, it is the order of the War Office, and not that of the Commander-in-Chief, that is the efficient authority, and in that case the latter is at least useless; but if the Secretary at War or Treasury should refuse to concur with the Commander-in-Chief, and should not sanction the arrangement which he had proposed or promulgated, then the order of the Commander-in-Chief is powerless, and would not indemnify the persons who might have acted under it; and it is obvious that nothing can tend more directly to lower the authority of any Officer than his issuing orders which he has not legally the power to enforce."[1]

38. If the Constitutional rule be that which is thus laid down by Lord Palmerston—and no one conversant with the subject can deny it—what can justify the inauguration of a new system of Military Finance, built up from the analogy of India, or some other conquered or despotic country, but in utter violation of all Constitutional principles? of a system in which — though the Commander-in-Chief is not to have any *direct* power over Finance, as that might excite attention or surprise—he is to have an *indirect* power over all the Financial Officers in the Army as being, under their Military Commission, bound to obey him? Either our Constitutional Rule must be altered, and the Commander-in-Chief made a responsible Minister of the Treasury Board, or these arrangements be reconsidered.[2]

Inauguration of a new system.

39. It follows, therefore, that the Commander-in-Chief has no Administrative or Financial duty to discharge, except to offer advice—at the request of the Responsible Ministers — as to the number of men, or the amount or nature of the force to be kept up at any place or station; the decision of these important questions, both of Policy and Finance, rests solely with the responsible Ministers of the Crown.[3] Given an Army supported by Parliament, and the office of Commander-in-Chief from the Crown, the duties

The amount of the force to be armed to be decided by the Ministry.

---

[1] Memorandum, Appendix CXLII ; and vol I, Chap VII, par. 5

[2] See Chap. XIX., pars 61, 63, and Chap XXIX, pars 52-69

[3] Chap V, par 8; Chap VII, par 8 In peace Parliament itself settled the numbers, Chap XIII., pars 3-5, but the King in War, Chap VI par. 3

of that Officer will be found to range themselves under one or other of the divisions afterwards enumerated; such duties being discharged by delegation from the Crown, acting upon the advice of responsible Ministers.

40. Now the limit of interference with the Commander-in-Chief on the part of the responsible Minister was laid down by the Royal Warrant of 11th October, 1861,[1] under the advice of the late Sir George Lewis. *Delegation of duty to the Commander-in-Chief.* The Military command and discipline of the Army, and also the appointments and promotions therein, are declared by that instrument to be vested in the Commander-in-Chief. All powers relating to these matters are to be exercised, and all the business to be transacted, by the Commander-in-Chief in his Office, subject, however, to the general control of the Crown over the Government of the Army, and the responsibility of the Secretary of State for the exercise of the Royal prerogative.

41. Nothing need be said to justify an instrument adopted under the advice of the late Sir George Lewis; but it *As to the Command of the Army* may be observed that it is the *command* of the Army, and the supposed separation or severance of it from the office or control of the Responsible Ministers, by placing it in the hands of an executive Military Officer commissioned by the Crown, that occasion the jealousy of Parliament. The Constitutional objections to the office of a Commander-in-Chief arise from the power which, under the Mutiny Acts and Articles of War, is vested in him to *command* the Army—a power absolute, according to the terms of the Officers' Commissions[2] and the Soldiers' enlistment[3]—to be obeyed implicitly according to the usage of the Service, and inflexibly according to the ruling of the late Lord Mansfield; and no doubt, looking at the Army in the aspect of the third power in the State,[4] the delegation of such power to *one* man opens up questions of grave import.

---

[1] Warrant of 1861, Appendix CXLI. This Warrant was drawn by the late Sir Geo. Lewis himself; and I am not aware that it came under the cognisance of any official (save the author), until it had been submitted to a section of the Cabinet, see Organisation Report, 1860, and Sir Jas Graham's Evidence before the Select Committee on the Admiralty, *passim.*

[2] Chap XVI, pars. 10-22.　　　　[3] Chap XV, par 112

[4] Chap II, pars 22-25; Chap IX, pars 1, 2, 11; Chap. XVI., pars. 4, 66.

42. If the Officer in Chief Command accepts implicitly,[1] and in the best faith, the Constitutional doctrine that all Military Power must be based on and emanate from the Civil Power, and that the Commands of the Sovereign to the Army can *only* be conveyed to the Commander-in-Chief through the channel of Responsible Ministers,[2] then the danger resulting from such an appointment is at an end. The Army then is in union with the Civil Institutions, and may—as Lord Hardinge asserted[3]—add strength to them.

If the Civil supremacy be honestly accepted, the Command it innocuous.

43. With regard to the *discipline* of the Army, it is nothing singular to entrust it to the head of the Military profession; for the discipline of every professional body is entrusted by usage to its own members. Subject, therefore, to excess of punishment on the one hand, or to the toleration of licentiousness—a danger overlooked by modern Army philanthropists, but which is far more terrible to the State—on the other, by the Commander-in-Chief, there is no reason why the Army should form an exception to this general principle, or why the Civil Minister should interfere.[4]

As to the discipline of the Army

44. The selection for Military employment, and the promotion therein, have always been made or influenced by Officers in subordinate or supreme Command. In many instances all that the Ministers of the Crown did was to register or record the Commissions.[5] The object of appointing a Commander-in-Chief was to secure greater efficiency, and that mainly by placing some check or control upon unworthy Political appointments or promotions. As, therefore, the Commander-in-Chief is responsible to the Secretary of State for the Military efficiency of the Army, he is entrusted (subject, of course, to the Constitutional rules that govern the admission of persons into the Military service of the Crown), with

As to first Appointments.

---

[1] 'Military Organization Report, 1860,' p. xix. and Evidence, and Sir James Graham's Evidence, Question 1071, Admiralty Committee, 1861
[2] Chap. XVII., pars. 55–64.   [3] Chap. XIV., par. 167
[4] Church Discipline Act, 3 & 4 Vic., c. 86, Medical Practitioners, 21 & 22 Vic., c 90.   [5] See Chap XVI., pars 23 26

the selection of the *personnel*, both as to Officers and men ; and it rests with him and his Officers to examine into the qualifications of all candidates, and to procure their Commissions or Enlistments for the Service.[1]

45. To insure professional merit—not political influence—leading to promotion in the Army, it is essential that the power of promotion should be held by the Commander-in-Chief, to stimulate the services of deserving Officers.[2]   There has never been any time in which this power of rewarding merit in *actual* service has been withheld from Officers in Chief Command.   Cromwell made it known that *he* could not please such a multiple and discordant body as Parliament, and, jealous as that assembly was of all power not exercised within its own walls, it was induced—if not obliged—to entrust the promotion of Officers to their Commanders   Human nature is much the same now as then, and if the power of promotion were taken away from the Commander-in-Chief his usefulness would be at an end. "I am quite positive," said Lord F. Somerset, "that the Commander-in-Chief could not maintain the discipline of the Army if the Officers had to look to any one but him for their advancement."[3]   Upon the same principle, the promotion of Privates to the several grades of non-commissioned Officers in a Regiment is left with the Lieutenant-Colonel in command.

As to Promotion.

A D 1833 Power held to be essential.

46. As the Rewards, so the Punishments, must rest primarily with the Commander-in-Chief.   Given by the Civil Power, the Mutiny Act, and the authority to hold Courts-martial, it is for the Commander-in-Chief to determine whether a Court shall be assembled, or what other punishment awarded.   If a Court be necessary, the selection of the members to compose it rests, as we have seen, with the Commander-in-Chief, and the sentence, when given, comes before him either as confirming Officer, or (where the Crown is confirming Officer) to make to Her Majesty such recommendation upon it

Military Punishments.

---

[1] Lord F Somerset, Questions 1918, 1919, 'Army and Navy Appointments, 1833'
[2] Chap. XVI , par 66 *et seq*
[3] 'Army and Navy Appointments, 1833,' Question 1905

as he sees fit. Speaking of the Power of Life or Death held by the Commander-in-Chief in India, Sir James Macdonald justified it in these remarkable words:—"That if he held not this power, he might find himself at any *moment*—instead of commanding an Army—in command of an *armed mob.*"[1]

47. And, lastly, when the responsible Ministers of the Crown have decided where, how, and when the Army is to be employed, it is for the Commander-in-Chief to offer his recommendation as to the General Officers to be entrusted with the Command and as to the Regiments that are to be engaged in the Service, but for this advice, if adopted by the Crown, the Ministers alone are responsible to Parliament

Selection for Service.

48. Granting that a large force should always be maintained, then it cannot, I think, be fairly doubted by any Statesman, that the separation of the "Command and Government of the Army" from the "Civil Administration" of it *was* a wise and Constitutional measure for Mr. Fox to advocate, and for Mr. Pitt to adopt, in 1793. What, even at that period, would have been the effect upon our Political Rights of a large increase in the Standing Army, and of the continuance of that Political Leaven under which various appointments to it were made, it is not easy to predicate; but whatever might have been the effect then, it is clear that the abolition of the Commander-in-Chief's office now could not possibly restore us to the *status quo* then existing. To let into the sphere of Political Influence the patronage of a vast Army would be to render the existence of the Army not only useless but intolerable under our Democracy.

Separation of the Government from the Administration of the Army

49. When, at the close of the War, in 1816, it was found to be impossible to reduce the Army to the 17,003 men at which it stood in 1793, the office of the Commander-in-Chief was maintained as one of the Departments[2] of the State. "The Secretary at War,

A.D 1816.

Office of Commander-in-Chief continued.

---

[1] 'Army Expenditure, 1850,' Question 2471
[2] Note M, Vol I, p 298

as was well known," said Lord Castlereagh, "has nothing more
to do with the discipline and regulation of the Army than any
other Member of the House. "Would the right hon. gentleman wish the office of Commander-in-Chief to be abolished
too? This Office was now more necessary than ever, and
the advantages that had arisen from it to our Army were
incalculable. Nothing had changed so much as the character
and discipline of our Military Force within the short period
that had passed since 1792.[1] Before that time, a British
Army, assembled under the same General, had no more
uniformity of movements, of discipline, and appearance in
its various Regiments than one composed of the troops of
different sovereign States. Let any one consider what was its
present state,—the facility with which it could perform all its
operations in concert, the perfect uniformity of tactics that it
possessed,—and he would acknowledge how much had been
done, and how necessary it was to continue an Establishment on
which this state of things depended "[2]

50 Granting,—therefore, the continuance of the office to
be a necessity, and therefore expedient,—by whom *To whom
and under what conditions should it be held? and—if should the
the duties of it have been correctly laid down—to Command be
whom can such a trust be confided? There is always a dis- granted*
position, coming from opposite quarters, to use the Army for
Political purposes; and (do all that can be done) it will always
be considered in reference to the *balance* of power in the State
"I have heard," said the Duke of Wharton to the House of
Lords[3] in 1724, "wise men say that if James II. had turned

---

[1] Extract from Sir H Taylor's Evidence before the Finance Committee, 1828,
p 258 —"I joined the army of the Duke of York in March, 1793, when it was
first on the Continent, and remained with it after the infantry came home until
1795; and during that period I saw not only the state in which the first part of the
army joined us, but also subsequent additions, which (with the exception of the
foot guards and a few other corps) was most disgraceful Nothing could be worse
in point of composition, in point of material, &c. I can hardly speak of it with
patience when I refer to the manner in which we were committed towards other services, even the most trifling, and even those of petty German princes, who had
only one regiment to send; we were ashamed of our service"
[2] 33 H. D (O. S), p, 998; and as to reduction of expenses, see 5 ib. (2), p 209
[3] 8 Parl Hist., p 388

out the old Officers, and made new ones among the *common soldiers*, King William would not easily have brought about his enterprise; at least, there would have been more bloodshed," adding another to many instances that are scattered throughout our Parliamentary history, showing that the Army—as at the Commonwealth—may be used against the liberties of the people.[1]

51. Is it not, therefore, to the interest of the Civil community that such a trust should be held by a Military person, "assured and well reported of holding good correspondence with the other great men of the State. and not by one factious or popular," having to make and maintain his character by Military prowess or political action?[2] and to the Army is it not of advantage that the dispenser of rewards and honours should be above seeking any for himself?—that his position should admit of no rivalry with theirs, and that from his near association with the Crown their exploits are looked upon from a Regal rather than a Personal point of view?[3]

The trust should be in a Military person, holding a good correspondence with other great men.

52. If a *non*-political person can be found for the command of the Army, is he to be entrusted with it without the active interference of the Parliamentary Minister who appointed him? Unless such be the case,—unless he is to discharge his duty sitting in an office not frequented by members of the Lower House seeking for Patronage—and in

Is the Parliamentary Minister to interfere?

---

[1] Chap. XVI, par 4, note 2, Chap XVIII., par 14, 2 Com Journ, p 135 From a miscellany Order Book from 1688 to 169⅔, that has come into my hands from the Judge-Advocate-General's office (where it has been for years misplaced), I find that William III on the 10th May, in the first year of his reign, appointed the Duke of Schomberg, the Earls of Devon and Monmouth, Lord Lumley, Thomas Wharton, William Harford, and three Generals, Commissioners for regulating and reforming all abuses, &c, in the Army They were to visit and review each Regiment—if necessary to disband it To inquire of the gentlemen of the county in which each Regiment was quartered, "what officers and soldiers have given any cause of being suspected to being disaffected to our Government" In case they should find "them unfit to serve in respect of their disaffection to our Service, the Commissioners were to disband them"—Pp 179-183 When was the Navy so dealt with?

[2] Chap XVIII, par 51.

[3] Would the Duke of Wellington have ever reached the highest rank in the Peerage, if the Commander-in-Chief had held the lowest? See Sir James Graham's evidence before the Admiralty Committee, 1861, Questions 1050-57

completo independence, guided only by Professional merit, the office may easily become Political by contact, and destructive to the State. All Military power is now concentrated in a manner wholly unknown in any previous period of our Constitutional History, and a complete Military Organization exists throughout the Country that might be effectively used for Political purposes. Under the system of selection for Military command, and to enable the Commander-in-Chief to discharge this (invidious) office, he has the character of each Officer brought before him half-yearly in the Confidential Reports of General Officers. Once give a Political character to his office, and what a cruel system of espionnage might readily be created throughout the Service, and upon the private character or affairs of any Officer in the United Kingdom.

53 Selection is the present popular theory under which Commands are to be disposed of; but if the in- strument for making this selection be changed [1] from

Commands to be given by selection

---

[1] Sir E Lugard, speaking as Secretary for Military Correspondence, of the Political influence brought to bear upon the Secretary of State for appointments and promotions in the Army, gave this Evidence before the Military Organisation Committee, 1860 —

"2240 Have you any opinion, from your experience with reference to the relative pressure for political considerations, upon the Secretary of State for the gift of Commissions, or with reference to first appointments, as compared with the pressure upon the Horse Guards?—A very strong opinion

"2241 Will you state it to the Committee?—I consider that the pressure upon the Secretary of State would be very great, the political pressure upon the Horse Guards is nil

"2242 From what you have seen (of course avoiding mentioning the names of any persons), have you any experience of political pressure brought to bear, even as matters now stand, upon the Secretary of State?—Yes, there are continually letters from Members of Parliament on subjects connected with the promotions and appointments in the Army, and I feel convinced that if the first appointments were with the Secretary of State, if he had more direct control over them, being a political officer, he would be obliged to give way in many instances where the Commander-in-Chief is not

"2243 *Sir De Lacy Evans* Is it from both Houses of Parliament, or from one, that these applications are made?—From both.

"2244 *Chairman* Avoiding the mention of names and periods, have you had experience in your own person of pressure from Members of Parliament?—I can hardly say pressure, because I am perfectly free from any political bias one way or another, but I have had applications in reference to matters of the kind

"2245 Personally addressed to yourself?—Yes

"2246 And your opinion is, that if in the last resort the Secretary of State

a Military to a Political Officer, importunities that are now not wholly unknown will greatly increase, and promotions will be given away, as Civil appointments are, to Constituents for Political services.[1] It will follow, therefore, that, as Lord Carteret foretold, a "Minister who distributes preferments at his pleasure may acquire such an influence in the Army as may be employed to secure himself from justice by the destruction of liberty; for unless it can be proved that no such Minister can ever exist—that corruption, ambition, and perfidy, have place only in the Military race—every argument that shows the danger of an Army dependent only on the General, will show the danger likewise of one dependent only on the Minister."[2]

54. In closing this Chapter it may be desirable to call the

Lord Palmer-
stone's rules
for the office
of Com-
mander in-
Chief.

attention of the reader to a Memorandum printed in the Appendix.[3] that was prepared by the late Lord Palmerston in 1827, when he held the office of Commander-in-Chief, laying down general rules for the guidance of those afterwards entrusted with that office.

---

determined upon first appointments, the pressure would be greater then in your office than it is now in the Horse Guards?—No doubt of it.

"2247 That is your fixed opinion?—That is my fixed opinion. The Commander-in-Chief is a permanent officer, he has nothing to do with political bias one way or the other, he never leaves office because the Government may change"

[1] In land transactions, the War Department knows quite enough of Solicitation to serve private interest—obviously at the public cost—to extend the patronage of the Secretary of State · Report on Civil Administration, 1837,' p 29.

[2] 11 Parl Hist, p 925   [3] Appendix CXLII

CHAPTER XXVII.

The Office of Judge-Advocate-General.

1. It has been already shown that, prior to the appointment of a Commander-in-Chief in 1793, the government of the Army was carried out by the Crown with the aid of a Board of General Officers, of which the Judge-Advocate-General for the time being acted as Secretary and Legal Adviser.[1] In this manner his office became secularized, and the holder of it involved in many questions *ultra* those that would come before him in his nominal character of a Judge. It was, I apprehend, to discharge the duty of defending the policy and action of the Military authorities taken under his advice as Secretary to the Board of General Officers that his presence in the House of Commons was originally needed.[2] But though the office of Secretary ceased with the Board, yet that of Legal Adviser to the Commander-in-Chief[3] remains.

[margin: Prior to 1793 Judge-Advocate-General acted as Secretary and Legal Adviser to Board of General Officers.]

2. The Powers of the Crown under the Mutiny Act for the government of the Army have been referred to in an earlier Chapter.[4] To insure their due execution according to the Law and Custom of War the Judge-Advocate-General is appointed, and, strange as it may appear, quits office with each change in the Administration. The office therefore is rather Administrative than Judicial; for the Military Organisation Committee of 1860 justified his position in Parliament[5] as a member of the Administration, though the House of Commons has at various times entertained a strong opinion that a Judge should not take part in Political controversies.[6]

[margin: Office is rather administrative than judicial.]

---

[1] Chap XXI., par. 13.

[2] Lord Hardinge's Evidence on Civil Administration, 1837, p 27.

[3] See Vol I, Chap IV, par. 67, and pp. 438, 447   Mr Mowbray's Evidence, C M Report, 1869, Question 4119   [4] Chap VIII   [5] P. xxi.

[6] 4 H D (O S), pp 284-541, 127 ib (3), p 993

3. The appointment of the Judge-Advocate-General is made
Appointment made by patent by Patent,[1] which confers upon him the office "according to the power and authority given and allowed in
and by the Mutiny Act of the 1st Geo. I.,[2] and according to
such other acts as shall from time to time be in force." The
duties which pertain to it are set forth in a Memorandum printed
in the Appendix.[3]

4. As Courts-martial are *sui generis*, the office of Judge-
Judge-Advo- cate General held respon- sible to Par- liament for the adminis tration of Military Law Advocate-General may be deemed so. The funda-
mental principle that the King cannot administer
Justice[4] in person is entirely ignored in the case of
Military Tribunals, the Sovereign being, in many instances, the Confirming Officer of their proceedings
This, like every other Prerogative, must, for the security of the
Subject, be exercised under the advice of a responsible Minister,
and hence the action of Parliament in recent years has been
to fix upon some one a definite responsibility in regard to the
Administration of Military Law,[5] and, to minimize responsibility,
the Judge-Advocate-General was, in 1806, made a subordinate
member of the Administration

---

[1] Appendix CXLIII

[2] It is difficult to explain, on any intelligible principle, why reference was or
is made to this Act of Parliament on the Judge-Advocate-General's patent   In
that year three Mutiny Acts appear to have been passed   The first (stat 2, c 3)
from 21th March, 1715, to 25th March, 1717, the second from 5th June, 1715, to
25th March, 1716, and the third from the 1st August, 1715, to 25th March, 1716
Neither of these Acts, so far as I can observe, confers any special powers on the
Judge-Advocate-General, but on Mr Byde's death in 1715, Mr Hughes' patent
contained in it a reference to the second Mutiny Act which has been continued
without alteration   See par 7 note 3

[3] Appendix CXLIV, and see the Evidence of Messrs Headlam and Mowbray
before the Court-martial Commission, 1869.   [4] Chitty, Prec, p 73, 74

[5] The Judge-Advocate-General has nothing to do with "Martial" Law, and the
proceedings of any Courts held under Martial Law are not sent to his office   Sir
D Dundas explained this to the Ceylon Committee   Thus, when questioned by
Mr Hume (5439), he said, "I have no knowledge of the matter more than the
Honourable Member has, or any other person who is competent to judge of a
point of Constitutional learning   Those things have nothing whatever to do with
the office I hold   The whole proceedings of the office I belong to are proceedings
under the Mutiny Act and the Articles of War, and you are questioning me as to
points with which I have nothing to do   5441 You are not aware of any precedents on the subject?—There are no precedents in my office, my office has nothing to do with the matter now inquired into   5442 Are you able to state to
the Committee, from any inquiry you have made, under what authority or in what
office, such proceedings can be found?—They are not in my office "

5. It must never be lost sight of that the only legitimate object of Military Tribunals is to aid the Crown to maintain the Discipline and Government of the Army, and that this is to be accomplished by upholding—so far as it can be done with justice—the authority of every Command.[1] There could not be a more dangerous rule to lay down than that the Crown, or indeed the General in Chief Command, is inflexibly bound by the findings of Courts-martial, so as to be obliged to act in accordance with their sentence of acquittal or punishment. The Officers have partialities and antipathies in favour of or against the accused, besides which their rule of professional duty or morality may be of a lower standard than the General deems it safe or expedient to recognize in his Command. The reader has only to examine the 'Records of the Indian Command of the Late General Sir Charles Napier,' [2] and the remarks on the Courts-martial submitted to him for confirmation, to be assured that these Tribunals are not infallible, but that their findings admit in many instances of revision from a General Officer, bearing a higher responsibility, and having a larger experience, than the members of the Court [3]

[sidenote: Courts-martial, Tribunals to aid and not to control the Crown or the General.]

6. As Military Law is generally *lex non scripta*, the Judge-Advocate-General is the adviser of the General in Chief Command, so that he may never enter into controversy with his subordinate, and by so doing suffer a legal defeat. Such a catastrophe would soon destroy all Military authority whatever. In matters of the first importance the Judge-Advocate-General therefore advises upon the case, and to prevent any possible miscarriage—on mere legal or technical grounds—frames the charges upon which the offender is to be arraigned. The facts being legally proved—that is, according to the law of evidence which rules in Courts-martial—of which again the Judge-Advocate-General

[sidenote: Office is that of Adviser to the General in Chief Command in all matters of discipline]

---

[1] Chap VIII *passim*, and pars 22, 42, and 65.

[2] Compiled by Mawson, and published at Calcutta, 1851 My attention was allied to this volume by Colonel Shadwell, C B

[3] Chap VIII , pars 22, 56, 65, and 66, and Chap XVI , par 129 *et seqq* , and in 2nd Report of Court-martial Commissioners (1869), p. viii Duke of Wellington's letter of 8th of March, 1814, Vol viii of 'Supplementary Despatches,' p 627

is the sole judge—the conviction is certain, and the authority of the General is upheld. Of course when the Judge-Advocate-General does not thus initiate proceedings the risk of error or miscarriage arises,—and it increases—according to the degree of experience which the General has in Military Law,—when he is cut off from this Counsel, and is acting with such advice.

7. The foundation of every proceeding by Court-martial is the Warrant of the Crown under the Countersign of the Secretary of State. In former years this warrant was addressed to the Judge-Advocate-General for the trial of persons at home, and to General Officers on Colonial or Foreign stations for the trial of persons abroad. In the first class of cases the Judge-Advocate-General or his deputy attended all Courts-martial held at Head-quarters[1]—in the Great Room at the Horse Guards; and in the other class, the proceedings were sent home—prior to 1768 to the Secretary-at-War;[2] and after that date to the Judge-Advocate-General—for submission to the Sovereign.

Warrants for holding Courts-martial

8. In the year 1704,[3] the channel of communication with the Sovereign was, as we have seen, the Judge-Advocate-General,[4] but in the year 1706 and for nearly a century afterwards, that duty was undertaken by the Secretary-at-War.[5] Upon the representation of the Judge-

Sentences to be submitted to the Sovereign.

---

[1] As to the office of Judge-Advocate-General, see 36th Report of Finance Committee, 1798, and 8th Report of Military Inquiry, p 215 19 H D. (O S), p 367

[2] Court-martial Book 130, 26th September to 12th November, 1766 In 1755, it was conceded that the Judge-Advocate should summon the witnesses —Mis Bk., p 325.

[3] See in the same year the Duke of Marlborough's Letter to the Judge-Advocate-General (Clarke) as to Mr Byde's succeeding him, vol 1. of Despatches, p 294.

[4] Vol I p 77, note 4

[5] Court-martial Book, p. 52 —

'*St James's,* 5 *Nov* 1706.

"This sentence of a Court-martial having been layd before the Queen, Her Majesty upon application made to her on behalf of the criminal, finding him an object of her mercy, is pleased to extend her gracious pardon to him

"Her Majesty does think fitt further to direct that in like cases for the future when the Judge-Advocate-General of the Forces shall lay before Her Majesty the sentence of a Court-martial, he do at the same time represent to her whether the person under condemnation is worthy of her favour or not, which however he is not to do without moving the Court-martial for their direction therein

"H St John"

And see 5 H D (O S), pp 648, 763

Advocate-General and the responsibility of the Secretary-at-War, the sentence was confirmed, and then promulgated by the Judge.

9. In 1806[1] the Judge-Advocate-General became a member of the Privy Council. He then took the pleasure of the Crown personally, and communicated the result to the Commander-in-Chief. This communication was promulgated by a General Order, but in May the practice was altered by declaring the sentence without mention of the Judge-Advocate in the Order.[2]

A D 1806.

Judge-Advocate-General became a responsible Minister.

10. It may be many years since a Judge-Advocate-General personally presided at a Court-martial,[3] but he is responsible for all Deputies acting under his delegation.[4] How these Deputies should discharge their duty is a matter for his direction, subject to the provision in the Articles of War, that a Judge-Advocate is never to act as prosecutor. When Lord Brougham[5] described the duties of the office the rule was otherwise, but few acting as Judge-Advocates availed themselves of their position to injure the prisoner. "The Judge-Advocate of a Court-martial, although certainly sometimes standing in the situation of a prosecutor, nevertheless, in all well-regulated Courts-martial, never forgets that he also stands between the prisoner and the Bench. He is rather, indeed, in the character of an assessor to the Court. On this point I might appeal to the highest authority present. By you, Sir,[6] these important functions were long, and earnestly, and constitutionally performed, and in a manner equally beneficial to the Army and the country. But I may appeal to another authority, from which no one will be inclined to dissent. A reverend Judge, Mr. Justice Bathurst, in the middle of the last century, laid it down as clear and indisputable, that the

Judge-Advocate presiding at a Court-martial.

---

[1] 6 H. D. (O S) 162, 11 ib, p 815, 6 ib (2) p 1223, and 8th Report of Military Enquiry (1809), pp 141, 142, 221   Appendix CXL

[2] Compare General Order, No 88, 22nd March, 1806, with General Order, No. 89, of 27th May, 1806   Vol 1. of Court-martial Decisions.

[3] Mr Villiers conducted the Court of Enquiry at Chelsea in 1855.   The Judge-Advocate-General had his office at the Horse Guards prior to 1794, and the General Courts-martial were held in the Great Room.

[4] Evidence of Mr Headlam before Court-martial Commissioners, 1869.

[5] Demerara Case, 11 H D. (2), p 973

[6] Mr Manners Sutton was Judge Advocate-General before he was Speaker.

office of a Judge-Advocate was to lay the proof on both sides before the Court, and that whenever the evidence was at all doubtful it was his duty to incline towards the prisoner."

A.D 1865

Duties laid down by Circular Memorandum

11 It was admitted that the Judge-Advocate at the trial of a prisoner should preside as the legal officer [1] to watch the proceedings, to see that justice is done to the prisoner,[2] and to assist the Court; but this position was authoritatively established under the sanction of the Secretary of State soon after Colonel Crawley's trial,[3]— probably the last occasion upon which any Deputy Judge-Advocate-General will ever act against the prisoner as a Counsel for the prosecution.[4]

In cases where the Sovereign is the confirming authority

12. The proceedings of all General Courts-martial, of which the Sovereign is the Confirming officer, are sent direct to the Judge-Advocate-General for his examination and approval.[5] If they are confirmed, it is upon his responsibility as a Minister of the Crown, for which he would be accountable in Parliament. In these cases the persons under sentence lose their legal remedy against the Sovereign as confirming Officer,[6] but hold one against the Minister in Parliament.

Judge-Advocate-General responsible only for the legality of the proceedings

13. The duty of the Judge-Advocate-General is confined to an examination into the legality of the proceedings: —the validity of the charges, the evidence of guilt, and the sentence with reference to the Statute Law. The expediency of carrying out the sentence or of

---

[1] 'Records of the Indian Command of General Sir Charles Napier.' Mawson, Calcutta, 1851 :—

" Head Quarters, 16th May, 1850

"The Deputy Judge-Advocate-General does not conduct a trial The Articles of War expressly charge the President of the Court with all the duties and details of conducting the trial He is to make the members take their seats according to their rank, he clears and reopens the Court when necessary, he preserves order, he collects the votes, no questions are put but through him, and by his permission or by that of the Court The Judge-Advocate cannot interfere with anything of his own authority in the privileges of a Court-martial, for which the President and the members are alone responsible "

[2] 137 H D (3), p 1837.   [3] Appendix CXLV.   [4] 173 H D (3), p. 1174

[5] See Appendix CXLIV Sir James Macdonald's Evidence before Committee on Army Expenditure, 1850, pp. 190-198, Military Organization, 1860, p 311 and Report on Courts martial, 1869   [6] Chap VIII, par 91

extending mercy, does not come within his province. In the former matters no one stands between him and Parliament—he bears his responsibility alone.

14. Considered in this aspect, there can be little doubt that the office should be held by a Lawyer of Independent position, and not by a Military Officer. But it may be worthy of consideration whether the office of Judge-Advocate-General should not be constituted as a permanent and not a political appointment—whether the Judge-Advocate should not act in matters of Military Law as the Queen's Advocate acts in matters of International Law, viz., in the character of Legal Adviser to the Government. The office, so constituted,[1] would lead up to the development of a Military Code, and the administration of Military Law on a firm basis. The Secretary of State would then represent the Prerogative of the Crown in all its attributes, acting upon the advice of the Law Officers of the Crown, the Advocate-General being one.

Independence of his office.

15. "Judges ought above all," said Lord Bacon, "to remember the conclusion of the Twelve Roman Tables,—'Salus populi suprema lex,'—and to know that Laws, except they be in order to that end, are but things captious and oracles not inspired. Let them also remember that Solomon's throne was supported by Lions on both sides—let *them* be Lions, but yet Lions under the Throne: being circumspect that they do not check or oppose any points of Sovereignty." No doubt, the Judge-Advocate-General may aid by experience, or weaken by ignorance—if not destroy—the discipline of the Army; but further, overlooking the oath to which every Officer on Court-martial duty is sworn, viz., to administer Military Law according *to conscience,* and the *custom of war* in like cases,[2] he may do evil without design, or any other desire than to uphold that which might be the duty of any other Judge—the strictest Rules of Law.

Counsel of Lord Bacon

---

[1] Until some change be made, would it be prudent to publish the 'Decisions of the Judge Advocate-General,' as the Royal Commissioners suggest?

[2] Chap VIII, par. 86.

CHAPTER XXVIII.

The Chaplain-General's Department.

1. UNDER this title it is intended to give some account of
Subject of
Chapter the provision made for the religious education of the
Soldier,[1] and for the public worship of Almighty God
in the Army. In suggesting the latter, the thoughts of the
reader will probably turn to the 'Book of Common Prayer;' but
he will find no mention whatever made of the Army in the
Liturgy, and he will think that this omission must be something more than accidental, because 'Prayers to be used at Sea
by Her Majesty's Navy' are there to be found.

2. The Prayers for the use of the Navy were inserted at
A.D. 1661-2.
———
Revision of
the Liturgy. the last revision of the Liturgy;[2] and, looking at the
feeling of all classes of the people towards the Army
at that period (A.D. 1662), it need not be a matter
of surprise that the clergy did not see fit to recognise the
Military Forces of the Crown as "the chief visible strength" of
the kingdom.[3] However, the inclusion of one and the exclusion of the other Service, furnishes evidence of the essential
difference—before adverted to in this Work—between the Army
and Navy in their Constitutional aspect towards the State.

3. But though the Statute Law, in establishing the 'Book of
A.D. 1662-3.
———
Daily prayers
enjoined
under the
Articles of
War Common Prayer,' was thus silent, the Articles of War
of 1662-3 prescribed the duty of every Chaplain to
be to read those Prayers daily to the Soldiers; thus,
"The Chaplains to the Troops of Guards and others
in Regiments shall every day read the Common Prayers of the

---

[1] See Note R R., in Appendix.   [2] Cardwell's Conferences, p. 384
[3] 4 Com Journ , p. 81.

Church of England to the Soldiers respectively under their charge, and to preach to them as often as with convenience shall be thought fit, and if any neglect his duty herein, he to be punished at discretion; and every Officer or Soldier absent from prayers shall for every absence lose a day's pay to His Majesty." [1]

4. Moreover, the King did his part in appointing Army Chaplains, for until the year 1796 a Chaplain formed as much part of the establishment of every Regiment as a Field Officer.   His appointment was made— frequently after purchase—on the nomination of the Colonel, and he held a Commission in the ordinary form, under Royal Sign Manual, to the particular Regiment to which he was appointed. [2]

Chaplains appointed to each Regiment.

5. The Articles issued "for the war against the French King," in April, 1666, were more specific regarding the "duties to God," and gave these directions as to public worship:—" (3). That the service of Almighty God be not neglected, it is ordained that prayers shall be orderly read every day to each troop of Our Guards, and every other of Our Regiment of Guards, Troops, or companies who have Chaplains allowed to them.   And once every week, on each Sunday or holyday, a sermon shall be preached, or some place of Scripture or catechisme expounded to them.   And every chaplain that omits his duty herein, and provides not some minister in orders to officiate for him, shall for the first offence forfeit half a week's pay, and for the second offence a week's pay, and for the third offence be cashiered; and all

A.D 1666
Provisions as to Public Worship.

---

[1] Article 18.

[2] In 1662 they appear to have been commissioned thus —

"Charles, &c , to Dr Herbert Astley, greeting   We do by these presents constitute and appoint you to be Chaplain of that Regiment of Horse raised or to be raised for our service, whereof our right trusty and right well-beloved cousin James Earl of Northampton is Colonel   You are therefore diligently to teach and instruct the officers and soldiers of the said regiment, who are to observe you as their Chaplain, and you are likewise to observe and follow such orders and directions as you shall from time to time receive from your said Colonel or other your superior officers of that regiment.   Given, &c., the 1st day of October, in the 14th year of our Reign.

"By His Majesty's Command,

"WILLIAM MORRICE "

Officers and Soldiers that shall often and wilfully absent themselves from publique prayers and sermons, and all such as shall abuse or profane any the places of God's worship, or the utensils or ornaments belonging or dedicated to God's worship, in any church or chappel, or shall offer violence to any chaplaine in the Army, or any other minister, shall be punished in the same manner, or otherwise at discretion, according to the nature and aggravation of the offence."

6 The direction for daily service was not of long continuance, for the Articles of 1673 made mention only of Sundays and public festivals and fasts. In the first statutory Articles of War issued in 1717-18 a still more general direction is to be found:—for all Officers and Soldiers to frequent diligently Divine Service in such places as shall be appointed for the Regiment; but no order is given as to the times at which such services are to be held. In both Articles pecuniary mulcts were to be inflicted on Soldiers (Officers being reprimanded by Court-martial) for absence, and by the Articles of 1717-18 the money thus levied was to be applied to the relief of the sick Soldiers of the Regiment.[1]

A.D 1673 and 1717

Directions of these Articles of War

7. In the Articles of War of 1748 the following additional Articles—having reference to the punishment of chaplains for misconduct—were inserted:—"(5). No chaplain who is commissioned to a Regiment, Company, Troop, *or Garrison*, shall absent himself from the said Regiment, Company, Troop, or Garrison (excepting in case of sickness or leave of absence) upon pain of being brought to a Court-martial, and punished as their judgment and the circumstances of his offence may require. (6.) Whatever chaplain to a Regiment, Troop, or Garrison shall be guilty of drunkenness, or of other scandalous or vicious behaviour derogating from the sacred character with which he is invested, shall, upon due proofs before a Court-martial, be discharged from his said office."

A.D 1748

Of these.

8. To carry down to the present time the account of military discipline as applicable to the subject under consideration, it may be noticed that the Articles of War for 1869 contain these provisions:—"(31.) Any Officer

A.D. 1869

Lastly of these

---

[1] 19 Rap and Tin 's England, p 192, note

or Soldier who, not having just impediment, shall not attend Divine Service in the place appointed for the assembling of the Corps to which he belongs; or who, being present, shall behave indecently or irreverently, or who shall offer violence to a chaplain of the Army, or to any other minister of God's Word, shall be liable, if an Officer, to such punishment as by a general Court-martial shall be awarded; and if a Soldier, to such punishment as by a general district or Garrison Court-martial shall be awarded. (33) Any commissioned chaplain who shall absent himself from his duty (excepting in case of sickness or leave of absence) shall be brought before a general Court-martial, and punished as the circumstances of his offence may require (34.) Any commissioned chaplain who shall be guilty of misconduct or vicious behaviour derogating from the sacred character with which he is invested, shall on conviction before a general Court-martial, be discharged from his office "

9 But in addition to the Chaplains upon the establishment of Regiments, each Fortress or Garrison had in many instances a Chaplain appointed by the Crown, either through the Governor or the Secretary at War, according to the nature of his duties. Of these appointments, at home and abroad, made through the Secretary at War, a return was laid before the Commissioners of Military Inquiry in 1807, and the Chaplains' duties were thus described — *Chaplains to Garrisons and Forts.*

10 The duties of these Chaplains consist in performing Divine Service to the Troops at the respective stations, and in executing all the other ordinary functions of a parochial minister The Garrison Chaplains are expected either to perform their duty in person, or otherwise to provide for the due execution thereof *Their duties*

The Chaplains to the Garrisons in Great Britain receive their salaries by half-yearly warrants, under the Royal Sign Manual, payable to the Governors of the respective Garrisons. The salaries of Garrison Chaplains on foreign stations are either paid to them on the station under the orders of the General commanding, or issued from the Pay Office under warrants prepared in the Department of the Secretary at War, at the option of the individual.[1] In the year 1798 there were fifteen home and thirteen colonial Garrison Chaplains.

11. In some of the older fortresses which the Sovereign used for occasional residence—as the Tower of London, Dover Castle, or Tynemouth Castle—the churches therein partake of the character of Royal chapels, and the fortresses of Royal Peculiars. In these and similar instances the Chaplains ministered to the Soldiers as to the other inmates of the fortress, and discharged towards them the duties of parochial minister. Formerly their stipends came out of the Royal revenue, but on the appropriation of supplies were transferred to Army votes.[2]

Chaplains in Royal Castles.

12. It is, perhaps, not to be wondered at that the system of Regimental Chaplains failed; for, prior to its abolition, the Army—comparatively small in number—was quartered in fortress or Garrison towns having established Chaplains; or any Regiment not so quartered was scattered over the country upon billets, and as inmates for some months, of the same house, the Soldiers came under the spiritual care of the Parochial Incumbent. As the Troops in Garrison were ministered to by the Garrison Chaplains, and the men on billet by the Parochial Clergy, there was left little duty for the Regimental Chaplain to perform in time of peace.

Regimental Chaplaincy System failed at home.

13. When the Army went into foreign quarters, or into the field, these Chaplains were really needed, and we have evidence that in the Duke of Marlborough's campaigns they were actually present, and of service.[3] But at the close of the last century their declension from duty was lamentable, and in describing it the Commissioners of Military Inquiry, in 1807, wrote thus:[4]—"At what period a relaxation in the attendance of Chaplains with their Regiments first began to prevail, it may be difficult and perhaps useless to ascertain; the indulgence of leave of absence seems to have gained ground

Also for Foreign Service

---

[1] 7th Report, p. 105

[2] The Chaplain of the Tower, though never in the Army, is paid out of the Distinguished Service 'Vote,' on which the Tower Garrison is borne.

[3] Coxe's Life, Vol. 1, pp. 386, 399 ; Despatches, vol. 1, p. 317

[4] 7th Report on Military Enquiry, p. 21

insensibly, till at length, notwithstanding the Articles of War on this head, the appointment became apparently a sinecure. The duty of Chaplain was usually performed by deputy, who was paid by his employer according to no certain rule, sometimes he received two shillings and sixpence per diem, but generally his remuneration depended on agreement, and not unfrequently on the discretion of the Commanding Officer. So universal indeed was the neglect of attendance, that, in 1793, when an Army was sent from this country to Flanders, there was only one Regimental Chaplain present with his Corps, the Army was, however, accompanied by four or five other clergymen, who acted as deputies to their respective employers.

14. Reprehensible as this instance of neglect of attendance in the Chaplains may appear, it was soon after followed by another still more extraordinary. In 1795, when General Sir Ralph Abercromby was preparing to proceed with a considerable force to the West Indies, he directed an order to be addressed to all the Chaplains of the Regiments under his Command, requiring their personal attendance at his then head-quarters, in order to settle amongst themselves what number of them should accompany the Troops on that expedition; but it is stated, that, relying on some promise made or implied when they purchased their Commissions that Personal Service would never be demanded of them, provided they assented to the usual deduction from their pay to remunerate a deputy, *no Chaplain* appeared to the General's summons." *A D 1795.*

On Abercromby's Expedition

15. The Chaplains were under no Episcopal Jurisdiction, nor was their conduct subject to the Revision of any Ecclesiastical Superior; therefore the first remedy proposed was the appointment of a Chaplain-General and the issue of a warrant for the reformation of the Chaplains' Department.[1] Accordingly, on *No Episcopal superintendence.*

Warrant of September, 1795

---

[1] The Reverend John Gamble was appointed Chaplain-General by a Commission in these words (7th Report, p. 93, Appendix) —

"George the Third, &c , to our trusty and well beloved John Gamble, Clerk, greeting We, reposing especial trust and confidence in your piety, learning, and prudence, do by these presents constitute and appoint you to be Chaplain General

the 23rd September, 1796, a Royal Warrant was issued for the re-organisation of the clerical duty in the Army, under which all Regimental Chaplains who did not join their respective Corps within a given day had to retire on a reduced allowance.

16. The Warrant then went on to provide[1] that,—"No Chaplain should appoint a deputy; no Chaplaincy becoming vacant by death or resignation should be again filled up; no sale, exchange, or transfer of Commissions by the present Chaplains should be permitted after the 25th of December, 1796, unless the application for that purpose should have been previously made; and in this interval that no Chaplaincy should be sold for more than was given for it, nor should the purchaser have any claim to sell the same again.

Sales of Chaplains' Commissions prohibited

17. In order to provide for the regular performance of religious duties in future among the Regiments whose Chaplains thus retired, the Warrant provided, first, for Foreign Service thus; that wherever an Army was formed, or a body of Troops ordered for Service abroad, and in all Garrisons or stations where several Regiments were near together, Chaplains should be appointed according to the number of Corps, in the proportion of one to each brigade, or to every three or four Regiments.

Future vacancies.

18. For Regiments on Foreign Service in separate stations, or not more than two in one place or near together, an efficient Chaplain was to be appointed. to be borne on the staff of the different Armies and Garrisons, and paid monthly from the agents of their respective Commanders-in-Chief or Governors.

On Foreign Service.

19 Then for every barrack in the British dominions a

---

of our land Forces raised, and to be raised, for our Service You are, therefore, carefully and diligently to discharge the duty of Chaplain-General, by doing and performing all and all manner of things thereunto belonging, and you are to observe and follow such orders and directions from time to time as you shall receive from us, or any your superior Officer, according to the Rules and Discipline of War Given at our Court at Saint James's, the 21st September, 1796 In, &c

"By His Majesty's Command,

'PORTLAND,'

[1] Chapl. Regulations, pp 8-12.

neighbouring clergyman was to be employed *as the curate* to perform Divine Service every Sunday, and to be paid 25*l.* per annum. The Commanding Officer of every ^{At home} separate Regiment in quarters was to attend with his Regiment at some parish church; or to employ a neighbouring clergyman to perform Divine Service to the men. As a remuneration, he was to empower the clergyman whose parish church he had attended, or who had done the duty of the Regiment, to draw on the Agent for such sum as the Colonel might think a just compensation, not exceeding 10*s.* per week for the actual time of service performed."

20. And that the (Ecclesiastical) discipline, as affecting the Commissioned Chaplains, might be complete, the concluding paragraph of the Warrant was in these words —"Lastly, we do hereby subject all regular Chaplains desiring to be continued in our Service to the *orders* of the *person* whom we shall hereafter appoint to be Chaplain-General of our Army, and who is to *govern himself* by such instructions as we shall from time to time think fit to give him *through our Secretary at War.*" *(Ecclesiastical discipline under Secretary at War)*

21. A Letter of Service, the usual credential of a General Officer, was issued to the Chaplain-General, and upon the same day, 14th December, 1796, the Secretary at War conferred upon him authority[1] to call upon the Chaplains (receiving pay) for such testimonials or explanatory documents as he should judge necessary. When found satisfactory, the Chaplain-General was to transmit the accounts to the Agent, by whom the salaries or gratuities were to be paid. A circular was also issued to the Officers in command, apprising them of the Chaplain-General's appointment, and directing them "to send all requisitions and all complaints of neglect of duty to the Chaplain-General (under cover to the War Office), who will lay the same before *me* in order that such directions as shall appear necessary may be given thereupon," thus constituting the Secretary at War a lay bishop. *(Functions of the Chaplain General under the Secretary at War)*

22. The payments made to the Parochial Clergy were not

---

[1] 7th Report, pp 47-9

however to be considered as inclusive of surplice fees [1] (for the occasional duties of marriage, baptism, and burial), but "only for such duties as the Regimental Chaplain could have performed had he been present with his Regiment. As in England such occasional duties must always have been performed by the Parochial Minister, or with his consent, the fees, when required, were paid to him :—on the two former occasions by the parties themselves, and on the latter by the Captains of Troops or Companies, as one of the articles for which they receive a contingent allowance

Surplice fees to be received by Parochial Clergy

23. Such was the niggardly system inaugurated in 1796-7, and the result of it, after it had been some time in operation, is thus reported to the Secretary at War by the Chaplain-General, in June, 1805 : [2]—

Result of the system of 1796.

24. "The largest allowance permitted where a separate service solely for the use of the Military is not actually performed, is 10s. a-week for one Regiment, and if the Regiment be quartered in different cantonments, and the Commanding Officer thinks fit to represent the expediency, there can be no objection to this sum being *divided* in such manner as may appear proper for the remuneration of *more than one clergyman* Seldom, however, except in fixed Military stations, or unless a separate service is performed, is the full extent of the above sum required, for when a Regiment is so dispersed in cities, towns, and large villages, that the Soldiers, without any inconvenience to the parishioners, or increase of duty to the clergyman, can attend the usual parochial service, it has always been considered that they have a right so to do.

Payment to Clergy when no separate Service was given

25. "To such clergymen as do actually officiate by a separate service it has been found expedient to augment the stipend from 26l. to 40l per annum; but in every case where this allowance is made the strictest attention is paid that the words 'separate service performed solely for the use of the Military' be introduced into the Certificate; the Certificate to be signed by the Commanding Officer, whose signature, if of the rank of a General Officer, is considered sufficient, but

When a separate Service was given

[1] 7th Report, p 70   [2] Chapl Regulations, p 96

it of inferior rank the signature of the Paymaster to a Regimental Certificate, or of the Barrackmaster for one of Troops in barracks must be added.   In the case of Troops encamped, one or more neighbouring clergymen are employed to officiate, and are paid according to the extent of the duty required, generally from one to two guineas a-week during the term of the encampment   In all Garrisons where a Chaplain is borne on the establishment, the duty must be either performed by himself in person, or by a Deputy approved by the Commanding Officer, and paid by the Chaplain, without any further expense being incurred by Government for clerical services at such stations."

26. But these arrangements, though satisfactory to the Chaplain-General, were not regarded in the same light by the Commander-in-Chief, and—to his honour be it said—he was urgent upon the Government to make a better provision for the Spiritual wants of the Army. [1]—"His Royal Highness noticed with much concern that very inadequate provision was made for this branch of the Service, in reference to the various embarkations which took place in the course of the year 1805; viz., the armaments under the commands of Sir James Craig and Lord Cathcart, and Sir David Baird.   Sir James Craig embarked in the month of April, in command of a Corps consisting of about 4000 men (it is not on this occasion necessary to be strictly accurate as to the exact numbers), with one Chaplain.   Lord Cathcart embarked in October with a Corps of 14,000 men, with one Chaplain; and it appears that Sir David Baird's Corps, consisting of nearly 4600 men, was actually unattended by any clerical Officer of any description."

Arrangements unsatisfactory to the Commander in-Chief

27. In June, 1806, he therefore wrote, "expressing his earnest desire that means should be taken to insure the proper attendance of Chaplains with every portion of His Majesty's Troops ordered for actual service [2]   He recommended that a Chaplain should be appointed to each Brigade on its being ordered to prepare for Foreign Service,

A D 1806

His remonstrance to the Secretary at War

---

[1] 7th Report, p 119   [2] Ib, p 111

that the Chaplains so appointed should be attached to their respective Brigades, and on all occasions do duty with them, on the same footing as other Staff Officers; that, with a view of rendering the appointments objects of competition with gentlemen of respectability in their profession, who, by their example and precept, may most effectually promote a due regard to religion and morality (*the best foundation of the discipline of an Army*, and in the Soldier's mind the most powerful and resolute *discharge of his duty*) the Commander-in-Chief was induced to recommend that their pay, while so employed, should be equal to that of a Major of Infantry."

28. The Commander-in-Chief had the mortification of perceiving that his letter produced no effect, inasmuch as no better provision was made for this branch of the Service in the armaments which took place during the year 1807, and at the commencement of the year 1808, than had been allotted to those before alluded to of the year 1805 With the Corps assembled in South America (being the united commands of the Brigadier-Generals Sir Samuel Auchmuty and R. Craufurd), consisting of upwards of 8000 men, or with Major-General Fraser's Corps, which landed in Egypt in the month of April, 1807, consisting of 6600 men, no Chaplain appears to have been sent With the Corps which embarked in the month of August, on the expedition against Zealand, under the command of Lieutenant-General Lord Cathcart, of which the portion of British amounted to 14,000 men, there appears to have been one British Chaplain With the expedition against the Island of Madeira, in October, under the command of Major-General Beresford, consisting of 3400 men, there was no Chaplain, nor does there appear to have been any Chaplain with the Troops, amounting to upwards of 7000, which embarked from Sicily in the month of November, under the orders of Lieutenant-General Sir John Moore.

The same was disregarded in 1807

29. In February, 1808, Major-General Spencer proceeded on Service, with a Corps of 4000 men, without a Chaplain, and in April Lieutenant-General Sir John Moore went into the Baltic with a Corps, of which 5500 were British, accompanied by one Chaplain The Corps, consisting of 8800 men, which subsequently proceeded on Service under

The like in 1808

the command of Lieutenant-General Sir Arthur Wellesley went without any clerical Officer of any description

30 These circumstances—and a very serious consideration as to the Troops in India, in which country no June, 1808, a further remonstrance Chaplains were attached to His Majesty's Army— induced the Commander-in-Chief to address a further brief remonstrance to the Secretary at War, and the evil of having to select novices—to act as Chaplains with the Troops proceeding upon Foreign Stations—was strongly pressed on the notice of the Government.

31. The Commander-in-Chief desired that the subject should be submitted " to the consideration of His Majesty's The substance of it as to Foreign Service Ministers, not only to secure the requisite number of Chaplains being in future attached to our Troops when employed on Foreign Service, but likewise that this arrangement might be extended to those at home; that a certain proportion, competent and in every respect efficient to the duty, should thereafter be attached to the Troops in Great Britain and Ireland, and be considered as belonging exclusively to the Staff of the Army."

32 The existing arrangements were in his view insufficient, for, "though they might ensure that Divine Service was As to Home Service. generally read to the Troops on Sunday (which however remained to be proved), there was no adequate provision made for the discharge of *other* duties, which cannot certainly be looked upon as less important, nor were they calculated to establish that constant intercourse and communication between the Chaplain and the Soldier which is necessary to render the service of the former of real essential benefit, or to impress the minds and conduct of the latter with that salutary influence which sentiments of religion and morality, when inculcated by persons duly authorised and specially appointed to that duty, cannot fail to produce. Such a measure was calculated to ensure the good conduct, to raise the character of the Soldier, and so to strengthen the discipline of the Army."[1]

33. When the Commissioners of Military Inquiry called on

----

[1] 7th Report p 113

the Commander-in-Chief for an explanation of his reasons for

condemning the new system, and urging an increase of expenditure, he justified his representations by the facts that have been previously given. Then referring to the spiritual provision made for the Troops at home, he expressed himself upon that subject in these words:— " His Royal Highness cannot conceive that Troops in regular Garrisons, or when assembled in considerable bodies, should depend on the casual attendance of the Parochial Clergy, though these means may with propriety be resorted to in instances of small detached Corps; nor does His Royal Highness consider that the clerical duties of the Army can be performed with efficacy, and in a mode calculated to produce the greatest and most beneficial effect on the minds of the Soldiers, except by Chaplains personally connected with them; and in recommending a liberal provision for the Chaplains of the Army, the Commander-in-Chief has not been less influenced by considerations founded on the good of the Service—which would be materially promoted by the respectability of the persons so employed—than by a due attention to the fair pretensions of those gentlemen—with reference to the great expenses of scholastic education, and other preparations for their situations in life—and to the importance of the duties which they are required to discharge."

34. These applications resulted in the abolition of Gar-

rison Chaplains, and the appointment,[1] through the

two Archbishops and Bishop of London, of Staff Chaplains[2] in sufficient number fairly to discharge their duty with the Troops in large detachments, either at home or abroad. After the war the religious superintendence

---

[1] Extract from Letter of Service of September, 1831, to Principal Chaplain, $\frac{35146}{12}$ —" You will continue to act as Secretary to the Prelates in the nomination of persons for the appointment of Chaplain to the Forces, submitting to their Lordships such testimonials as they may call for as to the qualifications of the candidates, and requiring their directions upon all points which they may deem necessary to be attended to in the consideration of the several cases brought before them "

[2] See Horse Guards Circular, 8th November, 1811, as to Service and Sermon

of the Troops came gradually into the hands of the Parochial Clergy, and in 1829 the office of Chaplain-General was abolished, the duties of the office being discharged by the Principal or senior Chaplain.[1] The number of Chaplains was subsequently so diminished that, in July, 1848, there were only five Staff Chaplains in Commission.

35. But during the period embraced in the last paragraph a system of "Registers of Births, Deaths, and Marriages" *Regimental Registers established.* for each Regiment was established under the orders of the Commander-in-Chief,[2] which is at present in operation, and might, if sanctioned by Parliament, afford valuable evidence of these events when they occur out of the United Kingdom.

36. In every Regiment and Battalion a Register is to be kept, in which the marriage of every Non-commissioned Officer and Private, and the baptism and age *Of Marriages and Baptisms in Great Britain* of every legitimate child born of parents belonging thereto are to be recorded, and each registry is to be certified by the signature of the Adjutant. As in Great Britain a Soldier's marriage may not, as the law now stands, be solemnized by a Chaplain to the Forces, each Soldier is specially ordered to ask, at the time of marriage, for a certificate from the Officiating Clergyman, to be brought to the Adjutant, for insertion in the Regimental Register. The Adjutant is to sign his name to the Registry, as giving the contents of the certificate produced.

37. When a Soldier in the field,[3] on the continent of Europe, or beyond sea, is married, the Chaplain to the *Of the same abroad.* Forces is to certify the marriage with his signature, and to require the same from the witnesses, in the Regimental Register. When a Soldier is married in any of Her Majesty's Garrisons or Settlements abroad, it is the duty of the Commanding Officer of the Regiment to take

---

[1] See Circular, 29th July, 1830, as to Chaplains' Department

[2] See General Orders, 318, of 1st July, 1816, and 415, of 24th May, 1824, and the Regulations for the government of the Army down to 1868

[3] 52 Geo III, c 116

precaution that the Local Regulations relative to marriage are carefully regarded. If the ceremony be solemnized by a Chaplain to the Forces, or clergyman usually officiating, he is to certify the marriage with his signature in the Register of the Corps to which the Soldier belongs, notwithstanding the same may have been recorded in any parochial or Garrison Register. If the marriage take place in some Parish Church, or by a clergyman not usually officiating to the Troops, the Soldier is to apply at the time for a certificate of his marriage, to be recorded in the same way as before mentioned as to marriages in Great Britain.

38. The Register should contain the following particulars, viz.:—1. The rank, and Christian and Surname of the Soldier, specifying whether bachelor or widower. 2. The Christian and surname of the woman, specifying whether spinster or widow. 3. The place of marriage, specifying parish, county, &c, &c. 4. The date of marriage. 5. The signatures of the parties married. 6 The signatures of the two witnesses present at the ceremony. 7. The signature of the Chaplain or officiating clergyman by whom the marriage was solemnized. 8. The certificate of the Adjutant that the Registry is correct.

Contents of Marriage Register

39. In cases of baptism, the parties are to bring without delay to the Adjutant, for the purpose of registry, an account, containing —1. The date of the child's birth. 2. The place and date of its baptism. 3. The Christian name of the child. 4. The Christian and surname of the parents. 5. The rank of the father. 6. The name of the Chaplain or other clergyman by whom the ceremony was performed

Contents of Baptismal Register

40. The Regulations are not to be construed as superseding the necessity of general Registers kept by the Chaplains to the Forces, or other Clergyman in any of Her Majesty's Foreign Garrisons or Settlements, which are to be transmitted to the Chaplain-General immediately after the 1st of January and July in each year, duly signed by themselves, and by the Officer Commanding each station.

Registers to be sent to Chaplain-General

41. A general recommendation is contained in the Regula-

tions that Officers who may be married, or have children baptized on Foreign Service, should avail themselves of the Regimental Register. There are circumstances in which no regular or permanent record of such marriage or baptism would otherwise be found. It is of great importance that the objects which these orders are intended to answer, both in a National and Moral point of view, should be fully understood; and that every Soldier should be sensible, that while it is calculated to prevent imposition, it affords the most ready means of obtaining for his legitimate offspring any benefit from the Royal Military Asylum, and from other Public Establishments which have been formed for the relief of the wives and the children of Soldiers. In many cases, Civil as well as Military, the Regimental Register may prove the only record in existence. Instances have occurred in which property to a considerable amount has descended to the children of private Soldiers, and of which they have been unable to obtain possession from the want of satisfactory evidence of their parents' marriage, which the Regimental Register is calculated to afford.

Advantages to be derived from the Registers.

42. The record of an Officer's or Soldier's death, of his last will and testament, and of his personal estate as realised under the provisions of the Regimental Debts Act, 1863, is to be found in the Pay List and Muster Roll of the Regiments which are sent in to the War Office quarterly. To enable all inquiries to be readily answered, these facts are extracted into a Register, a duty (formerly discharged by the Muster-Master-General's Office, and then paid for by fees on enquiry or search) which, under the present practice, gives the Public gratuitous information in answer to inquiries.

Record of death, &c.

43. Before quitting the subject, it is open to the suggestion whether it would not be just and expedient to give statutory authority to the Commissioned Chaplains to perform all the "Occasional Offices of the Church" for the Officers and men under their spiritual charge, and whether by the same authority, these records (of as much authenticity as extra Parochial Registers) should not be made legal evidence.[1]

Legislative sanction needed.

---

[1] 52 Geo III, c 116, 6 & 7 Wm IV, c. 86, 3 & 4 Vic, c 92

When the Troops are abroad, or wherever the parochial system does not extend, these offices of baptism, marriage, and burial, can only be performed by the Army Chaplains, and hence the necessity of Legislative sanction to give legal validity to their official acts, and to the Registries kept under the authority of the Queen's Regulations.[1] In England the case may be somewhat different baptism may be administered by an Army Chaplain, and no fee could, it is presumed, be claimed by the Parish Incumbent.[2] As to marriages, the Garrison Chapel might be registered under one or other of the Acts quoted in the note,[3] or all marriages of Soldiers in pay that were performed by the Commissioned Chaplains of Her Majesty's Army declared valid. As to burials, as no ground is consecrated by the Bishop against the wishes of the Incumbent, it is not possible to bury, save under terms of arrangement with the Parish authorities.

44. Of all persons that regard authority and competency,

Increase the use and influence of the Chaplains soldiers are the most sensitive. If their own Chaplains have not full legal sanction for all the offices of religion, they may mistrust their mission altogether. In districts extra Parochial, under the 31 and 32 Vic., c. 83, it appears only reasonable that this authority should be conferred upon them.

45. But to resume the more immediate subject of this

A.D 1844
Office of Principal Chaplain revived Chapter. in April, 1844, it was deemed expedient to make a new arrangement,[4] providing more effectually for the religious instruction of the Army, and with that view, the present Chaplain-General was appointed as the Principal Chaplain. The records of the Chaplain's Department were delivered over to him, and the Letter of Service indicated the outline of his duties in these terms.—

[1] 4 Geo. IV, c 91, Waldegrave Peerage, 4 Clark and Fin, 652, 12 & 13 Vic, c 68, 21 & 22 Vic, c 46, sec 2

[2] Burdeaux v Lancaster, 12 Mod Rep, p 172, Hobart's Reports, p 175

[3] 4 Geo. IV, c 76, 6 & 7 Wm IV c 85, 1 Vic, c 22, 3 & 4 Vic, c 72.

[4] $\frac{99972}{9}$

46. "In the first place he was to procure for the Archbishops of Canterbury and York and the Bishop of London such testimonials, as they might require with a view to the nomination of persons appointed for the first time to be Chaplains to the Forces, and to take their directions upon all points which they might deem necessary to be attended to in the consideration of the several cases brought under their notice. Then he was to communicate with the Secretary at War on all points relating to the promotion, exchange, increase of salary, or any fresh disposal of the services of a clergyman whose first nomination had previously been sanctioned before any such fresh nomination or succession be made, in order that the necessity for continuing the appointments or increasing the salary might first of all be decided upon by the Secretary at War.

Duties as defined by Letter of Service. First appointments and promotions of Chaplains.

47. "He was to adopt measures for becoming acquainted with the mode in which divine service was performed to the troops at home and in the colonies, and to suggest from time to time such arrangements as might appear to him to be desirable with a view to the Spiritual Welfare of the Forces at all Stations; exercising a general superintendence in all matters having reference to the spiritual instruction of the troops, and the provision of religious books for their use.

General superintendence of religious worship

48. "Whenever the Churches at any place in Great Britain and Ireland, in which troops were stationed for any length of time, did not afford sufficient accommodation for them, and it became necessary for the first time to provide for the performance of divine service or for attendance on the sick in hospital, the Principal Chaplain was required to ascertain, for the Secretary at War's information, that the officiating clergyman proposed was properly qualified, and if approved, he was to explain the duties to be performed before authorizing him to commence his functions. He was warned to exercise great caution and discretion in his recommendation of candidates, because of the different sects of which a regiment in her Majesty's service is generally composed."

Select Clergymen for duty

49. The concluding paragraph of his Instructions was expressed in these words:—"As I attach great importance to the duties of visiting the sick in hospital and

Visitation of the sick in Hospital

the supervision of the schools which have been established for the education of the children of the Soldiers, I shall be prepared to receive and consider any suggestion which you may be enabled to submit in respect to these points; and it being essential that these duties should be performed with a due regard to regularity as well as discipline, it might be expedient that the periodical visits should be recorded in a register to be established for that specific purpose."

50. In July, 1846, the title of Chaplain-General was revived, and the appointment conferred upon the present holder of that office, under Commission and a Letter of Service directing him to follow the Instructions of April, 1844. The emolument of the office was also increased, for reasons thus forcibly set forth by Lord Herbert:[1]—— "The Chaplain-General is at the head of a vast number of clergy ministering both at home and abroad to the spiritual wants of the troops, and the office is in the nature of an archdeaconry, with a jurisdiction far more extensive than any that attaches to that office in England."

A.D 1846.

Office of Chaplain-General revived

51. Hitherto the provision made for the spiritual wants of the members of the Church of England only has been noticed; and, indeed, in the earlier history of the Army, all Roman Catholics were, as far as possible, excluded from the Military Service Still they were found there; and in 1705 their presence is traced in an order issued by St. John, interdicting the officers of the Roman Church from attending "mass" at the houses of the French prisoners at Lichfield[2]

As to the Clergy of the Church of Rome

52. From the commencement of the present century—if not earlier— members of the Roman Catholic Church have been admitted into the Army with the cognizance of the Crown,[3] and from the year 1802 they, in common with others who dissent from the Established Church, have been exempt from attending the worship of the Church of England,

Roman Catholics in the Army

---

[1] 'Report of Army Expenditure, 1850,' p 25
[2] War Office Letter Bk. 133, p 290   [3] Marshall, p 59, 57 Geo. III, c. 92.

and permitted, when military duty does not interfere, to attend the worship of their own Church.[1]

53. Liberty of conscience was a great thing gained. It might, however, bring with it the spirit of religious proselytism, and therefore, in May, 1811, by General Order from the Commander-in-Chief, all Officers (except Military Chaplains) were forbidden to circulate religious tracts among the Soldiers. Having regard to the Fanatics in the Army of the Commonwealth, some caution must always be needed against the alloy of religious error.

*A.D 1802.
Freedom of worship to the three Churches allowed.*

54. Hitherto the services of the Roman Catholic Clergy had been gratuitous, and though the Presbyterian Clergy had been paid in Scotland, no general provision had been made for the payment of any allowance to them out of Scotland, or to the Roman Catholic Clergy anywhere. Therefore, in 1836, the Ministry of Lord Melbourne sanctioned the payment of the Presbyterian and Roman Catholic Clergy for services wherever rendered to the Troops (to the satisfaction of the Commanding Officer),[2] but issued no general Regulation to that effect.

*A.D 1836.
Payment to the Clergy of the three Churches commenced*

55. From that period to the present the progress of religious toleration or encouragement has been moving in the direction of placing the Churches of England Scotland and Rome upon a footing of equality in the Army. In 1854, upon the approach of the Crimean War, Lord Herbert approved of each of the three denominations being paid on a Capitation Rate;[3] and, after the War (1858),[4] General Peel, in a greater spirit of liberality, placed nineteen Roman Catholic and five Presbyterian Clergy on the Establishment of the Army as Commissioned Chaplains, and on the same footing with regard to allowances.[5] The Army Chaplains. who in 1857-8 numbered 22 Commissioned and 34 Assistant Chaplains, for the year 1869-70 consist of 80 Commissioned Chaplains.

All Chaplains put on a footing of equality

---

[1] 19 H D (O S , pp. 368, 385, and General Orders of 1811, p 84   [2] $\frac{72333}{2}$.

[3] Addenda to War Office Regulations, p 126

[4] See the approval of the Chaplains during the War, 141 H D (3), p 877

[5] Circular, 30th Nov., 1858 (283), Royal Warrants, 5th November, 1858, 16th November, 1859, 16th May, 1861, and 13th July, 1861

There has also been an allowance in the latter year of 19,368*l*
to officiating Clergy of these Churches.[1]

56. As places of Public Worship, some Consecrated churches
—as at Woolwich, Aldershot, and the older fortresses
—exist which are dedicated to the exclusive service
of the Church of England, by the deed of the Secretary of State and the Act of the Bishop But in the United
Kingdom and the Channel Islands 26 Churches or Chapels,
and 28 Chapel Schools are available for the general Public
Worship of the Army according to the order of the three
Churches. Military Burial Grounds have also been consecrated
or set aside for the interment of Soldiers.

As to Churches and Chapels at Military Stations.

57. Although, as we have seen, Chaplains have been attached to the Army from 1662, in one scheme or
another, for the performance of religious worship according to the rites and ceremonies of the Church
of England, no system has been established by which these
Clergymen are placed in a defined relationship towards the
Bishop of the diocese or the Parochial Clergy in whose diocese
or parish they may administer the Sacraments

Church of England Chaplains no Parochial status.

58. From Ireland the chief difficulty has arisen, and there
the Chaplains of the Church of England on more occasions than one have been objected to by the Irish
Clergy as intruders. In 1867, Mr. Craig, the Military
Chaplain in charge of the Troops within Richmond Barracks,
was prohibited by the Ecclesiastical Court in Dublin from
performing Divine Service or administering the Sacraments
there.[2]

A D 1867
Case in Ire-land of Wells v. Craig

59 Two advantages, however, resulted from this judgment.
First, that of placing the Army Chaplains of the
Church of England under the Episcopal superintendence of His Grace the Archbishop of Canterbury, and then
of procuring the sanction of Parliament to afford them greater
facilities for their ministrations, by the Army Chaplains Act
1868.[3]

Advantages resulting from it.

---

[1] Returns (135), 1859, and (187), 1865

[2] Appendix CXLVI

[3] 31 & 32 Vic , c 83.

60. This Act enables the Crown to set out by metes and bounds a precinct, and to declare the station, for all Substance of Army Chaplains Act. Districts to be set out the Ecclesiastical purposes of the Act, to be an extra-parochial district. The Secretary of State may then appoint any Army Chaplain to perform his functions in any such district; and during the continuance of his appointment he shall for all Ecclesiastical purposes be and be adjudged the Chaplain of an extra-parochial place within the provisions of the Act.

61. A Chapel consecrated for the performance therein of Divine Service, according to the Rites and Cere- Chapels consecrated or certified for Public Worship. monies of the said United Church, shall be, for the purposes of the Act, an extra-parochial Chapel. And where a Building shall have been certified, under the hand of the Secretary of State, to the Bishop of the Diocese, as used or intended to be used by Her Majesty's Military Forces as an unconsecrated Chapel for the purpose of Divine Worship according to the Rites and Ceremonies of the said United Church, the Secretary of State may appoint an Army Chaplain to perform all his functions therein. If at any time the building shall cease to be used for the purpose aforesaid, the Secretary of State shall certify such fact to the Bishop, and thereupon the provisions of the Act shall no longer apply to such building.

62. Her Majesty in Council, upon the recommendation of the Secretary of State, may declare all or any of the Exclusive Episcopal jurisdiction by Order in Council extra-parochial districts to be under the exclusive jurisdiction of any Archbishop or Bishop as may be named in the Order; and thereupon such Archbishop or Bishop may exercise over any Army Chaplain appointed to officiate within any such extra-parochial district all the powers and authority which he is by law authorized to exercise over any clerk in Holy Orders holding any preferment within his diocese. The previous consent in writing of the Archbishop or Bishop is needed before making the Order, and until revoked, all other Ecclesiastical jurisdiction in respect of the extra-parochial districts, wholly ceases.

---

[1] 1 & 2 Vic., c 106, sec 108; 3 & 4 Vic., c 86, sec. 22

63. Hitherto the plan has been—though the dawn of better

Improvement on the old system

times is visible—the admission of the Clergy of the English Church into the Pastoral office of an Army Chaplain, with the practical abjuration of all Episcopal authority over them; the adoption of a system utterly untenable according to the rule and order of the Church of England. Each Church should have fair play at least—if no favour be given to it; but to divorce the Episcopalian Clergy from the counsel and direction of their Ordinary is scarcely such. As affecting the efficiency of the Chaplains, the question is not unimportant; for every one—in any way connected with the Service—ought to cherish highly "the moral discipline of the Army."[1]

64. "The troops of France, of Prussia, or of Austria"—

The Army represents the National character

observed an eloquent writer—"never go beyond the limits of their own country, except to make war. Their wars too are all carried on against nations either Christian or Mahomedan, the whole of whom have attained to a certain degree of civilization, and with whose religious opinions there is neither desire nor opportunity to interfere. Our troops, on the contrary, go forth sometimes to fight, but much more frequently to protect and control millions of heathens whom they or their fathers have brought under subjection to the British Crown. If not a Missionary, therefore, in his own person, there is not a man in our ranks who, if he went aright, would fail to perceive that he should be a pioneer to the Missionary. Why has the dominion of India been granted by the Governor of the Universe to England? That a few individual Englishmen might acquire enormous fortunes, and a still greater number find employment, and earn a competency in that distant land? Certainly not, but that the victor should carry to the homes of the vanquished his juster laws, his fairer morals, his true faith: thus compensating by the benefits which he confers upon all generations, for the wrong which is done to one in depriving it of its natural right to self-government and a national existence. And how is this

---

[1] See an admirable article upon this subject in Vol 76 of the 'Quarterly Review' (1845), pp 387-423

to be done, if you employ throughout the heathen settlements a body of troops, among whom there is no ostensible appearance of any religious belief whatever, who by their daily lives outrage all the precepts of morality?" It is a matter, therefore, of more than ordinary importance to the character of Great Britain, that the General Commanding in India should be something more than a mere soldier—whatever his ability as such—but that he should also be a *gentleman*, not prone by his *personal conduct*, to violate the social decencies of life.

65 The Army Chaplains, as a class, do their duty admirably[1] In one Garrison at least, the Church is open daily for public and private worship, and all the Charities are heartily supported[2] In active service, where danger is to be met with, in ministering to the spiritual wants of dying men, these officers have been found.[3] Obviously the Service requires men of no mean endowments The confidence both of officers and men should be gained, to carry on their Mission with success; and when successful, their reward is great.[4]

Success of the Army Chaplain system

---

[1] 144 H D (3), p 877

[2] At Woolwich a short daily service has been established with success, and the beautiful church, erected at the instance of the late Lord Herbert, is always open for the use of the Garrison

[2] One Chaplain (at least) has a ball lodged in him, which he received in front while attending the wounded in China

[4] *Memorandum from the Society for Promoting Christian Knowledge —* ' The Fund of 'Clericus,' held in trust by this Society, was established by the late Archdeacon Owen, Chaplain-General The Archdeacon gave several donations in his lifetime, and left a sum of money at his death The amount of the Fund now, including accumulations of interest, is 12,638*l* 7*s* 11*d* Consols, producing an income of 379*l* 3*s* 4*d* per annum There is a balance to the credit of the Trust of 737*l* 5*s* 3*d* The object of the Trust is to supply Her Majesty's Land Forces with copies of the Book of Common Prayer, and such Religious Tracts as the Society may deem expedient "

CHAPTER XXIX.

THE CONSOLIDATED WAR OFFICE.

1. IN the previous Chapters an endeavour has been made to
Object of the present Chapter describe the Constitutional functions of the various Departments of the State entrusted with the "Civil Administration" and with the "Military Command" of the Army prior to the Crimean War; and to do this without anticipating in the narrative the description thereafter to be given of the changes initiated upon a political crisis during the Crimean War, and of their results.[1] This description remains to be given, and a justification to be offered for the expressions found in the Preface, in which the Department is designated as *Hybrid*, and referred to as discharging *functions vast, miscellaneous, and undefined.*

2. To assume that no alterations were needed, or that no
Changes made 1855 and their results. improvements could be suggested in Army Administration when the Chiefs of the old Departments were displaced and their functions undertaken by one Minister, is unnecessary. It is sufficient to say that the alterations needed were not those that were made, and that improvements then called for still remain to be commenced. Moreover, it may be asserted that from 1855 to 1861 the changes introduced have produced evils greater in degree than those remedied; while we appear, in 1869-70, *still* to be in pursuit of *organic* change

3. The Civil Administration of the Army broke down during

---

[1] See 136 H D (3), pp 940-1, 960, 1066, 1121; and see other Debates on the Administration of the Army at 133 ib, pp 1230-68, 1301-58, 135 ib, p 317, 137 ib., p 886, 138 ib, pp 420, 736, 140 ib, p 1023; 143 ib, p. 812

the Crimean War ; but as the Ministers of the Crown—and not the Generals in Command of the suffering Army— *Disasters during the Crimean War* were first heard in Parliament, the blame was attributed to a Military Department by its immediate suppression, and the Civil Minister was exalted by his installation to discharge the functions of the Master-General and Board of Ordnance.

4. Against such changes—as the Abolition of the Master-General, and the consolidation of the War Department *Warning of the Duke of Wellington against organic change* under one Civil head—the Duke of Wellington, in official intercourse, had solemnly warned the Ministry of Lord Melbourne in 1838, and of Earl Russell in 1849 [1] They both heeded his warning, or in deference to his great experience in War and Politics, abided by his advice. A few years sufficed —after he had passed away from us—to render his recorded opinions unavailing, and to raise up a "War Minister," with an annually increasing Military Expenditure

5. In endeavouring to trace out the reasons for these changes, made in defiance of the warnings of great experience, *Advantages to be gained* very much—from the time and circumstances under which the changes were made—unfortunately is left to conjecture.[2] As the Ordnance Department was abolished, and the War Office was increased in importance, we may not unreasonably presume that the main object of these measures was to develop the theory upon which that Office—rather than the Ordnance— was governed Extravagance was chargeable to the Ordnance as a Military Department, therefore a Civil one was to be substituted for it. The War Office was one of Law and Finance, therefore its employés should be Civilians trained officially for these duties The House of Commons, as voting the Supplies, ought to control Military Expenditure ; therefore the Civil Minister ought to be the emblem of economy.

6. Before examining (by results) how far those objects have

---

[1] See the Duke's Memoranda of 1838 and 1849, in Appendices CXLVII, CXLVIII

[2] See Earl Grey's motion of January, 1855, embracing the question of the neglect of the Ordnance Board, in not accepting the Price Candle Company's proposal to warm the Army by their "Candle Stoves," 136 H D (3) p 1074

been attained, the positive objections to consolidation must not

Objections to Consolidation considered be overlooked. Granting that "concentration is the policy of the present day"[1]—that policy assumes the capacity of the Minister's apprehension, and that he has actual knowledge, or the means of acquiring it, of the Department and of the work entrusted to him · otherwise it would be better, obviously,—to be without the Minister. But it will be seen that a large portion of the work of the War Department has been —and still is of necessity—carried through, without Ministerial control other than nominal.

7 The Census Tables will show to the Bishop of a Diocese

What are the duties dis charged or neglected? or the Rector of a parish the extent of his ministerial responsibility, and thus he may form an accurate estimate of the work that he leaves unfulfilled ; there is, however, no such exact test to satisfy a political servant of the State of the extent of his responsibility, or to show him that he does not accomplish by any given proportion the work entrusted to him. Certainly as having charge both of the Finance of the Army, and of the Constitutional Liberties of the People, the Secretary of State holds an office—having regard to the constant action of the Army upon those interests with which he is entrusted—where business can with less safety be left to take care of itself than in any other Department of the State.

8. At present, as the War Office is constituted, there is

The Minister in the power of the Permanent Staff good authority[2] for saying that the members of the permanent staff can let the Secretary of State see as much or as little of the business of his department as *they* please The vast number of papers shews it to be impossible for him to see all of them ; and as the selection is made by the heads of subdivisions, they have it in their own hands to say what papers, if not what proportion of them, shall or shall not be sent on to their Chief.

9. Dealing, for the present purpose of illustration, with

The vast extent of official work official returns, the comparison made in the year 1858 with the year 1853 shows the following results ·—In the year 1853 the War Office and Ordnance Board alone—

---

[1] Sir James Graham, Admiralty Report (Questions 843-912)
[2] Note J J , Appendix

without reference to the Treasury and other offices—having 5 Parliamentary Officers, and in the year 1858 the Secretary of State, having 1 Parliamentary Colleague, received and wrote letters as under .—

	Received	Wrote
In 1853	162,088	201,000
„ 1858	319,735	532,190
„ 1868	271,68	1

therefore it need scarcely be said that of these letters—written in the Secretary of State's name to persons in the highest and lowest ranks in the Civil, Military, or Political stations—his supervision and that of his Under Secretaries were purely nominal.

10. The principle of consolidation would, however, be carried too far when—to use again the words of the Commis- sioners of 1834[2]—"it trenches upon efficiency, renders the Department unwieldy, or destroys any of those checks which one department holds over another, or within itself." When absolute power was given to one Minister, the subordinate officers of the Ordnance and War Office suppressed, and certain duties of the Treasury absorbed, all these principles —if the matter is to be decided by antecedent testimony or by subsequent experience—were violated Evils of Consolidation

11. To deal with efficiency—which may be said to be a matter of opinion, not capable of definite proof,— whenever such an investigation shall be entered upon, the official acts of the abolished officers can and ought to be contrasted with those of the Secretary of State These papers would prove whether the labour of the latter Officer in each set of papers bore an equal, or what, comparison to the labours of those predecessors. In effect that it may be known, whether the Secretary of State has been able "personally to investigate all the *important* details of his Department," or rather whether the work has not been that of *irresponsible persons under him* (for to Parliament all his officials, called by any title, are irresponsible), to whom, as of necessity, the work has been "dele- (1) If it leads to in efficiency

---

[1] This return could only be arrived at by greater labour than I can command, but it is supposed to bear the same proportion to letters received as shown in 1858

[2] Chap XX, par 103

gated by a nominal chief," "having at best but an indifferent knowledge of what was going on in his Department."

12. The evil of such a system has shown itself in the distrust manifested by the Army against the War Department. In the first place, has it not come to be true that the Secretary of State, acting through his Department, has *no authority with the Army*, and is it not sought to remedy this state of feeling by filling the Principal Civil appointments in the War Office by Military Officers? Whatever may be the success of this measure, if for that purpose designed, it is clearly a departure from that *personnel* in the Civil Administration of the Army, which enjoyed the confidence of the Civil community, and of the Army.

Want of confidence in the Consolidated Department.
(i) By the Army

13. In the next place, the distrust of Parliament against the Department is shown (1) in the numberless petty details of Administration and Government with which the Notice and Order Books of the House of Commons are charged; (2) in the tone of censure or dictation assumed against the Minister, (3) in the motions for Committees or Commissions of Inquiry on matters of Military Administration within the ordinary competency of the Department to deal with

(ii) By Parliament

14. Lastly, in the distrust which each successive Secretary of State has manifested in the existing organisation of his Department, as evidenced by changes, by Committees of Inquiry, and by the introduction of novices in official matters from the outer world, rather than give promotion to the trained and experienced officers of the late Departments "The War Office and Parliament," said Lord Longford in the House of Lords, "has been very sensible of the necessity of watching Military Administration;" and, in proof of their vigilance, he mentioned that 17 Royal Commissions, 18 Select Committees, 19 Committees of Officers within the War Office, besides 35 Committees of Military Officers, had considered points of policy during the twelve years of its (the Consolidated Department's) existence.[1]

(iii) By each successive Secretary of State

15 That the Department is unwieldy—so that the right hand knows not what the left is doing, and therefore as a con-

---

[1] 188 H D (3) p 594

sequence, that too many or too few official acts are executed —recent events furnish the evidence. It is a sequence so obvious to such a consolidation that little doubt arises, and little proof need be given, as to its existence.

(2) If the Department be unwieldy

16 But the question, when considered with regard to the destruction of the Constitutional checks and safeguards existing from the time of the Revolution, assumes far higher importance. The time has not yet come that the leopard may lie down with the lamb,[1] or that a child may lead them. To those who think so, few warnings would avail; but to other readers I may venture to point out wherein these arrangements lessen our Constitutional safety.

(3) If it destroys the constitutional check or control previously existing

17. To trust the power of the sword to one or two men is in itself objectionable, and the more so as the Troops at home are massed together in vast bodies, rather than dispersed under separate Commands.[2] Whether dangerous or not, it has hitherto been deemed so, and our experience since 1855 is not sufficient warrant for us to laugh to scorn all the Constitutional arrangements of earlier periods Military Power is *now* shewn principally in Finance and Expenditure; but, at the promptings of Military Committees, its future development may soon find expression in usurping the Constitutional as well as the financial functions of the Ministers

Constitutional danger of placing all Military Power in one Minister

18. Several, rather than only one Member of the Cabinet,[3] were involved in the responsibility of Army Administration. If either of them lacked experience or wisdom, his action was soon stopped before he did any great mischief. In this arrangement the Country got the benefit described in Lord Bacon's aphorism . that "Counsellors are not commonly so united but that one Counsellor keepeth sentinel over another."[4] Here, therefore, was the first check which the

Various Members in the Cabinet responsible

---

[1] The experience that Statesmen had of an Army when it existed in the kingdom without a Civil Administration, is thus given by Sir W Morrice, who compared " The keeping of an Army on foot to a sheep s skin and a wolf s skin—which if they lie together, the former would lose its wool And again, if a sheep and a wolf be put into two separate grates, by one another, the sheep would pine and die at the sight of the other"—*Speech on Disbanding the Forces*, 30th August, 1660   [2] Chap XXVI , pars 2, 3

[3] I have seen the notes of three distinguished Statesmen then in the Cabinet on the Limited Enlistment Act, 1847 , but now the leverage used to move the present vast machine seldom rises higher than a Treasury Official and an Under-Secretary of State   [4] 28th Essay, p 194

Ministry and Parliament held upon the increase of Military Power or Expenditure under the arrangements of 1688.

19 That a Cabinet could hold in greater safety the preroga-

Constitu-
tional safety
in that ar
rangement.

tives of the Crown as to the Command of the Army than any one Member of it, admits of no controversy All questions of Prerogative are subject to flux and reflux at one time the Will of the Sovereign, and at another the aggressions of Parliament may—unless controlled—prevail. These elements of confusion have once broken loose, and therefore the State can never be wholly free from danger. What is one Minister—and that may be not the strongest in the Cabinet —against the adverse action of the House of Commons, either in Expenditure or in Prerogative, upon any question that stirs deeply—though erroneously—the National sympathy?[1]

20. In the Constitutional arrangements of 1688 the " Com-

The Consti-
tutional ar-
rangements
of 1688

mand" was wisely separated from the "Finance" of the Army; but in the arrangements of 1855 they were, either by design or inadvertence, so blended, that no definite line of policy was indicated.[2] The first theory— and that not by inadvertence, but deliberate intention—was to divorce the Responsible Minister from all responsibility in regard to the Command and Discipline of the Army. Until this monstrous theory was embodied in the Secretary of State's patent, no Official Act of any Constitutional Minister ever sanctioned such a doctrine.[3]

21. But by turning the Secretary of State into a Finance as

Secretary of
State not a
financial or
executive
officer

well as into an Executive Officer, an incongruous ar- rangement was made. No doubt an able man can undertake any duty to which he is educated; but this Country has enough of Constitutional history to learn from it— (1) that certain definite duties are usually attached to an Esta- blished Officer of the State, and (2) that the Secretary of State is no more a Finance Officer than the Lord Chancellor is a Fiscal one. No doubt, if advantage could be shown to result from changing the duties of either Minister, little could be said

---

[1] As to the Expenditure of the reformed House of Commons on the Army and Navy, see General Peel's speech, 182 H D ('3), pp 1203-7 As to Prerogative, instance Col Crawley's case and Sergeant-Major Lilley's See Chap XIX , par. 13

[2] Chap XIX , pars 4 16, Chap XXI, pars 33, 3o, 43, and Chap. XXVI

[3] 'Organization Report, 1860,' pp 572-3

against it. but the onus of proof would rest on those who originated such a change.

22. Now by the union of the varied functions of Secretary of State—of the Treasury—of the Principal Officers of the Ordnance,—and of the Secretary at War, in *one* man, these securities of a high Constitutional character are gone.   *One* man—or rather others in his name—can, without control, by the stroke of a pen, issue arms for (say) a million of men, out of the Reserve Stores can in the Queen's name send the whole Army to any part of the United Kingdom, or, if transports be at hand, to any part of the World, for any purpose, and under any Officer whom he appoints to command; and, lastly, may sell Dover Castle and the whole defensive works of the Kingdom, as defences, for any sum and to any person (not an alien) that he pleases.   These facts being admitted, what answer is it to say that in this *one* man and his employés, the Crown and Parliament have *such* confidence that all check and control ought to be dispensed with. To this suggestion the reply is obvious, and may be given almost in the words of Mr. Fox, that until 1855 " the Constitution knew no such confidence." [1] " The Executive Government may," as Lord Grey admitted, " ask for the confidence of the House of Commons to provide for the security and defence of the community," [2] but how are these objects secured by the cession of these extravagant powers to the nominal or actual Head of any Department ?

Union of functions destroys or lessens (1) Constitutional responsibility

23. By the same union of duties, that financial check which the separate Departments held one against the other, or which the Ordnance Department—with separate Parliamentary Officers—held within itself, and which it had cost so much time, experience, and care to bring to perfection, was absolutely destroyed.   In the chaos of destruction first principles were forgotten.   The Consolidated Department was deemed a new department, and its records—which, as to the Ordnance are continuous from Elizabeth's reign, and as to the War Office from Charles II.'s reign, and, in fact, were continued from page to page on the change of dynasty from the

(2) Financial control

---

[1] 29 Parl Hist., p 245   [2] Ib , p. 684

House of Stuart to the House of Orange—were practically abandoned, and a new series from 1855 commenced.

24. The different phases through which the War Department

Changes from 1854 to 1868

has gone since 1854 to the accession of the present Ministry are shown in the Official Record which is printed in the Appendix.[1] The Crown having appointed a fourth Secretary of State in June, 1854, that Minister, in February, 1855, assumed the duties of the Secretary at War's Office, and in May of the same year the Ordnance Board was dissolved. In Burke's time it had been saved because of the alleged efficiency of the newly appointed Master-General (the Duke of Richmond); but no such plea was—though it might have been—urged for Lord Raglan in 1855. The Lieutenant-General was informed that the Government intended to abolish the Board, and to conduct the *civil business* under the Secretary of State, while the Military Command of the Artillery was transferred to the Commander-in-Chief.[2] The transfer of the Ordnance property was made by the 18 & 19 Vic., c. 117.

25. However, the business of the Ordnance and War Offices

Accumulation of general duties

was not deemed enough for the War Minister, and therefore the Commissariat business from the Treasury —part of the Audit business from the Audit Board— the Militia and other Reserve Forces from the Home Office— the Clothing business from the Colonels and their agents—and part of the business of the Colonial Office—were sent to the War Department. Added to which (verifying Sidney Smith's prophecy[3]), a Small Arms Factory was established at Enfield,[4] and later in time a Clothing Factory at Pimlico.[5]

26. The increase to the War Department, as consequent

Staff of the War Department increased by transfer from other offices

upon these arrangements, may be thus stated —

(1.) By transfer from Colonial Office with the duties attaching to the Department of the Secretary of State for War when combined with that of the Colonies, viz., 4 clerks.

(2.) By transfer from Home Office of the duties attaching to that Department, in connection with the organizing of the Militia, occupying 4 clerks.

---

[1] Appendix CXLIX. $\frac{20106}{9}$.   [3] Vol. iii of his Works (1840), p. 228, and 165
H D (3), p 1091   [4] Appendix CXXIV   [5] Note W W, Appendix.

(3) By transfer from Audit Office, for the examination of Non-Effective payments, and the Commissariat Cash and Store, Accounts,—23 clerks.

(4.) By creation of a branch for the Ordnance Solicitor, owing to the increased business of the Consolidated Department, and the discontinuance of reference to the Treasury Solicitor by the Commissariat and old War Office branches,—4 clerks.

(5.) By the forming of a Clothing Branch to take up the duties formerly entrusted to the Colonels of Regiments and Agents in supplying clothing and necessaries to the Army, which relieved the agents of labour and responsibility, but added to the War Department,—22 clerks.

27. If, therefore, in the opinion of the Duke of Wellington— ' no bad judge and no bad administrator" (to cite the words and opinion of Sir James Graham)—the work only of the War and Ordnance Offices was too much for one Board of several Ministers to execute efficiently, what would be said by any good administrator of entrusting such a mass of work and of expenditure to one Secretary of State? *(margin: Effective Ministerial supervision impossible)*

28. Take, for illustration, but *one* branch of the Ordnance business, viz., the Manufacturing Departments. Have not immense works and shops been suffered to grow up under the Crown, in defiance of all the rules of political economy and sound financial administration. "When I look at the Army Estimates,[1] I find (said Sir James Graham), " they have 12,000 men in day-pay." Is it possible that the control of the Secretary of State over such commercial operations can have been more than nominal? *(margin: An illustration)*

29. But all the business of the Consolidated Department was to be essentially Civil, for even matters relating to the Command and Discipline of the Army were, by the terms of the Secretary of State's Patent, to be *absolutely* excluded from his Department. Taking the model of every Secretary of State's, and of the old Secretary at War's Office, all the employés would be Civil (and not Military), because they were, as the Secretary of State's Staff, to be a check upon the Military element in the State as represented by the Commander-in-Chief. *(margin: All the Civil business was to be placed under the Secretary of State)*

---

[1] Admiralty Report 1861. p. 125

30. In time of Peace the defence of the country (and therein the erection of forts), lies within the province of the Secretary of State, with which the Commander-in-Chief has no function--save to give his advice on the subject, if asked for it--and therefore the Engineer Corps, as scientific constructors, were needed in the Secretary of State's Office. Some of these Officers were necessarily retained in the War Department; but, with the exception of Ordnance Officers, the Secretary of State was served by a Civil Staff up to 1858.

except Engineer Officers or Constructors.

31. Now, in the ten years succeeding, a vast change in this respect has been made. In the first place, in 1858 and 1861, a large proportion of the Secretary of State's Civil Staff was sent over to the allegiance of the Commander-in-Chief, as Officers; and hence small trace is to be found in the Secretary of State's Office, of the Civil branches of the Commissariat or of the Ordnance. So far the balance has plainly been turned against the Civil and in favour of the Military Administration of the Army. But further, during the same period the highest permanent appointments of the War Office have been filled by Military Officers, either *ordered* to do duty as in the Harwich case [1]--for a limited period of 5 years, and then to return to the Commander-in-Chief's command--or for life. From these facts it is, therefore, plain that the (Civil) Administration of the Army prior and subsequent to 1858 are essentially different, that the changes of 1855--instead of leading, as they were designed to do, to Civil--have produced Military control, under the nominal superintendence of a Secretary of State, not always a Civilian.[2]

Changes from 1858 in the Staff of the Secretary of State

32. How little the War Office is now trusted (how far it can be trusted will be shewn hereafter) as a Civil and Finance Department of the State cannot be better illustrated than by reference to a speech made by the late Chancellor of the Exchequer in the House of Commons in March, 1869. Having laid down the axiom that it was the duty of the Treasury to control Public Expenditure, he objected--with obvious reason in the objection--to one of the Members of the Treasury Board passing his Departmental time at the War Office, "because *those who are surrounded by Military men* are less likely to check

War Office no longer a Civil and Financial Department.

---

[1] Vol I , Chap IX , par 8, Chap. XVI , par 15   [2] Chap XVII., par 62

Military Expenditure than those who pass their official hours at the Treasury, where the habit is to criticise and object to every item of expenditure that comes before them"[1]—a fact that is undisputed, and yet overlooked in its consequences.

33. This fact—of no mean importance, having reference to the Constitutional functions of the Secretary of State—has a more direct bearing upon the Finance of the Army. It has been already shown that the Treasury has not the same organs of sight and action that it formerly had,[2] that the Store Officers of the Ordnance no longer supply independent information to the Cabinet, and that many of the duties of the Audit Board are discharged by the Secretary of State's Staff. These premises being admitted, the importance of having the Secretary of State removed from " the danger " (as Lord Bacon[3] puts it) " of being counselled more for the good of them that counsel than of him that is counselled," is great.

Great importance of them.

34. Such being the character of the Secretary of State's Staff, its influence is obviously reflected in his official acts. In matters supplementary to his office, such as Commissions or Committees of Inquiry directed to gentlemen inside or outside his department, the same Military bias is observable. In the former matters the Crown, under the advice of the Secretary of State, accepts as Royal Commissioners such names as the Secretary of State deems it right to submit : in the latter, he acts on his own responsibility. In earlier times, Statesmen worked these Commissions; the Military element, though represented, was never predominant. Such information as Military Officers could give, they gave as witnesses; but in the greater matters of Military Administration or Policy, the Crown was counselled by Responsible Ministers—men of large and varied experience in Public Affairs. To clothe Military Officers—not always of high rank or attainment—with the disguise of Royal Commissioners, under the impression that their views will be less professional or more readily accepted by Parliament, may be attempted, but will soon be exposed.[4]

The Military element in the Commissions of Inquiry appointed by the Crown

---

[1] Mr. Ward Hunt's Speech, 194 H D (3), p. 858 Chap XXI., par 46
[2] Chap XIX., pars 24 and 56   [3] Essays, p 21
[4] Contrast the Commission on Civil Administration in 1837 with the Supply and Transport Commission of 1867 The one consisted of Earl Grey, Lord Palmerston,

35 But the Civil Department for the Administration of the Army was originally designed—to secure economy—to preserve an effectual check upon Military Expenditure—and to insure to the Commons complete responsibility for the Expenditure of the Public Treasure. How one Minister could effectually control such elements as the House of Commons and the Army, united in a common cause of Public Expenditure, was not shown before 1855, nor can it be proved since, having any regard to the facts shown in the accounts presented to Parliament.[1]

Consolidation was to secure economy

36. When the idea was conceived of entrusting to an *Under-Secretary of State* the task of moving and explaining the Estimates for the entire Military Expenditure of the United Kingdom, it was entirely original. Probably in a Free State it was without precedent that one Responsible Minister of the Crown should take under his charge (say) one-third part[2] of the whole taxation of the people, after deducting Consolidated Fund charges, and apply it, upon his own responsibility, to the Expenditure of the Army. The experiment has been a costly one, if a comparison be made of our Military Expenditure for each of the last twenty years, which is shown in recent Parliamentary Returns[3]

A sum equal to one third of the whole National Expenditure under one Minister

37. Dividing the total into four quinquennial periods, it shows a vast increase in the expenditure. Of course wars and rumours of wars have caused many expenses in these periods; but to take two normal years (say) 1853-4 against 1868-9, the total cost of the first was 10,114,449*l.*, as against 15,455,400*l.*, in the other year. An epitome of these Estimates is to be found in the Appendix, for which the reader is indebted to the Estimate branch of the Department.[4]

Result of the arrangement

Earl Russell, Lord Strafford, Lord Monteagle, and Lord Broughton (five eminent Statesmen and one General Officer), the other of three Generals and three Colonels, with one Civilian from the War Office added during the inquiry, and yet the Report of the last Commission would, as supplementary to the policy of 1858, work a greater revolution than ever was suggested in the Report of 1837 The Defence Commission (on which 7,000,000*l.* were spent) consisted of six Naval and Military Officers, and one Civilian, and the Prize Money Commission of four Military Officers and one Civilian

[1] Par 19 *ante*, and note thereto   Chap XIX , pars 13 to 16
[2] See 'Statesman's Year Book,' 1869, p. 246.
[3] See Statement on opposite page, and Parl Returns, 1859, Sess 2 (88), 1868 (412), 1869 (431)   [4] Appendices CL., CLI

38 This increase may be accounted for if the mere fact of the expenditure having been made be deemed satisfactory. The items that have become new annual charges since 1859 with the increase of pay have added upwards of one million pounds—a vast sum—as a *permanent*

Items of increased expenditure

ESTIMATE AND EXPENDITURE [1] FOR THE REGULAR ARMY (EXCLUSIVE OF THE AUXILIARY FORCES AND THE CHARGE FOR REGIMENTS SERVING IN INDIA) FOR THE PERIOD FROM 1ST APRIL, 1847, TO 31ST MARCH, 1868

	REGULAR FORCES			
	Estimate		Expenditure	
	Effective	Non-Effective	Effective	Non Effective
1847–48	£7,775,723	2,348,047	7,780,380	2,357.035
1848–49	7,656,402	2,336,684	7,612,579	2,316,635
1849–50	6,895,662	2,294,087	6,629,210	2,267,114
1850–51	6,591,883	2,264,212	6,422,379	2,271,623
1851–52 ..	6,961,296	2,227,640	6,901,748	2,201,707
1852–53 .	6,998,780	2,197,369	6,999,365	2,158,169
	£35,104,023	11,319,992	34,565,281	11,215,248
1853–54	7,322,152	2,186,768	7,205,701	2,143,646
1854–55	12,178,468	2,165,716	11,641,390	2,069,856
1855–56	26,937,212	2,147,864	26,963,531	2,151,961
1856–57	17,171,478	2,195,974	17,303,191	2,073,563
1857–58 .	10,015,091	2,187,875	9,887,979	2,202,947
	£73,624,401	10,884,197	73,001,792	10,641,976
1858–59	9,537,068	2,202,568	9,018,967	2,095,315
1859–60	10,866,666	2,107,454	11,181,508	2,061,022
1860–61	13,228,396	2,082,123	13,192,066	2,030,558
1861–62	13,277,696	2,069,308	13,005,905	2,039,857
1862–63	12,318,250	2,081,858	11,632,989	2,052,295
	£59,228,076	10,546,311	58,031,135	10,279,017
1863–64	11,383,162	2,103,552	11,051,098	2,046,303
1864–65	10,762,382	2,074,944	10,637,756	2,047,417
1865–66	10,272,907	2,077,800	10,115,998	2,046,164
1866–67	10,299,409	2,088,300	10,437,017	2,065,293
1867–68	13,745,817	2,104,000	13,919,172	2,055,841
	£56,463,677	10,448,596	56,161,041	10,261,018
Total	£232,195,900	45,547,143	229,539,929	44,794,324

[1] I am indebted to Mr Hanby of the War Office for this statement.

charge to the future Estimates, while the expenditure on works,[1] independently of the loan of 7,400,000*l.* for the Fortifications of 1860-9, and upon armament,[2] have greatly increased since the Consolidated Office was established.

Cost of superintending Staff

39. The want of a Superintending Staff cannot be alleged as a ground of complaint against the liberality of the Commons; for the House has steadily voted increased Establishment charges from 1853-4 to 1868-9,[3] as shown by the

---

[1] STATEMENT SHOWING THE SUMS VOTED FOR WORKS AND BUILDINGS FROM 1852-3 TO 1869-70.

Voted in		£	Voted in		£
1851-52	.	470,347	Brought forward		2,347,851
1852-53	.	449,028	1861-62	.	1,027,751
1853-54	..	695,655	1862-63	.	999,574
1854-55	.	932,821	1863-64	.	796,906
		2,347,851	1864-65		735,272
1855-56	..	1,387,500	1865-66	.	765,417
1856-57	.	1,839,069	1866-67	..	819,174
1857-58	..	938,586	1867-68	.	755,038
1858-59		1,053,607	1868-69	..	867,903
1859-60		1,518,021	1869-70	..	785,594
1860-61	.	1,559,462			16,028,874

Total	..	.	£18,376,725
Add Defence Works, under 30 & 31 Vict. c. 145	..	.	£7,470,000
Total		.	£25,846,725

Since 1859-60 the Secretary of State has invested little under 1,500,000*l.* in land, to resist war and invasion.

[2] 19,000,000*l.* up to July, 1868 Major Anson, 193 H. D (3), p 762

[3] COST OF THE WAR OFFICE AND HORSE GUARDS ESTABLISHMENTS, *bringing into comparison all items that have at any time been taken as Administration of the Army* (EXCLUDING, HOWEVER, THE EXPENDITURE OF THE TOPOGRAPHICAL DEPARTMENT EXCEPT THE DIRECTOR'S PAY)

[Taken from *Estimates—not Expenditure*]

	£			£
1853-54 War Office	115,173	1858-59 War Office	..	157,867
„ Horse Guards	. 26,018	„ Horse Guards	.	41,747
	£141,191			£199,614
1856-57 War Office .	159,301	1863-64 War Office		170,429
„ Horse Guards	45,735	„ Horse Guards		48,729
	£205,036			£219,158
1857-58 War Office	160,939	1868-69 War Office† .		191,227
„ Horse Guards	42,724	„ Horse Guards	.	49,535
	£203,663			£240,762

* The italics explain the difference between this Statement and (No 1) printed in the Appendix.
† The Superannuation Vote in the year 1866-7 showed an increase of 4000*l.*, and contained a List of Pensions granted to Clerks in the War Office at Pall Mall, alone amounting to 10,400*l* per annum

comparison of 141,191*l.* against 240,762*l.*, in addition to a large increase to the superannuation votes, made by the supercession of Civilians for Military assistants in the years 1866-7. If these statements are to be relied upon,[1] it would appear that the experience of those witnesses who, in 1837, warned the Government against change, led them to right conclusions in predicting that no *economy* would be effected by breaking down the subordinate Departments, which served as outworks to the Treasury.

40. But it may be pertinent to inquire whether the two facts standing in juxtaposition have any, and what, influence upon each other?—whether Military Expenditure has been permitted to increase because the *personnel* of the War Department has become military? and whether Parliament has lost that check and control which the Duke of Wellington deemed so necessary for economy?[2]

Are the two facts of a Military Control and Increased Expenditure connected?

41. No doubt, after a War Expenditure and War Establishment have been sanctioned for some time, it needs all the power of Civil Control to reduce both to the normal condition of Peace. It is open to remark, without touching upon the policy of either measure, that the Irish Church would never have been disestablished nor the Revised Code issued, if the Irish Clergy had formed the Parliament or schoolmasters the Privy Council; and it may well be questioned whether Parliament has, from a Military Administration, the same zeal for the reduction of the Army that would be given by a Civil Administration. At any rate, in the former, a class feeling has to be overcome in those enlisted under the Civil Minister, or it will turn in favour of the Army.

Difficulty of reducing War Expenditure

42. The Commander-in-Chief rightly insists upon efficiency both in men and *materiel*, leaving it to the Civil Minister—as responsible for Finance—to limit the expense within the total sum that he is prepared to submit on estimate to Parliament. Of course, if the Minister be too feeble to execute his function, the blame does

Action of Commander-in-Chief and Master-General on Expenditure

---

[1] I have no reason to doubt their truth, but having accepted them from others —the best authorities—they must be so accepted by the reader.

[2] See Chap XXI, pars. 44, 45, *et passim.*

not rest with the Commander-in-Chief. Meanwhile the action of the Master-General has been lost. As a responsible Minister of Finance, as well as a great General, he could and would uphold the authority of his Civil employés against Military Officers in a manner that is totally unknown where the Generals are, as now, to reign supreme. Operating, through a perfectly trained Staff, upon supplies and works, the action of the Master-General towards economy, though it affected the status or character, did not touch the personal interests of the Military. "I know enough," wrote the Duke of Wellington,[1] as Master-General, " of the character of General Officers in general, and of Sir John Keane in particular, to be very certain. . . . that if there should be no check upon him there will be no end of his dislocation of Stores and Magazines. . . . Two days after his order was given it was countermanded, but the expense incurred was 72*l.* All that I wish is, that General Officers should be obliged to consider a little of the real necessity for such orders before they issue them, and that they should feel that there is a Department interested in the review of the necessity for such orders after they have been carried into execution."

43. Neither would the Master-General suffer any Military

Master General upheld in Independent Control Officer to interfere with the duty laid down for the Ordnance Officers abroad ; and no difference of rank, between the General and the Civil *employé*, induced him to sacrifice the man of lower social grade who had, to the best of his ability, protected the public interests, to keep on *good terms* with the General. When the Commander of the Forces in the Leeward Islands ventured to interfere with the Ordnance Expenditure, the Duke of Wellington reminded him that the Board was responsible for it to Parliament, and therefore no authority but the Master-General's should be obeyed.[2] He administered such a reprimand to the Military officer that the civil subordinates did not *fear* to serve the Public *honestly.*

44. At home the increase in the same class of Expenditure

Ordnance Expenditure at home has been immense, and it is not sufficient to say that the same sum, if spent on works by the Master-General, would have been expended under the superin-

---

[1] Supplementary Despatches, vol ii. p 239.
[2] Memorandum to Mr. Griffin, 1824, vol ii , ib , p. 252

tendence of the same Engineer Officers—for their ability is pre-eminent—as the Secretary of State has employed. It is not needful to gainsay their competency, and it would be most ungenerous to do so,[1] but—to use analogy—as justice is administered under the direct sanction of the highest legal authority, and would not be satisfactory to the Civil community if it were otherwise, so the people have a right, through Parliament, to ask that the National Defences of the Realm — in Forts, to stand for ever, and an Armament for long use—should be, as formerly, entrusted to an Officer of the widest experience, directly responsible to Parliament as well as to the Crown, and who, by long active service, has gained Public confidence, so as to earn a seat in the Cabinet as the representative of the honourable profession of Arms.[2]

45. Of course, judging from our experience of the actual expenditure of the Ordnance Board, it is open to argument whether this vast expenditure would ever have been incurred by the Master-General. No doubt, in matters of professional importance, a Civil Minister is more in the hands of his advisers than the Master-General would have been. "The responsibility of a Civilian," said Sir James Graham,[3] "is great who takes a decided step in opposition to the best professional advice, if the question be of a professional nature." And this may account for the readiness with which an expenditure has been proposed to Parliament during the last ten years, so much in excess of any expenditure in a like antecedent period. Certainly, the two facts should be borne in mind when an attempt is made to account for one of them.

Would it have been incurred by a Master-General?

46. But the Consolidated Department has had advantages in the selection of Ministers, that can never recur, because the race of statesmen who have served in the separate Departments (as in the War Office or

Ministers hitherto in charge of the Consolidated Department,

---

[1] There is no one (Officer or Civilian) to whom the public are more indebted for the Fortification Works of 1860 than Colonel Jervois, C B , Royal Engineers. His moral courage, tact, and skill throughout all the political controversies in good or ill report, have been unfailing He has steadily persevered, and had he not done so the scheme must long since have broken down from mere inertia

[2] 'Organization Report, 1860' (Questions 6615 30)

[3] 'Admiralty Report, 1861' (Question 1043)

Ordnance) are leaving political life. Therefore each Secretary of State hereafter to be placed at the head of the Department will come probably into office a complete novice to the detail of a very vast Administration, or with the superficial information that may have been gathered up as an Under Secretary; at any rate, without that complete knowledge which it was possible to obtain by serving as an Ordnance Board Officer, or the office of Secretary at War.

47. The strain upon the official resources of the Department since 1855 has been great. The Chiefs of the Consolidated Office frequently have been changed in Ministerial arrangements;[1] and, in addition to the confusion resulting from forming two antagonistic into one homogeneous department, the opportunity has been taken to weaken the traditions of each office This has been done by placing in Control of various branches of the Department—as before observed upon—Military men, not conversant with Civil Administration, and having little sympathy with the Constitutional action or the financial checks of the Department towards the Army; whose desire would be "to bring the Horse Guards into the War Office,"[2] and thus to ignore or root out the old practices of Law and Finance, under which the Army has been administered, rather than be instructed in them for the five years during which they are to assume Civil functions. Besides

Strain upon the official resources of the Department

---

[1] The Seals of the Consolidated Department have been held by Earl Dalhousie in 1855, General Peel, 1858, Lord Herbert, 1859, Sir Geo. Lewis, 1861; Earl De Grey and Ripon, 1863, Marquis of Hartington, 1866, General Peel, 1866, Sir John Pakington, 1867, Mr Cardwell, 1868. The changes in the Political Undersecretaries, even more frequent, have been. Mr F Peel, 1855, Sir John Ramsden, 1857; Lord Hardinge, 1858, Earl of Rosslyn, 1859, Earl De Grey and Ripon, 1859, Lord Northbrook, 1861, Earl De Grey and Ripon, 1861, Marquis of Hartington, 1863, Lord Dufferin, 1866, Lord Longford, 1866, and Lord Northbrook in 1868 The Secretary at War's Office was, from 1809 to 1851, practically under one permanent chief—The Right Honourable L. Sullivan—who entered the War Office in 1809 with his brother-in-law, the late Lord Palmerston Lord Palmerston left the office as Secretary at War in 1828, and Mr Sullivan as Deputy in 1851.

[2] 'Organization Report, 1860,' Lord Herbert's Evidence, Question 6610, 7092. Much as of old—

> "Scandit fatalis machina muros,
> Feta armis"

And with much the same result,—

> "Ceduntur vigiles portisque patentibus omnes
> Accipiunt socios, atque agmina conscia jungunt "—Æn Lib II, l. 237, 267

being directly prejudicial to the Public Interests, such arrangements are discouraging in the highest degree to intelligent men who—in some instances with high intellectual endowments—have been invited by competitive examination to form the Secretary of State's Department, under the reasonable hope of holding those Staff appointments which Constitutional usage had hitherto assigned to Civilians, but who—from no fault of theirs—find themselves bearing the opprobrium of serving in a Department recently styled in Parliament, the "best abused" in the State.

48. No doubt it is open to the Government, both to supersede the Civil by the Military class in all employments of the State, and to give Military command to Civilians—if it be thought that efficiency or economy would be promoted thereby.[1] "If," said Sir James Graham (speaking of the Civil Service of the Admiralty, and the employment of sailors therein), "they have to superintend all the details of the Civil Service, which past habits have not made familiar to them, I think they have not an equal chance with Civilians. You cannot expect that they will render the same service, any more than if you send a Civilian to command the Fleet—he would be found extremely deficient." Of the financial results of the first alternative, the Army Administration of the last ten years affords some experience, but other Political considerations arise. Surely no Statesman would so totally disregard History as advisedly to abolish control, or—which in other words is the same thing—to establish a dual Military Government, one in the War Office and the other in the Horse Guards.

49. Possibly men of certain Professions might be disposed to act against the growth of their own numbers, or to curtail the advantages of their own class; but not so the Military profession. Allegiance to the authority and command of their Chief is too great and too loyal to permit them to act against his interest or influence, either in thwarting his wishes or in controverting his proposals. Nor does this feeling wholly centre in one Superior, for the regard to Rank and Seniority is such that there is but little exaggeration

Change of the Personnel

Control by Military agency

---

[1] 'Admiralty Report, 1861,' Question 1046.

in Shakspeare's description of it when Cassio expresses his hopes of salvation—"No offence to the General"—and insists upon being saved, in regard to his *rank* of Lieutenant, "before the Antient."[1] It is difficult to get a Subordinate, acting with a Superior, Officer, to express any opinion or to take any action adverse to his views—a defect now notorious, but one that, by anticipation of its development, was presented to the notice of the Commissioners of 1837.

50. The principle of dual Government—that is of two departments doing the same thing by mutual agreement—has really found development in Army Administration *since* the Crimean War, as before that epoch the action of each separate Department was defined, and the duties distinct. Of course the independent functions of Audit and Expenditure, as of the Houses of Lords and Commons, would become dual acts if the two Departments or Houses should blend their functions together. "The duty of an Auditor should be to pass in review the acts of an Accountant *when* completed; but if the Auditor is converted into an Adviser and Officer of the Executive, he ceases to be an independent check."[2] The Departments, as originally constituted, were, for these purposes of *independent control*, exercised by the Secretary of War and Secretary of State through *Civil* servants. The government is dual, so long as the expending and controlling Departments are constituted of Military Officers, for the control designed by the Constitution is consequently lost. "The habits of Military men tend to give them," said Mr. Gladstone, in a recent debate, "a mode of viewing affairs which is a Soldier's and not a Civilian's,"[3] and for that reason his Ministry deliberately refused to sanction the conversion of a Civil into a Military appointment. Rightly constituted, there ought to be no more dual government between the War Office and the Horse Guards than there is between the Home Office and the Commissioner of Police, or the Houses of Lords and Commons.

Dual government since the Crimean War.

[1] 'Othello,' Act II, Scene 3. See the Evidence of Sir James Graham before the Admiralty Court, 1861 (Questions 836, 837), and pp 143, 144

[2] Mr. Romilly's Paper in 'Report on Public Moneys, 1857,' pp. 53 and 57.

[3] 194 H. D (3), p 758

51. Probably no Public Document can afford a better illustration of the great difference of opinion that may be found to exist on subjects of Military Administration, between the Military advisers of the War Minister and the Civilian advisers of the Treasury, than the Correspondence laid before Parliament on the 30th of March, 1868, on the subject of "the Formation of the Department of Control,"[1] a subject by far the most important that has been submitted to the notice of Parliament upon "Army affairs" in the present century.

The Control Scheme.

52. In June, 1866, it appeared expedient to the Secretary of State (Lord Hartington) to submit to a Board of Military Officers, under the presidency of Lord Strathnairn, the consideration of the subject of the Transport duties of the Army *in the Field*; and for such a strictly professional inquiry—involving no Constitutional questions of *any* kind, but only the best arrangement to be made for a specific service in time of War—the Board was fairly constituted, and might have been entitled to the confidence of Parliament.[2]

1866.

Board of Military Officers appointed.

53. After the Seals of Office were transferred to another Minister,[3] the Board sought for, and obtained from him, a roving Commission of Enquiry, without any more definite instructions than a general approval of general principles, and an authority to report in detail the changes recommended. Neither the general principles nor the changes recommended were very clearly defined in the preliminary Report of the Board, and therefore the grant to the Commissioners of enlarged Powers was an act of official confidence towards the Military Officers composing it, but one to which neither the Crown nor Parliament were any parties.

Extended Powers given to them.

54. Regarding the subjects ultimately reported upon, these Officers had less claim to attention than *any* Royal Commission, or Parliamentary Committee, that had

Qualification of the Committee

---

[1] Sessional, No 373

[2] Transport Committee Report presented to Parliament 1867

[3] Extract from Report —"The President, General Lord Strathnairn, in company with Lieutenant-General Sir Hope Grant, communicated personally with the Secretary of State for War, and obtained his sanction for making a complete and exhaustive inquiry."—p. xi Surely, if the Sea Lord at the Admiralty handed over that Department to a Board of Naval Officers, their proceedings would not be held to have the sanction of a Civil Minister?

ever previously dealt with similar matters. In contrast with the Commissions of 1833 and 1837—that were composed of great Statesmen,[1] who collected the evidence of eminent Military Commanders—it must be noticed that these *quasi* Commissioners were all Military employés, and their witnesses, as a rule, subordinates under the Commander-in-Chief or the War Office. Probably, neither the Commissioners nor the Witnesses were familiar with Constitutional questions; for that aspect of the question—as a strange contrast to the proceedings of former Commissions—was wholly and entirely overlooked.

55. Their Report of March, 1867, as an official document is unique. Probably no Public document ever drawn by a British officer (Commissariat or Combatant), or ever accepted by any Minister, can bear comparison with this Report in these two features, viz., an entire absence from its pages of all Constitutional considerations, and of all knowledge relating to the Civil Administration of the Army. One idea, and only one, appears to have prevailed—to get under the control of Military authority all the Public Treasure either held by Constitutional officers, or hereafter to be appropriated, for Military service. All Civil servants hitherto entrusted with its guardianship, and owning a definite allegiance to the Minister—as distinguished from Military authority— being superseded. "As a matter of National importance," the Report recommended "that the reorganization should be carried out with every consideration for the fair claims of every one," and then added:[2]—"The Committee cannot be insensible to the magnitude of the changes involved in the scheme which they recommend, but they deem it their duty to record their opinion that these changes are but a *consequence* of the *concentration* which took place when the Administration of the Army was placed under the supreme control and responsibility of a War Minister."[3]

56. The Report was submitted to Parliament in May or June

[margin note: 1867 · Report of the Board]

---

[1] Par. 60, and note.　　　　　　　　[2] Par 140

[3] The counter Reports of the Departmental Officers—the other side of the controversy — have never been laid before Parliament, though referred to in debate

of the same year, and was rightly described by a Member of the present Cabinet (who certainly showed far more knowledge of its contents than any other Member of the Commons) "as little short of Revolutionary."[1] Such a description is not an exaggeration; but so utterly incomprehensible, or uninviting are the details of Army Administration to the Commons, or so little do they appreciate Burke's axiom,—"that confidence, of all Public virtues, is the most dangerous, and jealousy in the House of Commons, of all Public vices, the most tolerable, especially when the number and the charge of Standing Armies in time of Peace is the question"[2] —that the House at one time during the discussion "consisted only of 9 Soldiers, 2 Officials, and 2 independent Members."[3]

Submitted to Parliament in May, 1867

57. To examine the detail of the Scheme on these pages would be unnecessary, as the Report is readily accessible to every one seeking for Parliamentary information.[4] The scheme, leaving the supply of an Army in the Field— the only point referred to the Committee—dealt, in effect, with the whole Military Finance of the Country;[5] and its object was to make Military authority supreme at all times, by assimilating the System of Finance in Great Britain to that in vogue in India and France. Of course, at the top of the pinnacle was to be placed a Military Officer, of such rank and position " as would serve as an example to the best class of Military Officers to volunteer for Service in the Department:"[6] thus creating a vast Military Organization for the expenditure of Public Money without any *direct* responsibility to Parliament, or any definite relationship to the Crown—in effect, a system of Military finance without the Constitutional arrangements that existed in the late Ordnance Board.

Outline of the Scheme

58. What, therefore, were to be the powers or responsibilities of this Military Officer towards the Crown, as represented by the Commander-in-Chief, or towards Parliament, as represented by the Finance Ministers, were wholly undefined either in the Report itself, or in any Order in Council,

Comptroller in Chief.

---

[1] 187 H. D. (3), p. 1694.   [2] Works, vol. v. p. 4.
[3] 183 H. D. (3), p. 945   [4] Note [1], p. 12.
[5] See Debates in 187 H. D. (3), 1687-1694, 188 ib., p. 594, 193 ib., pp. 922, 1266.   [6] Par 131.

or in any other Official Document; but in Her Majesty's Speech from the Throne, in July, 1868, the Country was informed that a "considerable Reform had been made by the appointment of a Comptroller, combining thereby the various Departments of Military Supply under this *one* authority."[1]

59. The Secretary of State and the Commander-in-Chief being thus superseded, the reader must be informed

The Departments having the custody and expenditure of the Public Treasure placed under him

that the several Departments placed under this *one* authority embraced those that acted as the custodians or expenders of the Public Treasure. Therefore, to place these under the control of *one* man—neither a responsible Minister, nor a Civil employé under such a Minister, but—a Military Officer beyond control, and therefore—as some Members contended in Parliament—irresponsible to anyone (but the Crown?), would be a complete anomaly in this, though not unknown in Despotic or Conquered countries.

60. The experience of great men—versed in the art of War,

Experience adverse to the Control System

as well as in the details of Military Administration—has been quoted elsewhere to shew that, in their opinion the duties of Commissariat and Store Officers cannot, *with safety to the Public interests*, be entrusted to the same Officer or to the same Department. But this Report—based on evidence[2] taken from selected witnesses of little service or ex-

---

[1] 193 H. D (3), pp 1242, 1939, and Mr Disraeli's Address in 'The Times' of 3rd October, 1868, as to the Barrack Scheme, Chap XII., par 14 *ante*

[2] The witnesses examined in 1836-7 were 9 in number, 7 of whom were as under —Sir John Burrow Bart (the Secretary to the Admiralty); Captain the Hon George Elliott, R N. (Lord of Admiralty), The Right Hon Sir James Kempt (Master-General of Ordnance, 1831-4), the Duke of Richmond (Chairman of the Royal Commissioners of 1833), Sir Henry Hardinge (Clerk to Ordnance, 1823-8, Secretary at War, 1828-30, and Commander-in-Chief, 1852); Sir Hussey Vivian (Master-General of the Ordnance), and the Duke of Wellington (Master-General of the Ordnance, 1819-27, and Commander-in Chief in 1828-9) None of these witnesses were, or indeed could be, benefited by the Report of the Commissioners, and all the Soldiers were men of large experience in War and Civil Administration

The witnesses of 1866-7 were 28, and may be classified as having places either to gain in the new, or to lose in the established system With few exceptions, they are comparatively unknown, and no attentive reader of the Blue Book will fail to notice that after they are drawn out, by the questions put to them, to assert all that they can of their *own actual service in war* or *experience* in *civil* administration, what a very limited acquaintance with either is thought by some to justify a War Minister both in changing official servants and in destroying an approved system possessing at least this great superiority over any new scheme, that of "being established, and of being understood"   "The

perience, and, moreover. whose disinterestedness may possibly be questioned by reason of their subsequent advancement or employment in connection with the control scheme, presenting in all respects a marked contrast to the witnesses of 1837 [1]— proposed to accumulate other duties, as of Barrack, Transport, and Army Finance, on the same Officer, and—to make the confusion complete—to select, ultimately, candidates from Combatant Officers (if they will give up Command) for these duties. Concentration in a Department leads—as this Chapter shows— to the destruction of all efficient Financial checks; but, as brought to perfection to protect the Public Treasure against the Military element in the State, it is not likely that a Board of Military Officers would *very* scrupulously uphold them.

61. The effect of their scheme would be to annihilate these altogether. Discarding the experience of History, and proceeding on the theory that every Officer commanding in Garrison or abroad is not only as wise as a serpent but as harmless as a dove, the control of the Responsible Minister, financial or constitutional, would (no doubt) be an impertinence. Therefore, to prevent this interference, or possibly to prevent friction, the Minister and the General—where the Minister is not, as in some instances, altogether ignored—are placed on a footing of equality. Thus the Control "Department" is to have "direct responsibility to the Secretary of State, and to the General or other

Government and the Responsibility placed on a footing of equality in Administration.

"The complete and exhaustive inquiry on the whole subject of transport and supply of an army in the field," was made by the Committee, thus —

A	As to Carriages and Transport—3 Carriers and 2 Officers from the Royal Carriage Department	5
B	As to Stores--1 Purveyor, 3 Commissariat, 6 Store, 2 Artillery, and 3 Engineer Officers	15
C	As to Barracks, &c.—2 Medical and 1 Line Officers . .	3
D.	As to Civil Administration—The Directors of Ordnance and Stores, 1 Civilian, and 1 Line and 1 Indian General Officers	5
	Total . ..	28

As to the witnesses: in Class B, they were available for employment in the new system, the pay of which the Committee recommended should be increased (par 134), and some are so employed, in Class D, the 2 Directors (both distinguished Officers in the Artillery and Naval Services) were superadded, and the 2 General Officers were appointed Comptroller and Deputy-Comptroller

[1] Chaps VII and XII

Officer Commanding, for the completeness and efficiency of such Services."[1]   The Control "Officer" at each station is to bear this responsibility, (1), "that all supplies are of proper quality, sufficient in quantity, and distributed in conformity with established Regulations, or *with the orders of the General*"[2] and (2), "that all issues of money and stores are duly authorised by Parliamentary Estimate or Regulation, *or by the General Officer Commanding;*"[3] and lastly, as the result of these arrangements, the Report observes that "both Minister for War and General Officers will be able to entrust greater powers and give more confidence to a Comptroller than they can under the present system to the several Heads of Departments."[4]

62. But at each Station, at home or abroad, this equality ceases, to the prejudice of the Minister; for the Comp-troller is to be "the agent of the *General Officer*[5] for the supply of the Troops under his command," to whom, of course, "he was to be strictly subordinate,[6] having no power of reporting to the Secretary of State "as to supply or expenditure" except through the General Officer[7] in the first instance, and then through the Chief Comptroller,[8] "thus confining to one source the financial information now supplied by three, whereby unnecessary correspondence and sometimes confusion are caused."[9]

At the Station the General absolutely supreme

63. But as the Auditors might, if no other financial authority did, object to these arrangements and refuse to pass an Expenditure not expressly sanctioned by a Parliamentary Minister, the Committee—ready with an expedient to meet the dilemma in which the Barrack-Master General was placed by having to account[10]—recommend (1) that the functions of the Auditors should, "without further loss of time, be defined by regulations: due care being taken *to strictly* limit these duties so as not *to interfere* or clash with the functions of Control, or with any executive duties of the Service;"[11] and (2) that, "to carry out the system thoroughly," the payments made under the directions of the Comptroller should be locally audited by him "with the clerical aid of Non-commissioned Officers and

Audit regulations to be reversed

---

[1] Par 12   [2] Par. 20.   [3] Par 24
[4] Par 33   [5] Pars 15, 20   [6] Par. 143.
[7] Chap XIX, pars 24-48, and Chap XX., par 21
[8] Par. 23.   [9] Par 28   [10] Chap XII., par 28, *ante.*   [11] Par 30.

Soldiers."[1] So that—waiving all Constitutional objections—the system would lead to the re-development of those frauds in Army Administration that from the year 1688 have been suppressed by the vigilance of Parliament.[2]

64. "Men,' remarks Dr. Whewell, "have often committed thefts, frauds, and impositions, thinking their actions right, though they were such as all moralists would condemn as wrong;"[3] and he then shows how these may proceed from ignorance, and comments upon the maxim "that unavoidable error removes the blame of the actions which it causes."[4] Now, this Report proposes to extend the system of unavoidable error to every Military Station, by placing upon the Control Officer more duties than he can possibly discharge either with accuracy or fidelity to the Public, at the same time that it throws him under the heel of the General, who may repudiate all responsibility of disaster in the field, arising from the want of administrative knowledge; for *his* time is to be given "for consideration of purely Military and strategical duties of Command."[5] The greatest art of war—the sustentation of an Army in a hostile country—is far beyond the capacity of a modern General, according to the type of this Committee.

Inauguration of error

65. But had their recommendations been confined to the exigences of War, this Report might have been accepted—as made with no other end or aim than the Public welfare. In War, our people are as ready to make sacrifices of their money, and of their Constitutional rights, as the people of France; but considerations of War are not involved in "Barrack damages," or in placing the Public Treasure in the hands of irresponsible persons—or of surrendering all Financial control into the hands of Military Officers at home and in *the time of Peace.* No doubt, when your own or the adjacent house is on fire, or war is raging, you readily let the Fireman or Soldier destroy your property for the Public good; but there must be the fire or the war to satisfy you that this

Recommendations do not relate to Peace.

---

[1] Pars 27, 31   [2] Chap VII., pars 14, 21, 28, 50, 63, *et passim*
[3] 'Elements of Morality,' Bk II., chap xiv, p 268
[4] Ib., chap xviii, p 344   [5] Par 33

destruction is essential to safety. Martial Law being granted, the authority of the General Officer is and must be supreme in the district; but *hitherto* in Great Britain no Minister has, in time of Peace, ever resigned his supremacy in favour of the Army.[1] Indeed to accept the proposition—come from what quarter it may—that the Army *in Peace and at home* is to hold the same position as *in War or abroad* renders, no doubt, the Army supreme (as in France or Prussia), but it would destroy our *Constitutional* Government.

66. The history of the Barrack Department has already been given.[2] Its functions relate essentially to the Army in the time of Peace, for obviously in War the Army is abroad and the Reserve Forces in Home quarters. The value of the Public property in Barracks cannot be estimated under several millions sterling, yearly upon the increase by reason of the Palatial residences in which it is now deemed right to lodge the Soldier.[3] It is one of the functions of the Barrack Department to preserve this property on behalf of the Public, from destruction by Military occupation, and, as between the Public and the Military, to assess against the latter the damage which they have wantonly done during their residence.[4] However, the Army, as represented by the Barrackmaster-General and his staff of Military assistants, once got this Public property into their own hands by superseding the Ordnance Department;[5] and on the present occasion, when the supply of *an Army in the Field* was the subject referred to, the Committee appeared to think an appropriate one for the abolition of this (obnoxious) Civil Department.

As to the Abolition of the Barrack Department.

67. On what evidence their recommendation was based may possibly be known to the Committee; but whether the information which they obtained and published is accurate, may very reasonably be doubted, when it is compared

Upon what evidence?

---

[1] Chap XVIII , pars 1-13 [2] Chap XII , *ante*
[3] Vol. I., p. 223, note (*ante*). The Marine Barracks at Eastney far exceed the Guards' Barracks at Chelsea in extravagance of Building
[4] See General Order of 31st December, 1827, by the Duke of Wellington as Commander-in-Chief, and Chapter XX , par 44 *ante*
[5] Chap XII , pars 12, 19, 23, 30, 38, 44

with the explanations and emphatic contradictions given to the Published Evidence by the most competent authority on the subject, whose letter of remonstrance is printed in the Appendix.[1] Certainly, if advanced years or gallant service in the field (before any Member of the Committee was even commissioned), or an unblemished character—during forty-three years of official service, or the thought that his family have yielded to the Army many Officers that have fallen in the Service—are considerations to actuate honourable men—such evidence as has been published might have been withheld, or these protests appended to it.[2]

68. Of course, other recommendations of the Committee are equally at variance with experience. The Ordnance Department, as a matter of fact, was constituted primarily for the Navy before the Army existed;[3] and it is deemed essential by far higher authorities than the Committee rely upon, that the supply of the two Services should be combined not only for reasons of Finance, but of Defence.[4] These reasons, however, pass unnoticed. "The good organization of the Army is not to be deranged or set aside by consideration of the secondary purposes, for the alleged advantage that may be derived by the Navy from the existing system:"[5] showing how possible it is for military officers to exaggerate the importance of the Army in the second Line of Defence, and to ignore (if permitted to do so) our National Force—and the first Line of Defence—the Royal Navy.[6]

As to the Repudiation of the duties incident to Naval Ordnance.

[1] Appendix CLII

[2] Colonel Smith, C.B., the late Barrackmaster at Aldershot, is universally known and respected in the Army, but, for the information of the general reader, I may observe that he is the surviving brother of Sir H. Smith of Aliwal, Bart., and that he entered the Army and served in the Rifle Brigade from 1808 to the end of the War which closed with Waterloo. His Peninsula Medal has *Ten Clasps*

[3] Chap. IV, par. 60., Chap XX, par 7

[4] Appendix CXLVIII   [5] Par. 115

[6] Again—the Committee would recur to a system that was originated by the Secretary of War, against the Ordnance Department, but deliberately condemned in 1822 on the grounds both of expense and inconvenience, viz., the Division of Army and Ordnance Stores as to which see Chap. XIX., pars. 21, 27, and Report of Committee, pars 102-113

69. "Wonderful is the case of Boldness in Civil business,"
said Lord Bacon. "What first, Boldness—what second
and third, Boldness. And yet Boldness is a Child of
Ignorance far inferior to other parts; but, nevertheless, it doth
fascinate and bind hand and foot those that are either shallow in
judgment or weak in courage, which are the greatest part; yea,
and prevaileth with wise men in weak times: therefore, we see
it hath done wonders in popular States, but with Senates and
Princes less. And men ever open *the first entrances* of bold
persons into action *than look* after—for Boldness is *an ill
keeper* of *promise*." "Weak times" must indeed prevail when
—with the Counsels of the Great Soldier still ringing in their
ears—Statesmen can be found to endorse with approval such
a scheme as this Report foreshadows for the destruction of
the "Civil Administration of the Army." The resemblance
to the features of the prototype—the Barrackmaster's Scheme
of 1793-8,[1] is plain. In both, the Military was to prevail over
the Financial Element—Constitutional responsibility was to be
repudiated—trained officers to be superseded—and the Public
Treasure to be expended upon the order of General Officers,
in effect, avowed in one, and acted upon (with such scandalous
results) in the other instance. The abolition of the Home
and the substitution of the Foreign System in Great Britain,
under which Military Officers can exercise Power over the
National expenditure, was to be the rule of administration.
Certainly, to introduce the Military Policy of Despotic France[2]
or Conquered India into the Parliamentary System of England
was bold; but, true to Lord Bacon's description of Boldness,[3]
the scheme wanted "the ground of Science," and could not
hold out.

70. To break down any of the Constitutional arrangements
under which the relationship of the Army to the Civil
Government is regulated, must ever be attended with
great risk; and, no doubt, the changes of 1855, and of subsequent

Boldness in Civil business.

Interference of the Treasury.

---

[1] Chap XII *ante;* but the original papers of 1793-8 should be read, in contrast
with the Report of 1867.

[2] See the Paper on the French System, Note X X, Appendix

[3] Essay XII, on Boldness

dates, have been, in many respects, grave Political errors; but, upon the occasion referred to in the correspondence, the error would have been irretrievable, had not the Treasury come forward and protected the Public from the proposals of the " War Minister." At present, there is something left of the Constitutional action of the Department, though it has been severely weakened. It is quite possible for a courageous and sagacious Minister to replace much that has been too hastily if not ruthlessly destroyed; to restore the functions held in former times by the Treasury, the Ordnance Board, and the Secretary at War, for the security of the Treasure and Liberties of the People; to replace the present Administrative Officers of the Army in those former relationships towards the Crown and Parliament that were sanctioned by the great men who—not less as Soldiers than as Statesmen—warned us against the evils that have resulted from a total disregard of their wise counsels.

71. Before the Crimean War, all the Public Treasure was —as a rule with few exceptions—held and disbursed by Civilians, acting either directly or indirectly through the Treasury—subordinate, and accountable to one Master —a Responsible Minister of the Crown. The risk of loss was small; but even that risk was diminished as much as possible by taking Bonds in most instances, and in others by paying, whenever it was practicable, through the Paymaster-General in London, so that the Public employé should not touch money, but only put in motion a machinery for paying it to the Creditor under a proper authentication of debt. These rules —not from necessity, or, so far as can be proved, for the Public advantage—have been somewhat relaxed. To establish Local Paymasters, and to send down specie to outlying Stations, might have been a matter of Public necessity in Charles II.'s reign, when the Bank of England did not exist, and the Crown only could move Treasure under Military escort; but now to scatter broadcast, or to place it in the hand of Local Accountants, without the security directed by Parliament, involves different considerations. Surely it is unwise to repudiate that safety which the established practice of a great Department has secured in many instances to the Public?

[Side note:] Public Treasure held and disbursed under Bond.

72. The future of the Civil Administration of the Army, and the position that the Army is to hold in the State, are not subjects of *secondary* importance at the present time, for the small cloud that first appeared on the Political horizon during the Eastern campaign has largely increased. The evils of destroying Constitutional Departments and of superseding trained officials by novices in Civil employment[1] are already—even in time of peace—bearing their fruits in increased expenditure, and the Political danger of pla_ing with edged tools is apparent. The action of Parliament, and especially of the Commons, from the Revolution to modern times, was adverse to a Standing Army; but since the Crimean War, from the weakness of the Departments, the House of Commons and the Public Press, at the instance of Military correspondents[2] have taken the "Army affairs"—in matters *personal* to particular Officers or services—specially under their guardianship, the one reacting upon the other. The effects have been—what might have been expected from a Popular Assembly—increased expenditure and a relaxation of discipline.[3]   Every grievance, real or imaginary, to a Regiment

The future of Army Administration and of the Army.

---

[1] Chap XXI., par 52, note [3].   [2] Chap. VIII. par 51
[3] The House of Commons, on the 15th March, 1867, by a majority of 108 to 107 Members—not one Member of the late Council voting in the former number—affirmed the principle that the discipline of the Army in Service was to be under one rule of Punishment in Peace, and another in War. In effect, that our own countrymen throughout the world were to be unprotected, but that Foreigners in arms against us were to be protected—by the powers given to the Commanding Officer to inflict corporal punishment on Criminal Soldiers, 185 H D (3) Of course, Discipline must rapidly deteriorate—"You may have an Army without discipline—or you may have no Army at all," said the Duke of Wellington, "but if you are to have an Army in a state of discipline and in a state of efficiency, and I must say in a state of decent comfort, I have not a notion how you are to go on without having corporal punishment" But he objected upon higher grounds to the distinction between Home and Foreign Service "The great object of those commanding His Majesty's Troops and of the officers at the head of His Majesty's Army has invariably been to consider and represent Service abroad as an honour and an advantage—not one Service abroad only, but every Service abroad, and it would be a very unfortunate circumstance if a punishment pronounced by the Government and Parliament to be an improper punishment, should be inflicted upon those who are to perform the Service abroad, which it has been the object and duty of those at the head of the Army to represent as a Service of honour and advantage Now I have gone so far upon this subject of considering Service abroad as an advantage, that I can mention more than one instance in which,

or to an individual, first appears in an anonymous communication, and then is reproduced in Parliament by some Member having a capacity for questions.[1] The time, therefore, appears to have passed away "when the Army, once voted, is to be left to the management of the Crown." Standing between the Crown and Parliament, as outbidding competitors for its favour, the Army is sure to profit by these overtures, and at the cost of both.

73. In past Wars, save those of the Rebellion, the people have had but meagre accounts of the heroic deeds of our Countrymen; in future Wars, now that all independent sources of information[2] are cut off from the official channels of the Commissariat and Ordnance officers, a special reporter to the Public Press will be a necessity, and may be again assisted by the Treasury[3] to keep up with the Army. During the Crimean War, Pensions were increased and an extravagant suggestion made for an increase of Pay for Service in the Field.[4] Such things must be expected, unless the Public Treasure be in stronger keeping during the next War. Certainly, it is a notable sign of the times that when half a million sterling was added to the permanent burthens of the People, in 1867, to increase the pay of the Soldier in time of Peace, the House of Commons hailed it with cheers, and accepted the proposal of the popular Statesman without one dissentient voice.[5]

As to future Wars

74. No one had a wider experience with all Soldiers in all Services and in all regions than the Duke of Wellington,[6] while no man was ever less of an alarmist

Counsels of the Duke of Wellington

---

when regiments have misbehaved, and it has been proposed to send them abroad, I have said ' No, by no means, do anything rather than that,' because when you send a regiment abroad, you must represe·t it, and you must endeavour to have it felt, as being an honour, and particularly in time of war. If it should ever unfortunately be deemed anything like a disgrace, it would be the greatest misfortune that could happen to the Army and to the Public "—*Evidence on Military Punishments* (1836), Questions 5851-5846 The vote has at present resulted in 32 & 33 Vic , c 95, which is opposed to the Policy discussed at Vol I., p 405, *ante*

[1] 188 H D (3), pp 1191, 1492, 1523, 189 ib , p 1450   [2] Chap XIX , par 24
[3] 136 H D (3), pp 950, 1120.   [4] Vol I , p 107   [5] 185 H D (3), p. 1469
[6] As one of many instances, see his letters as to his leaving Paris in Nov 1814, to escape assassination, vol ix Supplementary Despatches, pp 422-4

than the "Iron Duke;" but *he* never invited Parliament or
the Crown to a blind confidence in an armed host, or to trust
all Military Finance to Commanding Officers.   On the contrary, his warnings were ever and anon directed—to the danger
always present, though latent, with an Army — against its possible aggression, on the resources, or even on the lives, of his
fellow-countrymen;[1] and, against the disturbance of that
balance of power over the Army that is held by the Crown
on the one hand and the Commons on the other.   "The
seeming wise," said Lord Bacon,[2] "find ease to be of the
negative side; for when propositions are denied, there is an end
of them."   In that spirit his experience may be disregarded,
and a fool's paradise indulged in.

75. The action of the Military Element upon those Civil
Departments of the State that stand between Parliament and the Army as the Custodian of the Public
Treasure, is, and ever must be, continuous, unless,
indeed, the precepts of the Baptist addressed to the Roman
have no application to any other Soldiery;[3] therefore it is
impossible to trace the progress of that element in our free
State after the downfall of the Military rule of the Stuarts,
without admitting the political sagacity of those Statesmen
who, as the best measure of security, designed to hold the
Army within the fixed and settled boundaries laid down by
its Civil Administration.   These, after remaining intact for
nearly a century, were first broken in upon by Burke's Act,
which released the Colonel from personal financial responsibility
for his Regiment.   Then, for the erection of barracks (for 200,000
men) in 1793, the Barrackmaster-General and Secretary at
War superseded the Board of Ordnance.   After this came the
appointment and the employment of the Commander-in-Chief
as a Military Minister for the defence of the Realm.   In 1806,
Mr. Wyndham's measure gave the Army a settled claim on the
Public Revenue, and rendered the reduction of it to the limit
of 1793 all but impossible.

Security in Civil Administration of the Army.

---

[1] Chap XV, par. 161, Chap XVII., par. 44.   [2] Essay xxvii.
[3] Chap XIX, par. 1-16.

76. The measures of 1833 [1] weakened the controlling power of the Treasury over Military expenditure, trusting to the false security of checking it through a popular assembly such as the House of Commons; but the progress of the Army towards the Public Treasure, though thus aided, was slow until 1855; for the line of demarcation between Finance and Law on the one hand and Military Command and Government on the other was till then well and clearly defined. That line being destroyed, the Army has made rapid strides. In 1854 the Treasury was again weakened, by the transfer of their Finance Servants to the War Minister.[2] Soon they were changed into Soldiers and placed under Military Command. Then the War Minister ceased to regard his functions as purely civil and financial, and the Public Treasure of the Ordnance was placed in the hands of Military Officers. No sanction from Parliament has ever been sought for in these organic changes, but the War Office is denounced in the House of Commons (by a highly competent authority)[3] as filled with Military men and hence,—upon the Constitutional ground before stated by Mr. Fox—not entitled to the confidence of Parliament in financial matters.[4]

Progress of the Army towards the Public Treasure

77. After all that has been done to give the Commander-in-Chief authority over Military Administrative Officers holding the Public Treasure, do the arrangements of 1858 and 1861—violating, as they do, the Constitutional Policy of the State—satisfy the alleged requirements of the Military Service according to the modern theory?[5] "All these Departments," said Lord Strathnairn,[6] "are under the War Office, and their duties bring them into constant relations at Military Stations with others—the Troops and their Commanders. But these relations are not defined by any rules or organization. The result is friction, I may say dissensions, amongst the Departments themselves, and undefined, doubtful, subordination to the Commander-in-Chief. I need not dwell on the danger of undefined

But are the present Administrative arrangements satisfactory?

---

[1] Chap XIX., pars 25-34.   [2] Chap XIX , pars. 35-53   [3] Par 32 *ante*
[4] Chap XXI , par 46.   [5] 193 H. D (3), p 1240   [6] 188 H D (3), p 599.

authority in the Commander-in-Chief at *any* time, but particularly in operations in the field and in troubled times." In the time of War no one for a moment gainsays the doctrine that the Officer Commanding in the Field must and ought to be supreme—but Peace is the rule, War the exception, in point of time.

78. It is, therefore, to remedy this division of authority—to render the General *at all times* supreme over the Administrative Officers of the Army—that the control scheme was to be inaugurated. "The duty of the Controller is," continued the speaker, "that, acting under the General Commanding, he should carry out all the War Office regulations required for the Service relating to the Administrative Departments, . . . and to carry out any measure which the Commander-in-Chief on his responsibility may consider necessary for *the good* of the Service or the success of *an* operation." Contrast this with the Constitutional language—found elsewhere—of the great Duke, and what next follows with his conduct. "The Duke of Wellington was," said Sir J. M'Niell, "in a great measure his own Quartermaster, his own Adjutant-General, and, in a still larger measure, his own Commissary-General;"[1] but a General of the modern stamp must, "in a partial revolutionary movement," telegraph to the War Office[2] for the assistance of a Commissariat officer, to save him delay and trouble in moving the handful of Troops that were to be put in motion on this occasion. Truth, however, requires that it should be stated that this Officer did not interfere with the arrangements made by the Administrative Officers acting under the system which this circumstance was cited to condemn.

The Control Department the suggested remedy

79. Hitherto, the Army has been officered by men who, as a rule, would disdain to take advantage of its weak administration. But how long this forbearance may last in the present aspect of changes, it is not possible to predict. Once alter—by lowering—the social status of officers, have the Army led by needy adventurers, and its Civil Administration would soon be

The Officers of the Regular Army of a higher social Status than those who serve in the Administrative Corps

---

[1] Lord Strathnairn's Statement, 188 H D (3), p. 601
[2] 'Organization Report, 1860,' p 233.

destroyed by their importunity to fill its appointments[1]   The expedient of inviting Combatant Officers to leave the front ranks of the Army for the rearward employments of Administration, was first suggested to the Regular Army at a period coeval with the extinction of the Indian Army, in which the employment of Officers in Civil duties had been extensively practised since the time when Burke described it as breaking down discipline and destroying the high character of the Military Service.   In India it was originally a necessity from the paucity of European Population, and the absence of a Civil Service.   The result of holding out such employment as Prizes could not affect in India, as it would in England, the Constitutional relationships of the Army to the State.   Besides, here a Civil Service exists, and as Tradesmen volunteer as Officers and Soldiers, the martial spirit of the higher orders does not need .(if it would receive) a stimulant by inviting Gentlemen into the Ranks, by promising, for a little extra pay, to turn them into Commissaries or Storekeepers.   In the face of experience, it is impossible to deny that men did enter the Indian Army with the hope, not of Military, but—reversing the career and ambition of the great Clive[2]—of Civil employment.   As a rule, however, these men were of a different stamp to the Officers of the Regular Forces, and it may be fairly questioned whether it is expedient to revive this system, now that it has ceased with the Indian Army, or to attempt to introduce it, and the class of men it attracts, into the Queen's Army.[3]

---

[1] For the appointment of Deputy-Governor of Cold Bath Fields Prison, vacant in June 1869, with a salary of 250*l* rising to 300*l* by 10*l* per annum, with residence, coals, and gas—there were *ninety-five* applicants   Of these, *forty-six* were Commissioned Officers, and *two* Non-Commissioned Officers   Of the Commissioned Officers *eighteen* were in active service at the time they applied.

[2] Macaulay's Works, vol iii, p 117

[3] The Generals of the present and of the last century have essentially different views towards the Civil Polity of the Army   So long as officers came into the Army from the great public schools, such as Winchester, Eton, and Harrow, their tone of mind in after time was very different from men educated under Military discipline at Sandhurst, and receiving, as a stimulant to their loyalty, a dole of money on the King's birthday to drink his health   When Sandhurst was established, Mr Grey and others foretold that its effects would be such as they have shown themselves to be in this respect,—the production of Soldiers with class interests

CONCLUSION.

80. "Army Affairs" in time of Peace have never since the Commonwealth so engaged the attention of the "Commons" as they have done from 1855. It is a consequence which was predicted by the Nestor of our age, when he warned the Statesmen of his era against making the recent changes adverted to in this Chapter. The course of Military Administration would be altered, and power would be transferred from the Crown to the House of Commons.[1] With hope—such as the alliance of the Army to a weak Political Party may inspire—what overtures may not be made to the Military element in the State, unless Statesmen bear keenly in remembrance the National degradation[2] resulting from such a policy? Therefore, hitherto, with few exceptions, Army Affairs in time of Peace have not been made, nor ought to be, a matter of Party Politics;[3] certainly in the latter conviction this Work has been undertaken, that—to avert danger—a beacon may be held up to warn off the great Statesmen by whom the vessel of the State may be guided, from some of the shoals and quicksands that surround the Administration and Government of the Army. It is possible to feel (as I do) towards the Army—what Sir James Graham's example in regard to the Navy proves—the very highest admiration for the character of the Service, and yet firmly to express the conviction that its Civil Administration ought not to be destroyed, or handed over to Military officers, who do not, as a class, make the best administrators of Civil Affairs, although they may be those of their

---

[1] Duke of Wellington to Lords Fitzroy Somerset and Melbourne (Appendix CXLVII.)

[2] The entries in the Journals of the House of Commons, from the 4th May, 1461, vol. ii, p 133 (the date of the first direct communication of the Commons to the Army), unto the entry of the 19th April, 1653 vol vii, p. 280, which was expunged by order of Parliament of 7th January, 1659, contain a record of events that may very easily be repeated if the Members of that House will facilitate them, by absorbing the Power of the Crown

[3] Mr. Disraeli's printed Address to the Electors of Buckinghamshire of 1st Oct., 1868, 'Times.' of the 3rd Oct.

own profession [1] Hitherto it has not been any one's duty to deal with the Administration and Government of the Army at any length in volumes like the present; and, therefore, much of the information which they contain has been necessarily drawn from Original Official Sources. Possibly I may be thought to unfold the subject in an aspect too exclusively Constitutional. If that be so, it must be borne in mind that of late this aspect—though of fundamental importance—appears to have been little considered, while the Official Records of the War Department prove to demonstration that the distinguished men who surrounded the Throne and governed both the Country and the Army prior to the Crimean War did not overlook the *ultimate* consequences that may be found to result to the *safety of the State* from disturbing the relationship in which the Army stands to the Parliament in matters of Expenditure, and to the Crown in matters of Government. Some of these were men of unexampled experience as Soldiers and Statesmen, but they refused—and that advisedly—to assimilate our Military Institutions to those of Continental States, while they adhered—and that deliberately—to the rules of Army administration and government under which our Royal Forces have been ever victorious abroad, and loyally non-aggressive at home. These rules—*if we may now wisely abandon them*—are at least worth recording, in grateful remembrance of the safety which (since the Revolution of 1688) they have afforded to the Crown and people of this Realm, and as an example to others, if not to ourselves, how Constitutional Freedom and Public Treasure, in the presence of a Standing Army in time of peace, may be—as hitherto they have been—preserved by us from Military Influence. In this belief, I have thought it no unworthy task for a Civil servant of the Crown (as he may be able) to preserve the history of those Constitutional arrangements which great Statesmen have planned, and great Generals have approved. No doubt, the Civil administration of the Army—like every other organization—may need revision; but, as the Army is a Political power which, of all others, it is the least prudent to trifle with, such reorganization—even if suggested by the Army—should

---

[1] 'Admiralty Report, 1861,' Questions 1044, 1045, and Vol., I, p. 388 *ante.*

surely — unless the time be indeed come for responsible Ministers to repudiate all responsibility—be the work of Statesmen; that the Constituencies may hold a substantial guarantee, in a measure so critical, that no encroachment will be allowed on the part of the Army, either on the Prerogatives of the Crown or on the Functions of Parliament. To aid the future by the experience of the past is therefore another object that I have kept steadily in view; and, should the Work be found of any use to Students of Constitutional History, I shall be amply rewarded for the labour which—in addition to other duties— it has occasioned me

APPENDIX.

NOTES.

(S.)

Chapter XV., par 107.

ON THE EMPLOYMENT OF FOREIGN SOLDIERS.

THE people of the United Kingdom have always been jealous, and not without reason—of the employment of Foreign Soldiers *within the Realm*—a distinction that should be noticed as against their employment *out* of the Realm—as *on the Continent* in British pay, a measure which has never met with the same objection.

The employment of Foreign Troops within the Realm may, for the present purpose, be traced back to the Dutch Guards[1] that accompanied William III., coming to take possession of the Throne of England. At that time General Ginkell was sent against the Mutineers in 'England,' and though the orders (printed in Appendix XXXV.) are in English, many other orders and letters in the War Office, at that date, are found in the *French* Language.

The Regal policy of sending British Troops abroad—as the Scots Guards were sent—then originated[2]—and of holding the Country in check by Foreign Troops.

The Crown having the right to make Treaties of Alliance, contracted thereby with Foreign Powers for the supply of Troops[3] That these Troops might be useful for all purposes of defence, the Treaty placed them at the absolute disposal of the Crown, and hence they could be ordered to Great Britain, upon the requisition of the King. In this manner 12,000 Hessians were within call of England at any time, from 1728[4] to 1787,[5] if not to a later period.

But apart from Treaty, as the Throne of England was held by the Sovereign of Hanover, the Hanoverian Troops could be brought

---

[1] Vol I, Appendix XXVIII   [2] Ib, Appendix XXXIII

[3] Treaties for Hessians, see 25 Com Journ, pp 23, 24 Treaties in force in 1694, and the list of Foreign Troops (317-640) employed, 11 Com Journ, pp 24, 179, 347, 12 Com. Journ., p 86 Treaties of 1702, see 14 Com Journ., pp. 14, 17, 24, 405-7, 8 Parl Hist., p 929   [4] Ib, p 643.

[5] Chap XIII, par. 42, and Vol vi of Mahon's England, pp 130, 131

over to this country, by order of the King, without the sanction of Parliament This was done in the year 1742,[1] and at subsequent periods, when English Troops were in Flanders.[2]

No doubt in the year 1745 the presence of Hanoverian, Dutch, and Hessian Troops within the Kingdom, materially strengthened the Government, and enabled the King and his Ministers to put down the rebellion. However, no sooner was it put down, and an address of congratulation moved (in April 1746), than British Troops were again sent to Flanders, although several Peers raised their voices and protested in Parliament against it.[3]

The frequent visitation of Foreign Troops to these shores stimulated Parliament, in 1756-7, to reorganize the Militia.[4] Since this National Force has existed, the Realm has been freed from the presence of Foreigners as protectors, and it has been deemed necessary for the Crown to seek the sanction of Parliament to legalize their employment.

The first occasion for the interference of Parliament arose in the year 1756, when the innholders objected to receive the Billets of Foreign Troops, and the Crown was advised that there was no legal power of billeting them. An appeal was made to Parliament, and the 30 Geo. II., c 2, was passed to declare that the Foreign Troops (brought over for the defence of Great Britain) should be quartered in same manner as the British Troops.[5]

This, however, only met one of the difficulties that were incident to the presence of Foreign Troops without statutory authority, for in January, 1757, the Secretary at War was advised[6] "that as a British Minister he had no power to proceed against a deserter from these Forces, but that His Majesty, as Commander-in Chief of these Forces, might order the man to be conveyed to his corps, if in England, or if gone abroad to be sent there without any offence against the laws of this country," but that he could do nothing more.

The first Act[7] directly sanctioning the employment of Foreigners as part of the Military Forces of the Crown was 29 Geo. II. c. 5. The Troops raised under it were to be for special service in America, and the preamble of the Act states the circumstances giving rise to their employment thus—(1) "that for the better defence of the (American) colonies it has been proposed to raise a regiment there, and to enlist as soldiers any of the Foreign inhabitants

---

[1] 12 Parl Hist, pp 940-1180, Vol. iii of Mahon's England, pp 245, 272.

[2] Ib., p 906, 13 ib, pp 232, 274, 388, 462-68, 1201, 1247   [3] Ib, p 1414

[4] 15 Parl Hist, pp 699-706   [5] Bk 721, p 115
Bk. 721, p 116   [7] 15 Parl Hist, p 699

of the said colonies, who, with the inhabitants, shall voluntarily enter themselves in His Majesty's Service as Soldiers, which Foreigners cannot so well be raised or trained without the assistance of some officers. (2) That it was expedient to facilitate the speedy raising of such regiment, and to *enable* a certain number of Foreign Protestants who have served abroad as officers or engineers to serve and receive pay *as officers* in such regiments or as engineers in America."

It was then enacted[1] that all such Foreign Protestants who should receive commissions from His Majesty to be officers, &c. (which commissions it should be left for His Majesty to grant), and should take the oaths, &c, therein prescribed, should and might serve and receive pay as *officers* in the said regiment, or as engineers in America[2]

The policy of employing Foreign *Soldiers* was not objected to when this Bill came before Parliament, but that of commissioning Foreign *Officers* was deemed highly unconstitutional. Indeed, the argument against keeping up a large National Army was its inutility for Continental Wars, the German market for Soldiers to fight these wars being always open to England. "I shall never be for carrying on a war," said Lord Egmont,[3] "upon the Continent of Europe, by a large body of National Troops, because we can always get Foreign Troops to hire. This should be our adopted method in any war upon the Continent of Europe."

Hitherto the Crown had never expressly asked the sanction of Parliament to employ Foreign Troops, other than by confirmation of a Treaty, under which they were engaged, but when in 1775 the Crown sent some Hessian Troops to garrison Gibraltar and Minorca, without the direct sanction of Parliament, the legality of the measure was expressly challenged by the Duke of Manchester in the House of Lords, and, by Mr. Marsham in the House of Commons,[4] and the Ministers met the objection by a proposal—which was not accepted—that a Bill of Indemnity should be passed.

In 1782 these Troops were brought to this country, for a temporary purpose, and therefore the 22 Geo III. c 26, was passed to enable the Crown to billet them.[5]

---

[1] Two years' service naturalized them in America by 2 Geo III, c 25

[2] The regiment raised under this Act was subsequently numbered the "60th Regiment," and by 38 Geo III, c. 13, was increased by a 5th Battalion of 1000 men, who might be foreigners.

[3] 14 Parl Hist, p 1283, and various other debates, also 17 ib, p 169.

[4] 18 Parl. Hist, pp 811, 819, 1334.

[5] The Hessians were landed in the Isle of Wight in 1794, and Parliament protested against the measure, see 30 Parl Hist., pp 1310-63, 1424 37, and 31 ib, p 1

The next Act[1]—the 34 Geo. III. c. 43—sanctioning the employment of Foreigners, was of an exceptional character. At the outbreak of the war with revolutionary France, the Act was passed for a limited period, which expired with the Peace of Amiens, to sanction the engagement of subjects of the late King of France, who should be willing to enrol as Soldiers or accept commissions as officers from His Majesty (which *commissions* it should be lawful to grant) to serve as Officers or Engineers in Europe, *the Channel Islands*, or in any part of the late King's Dominions It protected those engaged from any penalties attaching to them as Papists under the 1 Geo. I. stat. 2, c. 47, sec. 3, but prohibited more than 5000 men ever being in England at one time, or ever being marched into the country any greater distance than five miles from the sea-coast. They were also to be governed by Special Articles of War.

In 1800 the 39 & 40 Geo. III., c. 100, authorized the Crown to take into its service 6000 Dutch subjects, and to grant commissions to Officers, and to enlist them as Soldiers, being liable to the ordinary Army Mutiny Act and Articles of War

Upon the recommencement of the War, in 1803, it was necessary to have recourse to the assistance of Foreigners. The preamble of the 44 Geo. III. states,[2] that "it had been deemed expedient by His Majesty, in order to provide in the speediest manner for the better defence and greater security of the United Kingdom, to permit certain Foreigners, now in Great Britain, *to enlist as* Soldiers, to form them into regiments, and to grant commissions or letters of service therein to certain Foreign Officers acquainted with their manners and language, and that it is proper that all persons who shall have advised His Majesty to enlist such Soldiers and grant such commissions or letters of service should be indemnified." The Statute then confirmed and indemnified the persons who had advised these Acts of the Crown.

The number of foreign troops to be raised was not—but of those to remain within the United Kingdom was—limited (to 10,000 men), and all the men raised were to be governed by such Articles of War as His Majesty should think fit to establish A large body of men was raised, and as their numbers in the United Kingdom exceeded 10,000 men another Act[3] was passed, to increase this limit to 16,000, and to indemnify those persons who had advised His Majesty to exceed the former one. These troops were made, like other troops in His Majesty's service, subject to the Army Mutiny

---

[1] See 31 Parl Hist, pp 373-93
[2] Cap 75, and see 2 H D (O S), pp 934, 944   [3] 46 Geo III, c 23

Act and Articles of War then in force; and they continued in pay till the Treaty of Vienna, and afterwards (by 55 Geo. III. c. 85) till the Treaty of Paris [1]

The numbers of foreign troops in English pay from 1804 to 1813, and the proportion that these numbers bore to the effective strength of the Army will be seen from the Table (A) following this Note, but if these numbers are compared to those of Foreign Troops employed in earlier wars, they will (I think) be found to be small Our Continental Wars were, I apprehend, usually fought with Foreign rather than with Native Troops [2]

Upon the outbreak of the War with Russia the 18 Vic, c. 2 (passed for a limited period, and expiring with the Peace), enabled Her Majesty to enlist in Her service persons not being natural-born subjects, and to grant commissions or letters of service to any such persons to serve as Officers. The Act provided that this force should not be employed in the United Kingdom, except for training, formation, and reserve, and that when so employed it should not exceed 10,000 within the United Kingdom, or be entitled to be billeted. The force was made liable to the Army Mutiny Act and Articles of War in the same manner to all intents and purposes as Her Majesty's Regular Forces are subject to the same.

Whether the Russian War was popular or expedient, is a question not to be entered upon here, but the debates [3] on the Bill upon which this Act was founded prove to demonstration that the proposal which it contained was not popular, though it was expedient No Continental War was ever previously carried on with so small a number of Foreign Troops, and consequently the nation never before realized the loss of human life so keenly or so appreciated the service of the National Troops as in the Crimean War

As the Army of the late East India Company [4] consisted in part of Foreigners, it was thought necessary, on the transfer of it to Her Majesty, to sanction the continuance of their employment by 24 & 25 Vic., c. 74, s. 2.

---

[1] As to their landing in 1814, see 28 H D (O S), p 39, and Lord Folkestone's motion about Foreign Troops, 21 ib., pp 907, 1240

[2] 21 H D (OS), pp 907, 1240, 1258

[3] 136 H D (3), pp 254, 344, 414, 430, House of Lords, pp 488 507, 629, 746, 774; and House of Commons, 141 ib, p 566, 142 ib., pp 798, 1152, 143 ib, p 1112, 146 ib., p 1343

[4] As to its early origin and history, see 'Report of the Royal Commissioners on the Memorials of Indian Officers,' p. 6 of Appendix.

(A) EFFECTIVE STRENGTH OF THE ARMY[1]—RANK AND FILE—FROM 1ST JANUARY, 1804, TO DECEMBER, 1813.

	1804 January 1	1805 January 1	1806 January 1	1807 January 1	1808 January 1	1809 January 1	1810 January 1	1811 January 25	1812 January 25
REGULARS—									
Cavalry	16,729	20,316	23,396	26,261	26,402	27,391	27,740	27,410	27,638
Artillery and Engineers	14,113	17,109	19,546	20,951	22,250	23,563	24,238	23,668	23,824
Infantry	119,751	124,531	142,177	152,245	177,775	183,223	185,474	183,516	192,423
	150,593	161,956	185,119	199,457	226,427	234,177	237,452	234,594	243,885
Foreign and Colonial	17,039	22,375	26,043	35,816	37,217	36,947	38,390	40,543	45,881
British	133,554	139,581	159,076	163,641	189,210	197,230	199,062	194,051	198,004
MILITIA	85,519	89,809	74,653	76,159	67,677	81,577	72,487	84,439	77,055

	1813 January 25	1813 September 25			1813 December 25	
REGULARS—			**BRITISH REGIMENTS—**			
Cavalry	28,931	29,504	Cavalry		26,611	
Artillery and Engineers	25,407	27,014	Foot Guards		8,852	
Infantry	201,538	204,279	Infantry		152,463	
	255,876	260,797			187,926	
Foreign and Colonial	52,757	53,729	**FOREIGN AND COLONIAL—**			
			Cavalry		4,471	
	203,119	207,068	Infantry		47,034	
					239,431	
MILITIA	71,055	69,866	MILITIA		63,059	
					302,490	

ARTILLERY.

Non-commissioned Officers and Men, including Foreign 26,402

[1] 69 Com. Journ., 1814, p 638.

(T.)

Chapter XV., par. 167.

MILITARY SAVINGS BANKS.

THESE institutions date from the year 1842, when Parliament passed the 5 & 6 Vic., c. 71, to sanction their establishment, and to guarantee a yearly rate of interest not exceeding 3*l.* 16*s.* per cent. to the depositors This Act was amended in 1845,[1] and when the Benefit Societies that existed in the Army prior to 1849 were dissolved under the 12 & 13 Vic., c 71,[2] the share due to each Soldier was added to his account, or a new account opened in his name in the Regimental Bank[3] The law was amended and consolidated by the 22 & 23 Vic., c. 20, and the Regulations issued under the Act bear date the 31st August, 1861.

The Act provides—that the Banks are established for the purpose of receiving money from " non-commissioned Officers and Soldiers, and deposits raised or paid for objects or purposes connected with them," as authorised by Her Majesty: that the rate of interest shall not exceed 3*l.* 15*s.*, nor " be paid on deposits exceeding 30*l.* in the year till the end of the year, nor exceeding 200*l*, and that the receipts of infants and married women shall be taken as discharges for deposits by them made."

Other provisions are made by the Regulations; that Non-commissioned Officers and Soldiers only can deposit, and the maximum is to be 30*l.* for one year, and 200*l.* as a total sum by each depositor. The Commanding Officer of each Troop or Company is to sign for each deposit paid in, and seven days' notice of withdrawal to be given to the Commanding Officer. If the Officer has strong grounds for believing that the Soldier intends to make an improper use of his money, he may suspend the issue of the deposit, and report the case for the decision of the General, or the Commander-in-Chief and Secretary at War.

The Serjeant's Mess Fund, in the name of the Serjeant-Major, and—with the consent of the Secretary at War—any other Regimental Fund, may be deposited, irrespective of amount.

Gratuities for long service and good conduct, or for distinguished

---

[1] 8 & 9 Vic., c. 27
[2] 3 & 4 Wm. IV (Lo and Personal) cxvii , 107 H D (J), p 878, and 109 ib, p 358
[3] Secs 2 and 3

conduct in the field, are to be invested in the Bank, under the special authority of the Secretary at War, but on the Soldier's discharge the deposit may be withdrawn without any special authority, and on his death added to his general effects. If an annuity is awarded to him, or he is promoted by grant of a Commission, or if he deserts, the gratuity is forfeited.

On the Soldier's discharge, the deposit may remain for six months at interest—on his desertion it is forfeited, and on his death it is added to his general effects. Each year the accounts are to be audited by the Secretary at War, and on his signature the Public become responsible for the amount of each deposit. They are annually laid before Parliament, and those of June, 1868, are annexed.

Account (Pursuant to Act 22 & 23 Vic, c. 20)

	£	s.	d.	£	s	d
Balance due by the Public on the 31st March, 1866		..		301,375	16	11
Deposits in Military Savings Banks during the year ended on the 31st March, 1867	156,501	13	11¼			
Amount received on account of Army Charitable Funds during the year ended on the 31st March, 1867	945	6	1½	157,447	0	0¾
Interest allowed during the year 1866-7 on Deposits in Military Savings Banks	6,417	17	10¾			
Interest allowed during the year 1866-7 on Army Charitable Funds	1,608	4	9¼	8,026	2	8
				466,848	19	7¾
Withdrawals from Military Savings Banks during the year 1866-7	171,990	3	3½			
Disbursements from Army Charitable Funds during the year 1866-7	2,658	19	7¾	177,649	2	11¼
Balance due by the Public on the 31st March, 1867				289,199	16	8½

Number of Accounts open on the 31st March, 1867   17,898

	£	s	d		£	s	d.
Net Amount paid over to the Commissioners for the Reduction of the National Debt on account of the Fund for Military Savings Banks (inclusive of Army Charitable Funds) for previous years, together with Dividends received thereon, and similarly invested up to the 31st March, 1866	325,025	9	3				
Deduct,—Produce of Stock sold in consequence of the Excess of Payments over Receipts in 1866-7	20,202	2	10½				
					304,823	6	4½
Add,—Further Dividends received on account of the Fund for Military Savings Banks up to the 5th April, 1867, and invested in further aid thereof . .					15,298	14	6
					320,122	0	10½
Add,—Further Dividends received and similarly invested up to the 5th April, 1868					11,044	18	7
Total Amount of the Fund for Military Savings Banks up to the date of this Account					331,166	19	5½

War Office, 27th June, 1868   J. S. PAKINGTON

(U.)

Chapter XVI , *par* 10.

ON THE SIGNATURE OF COMMISSIONS IN THE NAME OF THE SOVEREIGN.

IT was formerly the Constitutional practice, upon the intended absence of the Sovereign from the Realm, to issue Letters Patent, under the Great Seal, appointing Lords Justices to sign commissions and execute other acts of State during such absence.   An early instance of this is in the year 1633 (May 11), on the intended absence of King Charles I., and the last of such appointments was made in September 1821, when, prior to the departure of George IV. for Hanover, Letters Patent were issued, appointing certain of the Privy Council (named), "as Guardians and Justices of Our Realm, and Our Lieutenants within the same for the administration of Our Government during Our absence from Our said United Kingdom."

Under this Patent a commission to an officer in the Army ran in these words   "In the name of His Majesty."   Then followed the words.   "By the Lords Justices," and the signatures of four

margin note: When to be signed by Commissioners authorised (1) By Patent.

Lords were added. The counter-signature was that of "William Hamilton," as *Under* Secretary of State. In other respects the commission was in the usual form.[1]

(2) By Statute — Upon other occasions than those of the Sovereign's absence from the Realm, the authority of Parliament has been obtained for the authentication of the appointment of officers without the actual signature of the reigning Sovereign to their commissions.

The first occasion was in the year 1811,[2] during the illness of King George III., when the Regency Act (51 Geo III., c. 1) prescribed the form of the Royal Sign Manual of the Prince Regent, and declared, "That it should be as valid and effectual, and have the same force and effect as His Majesty's Royal Sign Manual, and be deemed and taken to be, to all intents and purposes, His Majesty's Royal Sign Manual, and be obeyed as such." The commissions issued under this Act were intituled "In the name and on behalf of His Majesty," and otherwise proceeded in the usual form.

Again, in the year 1830, during the illness of George IV., an Act (11 Geo. IV., and Wm. IV., c 23) was passed to authorize the Royal Sign Manual being affixed, in His Majesty's presence and by His Majesty's command, to (*inter alia*) commissions, and to declare that His Majesty's Royal Signature, so affixed, should be "valid and effectual," &c., (using the same words as having been set out from the 51 Geo. III., c 1.)

No commission (with the exception next mentioned) was to be signed unless it had been previously indorsed with a memorandum signed by three of the Great Officers of State, describing the nature and object of such commission; and the exception was in the 3rd section, which provided, "That in all commissions to officers in His Majesty's land forces, the memorandum to be indorsed thereon as aforesaid shall be signed by the Commander-in-Chief of His Majesty's forces, or by the General Commanding-in-Chief for the time being, and that no other signature shall be required to such memorandum."

No commission to any officer appears to have been signed under the statute, though the approval of a submission paper for the appointment of officers was signed by the Commissioners.

These two Acts were necessarily of temporary duration, but in the year 1862, the number of commissions needing the Royal Sign Manual having considerably increased, it was deemed right to pass

---

[1] As some of the Commissions purported to give rank from a date prior to that of the Letters Patent, and a doubt having been raised against the validity of this Act, a Royal Warrant was issued on the return of the King, dated 10th November, 1821, confirming the rank named in the several Commissions.

[2] 22 H D (O S), pp 332-363

an Act of Parliament[1] "to enable Her Majesty to issue Commissions to the Officers of Her Majesty's Land Forces and Royal Marines, and to Adjutants and Quartermasters of the Militia and Volunteer Forces without affixing her Royal Sign Manual thereto."

After setting forth in the preamble that every Officer appointed or promoted by Her Majesty in Her Land Forces or Marines, and every Adjutant or Quartermaster in her Militia or Volunteer Forces, receives a Commission from Her Majesty with her Royal Sign Manual thereon, and that in the case of the Land Forces before such Commissions are prepared each Officer has been appointed or promoted by Her Majesty under her Royal Sign Manual to the Rank for which a Commission afterwards issues under Royal Sign Manual, and has been gazetted to his appointment or promotion, and has entered on his duties and received his pay, and that it was expedient to regulate from time to time the mode of authenticating the said Commissions granted by Her Majesty, the Act declared that it should be lawful for Her Majesty, by Order in Council, from time to time, as occasion might require, to direct that all or any Commissions for Officers prepared or to be prepared under the authority of Her Majesty's Royal Sign Manual might be afterwards issued without her Royal Sign Manual; but having thereon, in the case of Her Majesty's Land Forces, except as thereafter mentioned, the signatures of the Commander-in-Chief or the General Commanding-in-Chief, and of one of Her Majesty's Principal Secretaries of State, and in the case of the Royal Marines, of the Lords Commissioners of the Admiralty, and in the case of Military Chaplains, Commissariat and Store Officers, and of Adjutants and Quartermasters in the Militia and Volunteer Forces, of one of Her Majesty's said Principal Secretaries, and that every such Commission issued and signed in pursuance of such Order in Council should be conclusive evidence that the Officer named in any such Commission had been appointed or promoted by Her Majesty to the rank or office named therein.

In pursuance of the Act, an Order in Council was issued on the 7th day of June, 1862, to this effect —

1. That each Commission[2] thereafter issued to any Officer entering Her Majesty's Army, from Her Majesty's Indian Forces, under the regulations theretofore sanctioned by Her Majesty, should be signed by Her Majesty's General Commanding-in-Chief, and one of Her Majesty's Principal Secretaries of State, and such Commission should give rank in Her Majesty's Army,

Order in Council, 7th June, 1862.

---

[1] 25 Vic., c 4   [2] See Form A

from the date on which the Officer held similar rank in the Indian Forces. Her Majesty having been pleased to declare that the Commission given to every one upon first appointment to Her Majesty's Land Forces or Marines will be signed by Her Majesty.

2. It was further ordered — That all other Commissions required for Officers in Her Majesty's Service, on promotion or exchange, whether such promotion or exchange had been made or sanctioned by Her Majesty under Royal Sign Manual, before or after the passing of the Act, and all Commissions given for Adjutants and Quartermasters in the Militia and Volunteer Forces, should be signed, in the case of Her Majesty's Land Forces (except as in the Clause after-mentioned), by the Commander-in-Chief or the General Commanding-in-Chief,[1] and by one of Her Majesty's Principal Secretaries of State; and, in the case of the Royal Marines, by the Lords Commissioners of Her Majesty's Admiralty, and, in the case of Military Chaplains, Commissariat and Store Officers, and of Adjutants and Quartermasters in the Militia and Volunteer Forces, by one of Her Majesty's Principal Secretaries of State.

3 That every Commission signed in pursuance of the Order (except the Commissions referred to in Clause 1, and except all Commissions which should have been actually prepared under Sign Manual direction, bearing date prior to the 7th June), should refer to the Order in Council, and bear even date with the direction under Her Majesty's Royal Sign Manual, appointing or promoting the Officer [2]

4. That neither that Order, nor anything contained therein, should be construed to prevent Her Majesty from signing any Commission, or to prevent any Commission so signed from having the same validity and effect as if the Order had not been made.

In March, 1866, the signature of First Commissions having fallen

Order in Council of 12th March, 1866

into arrear, Her Majesty declared her will and pleasure that any such Commissions which on or before the 12th day of March, 1866, had been authorised under Her Majesty's

---

[1] This Commission will be, as to combatant Officers, in the Form B, set out in the Appendix, and as to Non-combatants, in the Form C and the Forms now in use

[2] In lieu of the concluding words, commencing in Forms B and C, with "Given at our Court," these words will be used—"In witness whereof the General Commanding-in-Chief and one of Her Majesty's Principal Secretaries of State (or two of the Commissioners for executing the Office of High Admiral, or one of Her Majesty's Principal Secretaries of State), in pursuance of the Order of Her Majesty's Most Honourable Privy Council, bearing date the 7th day of June, 1862, and by Command of Her Majesty, under Her Royal Sign Manual of even date herewith, hereunto subscribe(s) their (or his) names (or name) this

day of   , One thousand eight hundred and sixty-two."

Royal Sign Manual, but not signed by Her Majesty, should be issued and signed under the provisions of the Act Therefore another Order in Council was issued on the 12th March, 1866, declaring (1) that where, prior to the date thereof, any person had been first appointed to an office in Her Majesty's Land Forces or Marines under Her Majesty's Royal Sign Manual, but no Commission had been issued to him signed by Her Majesty, then that a Commission should be issued to every such person so appointed as aforesaid signed in manner following, that was to say —In any case of First Appointment to Her Majesty's Land Forces (except as in this Clause aftermentioned) by the Commander-in-Chief, or the Field-Marshal, or General Commanding-in-Chief, and by one of Her Majesty's Principal Secretaries of State, and in any case of First Appointment to the Royal Marines, by the Lords Commissioners of Her Majesty's Admiralty, and in any case of First Appointment as Military Chaplain, or Commissariat, or Store Officer, by one of Her Majesty's Principal Secretaries of State.

(2) That the Order should not prejudice or affect the Order of the 7th June, 1862, nor should the Order, or anything contained therein, be construed to prevent Her Majesty from signing any Commission, or to prevent any Commission so signed from having the same validity and effect as if the Order had not been made.

In the Appendix to the Order of the 7th June, 1862, these Forms were given —

A.

VICTORIA, by the Grace of God, of the United Kingdom of Great Britain and Ireland, Queen, Defender of the Faith, &c., &c, to our trusty and well-beloved A B., greeting ·—

We, reposing especial trust and confidence in your loyalty, courage, and good conduct, do by these presents, constitute and appoint you to hold the rank of   in Our Army, from[1]   , and We do hereby give and grant you full power and authority to command, and take your rank accordingly. You are, therefore, carefully and diligently to discharge the duty of   by doing and performing all and all manner of things thereunto belonging, and we do hereby command all Our Officers and Soldiers whom it may concern to acknowledge and

---

[1] The date from which he held similar rank in the Indian Forces

obey you as a   as aforesaid, and you are to observe and follow such Orders and Directions from time to time us you shall receive from Us or any your Superior Officer, according to the rules and discipline of War, in pursuance of the trust we hereby repose in you.

In witness whereof, the General Commanding-in-Chief and one of Her Majesty's Principal Secretaries of State, in pursuance of the Order of Her Majesty in Council, bearing date the 7th day of June, 1862, hereunto subscribe their names, this   day of   , One thousand eight hundred and sixty-two.

B.

VICTORIA, by the Grace of God, of the United Kingdom of Great Britain and Ireland, Queen, Defender of the Faith, &c., &c., to Our trusty and well-beloved   , greeting.—

We, *reposing especial trust and confidence in your loyalty, courage, and good conduct,* do by these presents constitute and appoint you to be an Officer in Our (1)[1]   from the You are, therefore, carefully and diligently to discharge your duty as such in the rank of (2)[2] *or in such higher rank as We may at any time hereafter promote you to,* exercising and well disciplining in Arms both the inferior Officers and Soldiers serving under you, and in using your best endeavours to keep them in good order and discipline, and We do hereby command them to obey you, as their Superior Officer, and you are to observe and follow such Orders and Directions from time to time as you shall receive from Us [in F and G, *Our High Admiral or Commissioners for executing the Office of High Admiral for the time being*] or any your Superior Officer, according to the rules and discipline of War, in pursuance of the trust hereby reposed in you

Given at Our Court, at   the   day of   18   in the   year of Our Reign.

By Her Majesty's Command.

---

[1] (1) to be filled in by —A, Cavalry, B Royal Artillery; C, Royal Engineers, D, Military Train, E, Infantry, F, Royal Marine Artillery; G, Royal Marines
[2] (2) Cornet (A); Lieutenant (B C F G), Ensign (D and E).

C

VICTORIA, by the Grace of God, of the United Kingdom of Great Britain and Ireland, Queen, Defender of the Faith, &c , to Our trusty and well-beloved   , greeting .—

We, *reposing trust and confidence in your loyalty* [*][1] *and good conduct,* do by these presents constitute and appoint you to be an Officer in the (1)[2]   Department of Our [Army (A)] from the   You are, therefore, carefully and diligently to discharge your duty as such in the rank of (2),[3]   *or in such higher rank as We may at any time hereafter promote you to,* by doing and performing all and all manner of things thereunto belonging.   And you are to observe and follow such Orders and Directions from time to time as you shall receive from Us (in A, *Our High Admiral or Commissioners for executing the Office of High Admiral for the time being*), or any your Superior Officer, according to the rules and discipline of War.

Given at Our Court, at   the
    day of   18   in the
    year of Our Reign.
      By Her Majesty's Command.

[*Countersigned by a Secretary of State; or, the Lords Commissioners of the Admiralty.*]

(V.)

Chapter XVI , par 46.

THE RESERVE FUND.

THE history of this Fund appeared to the Army Purchase Commissioners,[4] 1857, to be involved in some mystery, though Returns had been laid before Parliament in 1820[5] embracing these particu-

---

[1] [*]
b, c, Ability
a d, f, Integrity.
e, Piety.

To be filled in by, (1) —*a,* Commissariat, *b,* Medical, or (A), Royal Marines; *c,* Veterinary, *d,* Purveyors, *e,* Chaplains; *f,* Military Store.
(2). *a,* Deputy Assistant Commissary General, *b,* Assistant Surgeon, *c,* Veterinary Surgeon; *d,* Deputy Purveyor, *e,* Chaplain of the 4th Class, *f,* Deputy Assistant Superintendent of Stores

[2] See Note [1], p. 444
[3] See Note [2], p 414
[4] Pp. 66-74
[5] Feb. 22, Nos 75-79

lars —1st, an account, from 15th March, 1809, to 31st December, 1819, of all the Commissions sold, showing a total realization of 276,447*l.* 10*s*, and also an account of the Half-pay Fund for the like period, showing a balance of 423*l.* 18*s* 10*d* in the agent's hands, in dealing with 50,782*l* 5*s.* 5*d* realized by sales   If the sales in the first account produced any balance they were transferred to the Half-pay Fund, and out of the Half-pay Fund were paid "benevolences" to the widows and children of Officers, by order of the *Commander-in-Chief,* over and above the provision made for them *by Parliament*   By a later Return the account of the Half-pay Fund was brought down to December, 1855,[1] showing a balance of 217*l.* 13*s.* 10*d.* in the hands of the agents, and the benevolent objects of the Fund ceased at this period[2]

In or about the year 1823 another Fund originated, under the control of the Commander-in-Chief, which is now known as the "Reserve Fund"   In May, 1823, the Master-General of the Ordnance (the Duke of Wellington) obtained the sanction of the Treasury to allow a certain number of Artillery Officers to retire by sale of their Commissions at the Regulation price for the Line.[3] The purchasers had unattached Commissions   In 1824 the same system was extended to the Royal Engineers, and still later to the Royal Marines   In December, 1824, a Memorandum was submitted by the Commander-in-Chief to the King (apparently with the sanction of Lord Liverpool, but without the intervention of the War Office), for accelerating the promotion of Line Officers, by enabling Half-pay Commissions to be sold to Officers on the effective list of the Army.

For many years there had been an entire stagnation in Full-pay promotions. Majors had held that rank for twenty years, Captains from 18 to 21 years, Lieutenants from 14 to 17, and Ensigns from 9 to 12 years, and if the Army had been called into active operation these inefficient Officers must have been superseded.   These sales were to be made upon different terms to the officers selling, that is, the same price was to be *paid* by the purchasing, but the same *or a less price* was to be *received* by the selling Officers, as prescribed by the Regulations of 25th April, 1825.[4] The financial result of these measures was laid before the House of Commons in February, 1831,[5] and discussed before the Committee

---

[1] 'Army Reserve, 1857,' p. 468.   [2] Ib, p 74

[3] 'Army and Navy Appointments, 1833,' p 221.

[4] MS War Office Regulations, p 161, and see Sir H Taylor's Evidence before the Finance Committee, 1827, p 259, and Returns, p 278

[5] Nos. 326, 327, and vol. xiii of Sessional Papers, p. 59

on Army and Navy Appointments, 1833.[1]   In the Returns and Report laid before Parliament it appeared—1st, that 1005 Officers on half-pay had been bought out at an increased annual charge to the public of 6533l. 0s 10d. for future half-pay, against which a capital sum of 87,696l. 13s. 5d. was paid to the Exchequer up to 31st July, 1831,[2] and, 2ndly, that in the change from older to younger lives on the Half-pay List the cost to the public was 158,449l, and that capitalizing 6000l of the 6533l. at the further sum of 104,237l. made the total loss 262,686l. against 118,746l. (including the 87,690l) paid into the Exchequer.

Up to October, 1828, 81,000l. having then been paid to the Exchequer, Lord Hardinge, as Secretary at War, applied for the permission of the Treasury to use this sum in buying up Half-Pay Commissions by cancellation at a commuted price   This sanction was given, and when the first return was laid before Parliament, up to the 13th October, 1831, 199,683l. 14s. 9d had been issued to the agents of the Secretary at War to cancel 440 Half-pay Commissions, receiving 30,193l 16s. 6d. per annum[3]   The average income of each annuity was stated at 68l 12s. 5d, and the capital value at 1131l. 14s.   The sum paid to the Officer was 453l 16s. 7d, and the aggregate saving on the 440 Commissions cancelled[4] was estimated at 298,263l. 3s 4d

Later information, up to April in that year, was laid before the Select Committee of 1833.   The results were there stated[5] that 857 Officers of every class, holding 58,754l. 17s. 9d, had been commuted at 374,064l. 15s. 7d.,—the profit of each commutation being 694l 0s. 5d   The circumstances alleged by Lord Hardinge to justify this course were, no doubt, peculiar.   It was principally applied to Ensigns and Lieutenants, reduced after the peace in 1815, and who in some instances had not joined their Regiments, and in others done little service.[6]

Up to December, 1819, the balances of the sale and purchase account were from time to time paid to the credit of the public, through the Paymaster-General, but *from* that date they have been held by the agents of the Fund, applied under the orders of the Commander-in-Chief, and the balance invested in Exchequer Bills.[7]

Upon the augmentation of the Army in 1854, by the direct action of the Crown, rather than through the agency of gentlemen raising Regiments under Letters of Service, a large number of first

---

[1] 13 Sessional Papers, pp 224, 225   [2] P 33.   [3] P. 84.
[4] Ib   [5] Pp 227, 228
[6] See also these Returns and Papers —Vol xx (1826), pp 311, 351, 365, 375, vol xvii (1828), p 197, vol xxiv (1833), p 63, and see Chap XVI, par. 86.
[7] 'Army Purchase, 1857, pp. 68-72, 403-79.

Commissions came into the hands of the Commander-in-Chief for appointment. Under the old system these Commissions would have been at the disposal of the gentlemen raising the Regiments to meet recruiting expenses, but the Crown bore these and all other charges, Lord Herbert directed one hundred first Commissions to be sold, and the proceeds (45,000*l*) placed to the credit of the Reserve Fund, that at the reduction of the Army upon the close of the war their Half-pay might be commuted therewith [1]

At about the same period the Guards' Fund was created (as a separate Fund) by sale of first Commissions to extinguish the Supernumeraries which arise from the Pages of Honour to the Sovereign, being entitled to Commissions on their attaining 16 years of age [2]

The General Reserve Fund is therefore made up from the contributions of Line Officers, but its application has been devoted to other objects not in the same branch of the Service. The whole subject was therefore brought under the consideration of a Select Committee of the House of Commons in 1867, [3] and their Report presented to Parliament in May of the following year. [4] In the Revised Estimate for Vote 21, 1869-70, the Reserve Fund was included with this note.—

"The Receipts on the Reserve Fund Account are limited to the proceeds of the—

"(1.) Sale of the difference between the full value of an Infantry or Cavalry Commission, and that which an Officer is entitled to receive.

"(2) Sale of Commissions in succession to Officers placed on the Supernumerary, Seconded, and Half-pay Lists.

"(3.) Sale of every 3rd non-purchase vacancy in Foot Guards.

"(4.) Interest on the investments of the Fund."

/

(V.*)

Chapter XVI., par. 48.

RETIREMENTS OF NAVAL AND MILITARY COMMISSIONED OFFICERS UNDER THE 32 & 33 VIC. c. 31.

SINCE the first Volume of this work has been published, the 'Pensions Commutation Act, 1869,' [5] has been passed—founded upon a

---

[1] P 70.

[2] Ib pp. 72, 73, see 'Report on Military Organization, 1860,' *passim*, and Lord Palmerston's Evidence before the Finance Committee, 1828, p 147

[3] (453), 22nd July, 1867   [4] (298), 22nd May 1868   [5] 32 & 33 Vic., c 31

Recommendation contained in the Report of the Select Committee of the House of Commons on Army (System of Retirement) [1]

It is applicable only to officers and persons entitled to pensions out of the sums voted by Parliament to defray the charges of the Navy and Army services, not including non commissioned Officers and Soldiers of Her Majesty's Army and petty Officers and Seamen of Her Majesty's Navy, and the term "Pension"[2] is to include any half pay compensation allowance, superannuation or retirement allowance, or other payment of the like nature The Scheme of the Act is that the Treasury (in accordance with such regulations as they may from time to time make), on the application of any person to whom the Act applies, may commute his pension by the payment of a capital sum of money, calculated according to the estimated duration of the life of the pension-holder, subject to these provisions —

(1) In calculating the amount payable in respect of the commutation, the following rules shall be observed —

(a.) The age of the pension-holder shall be reckoned at the age he will attain on the birthday next succeeding his application for commutation

(b) In the case of impaired lives, years shall be added to the age of the pension-holder for the purpose of calculating the amount of commutation payable to him, and in like manner a deduction from age shall be made as an equivalent for the right to prospective increase of the pension to be commuted.

(c) In calculating the amount payable in respect of any pension, interest shall be reckoned at a rate of not less than 5*l.* per centum per annum

(2) Save as is in the Act expressly provided, the wife or children of a commuted officer shall not be deprived of any reversionary right to pension or compassionate allowance to which she or they may be entitled

(3) Where a commuted officer subsequently marries, his widow shall not be entitled to any pension, and no child of the officer, born after the date of such commutation, shall be entitled to compassionate allowance

(4) No application for commutation shall be received unless it

---

[1] Ordered to be printed 26th July, 1867 (482)

[2] Under the 22 Geo III, c 82, sec 30 the definition is, "any grant made more than once in three years" As to the Dead Weight Acts, passed after the Peninsular War, see 3 Geo IV, c. 51, and 9 Geo IV., c 79

be accompanied by a recommendation from the War Office or the Admiralty.

A Commutation Board is be formed, and report to the Treasury upon the cases of applicants for commutation in such manner as may be directed.

The Treasury are to make, alter, or revoke regulations as to the following matters —

(1.) The rules according to which applications for commutation are to be made, or, on payment of a prescribed fee, to be withdrawn.

(2) The tables according to which the duration of life of applicants for commutation is to be calculated for the purposes of this Act

(3.) The terms upon which pensions are to be commuted, and the cases in which commutation is to be refused [1]

If a commuted officer accepts any public employment, a deduction is to be made from the salary payable to him, equal to the amount which would have been abated from the pension if it had not been commuted [2]

It is not easy to foresee what may be the effect of this Act, and whether it will induce the Officer—as Mr Wyndham's Act induced the Soldier—to continue in the Service until a bonus on retirement can be obtained   Half-pay has not hitherto been assignable, upon the ground of public policy, because the Officer was at all times liable. having regard to his half-pay, to be called into Service. This Act ignores all such considerations, and may be cited as a reversal of the traditionary policy of the State, as to the pecuniary value of an Officer's Commission,[3] as to his liability to future Service,[4] and as to his ability to assign his half-pay [5]

(W.)

Chapter XVI , par 64

The Royal Military College at Sandhurst

This Institution, so far as the express sanction of Parliament was given to its establishment, dates from June, 1801   Prior to that time a School had been established at Great Marlow, Bucks , but the requirements of the Military Service extending, George III gave up a tract of Heath Land (part of the Hereditary Revenue of the Crown, at Sandhurst, Berks, and sent this message to the House of Commons [6]—

---

[1] Sec 7.   [2] Sec. 10,   [3] Chap XVI, par 58   [4] Ib , par 83
[5] Ib , par 98   [6] 35 Parl Hist , p 1446

"His Majesty thinks it proper to acquaint the House of Commons that an Establishment has been formed under His Majesty's directions for promoting the study of Military Science This Institution His Majesty is persuaded must conduce to the preservation and improvement of the skill and discipline which, combined with the native valour of British troops, have so often maintained the rights and asserted the honour of his kingdom His Majesty therefore recommends it to his faithful Commons to consider of making the provision that may be necessary for enabling His Majesty to accomplish in the most effectual manner an object of so much national importance"

At that time the command of the Royal Engineers being under the Master-General of the Ordnance, it was deemed necessary to train Line Officers for the special duties that might otherwise more properly have been intrusted to the Royal Engineers—as, the choice of camps,—the best mode of occupying, attacking, or defending them with a given force,—and the most ready and effectual means of affording assistance to a General in making his disposition by military plans rapidly designed Accordingly, that Line Officers might be trained to these duties to be performed under the Quarter-master General, and the Ordnance Corps superseded, this Institution was formed on the same model that had produced efficient officers for the Armies of France and Prussia.

It was from the date of this Establishment[1] under the charge of the Secretary at War—who ranked next to the President—the Commander-in-Chief—in the Council, and the Annual Estimates were moved by him An Estimate[2] was presented to the House for the expenditure of 67,000l. in three years for the purchase of land, and the erection of Buildings sufficient to hold the Professors and Scholars, consisting of two departments,—the Senior Department of thirty Officers, and the Junior Department of 250 Cadets The total annual estimate of expenditure being 20,245l. 8s 4½d., and of receipts 16,945l, leaving an annual balance of 3,300l 8s 4½d. to be borne by the public After an opposition from General Walpole and Mr Grey, a vote of 30,000l was taken " upon account," and the undertaking commenced

The Royal Warrant of 27th May, 1808, provides for a Governing body consisting (*inter alia*) of the Commander-in-Chief as president, the Secretary at War, the Quarter-Master-General the Adjutant-General, and the Governor of the College for the time being as Commissioners, and also for a Collegiate Board of resident officials

---

[1] The Tenth Report of Military Inquiry, 14th August, 1809.

[2] 56 Com Journ, p 878

2 G 2

acting under the Commissioners All the estates were to be held by Government and the Collegiate Board, but as the land had been purchased without any statutory power of holding it as a quasi corporation, the Act, 1862,[1] declared the College and the adjacent lands to be vested in His Majesty's Principal Secretary of State for the War Department, subject to the provisions of the Warrant, 1808.

In, or rather prior to the year 1858, it was suggested that every Candidate for a Commission should pass through a Military College, and that for this purpose the Woolwich Academy and Sandhurst College should be united as one Establishment for the Scientific Corps of the Army and Line. This view was strongly opposed in April, 1858,[2] upon the motion of Mr Monsell, and again in 1862[3] by Mr Selwyn (then Member of Parliament for Cambridge University), and was finally abandoned [4]

By the Regulations at present in force, the College continues to have two Divisions, and all the Candidates enter after a competitive examination. The Senior Division consists of officers five years at least in the Service, and who, in two years, must pass out on examination for Staff appointments in the Army,[5] the Junior Division —of Cadets, who enter between sixteen and nineteen years of age, under Regulations of the 5th September, 1867

In the Junior Division forty Cadets are educated free of all charge, and other students enter at various rates of charges The course of study is for eighteen months, but a pass for a commission may be sooner taken A certain number of Commissions without purchase, are assigned to the College, and given to those candidates having the highest order of merit Those candidates failing to obtain a Commission without purchase, but obtaining marks over the minimum qualification, have a prior claim to other candidates for purchase

(X.)

Chapter XVI , par 64

THE COUNCIL OF MILITARY EDUCATION

IN June, 1856, the late Lord Herbert brought the whole subject of Military Education before the House of Commons,[6] and the esta-

---

[1] 25 & 26 Vic , c 32   [2] 149 H D (3), p 1728   [3] 165 H D (3), p 1126
[4] See 'Military Organization Commission, 1860,' title, 'Military College,' and 'Report on Sandhurst by Select Committee of House of Commons, 1855' (317) 18th June, 1855   [5] Queen's Regulations, 1868
[6] 142 H D (3), p 990.

blishment in April, 1857, of this Council may be said to be the result which the Debate produced to the Army.

The general duties of the Council, exclusive of those appertaining to Army Schools, are as follows —

" 1 The recommendation to the Commander-in-Chief and to the Secretary of State for War of gentlemen for the appointment of examiners in the Army examinations

" 2 The recommendation to the Commander-in-Chief and to the Secretary of State for War of the persons who appear to them the best qualified for appointment to professorships and masterships at the Staff College, the Advanced Class of Artillery Officers, the Royal Military College, and, under certain limitations, at the Royal Military Academy

"To report to the same authorities, whenever it may appear desirable to discontinue the services of gentlemen holding the above appointments

"To investigate and report, when required to do so by the Commander-in-Chief, upon the qualifications of officers proposed to be appointed to posts of educational superintendence

" 3. To examine officers in certain subjects for direct appointments to the Staff.

" 4 To examine officers for admission to the Staff College , probationarily during residence , and for qualification for the general Staff on quitting the college

" 5 To examine officers of Artillery for admission to the Advanced Class, and for certificates on quitting it

" 6 To examine for admission to the Royal Military Academy, and for qualification for commissions in the Royal Artillery and Royal Engineers on quitting that Institution.

" 7 To examine for admission to the Royal Military College, Sandhurst, and for qualification for commissions in the Army at the termination of the course of instruction.

" 8 To examine candidates for direct commissions in the Cavalry, Guards, and Line, and for appointment to the Commissariat Department, to visit, whenever it may appear desirable, the educational departments of the Institutions above-named , and to report to the Commander-in-Chief on all questions connected either with the general education of candidates for the Army, or with the educational departments of the several Military Colleges." [1]

The Council consists of the Commander-in-Chief as ex officio President , a Vice-President and four members, of whom one is a civilian. Two Reports have been laid before Parliament by com-

---

[1] Extract from 2nd Report of the Council, 1865, p 3

n nd in 1860 and 1865, and the importance of professional education has not been lost sight of, for in 1866,[1] and again in May, 1868[2] the subject was brought before Parliament—when the Crown, upon the advice of Sir John Pakington, issued a Royal Commission on the 23rd day of June, 1868, to report on the subject as defined by the instructions addressed to the Commissioners

---

(Y.)

Chapter XVI, *par* 65

THE SCHOOL OF MUSKETRY AT HYTHE.

THE Enfield Rifle, 1853, was, in the year at which it bears date, introduced into the Service at the instance of Lord Hardinge,[3] then in command of the Army. The next object to attain, after the supply had been issued to the Troops, was to instruct them in the use of the new arm For this purpose land was purchased in the same year at Hythe, in Kent, and an "Establishment for a School of Musketry," at the annual expense of 1000*l*, was agreed upon by the Secretary at War

The Staff, and pay of the Staff, are not matters of sufficient interest to record here, but in June, 1853, the School was so far formed that men were ordered there (from each Battalion of the Guards and Rifle Brigade, and from two other Regiments), to undergo a course of instruction.

On the 13th August, 1855, the Commander-in-Chief issued Regulations for the organization of a permanent 'Corps of Instructors of Musketry," to act under the Commandant of the School at Hythe The Commandant and part of the Staff were always to be constantly at Hythe, and the others were to be detached to Depôt Battalions, or posted to Regiments or stations where instructors were most needed

These Regulations must be considered as annulled by the Royal Warrant of the 8th April, 1856,[4] which projected a more complete organization of the Corps. The Corps was enlarged, and district inspectors were appointed under the Commandant, who was made responsible that the troops were trained according to the approved system The men of the Corps of Instructors were to be discharged

---

[1] 182 H D (3), p 426   [2] 191 Hansard, p 1819
[3] 'Organization Report, 1860,' Lord Herbert, Qu 6504
[4] This was amended by 11th February, 1857

from their existing enlistment and re-enlisted into the Corps, to serve in any Regiment or Station that they from time to time may be posted to In each Regiment there were to be two Regimental Officers, a Captain Instructor and Subaltern Instructor, and from the Corps second and third class Serjeant Instructors When the Regiment enters upon Foreign Service the junior of each Rank goes to the Depôt

Early in the year 1861 the War Department made purchases of considerable extent of land at Fleetwood, and a northern School of Musketry was established there, under the Warrant of the 27th September, 1861, which revised the previous Warrants, both schools being under one Inspector-General of Musketry, responsible as heretofore for the efficiency of the Troops in the use of their rifles. The total expenditure in land and buildings at Fleetwood up to December, 1864, amounted to £60,681, and the annual Vote, limited in 1853 to 1000*l*, had in 1869-70 increased to 10,664*l*, besides the pay of the Instructors throughout the Army.

(Z.)

Chapter XVI., par 65

THE SCHOOL OF GUNNERY AT SHOEBURYNÈSS.

THE acquisition of land by the Board of Ordnance at Shoeburyness commenced in 1849, and the last purchase of the War Department was in 1860, for the purpose of enabling the Royal Artillery to exercise upon a large range. In addition to the land purchased, two large tracts of sea shore are leased, at 250*l*. from a private owner, and at 10*l*. from the Office of Woods The total outlay for land and buildings amounts to £127,511 up to the date of this Note

To free the land between high and low water mark from intrusion, and to preserve the use of the estate for Artillery practice, the 25 & 26 Vic , c 36, was passed, enabling the Secretary of State to mark out certain Artillery ranges, and to prohibit vessels from passing over the site under certain penalties to be recovered by a summary method. By General Order of the 1st April, 1859, the "School of Gunnery at Shoeburyness" was established for individual improvement, as well as for the advancement of Artillery Science in general. The Staff of the School was fixed at —" 1 Commandant and Superintendent ; 1 Field Officer and Chief Instructor, 3 Instructors in Gunnery, 1 Brigade Major ,

1 Adjutant and Quartermaster; 1 Captain Instructor (Carbine), 1 Schoolmaster, 1 Serjeant-Major; 1 Quartermaster Serjeant, 6 Serjeant Instructors, 1 Serjeant Conductor of Stores, 2 Orderly Room Clerks, 2 Storemen"

The broad outline of the system was thus described :—

" An Artilleryman should unite with proficiency in his own branch of the Service many of the qualifications of a Cavalry or Infantry Soldier, and it is therefore hoped that, while Officers will naturally use their utmost endeavours to train efficient Gunners, they will not lose sight of the great advantages to be derived from a thorough knowledge of the drills and manœuvres of both Services, in enabling them to conform with confidence and judgment to combined movements of all Arms. For the furthering of this object the directions contained in the recognised manuals are to be strictly adhered to, and it will be hereafter pointed out in a ' Course of Instruction' what portion of the Infantry manœuvres may be dispensed with by the Royal Artillery

" As an Infantry Soldier is not considered fit for the ranks as a duty-man until he is well versed in the proper management of his weapons, so an Artilleryman is to be considered a Recruit until he is properly instructed in the *essential* requisites of an Artillery Soldier. Commanding Officers of Artillery will therefore bear in mind that Gunners are not to be detailed by them for ' duty' until dismissed Gun Drill. Thus, if attached to a Brigade liable to coast duty, a course of Garrison Gun Drill must be completed. With a view to rendering this period of probation as short as possible, ' system' is absolutely necessary, and this system will be the subject of mature consideration by the Staff of the School of Gunnery.

" At all Artillery Stations opportunities are afforded for instruction in those mechanical operations (commonly called the Repository Course), which form such an essential portion of an Artilleryman's training, and Commanding Officers must adhere strictly to the distribution of time as allotted to the various departments of instruction, in order that uniformity of system may be maintained.

" The instruction in the management of Rifled Ordnance will form the subject of special arrangements, and will, in the first instance, be carried on under the immediate superintendence of the Staff of the School of Gunnery, and be gradually disseminated throughout the Corps. It would now be premature to enlarge on this portion of the subject "

On the formation of the School of Gunnery the Repository at Woolwich was to be placed entirely under the Commandant, with an Officer of the School to carry on, under his orders, the Gunnery instruction of the Garrison, and the Commandant was permitted, if necessary, to detail Subaltern Officers to assist this Officer in his duties.

The first Estimate was for an annual Vote of 1500*l*, and the last, for 1869-70, of 5871*l*

(A A.)

Chapter XVI, *par* 72

ROYAL MILITARY ACADEMY, WOOLWICH.

THE first Educational Establishment that was created by the Crown and sanctioned by a vote of public money was the Royal Military Academy at Woolwich, in 1741   Prior to this time, Artillery, as a science, is said to have been little understood, and that England had no Artillery Force of its own upon which the country could rely, all the duty of this branch of the Military Service being performed by Foreigners.[1] However that may have been, the "two old marching companies of Artillery" were augmented by a New Company, under a Royal Warrant of 21st of April, 1740,[2] and the Academy established

The Instruction of the Artillery Corps was not to be the only object for which such an Institution was to be founded. The members of the associated corps— the Engineers—were to be admitted to the same advantages. What the requirements for these Scientific Corps and their duties were, will be seen by referring to the Order in Council of 1683,[3] and it became apparent that the Public must furnish instruction in special subjects, to enable these corps to attain Military proficiency

The want of such instructions "for raw and unexperienced people belonging to the Military branch of the Ordnance in the several parts of mathematics necessary to qualify them for the service of the Artillery and the business of Engineers," was set forth to George II , and it was proposed to fit up a convenient Room at Woolwich Warren for a school or academy. This was sanctioned by Royal Warrant of 30th April, 1741 (under the countersign of

---

[1] See Mr Courtenay's (Surveyor-General to Ordnance) Speech, 24 Parl Hist , p 120   [2] 23 Com. Journ , p 579.   [3] Appendix XVI., p 461

Newcastle), and the Master-General of the Ordnance was authorised to appoint an able and skilful master and assistants, to make rules for the government of the school, and to provide instruments, books, and other necessaries at a total cost not exceeding 500*l.* per annum [1]

The sum of 500*l* appears to have been too small a limit, for it was increased to 1000*l.* per annum by a second Warrant of the 18th Nov., 1741, before the first Estimate was submitted to Parliament which (so far as the Academy is mentioned), was in these words [2]—"The charge of an Academy for the instruction of the inexperienced people belonging to the Military branch of this office, by His Majesty's Warrants of 30th April and 18th Nov, 1741—1000*l* "—a sum at which the Estimate continued to stand until the vote was increased to 1364*l* 14*s* in the year 1771 [3]

Rules appear to have been immediately framed and the Academy established the chief Master (Mr. John Muller) receiving 200*l*, and the second Master (Mr. Derham) 100*l.* per annum The course of study " to form good officers of Artillery and Perfect Engineers " was laid down with care, three days being given to theory and three days to practice in each week. During the lectures—which were to be open to the privates as well as to the officers—an officer of the Royal Artillery was to keep order ; but the *men* were to be instructed with the officers in practice under the directions of the Commanding officer of Artillery.

The front of a Polygon of the largest dimensions the ground would admit of was to be raised—as an earthwork—to be attacked every other and repaired every other summer, as instruction. An annual examination was to be held, and the scholars classed under certificates from the Chief Engineer, the Commanding Officer of Artillery, and the Chief Master of the School 1st, as the most distinguished, 2nd, as the most industrious, and 3rd, as those from whose proficiency little is to be expected.

" A Great and Solemn Exercise of Artillery was also to be performed " once a year in the presence of the Master-General and Board of Ordnance, and prizes given—of honour—to an Engineer Officer or Cadet, or—of money—to a private man

At the time when the Academy was opened, the Laboratory was upon a Peace Establishment, under the care of a Bombadier only, but in the year 1746 it was reformed, and the rules (as will be seen from the extracts given) made it subservient to the instruction of the Engineers and Artillery

Thus, for experiment,—" All Engineers, Officers, Bombadiers,

---

[1] ' Records of the Royal Military Academy, 1851 '　　[2] 24 Com. Journ , p 48
[3] ' Records of the Royal Military Academy,' p 2

Cadets, Gunners, and Matrosses, shall have free leave to improve themselves in the art of firewo'king . . . and whatsoever firework such Engineer. Officer, Bombadier, Cadet, Gunner, or Matross has made or fitted up, the Firemaster or his mate shall put the maker's name thereon before they are delivered into store, to the end that when they shall be tried, the Composer may have notice to see the merits or defects of his performance,"—and to secure the public service from loss—" no Engineer, Officer, Bombadier, Cadet, Gunner, or Matross, or any other person employed in the Laboratory, was to presume to take from thence any work which was composed either by themselves or others within the same."[1]

So, again, the Students of the Academy were to be instructed in the work of the Laboratory, the rules providing against any secret inventions being kept, to the detriment of the public service, for the benefit of the inventor, thus —"That the Firemaster and his mate, diligently, carefully, and properly instructed all Officers, Bombadiers, Cadets, Gunners, and Matrosses, and all others employed or to be employed in the Laboratory, in the whole art of making fire-works for real use as well as for triumph, and in every branch thereof, *without concealing any part* thereof, and that they do enter *fairly into a book all receipts of* composition, titled with the uses for which they are designed, with the manner of compounding, preparing, fitting, and working up all parts of fireworks, whether compositions, machines, or cases, and the said book *shall be an office book*, to be inspected by *all* such as are ordered to attend the Labora-tery, and *are* willing to be instructed therein "

In July, 1764, the School was styled the Royal Military Academy, and by Warrant of the Master-General on the 12th, a Lieutenant-Governor to the Academy (Capt. Pattison), was appointed to super-intend and see that the Regulations (which were then revised) were duly carried out. Barracks had been erected for the Cadets, and each on appointment had to proceed to Woolwich for attendance at the Academy, but the officers and privates of the Corps were no longer required to attend for instruction.

For many years there was no preliminary examination for the admission of Cadets, and young men were sometimes found without the elements of education, as "writing or reading." In the year 1772 a Cadet was returned to his father, that these and the rule of three might be taught to him before he came up for re-admission.[2] and to remedy this evil, and to insure a competent knowledge in the first four rules or arithmetic, the rule of three, the declension of

---

[1] 16th Report on Military Inquiry, p 69, and Chap. XX, par 43
[2] 'Records of the Royal Military Academy,' p. 22

the nouns, and conjugation of verbs by the Latin grammar,[1] a qualifying examination was sanctioned in 1774.

It would be useless to trace the history of the Royal Military Academy in further detail. It is sufficient to say that it was removed to sir Gregory Page's house on Woolwich Common, in or about the year 1783, which property the Ordnance purchased with the sanction of Parliament in that year for 18,000l.[2] At the present time the candidates, between sixteen and nineteen years of age, are admitted by competitive examination, under the Council of Military Education, and it has, like Sandhurst, assumed in recent years the aspect of a quasi benevolent establishment, the pupils being admitted on varying rates of charge according to the supposed means of the parents or their claims upon the Treasury

Every Candidate for examination must (besides his Register of Baptism) send such a Certificate of good *moral* character as shall be satisfactory to the Commander-in-Chief, and be examined by a Military Surgeon as to his physical ability. He is at liberty to remain three years to pass for his commission, but he may go up at any earlier period that he may be deemed qualified. He engages, upon admission, to abide by the orders of the Lieutenant-Governor, and the rules and discipline of the Service.[3]

With regard to Field Works, the Junior Officers of the Royal Engineers—before receiving their final commission and entering upon the general duties of the corps—pass through a course of practical instruction at Chatham, the Establishment of which is fixed by Royal Warrant of the 1st July, 1850.

The Officers of the Royal Artillery were invited by General Regimental Order of 2nd November, 1863, to qualify themselves for employment in connection with the Manufacturing departments, the Civil establishment of the Royal Military Academy, and generally for all appointments (not being Military Staff appointments) special to the Artillery Service. The mode of entering into this advanced class of instruction at Woolwich Arsenal is by competitive examination, and the candidates must have served six years and undergone a course of instruction at Shoeburyness

The instruction extends over two years, and embraces in succession the special duties of each manufacturing department (1) The Royal Gun Factories, (2) the Inspector of Artillery, (3) the Royal Small Arms Factories, (4) The Royal Carriage Department, (5) The Superintendent of Stores, (6) The Royal Laboratory The Professor of Applied Mathematics, and the several

[1] 'Records of the Royal Military Academy,' p 26
[2] 24 Parl Hist, p 120   [3] Circular, 1st May, 1868

Lecturers, proceed in corresponding order through their subjects
Periodical examinations are held,[1] and certificates given. The
instruction is gratuitous.

(B B.)

THE ARMY MEDICAL SCHOOL.

MEDICAL men have always been attached to each Regiment, and
received pay as regimental officers of the Army.[2] At the time of
their first appointment it would appear that charges for drugs were
made against the Crown, and to place these upon the footing of an
allowance the following Orders were[3] issued in 1673.—

"CHARLES R

"WHEREAS, for the preventing of the great and uncertain charge of
Apothecaries' bills of physic and internal medicines for sick soldiers,
We have thought fit to allow forty shillings a year to Richard
Whittle for providing of physic and internal medicines besides the
forty shillings for each company allowed to the Surgeon of the
Regiment of Our Foot Guards for external medicines yearly, which
said allowance of forty shillings yearly for physic or internal medicines is to commence from the twentieth of September last. Our
Will and Pleasure, therefore, is that you take notice thereof, and
give it in orders, that when the non-commissioned officers and private soldiers respectively shall be sick, the said Richard Whittle
may be applied to for internal medicines, as well as hurt men are
to apply to the Surgeon of the Regiment for external medicines,
when they need the same

"Given at Our Court at Whitehall, the 24th day of January,
1673.

By His Majesty's Command,

"ARLINGTON"

"*To Our Trusty and Well-beloved Colonel John
Russell, or other the Officer in Chief commanding Our Regiment of Foot Guards under his
command.*"

---

[1] The 2nd General Report by the Council of Military Education, 1865, p. 151.

[2] Pay before and after 1782, see 9th Report (1782), and 19th Report of Finance
Committee (1797), p 394   Warrant to improve the condition of Medical Officers
in May, 1804, Mis Bk., 1802, p. 257

[3] Mis Bk 512a, p. 76, and there is an entry of 13th July, 1673-4 suspending a surgeon for not having given tests of qualification under the late Act of
Parliament—Mis Bk, p 333

" CHARLES R

" WHEREAS, for the preventing of the great and uncertain charge of Apothecaries' bills of physic and internal medicines for sick soldiers, We have thought fit to allow twenty shillings a year for each Regimental Company of three score soldiers besides officers, to the respective Surgeons of Regiments, from the twentieth of September last, for providing and furnishing of physic and internal medicines, as well as there has been and is forty shillings yearly, for each such company allowed to the said Surgeons for external medicines for the respective requirements in which they serve. Our Will and Pleasure therefore is, that you take notice thereof, and that you give it in orders, that when the non-commissioned officers or private soldiers of your Regiment shall be sick or wounded, the Surgeon of your Regiment do provide physic or internal medicines, as well as external medicines for them

" Given at Our Court at Whitehall, the 24th day of January, 1673.

" By His Majesty's Command,

" ARLINGTON."

" *To Our Trusty and Well-beloved Colonel Sir*
  Charles Littleton, or the Officer in Chief com-
  manding Our most dear Brother James, Duke
  of York's Regiment'

In the year 1710 an Act (9 Anne, c. 8) was passed to renew the Mutiny Act, and for approving of medicines for the Army,[1] " to the end," as the enactment explained, " that His Majesty's Forces might be supplied with good and wholesome medicines, internal and external, and for preventing the loss and suffering of many officers and soldiers for want thereof" All Surgeons and Apothecaries in the Army were therefore bound to fit up their medicine chests at Apothecaries' Hall, and to have them examined and certified by the Master and Wardens of the Apothecaries' Company, and the Physician or Surgeon-General of the Army

This arrangement was terminated (if it continued so long) by the appointment of an Apothecary-General under patent, first granted on the 17th March, 1735, and afterwards renewed on the 19th January, 1747, in favour of Mr. Garnier, to obey the King and His superior officer for the time being, and to furnish good and wholesome medicaments to the Army. The pay was 10s a day,

---

[1] 9 Stat Realm, p. 390

but the principal emoluments were derived from the monopoly of supply, which was, up to June, 1807[1] (if not a later date), made by deputy.

The earliest trace of a distinct Administrative Organization is said to date from 1756, when Lord Barrington, as Secretary at War, was directed to establish an Hospital Board for the Medical Service of the Army, then intended to take the field, that under its direction this part of the Military Service (including medicines, hospital stores, and other requisite provision for the sick) might be carried into execution with ability, regularity, and despatch[2]

To limit[3] all contingent expenses for nurses and hospitals, or for sick men or recruits coming from the regiment, an allowance of 30*l* a year to each regiment of Foot in Great Britain, was sanctioned by the King on the 5th August, 1768, and Lord Barrington issued a circular to the colonels of the Infantry Regiments, " that as this allowance was sufficiently ample to bear any expense that can properly occur for the relief of the sick, and being considered an essential service to the regiments, His Majesty had no doubt of the Colonel's careful application of it to that service, agreeably to this most gracious intention,"[4] &c. Probably these arrangements continued on foot till the Army was supplied with medicines in kind by order in 1795.[5]

In October, 1793, the departments of Surgeon-General and Inspector of Regimental Infirmaries were separated, the two appointments being filled by Mr. Gunning and Mr. Keates. In January, 1794, Sir L Pepys was appointed Physician-General, and these three officers constituted the Medical Board until March, 1798, when it was dissolved

The arrangements then made were that each of these three officers should have a separate duty and responsibility[6] under Regulations then issued by the Secretary at War. The subsequent history of the Medical Department will be found fully set forth in the fifth Report of the Commissioners of Military Inquiry, whose Report was presented to Parliament in January, 1808

After the Crimean War a Royal Commission was issued on the 5th May, 1857 (to the late Lord Herbert and others), to inquire into the organization, government, and direction of the Medical Depart-

---

[1] See the 5th Report of the Commissioners of Military Inquiry (1807) as to the Army Medical Department, pp 218, 219, and see also 6th Report of the same.
[2] Sanitory Report, p. 421   [3] War Office Letter Bk 212, p 102
[4] On the same day each Regiment of Cavalry engaged on Coast Duty had an allowance of 20*l* per annum, to make up the deficiency arising on the charge for attendance and medicine, over the Regimental stoppage.—War Office Letter Bk 212, p 101   [5] Mis. Bk, p 495.   [6] 5th Rep., p 96

ment of the Army. An elaborate Report (undated) was presented
to Parliament in 1858, and from the recommendations contained in
it emanated the "Army Medical School to teach the specialties of
Military Medicine Surgery, Hygiène and Sanitary Science," which
could not be obtained in any Civil Medical School in the country.

Two model Hospitals were built, one at Netley, at the cost (in
land and building only) of £334,172, and another (the Herbert) at
Woolwich at the cost for the like items of £228,355, the one being
at £294, and the other at £314 per man[1] At the former Hospital the Army Medical School was established in 1863, under a
Senate appointed by the Secretary of State for War

By the first section of the Regulations of October, 1859, the
candidate, to enter this School,[2] must be unmarried and between
the ages of 26 and 21 inclusive, free from disease or any imperfec-
tion or disability that can interfere with the more efficient discharge
of his duty in any climate. He must also possess a Diploma in
Surgery, or a licence to practise it, as well as a Degree in Medicine,
or a licence to practise it in Great Britain or Ireland[3]

The candidates are then examined as to their educational attainments, and such candidates as pass may be arranged in three classes
of proficiency, and enter the School

While there, every student is required to conform to the rules
of discipline laid down by the Senate, and an allowance made to
each one of 5s with, or of 7s. a day without quarters. He has
to attend an entire course of practical instruction in (1) Hygiène,
(2) Clinical and Military Medicine, (3) the like Surgery, (4) Patho-
logy, and injuries incident to Military Service—these courses not
being of less than four months' duration At their conclusion, the
candidate, under the 8th Rule, has to pass an examination, of which
there are two in each year, by the Professors of the School; and, if
qualified, he will be considered eligible for a commission as Assistant
Surgeon.

In August, 1867, was founded a "Sidney Herbert Prize," in
connection with the School, for encouraging the study of Army
Medical Science. The trustees are Sir John Pakington, the Right
Honourable W. E. Gladstone, and Douglas Galton, Esq. The fund
consists of 1345l. 12s. 3d, 3l. per cent Consols, and the dividends
may be applied,—

"1st That one prize, to be called 'Sidney Herbert's Prize,'
shall be awarded at the end of each of the two sessions of the said
Army Medical School year to the candidate for a commission of

---

[1] Chap. XV, par. 167   [2] Warrant of 17th Oct, 1859
[3] 21 & 22 Vic, c. 90, sec 36.

Assistant Surgeon in the Army, who shall pass the best examination at the Examination for Commissions, in pursuance of the 8th rule of the 1st section of the said Royal Warrant, or of any rule to be substituted for the same 8th rule in case of the same being varied or superseded by any new rule respecting the matter of such 8th rule.

"2ndly. That such prize shall consist partly of a gold Medal and partly of a Gratuity in money, or wholly of a Gratuity in money, in the discretion of the said Secretary of State, or in any other form or way which such Secretary shall think fit to adopt or approve of

"3rdly. That the aggregate amount of dividends of the said Trust Fund accruing in each and every year shall be divided into two equal portions, and one of such portions shall be applied or disposed of in providing for, or as the prize to be awarded at the end of the session for the time being just ended or being about to end '.

The pay and promotion of Surgeons are regulated by Royal Warrant of the 1st October, 1858, and their duties by Regulations of 1859 and 30th January, 1864

(C C)

Chapter XVI, *par* 95.

ON THE PAYMENT OF HALF-PAY TO ANY OTHER PERSON THAN THE OFFICER OR HIS AGENT

To continue the subject opened in the text, in the first place, the Warrant of the 29th June, 1844[1] which is the authority for the payment of half-pay, runs in these terms. It declares that Warrant to be the "Establishment of half-pay officers from the 1st of April, 1844, and to continue in force until further orders." It then authorizes the Paymaster-General, "out of such moneys as are in, or shall come, to your hands for this use, you do pay unto the *several Officers* named in the following list, by quarterly payments or otherwise, the daily or annual rates of half-pay or of military allowances against their names respectively set down, from the 1st day of

(margin note:) A D. 1844 Warrant to Paymaster-General for payment of half-pay.

---

[1] Until this year this Warrant was issued annually to the Paymaster-General, but this Warrant is the last that has been issued by Her Majesty

April, 1844, or to the respective days on which any of them shall
die, or shall cease to be entitled thereto, upon their producing, or
Declaration required causing to be produced to you, declarations made and
signed by such of them as are, or shall be, resident within
Our United Kingdom of Great Britain or Ireland, before one of Our
Justices of the Peace, affirming that they are entitled to such daily
or annual allowances, and that they had not any other place or
employment of profit, Civil or Military, under us," &c (following
the terms of the Appropriation Act), "or, in the case of the absence
of any of the said reduced Officers out of Great Britain or Ireland,
then, upon producing, or causing to be produced, to you declarations
in writing of the purport above-mentioned, signed by the said Officers,
and made before, and attested by, a British Minister, Secretary of Em-
bassy, Secretary of Legation, or Consul, by a Notary Public, or by some
Magistrate or Magistrates, or other person competent to administer
such a declaration, specifying the place where such Officer shall
then be resident, or, in the case of the death of any such Officer,
upon declarations and certificates of some credible person, proving
to your satisfaction the time when, and the place where, the Officer
died, and that he had not, to the best of the knowledge and belief
of the person or persons signing such declarations or certificates,
any other place or employment as above-mentioned."

It then gives the Secretary at War authority to settle any
doubtful questions that may arise on the declarations
Secretary at War's autho- rity that are presented to the Paymaster-General, thus, " that
in all cases where such declarations, certificates, or other
documents may be deemed objectionable, on the ground of any
variation therein from the form prescribed, or of any erasures,
interlineations, omissions, or irregularities appearing therein, you
do accept the same notwithstanding such variation or defect, upon
Our approbation thereof being signified to you by a communication
from Our Secretary at War, such communication specifying in each
case the objection to which it is intended to be applied "

Lastly, it provides for payment to agents, &c., of the Officers,
Payment to Agents that in case the payment of any of the allowances borne
on this Establishment shall not be personally claimed by
the Officers themselves, the several persons respectively authorized
by the Officers or their representatives to receive the same, shall,
in writing under their hands, attest and declare that they verily
believe such declarations or certificates respectively to be genuine
and authentic And for so doing, this, with the *acquittances of the
said Officers*, or of their respective assigns or representatives, and
the declarations and certificates above-mentioned, shall be, as well
to you as to the Commissions for Auditing the Public Accounts and

all others whom it doth or may concern, a sufficient warrant and discharge "

The Annual Appropriation Act in declaring the rules under which half-pay shall be applied, provides — "That the rules hereafter prescribed shall be duly observed in the application of the said half-pay, (that is to say,) that no person shall have or receive any part of the same without making and subscribing a declaration to such purport and effect as shall be required in that behalf *by Her Majesty's Warrants directing the issue of the half-pay to be received,*[1] that no person shall have or receive any part of the same who was under the age of 16 years at the time when the Regiment, Troop, or Company," &c *(margin: Appropriation Act, 1867)*

The *Statutory* obligation imposed on the Officer of making an affidavit appears to have been by the Appropriation Act of 1799,[2] and Officers were also, for the first time, allowed to hold "Garrison and Staff Pay," with their half pay. The Act directed that the oath, the words of which were prescribed, should be taken *instead of the oath usually taken by Officers to entitle them to half-pay,* and that taking the oath, without taking any other, should "be sufficient to entitle the Officer to receive his half pay" *(margin: A D. 1766 / Oath imposed by Statute)*

The "oath usually taken" was prescribed by the Royal Warrant issued annually with the half-pay Establishment So long as the oath rested solely upon a Royal Warrant, the administration of it could be dispensed with by the same authority, and there are entries in the War Office books[3] showing that Royal Warrants were issued by the Secretary at War to the Paymaster-General, dispensing with affidavits from particular Officers *(margin: Prior thereto by Warrant)*

But from the time that the oath was imposed as a *statutory* obligation upon the Officer,[4] it became illegal in the Crown to dispense with it, and although the Appropriation Acts[5] have given a discretion to the Crown as to the *form* and *requisites* of the oath, such confidence would create a stronger obligation upon the Responsible Minister to provide in the form ample security that the money should be paid only to those Officers for whom it was voted by Parliament When half-pay has been issued without the affidavits prescribed by the statute, an indemnity to all persons concerned in the issue has been inserted in the Appropriation Act of the next year *(margin: Cannot be dispensed with / Statutory indemnity needed)*

---

[1] The words in Italics have been omitted from the Appropriation Act, since 1869, but the clause was adopted in 1821 (1 & 2 Geo. IV, c 122, sec 23)
[2] 39 Geo III, c 144 sec 24
[3] Mis Bk 522, p 99, January, 1716, but see Lord Barrington's refusal on legal grounds, L B, 1766, p 237   [4] Broom, Const Law, p 504
[5] See 1 & 2 Geo IV, c 122, s 24, and other instances

(D D.)

Chapter XVI, *par* 116.

ON THE MILITARY KNIGHTS OF ST GEORGE [1]

THE order of *Military Knights of Windsor* (previously to William IV's reign called the Poor Knights of Windsor) was originally founded by Edward III. (22nd year of his reign) for twenty-four poor Knights "impotent of themselves or inclining to poverty." Their endowments were provided out of the revenues of the Dean and Canons of St George's Chapel, Windsor, until the 22 Edward IV was passed, discharging the Dean and Canons from bearing all charges of the Knights

The present "foundation" rests wholly upon the will of Henry VIII. (3rd December, 1546), an Indenture of 4th August, 1547 (made in pursuance of the Will), and Rules executed by Elizabeth 30th August, 1559, for the regulation thereof

Estates were then conveyed to the Dean and Canons of St George, and a "continual charge" of 433*l.* 19*s* 6*d.* placed on the same for the Poor Knights [2]

Under these instruments were established 13 Poor Knights [3] (whereof one was to be the Governor of all the residue), "to be taken of gentlemen brought to necessity, such as have spent their lives in the service of the War, Garrisons, or other service of the Prince, having but little or nothing whereupon to live, to be continually chosen by Us, Our Heirs and Successors."

In Queen Anne's reign, they appear, from an entry in the War Office Books, [4] to have been admitted upon a Certificate of Qualification from the Secretary at War, thus —

"WHITEHALL, 1*st May*, 1706

"These are to certify the Right Reverend Bishop of Salisbury, Chancellor of the most noble Order of the Garter, or whom else it may concern, that Lieutenant Henry Phillips, late of Sir R Temple's Regiment, who has served for many years in the Army, and is now by age and other infirmities become unfit for further service, is recommended by His Grace the Duke of Marlborough to supply one of the vacancies of the Poor Knights of Windsor.

"H ST JOHN."

---

[1] 116 H D (3), p. 208, 130 ib., pp 1071, 1336, 133 ib, pp 210, 1305
[2] 422 Parl Proc. (H C), 3rd May, 1850
[3] Certificate of Secretary at War (St John), 1706, Mis Bk 519, p 55
[4] Mis Bk 519, p 55

The House in which they live were built within the Chapter Close in Mary's reign, and the residue of the estates having increased to 14 000*l* a year, an information was filed by the Attorney-General *v.* Dean and Canons of Windsor[1] for a proportionate increase of endowment, but the information was dismissed

In 1861 the 24 and 25 Vic, c 116, passed, giving them the profits of two suspended Canonries.

The income is 39*l* 9*s* 4*d* ordinary, and 60*l* more or less under 24 and 25 Vic, c. 116 The fees on appointment were 5*l* 5*s* 4*d*[2]

(E E.)

Chap XVI, par. 120

A SECONDED OFFICER

THIS Officer holds a Commission in the Army which is in abeyance —until he returns to actual Service The term originated (I apprehend) from the former practice upon the reduction of a Regiment, of dividing the Officers into two lists, the first embracing those Officers who were continued in pay and Service, and the other, or second list, those Officers formerly in the Regiment, and who were again to join it as vacancies arose on 'the death or retirement of Officers named in the first List[3] In 1787 we find the Secretary at War complaining of the injury which this forestalling of future promotion was to the Service.[4]

The present seconding system dates from the Treasury Minute of 23rd Dec, 1836, and applies to the Ordnance Corps principally The object of the system was to afford to various Departments of the *Government* the occasional Services of Ordnance Officers in Civil duties, and to enable the Master-General to consider such Officer—while he was thus withdrawn from the Service—as supernumerary and to fill up his vacancy until his return to Military duty, subject to these regulations[5] —

"That no officer of the Artillery or Engineers whose services shall be afforded to any civil department of the Government shall be considered supernumerary unless it be probable that the employment in which he is to be engaged will continue for two years

"That in every case in which the services of an Ordnance

---

[1] 24 Ben Rep, p 679   [2] 308 Parl Proc (H C), 23rd May, 1865
[3] Note G , Vol I p 369, *ante*   [4] 26 Parl Hist , p 1283, 29 ib , p 811
[5] Report on Promotion, 1858 (By Command)

Military Officer are applied for, it shall be submitted for the consideration of this Board whether the case come within this rule, and whether, in addition to the remuneration which is to be granted for performing the civil duties, he shall receive the whole or any part of his military pay.

"That if, during the continuance of his civil employment, he shall be promoted to a higher military rank, such promotion shall not carry with it any increase of military pay, the military pay and allowance of such higher rank not to be received until the cessation of the civil service.

' That upon the cessation of such civil service, and the return of the officer to his military duties, no promotion shall take place in the grade in which he is serving until the number shall be reduced by his being absorbed into the rank

"They further recommend that this arrangement, so far as relates to their being considered supernumeraries, and so for as relates to increased military pay on promotion, should apply to all officers, either of Artillery or Engineers, whose services may have been already given to any civil department, the duration of whose employment in such civil service shall have been greater than two years"

These rules were afterwards amended by Treasury Minute of 14th Dec, 1849, thus —

" *Memorandum as to the Conditions on which Officers of Engineers or Artillery may be employed in the Civil Service*

"1. *Officers Lent* —Officers may be lent for short periods, not exceeding two years, for temporary service. In this case the officers will receive the military pay (without extra pay or allowances) from the Ordnance and such emoluments from the department of the civil service in which they are employed as may be fixed at the time

"2. *Officers Seconded* —Officers whom it may be considered requisite to employ in the civil service for a period longer than two years are to be removed from the effective strength of the corps and placed on a seconded list as at present, for any time not exceeding ten years, after which they must either return to their corps or be dealt with as hereinbefore mentioned.

" Officers so situated *will retain their position in the corps as regards promotion*, but will receive no military pay, the whole of their emoluments being provided by the civil department in which they are employed

" In the event of application being made for the services of a subaltern officer, the Master-General is to determine, in each case, whether the officer has sufficient military service to allow of his absence from his military duties

"In the event of an application for this more permanent employment of an officer already lent to the civil service, the period of ten years for which he may be seconded is to commence, not from the time of his being lent, but from the time of his being seconded, so that the period of his absence may in this case extend altogether for a period of twelve years, but not longer

' 3 *Officers permanently employed in the Civil Service.*—Officers whom it may be desirable to continue in the civil service beyond the periods above stated, must (if they prefer remaining in the civil service to returning to their corps) retire permanently from the military service, and be placed on the retired list of the full-pay or half-pay of their actual rank, according to their military claims They will retain all the privileges of officers placed on the retired list in other respects, and also any claim which they may have acquired for pensions for their widows.

"During the period of their continuance in the civil service, the whole of their emoluments will be derived from the civil service, as in the case of seconded officers. On retiring from their civil employment, they will be entitled to receive their retired full-pay or half-pay from the Ordnance, as the case may be, together with such amount of superannuation from the civil service as they may have acquired a claim to, regard being always had to the amount of their retired military pay as directed by the 4 & 5 Wm IV c 24."

And again, by another Minute of 19th Oct., 1855 —

"1. That when the services of an officer of Royal Artillery or Engineers may be temporarily required in a civil department, and absence from his regular duties can be allowed without inconvenience to the military service, the Commander-in-Chief should grant him leave of absence for a period not exceeding six months, that in such case the officer should remain, in regard to rank, pay, and progressive promotion, in the same position as he would have been if granted leave of absence under ordinary circumstances on account of health or private affairs, and that the civil department employing such officer should make such addition to his military pay as will afford him adequate remuneration, when added to his pay, for the duty he may have to perform.

"2. In every case, and without exception, if the civil duty and employment lasts more than six months, and the officer prefers continuing in such employment, instead of going back to his military duty, he should be made supernumerary in his corps, *that he should nevertheless retain his rank with the progressive promotion in his corps to which his position may entitle him;* but that he should draw no military pay whatever, the whole of his remuneration being provided by the civil department in which he may be employed, that if, at the expiration of ten years, or earlier in case his civil employment should cease, he should return to his corps, he should, in such case, be considered as supernumerary, and fall into the first vacancy, but if, after the expiration of ten years, he should prefer remaining in his civil employment, he should then be placed on the retired list of his corps, and that on such officer first becoming supernumerary, his place in his corps should be filled up by an effective officer, so as to keep the corps always complete and efficient."

A Supernumerary draws pay from his Corps, and is an excess upon the Establishment.

(F F)

Chapter XVI, par 127

BREVET RANK

THE grant of Military Rank rests solely with the Crown,[1] but Regimental Rank was the only rank for many years known "Brevets," or grants of General Army Rank, were introduced at an early period in the reign of William III.

"With regard to the word 'Brevet' applied to the Army, as distinguished from Regimental promotion. it may be well to note that the first entry of a grant of Brevet Rank to be found in the books of the War Office occurs in 1692. It was a Commission granted by William III, who was then in Flanders, dated Brussels, 10th May, 1692, conferring a Brevet upon Francis Hawley, to command as Colonel of Dragoons, and in the same year Lieutenant Baron Spaar had a Brevet to command as Captain, and William Seymour and Henry Withers had Brevets to command as Colonels."[2]

Brevets were supposed to exempt an Officer from his Regimental duty, and therefore a Royal Order of 12th July, 1708, was issued in these words —

" ANNE R.[3]

"Whereas the granting Brevets to Officers for Rank in particular Regiments hath proved highly prejudicial to our Service in regard

---

[1] Bradley v Arthur, 4 Bar and Cres, p 304

[2] Extract from Report on Naval and Military Inquiry, 1833, p xxx

[3] Mis. Bk. 519 (Ink), p 23

the same hath very much suffered for want of Officers to do duty in their respective Regiments according to the posts for which they are Commissioned, and receive pay Our Will and Pleasure is that all Officers in every of the Regiments named in the margin shall from henceforth do duty in their respective Regiments, according to the posts and characters for which they have full Commissions and received pay notwithstanding any Brevet granted to them for superior posts or rank　Whereof all Officers concerned are hereby required to take notice and pay due regard and complyance to this Our order.

"Given at Our Court at Windsor, this 12th day of July, 1708, in the 7th year of Our reign.

"By Her Majesty's Command,

"R. WALPOLE."

This, by a subsequent Order of the 2nd August, 1708, was applied to all the other Regiments of the Service [1]

The evils of the Brevet system again appear in the subsequent orders of Queen Anne, dated the 1st of May, 1711, "to redress the many irregularties and abuses introduced into the Army," [2] and were dealt with in these words —

"As it has been observed that Brevets have been obtained since Our Order to the contrary, dated the 12th of July, 1708, which creates great inconveniencies, and tends very much to the prejudice of Our Service . To restore, therefore, that order and method which has been lost in the promotion of Officers in Our Army, it is Our express Will and Pleasure that no more Brevets be granted for the future on any pretence whatsoever."

During the Peninsular War the grant of Brevet rank was used for the well-merited promotion of many gallant Officers, for whose advancement in the Regiment vacancies either did not exist, or could not be filled in by the Commander-in-Chief. The Duke of Wellington [3] therefore represented the case to the Home authorities, and was authorised to name Regimental Officers for Brevet rank — a power first exercised after the Battle of Barrosa, when all the Majors who had commanded Corps were promoted to the Brevet rank of Lieutenant-Colonel

The first General Brevet took place in 1760, and the Brevets were used for the advancement of Officers as a class, [4] until the system was put a stop to. The whole subject of military employment and

---

[1] Mis Bk 519 (Ink), p 27　　　　　　　[2] Mis Bk 520, p 50
[3] 'Report of Naval and Military Inquiry, 1840,' p xxxvi , and p 123 of Evidence.
[4] 'Army and Ordnance Expenditure Report, 1851,' p 36

reward had been investigated by a Select Committee of the House of Commons in 1833 (Army and Navy Appointments), by Royal Commission on Naval and Military Promotion in 1840, a Committee of the House of Commons on Army Expenditure in 1850, and again by Royal Commission on Army Promotion in 1854, and this alteration was the result

The four last General Brevets brought an increased charge on the Estimates (1) of 11,376*l* 13*s*. 9*d* for the Brevet of 10th January, 1837, (2) of 6593*l*. 17*s* 6*d*, for the Brevet of 28th June, 1838, (3) of 14,998*l* 15*s*. 10*d* for the Brevet of 23rd November, 1841, (4) and of 20,064*l* 2*s* 6*d* for the Brevet of 9th November, 1846 Brevets were made on the responsibility of the Cabinet, and the only control that Parliament could exercise was that of refusing—through the House of Commons—to vote the Pay.[1]

(G G.)

Chapter XVII, par 55

AS TO A SENTRY OR SENTINEL

THERE are other cases requiring notice in which the Military are posted as sentries or guards over public property, or over prisoners, therein acting rather in substitution than in aid of the Civil power Of course in these instances a distinction must be made in the powers which the Military possess over persons who are subject to the Mutiny Act or alien prisoners of war, and over those who are " Civilians "

Over persons subject to the Mutiny Act the sentry or guard must exercise that control which his own duty under the Mutiny Act and Articles of War would require from him and would justify, as every sentry or guard is posted in the camp or garrison with definite orders, which proceed from the highest Military authority therein. These are assumed to be lawful orders within the 38th Article of War, binding on all within the camp or garrison, and therefore such as the sentry is bound to enforce Disobedience, either in the sentry or other such offender, would subject both to punishment If, therefore, any person subject to the Mutiny Act disobeys these orders, the sentry, or rather the officer of the guard upon the warning of the sentry, has authority, under the 18th and 19th

---

[1] See Lord Panmure's Evidence, ' Army Expenditure, 1850,' Questions 1714-21 1749, 1792-94

Articles of War, to place the offender in arrest or confinement, until released by the General, or tried by Court-martial.

What degree of force a sentry may use to capture or prevent escape in such a prisoner is open to controversy[1] In 1806 a corporal of the 58th Regiment was tried, but acquitted, for shooting at a deserter prisoner escaping from his escort.[2] In reference to such case, Sir Charles Napier remarks· "He suffered imprisonment and great anxiety of mind for doing that, which if he had not done, he would have been tried by Military law, degraded, and possibly flogged   Where the corporal shot a soldier—a man of his own society, by the laws of which *both* were bound to act, and which laws are given to us by the same authority which enacts the social laws—it was surely inconsistent and unjust that his life should depend upon the opinions of twelve jurors—men ignorant of our Military laws and customs."[3]

If a sentry be posted over prisoners of war, the rules of the service would, it is presumed, justify his shooting them to prevent their escape, for sentries who, in obedience to their Military orders, shot the French prisoners who were in England[4] attempting to escape were defended by the Secretary at War against the charge of murder or manslaughter.

Towards civilians it is presumed that a sentry, not being a peace officer, can only exercise the control or authority which is incident to an ordinary caretaker or gaoler   As a caretaker in charge, and in peaceable possession, of Crown property, with orders to prevent trespass or entry, he may, if it be a house or inclosure, defend this possession by force, using, however, only such force as is absolutely necessary to preserve the property from trespass,[5] and I have ventured to suggest in another place,[6] whether in some places this power is sufficient.   The law "will justify what it would otherwise consider as an assault, if such be necessary to put the party out of possession without outrage and violence, yet not a charge of beating, wounding, and knocking the party down"[7]

The Court of Queen's Bench, in Anne's reign, laid it down in a case still cited as law   "There is a force in law as in every trespass, *quare clausum fregit*   If one enters into any ground, in that case the owner must request him to depart before he can lay hands

---

[1] As to two Recruits killed at the Savoy in 1703-4, L B 132, p 121
[2] Bk 724, p 35   [3] 33 H D (O S), pp 930, 34 ib, pp 482, 492, 566
[4] Book 724, p 19   [5] King v Wilson, 3 Ad & Ell , p. 825
[6] Vol I , p 14, note [3]
[7] 1 Hale, P C , p 486, Gregory v Hill, 8 Ter Rep, p 300

on him to turn him out, for every *impositio manuum* is an assault and battery which cannot be justified upon the account of breaking the close in law without a request. The other is an actual force as in burglary, as breaking open a door or gate, and in that case it is lawful to oppose force to force; and if one breaks down the gate, or comes into my close, *vi et armis*, I need not request him to be gone, but may lay hands on him immediately, for it is but returning violence by violence; so if one comes forcibly and takes away my goods, I may oppose him without any more ado, for there is no time to make a request."[1]

To prevent an entry, the sentry may place himself before the person entering, and his doing so will be no assault,[2] but if the entry into an inclosure be made with a felonious intent, or, if the intruder[3] be escaping with stolen property, the sentry would not be justified in shooting him, though he had no other means of bringing the offender to justice[4]

Again, though a sentry may forcibly remove, and be assaulted by a trespasser, he has no authority for taking him into custody: all that he can do is to crave the aid of the Civil power, and hand the offender over to a peace officer.[5]

"To justify the use of a weapon in defence of his life, the person must satisfy the jury that the defence was necessary[6] that he did all he could to avoid it, and that it was necessary to protect his own life, or to protect himself from such serious bodily harm as would give a reasonable apprehension that his life was in immediate danger If he used the weapon, having no other means of resistance, and no means of escape, in such case, if he retreated as far as he could, he will be justified."

"But if," writes Lord Hale,[7] "a thief assault a true man, either abroad or in his house, to rob or kill him, the true man is not bound to give back, but may kill the assailant, and it is not felony"

Again the same author puts this case[8]—"that if A attempts a burglary upon the house of B, to the intent to kill him, or attempted to burn the house of B, if B, or any of his servants, or any one within the house, had shot or killed A, this had not been so

---

[1] Green *v* Goddard, 2 Salkeld, p 640　See Anderson *v* Warstall, 1 Car and Kir, p. 359; Holmes *v* Bagge, 1 Ell and Blac., p 786

[2] Innes *v* Wilie, 1 Car and Kir, p 262　　[3] R *v* Scully, 1 Car and P, p 319

[4] See R V Dodson, 3 Car and Kir, p 149

[5] See Price *v* Seeley, 10 Clar and Fin, p 29; Gordon *v* Gibbon, 3 Fos and Fin, p 609; Bell and Axton, 4 Fos and Fin, p 1022

[6] Reg *v* Smith, 8 Car & Pay, p 162　　　[7] 1 Pleas of the Crown, p 481

[8] Ib, p 487

much as a felony, for his house is his castle of defence, and therefore he may justify assembling persons for a safeguard of his house."

Far more important questions have arisen as to the proper instructions to be given to the Military who are permanently quartered in Civil or Military gaols, or are sent specially thereto in aid of the Governor. As early as 1778 the Admiralty asked Lord Barrington (the then Secretary at War) to issue special instructions that the Soldiers might act promptly, so as to prevent the escape of persons committed for trial on the charge of high treason or piracy under the (temporary) Act 17 Geo III. cap 9. The instructions in force were that they should act under the immediate direction of the Civil Magistrate, and Lord Barrington refusing to issue any other orders, Lord Thurlow,[1] on being consulted, wrote as follows —

"Every gaol-keeper is responsible for his prisoners, and punishable if they escape. It is therefore his authority and duty to impose sufficient constraint on their persons, and to guard his prison with sufficient force Where sufficient constraint (that is, ordinarily sufficient), is put on their persons, and reasonable circumspection is used, there is little danger of an escape[2] It seldom happens in experience, perhaps never, without singular negligence But if, notwithstanding all this precaution, prisoners (for high treason, as this case is) should rise upon their keeper, or otherwise attempt their escape, he is justified in using every degree of force which will be found necessary to suppress and retain them. And if any of them should be killed, it being otherwise absolutely impossible to suppress and retain them, the homicide will be justifiable, but merely by the necessity of the case, which makes it the more incumbent on the gaoler to see to the constant and ordinary restraint of their persons

"The prisons appointed by His Majesty in pursuance of the late Act are exactly equivalent to common gaols, and to be kept in the same manner Therefore firing upon the prisoners merely because they are found in the act of attempting to escape, whether it be by stratagem or even open resistance, is not justifiable there must be such necessity as is mentioned before.

"The keeper of such prison is to be considered as a Civil officer. He is indictable at common law for their negligent escape, which he

[1] Book 722, p 21.
[2] Rex v Thomas, 1 Russ on Crimes, p. 823. The Mutiny Act Council have passed an Ordnance authorizing the Guard to shoot at Prisoners escaping (17 Vic No 7, 1854)

is said in the case to have permitted. His assistants also act in a character merely Civil, and this is equally true whether he and they be or be not Soldiers   It is difficult therefore, to imagine what instructions can properly issue from Lord Barrington's office beyond those which his Lordship speaks of, as the common orders to the Military. It is certain that he would not be justified in issuing such orders as those proposed in the question. In what way he can safely comply with the requisition of the Lords of the Admiralty, is a question not to be answered without a more particular state of that requisition."

(H H.)

Chapter XVII , par 73.

THE COURTS-MARTIAL ON (1) COLONEL BRERETON AND (2) CAPTAIN WARRINGTON, FOR NEGLECT OF DUTY AT THE BRISTOL RIOTS.

(I) ON the 2nd January, 1832, His Majesty issued his warrant for a general Court martial, and Lieutenant-Colonel Brereton, (Inspecting Field Officer of the Recruiting Service), was arraigned before it upon eleven separate charges, of which the following outline is given

(1.) That having the command of the troops in Bristol, with directions (duly authorized) to be in communication with the Justices, and to arrange with them for their disposal in the event of the troops being required, and great disturbance and riot prevailing on the 29th October, 1831, by reason whereof the troops were called out by the Justice of the Peace (and the Riot Act having been read), the said Lieutenant Colonel was several times directed by the Justices of the Peace to use force for the dispersion of the rioters and the restoration or maintenance of the public peace, nevertheless, he, the said Lieutenant-Colonel, did not act with any vigour or effect in execution of such direction, but for the most part declined or neglected to comply, and conducted himself in a feeble and temporizing manner, calculated only to encourage the rioters in their violent proceedings

(2.) That on the 30th, when the Justice of the Peace required the troops to save the Mansion House, &c , then violently attacked by the mob, the Lieutenant-Colonel brought the same, and then withdrew part of them five miles from Bristol, contrary to the declared wishes of the Justice of the Peace, and in violation of his duty of guarding the peace of the city.

(3) That the Lieutenant Colonel stated as his reason that the men and horses were jaded and exhausted, whereas they were in an efficient state and fit for duty

(4) That he refused to recall the said troops, though the tumult and riot were increasing in an alarming manner, &c.

(5) That when the rioters were broken into one prison, and were going to attack another, and the Justice of the Peace required the Lieutenant-Colonel to employ force, he refused so to do.

(6) That when the Bishop's Palace was being attacked, and the Justice of the Peace required troops to save the said Palace, the Lieutenant-Colonel with troops entered the Palace Yard, but remained wholly inactive, and gave most peremptory orders to the troops not to use any violence to the rioters, but permitted them to carry off plunder.

(7) That when the city was in flames, and he was in personal command, he made no attempt whatever to arrest the progress of the same, but, on the contrary, he marched off his troops or a greater part thereof

(8) That on the arrival of the Yeomanry he neglected to avail himself of their services

(9) That having received from the Mayor at twelve o'clock on the night of the 30th a letter, " to consider himself fully authorized to take whatever steps, and to give whatever orders he might think fit to restore peace and preserve, as far as possible, the public peace," he, for four hours after, did not take any steps, &c, whatever, but retired to bed.

(10) That when called out of bed by a Justice of the Peace, at four o'clock the next morning (31st), and desired to march troops to the Queen's Square, he manifested great reluctance to comply

(11) That at various times when it was his duty to put down the rioters, he temporized with them, frequently shaking hands, &c.

"Such conduct as aforesaid evincing great want of the vigour and decision requisite for the duties in which he was engaged, being right disgraceful to his character as an officer, and prejudicial to good order and military discipline, and tending to destroy the confidence of the troops in their officers, and to reflect dishonour on His Majesty's service "

It was proved on the first charge " That the accused was directed by the Justice of the Peace to disperse the mob, clear the streets, and get the city quiet as soon as possible, that an officer asked permission to protect his men by firing, but the accused said, ' Let the rioters alone, and they will go to bed,' that ' he would patrol and be answerable for the peace of the city,' that ' he required from the Justice of the Peace an explicit order to fire,' and he was told that if it was necessary to fire, he must fire, and he was quite unrestricted from any use of fire-arms, &c , that he commanded his troops to clear the street without drawing swords, or using violence, but afterwards to use force "

On the second, third, and fourth charges—"That the Justices of the Peace strongly objected to the sending away of troops, and urged their being brought back, that the Mayor did not conceive the troops were under his command, or that Justices of the Peace were competent to give orders how the troops were to act, but that the wishes of the civil authorites were to be conveyed to the Lieutenant-Colonel, in order to their being carried into execution. that the Justice of the Peace told the rioters, in the hearing of the Lieutenant-Colonel, that the troops would fire, and told the Lieutenant-Colonel that the rioting must be put down His reply to the Justice of the Peace was that the troops should not fire, but that he must keep the rioters in good humour, as his men were not equal to contend with the mob

At this point in the proceedings, viz , after the Court had closed on the fourth day, the accused officer having privately called on the Acting Judge-Advocate-General, destroyed himself, after offering to withdraw his pleas of "Not Guilty," and to plead guilty

The Court-martial had been preceded by a Court of Enquiry, and, therefore, the facts (of which the military authorities were cognizant) clearly satisfied them that the civil magistrates had, in then orders, given the military officer complete power and authority to take all necessary measures for the suppression of the riot and the restoration of the public peace

(II). The Court-martial on Captain Warrington found him guilty of the three charges on which he was arraigned for neglect of duty, and he was dismissed the service

The only matter worthy of notice is contained in the following extract from the reply of the official prosecutor (Major-General Sir Charles Dalbiac, K.C H , then the Inspector-General of Cavalry) —

"The principle then which most alarms me in the prisoner's address to the Court, and which he has attempted to maintain in different parts of his defence, is, that the refusal of an officer to act without a magistrate is '*in strict accordance with the Rules of the Service*'

"Standing as I do here at the suit of my Sovereign, I should ill indeed acquit myself of the trust which has been reposed in me, were I not to record upon the proceedings of this Court, my most distinct and decided protest against the doctrine thus set up by the prisoner, a doctrine at variance with all the declared opinions of all our soundest Crown lawyers since the days of Elizabeth—a doctrine, not '*in strict accordance with,*' but *most decidedly opposed* to the orders and regulations of His Majesty's Service, as well as to the law of this land—a doctrine calculated not only to destroy the moral as well as the professional principles of the soldier, but to expose the person as well as the property of the subject to violence and to destruction—a doctrine which if admitted would enable every officer when placed in the command of His Majesty's troops for the suppression of tumult, to place the inertness of the Civil Power between himself and the personal responsibility of his station, and, under the protection of such inertness, to shelter himself from blame and disgrace."

The prosecutor then quoted Lord Ellenborough's opinion of 1801 (in the appendix) Sir James Mansfield's ruling in Burdett *v.* Abbott, and Sir N Tindal's charge to the Grand Jury at Bristol

---

(I I.)

Chapter XVIII, par 45

RECENT INSTANCES IN WHICH MARTIAL LAW HAS BEEN PRO-CLAIMED IN BRITISH COLONIES OR SETTLEMENTS, TAKEN (ACCORDING TO DATE) FROM PARLIAMENTARY RECORDS ON EACH CASE, AND ARRANGED UNDER THE NAME OF THE COLONY.

Martial Law has been declared in—

1	Barbadoes	1805 and 1816
2	Demerara	1823
3	Jamaica	1831-2,—1865
4	Canada	1837-8
5	Ceylon	1817 and 1848
6	Cephalonia	1848
7.	Cape of Good Hope	1834, 1849-51
8	Island of St. Vincent	1863

1 —BARBADOES,[1] 1805 and 1816

In May, 1805, the Governor (Lord Seaforth) proclaimed Martial Law from the 19th, to continue to the 21st, but afterwards prolonged it to the 25th May These proceedings were premature, and

---

[1] 'History of Barbadoes,' by Schomburgh, London, 1848

the Assembly presented an address to the Governor,[1] the substance
of which is given in these Resolutions :—

" 2nd. That the common law of the United Kingdom of Great
Britain and Ireland is in force in this Colony, unless altered by
British Acts of Parliament, or the Legislative Acts of this Island

' 3rd. That by the 26th clause of the existing Militia Act of this
Island, it is enacted, ' that whatever Articles of War or Military
laws shall be by the Governor or Commander-in-Chief of this island
and Council made by and with the advice and consent of the major
part of the Council of War here, shall not commence or begin until
an enemy, sufficient to cause an alarm to the whole island, appear in
sight here, and shall discontinue and lose their power so soon as
the enemy shall be gone out of sight of this Island, provided always
that the said laws be duly published, and a copy thereof hung up in
every court of guard for public view.'

" 4th That any attempt to proclaim Martial Law, otherwise than
during the existence of the circumstances in the above-recited clause
stated, and with the forms thereby prescribed, is highly unconstitutional, contrary to law, and subversive of the dearest rights of the
people "

In July following—the Governor having in the interval sent the
address to the Colonial Office—replied to the Assembly in these
words :—" I am instructed that the preservation of Her Majesty's
Prerogative of declaring Martial Law is essentially necessary towards
this end, as without that power no security can be had for the safety
of the Colony "

In April, 1816, a rebellion broke out, Martial Law was again
proclaimed,[2] and continued in force till 12th July, when all the
Judges, Justices of the Peace, and others holding public offices were
required to resume the exercise of their several functions   While
the Proclamation was in force the Court-Martial sentenced many of
the rebels to death [3]

2—DEMERARA,[4] 1823.

The rebellion commenced on the 18th, and on the 19th August,
1823, the Governor (with the sanction of the Court of Policy)
declared Martial Law,[5] which remained in force till 15th January,
1824; but on the 22nd August an amnesty was proclaimed, with

---

[1] 'History of Barbadoes,' by Schomburgh, London, 1848, p 362   [2] Ib , p 265
[3] Ib , p 396   [4] 23 Sess. Papers (1824), p. 365 *et seq*   [5] Ib , p 459.

a warning, "That those remaining in arms after 48 hours must be dealt with as rebels, and place little hope in mercy."[1]

The Rev. John Smith was put on his trial before a Court-martial on the 13th October. The acts upon which he was charged were alleged to have been done on the 17th to the 20th August, and those of latest date in defiance of the Proclamation. Documentary evidence of and from the 2nd November, 1817, was also laid before the Court, and, on the 24th November, 1823, he was sentenced to death; but the sentence was not executed, and he died in the Colonial gaol, on the 11th February, 1824.[2]

The legality of these proceedings gave rise to a celebrated debate in the Commons, upon the motion of Lord then Mr. Brougham, that an Address be presented to the Crown, setting forth, "That the House deem it their duty to declare that they contemplate with serious alarm and deep sorrow the violation of law and justice which is manifest in these unexampled proceedings,"[3] &c

In opening the discussion, Lord Brougham stated his view of the circumstances that would justify the Crown in declaring Martial Law.—"It is very true, that formerly the Crown sometimes issued Proclamations, by virtue of which Civil offences were tried before Military tribunals[4] The most remarkable instance of that description, and the nearest precedent to the case under our consideration, was the well-known Proclamation of the august, pious, and humane Philip and Mary, stigmatising as rebellion, and as an act which should subject the offender to be tried by a Court-martial, the having heretical, that is to say, Protestant, books in one's possession, and not giving them up without previously reading them Similar Proclamations, although not so extravagant in their character, were issued by Elizabeth, by James I, and (of a less violent nature) by Charles I, until at length the evil became so unbearable that there arose from it the celebrated Petition of Right

"Since that time no such thing as Martial Law has been recognised in this country, and Courts founded on Proclamations of Martial Law have been wholly unknown And here I beg to observe, that the particular grievances at which the Petition of Right was levelled, were only the trials under Martial Law of military persons, or of individuals accompanying, or in some manner connected, with Military persons. On the abolition of Martial Law, what was substituted? In those days, a Standing Army in time of peace was considered a solecism in the Constitution Accordingly, the whole

---

[1] 23 Sess Papers (1824), p 461   [2] Ib, p 517
[3] So few readers are possessed of Hansard's Debates, that I have felt it better to print these full extracts   [4] 11 H. D. (2), p 968

course of our legislation proceeded on the principle that no such establishment was recognised Afterwards came the Annual Mutiny Acts, and Courts-martial, which were held only under those Acts These Courts were restricted to the trial of Soldiers for Military offences , and the extent of their powers was pointed out and limited by law.

  "One word more, before I advert to the proceedings of the Court, on the nature of its jurisdiction [1] Suppose I were ready to admit that, on the pressure of a great emergency, such as invasion or rebellion, when there is no time for the slow and cumbrous proceedings of the Civil law, a Proclamation may justifiably be issued for excluding the ordinary tribunals, and directing that offences should be tried by a Military court such a proceeding might be justified by necessity , but it could rest on that alone Created by necessity, necessity must limit its continuance It would be the worst of all conceivable grievances—it would be a calamity unspeakable—if the whole law and constitution of England were suspended one hour longer than the most imperious necessity demanded I know that the Proclamation of Martial Law renders every man liable to be treated as a Soldier But the instant the necessity ceases, that instant the state of soldiership ought to cease, and the rights, with the relations, of civil life to be restored "

  But admitting, for the sake of argument, the power to declare Martial Law, and that its effect was to render every man liable to be treated as a Soldier, yet, in the instance before the House, Lord Brougham insisted on its needless duration —

  " When Mr Smith was about to be seized, he was first approached with the hollow demand of the Officer who apprehended him,[2] commanding him to join the Militia of the district To this he pleaded his inability to serve in that capacity, as well as an exemption founded on the rights of his clerical character. Under the pretext of this refusal his person was arrested, and his papers were demanded and taken possession of Amongst them was his private journal, a part of which was with the intention of being communicated to his employers alone, while the remaining part was intended for no human eye but his own In this state of imprisonment he was detained, although the revolt was then entirely quelled. That it was so quelled is ascertained from the despatches of General Murray to Earl Bathurst, dated the 26th of August At least the despatch of that date admits that public tranquillity was nearly restored , and at all events, by subsequent despatches of the 30th and 31st, it appears that no further disturbance had taken

---

[1] 11 H D (2), p 976   [2] Ib , pp 967, 968

place, nor was there from that time any insurrectionary movement whatever. At that period the Colony was in the enjoyment of its accustomed tranquillity, barring always those chances of relapse which in such a state of public feeling, and in such a structure of society, must be supposed always to exist, and to make the recurrence of irritation and tumult more or less probable. Martial Law, it will be recollected, was proclaimed on the 19th of August, and was continued to the 15th January following—five calendar months —although there is the most unquestionable proof that the revolt had subsided, and indeed that all appearance of it had vanished."

He then dwelt upon the fact that all danger from rebellion was over when the Court-martial commenced its sittings —

"The only justification of the Court-martial was this Proclamation[1] Had that Court sat at the moment of danger there would have been less ground for complaint against it But it did not assemble until the emergency had ceased, and it then sat for eight-and-twenty days. Suppose a necessity had existed at the commencement of the trial, but that in the course of the eight-and-twenty days it had ceased,—suppose a necessity had existed in the first week, who could predict that it would not cease before the second ? If it had ceased with the first week of the trial, what would have been the situation of the Governor? The sitting of the Court-martial at all could be justified only by the Proclamation of Martial Law, yet it became the duty of the Governor to revoke that Proclamation. Either, therefore, the Court-martial must be continued without any warrant or colour of law, or the Proclamation of Martial Law must be continued only to legalise the prolonged existence of the Court martial If, at any moment before its proceedings were brought to a close, the urgent pressure had ceased which alone justified their being instituted, according to the assumption I am making in favour of the Court, and for argument's sake, then to continue Martial Law an hour longer would have been the most grievous oppression, the plainest violation of all law, and to abrogate Martial Law would have been fatal to the continuance of the trial But the truth is, that the Court has no right even to this assumption, little beneficial as it proves; for long before the proceedings commenced all the pressure, if it ever existed, was entirely at an end "

Waiving these objections, he urged that the Court martial had no authority to try the prisoner for any act done *prior to* the date of the Proclamation

"The charges against Mr Smith are four[2] The first states that,

_____

[1] 9 H D (2), p 976   [2] Ib, p 990

long before the 18th of August he had promoted discontent and dissatisfaction amongst the slaves against their lawful masters. This charge was clearly beyond the jurisdiction of the Court, for it refers to matters before Martial Law was proclaimed, and consequently before Mr Smith could be amenable to that law. Supposing that, as a Court-martial, they had a right to try a clergyman for a Civil offence, which I utterly deny, it could only be on the principle of Martial Law having been proclaimed that they were entitled to do so The Proclamation might place him, and every other man in the Colony, in the situation of a Soldier; but if he was to be considered as a Soldier, it could only be after the 19th of August. Admitting, then, that the Rev. Mr. Smith was a Soldier under the Proclamation, he was not such on the 18th, on the 17th, nor at any time before the transactions which are called the Revolt of Demerara, and yet it was upon such a charge that the Court-martial thought proper, and indeed was obliged to try him, if it tried him at all But they had no more right, I contend, to try him for things done before the 19th in the character of a Soldier liable to Martial Law, than they would have to try a man who had enlisted to-day for acts which he had committed the day before yesterday, according to the same code of Military justice "

The speech of Sir James Mackintosh,[1] in support of the motion, is of greater value. Referring to Martial Law, he said —

"The only principle on which the law of England tolerates what is called Martial Law, is necessity, its introduction can be justified only by necessity; its continuance requires precisely the same justification of necessity, and if it survives the necessity on which alone it rests for a single minute, it becomes instantly a mere exercise of lawless violence When Foreign Invasion or Civil War renders it impossible for Courts of Law to sit, or to enforce the execution of their judgments, it becomes necessary to find some rude substitute for them, and to employ for that purpose the Military, which is the only remaining Force in the community While the laws are silenced by the noise of arms, the rulers of the Armed Force must punish, as equitably as they can, those crimes which threaten their own safety and that of society, but no longer: every moment beyond is usurpation, as soon as the laws can act. every other mode of punishing supposed crimes is itself an enormous crime If argument be not enough on this subject, if, indeed, the mere statement be not the evidence of its own truth, I appeal to the highest and most venerable authority known to our law. 'Martial Law,' says Sir Matthew Hale, 'is not a law, but

---

[1] 9 H. D (2), pp 1046-9, and vol. III of Works, p. 107

something indulged, rather than allowed, as a law. The necessity
of government, order, and discipline in an army is that only which
can give it countenance. *Necessitas, enim quod cogit defendit*
Secondly, this indulged law is only to extend to members of the
Army, or to those of the opposite Army, and never may be so much
indulged as to be exercised or executed upon others. Thirdly, the
exercise of Martial Law may not be permitted in time of peace,
when the King's Courts are (or may be) open."[1] The illustrious
Judge on this occasion appeals to the Petition of Right, which, fifty
years before, had declared all proceedings by Martial Law, in time
of peace, to be illegal. He carries the principle back to the cradle of
English liberty, and quotes the famous reversal of the attainder
of the Earl of Kent, in the first year of Edward III, as decisive of
the principle, that nothing but the necessity arising from the
absolute interruption of Civil Judicatures by arms can warrant the
exercise of what is called Martial Law Wherever and whenever
they are so interrupted, and as long as the interruption continues,
necessity justifies it. No other doctrine has ever been maintained
in this country since the solemn Parliamentary condemnation of
the usurpations of Charles I, which he was himself compelled to
sanction in the Petition of Right. In none of the revolutions or
rebellions which have since occurred has Martial Law been exercised,
however much, in some of them, the necessity might seem to exist
Even in those most deplorable of all commotions which tore Ireland
in pieces in the last years of the eighteenth century, in the midst
of ferocious revolt and cruel punishment, at the very moment of
legalising these martial jurisdictions, in 1799, the very Irish statute
which was passed for that purpose did homage to the ancient and
fundamental principles of the law, in the very act of departing from
them. The Irish Statute 39 Geo. III, c 2, after reciting that
Martial Law had been successfully exercised to the restoration of
peace so far as to permit the course of the Common Law partially to
take place, but that the Rebellion continued to rage in considerable
parts of the Kingdom, whereby it has become necessary for Parliament to interpose, goes on to enable the Lord-Lieutenant 'to punish
rebels by Courts-martial' This Statute is the most positive declaration that, where the Common Law can be exercised in some parts of
the country, Martial Law cannot be established in others, though
rebellion actually prevails in these others, without an extraordinary
interposition of the supreme Legislative authority itself.

"I have already quoted from Sir Matthew Hale his position
respecting the twofold operation of Martial Law, as it affects the

---

[1] Hale's Hist Com Law, c 11

Army of the Power which exercises it, and as it acts against the Army
of the enemy. That great Judge, happily unused to standing
Armies, and reasonably prejudiced against Military jurisdiction,
does not pursue his distinction through all its consequences, and
assigns a ground for the whole which will support only one of its
parts. 'The necessity of order and discipline in an Army' is,
according to him, the reason why the law tolerates this departure
from its most valuable rules, but this necessity only justifies the
exercise of Martial Law over the Army of our own State   One part
of it has since been annually taken out of the Common Law,
and provided for by the Mutiny Act, which subjects the Military
offences of Soldiers only to punishment by Military Courts, even in
time of peace   Hence we may now be said annually to legalise
Military Law, which, however, differs essentially from Martial
Law, in being confined to offences against Military discipline, and in
not extending to any persons but those who are members of the Army

"Martial Law exercised against enemies or rebels cannot depend
on the same principle, for it is certainly not intended to enforce or
preserve discipline among them   It seems to me to be only a more
regular and convenient mode of exercising the right to kill in war
a right originating in self defence, and limited to those cases where
such killing is necessary, as the means of insuring that end   Martial
Law put in force against rebels can only be excused as a mode of
more deliberately and equitably selecting the persons from whom
quarter ought to be withheld in a case where all have forfeited
their claim to it.   It is nothing more than a sort of better-regulated
decimation, founded upon choice, instead of chance, in order to
provide for the safety of the conquerors without the horrors of
undistinguished slaughter, it is justifiable only where it is an act
of mercy.   Thus the matter stands by the law of nations, but by
the law of England it cannot be exercised except where the jurisdiction of Courts of Justice is interrupted by violence   Did this
necessity exist at Demerara on the 13th of October, 1823 ?   Was it
on that day impossible for the Courts of Law to try offences ?   It is
clear that, if the case be tried by the law of England, and unless an
affirmative answer can be given to these questions of fact, the Court-
martial had no legal power to try Mr Smith.   Now, Sir, I must in
the first place remark, that General Murray has himself expressly
waived the plea of necessity, and takes merit to himself for having
brought Mr. Smith to trial before a Court-martial, as the most
probable mode of securing impartial justice; a statement which
would be clearly an attempt to obtain commendation under false
pretences, if he had no choice, and was compelled by absolute
necessity, to recur to Martial Law. 'In bringing *this man*

(Mr Smith) to trial, under present circumstances, I have endeavoured to secure to him the advantage of the most cool and dispassionate consideration, by framing a Court entirely of Officers of the Army, who, having no interest in the country, are without the bias of public opinion, which is at present so violent against Mr Smith'[1] This paragraph I conceive to be an admission, and almost a boast, that the trial by Court-martial was matter of choice, and therefore not of necessity.

"But the admission of Governor Murray, though conclusive against him, is not necessary to the argument; for my learned friend has already demonstrated that in fact, there was no necessity for a Court-martial on the 13th of October. From the 31st of August, it appears by General Murray's letters that no impediment existed to the ordinary course of law, no negroes were in arms, 'no war or battle's sound was heard' through the Colony. There remained, indeed, a few runaways in the forests behind; but we know from the best authorities,[2] that the forests were never free from bodies of these wretched and desperate men in those unhappy settlements in Guiana, where, under every Government, rebellion has as uniformly sprung from cruelty as pestilence has arisen from the marshes. Before the 4th of September even the detachment which pursued the deserters into the forest had returned into the Colony For six weeks, then, before the Court-martial was assembled, and for twelve weeks before that Court pronounced sentence of death on Mr Smith, all hostility had ceased, no necessity for their existence can be pretended, and every act which they did was an open and deliberate defiance of the law of England "

The principal speakers against the motion were Mr Scarlett, Mr Tindal, and Sir Jos Copley (A G), and the only matter of importance in Mr Scarlett's speech was his tacit admission,[3] "That he did not think it correct that the Court-martial should have been empowered or called on to try an offence which was committed before the institution of Martial Law." The same objection was thus dealt with by Mr Tindal [4]—

"It was said that Martial Law had been proclaimed on the 19th, and that the offence of Mr. Smith, if any had been committed, on the 17th, and then it was asked whether that law was to have an *ex-post facto* operation, and that under it all bygone offences were to be tried? He said, certainly not, it would not be lawful to try in this way an offence committed last year, or at any previous period, which gave it a character distinct and separate from the circum-

---

[1] Letter of General Murray to Lord Bathurst 21st October, 1823
[2] See Stedman, Bolingbroke, &c   [3] 9 H D (2), p 1069   [4] Ib., p 1239.

stances which occasioned the Proclamation of Martial Law. But here the case was different Mr. Smith was charged with having a guilty knowledge of meditated treason and rebellion on the 17th of August, and with having concealed that knowledge. On the 18th the negroes revolt, and in consequence Martial Law was the next day proclaimed. Was he not then drawing too nice and subtle distinctions—distinctions unworthy of the honourable and learned members on the other side—to say that the offence of concealing the knowledge of the treason on the 17th was a bygone offence, and not an offence cognisable by this Court-martial, there being then, under Martial Law, no other court in the Colony by which it could be tried "

3.—JAMAICA,[1] 1832—1865

On the 30th December, 1831, the Governor, with the unanimous opinion of the Council of War (summoned under the Militia Act, 50 Geo III., c. 17, sec 74), proclaimed Martial Law (which continued in force until the 5th Febru   , 1832) in these words .[2]—

"We do hereby strictly charge and command all and every the Commissioned and Warrant Officers and Private Men of Our Militia of Our said Island, to repair forthwith to their several and respective Regiments and Stations, and there to hold themselves in readiness to receive and obey all such Orders as shall from time to time be given to them by Our Captain General of Our Forces in Our said Island, or in his absence, by any superior Officer, upon pain of the highest displeasure, and of such pains and penalties as, by the Rules and Articles of War, established in Our said Island, are inflicted upon such persons as shall be guilty of disobedience of Orders."

The Governor, the Earl of Belmore, acted in the rank of Captain-General, gave his orders to the Major-General in command,[3] and placed the troops at his disposal [4]

The main facts of the Jamaica Rebellion, 1865, as pertinent to the prosecutions against the Governor of Jamaica (Edward Eyre, Esq), for proclaiming Martial Law, and against the Military Officer (Colonel Alexander Abercromby Nelson), for carrying it out, were briefly as follows .—

From the earliest period of our settling in Jamaica, the Governor,

---

[1] 47 Sess Papers (1831 2), pp 250, 283   [2] Ib , pp 250, 282, 283

[3] Ib , pp 277, 283.

[4] As to trials by Court-martial, see pp 287, 292 294, 295, 296

under certain circumstances, has had the power of declaring Martial Law, thus :—

"The Local Statute of 33 Charles II, c, 31, declared, "That upon every apprehension and appearance of any public danger or invasion, the Commander-in-Chief should forthwith call a Council of War, and, with their advice and consent, cause and command the Articles of War to be proclaimed at Port Royal and St. Jago de la Vega, and that then it shall and may be lawful for the said Commander-in-Chief to command the persons of any of His Majesty's liege subjects, as also their negroes, horses, and cattle, for all such service as may be for the public defence, and to pull down houses, cut down timber, command ships and boats, and generally to act and do, with full power and authority, all such things as he and the said Council of War may think necessary and expedient for His Majesty's service and the defence of this island "

This Act was, however, repealed by another Local Act (9 Vic. c 35), for consolidating and amending the Militia—which (amongst other things) first declared " that all Councils of War should consist of the Governor, or Commander-in-Chief for the time being, the Admiral, or Commander-in-Chief of Her Majesty's ships on this station, for the time being, the Captains, and if none, the Senior Officer in port, the several Members of the Privy Council of this Island for the time being, the Speaker, and Members of the Assembly, for the time being, General Officers of the Militia, and Field Officers of Regiments, not being Officers in her Majesty's Regular Troops, and that no other person whatsoever shall have a right to sit, debate, or vote thereat, and that not less than twenty-one of the above-mentioned persons be a quorum of a Council of War, " and then, in these words, enabled the Governor to declare Martial Law .—

" *And whereas* the appearance of public danger, by invasion or otherwise, may sometimes make the imposition of Martial Law necessary, yet, as from experience of the mischief and calamities attending it, it must ever be considered as amongst the greatest of evils *Be it therefore enacted,* That it shall not, in future, be declared or imposed but by the opinion and advice of a Council of War, as aforesaid , and at the end of thirty days from the time of such Martial Law being declared, it shall *ipso facto* determine, unless continued by the advice of a Council of War, consisting as aforesaid

"*And be it enacted,* That the Governor, or person exercising the functions of Governor, shall be authorised and empowered, by and with the advice of a Council of War, in the event of disturbance, or emergency of any kind, to declare any particular parish, distuct, or county of the island under Martial Law, and to exempt the [*other*] parts of the island from the operation of Martial Law, and whenever Martial Law shall be declared, or imposed by the authority aforesaid, or whenever the Militia, or any part thereof, shall be embodied for the purposes or under the provisions of this clause, pay shall be given to the Officers, warrant, and non-commissioned officers, and privates, in the following proportion." [The pay is here set out in the Act.]

A serious outbreak of the Negro population took place on the 11th October, in the parish of St Thomas, persons in authority being killed. A Council of War was assembled at Kingston, on the 12th, and sanctioned the proclamation (prepared by the Local Attorney-General) which was issued on the 13th in these words —

"VICTORIA,' &c

" To all our loving Subjects.

" Whereas we are certified of the committal of grievous trespasses and felonies within the parish of St Thomas-in-the-East of this our Island of Jamaica, and have reason for expecting that the same may be extended to the neighbouring parishes of the county of Surrey of our said island We do hereby, by the authority to us committed by the laws of this our island, declare and announce to all whom it may concern, that Martial Law shall prevail throughout the said county of Surrey, except in the city and parish of Kingston, and that our military forces shall have all power of exercising the rights of belligerents against such of the inhabitants of the said county, except as aforesaid, as our said Military forces may consider opposed to our Government, and the well-being of our loving subjects

" Given at Head-Quarter House, Kingston, on the thirteenth day of October, 1865 "

George W. Gordon, on the 17th October, went to the house of the General O'Connor in Kingston, and was there arrested by Governor Eyre and taken into custody on the 20th, and handed over to Colonel Nelson in Morant Bay, where Martial prevailed.

Various written and printed documents were sent with the prisoner, and the Governor, by word of mouth, gave instructions to Colonel Nelson to go over these, and, if he deemed the evidence sufficient, to frame such charges for trial by a Court-martial as he thought correct against the prisoner.

----

¹ Papers of February, 1866, Part i., p 17

Colonel Nelson, after devoting six hours to the perusal and selection of documents, drew up two charges, the 1st, of High Treason, the 2nd, with having complicity with certain parties engaged in rebellion, &c, at Morant Bay, on the 11th October, 1865. He then appointed a Court-martial for the trial of the prisoner, consisting of Lieutenant Brand, R N (President), Lieutenant Errington, R N , and Ensign Kelly of the 4th West India Regiment, and gave the charges, with the documents and notes of evidence, to the President.

The Court sat on the 21st of October, "at about 2 P M , and closed its sittings after day-light." It found the prisoner guilty, and sentenced him to death Late in the same evening the President handed the proceedings to Nelson, who, after carefully perusing, considered it clearly to be his duty "to approve and confirm them."

As the 22nd was Sunday, the execution was delayed, and, very early on that day, Nelson sent the Court-martial proceedings to General O'Connor, writing, "I have not furnished any report of the Court to the Governor, because, as he is now in Kingston, I apprehend all my reports should be made through you, my immediate Commanding Officer."

The General received the papers at 11 A M , and, after carefully considering the proceedings, the conviction, finding, and sentence of the Court martial, was of opinion "that the position of Colonel Nelson and the Colony called for prompt and immediate action" The proceedings were then sent by the General to the Governor, who wrote officially to General O'Connor, and privately to Nelson, on the 22nd instant (reaching the latter officer on the 23rd, before Gordon's execution), giving "his concurrence in the justice of the sentence, and the necessity of carrying it into effect " Nelson then appointed Monday, the 23rd, at 7 10 A.M , for the prisoner's execution, and his orders were obeyed On the 24th October, General O'Connor sent home to the military authorities the despatches of Nelson and Eyre, with a covering letter, expressing his approval therein

In framing this statement, I have endeavoured to follow, as closely as possible, the language of the various documents, and of the evidence of witnesses printed in Part II. of the Report of the Jamaica Royal Commissioners, 1866 The personal conduct of Colonel Nelson never raised a breath of suspicion but that he acted throughout with entire honesty, and with humane feelings. If he failed to appreciate the necessity of having legal evidence to convict a prisoner arraigned for his life—it was incident to his training for active military pursuits as a Soldier

The Proclamation was allowed to continue in operation during the 20 days, and then expired. On the 9th November, a Local Act of Indemnity (29 Vic., c 1), was passed in these terms .[1]—

It set out that, "being seduced by the insidious counsel of wickedly designing persons, many of the Queen's subjects conspired by force to overthrow the Constitution and Government established by law ; and in furtherance of such their purpose, did, with force, and in confederate multitude, commit, on the eleventh day of October, and on divers other days following, in the parish of St Thomas-in-the-East, many burglaries, robberies, arsons, murders, and other felonies, with treasonable purpose, in renunciation of their natural allegiance, and to the intent of the general massacre of all loyal and well-disposed subjects of the Queen here dwelling that upon being informed of such the aforesaid atrocities, the Governor, with the advice of a Council of War, and in order to prevent the extension of the said rebellious outbreak, proclaimed Martial Law that under God's providence, the military and naval forces of the Queen, with the loyal co-operation of others, Her Majesty's faithful subjects in this island, had arrested the spread of the rebellion, and saved the lives of law-abiding citizens from imminent general sacrifice ; and that military, naval, or civil authorities, necessarily employed in the prompt suppression of the atrocities aforesaid, might, according to the law of ordinary peace, be responsible in person or purse for acts done in good faith, for the purpose of restoring public peace, and quelling the rebellion aforesaid , and that it was expedient that all persons whosoever, in good faith and of loyal resolve, had acted for the crushing of the rebellious outbreak, should be indemnified and kept harmless for such their acts of loyalty "

It then enacted —

"First—That all personal actions, indictments, and proceedings, present or future, whatsoever, against such authorities, or officers, civil, military, or naval, or other persons acting as last aforesaid, for or by reason of any matter or thing commanded, ordered, directed, or done since the promulgation and publication of the proclamation of Martial Law aforesaid, whether done in any district in which Martial Law was proclaimed, or in any district in which Martial Law was not proclaimed, in furtherance of Martial Law, that is to say, on, from, and after the thirteenth day of October last past, and during the continuance of such Martial Law, in order to suppress the said insurrection and rebellion, and for the preserva-

---

[1] Papers of February, 1866, Part 1, p 175

tion of the public peace throughout the island, shall be discharged and made void, and that every person by whom such act, matter, or thing, shall have been advised, commanded, ordered, directed, or done for the purposes aforesaid, on, from, and since the said thirteenth day of October, and during the existence of such Martial Law, shall be freed, acquitted, discharged and indemnified, as well against the Queen's most gracious Majesty, her heirs and successors, as against all and every person or persons whomsoever

"Second—And it is hereby also enacted, That his Excellency Edward John Eyre, Esquire, Captain-General and Governor-in-Chief, and all officers and other persons who have acted under his authority, or have acted *bonâ fide* for the purposes and during the time aforesaid, whether such acts were done in any district in which Martial Law was proclaimed, or in any district in which Martial Law was not proclaimed, are hereby indemnified in respect of all acts, matters, and things done in order to put an end to the said rebellion; and all such acts so done are hereby made and declared to be lawful, and are confirmed

"Third—In order to prevent any doubt which might arise, whether any act alleged to have been done under the authority of the Governor, or to have been done *bonâ fide* in order to suppress and put an end to the said rebellion, was so done, it shall be lawful for the Governor for the time being to declare such acts to have been done under such authority, or *bonâ fide* for the purposes aforesaid, and such declaration, by any writing under the hand of the Governor for the time being shall in all cases, be conclusive evidence that such acts were so done respectively"

On the 6th February, 1867, an information was laid before the Chief Magistrate at Bow Street (acting under the 11 & 12 Vic, c 42, sec. 2, and the 24 & 25 Vic., c. 110, sec. 9), and a Warrant issued for the apprehension of Nelson, on the charge of wilful murder of George William Gordon, an inhabitant of Jamaica. On the 9th February, on receiving a private intimation that the Warrant had been issued, Nelson voluntarily surrendered himself, and was admitted to bail. He then appealed to the Military Authorities for protection, and on the 11th instant, the Solicitor to the War Department was instructed to undertake the conduct of his defence, and pay the expenses out of Army votes. The indictment was presented to the Grand Jury on the 16th April, 1867, and after the charge of the Lord Chief Justice, the Bill was thrown out. The removal of Gordon from Kingston, where Martial Law did *not* prevail, to Morant Bay, where it *did* prevail, the Chief Justice thought an illegal act in the Governor, but that Nelson, finding Gordon within the district, was not affected by this illegality, and

" it was no part of his duty to inquire how Gordon had been brought there." [1]

Whether Gordon was amenable to Martial Law was dependent on the fact of his having committed any offence against it " For a man cannot commit an offence against a law which law has no existence. If there is any one principle which in the exposition and application of the criminal law of this country is held more sacred than another, it is, that you cannot, by the *ex post facto* application of a law, make a man liable to it for an act done before the law came into existence. In like manner, if that which is already an offence is by Act of Parliament made a more serious crime and has a severer punishment attached to it, as where an act which was before a misdemeanour is constituted a felony, you cannot deal under the new law with an offence committed before the law was altered If, indeed, the matter is one of procedure only, a question of how a man shall be tried, this does not fall within the rule, but no one I imagine would seriously contend that the being subject to such a law as this so called Martial Law, and being tried before such a Court-martial, was merely a matter of procedure.'

The Governor was prosecuted under the 42 Geo III, c 85, and an indictment presented against him on the 2nd June, 1868, which, after the charge of Mr Justice Blackburn, the Grand Jury threw out On the question of Gordon's removal to Morant Bay, Mr Justice Blackburn, considering that by the General Law all crime is local and must be tried where it is committed, thought that the Governor might have been justified in bringing Gordon into the proclaimed district for trial [2]

For the conduct of the Military, the Governor was not to be deemed liable, their want of discipline was attributable to their Commanding Officers, and not to the Civil Officer. Nor was there, under the circumstances any obligation imposed on the Governor to rescind the proclamation of Martial Law before the expiration of the thirty days.

The opinion entertained by the Government as to the effect of the Indemnity Act was thus expressed in their despatch of the 18th June, 1866 —

" Her Majesty's Government have been advised by the Law Officers of the Crown that the effect of the Indemnity Act will not be to cover acts done either by the Governor or by subordinate officers, unless they are such as (in the case of the Governor) he may have reasonably and in good faith considered to be proper for the purpose of putting an end to the insurrection, or such as (in

---

[1] Papers of February, 1866, Part 1, p 118   [2] Pp 83-99

the case of subordinates) have been done under and in conformity with the orders of superior authority, or (if done without such orders) have been done in good faith and under a belief, reasonably entertained, that they were proper for the suppression of the insurrection, and for the preservation of the public peace in the island As regards all acts done by or under military authority, Her Majesty's Government are advised that the proclamation of Martial Law under the Island Statute of 1844 operated within the proclaimed district to give as complete an indemnity as the Indemnity Act itself"

The Bill against Governor Eyre having been thrown out, the question how far the Indemnity Act was a bar to criminal proceedings in England against the Governor was not considered, but Mr. Justice Blackburn expressed "a doubt whether when an act has been done which, according to the Imperial Legislature, would be triable as a crime in England, and you have a right to try that crime, whether the Colonial Legislature, although supreme in the Colony, could undo that crime which had become punishable by law here In one view, I take it, the law is pretty clear, that after a bill had been found here it would not have been competent to the Jamaica Legislature to pass any Act of Indemnity equivalent to a pardon"

As the Court of Parliament or Queen's Bench in England is the only tribunal for the trial of a Colonial Governor, a Local Indemnity is little needed for his protection in the Colony,[1] and if he is not to have the benefit of it in England the Act would be useless In the case of Phillips *v* Governor Eyre, the Queen's Bench held the Jamaica Act a bar to a civil action brought by a colonist for trial in Jamaica[2]

I need do no more than refer to the charges of Lord Chief Justice Cockburn[3] and of Mr. Justice Blackburn,[4] and to the case of Phillips *v* Eyre—4 Law Rep. (Q. B.), p. 242

---

4 —LOWER CANADA[5] 1837-8

On the 6th December, 1839, Lord Glenelg, the Secretary of State for the Colonies, wrote to the Governor in these terms—

"The first and highest prerogative and duty of the Crown, is the protection of those who maintain their allegiance against the

---

[1] See Lord Glenelg's despatch in 1836, Cape of Good Hope, *post*
[2] 4 Law Rep (Q. B.), p 242   [3] Ridgway, 1867
[4] Chapman and Hall, 1868   [5] 39 Parliamentary Papers (1837 8), p 422

enemies of order and peace To repress by arms any insurrection
or rebellion, to which the Civil power cannot be successfully opposed is, therefore, a legitimate exercise of the Royal authority and,
in the attainment of this object, the proclamation of Martial Law
may become indispensable

"It is superfluous to state with what caution and reserve this
ultimate resource should be resorted to, and that it ought to be
confined within the narrowest limits which the necessity of the case
will admit But if, unhappily, the case shall arise in any part of
Lower Canada, in which the protection of the loyal and peaceable
subjects of the Crown may require the adoption of this extreme
measure, it must not be declined."

On the 5th December, before this despatch reached the Colony,
the Executive Council (having before them the report of the Local
Law Officers upon the right of the Crown to declare Martial Law)
had sanctioned a proclamation issued by the Earl of Gosford, declaring Martial Law in the district of Montreal, in the province of
Lower Canada.

After a recital of the justifying circumstances, the proclamation[1]
ran in these words —

"Now therefore, I, Archibald Earl of Gosford, Governor-in-
Chief Captain-General in and over the said province of Lower
Canada, by and with the advice and consent of Her Majesty's Executive Council for this province, have issued orders to Lieutenant
General Sir John Colborne, commanding Her Majesty's forces in
the said province, and other Officers of Her Majesty's forces in the
same, to arrest and punish all persons acting, aiding, or in any
manner assisting in the said conspiracy and rebellion which now
exist within the said district of Montreal, and which have broken
out in the most daring and violent attacks upon Her Majesty's
forces, according to Martial Law, either by death, or otherwise, as
to them shall seem right and expedient for the punishment and
suppression of all rebels in the said district, of which all Her
Majesty's subjects in this province are hereby required to take
notice"

The proclamation was then sent to the Lieutenant-General (Sir
John Colborne), in command of Her Majesty's troops, with a letter
of instructions of the same date, in these terms.—

"That in all cases wherein the unlimited power with which you
are now invested can be exercised in co-operation with, or in subordination to, the ordinary laws of the land, and that in all cases
where from local circumstances, or from a prompt return to their

---

[1] 39 Parliamentary Papers (1837-8), p 447

allegiance, the deluded inhabitants of any part of that district display an honest contrition for their past offences, you will revert at once to the assistance of the Civil authorities, and impress upon a misguided people the conviction that Her Majesty's Government in this province is equally prompt to pardon the repentant and punish the incorrigible. These instructions will alleviate, in some degree, the apparent severity of a measure which the present painful emergency imposes on his Excellency and will relieve you from any responsibility that might otherwise arise out of the exercise, on all fitting occasions, of that leniency which his Excellency feels assured is so congenial to your feelings.

On the 7th December, Sir John Colborne reported the receipt of these instructions to the Horse Guards in these terms :—

"I beg to assure the General Commanding-in-Chief, that although the Governor-in-Chief has considered it necessary to declare the district of Montreal under Martial Law, I shall on every occasion avail myself of the assistance and advice of the Civil authorities in carrying into effect such measures as may be required to restore order and to protect the property of the loyal inhabitants."

These papers were submitted to the Law Officers of the Crown, for their Report,[1] who wrote as follows :—

"MY LORD,   *"Temple, January 16th,* 1838

"We have to acknowledge the receipt of a letter from your Lordship of yesterday's date, together with the copy of a letter addressed by the Earl of Gosford to the Attorney- and Solicitor-General of Lower Canada, and their reply on the subject of the power vested in the Governor of that Province to proclaim Martial Law. Your Lordship desires that we should take these papers into our consideration, and report to your Lordship our joint opinion, whether the views expressed by the Law Officers of the Crown, in Lower Canada, are correct in point of Law

"We have now the honour of reporting to your Lordship that, in our opinion, the Governor of Lower Canada has the power of proclaiming, in any district in which large bodies of the inhabitants are in open rebellion, that the Executive Government will proceed to enforce Martial Law. We must, however, add that in our opinion such proclamation confers no power on the Governor which he would not have possessed without it The object of it can only be to give notice to the inhabitants of the course which the Government is obliged to adopt for the purpose of restoring tranquillity. In any district in which, by reason of armed bodies of the inhabi-

---

[1] 39 Parliamentary Papers (1837-8), p 31.

tants being engaged in insurrection, the ordinary course of law cannot be maintained, we are of opinion that the Governor may, even without any proclamation, proceed to put down the rebellion by force of arms, as in case of foreign invasion, and for that purpose may lawfully put to death all persons engaged in the work of resistance, and this, as we conceive, is all that is meant by the language of the Statutes referred to in the Report of the Attorney- and Solicitor-General for Lower Canada, when they allude to the '*undoubted prerogative of His Majesty for the public safety to resort to the exercise of Martial Law against open enemies or traitors*' The right of resorting to such an extremity is a right arising from, and limited by the necessity of the case—*Quod necessitas cogit defendit.* For this reason we are of opinion that the prerogative does not extend beyond the case of persons taken in open resistance, and with whom, by reason of the suspension of the ordinary tribunals, it is impossible to deal according to the regular course of justice. When the regular Courts are open, so that Criminals might be delivered over to them to be dealt with according to Law, there is not, as we conceive, any right in the Crown to adopt any other course of proceeding. Such power can only be conferred by the Legislature, as was done by the Acts passed in consequence of the Irish Rebellions of 1798 and 1803, and also by the Irish Coercion Act of 1833

"From the foregoing observations, your Lordship will perceive that the question how far Martial Law, when in force, supersedes the ordinary Tribunals, can never, in our view of the case, arise Martial Law is stated by Lord Hale to be, in truth, no law, but something rather indulged than allowed as a Law, and it can only be tolerated because, by reason of open rebellion, the enforcing of any other Law has become impossible It cannot be said, in strictness, to supersede the ordinary tribunals, inasmuch as it only exists by reason of those tribunals having been already practically superseded It is hardly necessary for us to add that, in our view of the case, Martial Law can never be enforced for the ordinary purposes of Civil or even Criminal Justice, except in the latter so far as the necessity arising from actual resistance compels its adoption.

"I have, &c,

(Signed)   " J. CAMPBELL
                      " R M ROLFE"

Martial Law continued in force until the Governor of the Province recalled his proclamation of it on the 27th April, 1838.[1]

[1] 39 Parliamentary Papers (1837 8), p 532

5.—CEYLON,[1] 1848

The proclamation of the 29th July, 1848, put Martial Law in force until further orders, and called upon all Her Majesty's loyal subjects to remain peaceably in their homes, and on no account to join themselves to the said rebels   It was revoked on the 4th, and Martial Law was wholly to cease from the 10th October, 1848

For the trial of prisoners, the Civil Courts sat in districts beyond or out of the operation of Martial Law, and Courts-martial sat in the district within its operation [2]   The Civil Courts were slow, and the Courts-martial ready, to convict and punish the prisoners charged before them.[3]

In the cases tried by the Civil Courts, the offences were committed before, and in those by the Courts-martial the offences were committed after the " proclamation," and from particulars of the offences given at pages 242 and 262, it will be seen that high treason and minor offences against the ordinary Colonial Law were dealt with by the latter Courts

The Officer in command, Lieutenant-Colonel Drought, proclaimed (8th August, 1848) all the property of rebels to be forfeited, and all the moveable property of supposed (unconvicted) rebels, was sold or held by the public Officers [4]

A Local Act of Indemnity, framed on the model of the Irish Act of 1798, was passed,[5] and the Legislative Council and other of the principal inhabitants, by public addresses, thanked the Governor and the Naval and Military Officers for their vigorous conduct in the suppression of the outbreak, but on February 20th, 1849, the affairs of Ceylon were brought before the House of Commons by Mr Baillie, and the propriety of the conduct of Lord Torrington (the Governor) and of the authorities of Ceylon, in declaring Martial Law, and in their mode of carrying it out, was questioned.

A Committee of Enquiry was appointed by the House, and commenced it in 1849, continued it in 1850, and presented their Report to Parliament in March, 1850.[6] The evidence of Sir D Dundas (then Judge-Advocate-General) on the subject of Martial Law,[7] and the opinions of the late Sir Robert Peel may be referred to with great advantage [8]

In April, 1851, on the motion of Lord Torrington, the affairs of Ceylon came before the House of Lords,[9] when the Duke of Wellington spoke on the subject of Martial Law in these terms [10]—

---

[1] 36 Sess Papers (1849), p 181   [2] Ib , p 319   [3] 36 ib., pp 219, 220
[4] Ib , p 500   [5] Ib., p 267   [6] 12 Sess Papers, p 100   [7] Ib , p 176
[8] See Questions 5426-5533.   [9] 115 H D (3 , p 879   [10] Ib , pp 880, 881

" As to the remark which had been made about him, he would say a word in explanation   He contended that Martial Law was neither more nor less than the will of the General who commands the army   In fact, Martial Law meant no law at all.   Therefore the General who declared Martial Law, and commanded that it should be carried into execution, was bound to lay down distinctly the rules and regulations and limits according to which his will was to be carried out   Now he had, in another country, carried on Martial Law, that was to say, he had governed a large proportion of the population of a country by his own will.   But then, what did he do?   He declared that the country should be governed according to its own National Laws, and he carried into execution that will.   He governed the country strictly by the Laws of the Country, and he governed it with such moderation, he must say, that political servants and Judges who at first had fled or had been expelled, afterwards consented to act under his direction   The Judges sat in the Courts of Law conducting their Judicial business, and administering the Law under his direction "

6.—CEPHALONIA,[1] 1849.

On the 30th August, 1849, a Proclamation of Martial Law was made throughout those districts of the island[2] to which the late insurrectionary movement (marked by acts of atrocity) had extended, " and in all other districts to which it may extend," the Senate concurring in this course.

One prisoner (Vlacco) was brought to trial[3] before a Court-martial, on 17th October, 1849, for acts committed on the 28th, 29th, 30th, and 31st August 1849   Martial Law was taken off some districts on the 22nd; and an Amnesty proclaimed on 24th October, 1849[4]   Between 31st August and 27th October, 1849, there were sixty-eight Courts-martial, and in many the acts committed were alleged as prior to the Proclamation,[5] viz, 28th August, 1849, but the Legislature and Local Authorities voted Sir H. Ward (the Governor) testimonials.[6]

The conduct of the Governor and the Troops was approved by the Home Government,[7] but in the House of Commons Mr. Hume proposed, but failed to carry, an address to Her Majesty —

---

[1] 36 Sess Papers (1850), p 751

[2] English law did not prevail in this island, for, under the Treaty of Paris, England was only a Protector

[3] 36 Sess Papers (1850), p. 791   [4] Ib, p 766   [5] Ib, p 833

[6] Ib., p 865   [7] Ib, p 839

"That She will be graciously pleased to appoint a Royal Commission to proceed to the Ionian Islands, there, on the spot, to inquire into the causes of the disturbances that occurred in the Island of Cephalonia, and into the measures taken by Sir Henry G. Ward, the Lord High Commissioner, to restore peace, and into the manner in which forty-four persons were sentenced to death, and twenty-one of them executed, and also into the manner in which ninety-two persons were flogged and others banished from the Island without trial, and generally to institute inquiry into the causes of discontent in these Islands, and to recommend the best means of promoting their future peace and welfare "[1]

General Sir D. L. Evans[2] justified the conduct of the Governor, for the greatest mistake that could be committed in insurgent warfare, was to delay operations. By neglect a small insurrection might become a terrible war.

7.—CAPE OF GOOD HOPE.[3]

The border tribes having revolted and attacked the English settlers, Sir B. D'Urban, on the advice of the Attorney General, and with the unanimous assent of the Executive Council, placed the district under Martial Law, by the Proclamation[4] of the 3rd January, 1835, in these words —

"Whereas information has been received by me, that certain tribes, inhabiting the countries beyond the eastern frontiers of this Colony, have entered the districts of Albany and Somerset in several directions, and have committed, and still are committing, great outrage, devastation and murder therein, and it has become absolutely necessary to embody the inhabitants of the several districts of the eastern division of the Colony to aid His Majesty's Forces in the expulsion of the invaders now, therefore, in order to secure the efficient services of such inhabitants, and due obedience on their part to the orders of the Officer to whom I have entrusted the command of the combined Forces, until my assumption of the same in person, I do hereby order and direct, that from and after the promulgation of these presents, Martial Law shall be in force within the districts of Albany, Somerset, Uitenhage, Graaf Reinet, George, and Beaufort, for all cases and in all matters connected with the assembling and conducting the said combined forces, and shall continue to be in force until the expulsion of the said invaders, unless proclamation to that effect shall be previously made."

---

[1] 115 H D, p 980   [2] Ib., p 1001   [3] 39 Sess Papers (1835), p 648
[4] Ib, p. 660

Over certain districts Martial Law was revoked on the 17th June, 1835, and 9th July, 1836, and over the whole country on 18th August, 1836   On the 29th August, 1836, the Legislative Council passed an Act of Indemnity [1]—

" The said Governor, and also all persons acting under his order, direction, and authority, shall be, and they are jointly and severally hereby indemnified, freed, and discharged from and again t all actions, suits, prosecutions, and penalties whatsoever, for or on account or in respect of all or any acts, matters, and things whatso ever done, ordered, directed, or authorised by the said Governor, or by any person or persons acting under his order, direction, and authority, and within the said places or any of them, during the existence therein of such Martial Law as aforesaid   So only, and provided, that such acts, matters, and things shall have been done, ordered, directed, or authorised *boná fide*, in furtherance and in the execution of the objects for which Martial Law was proclaimed as aforesaid "

When this measure was submitted to the Colonial Office for con firmation, Lord Glenelg suggested amendments [2]   " I entirely concur in the opinion that it is proper that an Act of Indemnity should be passed for the protection of all persons who, in obedience to your orders, had carried Martial Law into execution in the eastern dis tricts during the late hostilities, but I am not satisfied of the pro priety of enacting such an ordnance in favour of yourself, because such an enactment appears necessarily to imply that His Majesty's representative is amenable to the Civil and Military tribunals of the colony,—an opinion to which I am unable to subscribe, and which, therefore, am unwilling to countenance   As Governor, you are responsible for acts done by you in that capacity to the King, to Parliament, and, in certain cases, to the Court of King's Bench at Westminster, but not to the Colonial tribunals

" I am also not satisfied that the concluding words of this ordin ance properly express the meaning which I am disposed to ascribe to the Local Legislature   Those words indemnify all persons for all acts done by them *boná fide*, in furtherance or in execution of the objects for which Martial Law was proclaimed   but many acts of wanton and unnecessary rigour, or even of injustice and cruelty, may possibly have been done *boná fide*, in furtherance of those objects   The expression ought, therefore, to have been " all acts necessarily or properly done," &c

" I have now to acquaint you, that His Majesty is pleased to direct that this ordinance shall continue in operation until his

[1] 39 Press Papers (1837), p 377   [2] Ib p 378

further pleasure shall be known, but I have received the King's commands to instruct you to propose to the Legislative Council the amendment of it, in those particulars which have been already noticed "

Martial Law was again declared[1] at the Cape in 1846 by three Proclamations. (1) By that of the 21st April the Governor proclaimed —" I do therefore order, proclaim, authorise, and declare, that from and after the promulgation hereof, Martial Law shall be, and the same is hereby declared thenceforth to be in force and operation in and throughout the eastern districts of this Colony, with and under all such powers, restraints, authority, demands, requisitions, services, and impressments as to Martial Law thereafter belong and appertain, and by and under the same, may be duly exercised and carried into effect, until this, my Proclamation, shall have been recalled or duly declared to be, and remain no longer in force and operation "

(2) By that of the 22nd April —" I do hereby proclaim and direct that from and after the promulgation of these presents, Martial Law shall be in force throughout the whole Colony for all cases, and in all matters connected with the assembling embodying, conducting, and supplying Her Majesty's forces, and the inhabitants who shall be enrolled and embodied for the purposes above recited "

(3) By the 25th April,—that for the protection of the Colony against devastation by invading hordes of armed Kafirs, and for the chastisement of the Kafir tribes engaged in hostility against Her Majesty's subjects, it was expedient and necessary that all levies of Burghers now called out and being made, or which should thereafter be made, under Martial Law throughout the Colony, should be efficiently and speedily mustered, and moved without delay to the Eastern frontier, there to render good service on Her Majesty's behalf in the common cause   and he did thereby call in and enjoin all officers and persons holding stations of authority under the Colonial Government, and engaged in Her Majesty's Civil Service in the Colony, to aid and assist, to the utmost of their power and ability, and by the exertion of the authority severally vested in them, in assembling, equipping, organising, and supplying the said Burgher levies, and in promoting their speedy movement through the intermediate districts or otherwise, towards the scene of service along the Eastern frontier

On the 13th January, a Proclamation was issued that Martial Law should cease, and on the 11th March 1847, the Colonial Legislature passed an Act of Indemnity

[1] 38 Sess Papers (1847) p 122

On the 25th of December, 1850, Martial Law was again proclaimed[1] in the districts of Albany, Uitenhage, Somerset, Cradock,
Graaf Reinet, Victoria, and Albert in order that the resources of
them and means may be appropriated with promptitude and vigour,
in the first instance to repel any inroad which may occur, as well as
hereafter to inflict signal retribution for the murders that have been
committed upon Her Majesty's soldiers.

As it was expedient that the whole force of the districts aforesaid should be assembled without any delay, the Proclamation
directed that all the male inhabitants thereof, between the ages of
18 and 50, excepting only those who, by their profession, or from
their infirmities, were exempt from Military service, should forthwith enrol themselves under their respective field-cornets or Officers
whom they desired to appoint. and that all Commanders stationed
upon the frontier line, and co operating with Her Majesty's Forces
in the general defence of these territories, were to place themselves
under the Command of Her Majesty's officers, being subject, however, to no punishment whatever, but by the direct authority of the
Commander-in-Chief.

Under this Proclamation forty-eight rebels were tried by Court-
martial in April, 1851, for offences committed (by some as early as
January preceding), and condemned to death. As the Governor (Sir
Harry Smith)[2] considered himself as acting under the Mutiny Act,
he doubted his power to commute the sentence without reference to
Her Majesty, and hence the subject was referred by him to the
Executive Committee of the Colony and the Local Attorney-
General of the Colony. The Opinion[3] of the latter is too prolix to be
set out verbatim

As these Kat River rebels are not Soldiers, nor subject to the
Mutiny Act and Articles of War, "the question," the Attorney-
General observes, "seems to him to be, whether a provision which
is in its terms restricted to Soldiers sentenced for Military crimes,
does in its spirit extend to persons sentenced by Court-martial
who are not Soldiers, and who are not charged with anything
which is by the Mutiny Act or Articles of War declared to be an
offence?

"In reference to this question, the Martial Law, which is
de facto (and, as some Colonial lawyers think, *de jure*) established
by the Governor's Proclamation, promulgated in times of danger
and rebellion, is a thing distinct altogether from the Military Law
created by the Mutiny Act and the Articles of War.

"By that species of Martial Law which, originating in public emergency, extends over all citizens, whether Soldiers or not, crimes and criminals which have no sort of connection with the Mutiny Act and Articles of War are brought under the jurisdiction, or at least under the power of Courts-martial " And it appeared to the Attorney-General " that the provisions of the Mutiny Act and Articles of War did not necessarily regulate either the sentences pronounced by Courts-martial against such criminals in regard to such crimes, or the powers of the Commander-in-Chief in regard to the commutation of such sentences.

" If the circumstances of the frontier were such as to allow of these Kat River rebels being put to hard labour upon public works within the divisions where Martial Law exists, there would be no greater difficulty in putting them to such hard labour there at once than in doing anything else whatever under Martial Law. The Martial Law now under consideration is not the well defined system created by the Mutiny Act and Articles of War, but a state of things in which, for securing the public safety, the Commander-in-Chief becomes a Dictator, exercising, upon his own responsibility, absolute power, trying criminals by whatever sort of tribunal he thinks fit, and punishing them in whatever manner he thinks fit Acting upon Martial Law as so described, the Commander-in-Chief could, of course, order the convicted rebels to be kept at hard labour, upon the same principle on which, had circumstances called for it, he might and would have ordered them to be shot "

The Attorney-General observed that " the need or not of an Act of Indemnity will, in general, distinguish between that Martial Law which is merely the will of the Commander-in-Chief, and that Military Law which is the Mutiny Act and Articles of War For anything done under the Mutiny Act or Articles of War no indemnity is needed The Act and Articles are law, and an indemnity becomes necessary only when that law and all other law has been exceeded Some lawyers in this Colony, as already observed, are of opinion that by the Colonial Law to suspend the ordinary law, and establish Martial Law, is an act competent to the Executive, and one for which no legislative sanction, previous or subsequent, is required. They view Martial Law as a branch of the ordinary law, and not as a foreign and disturbing force obeyed at the moment because irresistible, but punishable afterwards unless pardoned by the Legislature " The Attorney-General differed from this view of the Colonial Law, and " deems an Act of Indemnity essential in regard to every act against person or property, *primâ facie* actionable, of which the only justification capable of being pleaded in a Civil Court rests upon the Governor's Proclamation proclaiming Martial Law, and upon the authority of the Commander-

in-Chief acting under that Proclamation   In this view the sub
jecting of these rebels to imprisonment with hard labour would no
doubt require thereafter an Act of Indemnity, but the subjecting
of these rebels to imprisonment, not with hard labour, would require
an indemnity just as much.   Imprisonment *without* hard labour of
men not subject to the Mutiny Act would in strictness be as much
beyond the ordinary law as imprisonment *with* hard labour

"If," continues the Opinion, "these convicts cannot be detained
in the districts where Martial Law now exists, and where it will
hereafter continue to exist, some difficulty will arise.   Doubts may
exist whether the Civil Courts could recognise, in any shape,
Martial Law as created by Proclamation, and not by Ordinance
Greater doubts may exist whether the Civil Courts could recognise,
after the withdrawal of Martial Law, imprisonments awarded under
Martial Law, and in the course of being suffered in the districts
where Martial Law had once existed, and doubts yet greater may
exist whether the Civil Court in the Western divisions, where
Martial Law has not been proclaimed at all, could recognise, in
regard to prisoners brought there from the Martial Law districts,
the sentences of Courts-martial upon such persons as these Kat
River rebels   Questions of much delicacy might arise were such
prisoners to apply to the Supreme Court in Cape Town for their
liberation, or to kill or be killed in attempting to escape from a
convict station at this end of the Colony   Legislation would be
necessary in order to legalise effectually the imprisonment of all
non-military persons sentenced by Courts-martial or the Commander-
in-Chief during the existence of Martial Law, and kept in confine
ment, where Martial Law does not exist"

On the 3rd May, 1852, General Cathcart (who had succeeded
Sir Henry Smith as Governor) issued Regulations for the conduct of
the Government of Kaffraria while under Martial Law,[1] directing
all persons residing therein to obey the orders of the Chief Military
Authority, and of the Officers acting under him   He also commuted
the Court-martial sentence of death[2] to imprisonment for life, under
the powers of Martial Law, as well as those invested in him as
Governor

Martial Law was withdrawn[3] as to certain districts by Proclamation of 23rd March, 1853, but left in force in other districts, "for
the purpose of preserving the salutary power of trying by Courts-
martial, such rebels as might for some time yet to come surrender

---

[1] 51 Sess Papers (1852-3), pp 528, 639   [2] Ib, p 615
[3] 38 ib (1854-5), p 469

or fall into the hands of justice,"[1] and a Local Act of Indemnity[2] passed in these terms —

"That from and after the promulgation of this ordinance the said Sir Henry George Wakelyn Smith and the said Sir George Cathcart, and all parties acting under either of them, shall be and they are hereby jointly and severally indemnified, freed, and discharged from and against all actions, suits, and prosecutions whatsoever which might be brought or instituted in any of the Courts of this Colony for or on account of in respect of any acts, matters and things whatsoever done or to be done within any district or division of this Colony placed under Martial Law, during the existence of Martial Law therein, by the said Sir Henry George Wakelyn Smith and the said Sir George Cathcart respectively, or done or to be done in any such district or division by any person or persons acting under the said Sir Henry George Wakelyn Smith and the said Sir George Cathcart respectively, or under the Governor and Commander-in Chief for the time being, in any command or capacity, Military or Civil, which such person or persons may have exercised during the existence in such district or division of such Martial Law as aforesaid Provided always, and the indemnity hereby granted is granted upon this supposition and condition, that all such acts, matters, and things shall have been done or shall be done *bonâ fide*, necessarily, and properly in furtherance and execution of the objects for which Martial Law was proclaimed as aforesaid : Provided also, that every act, matter, or thing shall be presumed to have been done *bonâ fide*, necessarily, and properly, until the contrary shall be made to appear by the party complaining"

8.—Island of St Vincent,[3] 1862

On the 30th September, 1862, Martial Law was declared by the Lieutenant-Governor, with the advice and consent of the Executive Council,[4] and remained in force until the 20th October, 1864.[5]

"It will be necessary," wrote the Lieutenant Governor, to maintain Martial Law[6] until the capture of the principal offenders, and the return of the Force under Mr Stewart, but so soon as I am enabled to do so, I shall call the Legislature together, and I have every confidence that they will approve of the course taken, and indemnify me for the responsibility which I have found it necessary to assume Indeed, the state of popular feeling would support

---

[1] See recital of Local Act, 14th Feb, 1853
[2] 'Statute Law of Cape of Good Hope,' pp. 1042, 1043
[3] Sess Papers, (1863), p 509   [4] Ib, p 8.   [5] Ib, p 24   [6] Ib., p 9, par 23 .

measures of yet greater severity than those to which we have had resort "

The Council and House of Assembly each voted addresses of thanks to the Lieutenant-Governor and to the Naval and Military Authorities.[1]

During Martial Law no Courts-martial were assembled, but four men were killed and four men wounded during the riots. The persons arrested during Martial Law were subsequently tried by the Civil tribunals, and 127 convicted of felony.[2]

The Local Legislature passed a Local Act with a preamble, setting forth the facts, and enacting (so far as need be set out) · [3]—

" 1. The said Proclamation so issued on the 30th day of September, 1862, declaring the existence of Martial Law within this Colony, is hereby declared to have been lawfully issued and proclaimed, and is hereby ratified accordingly.

" 2. All persons who have been in any wise engaged in suppressing or endeavouring to suppress the said insurrection during the continuance and operation of the said Proclamation, declaring this Colony to have been under Martial Law as aforesaid, or in arresting, imprisoning, or confining, any person or persons concerned, or supposed to be concerned, in the said insurrection, shall be freed, discharged, and indemnified, as well as against the Queen's Majesty, her heirs and successors, as against all and every other person or persons, of, for, or concerning the killing, maiming, wounding, or hurting, arresting, confining, or imprisoning any person or persons during the said insurrection, and the continuance and operation of the said Proclamation.

" 3 To obviate any doubt which may arise, whether any act alleged to have been done in suppressing, or endeavouring to suppress, the said insurrection, was so done or otherwise, it shall be lawful for the said Lieutenant-Governor to declare such acts to have been done in suppressing, or endeavouring to suppress, the said insurrection, and such declaration in writing, bearing the signature of the said Lieutenant-Governor, shall be a sufficient discharge and indemnity to all persons concerned in such acts, and shall in all cases be conclusive evidence that such acts were done in suppressing, or endeavouring to suppress, the said insurrection "

On the Act being submitted to the Colonial Office, for the approval of Her Majesty, the Secretary of State (the Duke of Newcastle) replied thus [4]—

---

[1] Sess. Papers (1863), p 28   [2] Ib, p 72   [3] Ib, p 30
[4] Ib, p 158

"The first, second, and third Clauses of the Act will require alteration

"The first Clause declares the Proclamation of Martial Law to have been lawfully issued.   But this is not the fact, and ought not to have been so declared.   In proclaiming Martial Law the Executive Authority in fact declares itself obliged, for the protection of the community, to neglect law, trusting to the Legislature to relieve all who, in obedience to the constituted authority, may have acted in defence of the public safety, from the consequences of having acted unlawfully.   The Proclamation was right and necessary, but it was not strictly lawful, and to declare it so would be to endanger a most important constitutional principle

"I think that the indemnity contained in the second Clause is too wide   It would enable a person to escape punishment for the most wanton and unjustifiable acts, even to homicide, if it could be shown that he had been (or rather, I presume, that he was when the act was committed) 'in anywise engaged in suppressing, or endeavouring to suppress, the insurrection.'   And this, I observe, although the Lieutenant-Governor might have refused the certificate contemplated by the third Clause, which, although conclusive, is not a necessary part of the defence of the accused person.

"I annex the draft of an indemnity Clause which is taken from one in use in the Cape of Good Hope, and which I should wish to be substituted for the first, second, and third Clauses of the Indemnity Act, now under consideration   When this is done, I shall readily recommend that it should be left to its operation by Her Majesty."

(J J.)

Chapter XIX, par. 23

PARLIAMENTARY SUPERVISION OVER MILITARY EXPENDITURE BEFORE THE CRIMEAN WAR, AND AT THE PRESENT TIME

THE control of the military expenditure before the period of the Crimean War, by Officers of State holding ministerial appointments, was far more complete than it now is

Independently of the direct supervision of the Treasury over one branch of expenditure,—viz, the Commissariat,—the following Parliamentary officers were more or less concerned in the expenditure ; viz, the Secretary of State for War and Colonies, the Secretary at War, the Master-General of the Ordnance, the Surveyor-General of the Ordnance, and the Clerk of the Ordnance

The amount of the Army, Ordnance, and Commissariat, and Militia Estimates for 1853-4 (excluding services now borne on Civil Estimates), was 10,061,701*l* ; of this, the Secretary at War directly superintended 6,449,006*l* or $\frac{64}{100}$ths, the Treasury directly superintended 559,128*l* , or $\frac{6}{100}$ths, and the Ordnance with its three officers in the Ministry, of whom two were members of the House of Commons, superintended 3,053,567*l* , or $\frac{30}{100}$ths

The Estimates of 1868-9, similarly dissected, show a total of 15,230,800*l* , which would, under the old system, have been distributed as follows —

Secretary at War	£8,672,637 or $\frac{57}{100}$ths
Treasury	99 4,410 or $\frac{7}{100}$ths
Ordnance	5,558,753 or $\frac{36}{100}$ths

£15,230,800

That is to say, the proportion which the expenditure for services formerly looked after by Ordnance and Treasury Officers bears to the total expenditure has increased, whilst that appertaining to the Secretary at War has relatively diminished   This expenditure is now superintended by the Secretary of State for War

The cost of administering the Army in all its branches in 1853-4 was 141,191*l* , and in 1868-9, 240,762*l*

This military expenditure is made up of a mass of small details Under the former system it was possible for the several Parliamentary Ministers to master the details, and to be individually responsible for the conduct of their departments , under the present system the Secretary of State or Under-Secretary of State, who is the only Minister connected with the department in the House of Commons, frequently enters the department without any previous knowledge of its details, or, if he has detailed knowledge, it is only a partial knowledge connected with some one branch of the department only. He must consequently take his views from the permanent officers, and if he is not conversant with the business, they can, except in extreme cases, let him see as much or as little of the details as they please   they thus gradually acquire complete power in their several departments, and they are practically irresponsible   There is much truth in Lord Hardinge's observation, that "consolidation is bad when it prevents the head of the department from personally investigating all the important details, and this applies more particularly to a military department, because the Army is a great mass of small details."

The real strength of the financial check under the old system lay in the complete separation of the departments, and in the fact that the duties of the departments were not too extensive to be thoroughly investigated by the Parliamentary Chiefs, and that they were managed exclusively by Civilian agency. The Commissariat Officers of the Treasury were simply Civilians The Ordnance Department, which provided all the lodging and stores of the Army, was a Civil department, with Civil officers to administer it locally. They supplied the barracks, and controlled the lodging list, they provided the barrack furniture, and the fuel and light. No deviations from regulations were allowed without the previous sanction of the Board of Ordnance and the Treasury, these were much governed by the advice of their local Civilian Officers, who were independent of Military interests, and looked only to the necessities of the case, and not to the manner in which the various members of the Service could be pecuniarily benefited.

Besides this, an arrangement prevailed, which in recent changes has been gradually lost sight of, and the absence of which, at some future time, may lead to inconvenience, and possibly loss to the Government

The Board of Ordnance maintained at each station permanent local officials, these were the Storekeeper, who held a comparatively high official position as permanent Member of the Board of Respective Officers, and the Barrackmaster, who, though subordinate, had care of all buildings, and a knowledge of all lands and boundaries

There are always, and must be always, connected with property numerous local questions a knowledge of which can only be acquired by time, and yet which are of vast importance to the economical administration of the property, whether as regards the boundaries, or the letting or hiring of lands, or construction or alteration of buildings, or knowledge of local customs

The introduction of a Military instead of a Civilian Executive has caused these permanent officers gradually to disappear The storekeepers have been converted into a Military corps, and are moved from station to station according to a roster of service.

The appointment of Barrackmaster, formerly Local, has been converted into a moveable appointment

The Clerks of Works, who were a tolerably permanent body of men under the Board of Ordnance, are now moved according to roster, and it is proposed that they shall be dispensed with at no distant date, their work being performed by Officers of Royal Engineers and Military Foremen of Works

Moreover, the various departmental corps, which administer the supplies locally, and which at the time of the amalgamation of the Army Departments were purely Civil in their organization, have (with the exception of the Barrack Department) been converted into Military bodies, it follows, as a necessary consequence, that under the Royal Warrant, which defines the respective functions of the Secretary of State for War and the Commander in Chief, the detailed control over the discipline and management of these corps will rest with the latter. he thus becomes practically the arbiter of the Officers' advancement in their career, and of the stations at which they are to serve In fact, these corps must occupy a similar position to that occupied by the corps of Royal Engineers or Army Medical Department, in which the officer at the head of the corps is the Military Commandant under the Commander-in-Chief as well as directly responsible to the Secretary of State for the executive or financial duties committed to it.

At the same time, the bulk of the superior officers now employed in the War Office is Military, many hold their appointments for limited terms, and will return to their Military duties Their interests are therefore more identified with those of the Military, who apply for increased pay or allowances, or emoluments, or other benefits, than was the case under the old system

It follows that since the amalgamation, Military Officers have themselves been largely arbiters to influence the decision of the Secretary of State on the various demands for increased emoluments, as, for instance, for pay, for reduction of stoppages, for increase of rations of food, of accommodation, of fuel and light, for the condemnation of quarters, &c These applications come forward either directly or on appeals from the Horse Guards, who frequently urge the grant, of what is practically an increase of remuneration of Soldiers and Officers, upon the grounds of its being a boon to the Soldier or Officer, as much as on grounds of necessity, and whilst the application for each proposed concession is supported by the argument that it is small in itself, the aggregate of the numerous demands largely adds to the expenditure of the country

The Civilian Administrative Department of the War Office, whose duty it is to weigh the proposals for efficiency made by the Executive or Combatant departments of the Army against their probable cost, has by the constitution of the office been placed merely in the position of an advocate to fight the battle of the Public, before the Secretary of State as umpire, with a very powerful opponent in the person of the Commander-in-Chief, or other Military Officer, who urges the expenditure.

There has been no standard laid down to regulate the extent to which it is really necessary to extend the comforts of the Soldier, and each separate concession forms the basis of some fresh application

The result is, that whilst from 1853-4 to 1868-9 the increase of the number of men has been from 119,874 to 136,650, that is to say, the number in 1868-9 is barely one seventh more than it was in 1853-4, —

	1853-4	1868-9	Increase times nearly
The barrack stores were	47,829	116,000	2¼
Fuel and light	129,753	297,621	2⅓
Lodging money and rents	89,392	190,500	2⅕

In the next place, there is the conflict which is continually going on between efficiency and economy In time of war economy must give place to expenditure, since the necessary forces for the war and the necessary supplies for the forces must be had at any cost, or, rather, then the most liberal expenditure may be the truest economy

Conflict between efficiency and economy

In time of peace, expenditure should be subservient to economy to the fullest extent compatible with efficiency. In both peace and war there will exist a sort of wholesome opposition between economy and expenditure, both having regard to efficiency as their end.

The pressure which is put on the Secretary of State to incur expense for increase of efficiency is continual and enormous, for every zealous officer in any department of the Army, whether combatant or departmental, endeavours to introduce what he considers improvements in food, accommodation, equipments, and armaments, without any great regard to cost

Constant pressure to alter equipments and increase emoluments

The increases in the Estimates which have arisen from demands for increased efficiency are considerable The following instances show this tendency. Military instruction, such as instruction in musketry, gunnery, field works, good-shooting pay, &c, has increased from about 6000*l.* in 1855 to 76,000*l* in 1868 9 The cost of the educational establishments has increased from 72,331*l.* to 169,324*l* The cost of material of war, and experiments upon its improvement, have increased from 600,000*l* in 1853-4 to 1,550,000*l* in 1868-9

It is the function of the Secretary of State to weigh the advantages of the suggested improvement against the increased expense, and to decide how much should be adopted, or what emoluments should be given

Under the present organization, however, the Secretary of State is solely advised on questions of efficiency by Military Officers, whose tendencies are naturally on the side of efficiency, and the enormous mass of detail which an examination into any important question, of either emolument or efficiency, requires for its full bearings to be understood compels the Secretary of State to rely upon his professional advisers, who are the permanent officers in the department, for guidance in most of his decisions.

Thus it is that effective control over military expenditure by officers directly responsible to Parliament is now materially weaker than it was under the system which prevailed before the Crimean War, and it is a necessary consequence that under each successive Secretary of State the Parliamentary control will become less strong

November, 1868   DOUGLAS GALTON.

(K K.)

Chapter XX , *par* 36

THE STATUTORY POWERS FOR THE ACQUISITION AND MANAGEMENT OF LAND HELD BY THE LATE BOARD OF ORDNANCE

IN the previous Volume reference has been made[1] to the Statutory Powers given to the Crown and the Ordnance Board for the acquisition of land for defensive purposes It may be noticed further, that, under the apprehension of invasion, large arbitrary powers of taking land were conferred on the Lords Lieutenant, to be exercised with the consent of the Treasury, and the Act (43 Geo III , c. 55) which conferred them was in force during the war with France   During the same period the martello towers were built, and the Military Canal[2] was formed, the land for the latter being acquired under the powers conferred by the 47 Geo III , c 70   Other lands were acquired under public Vesting Acts—of which the 54 Geo. III , c 43, may be quoted as an illustration—passed whenever any extensive work of defence was to be undertaken   Though the possession and care of these various properties were with the Ordnance Department, the legal estate was outstanding in several persons, and it was deemed expedient, in the year 1821, to pass an Act[3] to vest the same in the principal Officers of the Ordnance Department, and to confer upon the Board powers of management and sale.

This Act was amended, and all the laws consolidated, by the 5 and 6 Vict , c 96 , the principal provisions of which relate to—

----

[1] Chap I , pars 22-26, Chap XI , par 26, Chap XII , par 47
[2] The Ordnance was not responsible for these   15th 'Report of Military Inquiry,' p 320
[3] 1 & 2 Geo IV c 69

1st. The vesting in the principal Officers of the Board all estates used for Ordnance purposes, and powers of sale and exchange in respect thereof.

2nd The power of compulsory purchase of lands needed for Ordnance purposes.

3rd The power of suing at Law or in Equity, as a *quasi* Corporation, in their official title, by their own Solicitor,[1] and without the sanction of the Attorney-General

4th Power to defend their possession, and other powers of management, &c

The principal provisions of the Defence Act, 1842, are these —
The 5th Section vested all estates (save those referred to in Sections 29 and 30) " which had been heretofore set apart for the use and service, or placed under the charge of the Ordnance or late Barrack Department, or set apart for or placed under the charge of any person or persons acting under the authority of or in trust for Her Majesty or of her royal predecessors, for the use and service of the said departments, or for Military defences, or held, used, or occupied, or purchased, vested, or taken by or in the name of or by any person or persons in trust for Her Majesty or her royal predecessors, or her or their heirs or successors, for the use and service of the said departments, or for the defence and security of the realm, either in fee or for any life or lives, or otherwise howsoever, and all erections and buildings then or thereafter to be erected and built thereon, together with the rights, members, easements, and appurtenances to the same respectively belonging, in the Principal Officers of Her Majesty's Ordnance and their successors in trust for Her Majesty, her heirs and successors, for the service of the said Ordnance Department, or for such other public service or services as Her said Majesty, her heirs or successors, shall from time to time by any Order in Council be pleased to

---

[1] There is a trace of the Attorney- and Solicitor-Generals having settled the purchase deeds of the Faversham Mills in 1759, but the Board of Ordnance have had a Solicitor on their establishment, and an assistant to him, for many years Mr Serjeant Adair was appointed to the office in 1782 by Mr Fox, and upon his death, in 1798, the Hon Spencer Perceval was appointed his successor by Lord Cornwallis The Messrs Smith (the authors of the 'Rejected Addresses') were the assistants, and their office absorbed the Solicitor's appointment Lord Abinger stated one of the objects of the 1 & 2 Geo IV, c 69, to be to enable the Board to manage the Ordnance property without being compelled to resort on every occasion to the Attorney- or Solicitor-General, and this power has been the means of effecting an annual saving of no inconsiderable sum, but it has placed the official Solicitor in an ambiguous position towards the Law Officers, when they desire to ignore the statutory powers which Parliament has advisedly conferred on the Department.—2 Cornwallis Papers, p 377, Doe and Legh *v* Roe, 8 Mee and Wels, p 580

direct" And the 6th Section declared that all estates thereafter
taken for the like purposes, should be held in the same manner

The 9th Section enabled "the said Principal Officers to contract for and purchase, for and on behalf of Her Majesty, lands,
tenements, or hereditaments, or to take or purchase any lease of the
same which should in their judgment be desirable to be purchased,
for and on behalf of the said Ordnance or Barrack services, or the
defence of the realm, upon such terms as to the said Principal
Officers should seem meet, and to enter into any contracts necessary
for that purpose," and by the 10th Section "all bodies politic or
corporate, ecclesiastical or civil, and all feoffees or trustees for
charitable or other public purposes, and all tenants for life and
tenants in tail, and the husbands, guardians, trustees, committees,
curators, or attorneys of such of the owners or proprietors of or
persons interested in any lands, tenements, and hereditaments,
which had been or might be thereafter agreed to be purchased or
taken for the use of the Ordnance Department, as should be femes
covert, infants, lunatics, idiots, or persons beyond the seas, or otherwise incapable of acting for themselves, were empowed to contract
or agree with the Principal Officers, either for the absolute sale or
exchange of any such lands, tenements, or hereditaments, or sale of
any reversion, or for the grant of any lease either for life or lives,
or for any term of years certain, therein, or for such period as the
exigency of the public service should require, and to convey, surrender, demise, or grant the same accordingly, and all the contracts, sales, conveyances, enfranchisements, surrenders, leases, and
agreements made in pursuance thereof, were declared valid and
effectual in law to all intents and purposes whatsoever, and a
complete bar to all dower, estates tail and other estates, rights,
titles, trusts, and interests whatsoever "

The compulsory powers were given in these terms   The
Principal Officers had power,[1] "to enter on, survey, and mark
out, or to cause to be surveyed and marked out, any lands, buildings, or other hereditaments or easements wanted for the service of the Ordnance Department, or for the defence of the
realm, and to treat and agree with the owner or owners of such
lands, buildings, hereditaments, or easements, or with any person or persons interested therein, either for the absolute purchase
thereof, or for the possession or use thereof during such time as
the exigence of the public service should require."

Under the 19th Section, "in case any such bodies or other
persons thereby authorised to contract on behalf of themselves or

---

others as aforesaid, or any other person or persons interested in any such lands, buildings, or other hereditaments so marked out and surveyed as aforesaid, should for the space of fourteen days next after notice in writing subscribed by or on behalf of the Principal Officers should have been given to the persons thereby authorised to contract on behalf of others, or interested themselves, as aforesaid, refuse or decline to treat or agree, or by reason of absence should be prevented from treating or agreeing with the Principal Officers, or should refuse to accept such sum of money as should be offered by the Principal Officers as the consideration for the absolute purchase, or such annual rent or sum as should be offered for the hire thereof (either for a time certain or for such period as the exigence of the public service might require), then the Principal Officers might require two or more Justices of the Peace, to put the Principal Officers, or any person appointed by them, into immediate possession of such lands, buildings, or other hereditaments, and the Justices should issue their Warrants under their hands and seals, commanding possession to be so delivered, and also issue their Warrants to the Sheriff to summon a Jury properly qualified, who should meet at some convenient time and place to be mentioned in such summons, and the said Justices might summon witnesses, and adjourn any such meeting if jurymen or witnesses did not attend, and the Jury, on hearing any witnesses and evidence that may be produced, should, on their oaths, find the compensation to be paid, either for the absolute purchase, or for the possession or use, as the case may be." The Section, however, contains a proviso, "that it shall not be lawful for the Principal Officers to use any lands, buildings, or hereditaments taken under compulsory process for the *barrack* service, or to erect *any barrack buildings thereon.*"

An appeal is given to the superior Courts by Section 20, and the 21st Section gives power to apportion the compensation between landlord and tenant thus :—"Any Jury impannelled to ascertain the compensation to be paid for any lands, buildings, or other hereditaments, under the Act, are required to ascertain and settle the proportion to be paid out of such compensation to any persons having any interest as lessees or tenants at will, or otherwise, and the proportion to be paid out of such compensation shall be returned on the verdict, but the Jury in any such case cannot alter the amount of the entire compensation awarded by any former verdict to be paid for such lands, buildings, or other hereditaments, but only the proportion thereof to be paid to the person or persons having separate interests therein."

A restraint—such as it is—is placed on the use of the compulsory powers by the 23rd section, declaring—"that no such lands, buildings, or other hereditaments shall be so taken without the consent of the owner thereof, or of any such person or persons as aforesaid, acting for or on behalf of the owner thereof, unless the necessity or expediency of taking the same shall be first certified by the Lord-Lieutenant, or two Deputy Lieutenants, and unless the taking of such lands, buildings, or other hereditaments be authorised by a warrant under the hand or hands of the Commissioners of Her Majesty's Treasury, or unless the enemy shall have actually invaded the United Kingdom at the time when such lands, buildings, or other hereditaments shall be so taken "

In apparent recognition of the Constitutional principle,[1] that the Crown only can hold a fort or fortress, the 24th Section provides that from lands taken for a temporary purpose, all buildings shall be removed by the Ordnance Board, but at the end of the section this proviso is found—"That nothing in this Act contained shall extend, or be construed to extend, to alter, prejudice, or affect any agreement which has been or shall or may be entered into by the said Principal Officers with any owner or owners of any such lands, buildings, or other hereditaments, or other person or persons acting on his, her, or their behalf, in relation to any such buildings or erections, but every such agreement shall remain valid and effectual in like manner as if this Act had not been passed" Placing it within the power of the Ordnance to agree to leave any fortress in the hands of a Subject.

The Defence Act, 1842, has—in regard to the powers at present under notice—been amended by later Acts. Under the 17 and 18 Vic., c 67, as amended by 22 Vic , c 12, common rights may be extinguished, and by the latter Act it is declared that the proviso in the 19th Section "shall not extend to prevent the erection of barracks on any lands taken as therein mentioned, and being within any fortress or garrison town or appurtenant to any fortification, or to prevent any buildings on any such lands being used as or for barracks" Statutory forms are also authorised for the conveyance of lands taken under the Defence Acts

The power given to the Board of Ordnance to sell all the fortresses of the Kingdom is not reconcileable with any Constitutional principle. The power is absolute and without any Constitutional control whatever The 12th Section runs in these words—"To sell, exchange, or in any manner dispose of, or to let or demise any of the messuages, buildings, *castles*, *forts*, *lines*, *or other fortifications*, manors, lands, tenements, or hereditaments respectively, vested in the Ordnance Board, with their respective ap-

---

[1] Chap I , par 13

purtenances, either by public auction or private contract, and to convey, surrender, assign, or make over, or to grant or demise the same respectively, to any person or persons who shall be willing to purchase or take the same, in exchange or otherwise respectively, and also to do any other act, matter, or thing in relation to any such messuages, buildings, *castles, forts, lines, or other fortifications,* manors, lands, tenements, and hereditaments, which shall by the *Principal Officers* be deemed beneficial to the public service, in relation thereto, or for the better management thereof, which might be done by any person having a *like* interest in any such like messuages, buildings, *castles, forts, lines, or other fortifications,* manors, lands, tenements, or hereditaments "

The control of the purchase-money was absolute, and when paid, as and to such persons as the Principal Officers named, the estates vested in the purchaser   Thus, by the 13th Section, "the moneys to arise and be produced by such sale or exchange, shall be paid by the purchasers, or the persons making such exchange, to such persons as the Principal Officers shall direct or appoint to receive the same, for the use of Her Majesty , and that the receipt of the Principal Officers for such moneys (indorsed on every such conveyance, surrender, or assignment as aforesaid) shall effectually discharge the purchasers, or persons by whom or on whose account the same shall be paid." And, under the 14th Section, "immediately after the payment of such purchase-money, and the execution of every such conveyance, surrender, and assignment as aforesaid, the purchasers, or the persons making such exchanges as aforesaid, shall be deemed and adjudged to stand seised and possessed of the messuages, buildings, *castles, forts, lines, or other fortifications,* manors, lands, tenements, and hereditaments so purchased or taken in exchange, and notwithstanding any defect in the title of the said Principal Officers thereto, freed and absolutely discharged of and from all and all manner of prior estates, leases, rights, titles, interests, charges, incumbrances, claims, and demands whatsoever which can or may be had, made, or set up, in, to, out of, or upon or in respect of the same messuages, buildings, *castles, forts, lines, or other fortifications,* manors, lands, tenements, or hereditaments, by any person or persons whomsoever, on any account whatever (save and except such estates, leases, rights, titles, interests, charges, incumbrances, claims, and demands whatsoever as in any such conveyance, surrender, deed of exchange, or assignment shall be accepted) "

There is nothing in this statute to prevent either the Ordnance in former years, or the Secretary of State in future ones, from selling all the fortresses in the three kingdoms, to any person or persons, or for any price To facilitate the sale, and to secure possession to the purchaser, Parliament has declared, that he shall have an absolute and indefeasible title " against the world, and that for his security " all adverse claims that can be raised against the Principal Officers under the title (Section 25), are to be paid out of the purchase-money.

Why the purchaser should be made so secure is not obvious The title of the Crown or of the Ordnance (as trustee for the Crown) needs no such assurance to make the property marketable That the Ordnance Board, as purchasers, should have an absolute and indefeasible title to the land purchased for the erection of fortifications, Parliament would readily concede, and in the Defence Act, 1860, such a provision was inserted, having a retrospective operation to all lands taken by the Secretary of State for public purposes [1]

The power to make voluntary grants of lands to particular individuals or corporations, is not, however, found upon this Act, and such grants (when made) would probably be held to be *ultra vires* It is a gift of the public treasure—equivalent to the money of a Parliamentary vote—to a particular person or corporation, which if submitted to the House of Commons *on estimate*, few Ministers would probably be found to propose, but this principle has not always been respected in making gratuitous grants of land. The Secretary of State is but a trustee, and when Parliament thinks fit to authorise the *gratuitous grant of public lands* to benevolent or praiseworthy objects, the power is conveyed in express terms, by Act of Parliament, as the Statute Book will show [2]

As necessary for management, the Ordnance Board were "authorised and empowered, to bring, prosecute, and maintain actions of ejectment, or other proceedings at law or in equity, for recovering possession of any lands, tenements, or hereditaments, vested in them by the Act of 1842, or otherwise howsoever, and to distrain or sue for any arrears of rent due for or in respect thereof under any parole or other demise from the said Principal Officers, and also to bring, prosecute, and maintain any other action or suit in respect of or in relation to such lands, tenements, or hereditaments last aforesaid, or of any trespass or encroachment committed thereon, or damage or injury done thereto, and also upon all covenants and contracts whatsoever made, to, or with the Principal Officers relat-

---

[1] Secs 36 and 46

[2] 3 Geo IV , c 72 , 4 & 5 Vic c 38, 15 & 16 Vic , c 49 , 17 & 18 Vic , c 112 The late Lord Herbert, in his last year of office, ruled against gratuitous grants, except under statutory authority

ing to the said Ordnance or Barrack Department, or the defence of the realm, and also to prosecute any other action, suit, or legal proceedings, civil or criminal, concerning the goods or chattels, stores, moneys, and other property, under the care, control, and disposition of the Principal Officers, and that in every such action, suit, or other proceedings the said Principal Officers for the time being shall be called 'The Principal Officers of Her Majesty's Ordnance,' without naming them or any of them, and no such action, suit, or other proceedings shall abate by the death, resignation, or removal of such principal Officers or any of them

"Nothing therein contained was to be taken to defeat or abridge in any such action, suit, or other proceedings, the legal rights, privileges, and prerogatives of Her Majesty, but that in all such actions, suits, or other proceedings, brought or instituted in the name and on behalf of the Principal Officers, and in all matters relating thereunto, it should be lawful for the Principal Officers to claim, exercise, and enjoy all the same rights, privileges, and prerogatives which had been theretofore claimed, exercised, and enjoyed in any action, suits, or other proceedings whatsoever in any Court of Law or Equity, by Her Majesty or her predecessors, in the same manner as if the subject-matter of the said suits or other proceedings were vested in the Crown, and as if the Crown were actually a party to such actions, suits, or other proceedings Her Majesty might also proceed by information in her Court of Exchequer, or by any other Crown process, legal or equitable, in any case in which such actions, suits, arbitrations, or other proceedings might have been otherwise instituted "[1]

And further, in regard to Crown property, the Board had authority given to act in these terms[2]—"To give any notice, make any claim or demand, and to depute or authorise any persons to make an entry which shall be requisite or expedient to be given or made by or on behalf of Her Majesty, with a view either to compel any tenant, lessee, or occupier of any part or parts of the said possessions of the Crown which are or may be by law vested in the Principal Officers, to quit or deliver up the possession thereof, or to compel the performance of any covenant, contract, or engagement in relation thereto, or to recover possession on non-performance of any covenant, contract, or agreement, or to compel the payment of any sum of money which ought to be paid in respect thereof, and to give any other notice, make any other claim or demand, and depute any persons to make any other entry which shall or may be requisite or expedient to be given or made by

---

[1] Sec 34   [2] Sec 36, see Doe and Legh v Roe, 8 Mee and Wels, p 580

or for or on behalf of Her Majesty, touching any of the said possessions which are or may be by law vested in the Principal Officers of Her Majesty's Ordnance."

In the Act of 1860, the Solicitor for the War Department was named officially to give or receive notices for the department in these terms[1]—"Any notice, summons, writ, or other document required to be served on the said Secretary of State, may be served by being delivered to the Solicitor for the War Department for the time being, or by being left for him thereat, and any notice, summons, writ, or other document required to be given by or on behalf of the said Secretary of State, shall be given under the hand of such Solicitor."

To facilitate the recovery of possession, in case properties are let to tenants, summary powers are given by the 22 Vic, c. 12, secs 5 and 6

Occasionally public rights interfere with the use of Ordnance property, and therefore the Defence Act, 1842, enables[2] the Department to stop up or divert any public or private footpaths, or bridle roads, on the condition that[3] "another path or road shall be provided and made in lieu thereof, at the expense of the Ordnance Department, and at such convenient distance therefrom as to the Principal Officers shall seem proper and necessary"[4]

As to lands taken under the Defence Act, 1860,[4] the powers are larger, for "the Secretary of State, without any writ being issued or other legal proceeding being adopted, may stop up or divert or alter the level of any highway, way, sewer, drain, or pipe, over, through, under, or adjoining any lands taken under the Act, he, if necessary, previously making, opening, or laying down another good and sufficient way, sewer, drain, or pipe, in lieu of that stopped up or diverted, and further, he may alter the course and level of any river not navigable, brook, stream, or watercourse, and any branch of any navigable river (such branch not itself being navigable) within or adjoining such lands, making compensation for any damage sustained by reason of the exercise of such powers, such compensation to be determined and paid in like manner as other compensation under the Act, or as near thereto as circumstances admit"

All the powers of the 1842 Act were transferred to the Secretary of State for the War Department, after his appointment in 1855 by the 18 and 19 Vic, c 117, and are now exerciseable by him In 1860 additional powers were conferred—(1st) By the 23 and 24 Vic, c 106, which enabled him to use the Lands

---

[1] Sec 4)   [2] Sec 16   [3] Sec 17   [4] Secs 40 and 41

Clauses Act, 1845, and (2) The Defence Act, 1860 (c 112), which amends the Act of 1842, and enabled the Secretary of State to acquire lands and building rights with greater facility than under the Act of 1842 [1]

The scheme of this Act was to enable the Secretary of State to sign and deposit declarations setting forth the land he required. 1st. To purchase absolutely (Red), and 2nd To have kept free from buildings (Green) Notices were to be served on all persons interested, and compensation made to them by agreement and arbitration, or by a jury This being done, the Act provided, (1) as to the lands required and to be taken absolutely, that they should, 'from and after payment of the compensation for the same, be vested in the said Secretary of State, on behalf of Her Majesty, discharged of all estates, rights, and interests whatsoever," and (2), as to the other lands, as follows [2] —"From and after the service of the notices prescribed by the Act in relation to any lands required to be kept free from buildings and other obstructions, the following restrictions, powers, and consequences attached with reference to such lands No building or other structure (other than barns, hovels, or other like structures of wood), may be made or erected thereon The Secretary of State may at any time enter and pull down any buildings or structures (other than as aforesaid) thereon, and cut down and grub up all or any of the trees thereon, and remove or alter all or any of the banks, fences, hedges, and ditches thereon, and make underground or other drains therein, and generally level and clear the said lands, and do all such acts for levelling and clearing the same as may be deemed necessary or proper by the said Secretary of State, but in such manner, nevertheless, that evidence of the boundaries of the lands held by different owners may be preserved, no person may alter the level of the lands, or do any act which may prejudicially affect any work done on the lands under the authority of the Secretary of State "

By the 28 and 29 Vic, c 65, the words "barns, hovels, and other like structures of wood," [3] are to be construed to mean only such barns and hovels as are constructed altogether of wood and are used for the shelter of cattle or sheep, or for the storage of agricultural produce, or for some other like agricultural purpose

No doubt the powers conceded to the Ordnance Board by the Act of 1842 are unusually extensive; but the Bill was submitted

---

[1] Sec 30   [2] Sec 34, and see 4 Com Journ, p 123
[3] See Powell v Farmer, 18 C B (N S), p 168

with the sanction of the Law Officers of the Crown,[1] and escaped attention in Parliament The Secretary of State is (I presume) the sole[2] judge, under Section 16, of what land is needed for the "public service,"[3] and of the precise spot on which a battery should be placed Having placed a battery or a military prison on an estate available for building, there would be no remedy for nuisance, and the only protection open to the public is the forbearance with which such powers are used [4]

But the Powers reserved to the Ordnance Board by Private Acts were in many instances of the first importance to the pecuniary interests of Public Companies and others Take, for example, the Railways that enter Portsmouth and cross the Hilsea Lines, under a Local Act (8 & 9 Vict, c 199) Over these the Ordnance Board had conceded to them Powers, all but absolute, for taking up the Railway at any time, thereby destroying not only the Works erected on the Ordnance Land, but a link in their Railway the most important for the terminal traffic[5] A Public Company might readily concede to a Board of Parliamentary Officers, presided over by a Military Officer of the highest skill and of great Public Reputation and experience, such extravagant Powers, but have they or the Public anything like the same security—when these Powers are transferred to *one* Minister who, from the necessity of his position as a Civilian, acts under the inspiration or upon the advice of irresponsible officials?

The same remark is equally applicable to the holding of lands for the Public against Local and Personal interests A Scheme comes before Parliament for some Public Enterprise to benefit proprietors or a Local Community Public interests, as held by the War Department, are opposed to private interests as represented by a Company. Such a Board as the Ordnance might be left to decide from their own experience, whether the land required might be

---

[1] This was disputed in *Ex parte* Laws (see shorthand-writer's notes), but these entries of disbursements under date of 14th June, 1842, appear conclusive — " Paid fees to the Attorney-General with case and perusing, and considering New Ordnance Vesting and Services Act, and assistance in the House of Commons, and Clerk " 'For four consultations, and Clerk " " The like to the Solicitor-General ' The Bill was drawn by Mr Rowe There is no provision for payment of costs to the land-owner, as the Court of Exchequer held in the case before referred to, and the Judge censured the provision in the Act, which he, as the Law Officer, had approved in the Bill

[2] Stockton v Brown, 9 House of Lords Cases, p 250, Galloway v Corporation of London, 2 De Gex, Jones and Smale, p 228

[3] 18 & 19 Vic, c 117, sec 3, Sheppard v Bradford, 16 C B (N S), p 375

[4] King v Place, 4 Adol and Ell, p 0 Ibottson v Peat, 3 Hur and Col p 649

[5] 'Report on Fortifications, 1869,' p xxxv., and Evidence of Colonel Jervois, C B

sold, and what Conditions, if any, might fairly be imposed for the construction of Works. These representations to the Committees in either House could be supported by men of high Professional Rank, speaking not as Deputies for a Civil Minister but upon their own authority as Members of the Administration

As the terms upon which property should be taken are within the discretion of the Secretary of State, he may, by taking property *on lease*—in effect borrow money on long terminable annuity at a rate greatly in excess of the price which the Chancellor of the Exchequer would pay for the same annuities. An instance of this is found in the Parliamentary Papers (105) printed 13th March, 1863 There, a Builder agreed to erect the Pimlico Clothing Stores for the Secretary of State at his own cost, and the Secretary of State to accept the use of the building when so erected, and to grant an annuity (which was the effect of his Covenant) of 2906*l* per annum for seventy-eight years The Secretary of State had the option—which he never exercised—of redeeming the annuity by payment of the capital sum of 39,600*l* , and if these figures are compared with those shown on the grant of annuities by the Chancellor of the Exchequer, it will be shown that the lease is not an advantageous loan—to the Public

For protection of Commercial Harbours, sites for Batteries may be granted to the Secretary of State under 24 & 25 Vic. c 45

(L L.)

Chapter XX , *par* 41

The Ordnance Survey Acts

These Acts have reference, first to Ireland, and, secondly, to Great Britain , and are in outline as follows —

1st As to Ireland.

The 6 Geo IV , c 99, reciting (1), " That it was expedient, with a View to the more effectual Execution of a General Survey of Ireland, by and under the Directions of Officers appointed by the Master-General and Board of Ordnance, that the reputed Boundaries of the several Parishes and Townlands in Ireland should be ascertained and marked out, enacted That it should be lawful for the Lord-Lieutenant to ascertain and mark out the reputed Boundaries of all and every or any Barony, or other Division or Denomination of Land in Ireland, and to appoint Persons to be Surveyors for the carrying into effect the Purposes of the Act [1]

---

[1] Sec 7

(2) " Any Surveyor appointed under the Act, and any other Person acting in aid and under the Orders of such Surveyor, and any Officer or Person appointed by or acting under the Orders of the Ordnance was empowered to enter any Land or Ground of any Person or Persons whomsoever, for the Purpose of making any Survey authorized by the Act, or by the Order of the Ordnance, and for the Purpose of fixing any Object to be used in the Survey, or any Post, Stone, or Boundary Mark whatsoever, and to fix and place any such Object, Post, Stone, or Boundary Mark whatsoever in the Land or Ground, or upon any Tree or Post in the Land or Ground of any Person or Persons whomsoever, and to dig up any Ground for the Purpose of fixing any such Object, and to enter upon any Lands through which such Surveyor shall deem it necessary to carry any Boundary Line for the Purposes of the Act, at any Time or Times whatever, until the marking out of any reputed Boundary Line shall be completed. In every Case in which it shall be necessary to fix any such Object within any walled Garden, Orchard, or Pleasure Ground, the Surveyor must give Three Days' Notice to the Occupier of his Intention so to do, and such Occupier may employ any Person whom he may think fit to fix such Object, at such Time, in such Place, and in such Manner as the Surveyor shall direct. the Surveyor is to do as little Damage as may be, and to make Satisfaction to the Owners of and other Persons interested in the Lands and Grounds, or Trees, which may be hurt, for all Damages sustained in the Execution of this Act, in case the same shall be demanded [1]

(3) " For the Purpose of marking out the reputed Boundaries of any such Barony or other Divisions, the Surveyor, by Notice in Writing to any Collector of County Cess Charges and Grand Jury Rates, shall require the Attendance of any such Collector, at such Time (not being less than Ten Days after the Date of such Notice) and at such Place as shall be specified in such Notice, at which Time and Place the Collector shall attend upon the Surveyor accordingly, and aid and assist him in the Execution of the Act. in case there shall not be any Collector, or the Collector shall omit or neglect to attend at the Time and Place mentioned in the Notice, then the Surveyor, by like Notice, shall require any Two or more Inhabitants to attend in the Place and Stead of the Collector, and every such Inhabitant shall attend upon the Surveyor accordingly, and assist him in the Execution of the Act [2]

(4) " Such Surveyor, at the Time mentioned in the Notice, accompanied by the Collector, or by such Inhabitants as aforesaid, shall perambulate the Boundaries of such Townland, Parish, or

Division, for the Purpose of ascertaining the same according to the best of their Power and Information, and for that Purpose shall call on any Inhabitant to assist them in so doing, and when it shall appear to such Surveyor that the reputed Boundaries of any such Townland, Parish, or other Division, are sufficiently ascertained, the Boundaries shall be marked out by the Surveyor, in such substantial and durable Manner as he shall think fit, by putting down Posts, or Blocks of Wood or Stone, or by affixing Marks on or against any House, Tree, or Post, and with such distinguishing Letters or Figures as such Surveyor shall think fit and proper for the Occasion, and after such Boundaries shall be so ascertained and marked as aforesaid, the same shall be and be deemed the Boundaries of such Townlands, Parishes, or other Divisions respectively.'

(5) "Any Person obstructing the Surveyor in ascertaining and marking out of the Boundaries shall forfeit a Sum not exceeding Ten Pounds and not less than Two Pounds, in the Discretion of the Justice before whom such Offender shall be convicted²

(6) "The Act shall not extend, nor be deemed nor be construed to extend, to ascertain, define, alter, enlarge, increase, or decrease, nor in any Way to affect any Boundary or Boundaries of any Land, with relation to any Owner or Owners, or Claimant or Claimants of any such Land respectively, nor to affect the Title of any such Owner or Owners, or Claimant or Claimants respectively, in or to or with respect to any such Lands, but all Right and Title of any Owner or Claimant of any Land whatever, within any Townland, Parish, or Division, shall remain to all Intents and Purposes in like State and Condition as if this Act not been had or made "³

The Act then gives an appeal on the question of boundary to the Quarter Sessions, and inflicts penalties on Collectors and others making default under the Act

In the year 1854 an Act, 17 Vic, c. 17, was passed (which was amended by the 20 & 21 Vic, c. 45, and 22 & 23 Vic, c 8) to enable alterations to be made in settled boundaries by Surveyors, appointed by the Lord-Lieutenant, in cases where, in consequence of recent alterations in the course of rivers and other changes, it was necessary for the purpose of the Ordnance Survey, or for other public purpose, that a revision should be made

2nd As to Great Britain.

The 4 & 5 Vic, c 30,⁴ in the preamble makes mention of the Ordnance Survey in these terms —

" Whereas several Counties in that Part of the United Kingdom

---

¹ Sec 11   ² Sec 13   ³ Sec 15   ⁴ 56 H D. (3) p 529, 57 ib, p 511

called England have been surveyed by Officers appointed by the Master-General and Board of Ordnance, and it is expedient that general Surveys and Maps of England, Scotland, Berwick upon Tweed, and of the Isle of Man, should be made and completed by Officers in like Manner appointed, and that the Boundaries of the several Counties in England and Scotland, and of Berwick-upon-Tweed and of the Isle of Man, should be ascertained and marked out."

It then enacts —

"That for enabling the Ordnance to make and complete such Surveys and Maps of England, Scotland, Berwick-upon-Tweed, and the Isle of Man, in manner aforesaid, it shall be lawful for the Justices assembled at any Quarter Sessions, upon the Application in Writing of any Officer appointed by Ordnance for the Purposes of the Act, such Application to be transmitted to the Clerk of the Peace Fourteen Days at the least before the holding of the Court at which such Application shall be considered, who shall cause Notice of such Application to be inserted in the Newspapers in which County Advertisements are commonly inserted Seven Days at the least before the holding of such Court, to nominate and appoint Persons to aid and assist, when required, any Officer appointed as aforesaid in examining, ascertaining, and marking out the reputed Boundaries of each County, City, and other Places, Districts, and Divisions, in England, Scotland, Berwick-upon-Tweed, and the Isle of Man, and such Person shall act under and obey such Directions as he shall receive from the Officer appointed by the Ordnance to make such Surveys and Maps as aforesaid [1]

" Any Person appointed by the Justices as aforesaid, and any other Person acting in aid and under the Orders of such Person, and for any Officer or Person appointed by or acting under the Orders of the Ordnance, after Notice in Writing of the Intention of entering shall have been given to the Owner or Occupier may enter into and upon any Estate or Property of any County, or of any Body Politic or Corporate, Ecclesiastical or Civil, or into and upon any Land, Ground, or Heritages of any Person or Persons whomsoever, for the Purpose of making and carrying on any Survey authorized by the Act, or by the Order of the Ordnance, and for the Purpose of fixing any Mark or Object to be used in the Survey, or any Post, Stone, or Boundary Mark whatsoever, and to fix and place any such Object in any such Estate or Property, and to dig up any Ground, for the Purpose of fixing any such Object, and also may enter upon any Estates or Property through which any such Person

---

[1] See 1

appointed by the Justices as aforesaid, and any Officer or other Person appointed by the Ordnance, shall deem it necessary to carry out Boundary Line for the Purposes of the Act at any reasonable Time of the Day, until the surveying, ascertaining, and marking out of any reputed Boundary Line shall be completed according to the Directions of the Act." Provision is then made, as in Sect. 8 of the Irish Act (2 *ante*), with an appeal to the Quarter Sessions in any case of compensation for damage.[1]

"For the Purpose of surveying, ascertaining, and marking out the reputed Boundaries of any County, any Person appointed by the Justices, or any Officer appointed by the Ordnance within such County, by Notice in Writing to the Clerk of the Peace, may require his Attendance, either in the County or any adjoining County, at the Time (not being less than Twenty-one Days after the Date of Notice) and at the Place specified in the Notice, and to produce to such Person any Books, Maps, Papers, or other Documents, in his Custody or Possession as the Clerk of the Peace, which such Person may require for the Purpose of carrying the Act into execution, at which Time and Place the Clerk of the Peace is required to attend, and to aid and assist him in the Execution of the Act. In case it shall happen that there is no Clerk of the Peace for any such County or adjoining County, or being such any such Officer shall omit or neglect to attend at the Time and Place mentioned in the Notice, then the Person appointed shall by like Notice require any Two or more Inhabitants of any County to attend in the Place and Stead of the Clerk of the Peace; and every such Inhabitant to whom Notice shall be delivered shall attend accordingly, and assist in the Execution of the Purposes of the Act. No Clerk of the Peace shall be obliged to attend at such Time, Place or Manner as shall interfere with the proper Discharge of his ordinary Duties as Clerk of the Peace, nor shall he be called upon to produce any Books, Maps, Papers, or other Documents the Production of which can in any way injuriously affect the Interests of the County.[2]

"The Person appointed as aforesaid, shall at the Time mentioned, accompanied by the Clerk of the Peace, or by such Inhabitants as aforesaid, perambulate the Boundaries of the County, for the Purpose of surveying, ascertaining, and marking the same, according to the best of their Power and Information," and the Boundaries shall be set out and preserved as directed by Sects. 10 and 11 of the Irish Act [3]

The Act also contains a provision (nearly similar to the 15th

---

[1] See 2   [2] See 5   See 6.

Sect. of the Irish Act), that rights of property are not to be affected by the Survey. In other respects it contains nearly the same provisions that are to be found in the Irish Act, except that the expense of the English Survey is to be provided for by the Ordnance (Sect. 10), and of the Irish by the Lord Lieutenant (Sect. 17 of the Irish Act)

The Act has been continued from time to time, and is now dealt with by 'The Expiring Laws Act, 1867'

It was expedient for Parliament to declare that the rights of property shall not be affected by these Surveys or published plans, or serious difficulties might have arisen. The Ordnance Plan must not be taken to indicate the aspect of the land as to buildings, ways, or hedges at the date of its publication, or at any particular date, save that which can be shown by the original entries in the Surveyor's Book. For instance, the original survey might have been made in 1854, the plan dated in 1855, revised in 1856 up to that date, and published in 1857. In many instances the books of original and revised survey may be forthcoming, but if not the plan cannot be relied on as evidence of the state of any building or roadway at any precise time anterior to the publication of the plan.[1]

(M M.)

Chapter XX, par 86.

Mr. Snider's Case.

The case of the late Mr Jacob Snider, junior, presents many of the features that occasion difficulty and misunderstanding in settling a claim for alleged invention. His transactions with the War Department,—two only in number and entirely distinct from each other,—may therefore be worthy of a brief notice.

The first transaction was as follows —Having in 1858-9 come from America to introduce the Mont Storm Rifle to the notice of European Governments, as an agent[2] of the inventor or owner, he brought that arm to the War Department. All that need be mentioned of this transaction are two facts. (1) that the arm was not adopted, and (2) that Mr. Snider incurred a liability for stores supplied to him by the public of 1l. 2s 2d., which he never discharged. No doubt, official applications were addressed to him

---

[1] As to the admission of Public Surveys, see Starkie on Evidence, 1853, p 284. Hammond v Bradstreet, 10 Exch Case, p 397, as to the tithe, plans, &c, Freeman v Reade 32 Law Journ (M C), 226

[2] He was, if I mistake not, a naturalist and stuffed birds.

by letter, which remained unnoticed, and the legal agent of the War Department, on the 10th August, 1861, requested payment by a letter which contained an intimation that, if the debt were not paid, legal proceedings must be taken, but with the same result Mr. Snider, junior, had disappeared from England, and his address was unknown, therefore no legal proceedings were taken ; and the debt was written off as bad in 1861-2. In this transaction the public lost 1*l* 2*s* 2*d*, with some time and trouble, but certainly nothing was done of which Mr. Snider, junior, ever had any right to complain.

The second transaction arose out of these circumstances.—In August 1864, the War Department issued an Advertisement to the Gun Trade for the best method of converting the Enfield Rifle into a Breech-loader, at a cost not exceeding 1*l*. an arm. Specimen arms were to be sent to the War Office on the 2nd September, and the Secretary of State reserved to himself the power of selecting such of the plans as "appeared promising" He also offered to deliver out of store six rifles, and to pay for their conversion, and for 1000 rounds of ammunition, the sum of 20*l*

Mr. Snider came into communication with the War Department, in reply to this advertisement; and on the 30th January, 1865, he delivered in six arms—converted under the principle of a patent of 1862—and received 20*l*. for their conversion [1] As these arms "appeared promising," the Government, in November, 1865, at Mr. Snider's suggestion, undertook the conversion of ten Rifles at Enfield, permitting him—if he saw fit to do so—to superintend the conversion, and to accept from the Enfield officials any suggestions that would improve the arm

This arrangement saved Mr. Snider the expense of manufacture, but,—as it was afterwards made the basis of two claims, put forward by Snider in a letter of the 28th June, 1866, for *personal services* rendered to the War Department, viz, 1st, for models and plans furnished to the factories, 300*l*., 2nd, for eight months' service from the 18th Nov, 1865, at 300*l* a month, viz, 2400*l*,—the facts stated are important It must also be noticed that if the Patent could only be put into successful operation under such personal superintendence, it was invalid, or if valid, the owners, and not the Government, ought to have borne Mr. Snider's expenses. However, waiving these points, and to ascertain what time and service had really been given to the public by Mr. Snider—as he declined to give any account—a return of his attendances there was called for from the Factories.

---

[1] There were other Patents in relation to the arm, but this was the *only* essential one

The Superintendent at Enfield wrote thus :—

"I had not seen Mr. Snider for seven years before his first official visit to me on the 24th Nov., 1865, in connection with the order I had received to convert ten Enfield Rifles into Breech-loaders on his plan. His subsequent visits were on the following dates.—30th Nov., 11th Dec., with drawings; 14th ditto, 22nd ditto, 4th Jan., 1866, with drawings of a small-bore 12th ditto, 19th ditto, and probably twice or three times more."

The Superintendent at the Laboratory wrote :—

"I have received no assistance whatever from Mr. Snider. He has attended the experiments on many occasions (I cannot say how many); but I have never required his attendance."

The President of the Select Committee thus :—

"It does not appear from the notes of the Sub-Committee that Mr. Snider has personally attended their experiments more than three times, viz., on 10/4/66, 1/6/66, and 22/6/66; he may possibly have been present on one or two occasions when it was not noted. Captain Hole feels confident that he has not been present six times."

Now for these *personal services* (such as they were) the sum of 1000*l* was awarded by the Secretary of State, on the 10th Aug 1866, which was accepted by Mr. Snider through his Solicitors, and paid to him on the 27th Sept., 1866 [2]

But his claims as an *Inventor* had to be investigated, and these stood upon less intelligible grounds, for in July, 1866, when the Secretary of State (in anticipation of a favourable result to experiments then pending), caused the title to the Patent of 1862 to be investigated, these facts appeared,—that when Snider visited France he took out, in Jan., 1862, a joint Patent with Francis E Schneider, of Strasbourg. That in July, 1863, Snider sold his moiety, but in December, 1864, under a General Power of Attorney, held by him for the sale of Schneider's moiety, Snider bought that moiety for 300*l*, in the name of and with another party, thus becoming the owner of one-fourth of the Patent at what (as both buyer and seller) he deemed a fair and honest price. For the convenience of these parties their moiety was vested in the owner of the first moiety, and all negociations with the War Department were carried on by Snider and his Partner through the Solicitors of this owner.

Such, in the best aspect of it, was Mr. Snider's claim as an Inventor and Patentee; but as some persons appeared to impugn the validity of that Patent, and others to set up claims under it, all the papers within the cognizance of the Department that related *in any way to the Breech-loading Arm* were laid before the Law Officers (Lord Cairns

d Sr W. Bovill) that they might advise on the rights of the
various persons claiming reward in regard to an Arm then *universally* known *only* by Mr. Snider's name

Now, the advice of the Law Officers given in September—therefore, after due deliberation—was plain, viz, that the War Department ought *not* to decide upon the conflicting claims either as to the legal merits of the Invention, or the legal rights of the parties, or to recognize the claims *of Mr. Snider or of any person*, to the exclusion of others   If, however, the disputants could agree to a holder of the reward, the amount might then be paid to such person, and the rights of the several persons left to the decision of the proper tribunals

This Opinion will perhaps satisfy many that Mr. Snider had no *peculiar* merit or claim upon the English Government as an Inventor or Patentee.

The owners of the Patent claimed 120,000*l.* of the Government for the use of it   this value being enhanced, if not wholly created, by the acts of the Government subsequent to the issue of their advertisement in August, 1864   The War Department having borne all the expenses of conversion (unless 20*l* for six arms and ammunition was not a fair equivalent), what reward should be given for the use that the Crown proposed to make of the principle of conversion developed in the Patent of 1862?

The Secretary of State (General Peel) thought 15,000*l.*—which (I think) will be found to be the largest reward ever paid for any invention of a similar character—ample; and, after arrangements and compromises entered into by the several claimants, this sum was paid, and it so happened that the *first* instalment of the reward was received at the Cannon Street Railway Station, by Snider's Partner on his way to the Emperor of the French,—the adoption of the Invention by the English Government having given a marketable value to the arm, and enabled the Patentees to offer it with confidence to every other Court in Europe   The balance of the reward was paid in due course, and thus ended Mr. Snider's second transaction with the War Department.

Probably no case has been more widely or erroneously circulated than that forming the subject of this present Note, for Mr. Snider was in debt, and immediately preceding his death (on the 27th Sept, 1865), wrote to a public Journal,[1] which gave a large circulation to the falsehood, stating, as a grievance, that "he was sued and judgment obtained by the Government for the sum of 1*l* 2*s* 2*d.*,"

---

[1] See 'Times' of these dates —1866, October 17th, 20th, 27th, 31st, November 1st, 1865, April 26th and 30th (money articles)

that he would send the writ on, but that he could not c a
give active search enough among his papers to find it, though he
had it somewhere with many notes urging payment." As he
asserted in the same letter that "he left England *early* in 1861,
and returned in 1863," it was all but certain, having reference to
the dates of his absence, and of the alleged legal proceedings, that
this statement,—which was also explicitly denied by the Secretary
of State's authority,—was untrue   However, these letters, written
with the object of enhancing his reward, utterly failed of success
for though they might have misled a portion of the public for a
time, they did not enhance by one iota the amount of Public
money which the Secretary of State thought proper to award
him.

(N N.)

Chapter XX., par 36

LIST OF ACTS VESTING LAND IN THE CROWN AND ORDNANCE BOARD.

7 Anne, c. 26	⎫ Vesting Acts Portsmouth, Chatham, and
8 Anne, c. 21 .	⎬ Harwich.
9 Geo. 1, c 32 .	Exchange of land at Portsmouth
31 Geo II., c. 39 .. ⎫	Vesting Acts Portsmouth, Chatham, and
32 Geo II., c. 30 ⎬	Plymouth.
31 Geo. II., c. 38 ⎫	Vesting Acts . Milford and Pembroke
32 Geo. II., c. 26 .. ⎬	
2 Geo III., c 37 . ⎫	Vesting Acts . Coasts of Kent, Sussex, and
4 Geo. III., c. 35 .. ⎬	Southampton.
6 Geo. III , c. 103	Improvement of Plymouth Dockyard.
31 Geo. II., c 39 ..	Ordnance Vesting Act Portsmouth, Chatham, and Plymouth.
33 Geo. II. .. .	Act relating to Gunpowder Magazine, Purfleet, and relating to preceding Act.
2 Geo. III , c. 37 ..	Vesting Act. Kent, Sussex, and Southampton.
20 Geo. III., c. 33 ..	Vesting Act: Plymouth and Sheerness, Defence of Thames, Gravesend, and Tilbury Fort.
21 Geo. III., c 10 ..	Same subject.
21 Geo. III , c. 61 .	Amending 20 Geo. III., c. 38, as to Plymouth.

(O O.)

Chapter XXI., *par* 49

A List of the Principal Statutes conferring Power on the late Secretary at War.

The Militia Acts of England (1802), *Ireland* (1809), *and Scotland* (1802)

An Act[1] to repeal an Act, made in the twenty-third year of King George the Third (Mr. Burke's Act), for the better regulation of the Office of Paymaster General of His Majesty's Forces, and the more regular payment of the Army, and for the more effectually regulating the said Office

An Act[2] for the more convenient payment of Half-pay and Pensions, and other allowances to Officers and widows of Officers, and to Persons upon the Compassionate List

An Act[3] to repeal so much of an Act passed in the forty fifth year of George the Third, for regulating the Office of Paymaster-General, as requires certain Accounts to be examined and settled within certain periods by the Secretary at War, and enabling His Majesty to make Orders for examining and settling such Accounts.

An Act[4] to authorise the allowing Officers to retire on Half-pay or other allowances, under certain restrictions

An Act[5] to extend the provisions of 51 Geo III., c 103, relating to the Half-pay and Allowance of Officers retiring from Service, and to authorize the allowing to Foreign Officers wounded the like Pensions and Allowances as are given to British Officers under the like circumstances.

An Act[6] to amend several Acts relating to the Militia, and to enlisting of the Militia into His Majesty's Regular Forces

An Act[7] to repeal 54 Geo. III., c 151, and 55 Geo. III. c 170 relating to the Office of the Agent-General, and for transferring the duties of the said Office to the Offices of the Paymaster General and Secretary at War.

An Act[8] for regulating the payment of Regimental debts, and the distribution of the effects of Officers and Soldiers dying in Service, and the receipt of sums due to Soldiers

---

[1] 15 Geo III c. 58   [2] 17 Geo III (Sess 2), c 25
[3] 48 Geo III., c. 128   [4] 51 Geo. III., c 103   [5] 52 Geo III , c 151
[6] 53 Geo III , c 81   [7] 57 Geo III , c 11   [8] 58 Geo III , c 73

An Act[1] to amend 59 Geo. III, c. 73, and 1 Geo IV c 81, for regulating the payment of Regimental Debts, and the distribution of the effects of Officers and Soldiers dying in Service, and the receipt of sums due to Soldiers, and for punishing Mutiny and Desertion of Officers and Soldiers in the Service of the East India Company

An Act[2] to consolidate and amend several Acts relating to the Royal Hospitals for Soldiers at Chelsea and Kilmainham.

An Act[3] to amend 52 Geo. III., c 171, so far as the same relates to the Retired Allowances of Quartermasters of Cavalry and Infantry

An Act[4] to make further Regulations with respect to Army Pensions

An Act[5] respecting the Transfer of certain Funds to the Secretary at War and the Paymaster-General.

An Act[6] to amend the Laws relating to the Payment of Out-Pensioners of Chelsea Hospital.

An Act[7] for rendering more effective the Services of such Out-Pensioners of Chelsea Hospital as shall be called out to assist in preserving the Public Peace.

An Act[8] to attach certain Conditions to the Construction of future Railways authorised or to be authorised by any Act of the present or succeeding Sessions of Parliament, and for other purposes in relation to Railways.

An Act[9] to regulate the Stations of Soldiers during Parliamentary Elections

An Act[10] for consolidating the Offices of Paymasters of Exchequer Bills and Paymasters of Civil Services with the Office of Paymaster-General, and for making other Provisions in regard to the Consolidated Offices

An Act[11] to consolidate and amend the Laws relating to the Militia in England.

An Act[12] to amend the Laws relating to Militia in England and Wales.

An Act[13] for further regulating the Payment of the Out-Pensioners of Greenwich and Chelsea Hospitals.

An Act[14] to defray the Charge of the Pay, Clothing, and Contingent and other Expenses of the Disembodied Militia in Great Britain and Ireland; to grant Allowances in certain cases to Sub-

[1] 6 Geo IV, c. 61   [2] 7 Geo IV, c 16   [3] 7 Geo IV, c 81
[4] 1 Wm IV, c 41   [5] 1 & 2 Vic, c 39   [6] 5 & 6 Vic, c 70
[7] 6 & 7 Vic c 95   [8] 7 & 8 Vic, c 85   [9] 10 Vic, c 21.
[10] 11 & 12 Vic, c 55   [11] 15 & 16 Vic, c 50   [12] 17 & 18 Vic, c. 105
[13] 19 Vic, c 15   [14] 18 & 19 Vic, c. 123.

altern Officers, Adjutants, Paymasters, Quartermasters, Surgeons,
Assistant-Surgeons, and Surgeon's Mates of the Militia, and to
authorise the Employment of the Non-commissioned Officers

An Act[1] to amend and consolidate the Laws relating to Military
Savings Banks

An Act[2] further to amend the Laws relating to the Militia

An Act[3] to provide for the Establishment of a Reserve Force of
Men, who have been in Her Majesty's Service.

An Act[4] to amend the Laws relating to the Militia

An Act[5] to facilitate internal communication in Ireland, by
means of Tramroads or Tramways.

An Act[6] for punishing Mutiny and Desertion, and for the
better Payment of the Army and their Quarters.

And Rules and Articles of War made under such last-mentioned
Act.

(P P.)

Chapter XXII, par. 66

Explanation of the Functions of the Board of Commissioners of the Royal Hospital at Chelsea, in respect to Pension and Prize Money[7]

The Institution of the Royal Hospital at Chelsea, for the relief of
"aged, maimed, and infirm land Soldiers," dates back to the year
1681, in the reign of King Charles II[8] The Board for managing
its affairs was first constituted by Patent, under the Great Seal of
William and Mary, 3 March, 1691, and consisted of three Commissioners, of whom the then Paymaster-General of the Forces was
one. It has since been repeatedly re-constituted under various
Patents, with a varying number of Members, but care has been
always taken to retain on the Board the Paymaster General for the
time being, who has officiated as its Chairman and Parliamentary
representative, and who has therefore been primarily responsible
for its proceedings. As at present constituted, the Board consists of

[1] 22 & 23 Vic , c 20 [2] 22 & 23 Vic , c 38 [3] 22 & 23 Vic , c 12
[4] 23 & 24 Vic , c 94 [5] 23 & 24 Vic., c 152 [6] 25 Vic , c 5
[7] I am indebted for this Note to Major-General Hutt, C B , the Secretary to the
Royal Commissioners.
[8] See an account of it, Lyson's 'Environs of London,' and 37 Ann Reg , p 116.

Commissioners, chosen from Civilians holding high offices of State, assisted by members of Military rank and experience, and its mixed character has been designed to ensure, at once, economy to the National Revenue, due control to the Crown, and justice to the faithful and deserving Soldier.

The operations of the Commissioners were at first confined to the management of the internal affairs of the Hospital, which was perhaps originally intended to accommodate within its walls the whole of the Pensioners, but as the number of deserving applicants for the Royal Bounty was immediately found to be in excess of the accommodation afforded by the building, the system of out-pensions became a matter of necessity, and the Commissioners were charged with the duty of awarding and paying these also, out of funds provided for the purpose by deductions from the pay of the Troops, and some provision, in addition, by the Crown. All such deductions have since ceased to be exacted, and the whole of the necessary funds for the support of the Pensioners are now annually provided by the liberality of Parliament.

The Commissioners appear to have been first clothed with Statutory authority in the year 1754, by the Act 27 George II, c 1, but their functions have since been acknowledged in various Statutes, the general law under which they act being set forth in 7 George IV., c. 16, the provisions of which have been very little varied by any later enactment

Pensions are granted in the way of Grace or Bounty from the Crown, for the Army possesses no *legal right* to such gifts. The general regulations under which they are granted are set forth in Warrants issued by the Crown to the Board of Commissioners, through the Secretary of State for War, such Warrants constituting the authority regulating the rates of pension, after the Commissioners have given due consideration to the length of the Soldier's service, the nature of his wounds, or other disabilities, the climate in which he has served, and the character borne at the time of his discharge In those rare instances which cannot be provided for by General Rules, the Commissioners may fix the rate of pension, but must submit their recommendation to the approval of the Secretary of State for War (representing the Crown); who is moreover charged with the duty of interpreting any passages in the Royal Warrants that may admit of doubt

Permanent Pensions are granted to Soldiers who have completed the full term of Service in the Army, or who, without completing the full term, have been discharged, owing to inability to serve by reason of wounds or injuries received in action, or who have become incapable of earning a livelihood on account of blindness, &c. &c. attributable to the Service, or by reason of other disabilities contracted by the Service after a minimum term spent therein, temporary pensions are given to men, not in these classes, rendered unable to serve owing to disabilities contracted while in the Army. The Board of Chelsea Hospital is moved in the first instance by the receipt from the Adjutant-General, or other competent authority, of the Soldiers' Discharge Documents, which set forth the length and character of his service, the reasons assigned for his proposed discharge, the medical reports upon the state of his health, and all other necessary information, and subsequently to discharge, Pensioners may apply to the Commissioners for increase of rate, where the maximum has not been already granted, or for renewal of temporary pensions, should sufficient grounds exist for further bounty, such applications being considered by the Board with the assistance of Reports specially procured from the local Staff Officers and local Medical Authorities.

Up to the years 1842-3, the actual payment of the money awarded as pension was made by the Chelsea Board, through the Excise Officers, Chief Constables of Police, and others, stationed throughout the United Kingdom, but at this time it was considered that the work of payment could be more conveniently performed by Officers on half-pay, resident in districts assigned—now known as Staff Officers of Pensioners—to receive their appointments from the Secretary of State for War. The Commissioners, however, continue to be alone responsible for the admission and continuance of persons on the Pension List. This is made clear by the Act of 19 Victoria, c. 15, which, while authorizing the Secretary at War to make regulations for the management and payment of the Pensioners, expressly declares that nothing in the Act contained "shall be held to interfere with the powers of the Chelsea Commissioners in regard to granting, increasing, reducing, suspending, taking away or restoring of pension, or to abridge, take away, or interfere with any power, authority, or duty of the said Commissioners other than by the Act is expressly provided."

The total number of pensions at present provided for exceeds 60,000, varying from year to year with the exigencies of the Service.

The internal management of the Hospital is regulated by Warrants addressed to the Commissioners by the Crown, fixing the rates of allowance for the several Officers and Pensioners, the duties they have severally to perform, and the conditions of admission. Originally intended, as is supposed, for the accommodation of all Pensioners at a time when the Military Forces of the Crown were of small numbers, the Establishment has, since the great extension of Out-pensioners, been filled by a selection of the most meritorious of this class, who must be of good character, have shown good service, and, as a general rule, have attained to advanced years. The building affords accommodation to about 540 (exclusive of Officers). and the helpless character of the inmates is best shown by the circumstances that their average age approaches 70 years, that nearly 100 are constantly found fit subjects for the Infirmary, and that the deaths fall little short of the same number annually. Preference is given to Candidates who have no families dependent upon them, and no person to take care of them; and to such men—requiring for the most part nursing, generous diet, and medical treatment—the rate of Out-pension would be wholly inadequate for support and comfort, nor would the cost of In-pension, though somewhat higher, suffice to procure for them, individually, homes and treatment suited to their circumstances, and merited by their services to the country. During the period of residence the Out-pension of course ceases, but the men are freely permitted to revert to it, and leave the Establishment should they so desire,—a course seldom pursued.

The connection of this Board with the payment of *Army Prize Money* had its origin in the beginning of the present century, when, owing to the loss of vast sums remaining from time to time in the hands of Agents appointed to distribute Prize Money on the occasion of each capture, Acts of Parliament were procured directing that all unclaimed shares should then and thenceforward be collected into a common fund, and devoted to a common purpose. The Commissioners of Chelsea Hospital were appointed the recipients of such shares, which they were to refund to those entitled thereto, if claimed within a given time, and if not claimed, to devote to the general purposes of the Hospital. By subsequent Acts it was designed that future Grants of Prize Money should be given to the Commissioners themselves for distribution, with a like provision respecting unclaimed shares, but since that time most of the booty taken in War by the Army has been captured in India, and the Prize Money granted in consequence has been necessarily made over to the late Honourable East India Company, or in more recent years to the Secretary of State for India, for distribution. The unclaimed shares of these grants, belonging to Her Majesty's Army, and all shares of this character claimed out of India, pass through the hands of the Chelsea Board, and become liable to the same provisions of law as those grants made direct by the Crown to the

Commissioners themselves   The law affecting the distribution and the duties of the Commissioners in connection therewith are for the most part to be found in 2 Wm. IV, c. 53, the provisions of which have been very little modified by any later Act   The Commissioners present annually to Parliament a statement of their operations, and from the one submitted for the year ended 31st December, 1868, it appears that they had, up to that date, and from the commencement of their operations, received shares amounting to 1,585,234*l.* 0*s* 8*d*, of which the sum of 1,103,954*l* 7*s* 11*d* was refunded to claimants   They also paid in aid of the Pension Votes 642,382*l* 1*s* 11*d*, the interest derived from temporary investments out of the fund enabling them to apply to the purposes directed a larger amount than they had originally received.

(Q Q.)

Chapter XXII, par 66.

THE PATRIOTIC FUND.

I HAVE noticed the fact that our earlier European Wars, after the Revolution, were carried on by the hire of Soldiers upon the Continent, and that by this policy the country was relieved from finding employment for discharged Soldiers at the close of the War[1] Another advantage was, that non effective charges *did not* appear in the Army Estimates for many subsequent years, as Pensions did not arise in favour of the Foreigner.   However, in some Wars, as in that unfortunate one against America, we were obliged to depend more upon our National than upon Foreign Troops, and on those occasions the public spirit of the people manifested itself by raising subscriptions for the wounded and disabled officers and men

At the commencement of the great War against Napoleon, the Underwriters at Lloyd's held a meeting in July, 1803, to raise such a fund, and they set a noble example by giving 20,000*l*, 3*l*, per cent, from the Common Stock of the House, as the first subscription.   This was followed by the Merchants of the City of London, and before the same month closed 150,000*l.* was raised.   The distribution was made by a Committee to the Navy and Army, and proceeded from a patriotic rather than a purely benevolent motive,

---

[1] Vol I, Chap XIII, par 7, and see Note S

to swords were voted to brave Officers, as well as money granted to
wounded Officers or Men [1]

Such being the feeling of the Merchants towards the Navy and
Army, Sir H. Popham thought that it called for some recognition
from the Navy, and, therefore, after his descent upon Buenos
Ayres, he opened a direct communication with the Committee, and
pointed out to the Merchants of London the advantages that would
result to commerce from his conquests.

The War in the Crimea attracted a deeper interest than any
other Foreign War undertaken by this country. The heroism
and patient endurance of the officers and men, the large proportion
of native Troops that were in the Pay of this country, the flood of
information through newspapers and telegraphs that was opened
upon us from the Crimea, brought the whole scene home in a
manner unknown to any other, or to our own people, in any previous
War. Consequently, so soon as any blood was shed, a Subscription
List was at once opened,—but in this instance under the Royal
sanction and with Royal Commissioners as the directing Agents

The Patriotic Fund for the Russian War was constituted under
Letters Patent of the 7th October, 1854, and the objects for which
it was raised are set forth in the recitals nearly in these words

The recitals state that "many soldiers, sailors, and marines,
serving in Our Armies and Fleets, have gallantly fallen in battle, or
by other casualties during war and many who shall hereafter be
engaged in conflict, or in the further prosecution of hostilities, may
also nobly sacrifice their lives in Our Service, while protecting the
invaded liberties of Our Ally, and repressing the lawless ambition
of Our enemies "

That ' many of Our loving subjects throughout Our Kingdom
and Dominions, actuated by a just sense of the sacred rights of those
who fall in their country's service and in support of Our just cause
of war, are anxiously desirous of testifying their loyalty by a just
and generous benevolence towards the widows and orphans of those
of Our soldiers, sailors, and marines who have been so killed, or
who may hereafter die amidst the ravages and casualties of war,
and also by their gifts and subscriptions to contribute a portion of
those means with which Our Nation has been blessed towards the
succouring, educating, and relieving those, who, by the loss of their
husbands and parents in battle, or by death on active Service in the
present war, are unable to maintain or to support themselves."

---

[1] See generally as to the Fund, 39 Ann Reg, p 14 · 45 ib., pp 408-18, 47 ib,
pp 391, 402, 435, 49 ib, p 13   [2] 49 Ann. Reg, p 43

" That public measures should be taken for the safe keeping and beneficial application of the several sums of money which may be given, subscribed, or collected, for all or any of the several purposes aforesaid and also for the purpose of securing such prompt and authentic information as may be required, to aid the just and faithful distribution of the said several sums of money, when so received."

The Letters Patent then set forth that " Her Majesty, being earnestly desirous, in lasting memory of those who have faithfully fallen in Our service, to encourage the loyal and hearty benevolence of Our loving subjects, which may hereafter be directed towards the Widows and Orphans of the Soldiers, Sailors, and Marines of Our Forces, who may now or hereafter be serving abroad in Our Armies and Fleets, or in services connected with Our present hostilities," thereby appointed Commissioners " to make full and diligent inquiry into the best mode of aiding the loyalty and benevolence of Our loving subjects, and of ascertaining the best means by which the gifts, subscriptions, and contributions of Our loving subjects can be best applied, according to the generous intentions of the donors thereof, and from time to time to apply the same as you, Our Commissioners, or any three or more of you, shall think fit or direct, either for the immediate relief of such special objects or destitution as may come within the meaning and purpose of such benevolence, or, for any of the purposes aforesaid, to increase, extend, or make additions to any of Our Royal or other charitable institutions already founded for similar purposes within Our United Kingdom. And further, to apply, or to order and direct the application of, all such moneys in such manner as to you Our Commissioners, or to any three or more of you, shall seem fit in the premises, so that you do in all things secure the most impartial and beneficent distribution of all such sums as may hereafter and from time to time be received under or by virtue of this Our Royal Commission."

Under this Commission a sum amounting to 1,460,000*l*, or thereabouts, was collected from all parts of the empire Our fellow-subjects at the world's end setting a noble example of liberality, and showing themselves members of the Anglo-Saxon brotherhood by the highest evidence of kinship, their sympathy in the loss of life caused by a devastating war.

Much of this sum has been carefully distributed to the relief of many deserving claimants, but as some permanent endowments have been created for the Army and Navy in future years, an account of these may be useful to the reader.

Now the Schedule to the Patriotic Fund Act, 1867 (which will be referred to hereafter), gives the detail of and confirms these specific appropriations made by the Royal Commissioners to increase and extend institutions existing in the United Kingdom at the date of the Letters Patent.

"1. The sum of 2747*l.* 5*s.* 1*d.* now 3*l.* per centum held under the trusts, declared by a deed poll of the 9th of February, 1857, to secure in perpetuity, on the nomination of the Royal Commissioners, the admission of thirteen Boys, sons of Soldiers, Sailors, or Marines, of Her Majesty's Service, into the Royal, Naval, and Military Free School at Devonport.

"2 The sum of 2747*l.* 5*s* 1*d.* new 3*l.* per centum, held under the trusts, declared by a deed poll of the 18th of February, 1857, to secure in perpetuity, on the nomination of the Royal Commissioners, the admission of eleven Boys, the sons of Soldiers, Sailors, or Marines of Her Majesty's Service, into the Royal Seamen and Marines' Orphan School, Portsea.

"3 The sum of 25,000*l.* paid to the Governors of Wellington College, upon an agreement confirmed by a bye law of the said Governors of the 27th of February, 1857, to secure in perpetuity, on the nomination of the Royal Commissioners, the admission of eighteen Boys, children of deceased Commissioned Officers in Her Majesty's Army, into the College.

"4 The sum of 1000*l.* paid to the Treasurer of the Cambridge Asylum at Kingston-on-Thames towards building, and 2116*l* 8*s.* 1*d.* new 3*l.* per centum held under the trusts, declared by a deed poll of the 3rd of September, 1857, to secure in perpetuity, on the nomination of the Royal Commissioners, the admission of five women, Widows of Soldiers, into the Cambridge Asylum

"5 The sum of 5000*l* sterling paid to the Treasurer of the Royal Naval Female School at St Margaret's, Isleworth, for the general purposes of the Institution, and held under a deed of covenant of the 16th April, 1857, to secure in perpetuity, on the nomination of the Royal Commissioners, the admission of five pupils into the School upon the terms and conditions mentioned in the Indenture

"6 The sum of 8000*l.* paid to the Royal Naval School, New Cross, for the general purposes of the Institution under the sanction of Parliament, to secure the admission in perpetuity, on the nomination of the Royal Commissioners, of seven pupils, sons of Naval or Marine Officers, upon the terms and conditions specified in the 23 & 24 Vic, c. 104 (local and personal)"

These appropriations were made in pursuance of the Resolution of the Executive Commissioners, dated May, 1856, the substance of which, as to *other* endowments, was in these words:—

"The Commissioners having, by Scale of Allowances adopted at the last meeting, made liberal and proper provision, firstly, for the Widows and Orphans, for Non-commissioned Officers, and Petty Officers, Privates, and Seamen, and secondly, for Widows and Orphans of Officers to the rank of Colonel inclusive, deemed it essential, in making further provision for these immediate objects of their care, to adopt such measures as would confer enduring benefits on the two Services. It was therefore determined to effect the endowment of Institutions for the benefit of the Children of Soldiers, Sailors, and Marines, and by the purchase of presentations to already existing Asylums and Schools for similar objects, all which, whilst strictly within the terms of the Royal Commission, which authorises the Commissioners to apply portions of the Fund —'To increase, extend, or make additions to any of our Royal or other charitable Institutions already founded for similar purposes, viz, succouring, educating, and relieving those who by the loss of their husbands or parents in battle, or by death on active service in the present War, are unable to maintain or to support themselves,'—would also be in accordance with the known wish of many of the subscribers, and be an enduring memorial of the loyalty, patriotism, and sympathy manifested by all classes during the late war.

"Resolved, that there shall be a perpetual endowment of 5000*l* per annum for the education and maintenance of about 300 Daughters of Soldiers, Sailors, and Marines and that 140,000*l* be allotted to the purchase or erection of a suitable house with grounds, and 20,000*l* for furniture and other necessaries—making together 160,000*l*.

"That there shall be a perpetual endowment for a School for about 100 Boys, the Sons of Soldiers, Sailors, and Marines. This it is estimated will cost 25,000*l* beyond the allowances under the Scale, for the Boys at present provided for

"That the interest of the above-mentioned sums shall be set apart for the education and maintenance of 300 Girls, and about 100 Boys; but, until Schools are in full operation, the interest shall go into the general Fund.

' Resolved, that it be referred to a Committee to consider and report whether two or more Schools should be purchased or erected, or whether the Funds should be applied in any other and what manner, and whether it will be advisable to lessen or increase the number of Girls or Boys to be provided for as assumed "

From these Resolutions originated the Royal Victoria Patriotic Asylum, at Wanstead, for the Daughters of Soldiers, Sailors, and Marines, elected thereto by the Royal Commissioners

The site of this School was purchased on the 24th June, 1857, from Earl Spencer, for 3300*l.*, and was conveyed to three of the Commissioners as Trustees for the Fund, and a building was erected at the cost of (say) 70,000*l.* For the perpetual endowment of the School the Commissioners, by letter of 19th June, 1860, directed the Paymaster-General to open a separate account in his books, to be called the Royal Victoria Patriotic Asylum Account, and to transfer from the General Account of the Patriotic Fund to this special account 2273*l.* 5*s.* cash, and the following securities :—

	£	s	d		£	s	d
London and Greenwich Railway Loan, 4 per Cent	50,000	0	0	cost	50,062	10	0
Canada Government 6 per Cent Debentures	30,000	0	0	,,	32,750	0	0
New Brunswick Government 6 per Cent. Debentures	7,000	0	0	,,	7,075	0	0
Nova Scotia Government 6 per Cent Debentures	2,000	0	0	,,	2,092	10	0
New South Wales Government 5 per Cent Debentures	20,000	0	0	,,	19,887	10	0
South Australian 6 per Cent Debentures	10,000	0	0	,,	10,300	0	0
Victoria Government 6 per Cent Debentures	20,000	0	0	,,	22,087	10	0
	139,000	0	0		144,255	0	0

With reference to an endowed Boys' School the Commissioners have always had it in contemplation to establish one in perpetuity, and for that object a Fund was set aside at the ninth meeting of the Royal Commissioners, 13th March, 1857, by the following resolution —

"Resolved—It will be impossible to carry out their plan as sanctioned at last Meeting, of purchasing nominations in the Government Asylums for 100 Boys in perpetuity, but that to secure for the future the sum of 25,000*l.*, that sum to be now set aside as a permanent and separate Fund for the maintenance and education of Sons of Soldiers, Sailors, and Marines, and that interest be added from time to time, to accumulate with capital, until the Royal Commissioners shall direct to the contrary "

And the following entry in Appendix A (page 7) to the Commissioners' 6th Report to Her Majesty (June, 1866) is found :—

"SECURITIES OF BOYS' SCHOOL ACCOUNT

	£	s.	d
"East India 4 per Cent Debentures	32,000	0	0
New 3 per Cent. Annuities . .	6,427	0	0 "

In the mean while the Commissioners are carrying on two Boys' Schools at the expense of the General Fund upon leasehold premises held at Chipping Barnet, by indenture of 25th August, 1858, for the residue of an unexpired term of twenty-one years from 29th September, 1856, and at East Hill, Wandsworth, by indenture of 18th July, 1861, for a term of nine years to expire at Midsummer, 1870.

From the Report of Mr Finlaison (see Commissioners' Report of 1866), it appeared that, independently of the two special appropriations in favour of the "Royal Victoria Patriotic Asylum, and the Boys' School Account," there was on the General Fund a then *present* available surplus of 86,804*l*, and a probable *future* surplus of 161,304*l*, for which no objects—coming within the terms of the Royal Commission, and the rules from time to time laid down by Her Majesty's Commissioners—could be found

It therefore became necessary to apply to Parliament for powers granting the surplus to other than the original objects, after those objects were satisfied   Thus the Patriotic Fund Act, 1867,[1] provided that this Fund should be applied as follows :—

"First, in relief of Widows, and maintenance, education, training, and advancement, of Children of Soldiers, Seamen, and Marines of Our Army and Navy who lost their lives in battle in the late War with Russia, or in consequence of wounds received in or by or in consequence of other casualties sustained in or disease contracted in that War.

"Secondly, in maintenance, education, training, and advancement of Children of Soldiers, Seamen, and Marines, of Our Army and Navy who had lost or should thereafter lose their lives in battle or in any other War, or in consequence of wounds received in or by or in consequence of other casualties sustained in or disease contracted in any other War

"Thirdly, in maintenance, education, training, and advancement of Children of other Soldiers, Seamen, and Marines of our Army and Navy who had lost or should hereafter lose their

---

[1] 30 & 31 Vic , c 98

lives in the service of the Crown, or by or in consequence of casualties sustained or disease contracted in the Service of the Crown.'

As the estates and property of the Fund were likely to get outstanding in the legal or personal representatives of the Commissioners, a power was given to the Crown[1] to appoint, by Letters Patent, the First Lord of the Admiralty, the Secretary of State for War, and the Paymaster-General, the official trustees of the real and personal property of the Royal Commissioners, and power was given to the official trustees to institute suits and proceedings without abatement thereof by the death or resignation of office.

The rights of patronage and nomination to the Schools and charities were preserved and continued to the Royal Commissioners appointed from time to time by supplementary patent. But when the number of Commissioners is reduced below twelve, then these rights may be exercised by such person or persons as Her Majesty by Royal Warrant may be pleased to direct.

The Supplementary Patent is dated the 26th March, 1868, and declares that nothing in it shall prejudicially affect the claims of any person under any grant or arrangement theretofore made by the Commissioners acting under the original Commission

It, however, revoked and determined the following parts of the original Commission —

"1st. So much thereof as related to the appointment of Secretaries, and to the filling up of vacancies in those offices.

"2ndly. That part thereof, commanding the Paymaster-General to open and keep a separate Account at the Bank of England.

"3rdly. So much thereof as relates to the Audit of Accounts, disbursements, and payments"

But in all other respects the original Commission was confirmed, "subject to the provisions of the supplementary Commission, and the same is to be read and have effect with the supplementary Commission as one Commission."

(R R.)

THE ROYAL MILITARY ASYLUM.

Chapter XXII, par. 66

The only provision made for the orphan children of soldiers is that

---

[1] 30 & 31 Vic, c 98

of educating some of them in the Royal Military Asylum and Hibernian School.

In the year 1800, the Duke of York, as President of the Institution or Commander-in-Chief, by circular letter of 20th December, addressed to the colonels of regiments, proposed to them to defray the annual charge of an institution for the maintenance and education of the orphans of soldiers, and of such children as are unavoidably left behind on embarkation for Foreign Service, in part by a voluntary subscription of one day's pay from all ranks of the Army, and the residue was to be obtained by subscription from the Civil community[1] The sum of 3061*l.* 13*s* 1*d.* was immediately raised from, but in part returned to the Army, as the House of Commons was ready to make the necessary grants for the maintenance of such an institution, which may be said to have had its origin in a Royal Warrant of the 24th June, 1801,[2] appointing Commissioners for the Asylum established for the maintenance and education of orphan and other children of the non-commissioned officers and soldiers of the Army; and the Commissioners were ordered to prepare rules and regulations for the good government thereof.

The Asylum was built by the Barrackmaster-General at an extravagant cost of 105,000*l.* upon a leasehold estate of fifty years' term. The children were first admitted in August, 1803, when the school-teaching was commenced For many years the Asylum was regulated by the Royal Warrant of 26th April, 1805, which provided that 700 boys and 300 girls should be educated therein.[3]

The Commissioners appointed in 1805 were the four younger sons of George III , and certain *ex officio* Commissioners (as the Commander-in-Chief, Secretary at War, Bishops of London and Winchester, the Paymaster-General, the Master-General of the Ordnance, the Quartermaster, Adjutant-General, the Barrackmaster, Inspector of Recruiting Colonels of two Regiments of Life Guards, the Judge-Advocate, the Chaplain-General, and the Deputy Secretary at War), who were to hold four Quarterly Boards for the Officers of the Asylum, and to admit children, giving a preference according to the following rules of selection :—

"1st To orphans

"2nd. To those whose fathers have been killed, or have died on Foreign Service[4]

---

[1] $\frac{132021}{1-7}$ (O. S).   [2] 19th Report of Military Inquiry, 1812, p. 457

[3] Ib., p. 396   [4] "Or Home Service' in the Royal Hibernian School, 1846

"3rd To those who have lost their mothers, and whose fathers
are absent on duty abroad "

"4th To those whose fathers are ordered on Foreign Service,
or whose parents have other children to maintain "

The number of children admitted in each year has varied
considerably   It was largely increased until the close of the
French War. thus, by Royal Warrant of 24th February, 1809,
the numbers were extended to 712 boys, and 348 girls and in 1810,
the total number of children was made up to 1300. By Royal
Warrant of 25th January, 1816, a building to hold 400 children
was erected at Southampton, and that number appointed as inmates [1]

The reductions commenced in 1819 and in August, 1821, the
admissions were limited to children who had lost one or both
parents   In 1822 the limit was to be 1000 children, and only one
admission for two vacancies was allowed   In 1830 and 1831 the
limits were to be 600 boys and 200 girls   In 1833-4, children who
had lost both parents were admitted, but vacancies arose in January,
1838, when the terms of admission were enlarged, and the number
of boys was limited to 350.

In 1840, the Southampton Establishment was closed, and no
girls were afterwards admitted into Chelsea   Up to that date the
number of children admitted, both into Chelsea and Southampton,
stood as follows —

	Boys.	Girls.	Total.
In the Asylum	345	14	359
Had died	264	98	362
Deserted	10	.	10
Been apprenticed . . .	1622	1385	3007
Discharged with gratuities.. .	470	795	1265
Given up to Parents .	1303	241	1514
Detained by same .. .	177	39	216
Volunteered for the Army .	1957	.	1957
	6148	2572	8720

[1] 'Finance Report, 1817,' pp 59, 60 , ib., 1818, p 18

The number of children which then might be accommodated at Chelsea amounted to 1250

The total expense of the Asylum from 1801 to 1831 was 794,157*l.* In 1848, Parliament sanctioned the use of 30,000*l*, part of the unclaimed Prize Money, for the purchase of Lord Cadogan's estate, on which the Asylum had been built [1]

In the year 1846 two important changes were made, that are best explained in the order of date—(1) the establishment of a Normal School at the Asylum by Royal Warrant of the 21st November, 1846, and (2) the revision of the Asylum by another Warrant of the 21st December, 1846.

With reference to the Normal School, it may be observed that regimental schools had been established for many years anterior to 1846. The earliest trace of these institutions, that I am aware of, is to be found in the Bedford Militia, in which regiment the late Mr Samuel Whitbread, M P, when the Lieutenant-Colonel, established a school in November, 1809. Out of this act arose a lengthened litigation,[2] which, so far as need be mentioned here, determined that a Commanding Officer could not of his own authority order his men (1) to go to school, or (2) to pay the schoolmaster

However, in August, 1811, the Duke of York submitted to the Secretary at War a proposal to establish schools throughout the Service for the education of young soldiers and soldiers' children upon the principle of Dr Bell, as adopted with much success at the Royal Military Asylum, which proposal was accepted by the Treasury, and provision of 20,000*l.* made in the Estimates of 1812 for these schools.[3]

The schoolmaster for each regiment was to be an attested soldier, selected by the Colonel, and placed on the strength of the Regiment as a Sergeant-Schoolmaster,[4] with the same pay and allowances as a Paymaster-Sergeant   In the half-yearly accounts 10*l* was to be allowed for stationery and other incidental expenses of the School.

From these arrangements it became the duty of all soldiers subsequently enlisting into the Army to attend school, and it was within the competency of the Crown, acting through the Com-

---

[1] 11 & 12 Vic., c 103, see the Army Expenditure, 1850, and Report of 1851.

[2] Warden *v* Bailey, 4 Taun Rep, p 67, and Bailey *v* Warden, 4 Mar. and Sel, p 400, 21 H D. (O S), p 1201.

[3] 21 H. D. (O S.), p 894, and General Lefroy's Report of 1859, and Horse Guards Circular, 14th November, 1811

[4] See Warrant of 2nd July, 1846 creating the Rank

mander-in-Chief, to order them as part of their duty to do so to
enable them to become efficient soldiers. However, a doubt having
been raised upon the point it was covered by inserting the following clause in the Articles of War for 1859 —

"(32.) Any non-commissioned officer or soldier who, without
due cause or without leave from his commanding officer, shall
absent himself from the garrison or regimental school when duly
ordered to attend there, shall be liable to be tried before a Court-
martial for disobedience of orders, or be subject to such punishment
as it may be competent for his commanding officer to award.'

Libraries followed after a long interval, and were (if I mistake
not) first established in August, 1838,[1] by a grant from the Treasury
of 20*l* for each of the 50 larger military stations, and of 10*l* to each
of 108 smaller stations. The General Order of the 5th February,
18.0, laid down the regulations for their management, and for the
eleven years, from 1846-7 to 1856-7, the average annual cost to
the public was 7234*l* per annum.[2]

The Normal School at Chelsea was established by Royal Warrant
of November, 1846, to instruct Regimental and other Schoolmasters
for the Army, and as a model school—after which all military
schools should be formed. It was opened in March, 1847.

The students enter by competitive examinations twice a-year,
their age being between nineteen and twenty-five, and their
standard of height five feet and four inches. Civilians give a bond
in 50*l* that they will enlist as schoolmasters for general service in
the Army. Their education is gratuitous.

The Model School was raised in numbers to 500 boys, ranging in
age from six to sixteen years, though the average age is eleven.
The children are organised for military purposes in six companies,
and for the purposes of education into five schools, under as many
masters.

The Royal Military Asylum was in a certain manner re-
organized by Warrant of the 21st December, 1846, and the Asylum
was placed under the management of a Board, five of whom (the
Commander-in-Chief, the Secretary at War, Paymaster, Quartermaster, and Adjutant-Generals, or Governor of Chelsea Hospital
being one) were to form a quorum, and the School was to be under
a Committee consisting of the Secretary and Deputy-Secretary at
War, the Bishop of London, Paymaster General, Judge-Advocate
General, and Quartermaster-General, who were to give directions
relating to education.

---

[1] 46 H D (3), p 1126 [2] Lenoy, p 51

(S S.)

Chapter XXII, par. 66.

THE ROYAL HIBERNIAN MILITARY SCHOOL.

THIS Institution, which may be said to date from Her Majesty's Letters Patent of the 9th December, 1846, arose out of the Hibernian Society, which had previously existed as an exclusively "Protestant" establishment.

This Society was originally founded in 1764 by private subscription for the education of twenty children at Oxmantown,[1] in consequence of the great distress to which the families of Soldiers on Foreign Stations were reduced. In subsequent years the Irish Parliament made grants for the erection of schools in Phoenix Park, part of which (consisting of thirty-three and a-half acres) had been granted to the Society by the Crown. The Society was first incorporated by Letters Patent of the 14th July, 1769, and another Charter granted on the 8th February, 1808, for the education of children, elected upon the same rules of preference that had been laid down in 1805 for the Royal Military Asylum.

The school buildings were calculated to contain 600 children, and the Society was possessed of funded property (the gift of private benefactors), yielding an income of 280*l.*, but from the year 1784 the maintenance of the School was principally derived from Parliament, the total of these grants from the Union to 1829 inclusive amounting to 243,531*l.*

In 1829, the Select Committee on the Irish Estimates thought it desirable that the School should be brought under the direct control of the Secretary at War, and voted in the same Estimate with the Military Asylum at Chelsea, but it was objected to by the governing body in Ireland, and nothing further was done beyond limiting the future admissions to 300 children.

In 1818 its exclusively Protestant character was again asserted by the Charter of the 5th December, 1818, which authorized the Commissioners to appoint fit and able artificers to teach the children such trades as the Society might see fit: and the first relaxation of the rules, which obliged the children to learn the Catechism of the

---

[1] See further, 'Army Expenditure, 1850.'

Church of England, and attend its services, was granted by the Charter of Her Majesty, bearing date 4th March, 1841.

The ' Royal Hibernian Military School" was established under that title by the Royal Charter of the 19th December, 1846,[1] which appointed—as the new Governors—the Lord-Lieutenant for the time being, and several other persons (being, with two or three exceptions, Military Officers). The Governors have the general management of the School, the appointment of masters and artificers, and also of the Protestant resident chaplains for the instruction of such of the children as shall be Protestants of the Church as Established in Ireland

The Charter gives exemption to the children of Roman Catholic and Dissenting parents from attending this instruction, and enables the Governors to appoint chaplains or teachers of these persuasions to visit the School and instruct the children

The parents or friends applying for the admission of children are required to sign a consent to the children remaining in the School as long as the Governors see fit, and to their being disposed of—when of proper ages—with their own consent, at the discretion of the Governors as apprentices or servants, or, if boys, of their enlisting into the Army.

The Rules and Regulations at present in force bear date of the 1st of January, 1854, and the last Estimate shows the school to contain 410 boys, and to be maintained at an annual cost of 11,778*l*. With the altered arrangements made for the Church of Ireland some modification may be required in the existing Charter of this Institution.

(T T.)

Chapter XXIII., par 12

UPON THE STATUTE LAW REGULATING THE TAKING AND GIVING SECURITIES BY PUBLIC ACCOUNTANTS.

The Acts—50 Geo. III., c. 85, and 52nd Geo III., c. 66—direct that all Persons holding Situations of Public Trust shall give Security for the due performance of their duty in a Bond, with two Sureties, for such amount as the Head of the Department under which they

---

[1] See Commons' Return, 23 May, 1858 p. (294), and 12th March, 1861, p. (98).

are employed shall require, according to the nature of the trust
reposed in them, these Sureties are required to be named to and
approved by the Head of the Department, and the Bond is to be
executed by the respective Persons within the undermentioned
periods, according to the Location of the Party appointed, when
receiving the notification of Appointment, viz —

Within 1 Month, if the Officer shall be in England or Wales,
    2 Months, if in Scotland,
    3 Months, if in Ireland;
    6 Months, if in Europe or America, or the West Indies,
    9 Months, if in Africa,
    18 Months, if in the East Indies, or any other part of Asia,
    10 Months, if on the High Seas, or within three Months
        after his arrival in England.

The amount of the Security is to be approved by the Lords Commissioners of the Treasury, or the Head of the Department to which
the Party appointed belongs.

Persons neglecting to give Security forfeit the Appointment or
Commission in respect of which the Security ought to have been
given.

In the event of the Death or Bankruptcy of any Surety, a
written notice of such Death or Bankruptcy is to be sent to the
Head of the Department within certain periods, viz —

Within 4 Months, if in Great Britain or Ireland, if on the High
      Seas,
    4 Months, after their arrival in Great Britain or Ireland,
    12 Months, if beyond the Seas, except in the East Indies,
      or beyond the Cape of Good Hope,
    18 Months, if in the East Indies, or in any part beyond
      the Cape of Good Hope, unless he arrive in
      Great Britain or Ireland sooner, then within
      four Months after such arrival.

Persons neglecting to give this notice, are to forfeit a fourth of the
Sum, to be recovered in due course of Law, for which the Surety,
so Dead or become Bankrupt, shall have given Security; and the
Appointment also will be forfeited unless new Security be given
within the time prescribed for giving the original Security.

These Bonds were formerly registered against the lands in
England of the several parties under the 2 Vic, c 11; 18 & 19 Vic.,
c. 15, and 22 & 23 Vic, c 35, sec 22, and in Ireland under 7 & 8
Vic., c 90, and satisfaction could be entered on the Registry under
23 & 24 Vic, c 115

Under the present Law—28 & 29 Vic., c 104, secs 48 and 49—no Registry in England is to avail until execution has been issued on the Bond.

Under the provisions of later Acts, in lieu of giving Bonds with Security, the same persons may transfer Public Funds in the Books of the Bank of England, or deposit there Exchequer Bills to the joint account of the person appointed and the head of the Department to which he belongs

Until default, the Dividend may be received by the person appointed, but the Funds cannot be transferred without a Certificate from the Head of the Department.

Upon a Certificate that the Revenue has been damnified by the person appointed, the Head of the Department alone may realise, by sale of the proceeds or Exchequer Bills, the amount of the loss. When no claim is raised against the Fund, it is re-transferred or re delivered to the personal representative of the party appointed.

A jurisdiction is given to the Common Law Judges to decide any question of loss or damage between the Head of the Department and the person appointed. Their decision is final, unless they direct an issue to be tried before a Jury. Any Public Funds, therefore, that are transferable on the Books of the Banks of England or Ireland, as Stock of the East India Government, are accepted by the Treasury as security under these Acts.[2]

(U U.)

Chapter XXV., par 24

The Most Honourable Order of the Bath.

This Order, which was instituted and ordered by Letters Patent of the 18th May, 1725, as a Military Order of Knighthood, was reformed by Letters Patent of the 14th April, 1847, the substance of which were in these words.[3]—

" We do hereby further ordain, direct, and appoint, that the said Order shall henceforth be known and described by the style and designation of the Most Honourable Order of the Bath.

---

[1] 5 Geo IV , c 53 , 6 & 7 William IV , c 28 , 1 & 2 Vic , c 61

[2] 22 & 24 Vic., c 38, sec. 10, Colne Railway Journ Rep , p 528 , and Cockburn v Peel, 3 De Gex Fish and Jones, p 171

[3] 'London Gazette,' 25th May, 1847, No 1947

" And that the said Order shall consist of the Sovereign and Great Master, and of nine hundred and fifty-two Companions or Members, to be divided into three such classes as hereinafter mentioned.

" And that We, Our Heirs and Successors, Kings or Queens Regnant of the United Kingdom aforesaid, shall be Sovereigns of the said Order.

" And that a Prince of the Blood Royal, or such other exalted personage as We, Our Heirs and Successors, shall hereafter appoint, shall be Great Master of the said Order, and shall, in virtue thereof, be the First or Principal Knight Grand Cross of the said Order.

" And that the said nine hundred and fifty-two Members shall be divided into three classes and that of the said three classes, the first or highest class shall consist of seventy-five Members, to be styled or designated Knights Grand Cross of the said Order, and that the second class shall consist of one hundred and fifty-two Members, to be styled and designated Knights Commanders of the said Order, and that the third or lowest class shall consist of seven hundred and twenty-five Members, to be styled and designated Companions of the said Order.

" Provided, nevertheless, and We do further ordain, direct, and appoint, that if at any time hereafter any occasion should arise, rendering expedient any increase to the number of Members comprised in all or any of the classes of the said Order, it shall be competent to Us, Our Heirs and Successors, by any Statute or Statutes to be hereafter made, to authorise any such increase of the number of Members of any such class or classes

" And that such persons only shall be competent to be Members of any of the said three classes, as shall possess the qualifications to be for that purpose defined in any Statute or Statutes to be hereafter made, in the manner and form for that purpose prescribed in and by the said recited Letters Patent

" Provided always, that no such Statute so to be made as aforesaid shall be of any force or authority, unless before the actual making and promulgation thereof We shall have signified to the Great Master of the said Order, by a Warrant under our Signet and Sign Manual, countersigned by one of Our Principal Secretaries of State, Our pleasure that the same should be so made and promulgated.

" And we do further direct, ordain, and appoint, that when and so often as any person shall hereafter be appointed to be a Member of the said Order, such appointment shall be made in the manner following, that is to say, that the name of every such candidate being laid before Us, or Our Heirs and Successors, by one of Our or their Principal Secretaries of State, the pleasure of Us, or our Heirs and Successors, respecting the appointment of any such candidate, shall by Us or Them be thereupon signified to such Secretary of State, and when and so often as We, or Our Heirs and Successors, shall so have signified Our pleasure in favour of the appointment of any such candidate, it shall be the duty of such Our or Their Secretary of State to prepare, for the approbation and signature of Us, or Our Heirs and Successors, a Warrant, addressed to the Great Master of the said Order for the time being, for the appointment of any such candidate, which Warrant, being first countersigned by the Secretary of State preparing the same, shall be the full and final authority to the said Great Master for preparing for the signature of Us, or Our Heirs and Successors, and for laying before Us or Them to be signed, and for sealing with the seal of the said Order when so signed, a grant or authority from Us, or Our Heirs and Successors, to each and every such candidate to be a Member of the said Order, and to have, exercise, and enjoy all the dignity, rank, and privileges thereunto appertaining, according to the class to which each such candidate shall so be appointed

"In witness whereof We have caused these Our Letters to be made Patent. Witness Ourself, at Westminster, the fourteenth day of April, in the tenth year of Our reign"

Statutes of the Order were issued with the Letters Patent, but these were revoked by Statutes of the 31st January, 1859, of which the most important are as follows —

"Second —That the said Most Honourable Order shall consist of the Sovereign, a Great Master, and *three* several classes, viz. —

> Knights Grand Cross,
> Knights Commanders, and
> Companions.

" Third —We, Our Heirs and Successors, Kings and Queens Regnant of this United Kingdom, are and for ever shall be Sovereigns of this Most Honourable Order, to whom doth and shall belong all power of annulling, *interpreting*, explaining, or augmenting these and every part of these Statutes

"Fifth —That this Most Honourable Order shall contain three classes, styled respectively, 'Knights Grand Cross,' 'Knights Commanders,' and 'Companions.' That *each and every* of these *three* classes shall likewise *contain two subdivisions*, whereof the first shall be styled '*Military*,' and the second '*Civil*,' each of which subdivisions shall be composed partly of Ordinary and partly of Honorary Members.

"Seventh.—That the *Military* Division of the First Class, or Knights Grand Cross, shall not exceed *fifty* in number, and that no person shall be appointed to this division who doth not, at the time of his nomination, actually *hold a commission in Our Army* or in Our Indian Military Forces, of or above the rank of Major-General, or *a commission in Our Navy, of or above the rank of Rear-Admiral*

"Eighth.—That the *Civil* Division of *the First Class*, or Knights Grand Cross, shall *not* exceed twenty-five in number; and that no persons shall be nominated thereto, or to either of the two other Civil Divisions of this Order, who shall not by *their personal services* to Our Crown, or *by the performance of public duties*, have merited Our Royal favour.

"Ninth.—It is ordained that the Military Division of the Second Class, or Knights Commanders, may be increased to One hundred and twenty-three in number, and that no person shall be appointed thereto who doth not at the time of his nomination actually hold a Commission in Our Army or Marines, or in Our Indian Military Forces, of or above the rank of Colonel, or a Commission in Our Navy of or above the rank of Captain, or a Commission of equivalent or higher rank in the Commissariat Service of Our Army or Indian Military Forces, or in the Medical Service of our Army, Navy, or Indian Military or Naval Forces

"Tenth.—It is ordained that the Civil Division of the Second Class, or Knights Commanders, may be increased to Sixty in number, and that no person shall be appointed thereto, who would not according to the provisions contained in the Eighth of the aforesaid Statutes of Our said Order, be qualified for being nominated to be of the Civil Division of the First Class, or Knights Grand Cross of the said Order.

"Eleventh.—It is ordained that the Military Division of the Third Class, or Companions, may be increased to Six hundred and ninety, and shall not, except under special and temporary exigencies, exceed that number, and that no person shall be nominated thereto who doth not actually hold, at the time of his nomination, a Commission in Our Army, or Marines, or in our Indian Military Forces, of or above the rank of Major, or a Commission in Our Navy, or in Our Indian Naval Forces, of or above the rank of Commander, or a Commission of *equivalent or higher rank in the Commissariat Service of Our Army*, or Indian Military Forces, or in the Medical Service of Our Army, Navy, or Indian Military and Naval Forces, nor shall any person be admitted into this Division unless his services have been

...ed by the especial mention of his name in despatches as having distinguished himself by his valour and conduct in action against the enemy, in the Command of a Ship of War, or of Our Troops, or at the head of a Military Department, or as having by some Active Service, under his immediate conduct and direction, contributed to the success of any such action, provided, nevertheless, and We do hereby declare that this last-mentioned regulation shall not be applicable to Commissariat and Medical Officers, and instead thereof We further declare that no Commissariat or Medical Officer shall be competent to be an ordinary Member of the Military Division of the Second and Third Classes of the said Order, unless it shall appear to Us that by his meritorious services in actual war, in providing for the wants of Our Army, or of Our Indian Military Forces, or in taking care of the sick or wounded Officers, Soldiers, and Seamen of Our Army and Navy, or of Our Indian Military and Naval Forces, he has deserved such distinction

"Twelfth —That the Civil Division of the Third Class, or Companions, shall not exceed two hundred in number, and that no person shall be appointed thereto who would not, according to the provisions hereinbefore contained, be qualified for being nominated to be of the Civil Division of the Second Class, or Knights Commanders of the said Order.

"Thirteenth —That the Honorary Members of the Order shall consist of Foreign persons upon whom We may think fit to confer the honour of being received into the Military and Civil Divisions of the several Classes of this Order; and that the number of such Honorary Members may consist of as many Foreign persons as We, Our Heirs and Successors, shall think fit to appoint.

"Fourteenth —That although We have deemed it expedient in the foregoing Statutes to prescribe and limit the numbers which shall constitute each class and each division of this Most Honourable Order, nevertheless, inasmuch as We are pleased to regard not merely the present but the future exigencies of this Our Realm, so We have thought fit to provide for distant contingencies · therefore, in the event of any future wars or of any actions or services, civil or military, meriting peculiar honour and reward, it shall be lawful for Us, Our Heirs and Successors, in virtue of the powers to Us and Them reserved in and by the said recited Letters Patent of the tenth year of Our Reign, to increase the numbers in any of the said classes, and in any of the said divisions, and to assign a place in any such divisions to any of Our Officers, Naval and Military, whose rank in Our Service would not qualify him for holding a place therein according to the provisions hereinbefore in that behalf made

"Eighteenth,—That in all solemn ceremonials, and in all other places and assemblies whatsoever, the Knights Grand Cross of the Most Honourable Order shall have place and precedency next to and immediately after Baronets, and that the Knights Commanders of this Order shall have place and precedency next to and immediately after the Knights Grand Cross of Our Most Distinguished Order of Saint Michael and Saint George, and that the Companions of this Order shall have place and precedency of the Cavaliers and Companions of Our Most Distinguished Order of Saint Michael and Saint George, and before all Esquires of these Our Realms, nevertheless, We are pleased to declare, that nothing contained in this Statute shall be taken or construed to diminish the privileges or precedency reserved in the seventeenth Statute to the Members of this Most Honourable Order nominated or appointed previously to the date of these presents. And that (with the exception of the Great Master of this Most Honourable Order, and of the Members of the Royal Family), the Knights Grand Cross, Knights Commanders and Companions of this Order, shall take rank among each other according to the dates of their respective nominations in the Classes of this Order to which they severally belong.

"Twenty-second,—It is ordained, that on the promotion of a Member of the Second or Third Classes of this Most Honourable Order, to a higher class of the same division of the said Order to which he has been already admitted, the insignia of such lower class theretofore worn by him shall be returned to the Registrar and Secretary of the Order, and be by him deposited with the Chamberlain of Our Household, and the Registrar and Secretary of the Order, for the time being, is hereby authorized, empowered, and directed to ask, demand and receive from such Members as have already been promoted, or that hereafter may be promoted, as aforesaid, the Insignia of the Order theretofore worn by such promoted Member. Provided, nevertheless, and it is further ordained, that if any person who shall have been admitted to be a Member of the second or of the third class of the Military division of this Order, shall subsequently be admitted to be a Member of the higher class of the Civil Division thereof or if any person who shall have been admitted to be a Member of the second or of the third class of the Civil Division of this Order, shall subsequently be admitted to be a Member of a higher class of the Military Division thereof, such person shall be entitled to retain and wear the insignia of such inferior class in addition to the insignia of such higher class, although by the acceptance of such higher rank in the said Order he shall have vacated his place as a Member of such lower class thereof

"Twenty-fifth —In order to make such additional provisions as

shall effectually preserve pure this Most Honourable Order, it is
o ained, that if any Knight Grand Cross, Knight Commander or
Companion of this Order be convicted of treason, cowardice, felony,
or of any infamous crime derogatory to his honour as a Knight or a
Gentleman, or if he be accused of any such offence, and doth not,
after a reasonable time, surrender himself to be tried for the same,
he shall forthwith be degraded from the Order by an especial
Ordnance issued for that purpose, signed by the Sovereign, and
sealed with the Seal of this Order. It is hereby further declared,
that We, Our Heirs and Successors, Sovereigns of this Order, are
and for ever shall be sole judges of the circumstances demanding
such degradation and expulsion, moreover, the Sovereign shall at
all times have power to restore to this Most Honourable Order, such
Members thereof as may at any time have been expelled."

Other Statutes were issued on the 24th June, 1861, that substituted 9, 10, and 11, as printed above, for those of the same numbers
printed in the Statutes of January, 1859.

(V V.)

Chapter XXV, *par.* 24

THE VICTORIA CROSS

As supplementary to the Order of the Bath, a new decoration for
valour, to be bestowed on the Officers and Men of Naval and Military
Services, was instituted by Royal Warrant of the 29th January,
1856, of which the principal clauses are as follows —

"Firstly That the distinction shall be styled and designated 'The
Victoria Cross,' and shall consist of a Maltese Cross of Bronze, with
Our Royal Crest in the centre, and underneath which an escroll,
bearing this inscription, 'For Valour.'

"Fourthly That any one who, after having received the Cross,
shall again perform an act of bravery, which, if he had not received
such Cross, would have entitled him to it, such further act shall be
recorded by a Bar attached to the riband by which the Cross is suspended, and for every additional act of bravery an additional bar
may be added

"Fifthly That the Cross shall only be awarded to those Officers
or Men who have served Us in the presence of the enemy, and shall
have then performed some signal act of valour, or devotion to their
country.

"Sixthly. With a view to place all persons on a perfectly equal footing in relation to eligibility for the Decoration, that neither rank, nor long service, nor wounds, nor any other circumstance or condition whatsoever, save the merit of conspicuous bravery, shall be held to establish a sufficient claim to the honour.

"Seventhly. That the Decoration may be conferred on the spot where the act to be rewarded by the grant of such Decoration has been performed, under the following circumstances:—

"(I) When the Fleet or Army, in which such act has been performed, is under the eye and command of an Admiral or General Officer commanding the Forces

"(II) Where the Naval or Military force is under the eye and command of an Admiral or Commodore commanding a squadron or detached naval force, or of a General commanding a corps, or division or brigade on a distinct and detached service, when such Admiral, Commodore, or General Officer shall have the power of conferring the Decoration on the spot, subject to confirmation by Us.

"Eighthly. Where such act shall not have been performed in sight of a Commanding Officer as aforesaid, then the claimant for the honour shall prove the act to the satisfaction of the Captain or Officer commanding his ship, or to the Officer commanding the regiment to which the claimant belongs, and such Captain or such Commanding Officer shall report the same through the usual channel to the Admiral or Commodore commanding the force employed on the service, or to the Officer commanding the forces in the field, who shall call for such description and attestation of the act as he may think requisite, and on approval shall recommend the grant of the Decoration.

"Ninthly. That every person selected for the Cross, under Rule Seven, shall be publicly decorated before the Naval or Military force or body to which he belongs, and with which the act of bravery for which he is to be rewarded shall have been performed, and his name shall be recorded in a General Order, together with the cause of his especial distinction.

"Tenthly That every person selected under Rule Eight shall receive his Decoration as soon as possible, and his name shall likewise appear in a General Order as above required, such General Order to be issued by the Naval or Military Commander of the Forces employed on the service.

"Twelfthly. That as cases may arise not falling within the rules above specified, or in which a claim, though well founded, may not have been established on the spot, We will, on the joint submission of Our Secretary of State for War and of Our Commander-in-Chief of Our Army, or on that of Our Lord High Admiral or Lords Commissioners of the Admiralty in the case of the Navy, confer the Decoration, but never without conclusive proof of the performance of the act or bravery for which the claim is made

"Thirteenthly That, in the event of a gallant and daring act having been performed by a squadron, ship's company, a detached body of Seamen and Marines, not under fifty in number, or by a brigade, regiment, troop, or company, in which the Admiral, General, or other Officer commanding such forces, may deem that all are equally brave and distinguished, and that no special selection can be made by them then in such case, the Admiral, General, or other Officer commanding, may direct, that for any such body of Seamen or Marines, or for every troop or company of Soldiers, one Officer shall be selected by the Officers engaged for the Decoration, and in like manner one Petty Officer or Non-commissioned Officer shall be selected by the Petty Officers and Non-commissioned Officers engaged; and two Seamen or Private Soldiers or Marines shall be selected by the Seamen, or Private Soldiers, or Marines, engaged respectively, for the Decoration, and the names of those selected shall be transmitted by the Senior Officer in command of the Naval force, brigade, regiment, troop, or company, to the Admiral or General Officer commanding, who shall in due manner confer the Decoration as if the acts were done under his own eye

"Fourteenthly. That every Warrant Officer, Petty Officer, Seaman, or Marine, or Non-commissioned Officer or Soldier, who shall have received the Cross, shall, from the date of the act by which the Decoration has been gained, be entitled to a Special Pension of Ten Pounds a-year, and each additional Bar conferred under Rule Four on such Warrant or Petty Officers, or Non-commissioned Officers or Men, shall carry with it an Additional Pension of Five Pounds per annum.

"Fifteenthly In order to make such additional provision as shall effectually preserve pure this most honourable distinction, it is ordained, that if any person on whom such distinction shall be conferred, be convicted of treason, cowardice, felony, or of any infamous crime, or if he be accused of any such offence, and doth not after a reasonable time surrender himself to be tried for the same, his name shall forthwith be erased from the registry of individuals upon whom the said Decoration shall have been conferred by an especial Warrant under Our Royal Sign Manual, and the Pension conferred under Rule Fourteen shall cease and determine from the date of such Warrant. It is hereby further declared that We, Our Heirs and Successors, shall be the sole judges of the circumstance demanding such expulsion, moreover, We shall at all times have power to restore such persons as may at any time have been expelled, both to the enjoyment of the Decoration and Pensions.

"Given at Our Court at Buckingham Palace, this twenty-ninth of January in the nineteenth year of Our Reign, and in the year of Our Lord One thousand eight hundred and fifty-six

' By Her Majesty's Command,

"PANMURE."

(W W.)

Chapter XXIX., *par.* 25

ON THE ARMY CLOTHING SYSTEM

THE Clothing and Equipments for the Army, except the Household Cavalry and Ordnance Corps, were from the earliest period[1] up to 1855 supplied by the Colonel, who received a fixed sum for every man on the Establishment, which was called off-reckonings.

The Colonel was bound to supply clothing according to patterns sealed by a Board of General Officers appointed by the Sovereign, and who considered any complaints made by Regiments respecting the Clothing The Clothing for the Household Cavalry was supplied in the same manner up to 1780, when the system was altered by Royal Warrant, and a fixed sum granted for every man, which forms a fund, out of which the Clothing and Equipment is supplied by the Lieutenant-Colonel, acting under the orders of the Goldstick, who is Colonel of the Regiment. The whole Fund is expended upon Clothing and Equipment, no profit is derived by the Colonel, who receives a fixed annual rate of pay. No change has been made in this system.

The Clothing for the Ordnance Corps and Colonial Regiments (except West India Regiments supplied by the Colonel) has always been provided by the Board of Ordnance by contract.

The system under which the Colonel furnished the supplies was established during the reign of Queen Anne, and has at various periods formed the subject of inquiry by Royal Commissions and Parliamentary Committees

The earliest Regulations for the Clothing under this system are dated 14th January, 1707, and the first Article states, "The sole responsibility of the Colonel for the Pay and Equipment of his Regiment is the principle of Military Finance, who is held respon-

---

[1] Regulations of James II., W O Bk 795, pp. 135-9.

...ible in his fortune and in his character for the discharge of his duty in providing the supplies of his Regiment."

The earliest inquiry into the system took place in 1776, by a Committee of the House of Commons, to ascertain the average profits of each Colonel from 1700 to 1745

The Commissioners of Accounts in 1783 recommended that the Board of General Officers should make the contracts for the Clothing.

The Finance Committee of 1798 recommended that the Army should be clothed by a single contract made by the Executive Government

The Commissioners of Military Inquiry in 1807, did not concur in either of the proposals made in 1783 and 1798, but recommended that the Colonels should continue to provide the clothing of their respective Regiments.

No further inquiry took place till 1833, when the Parliamentary Committee on Army and Navy Appointments entered into a long and minute examination of the system, and did not recommend any changes

The Parliamentary Committee upon Army and Ordnance Expenditure in 1849 came to the same conclusion

No further inquiry took place till 1854, when the Crimean War broke out, and large augmentations were made to the Army. The off-reckonings were granted upon every increase of Establishment, without any reference to the numbers actually effective, and these being considerably below the Establishment, it became apparent that the public were paying the Colonels to clothe men who were never in existence After very careful inquiry, Mr Sidney Herbert, then Secretary at War, considered it necessary, in the interests of the public, to abolish the off-reckonings, and to give the Colonels a fixed sum in lieu of any profits upon clothing, but the Colonel continued to appoint his own clothier, and to be responsible for the supply, the public paying the cost price charged by the clothier to the Colonel   The Board of General Officers was maintained

This change was promulgated to the Army by Royal Warrant, dated 6th June, 1854

In 1855 the Board of Ordnance was abolished, and the various Departments for the Administration of the Army were consolidated It then became necessary to reconsider the Clothing arrangements. The system adopted by Mr. Sidney Herbert withdrew from the Colonel all profit, but left him still to provide the Clothing, and the public derived no advantage by competition in the trade

It was accordingly determined by Lord Palmerston's Government to provide all Clothing, except the Household Cavalry, by public contract, and a Clothing Department was established at the War Office for this duty. The Royal Warrants of 21st June, 18 , relieved the Colonels, and consequently the Army Agents, from all duties connected with Clothing, and abolished the Board of General Officers. In 1857 a Government Factory was established at Woolwich, for the purpose of making Clothing for the Royal Artillery and Engineers, which had hitherto been made by contract.

The Parliamentary Committee on Public Contracts inquired into the working of this Establishment, and in the Appendix No 7, to the third, fourth, and fifth Reports, 1858, will be found a comparison of actual cost with contract prices. This statement shows that in ten months there was a saving of 15,254*l*, out of which the cost of buildings amounting to 12,600*l* was defrayed leaving a net saving of 2654*l*.

At the same time a small Establishment was created in London for making the Clothing of the Foot Guards and a few Regiments of the Line, which had been made by contract since 1855.

In Appendix No. 7, Form A, to the third, fourth, and fifth Reports of the Contract Committee the results of the working of this Establishment are given. There is a saving of 4289*l*. In consequence of those results it was determined to extend the manufacture of clothing by Government, and in 1862 the Royal Army Clothing Factory at Pimlico was completed. According to the latest returns the tunic which cost in 1857, by contract, 1*l* 1*s* 6*d*. is now manufactured in the Factory for 16*s*. 6*d*. An annual balance sheet is laid before Parliament, showing the exact expenditure, and the abstract of the last balance sheet herewith annexed shows the total outlay upon the Establishment. Clothing to a considerable extent is still made by contract, so that a check is exercised over the cost of production in the Factory.

Necessaries for recruits were paid for out of the bounty, and were supplied by the Recruiting Officer. This system led to a great evil; the recruit was charged so high a price for the articles that he rarely received any balance of his bounty, and in many cases joined the Regiment in debt. The Royal Warrant of February, 1857, changed this system, and the recruit is now supplied with articles from the Public Stores, and the reduced bounty is paid to him without any deduction.

Necessaries for old Soldiers, and paid for by them, were, until 1862, furnished by the Commanding Officer, but in 1862 arrangements were made to issue the articles from the Public Stores on repayment.

7th August, 1869.   GEORGE RAMSAY.

Royal Army Clothing Factory, Pimlico.

BALANCE SHEET of the Royal Army Clothing Factory, Pimlico,
for 1867-8

Dr.	£	s	d	£	s	d		£	s	d	£	s	d
To ... of Buildings — (Cost of purchase)	30,000	0	0				By Balance.— Buildings (Original purchase) .	30,000	0	0			
... to 31st Mar 1867 .	3,597	15	2				Add—Additions, to 31st March, 1867 .	3,597	15	2			
,, Machinery .	3,045	18	0				,, ,, during 1867-68 .	—			33,597	15	2
,, Tools and Implements .	181	13	1										
,, Stock of Materials	1,290	1	10¼										
,, S of manufactured Goods	870	11	11½				Machinery on 1st April, 1867 .	3,045	18	0			
,, Finished Goods for Appropriation	70	3	0				Deduct — Depreciation at 10 per cent.	304	11	9	2,741	6	3
,, Miscellaneous Stores .	2,500	15	2½	41,615	2	1½							
To Purchases — Buildings (New) .	—						Add — Additions during 1867-68, per contra .	—					
Machinery (New) .	—												
Tools and Implements .	76	5	1	76	5	1	Tools and Implements on 1st Apr, 1867 .	181	13	1			
To Repairs to Buildings	—						Deduct — Depreciation at 10 per cent.	18	3	4			
,, ,, Machinery	45	18	1										
,, ,, Tools and Implements	2	12	1	48	10	2				163	9	9			
To Contract Clothing received from Storekeeper for Appropriation	40,415	3	4				Add — Additions during 1867-68 per contra . .	76	5	1	239	14	10
Materials .	245,612	3	6½										
Miscellaneous Stores	615	14	7½	286,643	1	6	Materials in hand	—					
To Charges & Expenses Cost of Inspection of Material .	366	0	0				Finished Goods and Contract Clothing waiting Appropriation .	—					
Wages . .	41,944	17	9½										
Cutting . .	5,554	6	6½				Finished Goods and Contract Clothing Re-Issued to Storekeeper .	40,485	7	1			
Ground Rent .	356	0	0										
Water Rate .	49	13	4										
Insurance .	78	0	0				Miscellaneous Stores	2,142	18	9	42,628	5	10
Salaries .	750	0	0										
Medical Attendance	85	5	0										
Lodging Allowances .	33	6	0				By Production of Articles manufactured during the year . .	267,857	12	8½			
Rental Value of Officers' Quarters .	100	0	0										
Police .	298	3	2				By Alterations and Repairs during the year	1,644	8	1½			
Gas .	442	16	4										
Fuel .	212	7	9½				By Garments issued, Cut and Basted .	2,807	9	3½			
Stationery (not purchased on spot)	80	0	0										
Interest on Invested Capital .	1,454	1	6				By Semi-manufactured Goods . . .	8,920	4	11½			
,, ,, Working ,,	869	0	0										
Miscellaneous	46	19	0				By Materials Re-issued to Store Department, &c.	9,467	13	9½			
To Annual Charge to repay the original outlay on Purchase of Lease in 75 years, at 3½ per cent. Compound Interest .	86	2	0										
To Annual Charge to repay Additions to Buildings on 31st March, 1867, in 73 years, at 3½ per cent. Compound Interest .	19	12	2	53,172	17	0½	By value of Cuttings issued to Storekeeper, and sold during the year	4,645	5	0	302,318	13	10½
				381,555	15	11½					381,555	15	11½

H W S Whiffin
Chief Auditor of Army Accounts.

J H Hudson,
Superintendent

(X X)

Chapter XXIX., *par.* 69

THE *INTENDANCE MILITAIRE* AND THE ARMY CONTROL DEPARTMENT.

THE French Intendance has manifestly been to a considerable extent the model for the Army Control Department as proposed by Lord Strathnairn's Committee on the Transport and Supply Departments of the Army[1] The "prevailing Military character" of the Department,[2] the relative Military rank proposed for its members,[3] its exclusive recruitment by Military Officers,[4] the pensioning of Officers of existing Departments,[5] are all characteristics of the Intendance, or of the manner in which it was formed While so much unqualified praise is given to the French Service,[6] it is worth while, and not without interest, to see what has been said on the other side of the question by competent judges

The thirty-ninth paragraph of the Committee's Report recommends that, " . . as soon as the qualified Officers of the existing Departments shall have been absorbed, the Department of Control should be recruited exclusively from Military Officers " The principle involved in this recommendation exists in France, where it is much attacked. The circumstances which led to its adoption are described by the well-known Worms de Romilly (then Sub-Intendant of the Second Class) in 'Quelques Réflexions sur l'Organisation de l'Intendance Militaire' (Paris, 1850). He says.—"The Intendance was formed of two corps—the Inspectors of Musters and the War Commissariat, but when the amalgamation was effected, sufficient thought was not bestowed upon the future recruiting of the new arm, which was very imperfectly constituted, and deprived at starting of means of action commensurate with the importance of the functions attributed to it. When the Inspection and the Commissariat were united, the Administration was not liked by the Army. Control and command rarely accord . . . In the hope of terminating bad feeling, the notion of a *rapprochement* was taken up; a sort of compromise was adopted, and it was thought that by recruiting the Intendance from the Army alone, and admitting Army men to all the administrative functions, harmony might in a little time be established. This project was put in execution. Little was thought of the future in the face of the difficulties of the moment. Con-

---

[1] Report, *notes*, pp xl., xiii , xiv , xli., &c.   [2] Ib., p xli , *note*

[3] Ib , p xvii., § 35, and App I   [4] Ib , p xvii , § 39, and p xx., §§ 48, 50

[5] Ib., p xli., § 135   [6] Ib , p xiii , *note*

formably with the Ordonnance which now regulates the organization of the Intendance, no one can enter the corps until he has attained the rank of Captain. A Captain is qualified to become an *Adjoint* of the Second Class, a Chef de Bataillon to become an Adjoint of the First Class, a Lieutenant-Colonel a Sub-Intendant of the Second Class, and a Colonel a Sub Intendant of the First Class The result of this mode of recruiting is, that, as it is extremely difficult for individuals to rise to the level of the employment to which they are called without practical preparation, the newly promoted are at least as embarrassed as the members of the Intendance would be if posted to regiments to fill substantively their relative ranks "

The following passages are from General Trochu's well-known book 'L'Armée Française en 1867' (9th edition), and form an instructive commentary upon the observations of Worms de Romilly, and the proposal of the Committee —"In France, after the campaigns of the Republic and the Empire, men whose experience was considerable united for the purpose of endowing the Army with a system of Military Administration, the principles and mechanism of which had a high practical value in reference to war   . . In the system of these great administrators, the *direction* and the *control* of the various services were carried on side by side, without being confounded one with the other.   . . The Directors, the Controllers, and the Executive Officers, were men of business, who had been initiated in business from the first step of their careers, and educated from an early period for the performance of their functions in the Army by actual duty, by exchanges, and by being specially brought into contact in every way with the details of those functions They lived from the age of eighteen to twenty in the atmosphere of transactions having particular application to the administration of the Army . . . The members of the Control Department and the Agents of the Administrative Services commenced their career as students, learning from their youth what was always to be their speciality [1] Under the system which prevails now-a-days, all these functionaries, without exception, before entering upon their business calling have been, during long years—the years of youth, during which men learn and study with most fruit—Officers and *Sous-Officiers* in the Army! In such cases an examination takes the place of ten or fifteen years of practical and professional experience What do I say?—of thirty or forty years of such practical experience, since we see Generals of Brigade, most frequently at the last

---

[1] The Ordonnance of 29th July, 1817, creating the Intendance, had a provision for ten Students, whose numbers were increased to twenty by the Ordonnance of 27th September, 1820 The students were suppressed by the Ordonnance of 18th September, 1822.

hour of their career, become Intendant-Generals; that is to say, the arbiters for the next war of the existence of our troops in the field!

"It is in vain, I think, to seek in the whole scope of the public affairs of France a more astonishing example of a blunder."

General Trochu mentions that in the Italian campaign divisions of the Army were often without bread or biscuit, and adds that, if the system goes on, he sees nothing for it but to attach suttlers to the head-quarters of each division to undertake the supplies under the orders of the Control Department instancing the case of a well-known Marseilles house which in the Crimean War came to the assistance of a paralysed department and appeared to create abundance in the Army, rendering all its operations possible, while giving the country money and making an enormous fortune for itself. He goes on —"At present all the functionaries of the French Military Administration, great and small, have the Army for a common origin. They retain the instincts, the prejudices, and the sympathies of the profession in which the first and often the greater part of their life has been passed. . . . I think I have shown that by the manner in which the Control Department is recruited, it loses much of the speciality desirable in view of the immense extent of the business to which it is called upon to attend, particularly on active service."

Now that Marshals Bugeaud and Niel have passed away, General Trochu is perhaps the highest living authority on such a subject.

Lord Strathnairn's Committee, however, represents " the present Intendance " to be " a corps admittedly well adapted to secure at once administrative efficiency and economy," and says that, by means of its exclusive recruitment from among Military Officers, " the administration of the Army is conducted by Officers in the vigour of life, possessed of superior professional attainments, and trained to the performance of their special duties." [1]

We have thus seen the opinions of the Intendance itself, and of the combatant branches, those of the Medical Department coincide, and are, if possible, more decidedly expressed. Some articles which have recently appeared in ' Gazette Hebdomadaire,' on the medical statistics of the French Army, have attracted much attention It is recorded as an extraordinary fact that, while in the English Army 33 9 per cent, and in the American forces 40 2 per cent, of surgical operations in war prove fatal, in the French the corresponding proportions are enormously greater, having been in the Crimea 72·8, and in the Italian campaign 63 9 per cent. The cardinal cause assigned for this mortality is "the supremacy, the omnipotence of the Intendance Militaire, which from a medical

[1] Report, p xiii, note

point of view is in a condition of absolute incapacity" It is shown that in the Italian campaign instead of providing the army from the resources of the country in which it lay, by payment to friends and plunder of enemies, immense quantities of flour, rice, coffee, sugar, &c, were brought from France, and idly accumulated in Store at Genoa in consequence of a failure in the means of transport. The Surgeon-in-Chief of the Guards wrote from Alexandria on 19th May, 1859, "No litters, no ambulances, no waggons, I have begged hard for chloroform and perchloride of iron, nothing has as yet been given me" He writes again from Valeggio on July 7th, "For the last fortnight some regiments have only once or twice had bread, and even then it was mouldy and of a very bad quality. Wine has completely failed. there has scarcely been any issue of it" From Montebello, on May 24th, the Surgeon-in-Chief of the First Corps d'Armée reported that " in consequence of the inexperience, or the numerous pre-occupations of the Intendance, nearly 800 wounded have been fed for four days by private charity. The want of medicines in regiments and field hospitals continues." From Castiglione, on July 2nd, an officer wrote to the Emperor himself " Sire, the wounded of Solferino (June 25th), who are crowded here, have not yet had their wounds dressed for want of supplies. We have lint, but no linen, no shirts, no sugar, no provisions" These are a few extracts from the official correspondence on the subject So much for the incapacity of the administrative corps, and now as to the contest of authority arising out of the relative military rank. The following is reported by an eye-witness.[1] —

At Milan in 1859, the Surgeon-in Chief of the Hospitals of the city had thought it his duty at the end of the campaign to write a letter of thanks to his colleagues of the town, who had assisted in the care of the wounded One morning all the military surgeons present at Milan were, with their assistants, and the civil surgeons attached to the hospitals, summoned before the Sub-Intendant, who commenced to read from a paper as follows:—"A Military Surgeon has thought proper to address a circular—" "Pardon me," said the Surgeon-in Chief, "the letter, which was written with my own hand, was not a circular" "You are placed in arrest for a fortnight for that observation," was the reply of the Sub Intendant

The Ordonnances of the 29th July, 1817, 18th September, 1822, and 19th June, 1829, ruled that the Intendance should form portion of the General Staff of the French Army Baron Bardin, a General Officer, author of a 'Dictionnaire de l'Armée de Terre,' observes that " These Ordonnances fell, in this respect, into a contradiction, since they declared at the same time that the Intendance should remain independent of General Officers It is impossible to form

<hr>

[1] 'Revue des Cours Scientifiques, 1869,' p 722

position of a Military aggregate, in which everything is hierarchical, and at the same time decline submission to individuals holding superior ranks and positions. The Intendants wished to be Military men without recognizing Military command, to be in the Army without being of the Army, to be an Administrative Army quite distinct from the Combatant Army. How imprudent was this! The Intendance thus sowed the seeds of rivalries and troubles, which bid fair to be fatal to its aims, especially in the field.'

As regards the relative rank[1] and Military positions proposed to be assigned to the Control Department, General Trochu has the following remarks upon the subject of the similar rules existing in the French Service:—"In order usefully to fulfil the duties of its difficult calling, and in order to obtain respect for that calling, the Control Department has been desirous, with good show of reason, that it should have a special standing with reference to the Army. It has thought to obtain this by assimilating its various ranks to ours, from General of Division down to Captain, with all the prerogatives that attach to them. . . In my opinion, it has made a mistake . . . *The Control Department holds directly from the State a high and necessary mission, which it should pursue with an absolute independence. It is in the plenitude of this special independence that the Department should seek for the consideration and respect which are indispensable to it, and which are its due.* But it has—while creating, up to a certain point, an antagonism—sought to obtain such consideration and respect by Military rank and the Military prerogatives attaching to such rank; prerogatives which the Combatant Branch, often with some warmth, does not fail to contest and to render unpleasant."

The following remarks on the same subject are from the 'Réponse d'un Officier Inférieur' (Paris, 1867), a remarkable pamphlet which was called forth by General Trochu's work, and has obtained much notoriety.—"We cannot close our observations on Military Administration without speaking in detail of an arrangement of which the utility is much questioned; the assimilation of the hierarchy of the Intendance to the Military hierarchy, as follows:— The Adjoint, Second Class, ranking as Captain, the Adjoint, First Class, as Chef d'Escadron, the Sub-Intendant Second Class, as Lieutenant-Colonel; the Sub-Intendant, First Class, as Colonel, and the Intendant, as Field-Marshal." And he concludes "that the assimilation of any hierarchy whatever to the Military hierarchy is useless, and consequently hurtful."

<hr>

[1] Report, p. xvii., § 35. Controller relative rank of Brigadier General, and when with an Army in the field, Major-General. Deputy Controller relative rank of Colonel. Assistant-Controller of two classes, ranking respectively as Lieutenant Colonel and Major.

This "assimilation" of ranks has been periodically established, modified, and suppressed, in the French Intendance. The difficulties it has caused and the consequent changes that have been made, have been numerous. The Intendance was established by an Ordonnance of 29th July, 1817, which, in its 11th and 16th articles, contains the origin of the assimilation.[1] The 32nd article of the Ordonnance of 18th September, 1822, reorganizing the Department, abolishes the relative rank in the following terms —" The functions of the Intendance being solely administrative, confer no rank in the Army All assimilations previously established are abrogated." The Ordonnance of 10th June, 1835, which again reorganized the Intendance, re-establishes relative rank, and the preamble of that Ordonnance is worthy of remark, as showing to some extent the reasons for the measure, and bearing out the observations of Worms de Romilly, before given. It is as follows —" Considering that the Intendance forms part of the General Staff of the Army, and that the recruiting of the Corps is exclusively confined to the Officers of all branches of the Army —wishing, in consequence, to establish a more complete harmony between the organization of the Intendance and that of the other special Corps of the Army," &c , &c

It is observed in the 'Réponse d'un Officier Inférieur,' that this last assimilation "soon gave rise to pretensions which drew from the Minister of War, on 30th March, 1837, the decision that the Ordonnance of 10th June, 1835, in instituting a correspondence between Military ranks and those of the Intendance, had for its object the regulation of the steps to be taken in regard to the admission of Officers of all arms of the Service into the Intendance, and that it had not the effect of assigning them an assimilation of ranks, properly so called."

As regards the pensioning of Officers of existing Departments,[2] it is curious to trace the history of the French Corps in this respect The Intendance was, as has been said, established by an Ordonnance of 29th July, 1817, the 1st Article of which suppressed the previously existing Corps of Inspectors of Musters and Commissaries of War The 6th Article of the same Ordonnance laid down that the new corps was to be formed solely from the two old corps thus suppressed, but occasion was taken for weeding those corps and introducing new blood The result was that upwards of a hundred members of the abolished services were dismissed or forced

---

[1] " The Intendants, Sub-Intendants, and Adjoints will be classed, in order of precedence and for military honours, as follows —Intendants with Field Marshals , Sub-Intendants with Colonels , Adjoints, first and second class, with Chefs de Batalhon,—with some modifications after ten years' service "

[2] Report, p xlii , § 135

to retire, and thus, as a French writer has observed, 'its cradle was surrounded by antagonists" The subject was subsequently debated in the Chamber of Deputies in two consecutive years, and an attack was made upon the Minister for War, whose proceedings, in regard to the Intendance, it was said, "the English Parliament would never have tolerated." The result was that it was found necessary to issue the Ordonnance of 27th September, 1820, providing for the gradual re employment of the Officers who had been dismissed or pensioned They were for that purpose formed into an "auxiliary cadre," consisting of a hundred Officers, to whom were assigned one-half of the future promotions occurring in the Intendance, the other half being filled up within the Intendance itself This provision was confirmed by the Ordonnance of 11th December, 1830 (Article 5), and it will thus be seen that, within three years of the wholesale pensioning which has been described, the Minister for War found himself obliged to recal the pensioned Officers to active service, and that thirteen years after the original formation of the Intendance they had not been all disposed of

The following tabular Statement[1] shows the changes that have taken place from time to time since 1817, in the ranks and numbers of the Intendance Militaire of France —

DATE	Intendant General	Intendant	Sub-Intendant.				Adjoint Sub-Intendant.		Adjoints to the Intendance	Adjoints to the Intendance		Students	Total
			1st Class.	2nd Class	3rd Class.	4th Class.	1st Class	2nd Class.		1st Class.	2nd Class		
29th July, 1817		35	15	45	60	60	15	20				10	260
17th Jan , 1821		35	66	67	67	.	40					20	295
18th Sept , 1822	..	25	35	50	100		35						245
26th Dec , 1827		25	35	50	100		10	15					235
10th June, 1829		20	35	50	80				25				210
10th June, 1835		25	75	75						30	20		245
1862	8	26	48	98						53	18		251
1864, 1869	8	26	50	100		.				56	24		264

[1] I am indebted for this paper to an official friend, who desires his name may be withheld

ILLUSTRATIONS.

(LXXIX.)

Chapter XV., pars. 1 and 9

ROYAL WARRANTS[1] AS TO THE DRAFTING OF TROOPS FOR SERVICE IN MINORCA.

"GEORGE R

"WHEREAS, our trusty and well-beloved Commander James O'Hara hath most humbly represented unto us that upon his arrival at Port Mahon, in the month of September last, he found several men there that had served in the Regiment under his Command for twenty years or upwards who in pursuance to the 8th Article of Our Instructions to Our Governor of Our Island of Minorca, bearing date the 20th day of May last past, directing the manner of Relieving our Four Regiments of Foot in Garrison in that Our Island, had drawn Lots for filling up the Relieving Regiments to their established numbers, and were accordingly turned over to complete the said Regiments, by which means, after a long absence from their native country, they have no prospect of seeing the same in many years to come, unless We shall be pleased in consequence of their past Services to revoke and annul the said 8th Article of Our before-mentioned Instructions, importing that the Non-Commissioned Officers and Private Men to be draughted out of the remaining Ten Companies of the Regiments to be relieved to complete the Relieving Regiments should be such as were fit for Service and willing to stay upon the Island, but in case there should not be a sufficient number of Volunteers, then the remainder to be taken by lots, and all the men of the Regiments to continue upon the Island who should be unserviceable to be exchanged in like manner, which we think but reasonable and fitting to grant Our Will and Pleasure is, and we do hereby revoke and annul the 8th Article of Our Orders and Instructions before mentioned, hereby authorizing and directing you to cause so many of the Non-Commissioned Officers and Private Men of the Four Regiments mentioned in the

---

[1] Bk 521, p 111

[2] Pp 72, 73

margin as had served longest, and upon whom the lot fell to be turned over into the Regiments commanded by Colonel James Otway, Colonel Cosby, Brigadier Bissett, and Colonel Charles Otway, to complete them to the numbers according to Establishment to be re-incorporated into the several Regiments and Companies out of which they were taken, the said Regiments and Companies re-delivering a like number of serviceable men from amongst those who were last entertained in Our Service in the respective Regiments, to fill up the Regiments remaining in Garrison, in Minorca And for so doing this shall be your sufficient Warrant

" Given at Our Court at St. James's, this 31st day of October, 1718, in the fifth year of Our Reign.

" By His Majesty's Command,

"R P"

" *To Our Governor, or Lieutenant Governor,*
or Officer Commanding-in-Chief Our
Forces in the Island of Minorca "

(LXXX.)

Chap XV., pars 12 and 16

BEATING ORDER FOR RAISING RECRUITS BY BEAT OF DRUM, AND NOTICE AS TO BOUNTY.

" GEORGE R

" THESE are to authorise you by Beat of Drum or otherwise to raise Volunteers in any County or part of this Our Kingdom of Great Britain, for a Regiment of Foot under your Command for Our Service, to consist of Ten Companies, of Two Sergeants, Two Corporals, One Drummer, and Forty Private Soldiers, including the Widows' Men in each Company. And when you shall have listed twenty Men fit for Service in any of the said Companies, you are to give notice to two of Our Justices of the Peace of the Town or County wherein the same are, who are hereby authorised and required to view the said Men and certify the day of their so doing, from which day the said Twenty Men and the Commissioned and Non-Commissioned Officers of such Companies are to enter into Our pay. And you are to cause the said Volunteers to be raised and levyed as aforesaid, to march under the command of such Commanding Officers as you shall direct to
appointed for the Rendezvous of Our said Regiment.

" And all Magistrates, &c

' Given at Our Court at St James's, this 23rd day of July, 1715, in the first year of Our Reign.

          "By His Majesty's Command,

                    "WM. PULTNEY"

' *To Our Trusty and Well-beloved Thomas Stanwix,*
Esq, Brigadier-General of Our Forces,
and Colonel of one of Our Regiments of
Foot, or to the Officer or Officers appointed
by him to raise Volunteers for that Regi-
ment."

(2.) NOTICE FOR LONDON GAZETTE.

               " *Whitehall, 26th July,* 1713

"WHEREAS, His Majesty has issued out new Commissions for the raising of several Regiments, Notice is hereby given, that every man who lists himself in any of the Regiments of Foot shall receive forty shillings levy money

---

"(3) Mr. Secretary Pulteney desires the above Advertisement may be inserted in this day's ' Gazette.'

            " I am, &c.,

" *Mr. Buckley* "   "JAMES TAYLOR."

(LXXXI.)

Chap. XV, *par* 14

PROPOSAL[1] FOR RAISING A REGIMENT FOR RANK, AND THE SECRETARY AT WAR'S REPORT THEREON.

(1) *Proposals humbly offered by John Apletre, Esq, in the Commission*
of the Peace for the Counties of Warwick and Worcester, and late
High-Sheriff of the last-named County

" 1. That with His Majesty's permission he will raise a Regiment of Foot, consisting of twelve companies, one whereof to be Grenadiers.
" 2. That he will raise, cloath, and arm them at his own charge.

---

[1] Letter Bk 133, p 77. It would appear from vol 1. of the 'Marlborough Despatches,' p 290, that this proposal was submitted to the Duke

"3. That the said Regiment shall not come into His Majesty' Pay till within one month after it shall be compleat, according to the English Establishment in the interim to be paid by the said Mr. Apletre

"4 That the nomination of the Officers in the said Regiment shall be in the said Mr Apletre, except the Lieut.-Colonel and Major.

"5 That the Officers so named shall be men of loyalty to His Majesty's Government, of probity, resolution, and every way quali fied to serve against His Majesty's enemies

"6. That the said Regiment shall be mustered on board any of His Majesty's Ships in the River, or el ewhere within the Kingdom

"J. APLETRE"

(2) Report of the Secretary of War thereon

"SIR,   "*Whitehall, September,* 1704

"In answer to your Letter of the 10th of August, about a proposal made by Apletre for raising a Regiment of Foot Soldiers, wherein was enclosed a List of the Captains named by him for the said Regiment, of whose qualifications and fitness being desired by you to inform myself, and to let you know my opinion how far I consider this proposal practicable and for His Majesty's Service, I have thereupon enquired into the characters of the Captains offered by him to serve in the said Regiment, and whom he undertakes, in his fifth proposition, shall be men of loyalty   The Gentlemen are all unknown to me, and the Certificates Mr. Apletre has provided in their behalf are herewith transmitted to you

"As to his second and third propositions, I am to observe to you that by this means His Majesty may save

	£.	s	d
"By the Levy Money for 658 effective Private Soldiers (the number of a Regiment in England, at 3*l* a man) the sum of . .	1974	0	0
"By one month's entire Pay of the Regiment, according to this Establishment .	1113	18	8
"And by the broken muster, which may amount to about half that sum .. .	556	19	4
"In all about	3644	13	0

Besides *the Arms which he will furnish at his own charge,* and which in other cases are delivered out of the Stores of the Ordnance.

"As to the cloathing, the Queen will save nothing by it, for desiring him to explain that article, I *find he expects to have the whole pay after they have been a month complete,* without deducting the off reckonings, so that this Regiment will be cloathed in the very same manner as all other Regiments are, the *off reckonings ever answering that charge* I send you likewise his proposal of giving 5000*l se urity,* the persons named are himself and three others, whom he offers to be Captains in his Regiment.

'You desire my opinion how far I consider this proposal practicable, and for His Majesty's Service In answer to which I can only say, that if the Gentlemen proposed for Officers are men of better substance and interest than ordinary, to which purpose I do not observe that any of the Certificates speak, there is no doubt but that this design is praticable. *Whether it be for His Majesty's Service to take this method of levying Forces was the sure way to save much,* more than what I mentioned above of the first charge, must be submitted to the judgment of those who are to determine this matter

"I am, &c., &c.,

"*To Mr. Secretary Hodges*"
"H. Sr. John."

(LXXXII.)

Chapter XV , par 15

(1) Royal Warrant, authorizing the Secretary at War to issue Beating Orders for One Year, and Beating Order of the Secretary of War in pursuance thereof.

"George R

"Whereas We deem it expedient that so many men shall be raised by beat of drum or otherwise, as shall be wanting, to recruit and fill up the respective troops or companies of our regiments of Cavalry and Infantry to the number allowed upon the Establishment, We do hereby authorize and empower our Secretary at War for the time being to issue Beating Orders to the Colonels of our said regiments of Cavalry and Infantry, or to the officers appointed by them, to raise men for such regiments, which Beating Orders, signed by our Secretary at War, shall be to the officer so employed a sufficient order and authority, as well as to all Magistrates,

Justices of the Peace and Constables, and all other our civil officers who may be required to be assisting in providing quarters, impressing carriages, and otherwise as there shall be occasion. And for so doing this our order shall be and continue in force for twelve months from the 25th day of the present month.[1]

"Given at our Court at Windsor, this 20th day of March 1829, in the first year of our reign.

"By His Majesty's Command,

"ROBERT PEEL."

---

(2) INFANTRY OR CAVALRY

"WHEREAS His Majesty by His Royal Order, bearing date the 20th day of March, 1829, has been pleased to empower the Secretary at War for the time being to grant Beating Orders to the Colonels of the several regiments of Cavalry and Infantry in His Majesty's Service

"These are therefore to authorise you by beat of drum, or otherwise, to raise so many men in any county within the United Kingdom of Great Britain and Ireland as are or shall be wanting to recruit and fill up the respective troops of the regiment of Infantry under your command, to the number allowed upon the Establishment

"And all Magistrates, Justices of the Peace, Constables, and all other civil officers whom it may concern, are hereby required to be assisting unto you in providing Quarters, impressing Carriages, and otherwise, as there shall be occasion; and for so doing, this order shall be and continue in force for twelve months from the 25th day of the present month.

"Given at the War Office, this 22nd day of March, 1829,

"H. HARDINGE."

"*To the Col. of ——— Regiment or to the Officer appointed by him to raise Troops for the Regiment.*"

---

[1] The day on which the Mutiny Act expired

(LXXXIII.)

Chapter XV., par. 20

LETTER OF SECRETARY AT WAR[1] ORDERING THE DISCHARGE OF A MAN FROM ILLEGAL ENLISTMENT, AND THAT COMPENSATION SHOULD BE MADE TO HIM.

"SIR,   " *Whitehall, 24th April*, 1705.

 I send you here enclosed the copy of an Affidavit of Jaspar Cotman, of Hampshire, Woolbuyer, made before the Mayor of Winchester, and two Justices of the Peace, relating to one Peter Bigwood, a servant of the said Cotmans, who has been lately forced into the Service by some Soldiers of the Company of your Regiment, marching under the command of Lieutenant Hays, to Portsmouth, and that he has been very much beat and abused by them. I am thereupon directed to acquaint you that Her Majesty does think fit that the said Peter Bigwood be forthwith discharged, and have some reparation made him, and that you give orders to the said Lieutenant Hays accordingly.

       " I am, Sir,
         " Your most humble Servant,
" *To Colonel Hamilton.*"   " H. St. John "

(LXXXIV)

Chapter XV , par. 32

SECRETARY AT WAR'S APPLICATION FOR CRIMINALS IN PRISON TO BE ENLISTED IN THE DUKE OF MARLBOROUGH'S REGIMENT.

"SIR,   " *Whitehall, 4th March*, 1706.

 My Lord, Duke of Marlborough, having received information of three persons, now in Northampton Gaol, named Richard Long, Edward Gardner, and —— Bryar, who are guilty of several no

---

[1] Letter Bk. 133, p 245, see also 10 Com Journ , p 836
[2] Letter Bk 135 p 169

torious Crimes, but having been convicted of Dear Stealing only, are like to be set at liberty again, unless they are listed as the Law directs, His Grace has therefore ordered an officer to go down to Northampton to receive and enlist them, and to that end you are desired to cause them to be secured in Northampton Gaol, untill such time as the officer shall arrive there, and to give him what assistance you can in Listing the said men.

"I am, Sir,

"Yours, &c.,

"*To the Mayor of Northampton.*"   "H Sr John."

(LXXXV.)

Chapter XV., par 46

Report of Sir R. Eyre[1] on the Enlistment of Soldiers by Military Officers.

"Captain Gooch, of Colonel Godfrey's Regiment, having listed several Volunteers at Coventry, which the Magistrates have forced from him, on pretence that Officers are restrained by the late Acts to the methods therein prescribed, humbly desires to know whether Officers by virtue of their Commissions and General Beating Orders as formerly are not empowered to entertain Volunteers, humbly conceiving the Act was intended for their assistance by new expedients, not to take away any power they had formerly.

"Sir,   "*Whitehall, 2 June,* 1709.

"I am of opinion, that there being in this Recruiting Act no restrictive clause that forbidds the Officers listing Volunteers as formerly, that they have the power, but, for my further satisfaction, I desire your Opinion upon this matter

"I am, Sir,

"Your most faithfull humble Servant,

"R. Walpole"

---

[1] Mis Bk 519 (MS), p 47

" *Opinion*

" Sir, " *Lincoln's Inn, 2 June,* 1709

" I think you have made a very right Judgment in this matter, for the Officers of the Army have certainly a Power to list and receive men into the Service as incident to their Commissions. And being under no restriction by any Act of Parliament, their listing is effectual to all purposes, and no civill Officer can discharge the person that has listed himself as a Volunteer.

' I am, with all respect,
' Sir,
' Your most obedient Servant,
" R EVAL."

(LXXXVI.)

Chapter XV, *par.* 51

REPORT[1] OF THE LAW OFFICERS ON THE RELEASE OF MEN IMPRESSED UNDER 29 GEO II., c 4

" *Case*

" SEVERAL of the men lately impressed under the 29 Geo II, c 4, have applyed for their Habeas Corpus returnable before the Judges at their Chambers in order to get discharged, alleging they are not objects within the meaning of the Act, notwithstanding the Commissioners empowered by the Act have thought them such, and have delivered them over to the Military Power as proper persons to serve His Majesty, by which means the Crown is put to great trouble and expense in opposing their discharge, and the intent of the said Act is thereby greatly evaded, Therefore, in order to prevent the same, and the ill consequences that immediately attend it, the Secretary at War hath directed Mr Francis to lay the said Act before Mr. Attorney- and Solicitor-General for their consideration and Opinion upon the following quære

" 1st Quære Can any and what step be taken for the preventing these men from obtaining their Habeas Corpus returnable before any Judge at Chambers before Term, and if not, what is the most advisable method for the Secretary at War to take herein for preventing the same for the future ?"

[1] Vol 721, p. 139

" *Report*

" *January 11th, 1757.*

" It has prevailed in usage for the Judges to grant the Habeas Corpus upon this and other Acts of Parliament of the like nature; but if a return be made to the Writ, alleging that the person who has sued it out is a proper object of the authority given to the Commissioners, I am of opinion that such Return may be supported in law, because it ought not to be judged of upon Affidavits, but upon the face of the Return itself The party is afterwards at liberty to bring an action for a false return, in which the whole matter will be inquired of, upon all proper evidence of the circumstances I know no other method of proceeding in this case, or by which the delays and inconveniences arising from the serving of such Writs in the execution of the Act in question can be prevented, unless the Legislature shall think fit by a new law to make the judgment of the Commissioners absolutely final, which I doubt would meet with great difficulties in Parliament.

" C. YORKE."

(LXXXVII.)

Chapter XV., par 61

(1) REPORT[1] OF SIR P. YORKE AS TO THE VALIDITY OF ENLISTMENT THOUGH THE OATH OF FIDELITY HAS NOT BEEN ADMINISTERED

' *Extract from Letter of 6 May, 1727.*

" LAST Wednesday, my Sergeant listed one James Mills of this City. Thursday morning he brought him to me, when the said Mills acknowledged to have freely and voluntarily enlisted himself, and said he had been formerly a Soldier in Colonel Chudleigh's Regiment, and now was willing to serve His Majesty again. Thursday and Friday he demanded and received his Pay, but on Friday, in the afternoon when the Sergeant would have carried him to be sworn before a Country Justice (those of this City having at all times made a scruple of swearing any of the Citizens), the said Mills, through the persuasions of his wife, refused to go, upon

---

[1] Letter Bk 721, p 19

which I ordered the Sergeant to put him upon the guard   Complaint being made to the Mayor, he sent on Saturday morning to demand him from the Guard, the man pretended he was in drink when he entertained, but owned that my Sergeant had not helped him to it. The Mayor insisted that no man could be deemed a Soldier before he had owned his free consent before a Civil Magistrate and I had no right to the man. took him from the Guard, and sent him to Bridewell; ever since I used my utmost endeavours to have the man delivered to me, but to no purpose, which has put me under a necessity of applying to you for redress'

"Sir,   "*Lincoln's Inn, May 25th*, 1727.

"I had the honor of a letter from you with the enclosed extract of one from an Officer who is recruiting in Bristol, concerning a dispute arisen there about a man enlisted, in which you are pleased to desire my opinion, whether a man who hath voluntarily enlisted when he was sober, and hath received pay, can be deemed a Soldier by law, though he hath not been sworn before a Civil Magistrate?

"Upon this question I am of opinion that persons so enlisted, and having received pay, is to all intents and purposes a Soldier, and that swearing before a Civil Magistrate is not necessary to make the enlisting effectual, but is required for other purposes. As to the dispute between the above-mentioned Officer and the Mayor of Bristol, I apprehend, if the case be truly noted in the enclosed Extract, that the Officer was in the right, and that the Mayor had no authority to take him out of the Service in the manner there represented.

"I am, &c,

"P YORKE."

(2) REPORT OF SIR DUDLEY RYDER TO THE SAME EFFECT.

"4 *Sept.*, 1740.

"I am of opinion, though A. B. has not taken the above Oath, yet he is a Soldier, and liable to be tried by a Court-martial according to the Act for punishing Mutiny and Desertion, &c., to suffer such punishment by the sentence of that Court as Soldiers are subject to

"D. RYDER.

(3) Report of Law Officers[1] in 1812 upon the same Question.

Chapter XV , par 61

" *Case.*

" By the Mutiny Acts and Articles of War of the years previous to 1811, Recruits upon enlistment swore to serve 'King George,' or King George III , for a term of years or until regularly discharged, as the case might be.   In the Mutiny Acts and Articles of War for 1811 the words 'his heirs and successors' were introduced   Doubts have been started whether, in the event of the death of the present King, those men who had sworn and engaged to serve King George III. could legally be held to the service of King George IV , and whether those who have sworn to serve King George could in like manner be detained in the service of a successor of a different name, or of a Queen who should ascend the throne, before the period of their service is expired

" The Opinion of the Attorney and Solicitor-General is required —

" Whether Recruits who have enlisted prior to the year 1811 will be liable to be detained in the service of a successor to His present Majesty until the expiration of the term for which they enlisted, or for any period after the King's demise ? "

" *Report.*

" *Upper Guildford St* , 14*th March*, 1812

" WE conceive that the act of enlisting precedes the oaths which, as far as they regard the service of the person taking them, are required as securities for his faithful performance of the duties thereof, but that he is completely enlisted before he takes the oaths for the period   See the Mutiny Act, 51 Geo. III . c 8, s. 74, which enacts that every person receiving enlisting money shall be deemed to be enlisted as a Soldier, subject to the relief afterwards granted to persons hastily enlisting themselves, and the following section, and also the 1st article of the 3rd section of the Articles of War, which directs the Oath of Fidelity.

" V Gibbs
" Thos. Plumer.'

---

[1] No 2 N S., p 194, see Statute 6 Anne, c 7, s 8

(LXXXVIII.)

Chapter XV , par 86

EXTRACT FROM COMMONS' JOURNALS AS TO STRENGTH OF
THE ARMY, BEFORE, UNDER, AND AFTER MR. WYNDHAM'S
ACT FOR LIMITED ENLISTMENTS.[1]

Mr Wyndham's Resolutions[2] were these—

I. That the effective strength of the Army was—

	Regulars.	Militia	Total
On the 1st of March, 1806	173,600	75,182	248,782
On the 1st of March, 1807	181,856	77,211	259,067

A reduction having in the mean time taken place, of a local corps of
3000 men and upwards, in the island of Ceylon

II. That the provisions of certain Acts of Parliament passed
during the year 1806 and having in view the better ordering of
the Army, and the improvement of the condition of non-commissioned officers and soldiers, took effect from the 24th of June in the
said year.

III. That from the 1st of July following, the number of recruits
raised for the Regular Army (exclusive of those raised for Foreign
and Colonial Corps, and 650 men for a regiment commanded by the
Hon Colonel Dillon) was—

		Rate per Annum
In the 1st period of three months, ending on the 1st of October, 1806	2,770	11,080
In the 2nd period, ending on the 1st of Jan , 1807	3,496	13,934
In the 3rd period, ending on the 1st of April, 1807	5,335	21,340
In the 4th period, ending on the 1st of July, 1807	6,078	24,312

IV. That on the 25th of October, 1806, the bounty to recruits
was reduced—

	s	d		s	d
For the Cavalry, from	13	8	to	8	3
For the Infantry ..	16	16	to	11	11

V That the number of recruits raised for the Regular Army
in Great Britain and Ireland, according to the Adjutant-General's
returns, was, in the first six months of

	By ordinary Recruiting.	Additional Force	Total.
1805	6,736	4,187	10,923
1806	4,949	4,834	10,783
1807	11,413		11,413

[1] 62 Com Journ , p 485.   [2] 9 Parl Deb., p 1218

VI　That, amongst the numbers raised in the first six months of 1805, are included 3089 raised by officers recruiting for rank

VII. That the men raised under the Additional Force Act were for Home Service only, and might be of any height not less than five feet two inches, and of any age between 18 and 45

VIII. That in the Regular Army no man could be received but between the ages of 18 and 30, and of a height not less than five feet four inches, the standard for men not entering for general service, but choosing their own Regiments, being five feet five inches, and for the Guards and Cavalry still higher

IX. That by Recruits raised by ordinary recruiting are meant men raised either at the Head quarters of Regiments, or by the recruiting districts late under the superintendence of the Inspector-General

X　That according to the War Office Return of Recruits for whom Bounty has been drawn as raised at the Head quarters of Regiments in Great Britain, and the Inspector-General's Return of the numbers raised by the recruiting districts, the produce of the ordinary recruiting was, during the first six months of

	At Headquarters of Regiments in Great Britain	By Recruiting Districts in Great Britain	By ditto in Ireland	Total
1805	.. 1,470	2,327	912	4,709
1806	1,084	1,957	953	3,994
1807	. 2,536	6,115	2,396	11,047

XI　That the number of men who volunteered from limited to unlimited service was, during six months—

Ending 1 July, 1805	2,225
„ 1 January, 1806	2,863
„ 1 July, 1806	2,413
„ 1 January, 1807	7,081

XII. That the number of men who deserted from the Army at home was, during the first six months of—

	In Great Britain	In Ireland
1805	1 in 202	1 in 204
1806	1 „ 217	1 „ 235
1807	1 „ 293	1 „ 205

XIII. That the number of men who deserted from the recruiting districts was, during the first six months of—

1805	1 in 10
1806	1 „ 10
1807 .	1 „ 12

Lord Castlereagh's Resolutions[1] were—

I. That the increase of 8,250 men, as stated, in the Regular Army, between March, 1806, and March, 1807, has been produced by 2908 men received from the Irish Militia, and 3542 under the Additional Force Act. Total, 6450 men, without which aids (deducting our losses in Egypt and South America, viz., 2185 men, which appear in the Effectives of the Army on the 1st of March, 1807) the Army would have decreased under the Regulations established in June, 1806, in the number of 379 men. That the Regular Army has been progressively increasing,[2] previous to the establishment of the new system of levying men, as follows, the amount being—

On the 1st of July, 1804	..	..	..	141,740
"	"	1805	.	.	.	162,997
"	"	1806	..	.	.	175,997

III. A. That the number of Recruits raised quarterly for the Regular Army, between the 1st March, 1805, and 1st March, 1806, when the repeal of the Additional Force Act was determined on, was (exclusive of Foreign and Colonial levies, and of men transferred from the Militia) as follows,—

			Number raised	Rate per Annum
1st Quarter ending July 1, 1805		.. 4,865	19,460
2nd " " December 1, 1805		. 4,252	17,008
3rd " " January 1, 1806 .		. 4,790	19,160
4th " " April 1, 1806		.. 6,096	24,384

III. B. That the number of men raised as above between the 1st of April, 1805, and the 1st of April, 1806, was 20,003; the number between July, 1806, and July, 1807, 17,689, being 2314 less than in the former year, whereas the number of boys included in the 17,689, exceeded by 1076 the number included in the 20,003, the preceding year's produce.

III. c. That the number of men obtained for Regular Service, including men transferred from the Militia (and exclusive of Foreign and Colonial levies) was, between July, 1805, and July, 1806, 33,693 men; between July, 1806, and July, 1807, 20,681

---

[1] 9 Parl Deb., pp 1220-22

[2] See 132 H D (3), 1378, for numbers enlisted yearly from 1794 to 1806, by ordinary mode of recruiting —

1794	.. 38,565	1799	. 41,316	1803	.. 11,253
1795	. 40,463	1800	. 17,829	1804	9,430
1796	16,366	1801	17,413	1805	. 11,677
1797	.. 16,096	1802	.. 7,403	1806	11,875
1798	21,457				

men, being 14,012 men less than in the preceding year, exclusive of the services of the men raised in the latter years being determinable in seven or ten years, according to the terms of their enlistment.

III D. That whilst the number of men levied in the latter year was less than the former, as stated in the preceding Resolutions, an annual additional charge of 450,000*l* in increased pay and pensions to the Army has been incurred, as an encouragement to induce men to enlist, being at the rate of about 25*l.* per man on the number of men raised within the year, and which expense must be hereafter largely increased, in proportion as the pensions on 14 and 21 years' service come into operation.

III. E That during the former year the recruiting parties did not exceed in number 405; that in the latter year they had been increased to 1113, exclusive of above 400 extra Recruiting Officers; and from the 8th of December, 1806, 54 second battalions have been recruiting, under an intimation that if they did not raise 400 men each in six months the battalions would be then reduced, and the Officers placed on half-pay, which extraordinary increase of the number of recruiting parties must be considered not only as highly prejudicial to the discipline and efficiency of the Army, but as so much expense incurred for the levy of men, as distinguished from the performance of regimental duty.

III. F. That whilst the number of men raised as above for the Regular Service has in the latter year been reduced, the proportion of desertions in the Army serving at home has been rather increased; the proportion being, in the five successive half-yearly periods, as follows :—

Desertions in the Army at Home :—

Jan 1805 to July 1805	..	..	.	1 in 194
July 1805 to Jan. 1806	.	..	.	1 „ 152
Jan 1806 to July 1806	..	.		1 „ 275
July 1806 to Jan 1807	.	.		1 „ 243
Jan 1807 to July 1807				1 „ 236

IV That the expense of levy money for General Service has been reduced; for cavalry, from 19*l.* to 15*l.* 4*s.* 6*d.*, and for Infantry from 22*l.* 8*s.* 0*d.* to 18*l.* 12*s.* 6*d.* But the term of service has also been reduced from service for life to service for ten and seven years, which supposes two additional periods of enlistment, and consequently two additional bounties in the course of a service of 21 years, exclusive of the additional pay and pensions as above referred to.

VI. That among the number raised in the first six months of

1807, being 11,413 men, 8035 have been raised by the 54 second battalions; that is, by Officers recruiting to avoid reduction

VII. and VIII. That with the exception of 6242 men transferred to garrison battalions, all men raised under the Army of Reserve and Additional Force Acts have been since enlisted into the Line, being of the age and height required by His Majesty's Regulations, and amongst the men so transferred to garrison battalions are included all men who did not choose to enter for General Service, without reference to age or height.

XI. That the men volunteering from limited to unlimited service, from 1st July, 1806, to 1st January, 1807, received ten guineas bounty for only extending their service from Local to General Service, whereas before that period (the bounty being the same) the men transferring themselves to the Line exchanged their Service, not only from Home to Foreign Service, but from Service limited in point of time to Service for life; and the men in the latter period who refused to transfer their services were ordered to be drafted into garrison battalions.

(LXXXIX.)

Chapter XV., par. 98.

REPORT [1] AS TO OBSERVANCE OF THE DIRECTIONS OF THE MUTINY ACT IN THE ENLISTMENT OF RECRUITS, AND UPON THE FOLLOWING QUESTIONS.

"1. WHETHER a Soldier can be attested with his own consent before the expiration of the twenty-four hours?

"2 Whether an attestation is good, and a man enlisting becomes a Regular Soldier if carried after his enlisting to any distance for the purpose of being attested, instead of being carried to some Justice next to or in the vicinity of the place where such person shall have enlisted?

"3. Whether a man so attested before a Magistrate not residing next to or in the vicinity of the place where he shall have enlisted, can be considered, if he quits or absconds, as a deserter?

"4. Whether an attestation is good after four days?

"5 Whether, if a man enlisted and not attested within four days runs away before attestation, he can be considered as a deserter?"

---

[1] Bk 1 (N S.), p 394

" *Report*

" *Lincoln's Inn, Jan 22, 1807*

' 1. We are of opinion that a Recruit cannot be attested, even with his own consent before the expiration of the twenty-four hours.

" 2. We incline to think the attestation would be good, and the man enlisting would become a Regular Soldier, though made before a Justice not residing, or being next to or in the vicinity of the place where such person was enlisted. But this may be doubted, and therefore, unless in case of necessity, we think the directions of the Act in this respect should be strictly observed.

" 3. We think such person so acting will be deemed a deserter

" 4. We think an attestation will not be good after four days

" 5. If there has been no attestation within four days, and the Recruit after that time runs away, we think he cannot be considered as a deserter.

" If this question supposes the man to have run away within four days, we think that he is to be considered as a deserter.

" V. GIBBS.
" THOS. PLUMER."

(XC.)

Chapter XV., par. 103.

REPORTS[1] AS TO THE ENLISTMENT OF APPRENTICES.

(1.) " *Statement*

" It sometimes happens that Recruiting Officers enlist apprentices

" *Query:* Whether such Recruits can be proceeded against as *Deserters* if they do not repair to their Regiment, Troop, or Company, when they are out of their time?"

" *Report.*

" *2nd July,* 1753

' We are of opinion they cannot. Their being permitted to serve their time without furlough or licence, will be deemed a waiver of an engagement, to the prejudice of their masters, whatever right might have been acquired by their original enlisting as against themselves.

" D. RYDER
" W. MURRAY"

---

[1] Bk. 721, p 168.

(2) "*Statement.*

"It often happens that apprentices enlist in the Army.

"Query 1. Whether apprentices so enlisting can be detained from their masters?

"2 Whether the law requires that upon being reclaimed by their masters they should be absolutely discharged from the Service, or only that they should have a temporary furlough, or leave of absence for the time of their apprenticeship?

"3 Whether persons who have been enlisted while apprentices, and dismissed with such a furlough or leave of absence, can be proceeded against as Deserters, if upon proper notice they do not repair to their Regiment, Troop, or Company, when their indentures are expired?"

"*Report.*

"*16th February,* 1760.

"1. I am of opinion they cannot, for an apprentice is not *sui juris,* or capable of contracting against his indentures, so that whether he contracts with a private person or with the Crown as a volunteer his contract in both cases is void, and the apprentice must be delivered up if he is reclaimed by his master.

"2. I think the apprentice must be absolutely discharged, because the enlisting is void by reason of the inability in the apprentice to enlist at all, provided always that he is demanded by his master, for if he gives him up, I think the enlisting good.

"The answer to the last Query will answer this likewise. When the apprentice is once dismissed upon the master's claim, he is discharged for ever [1]

"C Pratt."

(XC.*)

Chap. XV , *par.* 116

Two Orders—(1st) against Officers or Soldiers carry-in Bayonets except upon Duty [2], and (2ndly) against Soldiers carrying Ammunition, with a Note thereon.

"For the preventing of mischief that may happen by the carrying of Bayonetts, We do hereby strictly forbid all Officers and Soldiers, of what quality soever, within our pay and entertainment, to carry

---

[1] As to enrolment of apprentices in the Militia, see 42 Geo III , c 90, sec 49, 59 Geo III , c 24, sec 4, and 56 Geo. III , c 64 [2] Mis Bk , 1683 to 1697, p 111

a Dagger or Bayonett at any other time than when such Officers or Soldiers shall be upon duty, or under their Arms, upon pain of being punished at the discretion of a Court-Martiall. And the Officers and Commanders-in Chief of our several Regiments, Troops, and Companies, and Governors of our Garrisons, are hereby required to cause these our Commands to be forthwith read and published at the head of each respective Regiment, Troop, and Company, that all persons may give due obedience thereunto.

"Given at our Court at Whitehall this 4th day of March, 168⅞, &c

"By His Majesty's Command,

"W. B"

Note —It will be noticed that this order is put forth by the Secretary at War, and not by the Commander-in-Chief, as was the case when the same order was renewed by Horse Guards Circular, No. 105, 15th Nov., 1837.[1] So also is the Order of 4th August, 1686, as to the care of arms.

As the possession of ball-cartridge by every private in the Army is a fact attracting public notice,—now that a rifle may be easily loaded, and then discharged with felonious intent,—one or two references to the General Orders of the Army—so far as they bear upon the subject—may be useful. In the first place, it must be noticed, that all ammunition was issued by the Board of Ordnance twice a year to the Commanding Officer of the Regiment upon his requisition sent up through his Regimental Agent.[2]

It was distributed to the Captains, who were to give receipts for the same, and be held responsible for the care and expenditure of the ammunition so received[3] The Captains were daily to examine the men's arms and ammunition, and frequently to expose the latter to the sun and air[4]

An allowance of 10*l* a year being given to the Regiment for the carriage of ammunition, the expense of carriage was avoided by the Regiment returning the ammunition to the Ordnance on change of quarters This practice was forbidden by General Order of the 9th August, 1826, and a fair proportion of the ammunition was to be given to the men to be carried in their pouches, and the residue held by the Quartermaster.[5]

This order appears to have been misunderstood, and accordingly on the 14th March, 1827, the Duke of Wellington issued another

[1] 27 H D (31), p 875, and 'Organization Report, 1860,' p 5 W O Bk 795, p 88   [2] General Regulations of August, 1811, p 70
[3] P. 90.   [4] Pp 116, 238, 276, 286, 335
[5] General Regulations of 1822, p 527

General Order [1] (449), directing (*inter alia*) that all Regiments were to have *in the constant possession of the men* 10 rounds of Service ammunition, which were to be under the daily inspection of Officers of Companies. Upon emergent circumstances the supply was to be increased by 50 rounds per man, but this extra supply was to be returned when the emergency had ceased.

The object for issuing this order is explained by the Duke to Sir George Murray in a letter of 10th April, 1827. It was to prevent the accumulation of large resources of ammunition, and thereby the recurrence of accidents from explosion that had taken place in the Isle of Wight and elsewhere. Therefore it was necessary to state the minimum and maximum that each soldier should have in his possession [2] that the reserve might be regulated.

The present arrangements are as under :—

G. O., 94 —(*Specially issued 7th September,* 1869) REGIMENTAL SERVICE AMMUNITION.

"Henceforward the service ammunition of the Army is to be removed from the pouches, and placed in the regimental expense magazines.

"General Officers, commanding districts at home and stations abroad, will use their discretion should the state of the locality, in which the troops under their command are serving, be such as to require an exception to be made in this respect, in which case they will at once report the same to His Royal Highness the Field-Marshal Commanding-in-Chief.

"Proper care should be taken that a key of the magazine is at all times in possession of some responsible person in camp or barracks, with a view to the immediate issue of the ammunition if wanted on emergency.

"Guards and escorts, or parties detached in aid of the civil power, will invariably have the requisite quantity of ammunition served out to them before going on duty. This supply is to be collected after the duty has been performed, and returned into the magazine "

---

[1] General Regulations of 1822, p 546.
[2] Supplementary Despatches, vol iii, p 626

(XCI)

Chapter XV., *par.* 143.

ARMY OF RESERVE.

Statement A.

No. 1.

Number raised to 1st May, 1804, including Casualties [1] ..		45,492
Total raised in (say to July) 1804 [2] . . .	5,033	
Number raised from 1st January to 1st May, 1804 [3] . .	4,505	
Difference from May and June 1804 [4]		528
Total raised		46,020

No. 2.

CASUALTIES TO 1ST MAY, 1804 [5]

Rejected, Discharged, claimed by Civil Law, &c.	2,116
Deserters, claimed as Deserters from other Corps, &c.	5,651
Deaths	589
Total of Casualties to 1st May, 1804	8,356
Proportion of Balloted Men, English and Scotch (the Irish Casualties do not distinguish Balloted Men from Substitutes) .. .	266
Residue, Substitutes	8,090
Total of Balloted Men to 1st May, 1804 [6]	2,873
Deduct Casualties as above	266
Effective Balloted Men (see remark below)	2,607
Balloted Men who would not volunteer [7]	1,004
Balloted Men who did volunteer—suppose	1,603

---

[1] 'Military Transactions,' part i , p 60.   [2] Ib., part ii , p 136.
[3] Ib , part i., pp. 65-7.
[4] The proportions of Balloted Men and Substitutes in this number are not ascertained.   [5] 'Military Transactions,' part i., pp 65-7.
[6] Ib.   [7] Ib., part ii., p 8.

No. 3.

VOLUNTEERS TO THE LINE.

Return dated 15th March, 1806—Army of Reserve [1] { 1803	..	.	7,214
1804	..	..	9,920
1805	..	..	2,149
Ditto ditto from additional Force—1804 and 1805	..	..	8,154
Volunteers from *Limited* Service,[2] presumed to include, and to be confined to, Army of Reserve and Additional Force—return dated 10th August, 1807 { 1806	.		9,424
Six months to 24th June, 1807		.	1,831
Total from Army of Reserve and Additional Force		.	33,252
Total from Additional Force [3]	..	..	8,562
Residue, Volunteers from Army of Reserve [4]	..	..	24,690

No. 4.

Total raised, as above	..	.	46,020
Deduct, Casualties, as above ..	.	..	8,356
Effectives in the Army of Reserve ..	.	..	37,664
Deduct, Volunteers to the Line, as above ..	.	..	24,690
Residue to Garrison Battalions, but including Casualties after 1st May, 1804 [5]			12,974

No. 5.

Effectives of the Army of Reserve, as above	.	..	37,664
Of whom, Balloted Men, as above ..	.	.. 2,607	2,807
Irish *Recruits* [6]	..	200	
Substitutes ..	..	..	34,857

Statement B.

No. 1.

Number of Balloted Men [7] ..	.	..	2,873
Ditto of Substitutes, including 200 Recruits [8]	..	..	41,198
Total, including English and Scotch Casualties ..	..	..	44,071
Add, Irish Casualties [9]	..	.	1,4??
Total raised [10] ..	..	.	45,4??

[1] 61 Com Journ., p 628. [2] 62 Com. Journ., p. 897.
[3] 'Military Transactions,' part ii , p 11, written 1st June, 1809.
[4] The total in 'Military Transactions,' part ii., p 28, viz., 17,843, is taken from a return dated 31st January, 1805. [5] 'Military Transactions,' part ii, p 8.
[6] Ib , part i., p. 67 [7] Ib , p. 61. [8] Ib., p 67. [9] Ib. [10] Ib., p. 60

No 1 —(*continued*)

Brought Forward.—Total raised		..	45,492
Add (see statement)		..	528
Total raised	..		46,020
Balloted Men {as above		2,873}	
{add, from the above 528, say		50}	2,923
Substitutes, including 200 Recruits (Ireland)			43,097

No 2.

Casualties {Rejected, claimed by Civil Power, &c.		2,116
{Deserted, Deserters from other Corps, &c		5,651
		7,767
Of whom, Balloted Men		266
Substitutes		7,501
Deaths being ordinary Casualties, not included		
Total of Balloted Men, as above		2,923
Deduct Casualties		266
Balloted Men, Effective		2,657
Total of Substitutes, as above		43,097
Deduct Casualties		7,501
Substitutes, Effective		35,596
Balloted Men, ditto		2,657
Total Effective, previous to volunteering		38,253
Volunteered ..		24,691
Remained, and were formed into Garrison Battalions [1]		13,562

No 3.

ESTIMATE OF THE PERSONAL BOUNTY

	£
2657 Effective Balloted Men, at 17*l* 2*s*. each, viz , half the ordinary} price of a Substitute, and two guineas from Government ..}	45,434
200 Irish Recruits at 7 guineas [2]	1,470
35,396 Substitutes at 31*l* 1*s* , viz , 30*l* average price, and one} guinea from Government }	1,099,045
Total for Effectives	1,145,949

[1] 'Military Transactions,' part 1 p 61　　　　[2] 43 Geo III , c 50, sec 41

No. 3 —(*continued*)

Brought Forward —Total for Effectives	1,145,949
Deserted, or Deserters from other Corps, 5651, at 15*l* each, half the price of a Substitute[1]	84.765
Total of personal Bounty to the Army of Reserve	1,230,714
Bounty to 24,691 Volunteers to the Line, at 7*l* 12*s* 6*d* only[2]	188,268
Total for Army of Reserve and Volunteers to the Line	1,418,982

Army of Reserve, from July 1803, *to July* 1804, *when it merged in the Additional Force*

Total raised[3]		45,492
Add, viz, Total raised in 1804[4]	5,033	
Ditto ditto to 1st May 1804[5]	4,505	
		528
		46,020
Number of Balloted Men[6]	2,873	
Add, as above, the whole taken as Balloted Men	528	
		3,401
Irish Recruits for the Levy[7]		200
The residue, Substitutes		42,419
		46,020
Substitutes[8]	41,198	
Which number includes Irish Recruits[9]	200	
		40,998
But does not include Irish Casualties[10]		1,421
		42,419
Total, therefore, of Substitutes		42,419

[1] *No sum estimated for 2116 men rejected, claimed by Civil Law, &c*

[2] The Army of Reserve having merged in the Additional Force, the Volunteers are presumed to have received the same rate of Bounty, viz, nine guineas, as fixed in November, 1804, for Additional Force, after which, at least 7000 men volunteered from Army of Reserve

No sum taken for Ballot Expenses, paid by Government, which must have been very heavy. On the other hand, the Irish Levy Expenses, &c, must have been in Irish currency, and the average of 30*l* for a substitute, may possibly not have applied to Ireland, although no distinction is made in 'Military Transactions,' part 1, p 61

Deduct on this account, 118,982*l*, leaving 1,300,000*l*

[3] 'Military Transactions,' part 1, p 60   [4] Ib, part 11, p 136
[5] Ib, part 1, pp 65-7   [6] Ib p 61   [7] Ib, p. 67
[8] Ib, p 61   [9] Ib, p 67   [10] Ib

CASUALTIES

Rejected, discharged claimed by Civil Power, &c., &c [1] . .	2,116
Deserted, claimed as Deserters from other Corps, &c , &c [2]	5,651
	7,767
Of the above, Balloted Men [3] . . .	266
Residue, Substitutes . .	7,501
	7,767

Deaths, 589, being ordinary Casualties, are not taken as Deductions from the result of this Levy [4]

The Irish Casualties do not, in any manner, distinguish the Balloted Men from the Substitutes, &c. But out of 6776 men remaining effective, there were only 48 Balloted Men [5]

The English and Scotch Casualties do distinguish the Balloted Men from the Substitutes in the *Totals* of the Casualties, but not in the particular classes of Casualties.[6]

Thus the above 266 Casualties amongst the Balloted Men, may include some deaths, the effect of which is to *reduce* the number of Casualties by rejection or desertion amongst the *Substitutes.*

Total of Balloted Men, as above . .		3,401
Deduct, Casualties, as above .	266	
Men who would not volunteer [7] . .	1,004	
		1,270
Residue of Balloted Men, taken as having volunteered		2,131
Irish Recruits, ditto ditto		200
Substitutes, ditto ditto		17,222
Total volunteered [8]		19,553
Total of Substitutes, as above		42,419
Deduct, Casualties, as above . . . 7,501		
Volunteered . . . 17,222	24,723	
Substitutes who did not volunteer		17,696
Balloted Men who did not volunteer [9]		1,004
Total number of Men who did not volunteer . . .		18,700

---

[1] 'Military Transactions,' part I., pp 65-67.   [2] Ib.   [3] Ib.

[4] Ib.   [5] Ib , p 67   [6] Ib., pp 65, 66   [7] Ib., part II., p 8

[8] 61 Com. Journ , p 624   [9] 'Military Transactions, part II , p 8

Par 156.

Statement D. *Of Recruiting, from* 1803 *to* 1806

	1803	1804.		1805			1806.		
	Regular Army	Regular Army	Addl. Force	Regular Army		Addl. Force	Regular Army		Addl. Force
				Men.	Boys		Men	Boys.	
January	911	700		860	108	774	2080	850	1079
February	986	672		1109	173	831			1213
March	1075	489		1179	133	891			1287
April .	916	586		1011	77	542			890
May	605	647		964	136	608	2019		909
June .	1129	666		867	119	541			456
July ..	1827	689		778	152	528	827	91	
August	1262	1066		596	188	630	791 [1]	79	
September	696	857	133	698	144	538	899	93	
October	508	1272	451	620	115	653	1039	117	
November	593	910	481	731	84	900	955	109	
December	745	876	593	767	68	852	1077	199	
Totals	11,253	9430	1658	10,180	1497	8288	9687	1538	5834

The Returns for the Regular Army for 1803 and 1804, are taken from 'Military Transactions,' part II, p 78 The return of *Men* for first six months of 1806, is taken from part II., p. 134.

The other returns are taken from 62 Com. Journ , pp. 892, 898, 900, 63 Com Journ., pp 601, 610, 611.

No monthly distribution of Boys for the first six months of 1806 can be traced.

In the 'Military Transactions,' part II., p 78, the Return of Recruits for 1805 includes Boys, without distinguishing the proportion thereof The aggregate, 11,677, corresponds with the above.

---

[1] The above total for August, 1806, does not include 650 Men of Dillon's Levy, converted into the 101st Regiment, according to a Memorandum in the Return to the House of Commons They are included in the Return of Recruits, 'Military Transactions,' part II, p 134

In the 'Military Transactions,' part II, p. 136, there are two Returns of Additional Force for 1805 One states 8492, the other, as above, 8288. Neither the above Returns, nor those in 'Military Transactions,' part II., p 78, include about 3000 Men, raised, apparently in 1804 and 1805, for four new Levies in Ireland Vide note in page referred to.

Additional Force, raised under an Act of June, 1804, repealed in June, 1806.

Boys inlisted under a General Order of December, 1804.

Statement E *Of same, from 1807 to 1809.*

	1807			1808		1809			
	Extra Recruits.	Ordinary Recruiting		Ordinary Recruiting		Ordinary Recruiting			
						Unlimited Period		Limited Period	
	Men	Men	Boys.	Men	Boys.	Men	Boys.	Men	Boys
January			356	632	153				
February	440	4574	379	649	178	1976	522	792	169
March			370	901	194				
April			415	944	266				
May	622	4782	460	815	247	2336	451	1012	17o
June			341	912	196				
July			411	960	206				
August	708	3414	313	1083	234	1170	259	515	155
September			220	806	201				
October			175	887	221				
November	621	2599	221	804	161	1251	235	323	79
December			156	1084	229				
	2391	15,369	3817	10,477	2486	7033	1467	2642	578
						1467	578	7033	2642

Total, Unlimited Period   8500

Ditto Limited Period   9675   2220
Ditto Men   10,477   2045
Ditto Boys   2,486   2045

Grand Total, corresponding with the Adjutant-General's Return   12,963   ..   11,720

(XCII.)

Chapter XVI., par 36

LETTER[1] FROM SECRETARY AT WAR EXPRESSING GEO. I.s
AVERSION TO THE SALE OF COMMISSIONS.

" My LORD,   ' *Whitehall, 23rd March,* 17$\frac{16}{17}$.

    "Though it is scarce possible for any who has not applied
to the King to conceive the great aversion he always expresses upon
the mention of leave for any Officer to dispose of his Commission,
and every body is discouraged from speaking on that head, I could

not, however, resist your Lordship, and not only laid before His
Majesty your request in favour of Lieut. Moody, but as far as I was
able proposed his consent to it, which I could not obtain, His
Majesty being pleased to say that if by his own fault he was unfit to
serve, he should be tried and broke, and if he was rendered incapable
by the Service, he might be put upon half-pay and a reduced
Lieutenant put in his place, if this last proposal will be of any
service to your Lordship, if you please to send the name of any
half-pay Lieutenant upon the Establishment of Great Britain, I
doubt not but to obtain His Majesty's consent to it.

" I am,

"My Lord, your Lordship's, &c.,

" WM. PULTENEY."

" *Lord Irwin.*"

(XCIII.)

Chapter XVI , par 38.

ROYAL WARRANT [1] DISPOSING OF THE PROCEEDS OF THE SALE OF MAJOR COPE'S COMMISSION.

" GEORGE R.

" WHERFAS, the General Officers of Our Army, to whom We were
pleased to referr the Petition of Mrs. Anne Cope, wife of Major
Henry Cope, late of your Regiment, have, in obedience to Our commands, reported to Us, that out of the Summ of Nine hundred
pounds produced by the Sale of his Commission, and lodged in your
hands, there remains the summ of Three hundred eighty-three
pounds seventeen shillings and nine pence three farthings, after the
deduction of such summs as in their opinion are Regimentall or yet
doubtfull, and also after deducting the summ of One hundred pounds,
which was paid Mrs. Anne Cope upon a Report of their Board
(bearing date the 27th of July last) representing that Our Warrant
for Fifty pounds a year out of the said Major Henry Cope's pay for
her subsistence appeared to be then two years in arrear; And
whereas the said Mrs Anne Cope has been represented to Us to
have been very ill treated by her husband, the said Major Henry
Cope, and to be at present without any support; Our will and

---

[1] Mis Bk 51 3, p 140

pleasure therefore is, that you pay unto the said Mrs Anne Cope the aforesaid summ of Three hundred and eighty-three pounds seventeen shillings and nine pence three farthings, which We are graciously pleased to allow her for her future support and maintenance. And for so doing, this, with the acquittance of the said Mrs. Anne Cope, or of her Assigns, shall be to you and all others whom it may concern, a sufficient Warrant and Discharge.

" Given at Our Court of St. James's, this 24th day of June, 1721, in the Seventh year of our Reign.

"By His Majesty's Command,

" GEORGE TRABY."

" To our Trusty and Well-beloved Major General
Thomas Whetham."

(XCIV.)

Chapter XVI., par. 55.

ADVERTISEMENT[1] IN THE 'LONDON GAZETTE' AGAINST ILLEGAL AGENCY.

— " *Whitehall, 19th October,* 1711.

" WHEREAS, a scandalous advertisement has been twice published in the ' Post Boy,' ' That whoever has a mind to treat about the purchasing commissions in the Army, either in our regiments or others, might apply themselves to Mr. Pyne, at his coffee-house under Scotland Yard Gate, near Whitehall, and they should be further informed about it,' which being directly contrary to Her Majesty's express will and pleasure, some time since declared and signified, as well at home as to all her Generals abroad, against the sale of commissions upon any account whatsoever, it is thought fit to give this public notice to prevent any abuses or impositions that might happen therefrom; and whoever shall discover to Her Majesty's Secretary at War, at his office in Whitehall, the authors of the said advertisement, shall have due protection and encouragement."

---

[1] Mis. Bk. 519, p. 27.

(XCV.)

Chapter XVI , par. 57

GENERAL ORDER[1] (No. 807).

" *Horse Guards, S.W.,* 19*th February,* 1862

" WITH regard to the addition of twelve non-purchase Regiments of the Line to the British Army, His Royal Highness the General Commanding-in-Chief is pleased, with the concurrence of the Right Honourable the Secretaries of State for War and for India, to establish the following regulations —

" 1. In non-purchase Corps of the Line no Officers can sell their Commissions.

" Those who enter from the Indian Service retain their claim to Indian pension, and all others are entitled, with Her Majesty's approval, to retire on full or half-pay, according to the terms of Her Majesty's Warrants of the 14th October, 1858, and 28th March 1861

" 2 An Officer joining a purchase Regiment from the Indian Service will be placed on the same footing, in all respects, with the rest of the Officers of that Regiment.

" Having forfeited all claim to Indian pension, he will become entitled to retire on full-pay or half-pay, under the Warrants above specified.

" Non-purchase Officers of such Regiments have the privilege of receiving, subject to the consent in each case of the General Commanding-in-Chief, and of the Secretary of State for War (which is liable to be withheld if the retirement results from misconduct), an allowance, on retirement, of 100*l* for each year's service, whether in the British or Indian Army, provided the total amount does not exceed the price of the Commission resigned."

(XCVI)

Chapter XVI , par. 63

(1.) ORDER[2] OF QUEEN ANNE ABOUT PERSONS NOT OF AGE TO SERVE IN THE ARMY.

" HER MAJESTY, finding it very prejudicial to the Service to have

---

[1] See 166 II D (3), p 982.

[2] Mis Bk 519, p 29, and 11th May, 1711, p 50, vol ii Mackenzie's 'Cold-stream Guards,' p. 316

Commissions given to children and others unfit to do duty with their Regiments, is pleased to declare that for the future no person that is not of age sufficient to serve shall be admitted into any of of Her Majesty's Troops, except the children of Officers who have been slain or suffered extremely in the Service; in which case the merits of the father may make it reasonable to show that mark of Her Majesty's Royal favour to the son.   Her Majesty is pleased further to declare that, of those who are thus qualified there shall not be at any one time above two in a Regiment, and that when any Regiment shall be ordered upon Service these persons shall be removed into other Regiments that are left at home, out of which other Officers shall be taken to supply their room in that which goes abroad.

"Given at Whitehall, this 29th day of May, in the Fourth year of Her Majesty's Reign.

"By Her Majesty's Command,

"H. St John"

(2) Letter[1] from the Secretary at War to the Paymaster-General as to a Child in Commission

"Sir,   "*Whitehall, 28th Sept.*, 1711.

"Her Majesty having been pleased to grant Fitton Minshull, a child, a commission of Ensign in Brigadier Stanwix's Regiment of Foot, in order for the support of his mother and family, in consequence of the loss of his father and uncle, who died in the Service, and has likewise given him a furlough to be absent from his duty until further order; I am, therefore, to signify to you Her Majesty's pleasure that you pay unto the agent of that Regiment his subsistences from the time he was last paid, to be by him paid over to the mother of the said Ensign Minshull, and continue it from time to time, as it shall grow due, that the said pay may be applied to the purpose intended by Her Majesty.

"I am, &c,

"E Granville"

"*Mr. Brydges.*"

---

[1] Report of Commissioners, 'Naval and Military Enquiry,' p. 32

(XCVII.)

Chapter XVI., par. 93.

CORRESPONDENCE[1] WITH THE TREASURY AS TO THE APPROPRIA-
TION AND PAYMENT OF ARREARS OF HALF-PAY.

"SIR,   " *War Office,* 30*th October,* 1843.

"I have the honour to request that you will state to the Lords
Commissioners of the Treasury the following difficulty in which I
am placed, by the discussion in the House of Commons of a variation
in practice between the Secretary at War and the Lords of the
Admiralty, touching the half-pay of a lunatic officer.

"The Secretary at War has always considered the half-pay of an
officer as a personal grant, and when the officer has been Half pay a
incapable of managing his affairs has, in the first instance, Grant
appropriated such portion of his half-pay as was required for his
maintenance to such exclusive object; and if his immediate relatives
—his wife, his sister, &c.—were dependent on him, has issued the
remainder to them On the other hand, if the officer's means were
sufficient for himself and his immediate relatives, no part of the
half-pay has been issued

"The accumulation of unissued half-pay is paid to the officer if
he recovers, but if he dies insane is not issued at all. Accumulations.

"The right of the Secretary at War to detain the half- tions.
pay has been frequently disputed by relatives wishing to make a
property of a lunatic, by heirs having no claim but relationship,
and has been the subject of correspondence with the Com- Retained by
missioners acting under the Lord Chancellor, but the right War Office.
to consider half-pay at the disposal of the Crown has been successfully maintained, and doubtless it rests with the Secretary at War
to exercise a sound discretion as to the appropriation of that of a
lunatic officer.

"It is understood to be the practice of the Admiralty to issue the
half-pay of a lunatic officer to those who have the charge of him,
consequently there can be little or no accumulation, and whatever
there is is paid to his representatives at his death.

"But as the non-retention by the public of any part of the pay
of a lunatic naval officer stands unpleasantly contrasted with the
War Office practice, I desire the instructions of the Treasury.

---

[1] Letter to Treasury, Book D, p 173

" The present practice of the Navy is regulated by 11 Geo IV,
c 20, s 70, which authorizes payment of the half-pay of
a lunatic officer of Navy or Marines to the persons taking
charge of him, and this authority by statute is based upon the fact
of such officer not having been the subject of a Commission of
Lunacy, and, therefore, not having any *legal representative* to claim
that which is required for his maintenance.

Admiralty practice

" It may be assumed from hence that the Admiralty would, as a
matter of course, have made the issue to any one legally appointed
to take charge of the lunatic   If so, the broad ground which has
been always taken here regarding half-pay generally, has evidently
not been touched upon by the Admiralty.

" As already observed, the half-pay is by the War Office considered to be purely at the disposal of the Crown, and therefore not
issuable either to the Committee or to the heir of a lunatic, but
according to the discretion of the Secretary at War, who therefore
required no such Act[1] as that above quoted to enable him to issue it
for the manifest benefit of the officer, or to his immediate relations,
according to his obvious wishes when he was sane, neither has the
Secretary at War any fetter imposed upon the exercise of his judgment, since he has successfully maintained his position

" There is also another marked difference as to the appropriation
of the lunatic officer's pay, between the two services.

" If a lunatic naval officer is admitted into a naval asylum,
1s. 6d. a-day only is deducted from his pay as the charge of his
maintenance, whatever may be his rank, and the residue, if he has
no wife or children, is allowed to accumulate, and is paid at his
death to his legal representative.

" In the Army, if the officer is not married, and is maintained at
the public expense, the real charge of his maintenance is
applied in diminution of that expense, and at his death,
unless he has a parent, brother, or sister in distress the residue is
credited to the public.

Married lu-
natic Officer

" If, on the other hand, the charge for maintenance be greater
than the amount of half-pay, the public suffers the loss

" I can see no reasonable ground for charging a lunatic officer
with the expense incurred by the public in taking care of him as far
as his half-pay will meet that charge, unless he should happen to be
married, in which case the custom is to apply one-half of his pay for
his wife's maintenance

" As this subject has attracted public attention by a motion in
the House of Commons last session, and as I have now a case before

---

[1] This is not a correct view of the law.

me in which the accumulation of the officer's half-pay amounts to
800*l.*, and is claimed by a relation whose conduct has been the
reverse of humane towards the lunatic, I have directed the case to
be drawn out in the accompanying paper, and I shall, before I
decide upon that case, request to have the opinion of their Lordships
on the general question; and if any alteration be deemed to be
advisable, I have to request to be informed to what extent the Regulations of the Navy shall be adopted by the Army.

"I have, &c.,

(Signed)   "H. HARDINGE."

" *The Secretary of the Treasury.*"

The reply from the Treasury,[1] of the 9th May 1844, was in these
terms —

"My Lords entertain no doubt of the correctness of the view
which has been taken of this subject at the War Office, *Reply from Treasury*
viz., that half-pay is a personal grant to the officer, which *Treasury*
may be either given or withheld at the pleasure of the *Half pay a Personal*
Crown, and that the appropriation of the half-pay of a *Grant.*
lunatic military officer ought to be regulated at the discretion of the
Secretary at War, with reference to the circumstances of each particular case

"It appears to their Lordships that, in the exercise of this discretion, a liberal and indulgent consideration should be shown *Discretion of*
towards the lunatic officer and all connected with him *Secretary at War*
In the first place, a sufficient provision should be made for the wants
and comforts of the officer himself, in the next place, if any surplus
remains of the half-pay, regard should be had to the circumstances
of those who were dependent upon him, and in the habit of receiving
pecuniary aid from him while he was in the possession of his faculties, and (lastly) if there be any surplus at the decease of the
officer, it should be held available for the purpose of meeting any
well-supported claim that may be brought forward on the part of
his relatives

"On this last point it appears to my Lords that the Secretary at
War may be guided by the following general principles.— *Distribution of Accumula-*
"1st. If the deceased officer's half pay was rather of *tion.*
the nature of a reward for past services than of a retainer *1 Half pay*
for future employment, and there is reason to believe that *earned*
had he retained possession of his faculties he would not have been

[1] P 158.

again called upon to serve, the whole of the accumulated arrear may in that case be paid to his relatives who are dependent upon him for their maintenance, if there should be any such ; and if not, to his legal representative.

"2ndly. But in case the deceased officer cannot be considered as having *earned* his half-pay by actual service, and his surviving immediate relatives have means sufficient for their support independently of him, my Lords consider that the accumulated arrears of his half-pay should remain unissued according to the established rule.

2 If not earned.

"3rdly. Even under these latter circumstances, if the deceased officer should have relatives who were dependent upon him for support, the arrears of his half-pay may be paid to those relatives in the proportion in which they had been in the habit of receiving assistance from him, or in such other proportion as the Secretary at War may consider most proper.

3. Relatives dependent on Officer

"The other point in which the practice of the Navy is stated to differ from that of the Army is, that while 1*s.* 6*d.* a-day only is deducted from the half-pay of naval lunatic officers admitted into a naval asylum, the deduction in the case of military officers is proportioned to the real charge of their maintenance Their Lordships entirely concur in opinion with the Secretary at War that there is no reasonable ground for not charging a lunatic officer with the expense incurred in taking care of him One-half of the half-pay of lunatic naval officers admitted into Haslar Hospital was formerly deducted for their maintenance, but it having been ascertained that the actual cost did not equal that amount, the charge was reduced to 1*s.* 6*d.* a-day. If the last-mentioned deduction is not sufficient to cover the expense actually incurred for the maintenance of lunatic naval officers, it ought, in their Lordships' opinion, to be increased to the extent requisite for that purpose

Admiralty practice.

"My Lords have desired that, in any cases that may hereafter arise in the Commissariat, the views and intentions herein expressed may be applied with regard to the half-pay of a lunatic officer."

(XCVIII.)

Chapter XVII., par. 16.

LETTER [1] FROM SECRETARY AT WAR, STATING THAT THE LORD-ADVOCATE HAD BEEN INSTRUCTED TO ENTER A 'NOLLE PROSEQUI.'

"SIR,   " *Whitehall, 8th January,* 17$\frac{1}{19}$.

"I have, with your letter of the 29th past, received a copy of the Precognition taken by the Lord Provost of Edinburgh relating to the death of James Key by the riot at Leith, which I laid before His Royal Highness, who likewise received the same from the Duke of Roxburgh, and by His Royal Highness's directions his Grace has sent orders for a *Nolle Prosequi* in favour of the soldier, as the Lord Advocate proposed

"I am, Sir,

"Your most humble Servant,

"WM. PULTENEY."

"*Lieut.-General Carpenter.*"

(XCIX.)

Chapter XVII., par 16.

WARRANT [2] TO ENTER A 'NOLLE PROSEQUI' ON ANY PROSE-CUTION TAKEN AGAINST GENERAL STEARNE AND THE OFFICERS ACTING UNDER HIM IN THE CORK MUTINY, ON THE 13TH JUNE, 1717.

"GEORGE R.

"WHEREAS, it hath been represented unto Us —That on Thursday, the 13th day of June, in the third year of our Reign, about 200 soldiers of our Regiment of Foot, commanded by Brigadier-General Vezey, having mutinied at Cork, in Our Kingdom of Ireland, and seized the colours of their regiment, and marched with their arms into the country and encamped about a mile out of the town, and

---

[1] Letter Bk 147, p 32   [2] Mis Bk 521, p. 91

2 s 2

that Our trusty and well-beloved Brigadier-General Robert Stearne having arrived the day following at Cork from the country, as did some Forces from England, the Magistrates of Cork, justly apprehending that great violence and mischief might ensue, desired the assistance of the said General Stearne and the rest of the officers there to suppress the said mutiny, and that thereupon it was resolved to march a detachment of the said Forces to bring the said mutineers to reason, and that on the approach of the said Forces the said mutineers marched to and secured a pass in Dublin Ro called Glanmire Bridge, three miles from Cork, and that about four of the clock in the afternoon the said General Stearne, with the said detachment, came up with the mutineers, and sent Alderman Franklin of Cork and others to persuade them to submit, and that on their refusing so to do the said General Stearne ordered Captain Taylor to advance with his Grenadiers to terrify them, and that they accordingly so advanced, but the said mutineers being obstinate kept their post on the said bridge, attacked Captain Taylor and fired on his men, killing one of them and wounding another, and that 'Captain Taylor, thereupon returning the fire of the mutineers. killed four of them, on which the rest threw down their arms and fled,' and that by means thereof an entire stop was put to the said mutiny and that the said mutineers had concerted a place of rendezvous, with soldiers of other Regiments intending to mutiny, who when joined together would have made a considerable body, and that the same might have been of very dangerous consequence to Our loving subjects of the said Kingdom of Ireland, and would not have been suppressed or reduced without great bloodshed. And whereas, the zeal and conduct of the said General Stearne for Our service in the said action worthily deserves our Royal commendation and approbation. We do therefore by these presents commend and approve of the conduct and behaviour of the said General Stearne in the action of Glanmire Bridge aforesaid, and do declare that the suppression of the said mutineers tended greatly to the quiet and peace and preserving the lives and estates of several of Our loving subjects of the said kingdom, as also to the support of Our Royal Authority and Government, and that the conduct of the said General Stearne and what was done by his order was legal, 'and for preventing any ill-designing person or persons at any time or times hereafter, in Our name or in the names of Our successors or any of them, from calling in question or arraigning or prosecuting the said Brigadier-General Stearne, or any of the officers or soldiers employed in the suppression of the said mutiny, for the killing of any of the said mutineers, on pretence the same was committed and done in time of peace and contrary to law or on any other pretence whatsoever ; we do hereby, for Us, Our heirs and successors, direct, appoint, and strictly command, charge, and require Our and their Attorney-General for the time being of the same Kingdom of Ireland, as occasion shall be or require from time to time, and at all times hereafter, on every or any such prosecution or prosecutions as aforesaid to be commenced against the said Brigadier-General Stearne, or any of the said officers or soldiers employed as aforesaid in suppressing the said mutiny, for any the pretended murder or murders of any of the said mutineers killed in the said action, to cause to be entered in the name of Us or Our successors *Nolle Prosequi* to every such prosecution or prosecutions, and for so doing this shall be a sufficient warrant and authority to any such Attorney-General; and if occasion should require, We or Our successors shall and will renew such orders.'

"Given at Our Court at Kensington, this 11th day of June, 1718, in the Fourth year of Our Reign.

"By His Majesty's Command,

"J. Craggs."

(C.)

Chapter XVII., *pars* 8 and 17

ORDER[1] OF THE PRIVY COUNCIL FOR EMPLOYMENT OF TROOPS IN AID OF THE CIVIL POWER.

"*At Hampton Court, the 22nd of August, 1717.*

"*Present :—*

"THE KING'S MOST EXCELLENT MAJESTY.

Lord Chancellor.	Earl of Berkley.
Duke of Roxburgh	Viscount Stanhope.
Earl of Lincoln	Lord Onslow,
Earl of Sunderland.	Lord Chief Justice King.

"WHEREAS, the Commissioners of Our Customs have made a Presentment of the 10th July last to the Lords Commissioners of Our Treasury in the following words, viz. .—

"' We have had frequent complaints from our officers in several parts of the Coast of this Kingdom, that the Smugglers are now grown so very numerous and insolent that they appear in bodies

---

[1] From the Council Books

from twenty to thirty armed men, and in defiance of the officers of the Customs do forcibly run great quantities of goods to the great prejudice of the Revenue and the fair traders, a fresh instance whereof we have now before us from one of our officers at Stockton, who hath represented to us in his letter of the 7th instant (copy whereof is hereto annexed for your Lordships' more particular information) that upon notice of a considerable quantity of goods being run near that port, he applied to the Commanding Officer of two Troops of Dragoons now quartered there to assist him in securing the said goods, but was refused such assistance by the said Officer, notwithstanding the Clause in the Act of Frauds 14 Car. II [1] requires the same, such Commanding Officer alleging that he had no orders to assist any officer of the Customs in the execution of his duty, we have therefore thought it our duty to lay this matter before your Lordships, and humbly pray that you will please to be a means that the Military officers quartered not only in and about Stockton but also on other parts of the coast of this kingdom may be directed to assist the officers of the Customs as there shall be occasion in seizing uncustomed and prohibited goods.'

"His Majesty taking the same into consideration, is pleased with the advice of His Privy Council to order, and it is hereby ordered that His Majesty's Secretary at War do forthwith cause directions to be given to all Military Officers quartered at or near the sea coast throughout England as well as Scotland, that they be assisting to the Civil Magistrates when desired by them and the officers of the Customs, for the executing legal process and other matters relating to His Majesty's Service in hindering the exportation of Wool and illegal importation of French Silks, Brandy, and other goods, and preventing the evil practices complained of in these Presentments."

---

[1] The section of the Act is in these words —14 Car II, c 11, sec 30.—' And be it further enacted and ordained that all Officers belonging to the Admiralty, Captains and Commanders of Ships, Forts, Castles, and Blockhouses, as also all Justices of the Peace, Mayors, Sheriffs, Bailiffs, Constables, and Headboroughs, and all the King's Majesty's Officers, Ministers, and Subjects whatsoever whom it may concern, shall be aiding and assisting to all and every person and persons which are or shall be appointed by his Majesty to manage his Customs, and the Officers of his Majesty's Customs, and their respective Deputies in the due execution of all and every act and thing in and by this present Act required and enjoined, and all such who shall be aiding and assisting unto them in the due execution hereof shall be defended and saved harmless by virtue of this Act"

(CI.)

Chapter XVII , *pars.* 8 and 17.

WARRANT FOR TROOPS TO AID THE CUSTOMS AND CIVIL
POWER.[1]

"GEORGE R

[*Presentment set out as above.*]

"We have taken the same into consideration, and are pleased with
the advice of Our Privy Council to order, and We do hereby require
and command all the officers of Our Army wheresoever they are
now quartered, or shall hereafter quarter, on or near our sea coasts
throughout our Kingdom of Great Britain, to be aiding and assisting
to the Civil Magistrates when desired by them, and the officers of
our Customs, for the executing legal processes and other matters
relating to Our Service, in hindering the exportation of Wool and
illegal importation of French Silks, Brandy, and other goods, and
preventing the evil practices complained of in the said Presentment,
and for so doing this shall be to them and all others concerned a
sufficient warrant and direction

"Given at our Court at Hampton Court, this 10th day of September, 1717, in the Fourth year of our Reign

"By His Majesty's Command,

"J. CRAGGS"

(CII.)

Chapter XVII , *par* 20

LETTERS AND REPORTS[2] AS TO THE ACTION OF THE MILITARY
IN AID OF THE CIVIL POWER

(1.) *Letter of Lord Carteret (Secretary of State) to the Secretary
at War*

"SIR,   "*Whitehall, January 11th,* 172½.

"It having been humbly represented to His Majesty by the
Mayor and others, Justices of the Peace of Taunton, that great dis-

---

[1] From War Office Mis. Bk 521, p 34   [2] Mis. Bk. 523, p 161

oiders had lately been committed there by the labourers, and that the Civil Power was not sufficient to quell those disorders, and bring the offenders to Justice, without the assistance of the Military Power, and having since received several affidavits in proof of what the said Mayor and Justices have alledged, I have by His Majesty's command referred the same to the consideration of Mr. Attorney-General, who is of opinion that in such extraordinary cases it is both lawful and proper that the Military Power should interpose where the Civil Magistrate cannot otherwise be supported in the due execution of Justice   I herewith send you enclosed a copy of Mr. Attorney-General's Report upon this subject, with his Majesty's directions to you, that pursuant thereto you send the proper orders to the Commanding Officers in and about Taunton to give their assistance, according as the same shall be required by the Civil Magistrate, and 'in framing the said orders particular regard is to be had to the caution mentioned in the said Report,—that the soldiers should not interpose until such time as they shall be required by the Civil Magistrate to give their assistance.'

"I am,

"Your most humble Servant,

"CARTERET."

"*The Secretary at War.*"

<hr>

(2.) MR. ATTORNEY-GENERAL'S REPORT[1]—(par. 20).

"MAY IT PLEASE YOUR LORDSHIP,   "*10th January,* 1721

"In obedience to your Lordship's commands, signified to me by yours of the 6th instant, to peruse and consider the annext Affidavits and Papers relating to several Riots and great Disorders committed by the labourers at Taunton, and to report my opinion to your Lordship in such manner that yo _ Lordship might be enabled to return a proper answer to what is prayed by the Mayor and other Justices of the Peace of Taunton, of being supported by the Military Power, I have perused and considered the same, and do find thereby that there has been most enormous Ryots and extravagant Disorders, with great barbarity, committed by the several persons in the Affidavit mentioned, which is not necessary particularly to mention to your Lordship, because the Mayor and Justices of the Peace at Taunton appear to be fully apprized of the nature of the offences of the Criminals, and in what manner they ought to be punished, and with great zeal for His Majesty's service and the

---

[1] Bk. 721, p 3.

peace of the place, endeavoured to bring them to justice; but the Criminals have been rescued out of the hands of the Officers by so great a number of people, riotously assembled, that the strength of the Civil Power there is not sufficient to enforce the putting the Laws in execution, which occasioned the desire of Mr. Newton and Mr Gunston, two Justices of the Peace, in their letter of the 2nd of December last, that such orders may be given to the gentlemen of the Army then there to assist the Civil Magistrates in the execution of their respective offices, as may be necessary to preserve the peace of the Town and to bring the Offenders to Justice. I humbly certify to your Lordship that by the Law any person may justify the assistance of the Civil Magistrate or Officer in keeping the Peace or executing Legal Process when required by such Officer or Magistrate, without distinction whether such a person is a Civil or Military man, and therefore I am of opinion, orders may be legally given to the gentlemen of the Army at Taunton, that whenever a great Riot is committing, or any Warrant of any Justice of Peace, or other Legal Process is attempted to be executed on any Criminals or offenders, in order to bring them to Justice, and a rescue is endeavour'd to be made of such Criminal, or resistance made to the execution of such Warrant or Process, or to the Civil Magistrate or Officer executing such Process, or endeavouring to bring such offender to justice, that the Soldiers in such cases should give their assistance to such Civil Magistrate or Officer, with a caution that they should not at all interpose in any of these things, but at such times as they shall be desired by the Civil Magistrate or Officer, who best will judge when they stand in need of their assistance.

"All which is humbly submitted to your Lordship's great wisdom.

"ROBERT RAYMOND."

*"To the Right Hon. the Lord Carteret, one
of His Majesty's Principal Secretaries of
State"*

---

(3) LETTER[1] OF SECRETARY AT WAR TO THE ATTORNEY-
GENERAL—(*par.* 22).

"SIR, *"Whitehall, 19th October,* 1732.

"As the Mayors and Civil Magistrates of the Cities and Corporation Towns in Britain frequently send to my Office for a military assistance, as often as they apprehend their own strength is not

---

[1] Letter Bk. 159, pp 370, 371

sufficient to suppress riots and other disorders, when they happen amongst them   it has always been the practice of my predecessors, as well as my own, to give it them, by sending Troops of Horse or Dragoons, or Companies of Foot to their aid and assistance, with instructions for their behaviour, signed sometimes by the King, and at other times by the Secretary at War for the time being, copies of which I send you for your information   And, as the Commissioners of the Customs and Excise frequently do the like, I am to desire you will please to peruse both the orders, and send me your Opinion whether the said Orders may not be further extended with regard to the repelling force by force.

> " I am, with great respect, Sir,
> " Your most obedient and most humble Servant,
>
> " WM. STRICKLAND "

(4.) THE LIKE [1]—(*par* 18).

" SIR,   " *Whitehall, 6th December,* 1732

" I had the honour of your letter of the 20th of November, in which you desire to know when the clause about repelling force with force was first introduced in the Orders which have been given to the Troops from time to time, when sent to the assistance of the C vil Magistrates and Officers of the Customs, against the Owlers and Smugglers, and other occasions,   I have looked into all the Books of my Office, and send you enclosed extracts of the several Orders which have been issued from the time Mr Pulteney was Secretary at War, who was the first person we find to have given directions of that kind, and who has been followed in the same style by the other Secretarys at War succeeding him, till Mr. Pelham came in   And as I observed that those Orders which he counter-signed deviated in some manner from the others, I consulted him upon it, and he told me, that he conceived he had made the altera-tions to make it as conformable as he could to an Opinion which Lord Raymond gave, when his Lordship was Attorney-General, a copy of which I send you also for your information, the original having been by him sent to the Lord Carteret, when Secretary of State, and by his Lordship transmitted to the War Office   You will please to observe how Mr. Pelham's Orders have varied from his predecessors, which, as he told me, were so altered from time to time, according to the exigency of the Service

---

[1] Letter Bk. 159, p 374

"This is all I can find upon the subject, and desire, when you have fully considered it, that I may have your Opinion upon it.

"I am, with great truth and respect, Sir,

"Your most humble and most obedient Servant,

"WM. STRICKLAND."

---

(5) REPORT OF SIR P. YORKE ON LETTERS (3) AND (4)— (par 23).

"SIR,   "*Lincoln's Inn, 2nd January,* 1732.

"I have considered your two Letters relating to the form of the Orders usually given to the Officers of the Troops which from time to time have been sent to the assistance of the Civil Magistrates and Officers of the Revenues against Rioters and Smugglers, together with a Copy of a Report made by the Lord Raymond, when Attorney-General, to the Lord Carteret, then Secretary of State, on that subject, and Extracts of the several Orders of that kind which have been issued since January, 1716.

"The question, in which you desire to be satisfyed, is whether those Orders may not be further extended with regard to the repelling Force with Force.

"As to this point I do not find any direct Opinion given by Lord Raymond in his Report which was made on the particular occasion of great riots at Taunton, but his words are —

"'That orders may legally be given to the Gentlemen of the Army at Taunton that whenever a great Riot is committed, or any Warrant of a Justice of the Peace or other Legal Process is attempted to be executed on any Criminals in order to bring them to Justice, and a Rescue is endeavoured to be made of such Criminal, or Resistance made to the Execution of such Warrant or Process, which the Civil Power is not able to withstand, that at the request of the Civil Magistrate or Officer executing such Process, or endeavouring to bring such Offender to Justice, the Soldiers in such cases should give their assistance to such Civil Magistrate or Officer, with a caution that they should not at all interpose in any of these things but at such times as they shall be desired by the Civil Magistrate or Officer, who best will judge when they stand in need of their assistance   I observe that, in fact, these Orders have been variously penned in the Clause now under my consideration   From January, 1716, to January, 1723, the Clause runs in the affirmative, viz., "To

---

[1] Bk. 721, p 42

repell force with force in case the Civil Magistrate shall find it necessary, or to repell force with force in case it shall be found necessary."

"'From April, 1724, to May, 1732, they have sometimes run in the Affirmative, but generally, and for the most part, in the Negative viz "Not to repell force with force unless the Civil Magistrates (or the Civil Magistrates and Officers of the Customs) shall find it necessary,"

"'And in one instance during this period the Order is "To repell force with force, if it shall be found absolutely necessary, and not otherwise"'

"Upon consideration of the whole matter, I entirely concur in opinion with my Lord Raymond in his Report that the Officers of the Troops and the Soldiers should be directed not to interpose at all in any of those cases, but at such times as they shall be desired by the Civil Magistrates or Officers, *in which Officers of the Revenue must be included in case of running Goods.*

"But as to the Clause now in question, the forms whereof have differed in the manner before mentioned, I think it most advisable to express it, agreeably to some of the precedents, in general terms, viz 'Not to repell Force with Force, unless it shall be found absolutely necessary'

"I am with great respect, Sir,

"Your most obedient and most humble servant,

"P YORKE."

---

(6) WARRANT[1] OF THE SECRETARY AT WAR TO THE MILITARY OFFICER TO AID THE CIVIL POWER—(*par* 23).

"IT is His Majesty's Pleasure that you direct a Detachment of Commission and Non-Commission Officers and Private Men equal to one entire troop to be made from His own Royal Regiment of Dragoons under your Command, and cause the same to march forthwith from their present quarters (according to the Route annexed) to Lewis, there to be aiding and assisting to the Civil Magistrates and Officers of the Revenue in preventing the Owlers and Smugglers from Running of Goods upon that Coast, and in apprehending the said Owlers and Smugglers and seizing their Goods, in order to which His Majesty's further Will and Pleasure is that the said Detachment shall be Quartered in such Places as shall be concerted and thought convenient from time to time between the Commanding Officer of the said Detachment and the Collector of the Excise

---

[1] Bk 721, p 42

there for the more effectually answering the Purposes aforementioned, *but not to repell Force with Force unless thereunto required by the Civil Magistrates* Wherein the Civil Magistrates and all others concerned are to be assisting unto you in providing Quarters and pressing Carriages, and otherwise as there shall be occasion

"Given at Whitehall, this 12th day of May, 1733

"By His Majesty's Command

"WM. STRICKLAND"

"To Major General Gore, Colonel of His Majesty's
Own Royal Regiment of Dragoons, or to the
Officer Commanding in Chief the said Regiment and Detachment above mentioned"

(7) LETTER FROM THE TREASURY TO SECRETARY AT WAR - (par 23)

"SIR, "*Treasury Chambers, 21st May, 1736*

"His Majesty's Attorney and Solicitor-General having by their Report dated the 10th inst represented to the Lords Commissioners of His Majesty's Treasury that the Commissioners of the Customes had laid before them a Copy of the King's Warrant for Enabling the Military Power to assist the Civil Officers against Rioters and Smugglers, in order to make the same more explicit, and it being their opinion that in the room of the words [thereunto required by the Civil Magistrates] it may be proper to insert these words [it shall be found absolutely necessary] Their Lordships command me to transmit the said Report to you, with their desire that you will please to lay the same before His Majesty for His Approbation and direction therein

"I am, Sir,

"Your most obedient humble Servant,

"*The Secretary at War*" "J SCROPE."

(8) REPORT OF LAW OFFICERS—(par 23).

"*To the Right Honourable the Lords Commissioners of His Majesty's Treasury*

"MAY IT PLEASE YOUR LORDSHIPS,

"In Pursuance of your Lordships' Directions, the Commissioners of His Majesty's Customs have laid before us the Warrant hereunto

---

[1] Bk 121, p 39 [2] Ib

annexed, and likewise the Opinion of Lord Haid-'c'-o (... Attorney-General), a Copy of which is hereunto annexed

"And We are humbly of opinion that in the Room of *two* Words [thereunto required by the Civil Magistrates] it may be proper to insert these Words [it shall be found absolutely necessary], and We approve of the form of the said Warrant in every other part of it

"All which is humbly submitted to your Lordships' great Wisdom and Judgment.

"*May* 10*th*, 1735."

"J. WILLES,

"D. RYDER"

(9) LETTER[1] FROM LORD BARRINGTON, GIVING A GENERAL AUTHORITY FOR TROOPS TO AID THE CIVIL POWER —(*par* 24)

"SIR,   "*War Office*, 24*th September*, 1766

"The present riotous assemblings on account of the high prices of corn and provisions in many parts of the Kingdom having made it necessary for the Magistrates to call in a Military Force to their assistance, and there being reason to apprehend that the same disorder may continue and spread farther, I think it proper to send you enclosed an order for aiding and assisting the Civil Magistrates in the neighbourhood of your Quarters, in case they should have occasion, upon any riots or disturbances, to apply to you, and upon receipt of this, you will be pleased to wait on the Magistrates of the neighbourhood, and give them information of the directions you have received for the more early prevention of these disturbances.

"I am persuaded there is no occasion for me to caution you to take great care that the troops under your command do not at all interfere in any of these things but at such times as they shall be required by the Civil Magistrates, who best will judge when they stand in need of Military assistance.

"I have the honour to be, &c, &c,

"BARRINGTON.'

"*To Lieut-Colonel Kellet, or the Officer Commanding the Royal Regiment of Horse Guards at York.*"

Similar letter sent to 19 Commanding Officers of Regiments and Independent Companies

---

[1] Letter Bk 208, p 319   As to Sir P Francis being the author of the 'War Office Letters' at this period, see vol 1 of his 'Life,' by Parker and Merivale

(10.) LETTER[1] OF SERVICE TO COLONEL WARDE, TO COMMAND TROOPS IN AID OF THE CIVIL POWER.—(*par.* 24).

" SIR, *" Wa. Office, 3rd October, 1766.*

"The continued disturbances which have happened in the Western Counties having made it necessary to station a number of detachments both of Dragoons and Foot at different places in those counties, it is thought highly expedient that they should all be under the command of one Officer, of judgment and experience; and I am to acquaint you that the King has appointed you to take the care of this service. It is His Majesty's pleasure that you should immediately repair to Devizes, which is the most centrical place with respect to the different quarters of the Troops, as you will see by the disposition which I send you inclosed, and take upon you the command of the Troops specified therein. You are at liberty to make any alteration that you shall judge necessary in the present disposition for preserving the public peace, and to remove yourself to any other quarters, as occasion may require.

"You will be so good as to inform me from time to time of anything of consequence that may happen

" I have the honour to be, Sir, &c ,

" BARRINGTON.

"P S It is unnecessary for me to add that the Troops are never to be employed but in the usual manner upon requisition made by the Civil Magistrates and for their assistance.

" To Lieut -Colonel Warde of the 4th Dragoons,
at Winchester."

(11.) EXTRACT FROM LETTER TO THE MAGISTRATES BY THE SECRETARY OF STATE—(*par.* 27).[2]

" SIR, *" St. James's, 17th April, 1768.*

"Having already signified the King's pleasure to the Lord-Lieutenant of the County, with regard to the measures to be taken in general for preserving the Peace, I make no doubt but that either some steps have or will immediately be taken by him on that head. . . . . . . When I inform that every possible precaution is taken to support the dignity of your Office, that upon application from the Civil Magistrate to the Tower, Savoy, or the War Office,

---

Letter Bk. 208, p 384 [2] 'Junius's Letters,' vol 1, p 132, and vol II., p 120

---

he will find a Military Force ready to march to his assistance ..
to act according as he shall find it expedient and necessary, I need
not add that if the public peace is not preserved . .   . the
blame will be imputed to the want of prudent and spirited conduct
in the Civil Magistrate.   As I have no reason to doubt your caution
and discretion in not calling for Troops till they are wanted, so, on
the other hand, I hope you will not delay a moment calling for
their aid, and making use of them effectually where there is occasion,—that occasion always presents itself when the Civil Power is
trifled with and insulted.   Nor can a Military Force ever be employed to a more constitutional purpose than in support of the
authority and dignity of Magistracy

" I have, &c.,

·" WEYMOUTH."

" *To the Chairman of the Quarter Sessions,*
   " *Lambeth.*"

**(12.) EXTRACT FROM LETTER[1] OF 18TH APRIL, 1768, FROM
    SECRETARY AT WAR, LORD BARRINGTON, TO SECRETARY
    OF STATE, LORD WEYMOUTH.**

" I beg leave on this occasion (on application from the Newcastle Magistrates for Troops), though it is going a little out of my
province, to express a hope that whenever there shall be occasion to
employ Troops to suppress Riots, the Civil Magistrates will take
care that proper objects be seized and brought to punishment
according to Law, without which no disorders of that kind will be
quieted for any time, and the Forces will be continually wanted for
a most *odious* service, which nothing but necessity can justify."

**(13.) LETTER[2] FROM LORD BARRINGTON TO SURREY MAGIS-
    TRATES AS TO THE USE OF THE TROOPS AT ST. GEORGE'S
    FIELDS—(par. 27).**

" GENTLEMEN,   " *War Office, 29th April, 1768*

" I have just received your letter of this day's date, wherein
you desire the assistance of a few Horse to be quartered at the Inns
in the Borough this night, and in answer to it am to inform you that

---

[1] Letter Bk 211, p 317   [2] Ib , p. 354.

there are no Horse which can be ordered to quarter in Southwark in the manner you desire, but, if a military assistance should be necessary, by applying to the Commanding Officer at the Tower, the Savoy, or at the Tilt Yard, sufficient parties of the Foot Guards will be sent from any of those places. If you should judge that Horse are absolutely necessary, you may apply to the Commanding Officers of the Troops of Horse and Grenadier Guards, at the Horse Guards, Whitehall, who have orders to comply with such requisition as shall be made by the Civil Magistrates on this head.

"I am, Gentlemen, &c,

"BARRINGTON."

"*The Worshipful the Civil Magistrates of the County of Surrey.*"

(14.) LETTER[1] FROM LORD BARRINGTON TO GOLD-STICK-IN-WAITING, THANKING THE TROOPS FOR THEIR CONDUCT AT ST. GEORGE'S FIELDS[2]—(par. 28).

"My LORD,   "War Office, 11th May, 1768.

" Having this day had the honour of mentioning to the King the behaviour of the Detachments of the Troops of Horse and Grenadier Guards which have been employed yesterday, and the day before in assisting the Civil Magistrates and preserving the public peace, I have great pleasure in informing your Lordship that His Majesty highly approves of the conduct both of the Officers and Men, and means that his gracious approbation should be communicated to them through you.

"Employing the Troops on so disagreeable a service always gives me pain. The present unhappy Riots make it necessary, I am persuaded they see that necessity, and will continue, as they have done, to do their duty with alacrity. I beg you will be pleased to assure them that every possible regard shall be shown to them; their zeal and good behaviour upon this occasion deserve it, and in case any disagreeable circumstance should happen in the execution of their duty, they shall have every defence and protection that the law can authorize and this Office can give

"I have, &c.,

"BARRINGTON."

Gold-Stick-in-Waiting "

---

[1] Letter Bk. 211, p. 379

[2] See the 'Letters of Junius,' of the 19th May, 1768, vol iii, pp. 57, 436 (edition of 1812)

(15) NOTES[1] OF THE OPINION OF THE JUDGES ON THE ...
OF THE DEFENDANT IN THE KING *v.* SAMUEL GIL ...
ESQ, AT THE OLD BAILEY, 10TH JULY, 1765 (OR THE
AFFAIR IN ST. GEORGE'S FIELDS)—(*par.* 23)[2]

Mr. Justice Gould:—' This last Witness speaks to the material
Part of the Transaction To be sure Mr Serjeant Glynn opened
this Case, in my apprehension, perfectly agreeable to the Constitution.   For the Preservation of the Peace of this Country, independent of the Rules of the Common Law which puts—(a Chasm[3]—)
relative to this matter this Act of Parliament itself is a full Commission to the Magistrate, to the Civil Authority, to call in such
Persons of His Majesty's Subjects (for much like that is the Expression) in order to disperse and to pacify, as are of Age and
Ability, so that there is not an Exception of any Man in the
Kingdom, be he who he will, that is between 15 and 70 (for
there the Line is drawn by the Rules of the Common Law) but
he is bound to attend and give his assistance under the Direction
of the Civil Magistrate.   Brother Glynn, you have great Candour,
and consistent with that Knowledge which I am sensible you
possess of the Profession, I do appeal to you upon the State of the
Facts how the Matter stands in your Judgment."

Mr. Serjeant Glynn:—"Your Lordships will never find me
acting a Part against Humanity and Candour, and I am not now
pressing this Gentleman's Conviction: I opened the Law, that
where it was absolutely necessary for suppressing a riotous Mob,
that there the Magistrate is justified, the application therefore
of the Facts to the Law is the whole Question.   With respect to
myself I shall not say a word more about it "

Mr. Justice Gould —" This is clear Law, and laid down expressly
by Dalton, both in his 'Office of Sheriff,' and 'Office of Justice
of the Peace,' that the Sheriff as a Ministerial Officer, a Justice of
the Peace, and a Magistrate, whenever he has even an Apprehension that he is to be obstructed in his Duty, has a right to call
together such a Number of His Majesty's Subjects as he shall judge
competent, and not only that, but armed in such a Manner as he
shall judge fit, and Mr. Dalton quotes there a very material Case
under the Title of Riots.   That in the Reign of Henry the VII. the
Sheriff took 300 Men armed with Guns, Harbigeons, and such

---

[1] Bk. 722, p 45
[2] The evidence in this case is given at Vol II. of the 'Annual Register,' pp.
227-233   [3] Sic

... ..., and Complaint was made against the Sheriff for coming
... ... an armed Force to execute the King's Writ. And what
... the Court to it? They said he had a right to do it. So
... the first Volume of Lord Hale's 'Pleas of the Crown,' fol. 494,
... which takes notice of a temporary Act, just like this Riot Act
in some Degree and measure, that was passed in Queen Mary's Reign,
... is express Authority given to the Justice of Peace to arm
... the manner of an armed Force; to that Effect are the very Words
of the Act of Parliament here. What says my Lord Hale? *He
says, This is no more than he might have done at the Common Law*
And therefore that is the true Ground and Foundation upon which
all this stands And People are misled, in my Apprehension, by
a false Delusion hung out to them, as if there was an Idea of
Martial Law, or Military Power being to be called in, there is
no such Thing. Th3 *Justices of Peace have a right to call in any
Body of His Majesty's Subjects;* and if there were not Soldiers at
hand, they might collect Arms as they thought fit, and put into the
Hands of any of His Majesty's Subjects, whether they be of His
Majesty's Forces or not, but neither they, nor the others of them,
could be justified to go such Lengths, but *under a pressing Occasion,
or under the Command of a Civil Magistrate* From what I have read
upon this Occasion, I do think that while the Civil Magistrate
conducts himself with Humanity and Propriety upon an urgent
Occasion, when a riotous Mob are assembled together, and are
committing the utmost Excesses, and don't disperse, that he is
authorized by the Common Law, the great Object of which Law
is the Preservation of the Peace of this Kingdom, for without
Peace, how in the name of God is it possible for any of us to be
safe in our Persons, in our Liberties, which are more valuable than
our Lives, or in any Thing we can think of? For my part, upon
the State of this Evidence, as I have collected it, I have taken
upon me to speak first, I form this Opinion, that what this Gentleman has done is perfectly justifiable."

Lord Chief Baron Parker:—"I am of the same Opinion, Gentlemen, with my Brother Gould, and I take this to be so with respect
to the Common Law of the Kingdom, *supposing the Riot Act out of
the Case* By the Common Law it was the Duty of every Justice
of the Peace, of the Sheriff, of every Constable, and inferior
Officer, to lend his utmost Assistance to suppress Riots. It was not
only their Duty, but it was the Duty of every Subject in the
Kingdom to do it, and not only so, but if called upon, he was
punishable if he did not do it In Lord Popham, page 121, of
his own Works, whenever a Justice of Peace or Constable calls

upon other Persons to assist them, *they have a right, and may use them*, every Subject whatever so called upon, has a right to arm himself, he has a right to use those Arms for the Preservation of the Public Peace, *and to suppress the Riot*   And there is a farther Reason if occasion, he has a right to make use of them in his own Defence, and to repell Force by Force.   This is not only the Law as declared by Lord Popham, but another learned Judge, my Lord Chief Justice Anderson, who was Lord Chief Justice of the Common Pleas, reports a Meeting of all the Judges in England, in 1666, & '67, in Burton's Case   this was the Opinion of all the Judges in England, as reported by him,—that they may do it by the Common Law.   There were former Acts that gave pretty much the same Power as is given by the Riot Act, which I dare say some of you, Gentlemen, have had Curiosity to look into   I am old enough to remember the passing of that Law, and the Occasion of it.   I know whom it was drawn up by, perhaps two as able Men as ever served the Crown in this Kingdom, Sir Edward Northey who was Attorney General, and the late Lord Raymond   What does that Act provide? It provides that wherever there is a Riot, the Justices of the Peace are to go and read the Proclamation, if the Justices are obstructed in reading,—if after it is read, the Rioters do not depart within an Hour,—they are declared to be all Felons without the Benefit of Clergy.   Why it may be said upon this Occasion, 'It is very hard— perhaps there might be an innocent Spectator;' but the Law is expressly so.   I will put a similar Case and Instance to illustrate it.   Suppose a Man shoots at a Person against whom he has Malice and misses him, and kills another Man; it is murder, because there was a felonious and malicious Intent.   Suppose a Man is attacked by a Highwayman upon the Road, and in his own Defence draws a Pistol, shoots at the Highwayman, and kills another, an innocent Man; this is not Murder, nor Manslaughter, but mere Misadventure.   You are to consider whether there was a proper Foundation *for the Interposition*   According to one of the Witnesses, this Certain man seemed desirous of being the Occasion of Murder, contrary to what all the other Witnesses have said; but I have no Doubt at all upon the whole of the Evidence given for the Crown, but that this Gentleman has done no more than was his Duty to do, and he would have been answerable to the Public if he had not done it."

Mr. Justice Ashton :—'I am of the same Opinion, and whoever attends to the History of this Kingdom, and looks into the first Chapter of a Book written by an eminent Author, upon Riots, unlawful and rebellious Assemblies, will see the great Danger Hazard arising from them to this happy Constitution, to the

Security, and good Order of Government, the Happiness of Men in their Habitations and Preservation of their Property; and will, I have no Doubt, naturally concur with the most excellent Reason of the Law, and the Provision of the Statutes that are made to suppress such riotous Proceedings. In the Time of Richard the Second an Outrage at Dartmouth in Kent, originally only about paying a Groat, put in Hazard the Life of the King, the Overthrow of the Kingdom and the burning of this City. In the Time of Harry the Sixth a rebellious Mob brought to Death Richard Plantagenet Duke of York, after him Harry the Sixth, and Edward his Son, by not restraining the Rebellious Assembly in due Time. The Legislature have from Time to Time (upon which, as my Lord says, it does not alone depend) *from the 34th of Edward the Third* down to the present Time, made Acts to prevent *the Danger of the Continuance of Riots*, and for their instantaneous Suppression. In Edward the Third's time, Harry the Fourth, Harry the Fifth, Edward the Sixth, in Queen Mary, and during the whole Reign of Queen Elizabeth, there were Acts of Parliament worded very much into, almost the same as the present Statute of George the First; which Acts were alluded to by my Lord, and which *declared that if the Persons so unlawfully assembled, fortuned to be killed, slain, maimed, or hurt by the Magistrates in suppressing or taking them, such Magistrates shou'd be free, discharged, and unpunishable, as well against the King as against any other Persons, for maiming, killing, or hurting these People.* This Statute of George the First seems to be copied from these Acts of Parliament upon that great Occasion that my Lord remembers; and has taken Notice of the prodigious Riots that were then in the City. But however it does not stand alone upon that, the two Cases my Lord Chief P   n has been pleased to mention have received additional Weigh   om Lord Hale. In his first Volume, fol. 53, he recognises this,   says that by the Common Law all Persons who stand in Opposit   to the Sheriff or Civil Magistrate, *might be reduced by Force*, and all, if necessary, were bound to assist the Sheriff or Civil Magistrates to suppress Riots .   .   . by the Statutes of Harry the Fourth and Edward the Sixth   And if the Sheriff or Magistrate, or any Person coming in aid of them, was killed, it would be Murder in all the Rioters. The Person who is the Editor of that Book mentions it, and so does the Act of Parliament. Suppose this Brickbat taken notice of here, had killed the Magistrate doing his Duty, can there be a Doubt but that every Man so cautioned to disperse, would have been a Principal in that Murder, having disobeyed the Law, and continued in the Place upwards of an Hour afterwards? Then the only Question that remains is a Matter of Fact, for I don't find that there is any Difference between the very learned Couns l who opened this Matter, and myself, as to the Law, for he agrees with me that *where there is this Outrage, the Sheriff will his Posse any reduce it;* and as to calling in Men with red or white Coats, it makes no sort of Difference. Whom would you call in but those who are the more readily provided to do their Duty? A Soldier is not disqualified as a Subject, from doing his Duty to the Civil Magistracy. It comes now to this Question—that is, a Question of the Facts arising upon the Testimony here given,—Was there, or was there not, that necessity? was there such a Call that the Magistrate should bring any of the Military to exercise that Power the Law gives him to subdue the Riot? This is the Fact. Here is the *principal Person in the Kingdom besieged, the Door broke open on Monday, forced to be barred, the Marshal of the King's Bench with his Turnkey, who says he can hold out no longer, require them to come,—they find* 15,000 or 20,000 *What passing over the Causeway? No, hallowing, huzzaing, and throwing Stones at the Magistrates; Civilly desired to go,—refusing, persevering to the last—The Proclamation is read—They don't regard it—At the Time the Laws are going to be put in Execution, they pelt the Magistrate, they give him a Blow on the Head* And supposing, as is said, it was to be worse; *it is a known Thing that Magistrates are not bound to draw to the Wall;* No, that would be a Reflection upon the Laws of this Kingdom, if Magistrates were to yield, they are not bound by Law at all, but other Men are obliged to bear off till they are forced perhaps by necessity to make use of a Weapon that destroys a Man. The Magistrate is insulted and struck; the Mob will not retire upon fair Terms, *they are ordered to be fired upon,* Can there be an Instance of a more candid, fair, and more proper Behaviour in a Magistrate than is proved by two of the Prosecutor's own Witnesses in this Case of Redburn? Which I beg leave to say is the only thing we are trying I shall not take Notice of or mention the others — An unhappy Man is killed by this: it is expressly within the meaning of the Statute, it is warranted by the Law. If this is not a Necessity, one must return again, and look into the Rebellions that have been in this Kingdom The Magistrate has acted temperately and advisedly too, and was driven to the very last Necessity before he exercised that Authority which the Common Law and the Statutes of this Kingdom have entrusted him with, and I cannot conclude without saying, that it is a most melancholy thing to have a Magistrate seated at that Place to take his Trial for the Murder of a Man, when he himself has been discharging his Duty to prevent the Consequences of these riotous Attempts, dangerous to Government itself, to the Happiness of individuals, and all this at the Hazard of his own Life and Property. And therefore I concur with my Lord Chief Baron Parker. My Lord Hale repeats it in two other Places, to shew it was a Thing he was truly satisfied of. He says the same thing in folio 53, and 296."

Mr. Recorder :—" After the Subject has been so fully discussed by the learned Judges, I will only say one Word,—That upon the Evidence of the three Constables Nichol, Abbot, and Wells, and of Pennce, I am most clearly of Opinion with the learned Judges, that the was a riotous Assembly which it was the Duty of the Magistrates to attend to suppress, and to disperse the Multitude, and the Defendant was fully justified in giving the Order he did, under the Circumstances in which he did it."

---

(16) SECRETARY AT WAR'S ORDER[1] TO THE GUARDS TO ASSIST THE CIVIL POWER AT LORD GEORGE GORDON'S RIOTS— (par 32)

"Sir,   " War Office, 5th June, 1780.

"One of His Majesty's Principal Secretaries of State having transmitted to me information that numbers of people are assembled in the City of London in a tumultous manner and are actually committing great outrages there, and desiring that immediate orders may be given to the Commanding Officer at the Tower to afford the Civil Magistrate such assistance as he shall think proper to demand for restoring the public tranquillity, I do hereby signify to you His Majesty's pleasure that you hold yourself and the Troops under your command in readiness to assist the Civil Magistrate in case he shall require it, and that upon his requisition, and under his authority, you do order, from time to time, such of the said Troops as shall be thought necessary for the purpose before mentioned to march to the place or places which the Civil Magistrate shall point out.

"I am, Sir, &c,

"C JENKINSON."

"Office. Commanding the Foot Guards at
    the Tower."

---

[1] Bk, 238, p 259, see also pp 260-265, 269 277, 287, 290, 291, and App CIX., *post*

(17.) LETTER[1] FROM SECRETARY AT WAR TO THE SECRETARY
OF STATE AS TO CONDUCT OF THE MAGISTRATES AT LORD
GEORGE GORDON'S RIOTS—(*par.* 32).

"My Lord.   " *War Office, 6th June,* 1780.

"In the course of last night. I was honoured with your Lordship's letter, dated the 5th at midnight. Before the receipt of this,
every possible order had been given for Troops to be in readiness,
and a very large Military Force has continued to assemble through
the whole of yesterday and last night, ready to assist the Civil
Magistrates at their requisition in preserving the public peace.

"I can further add, it appears to me by reports made to me from
the Officers Commanding those Troops, that except in two instances
that happened in the Tower (and, by sending a larger Force into
that Garrison, this defect was remedied yesterday evening), there
has always been a number of Foot Guards ready to assist the Civil
Magistrate, and more than he has called for or appeared to want

"I have further to acquaint your Lordship that I have, with
Lord Amherst's concurrence, sent a special messenger with an order
for a Regiment of Dragoons to march without delay from Canterbury
to the neighbourhood of London.

"I have now the honour to enclose to your Lordship a Copy
of a Letter and Report transmitted to be by Major-General Win-
yard, the Field Officer in Staff Waiting for the Foot Guards, of
what happened in the course of yesterday and last night, and must
beg in the most serious manner to call your Lordship's attention to
some parts of that Letter and Report, wherein it appears that in
one instance the Civil Magistrate, having called for the Troops, was
not ready to attend them ; that in another instance, the Troops
having been called out, were left by the Magistrates exposed to the
fury of the populace, when the party, as I am informed was insulted
in a most extraordinary manner ; and that in two other instances,
after the Troops had marched to the places appointed for them,
several of the Magistrates refused to act.

"It is the duty of the Troops, my Lord, to act only under the
authority and by the direction of the Civil Magistrate. For this
reason they are under greater restraints than any other of His
Majesty's subjects, and when insulted are obliged to be more cau-
tious even in defending themselves. If, therefore, the Civil
Magistrate, after having called upon them, is not ready to attend
them, or abandons them before they return to their Quarters, or after
they arrive at the places to which they have been ordered, he refuses

---

[1] Letter Bk. 838, p 265, see also Appendix OIX , *post.*

to act, I leave it to your Lordship to judge in how defenceless and how disgraceful a situation the Military are left; and how much such a conduct as this tends even to encourage riots, and to bring matters to the last fatal extremity; and how much the Public Service as well as the Troops must suffer by it.

"I am forced to urge this matter the more strongly to your Lordship, as what I have now laid before you are not the first instances that have come to my knowledge of a conduct of the like kind in the Civil Magistrates.

"I have the honour to be

"My Lord, &c.,

"C. JENKINSON." [1]

"*Lord Viscount Stormont, &c., &c., &c.*"

(18.) REPORT [2] OF SIR JOHN SCOTT AND SIR JOHN MITFORD TO THE DUKE OF PORTLAND—(*par.* 50).

‹ MY LORD DUKE,   "*Lincoln's Inn*, 30th July, 1796.

"We are honoured with your Grace's letter of the 4th instant, transmitting to us copies of a correspondence which has passed between Lord De Dunstanville and Lieutenant-Colonel Montagu, and likewise of a letter from Lieutenant-Colonel Montagu to the Earl of Carnarvon, Colonel of the Wilts Militia, respecting the authority which is vested in magistrates to call for the assistance of the Military, under circumstances therein stated, and desiring our Opinion—

"1. Whether, in cases where there is reasonable ground of apprehension that the Civil power will not be sufficiently strong to preserve the public peace, or to prevent the rescue of prisoners legally committed, though no riot actually exists, Magistrates can legally call for the assistance of the Military?

"2. Whether the presence of the Magistrate is indispensably necessary upon all such occasions?

"3. Whether in case the Troops, as Militia, upon such service, should be marched to a distance from their quarters they can legally be billeted at the place they remove to, and enjoy the privileges and advantages to which they are entitled upon a regular march?

"Your Grace has also added for our information a copy of the

---

[1] For the subsequent Orders issued, see Appendix CIX, *post*.   [2] Bk. 723, p. 100.

then Attorney-General's Report in 1721, upon some disorders committed at Taunton.

"In answer to the *first* question which your Grace has proposed to us, we beg leave to observe, that the Military (including the Militia when drawn out and embodied, as well as His Majesty's Regular Forces), are subject to the provisions in the Annual Mutiny Bill, and to the powers which his Majesty has by his prerogative over the Military Force of the country, and, so far as is consistent with obedience to Military discipline and command, we apprehend the Civil Magistrates have the same power to call for the assistance of the Military as they have to call for the assistance of others of His Majesty's subjects *But we apprehend the Magistrates have no power to call for the assistance of the Military in cases in which they cannot call for the assistance of other of His Majesty's subjects*

"We think that where a Magistrate has reason to apprehend that the ordinary Civil power will not be sufficient for the preservation of the public peace, he may command all persons present to assist him in the preservation of the public peace, although no breach of the public peace shall have been actually committed, and if he shall know, or shall have been informed, that any riot, rout, or other assembly against the peace, has actually taken place, he may call all persons within his jurisdiction to attend him to the spot, and assist him in suppressing such riot, rout, or other assembly, and apprehending the offenders, and all persons so called upon are bound to give their assistance so far as is consistent with other duties of equal or superior obligation. But we apprehend the Magistrates cannot require from the Military any assistance repugnant to the obligations of their Military duty, such as to march from that part of the country in which they are stationed by their military orders, to another part of the country to which their military orders do not direct or authorise them to go

"We also apprehend that the Magistrates have no right to order any person of any description to assist in conveying to jail any person against whom they shall have issued a Warrant of Commitment, except the person or persons to whom such Warrant shall be directed, and we apprehend that such Warrant cannot be directed to any person except high constables or petty constables, without the consent of such person to act in the execution of the Warrant But where a Warrant of Commitment directed to a constable made by a Magistrate the constable may take such assistance as he shall think proper, and we apprehend His Majesty may give such orders to the Military as will enable them to afford to constables executing such Warrants such assistance as they could legally require or receive from other persons

"It seems to us, therefore, probable that the difficulties which
have occurred to the Magistrates of the county of Cornwall, and the
Officers of the Wilts Militia, which have induced your Grace to put
to us the questions contained in your Grace's letter, may probably
be, in a considerable degree, removed by such explicit orders given
by the proper Military Authority to the Commanding Officer of the
Regiment, and by the Commanding Officer of the Regiment to the
Commanding Officers of the several detachments, as we apprehend
have been given in similar cases.

' In answer to the *second* question put to us by your Grace, we
think the Magistrate cannot of his own authority order the Military
or any other person to assist in the preservation of the public peace,
unless he is personally present, except as he may command the
attendance upon him of all persons in such cases in which he has a
right to call out the power of the county, and so far we consider
the presence of the Magistrate as indispensably necessary on all
such occasions as are mentioned in your Grace's letter.

"In answer to your Grace's *third* question, we think if the
Troops upon any such Service as is therein supposed shall be
ordered to march to a distance from their quarters, under the
command of their proper Officers, by proper Military Authority,
they may be legally billeted at the place to which they may be so
removed, but we think that they cannot enjoy the privileges and
advantages to which they are usually entitled on a march unless
those orders shall be given for their march, under which the
Justices are authorised, by the Mutiny Bill, to issue Warrants for
that purpose.

" JOHN SCOTT.
" JOHN MITFORD."

(19.) EXTRACT FROM LETTER¹ OF LIEUT-COLONEL MONTAGU
OF AUGUST, 1796—(par 50).

"THE Collector of the Customs for this District has this day
waited on me by order of the Commissioners, to show me a copy
of a letter he received from them, dated the 14th of May, signifying
the Order given by the Secretary at War relative to the Revenue
Officers being assisted by the Soldiers quartered within the Western
District, and desiring the said Collector to report my answer

' It appears this Order was transmitted to the General Officer
then commanding the District, and was the cause of an Order the Com-

---

¹ Bk 723, p 105

manding Officer of the Wilts Militia received to that from Cene.
Morris I had long conceived the General Orders the Military .. .
time to time received from the War Office to assist the Civil Pow.
and the Revenue Officers were not sufficiently explained, and th. t
an assumed power in Officers of those Departments was too ofte.
the consequence of such General Orders, which were glaringly
illegal, to the abuse of the Military, without knowing where to lo..
for responsibility. It became necessary for me, when I found th..
Regiment under my command almost daily called on to do the duty
of excisemen and constables in a military capacity to inquire how
far the Military could act in such incompatible characters and on
the one part to request that you would officially explain the full
intent and meaning, or get explained, the General Orders for
assisting Revenue Officers; and on the other part I had conse (e)
to lay before the Secretary of State a correspondence between me
and Lord De Dunstanville, concerning the impropriety (as I deemed
it) of his Lordship ordering a party of the Wilts Militia to escort
felons to jail.

"This I strongly contended was an illegal act, because Military
cannot be commanded by any but Military Officers. Not that I was
inclined to dispute the authority of a Magistrate acting in person,
but that he cannot delegate his powers, be what they may. Nor is
there any necessity of a Magistrate straining such a point when he
is by law invested with such extraordinary powers of raising the
people of his district in a *posse comitatus* whenever he is impeded in
the execution of his duty, and can most assuredly call in a Soldier
to his aid, individually as a citizen, though not collectively as
military, much less delegate such a power to a stupid fellow of a
constable

"If, therefore, the points in question are carried to their full
extent it is the fault of those Magistrates who contend a right to
such illegal practice, for I never wished to take from a Magistrate
that which long custom has given them, though it is an assumed
power, because I believe, if confined to their personal attendance, it
may be productive of good; but I never subject myself to be commanded by a constable.

"Our Correspondence to this effect was accordingly laid before
the Duke of Portland, and afterwards more fully explained by Lord
Carnarvon, who was informed by his Grace that the Law Officers of
the Crown were the proper persons to decide the point in question,
and he should therefore desire their opinion. There this matter
stands

"Finding, however, the frequent demands upon the Military
under my command for the purpose of apprehending persons of

various descriptions by virtue of a Warrant granted by a Justice of the Peace, and thereby requiring the Military to do the duty of constables illegally, I was under the necessity of giving the following Regimental Orders —

"'No Officer or Non-commissioned Officer is in future to be concerned in marching, or causing to be marched, any party of Soldiers under their command to escort or convoy any person to jail, or other place of confinement, committed by a Magistrate, unless some one of His Majesty's Justices of the Peace, Sheriff, or Under Sheriff, attends in person, nor in any way to interfere or be concerned in any manner whatever by the Civil Power, unless authorised by the personal attendance of the Magistrate, whose power being delegated to a constable or inferior Officer, will not justify the actions of a military body, whether offensive or defensive, when acting under such illegal authority.

"'In respect to the aid and assistance required of the Wilts Militia by the Officer of Excise, the Commanding Officer is not at present capable of defining the general terms of the Order sent to the Regiment for that purpose. He must therefore beg the Officers on detachment to peruse the General Orders of the —— May as their guide. It is, however, necessary to observe that no Soldier can be permitted to quit his arms, or do any laborious work, or to search for any smuggled goods. Where it is necessary he should for that purpose lay down his arms for a moment. Nor on any account is a Soldier to be suffered to enter a boat, or be put on board a ship on any pretence whatever, but at all times to be connected and in military order.

"'If at any time an Excise Officer compels by threats or otherwise a Soldier to disobey this order, or gives or suffers to be given any spirituous liquor to a Soldier while on the execution of his duty, such exciseman is to be instantly reported to the Commanding Officer, that the complaint may be immediately laid before the Commissioners of Excise. Any Non-commissioned Officer coming to the knowledge of such or any other misconduct of an Excise Officer, and neglecting to report it immediately to his Officer, shall be reduced, and suffer such corporal punishment as by the sentence of a Court-martial shall be awarded.'

"By these Orders your Lordship will perceive I have not declined giving assistance to the Revenue Officers where the aid of Military was required to seize contraband goods, nor has there been an instance of refusal as yet to assist the Excise Officers except in two instances, as before stated, where a party was required to take the person and not the goods of a smuggler, by a Warrant from a Magistrate; and I contend still, the Military cannot act in such

cases legally, and I think a Magistrate must be little acquainted
with his duty and his powers to require it · but if a Magistrate or
an Excise Officer will sit at home, and fancy their under-Officers
are not sufficient, it is unpardonable, when a Magistrate has a power
of swearing in as many as he chooses to execute his orders But
the fact is, it is less trouble and less expense to call in Military aid,
without considering one moment the unpleasant situation a Military
Officer or Soldier may be brought into.

"I beg your Lordship will believe I have every inclination to
assist the Civil Power when I can do it with safety, and I only
want to have it explained, by proper authority, how far and in
what cases the Military are subject to the Order of the Civil
Department. When this is once decided by the Law Officers of the
Crown we shall know where to look for responsibility."

(20.) The like from Letter[1] of same. Received at the
  War Office, 16th November, 1796—(*par.* 50)

"I had the honor of receiving a copy of the Opinion given by the
Law Officers of the Crown relative to a correspondence originating
between Lord De Dunstanville and myself concerning the powers
vested in a Magistrate by Law to command the Military I beg
leave to observe the two first queries, as put by the Secretary of
State and answered by the Crown Law Servants, are perfectly clear
as stated in the copy of their reply, but I think the Secretary of
War's letter[2] to your Lordship is not a satisfactory explanation of
their reply to the first query, for it does not appear that a *request*
of a Magistrate or a requisition of a Constable acting under the
warrant of a Magistrate will indemnify the Military as a *Military
Body* In cases where a Magistrate finds it necessary to command
the aid of all persons *present*, should a *soldier* be one amongst the
persons present he may be equally obliged to aid and assist the
Magistrates (if it is not repugnant to the obligation of his military
station, which must depend on His Majesty's orders); but then such
soldier so commanded by a Magistrate is no longer in a military
capacity, or pointedly compelled to assist the Magistrate *because he
is a soldier*, but as a citizen accidentally present when the Magistrate
commands all *present* to assist *him*. In cases where a Magistrate has
a power by law to call all persons within his jurisdiction to attend
him, by the same rule he may call one and every other soldier

---

[1] Bk. 723, p 129 [2] This letter I am unable to trace in the War Office Book.

within that jurisdiction to his aid as citizens, provided His Majesty by orders dispenses for the time being with all military duty; but the Opinions of the Law Officers do not convey to me that any orders given to the Military to assist a Magistrate as military would be legal, but by the words of the Law Officers' Opinions ('His Majesty may give such orders to the Military as will *enable* them to afford to constables, &c., assistance') Now, the word 'enable' certainly only implies a liberty granted to leave their military duty, without which permission they would be exempt from that obedience due to a Magistrate as other citizens are by law bound to give on certain occasions, but it by no means appears that it is legal for the military to comply with any orders given them to assist the Civil power as a military body commanded by military officers Now, if a constable, supposing himself insufficient to execute a warrant under the authority of a Magistrate, had the power of demanding a military force of a Commanding Officer to assist him (as stated by the Secretary at War's letter), his powers would be greater than the Magistrate's, for it seems clearly decided a Magistrate has no such legal authority but in cases where the military are indiscriminately taken with other citizens, the Law Officers say, 'The constable may take such assistance as he shall think proper,' but this does not imply that he shall go ten miles to pointedly fix on the military force to aid him Nor does it appear that a Commanding Officer can *order* a military party to assist him, though he may by permission of His Majesty give *leave* to any number of soldiers to leave their military duty. But then and in that case another query might arise, whether or not an officer or soldier by virtue of their station are obliged to submit to the order of a constable legally, and whether by such virtue they are not legally exempt, and their assistance becomes optional.

" These are matters that still want explanation from the Secretary at War's letter, as we seem to construe the Opinions given by the Crown Lawyers in a different way

" Not long since, a constable came out of the country five miles from Penryn, having a warrant to execute and, without asking any permission of the Commanding Officer, took a soldier or two with him, which men were not to be accounted for at the time and place of exercise If, therefore, the military were at all subject to the call of the Civil power by law, I conceive it would greatly distress the Service I should, therefore, humbly conceive a soldier is as much exempt from the orders of the Civil power as he is from serving the office of Constable, and I believe it is perfectly inconsistent with law that any person should act in both capacities at the same moment

" In regard to the last query put by the Secretary of State, '
not at all applicable to the case. No one ever doubted the '
Commander-in-Chief of the District, could order the
march as you thought proper under the authority and
given you for that purpose, and that by such order the
marched would be entitled to all the advantages a Route
War Office would give.

" The query ought to have been, whether a Magistrate ordering
such troops to march *without the order,* or rather a *Route* from you,
were entitled to billets and all other usual advantages; however,
the answer implied *they are not* unless ordered by *Military authority,*
and *I* do not conceive I have such authority or any other Officer
but the Commandant of the District.

" Upon the whole it appears clearly decided by the best law
authority that a Magistrate has no more power or command over
Military than he has over other of His Majesty's subjects, and that
he cannot demand their aid as a *Military Body,* but indiscriminately
as a part of the persons present when such assistance is wanted, or
when a Magistrate is obliged to call all persons within his jurisdiction.

" That a constable, under a Magistrate's warrant, may also call to
his assistance any person he thinks proper, whether he is a soldier
or not, but not to compel any *Military Force* to act under his orders,
provided in both these cases His Majesty permits such Military to
be excused from their duty of that station, but that no Commanding
Officer can give *orders* for any party of Military to assist a constable,
though he may by His Majesty's orders give them *leave.* This I
understand to be the explanation of the Law Officers' Opinions,
which is to be our legal guide, and I should not think myself justified by such decision to order any party under my command to
march to aid the Civil power, but where a Magistrate attends in
person.

" But I shall not trouble your Lordship any longer, as I have no
doubt, upon your perusal of the answers to the queries put, you will
be of the same opinion."

---

(21) Further Report[1] of the Law Officers—(*par.* 50).

" My Lord Duke,   " *Lincoln's Inn, 19th December,* 1796.

" In obedience to the command communicated to us, we have
perused the several papers which your Grace has transmitted, and

---

[1] Bk. 732, pp 138-145.

have again considered the points on which we submitted our
Opinion on the 30th of July last, in answer to your Grace's letter of
the 8th of the same month, and more especially with the view to
which your Grace's letter of the 22nd November last requires us
particularly to direct our attention.

"The doubts entertained by the General of the Western District
we apprehend have been suggested to the War Office, in consequence
of the letter (without date) of Lieutenant-Colonel Montagu to his
Lordship.

"We have attentively and repeatedly perused that letter, and
we must acknowledge that we find great difficulty in satisfying
ourselves of the nature and full extent of the doubts which pressed
on the mind of Lieutenant-Colonel Montagu in his anxiety to
discharge with exactness his general duties as a Subject, and his
particular duties as a Soldier

"The first doubt which he appears to suggest is, 'Whether the
requisition of a Magistrate, or the requisition of a Constable acting
under the Warrant of a Magistrate, will indemnify the Military as a
Military Body,' or, to use his words in a subsequent passage, 'as
a Military Body commanded by Military Officers.'

"We apprehend that a Military body commanded by Military
Officers, acting in obedience to the lawful commands of a Magistrate,
either in assisting that Magistrate personally, or in assisting a
person acting under the Warrant of that Magistrate, will act
according to its duty if the Orders which that Military body has
received from its superior Officer warrants it in giving that
assistance.

"We know not in what manner we can more explicitly state
our opinion of the indemnity to a Military body so acting, than by
stating that its conduct will, in our opinion, be legal. Lieutenant-
Colonel Montagu seems to lay a stress on the words 'as a Military
Body,' and we apprehend that he has been led to the doubt which
he has suggested, by mistaking our meaning in our former Opinion,
given in our letter to your Grace of the 30th July last. We did
not mean by that letter to convey an opinion, and on re-perusal it
still appears to us not to convey an opinion, 'that a Soldier acting
in the assistance of a Civil Magistrate is no longer in a Military
capacity,' which Lieutenant-Colonel Montagu seems to consider as
a just conclusion to be drawn from the opinion expressed in that
letter.

"We conceive that the Military duty of a Soldier remains
whilst he acts under the orders of a Civil Magistrate; that he is
still necessarily subservient to Military discipline, and that the
command of the Magistrate cannot exempt him from that discipline,

and we beg leave to say that we cannot but think that this is
implied in the Opinion which we before submitted to your Grace,
although the misapprehension of that Opinion by Lieutenant-
Colonel Montagu leads us to fear that the language which we
used to express our sentiments was not so clear as it ought to have
been.

"Lieutenant-Colonel Montagu, pursuing the idea of our sentiments which he appears to have formed, has drawn this conclusion
as the result of our Opinion, 'that no Orders given to the Military
to assist a Magistrate as Military' (or, as he expresses himself in a
passage before alluded to, 'as a Military Body commanded by
Military Officers') can be legal

"We beg leave to say that we think that nothing in our former
letter to your Grace warrants this conclusion, which would necessarily lead in its consequences to the destruction of Military Discipline, and to exempt the Officers from all responsibility for the
conduct of their Soldiers whenever the Military shall be called upon
to assist the Civil Magistrate

"Lieutenant Colonel Montagu, pursuing the idea which he had
adopted, appears to us to have misunderstood the sense in which we
meant to use the word 'enable' in our former Opinion, which he
appears to consider as importing a liberty granted to Soldiers to
leave their Military duty. We think the passage in which the
word is used does not warrant this construction of the word We
certainly did not mean to use it in the sense in which it has been
understood by Lieutenant-Colonel Montagu, and, on the contrary,
we conceive that when His Majesty, and his Military Officers by his
command, authorise any Military Corps to act in the assistance of
the Civil Magistrate, they do not authorise the individuals composing that Corps to leave their Military duty, but require them, in
obedience to their Military duty, to afford assistance to the Civil
Magistrate in the exercise of his duty.

"Lieutenant-Colonel Montagu mentions a case, which he represents as highly inconvenient to the Military Service, the case of a
constable requiring Soldiers to assist him in executing a Warrant
without asking the permission of their Commanding Officer We
feel no difficulty in saying that we think the Soldiers who were
thus absent from their Military duty without leave were guilty of a
Military offence, for which the requisition of the constable afforded
them no lawful excuse, although the circumstances may have been
such as might induce their Commanding Officer to consider the
fault as not meriting very severe reprehension.

"From the whole of Lieutenant-Colonel Montagu's letter I
collect that he has formed a general opinion 'that no person can be

a Military character, assist a Civil Magistrate in the execution of the duty of that Magistrate,' and he has also at the close of his letter stated his further opinion, as the result, we presume, of what he had before stated, that no Orders of His Majesty, or of a superior Officer, would justify Lieutenant-Colonel Montagu in ordering any party 'under his command to march to aid the Civil Power, but where a Magistrate attended in person,' and that no Commanding Officer can give Orders for any party of Military to assist a constable, though he may, by His Majesty's Orders, give them leave.'

"The general opinion which Lieutenant-Colonel Montagu appears to have so formed we have already stated to be, in our opinion, erroneous; and we apprehend that Lieutenant-Colonel Montagu may, at the request of a Civil Magistrate, and in pursuance of Military Orders warranting his compliance with such request, order a party under his command to march to any spot to aid the Civil Power, although a Magistrate may not be on the spot at the time such Orders shall be given. Whether the Military party so sent upon duty, when arrived at the spot, can act in assisting the Civil power, must depend on the existence on the spot of a Civil Power to be assisted, and so far the presence of the Magistrate to warrant an act of the Military party may, in a variety of cases, be absolutely necessary. But if (for instance) on the spot the Military party should find a constable employed in convoying to prison persons committed by a Magistrate, and the constable should desire the assistance of the Military party to prevent a rescue, we apprehend the party may lawfully give that assistance so far as their Military Orders will warrant them in so doing, and we apprehend that Lieutenant-Colonel Montagu may, in obedience to the Orders which he may receive for that purpose, order a party of Military under his command to assist a constable in the lawful execution of the duty of such constable.

"We have entered into this long discussion of the subject of Lieutenant-Colonel Montagu's letter, in the hope of preventing any further misconception; at the same time that we doubt the propriety of our so doing and whether it was not our duty merely to report to your Grace on that head, that we adhered to the opinion expressed in our former letter, adding that we conceive His Majesty may by orders given to his Troops make assistance to the Civil Magistrate in the lawful execution of his Civil duty, a part of their Military duty, that the Troops acting at the requisition of the Magistrate in obedience to such orders would still be subject to Military discipline, and would therefore act as a Military body, commanded by Military Officers, and that the orders of the Civil

Magistrate would not warrant them in disobedience to the Order of their Military Commanders, acting in discharge of their Military duty.

"We understand that the usual Orders have been issued to the General of the Western District to give such Orders to the Troops under his command as may be necessary for rendering assistance to the Civil Magistrates in the exercise of their duty. We are not informed of the precise terms of those Orders, but we conclude from the letter of the Secretary at War of the 5th of September last, that they are very ample. Under these circumstances we cannot form any judgment whether any further Orders are, or are not, necessary. We can only venture to submit to your Grace how far it may be useful to repeat the Orders already given, with such particulars as may fully and directly apply to the subject upon which doubts have been suggested to the General, if the Orders already issued do not contain such particularities.

"In answer to that part of your Grace's letter which relates to the security of the Revenue Officers in the exercise of their duty, we submit that if the orders already given are not sufficiently explicit, it may be proper to give orders to the General to render them assistance in the execution of their duty in terms similar to those for the assistance of the Civil Magistrates, and we submit whether it may not be useful to state explicitly the extent in which the requisition of the Revenue Officer shall make it the duty of the Military Commander, as a Military Officer, to render that assistance. We apprehend the Military, in assisting the Revenue Officers, are protected by the authority given by law to those Officers and to their assistants, and that the Military, when employed in assisting the Revenue Officers, can have no legal warrant for their acts, but such as the Revenue Officers can give to any other person who may assist them in the execution of their duty.

> "JOHN SCOTT
> "JOHN MITFORD."

(22.) TWO QUESTIONS AND THE OPINION OF THE FOUR LEADING COUNSEL ON THE CIRCUIT, LAID BEFORE THE GRAND JURY OF THE COUNTY OF SOMERSET.

"*Taunton, March* 30, 1801.

"Q. MAY the Magistrates appoint constables at their pleasure, and how are they to be appointed? and can constables be appointed for the whole county? Can they appoint any of the military to be constables?"

"A. Magistrates may appoint special constables at their discretion, by administering to them the usual oath of constables, and, being so appointed, such constables may act as such in all cases Any person may be appointed constable, but whether it be advisable to appoint any of the military to that office is not a subject for our consideration "

" *Q.* Would it be prudent, in case of great necessity, for the military to act in the absence of the Magistrates and peace officers ? "

" *A* The duty of the Military is the same as that of all subjects, and they are alike bound to use the means in their power to maintain the public peace, though, in the absence of the Magistrates and constables, the prudence of their acting must depend on the occasions, and in cases of great necessity we have no doubt in saying that they ought to act.

"Robt. Dallas
"V Gibbs.
"John Lewis.
"Henry Tripp."

---

(23) Case submitted for the Opinion of the Attorney-General, as set out in His Majesty's Regulations for the Government of the Army.

"It frequently happens, upon the breaking out of riots or other disturbances, at a distance from the abode of any Magistrate, that the Officers commanding troops have expressed doubts how far, and under what circumstances, they should be justified in proceeding to suppress such riots and disturbances without the directions of a Magistrate or such other peace officers as are specified in the *Riot Act*

" Your Opinion is requested, Whether in case of any sudden riot or disturbance a constable or other peace officer, being under the degree of those described in the Riot Act, can call upon the Military to suppress such riot or disturbance; and how far, in the absence of any constable, or other peace officer at all, the military would be justified in proceeding to suppress any riot which might break out ? "

(24.) Report of the Attorney-General.

"*Lincoln's Inn, April* 1, 1801.

"I understand the *disturbances* here meant to be such as amount to the legal description of *riots* The word ' *disturbance* ' has no legal and appropriate meaning beyond a mere *breach of the peace*, which is not, however, the sense in which the word is used in this case, the case plainly importing a breach of the peace by an assembled multitude.

"In case of such *sudden riot and disturbance*, as above supposed, any of His Majesty's subjects, without the presence of a peace officer of any description, may arm themselves, and of course may use a degree of force to suppress such riot and disturbance.

"This was laid down in my Lord Chief Justice Popham's Reports 121, and Keeling 76, as having been resolved by all the Judges in the 39th of Queen Elizabeth, to be good law, and has certainly been recognized in Hawkins and other writers on the Crown Law, and by various Judges at different periods since.

"And what His Majesty's subjects *may* do, they *also ought* to do for the suppression of public tumult when an exigency may require that such means be resorted to.

"Whatever *any other class* of His Majesty's subjects may allowably do in this particular, *the Military way unquestionably do also.*

"By the common law, every description of peace officer may, and ought to do, not only all that in him lies towards the suppression of riots, but may, and ought to, command *all other persons* to assist therein.

"However, it is by all means advisable to procure a Justice of Peace to attend, *and for the Military to act under his immediate orders*, when such attendance, and the sanctions of such orders can be obtained, as it not only prevents any disposition to unnecessary violence on the part of those who act in repelling the tumult, but it induces also, from the known authority of such Magistrates, a more ready submission on the part of the rioters to the measures used for that purpose; but still in cases of *great and sudden emergency, the Military, as well as all other individuals, may act without their presence, or* without the presence of any other peace officer whatsoever.

(Signed)   "EDWARD LAW."

(CIII.)

Chapter XVII., par. 39

ORDER[1] FOR THE MILITIA TO AID THE CIVIL POWER.

"[COUNTY OF CARDIGAN]

" *To the Officer commanding the Cardigan Militia, at Aberystwyth.*

" WHEREAS, the Civil power has been invoked to apprehend the six persons charged with having feloniously and riotously taken down and demolished the dwelling-house of Augustus Brackenbury, gentleman, at the parish of Llanymython, in this county, we therefore request you will be pleased to attend, with the men under your command, provided with arms and ammunition, at the village of Llanymython, to-morrow morning at the hour of 9 o'clock, there to be in readiness to aid and assist the Civil power in the apprehending such persons under the authority and direction of such Justices as may be then and there assembled.

"Dated this 2nd day of June, 1826.

"W. C GILBERTSON,"

(*and four other Justices*).

(CIV.)

Chapter XVII., *par.* 43

VOLUNTEERS ACTING IN AID OF THE CIVIL POWER.

Memorandum; as originally issued on the 3rd *June, and as altered and re-issued on the* 13th *June,* 1867.[2]

"*War Office,* 13th *June,* 1867.

"1 QUESTIONS having arisen as to the power of the Civil Authority to call upon the Volunteer Force to act in aid of the Civil Power in suppression of riot or public commotion; and [doubts having been expressed] as to the duty of the members of the Volunteer Force, if so called upon, the following Circular is issued for the general information of *that* [the Volunteer] Force, in accordance with the opinion of the Law Officers of the Crown.

"2 Her Majesty's subjects are bound, in case of the existence of riots, to use all reasonable endeavours, according to the necessity of the occasion, to suppress and quell such riots, and members of the Volunteer Force are not exempted from this general obligation, *and they may, in common with all other Her Majesty's subjects, be required by the Civil Authority to act as Special Constables for such purposes but they must not, when so acting, appear in their Military Dress*

"3 The Civil Authority is not in any case entitled to call upon or order Volunteers to act as a Military Body [with or without arms] in the preservation of the peace.

-----

[1] No 361—Ordered by the House of Commons to be printed, 14th June, 1867

[2] The words in brackets stood in the original Memorandum of the 3rd June, but were omitted on the re-issue, on the 13th June, 1867, when those marked in Italics were inserted

"[4. Members of the Volunteer Force may, in common with all Her Majesty's subjects, be called upon and required by the Civil Authority to act as Special Constables, for the purpose of suppressing and quelling riots.]

"4. [5.] In cases of riots and disturbances not amounting to insurrection, and not having for their object the commission of felonious acts or the subversion of the Civil Government, Special Constables, whether *members of the* Volunteer[t.] *Force* or others, should [not] be armed with [or use any weapon other than] the ordinary constable's staff, [and in such cases no Volunteer should, when acting as a Special Constable, appear in his Military Dress].

"5. [6.] In cases of serious and dangerous riots and disturbances, [for instance, in case of insurrection or of riots having for their object the commission of felonious acts or the subversion of the Civil Government,] the Civil Authority may [call upon and] require Her Majesty's subjects generally, including *members of the* Volunteer[s] *Force* to arm themselves with and use [such] other weapons [of defence or attack as may be in their power and may be] suitable to the occasion, and such other weapons may be used accordingly by *members of the* [Her Majesty's subjects, including] Volunteer[s] *Force*, according to the necessity of the occasion

"[7 Firearms should be the last weapons so to be called into action, and should be resorted to only in cases when, without their use, it would be practically impossible to quell the disturbance]

"[8 All Her Majesty's subjects, including Volunteers, in acting either as Special Constables, or otherwise, for suppressing and quelling riots, are entitled to use and put in action such knowledge and practice of military discipline and organisation as they may possess, for the purpose of making their combined strength, and the use of such weapons as the occasion may justify, more effectual]

"[9. Her Majesty's subjects, including Volunteers, in cases in which it is proper for them to act for the suppression of riots, should act, if it be practicable, under the direction of the Civil Authority; but they will not be released from the obligation to use their reasonable endeavours for the suppression of riots and disturbances, according to the necessities of the occasion, if magistrates should not be present, or not within reach of immediate communication when any such occasion arises.]

"6. [10.] In the event of an attack upon their storehouses or armouries, members of the Volunteer Force may combine, and avail themselves of their *organization* [military discipline] to repel such attack and to defend such storehouses and armouries, and for such purposes may, if the necessity of the occasion require it, use arms

"LONGFORD "

(CV.)

Chapter XVII, par. 53.

DUTIES IN AID OF THE CIVIL POWER.—EXTRACTS FROM QUEEN'S REGULATIONS AND ORDERS FOR THE ARMY, 1868.

Paragraph 912 *contains the Case and Opinion printed, p* 649, *ante*

"913 WHEN Troops are called out in aid of the Civil Power at home the Officer Commanding at the station is immediately to report the same by telegraph to the Military Secretary for the information of the Commander-in-Chief, and is to forward a duplicate Report by the same channel to the Quartermaster-General. The Officer Commanding the party will report to the Military Secretary daily in writing, as well as to the Officer Commanding the station from which he has been detached, the progress or completion of the service on which he is employed. An immediate notification of every movement of the Troops is also to be made to the Quartermaster-General. *[margin: Calling out of Troops to be reported]*

"914. No Officer is to go out with Troops for the purpose of aiding in the suppression of riot, the maintenance of the public peace, or the execution of the law, except upon the requisition of a Magistrate, in writing, or in the cases of *great and sudden emergency* referred to in para 912 *[margin: Magistrate's requisition.]*

"915 The Officer Commanding the Troops is to move to the place to which he shall be directed by the Magistrate: he is to take care that the Troops march in regular military order, with the usual precautions, and that they are not scattered, detached, or posted in a situation in which they may not be able to act in their own defence. The Magistrate is to accompany the Troops, and the Officer is to remain near him. *[margin: Movement of the Troops.]*

"916. When the number of the Detachment shall be under twenty files, it is to be told off into four sections. If there should be more than twenty files, the Detachment is to be told off into more sections than four. *[margin: Detachments to be told off into four sections.]*

"917. All commands to the Troops are to be given by the Officer. The Troops are not, on any account, to fire excepting by word of command of their Officer, who is to exercise a humane discretion respecting the extent of the line of fire, and is not to give the word of command to fire, unless distinctly required to do so by the Magistrate. *[margin: Commands to be given by the Officer]*

"918 In order to guard against all misunderstanding, Officers commanding Troops or Detachments are, on every occasion in which they may be employed in the suppression *[margin: Fire of the Troops to be effective.]*

of riots, or in the enforcement of the law, to take the most effectual means, in conjunction with the Magistrates under whose orders they may be placed, for notifying beforehand, and explaining to the people opposed to them, that in the event of the Troops being ordered to fire, their fire will be effective

"919. If the Commanding Officer should be of opinion that a *Firing by files* slight effort would be sufficient to attain the object, he is *or sections.* to give the word of command to one or two specified files to fire   If a greater effort should be required, he is to give the word of command to one of the sections, told off as above ordered, to fire, the fire of the other sections being kept in reserve till necessary, and when required, the fire of each of them being given by the regular word of command of the Commanding Officer

"920   If there should be more Officers than one with the *When there* Detachment, and it should be necessary that more sections *are more* than one should fire at a time, the Commanding Officer *Officers than* *one* is to fix upon, and clearly indicate to the Troops, what Officer is to order any number of the sections to fire — such Officer is to receive his directions from the Commanding Officer, after the latter shall have received the requisition of the Magistrate to fire No other individual, excepting the one indicated by the Commanding Officer, is to give orders to any file, or section, to fire

"921. The firing is to cease the instant it is no longer neces- *Instructions* sary, whether the Magistrate may order the cessation or *as to firing* not.   Care is to be taken not to fire upon persons separated from the crowd   It is to be observed, that to fire over the heads of a crowd engaged in an illegal pursuit, would have the effect of favouring the most daring and the guilty, and might have the effect of sacrificing the less daring, and even the innocent.

"922   If firing should unfortunately be necessary, and should *Serious* be ordered by the Magistrate, Officers and Soldiers must *nature of the* *duty* feel that they have a serious duty to perform, and they must perform it with coolness and steadiness, and in such manner as to be able to discontinue their fire at the instant at which it shall be found that there is no longer occasion for it.

"923   Commanding Officers of Stations and Corps are, on the *Convict Esta-* requisition of governors of Convict Establishments in *blishments* their neighbourhood, to afford temporary assistance in aid of the Civil guard, in cases of emergency, such as a disposition on the part of the Convicts to mutiny   Reports of the demand of the governor and of the completion of the service are to be immediately made to the Military Secretary "

(CVI.)

Chapter XVIII, *par.* 13

REBELLION OF 1715.

" At the Court at St. James's, the 25th of July, 1715.

" *Present,*

THE KING'S MOST EXCELLENT MAJESTY,

H.R.H THE PRINCE OF WALES,

Lord Chancellor,	Earl of London,
Lord President,	Earl of Ilay,
Lord Steward,	Bishop of London,
Lord Chamberlain,	Lord Somers,
Duke of Montrose,	Lord Coningsby,
Duke of Roxburgh,	Mr. Comptroller,
Lord Great Chamberlain,	Mr. Vice-Chamberlain,
Earl of Dorsett,	Mr. Secretary Stanhope,
Earl of Manchester,	Chancellor of Exchequer,
Earl of Cholmondeley,	Mr. Walpole.

" This day the following Proclamation was read at the Board and approved, viz. —

" ' By the King, a PROCLAMATION for suppressing Rebellions and Rebellious Tumults

" ' *A Proclamation*

" ' GEORGE R.,

" ' WHEREAS of late, some of the meanest of our people have been, in divers parts of this Kingdom, seduced and stirred up to riots and tumults to the disturbance of the public peace, and the same are now carried into open rebellion, and a levying of war against us and our Royal authority by the said rebels, having not only declared the end of their rising in arms to be to a general purpose and that against law, but even proceeded with an Armed Force in many and distant places, to pull down, burn, and destroy, the houses and buildings of our good and peaceable subjects, and by their having declared for the Pretender, and actually resisted and engaged with force of arms such as by lawful authority were endeavouring to disperse them, and there is no room to doubt but these traitorous proceedings are promoted and encouraged by Papists, Nonjurors, and other persons disaffected to our Government in expectation of being supported from abroad. We have, therefore, thought fit to the suppressing and putting a speedy end to the said Rebellion, by and with the advice of our Privy Council, to issue this our Royal Proclamation, hereby declaring that all our Officers, Civil and Military, are by the duty of their several offices and commands, obliged to use their utmost endeavours, by force of arms if necessary, to suppress all such traitorous Rebellions, and that in like manner all the subjects of this Realm are bound by law to be aiding and assisting in the suppression of such Rebellions, or may act against such rebels without the presence of such Officer, if the presence of such Officer cannot be had, or if such Officer refuses or neglects to execute his duty, and that all our dutiful and loyal subjects may, without any express warrant or authority, act in defence of their houses, persons, or possessions, if attacked or assaulted by such rebels or riotous persons, and if any of the said rebels shall happen to be slain, either by the Civil or Military Officers, or our Troops, or other our loyal subjects acting as aforesaid in the defence of the laws of our Royal Authority, and the preservation of the public peace, such killing is justifiable, and they who do it are indemnified by law. And we, therefore, strictly charge and command all our Officers, as well Civil as Military, and all other our obedient and loyal subjects, that wheresoever they shall meet with the said rebels and traitors, so as aforesaid, in arms and open Rebellion against us, they do endeavour without delay to suppress them with their utmost force, and to treat them with that severity with which rebels and traitors found in actual War and Rebellion against the Crown may be treated.

"'Given at our Court at St. James's, the 25th day of July, 1715, in the first year of our Reign.'"

(CVII.)

Chapter XVIII, *par* 18.

REBELLION OF 1745.

" At the Court at Kensington, the 5th day of September, 1745

" *Present,*

THE KING'S MOST EXCELLENT MAJESTY,

Archbishop of Canterbury,	Earl of Harrington,
Lord Chancellor,	Earl of Bath,
Lord President,	Viscount Cobham,
Lord Steward,	Viscount Torrington,
Lord Chamberlain,	Lord Monson,
Duke of Bolton,	Lord Sandys,
Duke of Bedford,	Mr Vice-Chamberlain,
Duke of Newcastle,	Master of the Rolls,
Marquis of Tweeddale,	Lord Chief Justice Willes,
Earl of Pembroke,	Sir William Yonge,
Earl of Winchilsea,	Sir John Norris,
Earl of Cholmondeley,	Thomas Winnington, Esq.,
Earl of Granville,	Marshal Wade,
Earl Fitz Walter,	St John Rushout

" This day the following Proclamation was read at the Board and approved, viz —

" ' By the King, &c. &c &c

" ' GEORGE R ,

' ' WHEREAS the eldest Son of the Pretender hath presumed, in open violation of our Laws, to land in the north-west part of Scotland, and has assembled a considerable number of Traiterous and Rebellious Persons in Arms, who have set up a Standard in the name of the Pretender, and in an audacious manner have resisted and attacked some of our Forces, and are now advancing farther in that part of our Kingdom of Great Britain , and there is the greatest reason to apprehend that these wicked attempts have been encouraged, and may be supported by a foreign Force ' "

[Then the Statutes against Papists and Reputed Papists were recited and put in force, and the Proclamation ended thus]

" ' And we do hereby further strictly charge and command all our Judges and Justices of Peace, and other Magistrates that they do use their utmost endeavours to prevent and suppress all Riots, Tumults, and Unlawful Assemblies ; and to put in due and strict execution all Laws made for preventing, or for the more speedy and effectual suppressing and punishing the same, and that all our loving subjects be aiding and assisting therein."

(CVIII.)

Chapter XVIII., *pa*. 19.

REPORT[1] ON THE OPERATION OF THE INDEMNITY ACT (19 GEO 2, c 20)

"Query.

"WHETHER or no a sentence passed by the Lords of Session in Scotland against an Officer in December, 1746, for obeying the orders of H R.H the Duke in distressing and annoying the Rebells, and all those concerned in that unnatural rebellion, as aiders and abetters the preceding summer, though the act for which he was accused, tried, and condemned happened some time before the Act of Indemnity, I say is it in the power of the Scotch laws to put that sentence in execution upon his appearing in the country, notwithstanding there was a *Noli Prosequi* sent down to Edinburgh by His Majesty to stop all further proceedings ? But whether or no this *Noli Prosequi* set aside their sentence pronounced against him as the tryal was previous to it, if not, then the question is, If he is not liable to be apprehended upon his going into Scotland, and suffer a punishment agreeable to his former sentence ?

" CHAS. HAMILTON "

" Opinion.

"SIR,   *" Bath, 7th September,* 1751.

"I have perused and considered the Quære which you were pleased to desire my Opinion upon, and, so far as I am able to judge from the case, put very shortly and imperfectly, and in a matter to be governed principally by the Scots law, I am inclined to think the Officer cannot be apprehended and punished in Scotland by virtue of the sentence passed on him there in the year 1746 But the particular nature of the charge against him, or of the sentence,

---

o, of the proceedings in the *Noli Prosequi* not being stated, and the precise effect of the *Noli Prosequi* in Scotland depending on the Scots Law, I cannot form such a judgment upon it as I could advise the Captain to rely upon, and should think his best way would be to take the Opinion of the Lord Advocate of Scotland upon the whole matter.

'I am, &c.,

' *The Rt Hon Henry Fox, Esq.*" "D. RYDER."

(CIX.)

Chapter XVIII, *par.* 20.

RIOTS OF LORD GEORGE GORDON [1]

" At the Court of St. James's, the 7th of June, 1780.

" *Present,*

THE KING'S MOST EXCELLENT MAJESTY

Lord President,	Viscount Falmouth,
Duke of Northumberland,	Viscount Hinchingbrook,
Lord Chamberlain,	Lord North,
Earl of Denbigh,	Lord Onslow,
Earl of Sandwich,	Lord Edgcumbe,
Earl of Hillsborough,	Lord Amherst,
Lord Charles Spencer,	Mr. Speaker,
Lord George Germain,	Jas Stuart Mackenzie, Esq.,
Viscount Townshend,	Richard Rigby, Esq,
Viscount Stormont,	Charles Jenkinson, Esq

" This day the following Proclamation was read at the Board and approved, viz —

" ' GEORGE R,

" ' WHEREAS a great number of disorderly persons have assembled themselves together in a riotous and tumultuous manner, and have been guilty of many acts of treason and rebellion, having made an assault on the gaol at Newgate, set loose the prisoners confined

---

[1] As to the prior orders of the Secretary at War, see Appendix CIL (16 and 17), *ante*

therein, and set fire to and destroyed the said prison, And, where-as, houses are now pulling down in several parts of our Cities of London and Westminster, and liberties thereof, and fires kindled for consuming the materials and furniture of the same whereby it is become absolutely necessary to use the most effectual means to quiet such disturbances, to preserve the lives and properties of individuals, and to restore the peace of the country; We, therefore, taking the same into our most serious consideration, have thought fit, by and with the advice of our Privy Council, to issue this our Royal Proclamation, hereby strictly charging and exhorting all our loving subjects to preserve the peace, and to keep themselves their servants and apprentices, quietly within their respective dwellings, to the end that all well-disposed persons may avoid those mischiefs which the continuance of such riotous proceedings may bring upon the guilty. And as it is necessary, from the circumstances before-mentioned to employ the Military Force, with which we are by law entrusted for the immediate suppression of such rebellious and traitorous attempts, now making against the peace and dignity of our Crown and the safety of the lives and properties of our subjects, We have, therefore, issued the most direct and effectual orders to all our Officers, by an immediate exertion of their utmost force, to repress the same, of which all persons are to take notice.

"'Given at Our Court of St James's, the Seventh Day of June, One Thousand Seven Hundred and Eighty, in the Twentieth Year of Our Reign.

"'GOD SAVE THE KING'"

On the same day the following General Orders were issued to the Officers and Commanders of all His Majesty's Forces in Great Britain.—

"*General Orders.*

"*Adjutant General's Office, June* 7, 1780

"In obedience to an Order of the King in Council, the Military to act without waiting for directions from the Civil Magistrate, and to use force for dispersing the illegal and tumultuous assemblies of the people.

"WM. AMHERST, *Adjutant-General*"

(CX.)

Chapter XVIII., par. 28

1st PROCLAMATION[1] OF LORD CAMDEN IN THE IRISH
REBELLION OF 1798.

"WHEREAS a traitorous conspiracy, existing within this Kingdom,
for the subversion of the authority of His Majesty, and the Parliament, and for the destruction of the established Constitution and
Government, hath considerably extended itself, and hath broken
out into acts of open violence and rebellion.

"We have, therefore, by and with the advice of His Majesty's
Privy Council, issued the most direct and positive orders to the
Officers commanding His Majesty's Forces, to employ them with
the utmost vigour and decision for the immediate suppression
thereof, and also to recover the arms which have been traitorously
forced from His Majesty's peaceable and loyal subjects, and to
disarm the rebels, and all persons disaffected to His Majesty's
Government, by the most summary and effectual measures.

"And we do hereby strictly charge and command all His
Majesty's peaceable and loyal subjects, on their allegiance, to aid
and assist, to the utmost of their power, His Majesty's forces in the
execution of their duty, to whom we have given it strictly in command to afford full protection to them from all acts of violence
which shall be attempted against their persons or properties.

"Given at the Council Chamber in Dublin, the 30th day of
March, 1798

"GOD SAVE THE KING."

(CXI.)

Chapter XVIII, par. 29.

2ND PROCLAMATION[2] OF LORD CAMDEN.

"His Excellency, the Lord-Lieutenant, by and with the advice of
the Privy Council, has issued orders to all the General Officers
commanding His Majesty's forces, to punish all persons acting,
aiding, or in any manner assisting in the rebellion which now
exists within this Kingdom, and has broken out in the most daring

---

[1] 40 Ann Reg, p 230.   [2] Ib., p 233

and violent attacks upon His Majesty's forces, according to Martial
Law, either by death or otherwise, as to them shall seem right and
expedient, for the punishment and suppression of all rebels in the
several districts, of which all His Majesty's subjects are hereby required to take notice.

"Given at the Council Chamber in Dublin, the 24th day of
May, 1798.

"GOD SAVE THE KING"

(CXII.)

Chapter XVIII., par. 44

CORRESPONDENCE[1] BETWEEN THE LATE DUKE OF WELLINGTON
AND LORD CASTLEREAGH AS TO THE EXECUTION OF
MARTIAL LAW UPON OFFENDERS IN THE BRITISH ARMY
IN 1809.

(1.) SIR ARTHUR WELLESLEY TO LORD CASTLEREAGH.

(*Extracts.*)

"*Ab. antes.* 17*th June,* 1809.

"I cannot, with propriety, omit to draw your attention again to
the state of discipline of the Army, which is a subject of serious concern to me, and well deserves the consideration of His Majesty's
Ministers.

"In the first place, I am convinced that the law is not strong
enough to maintain discipline in an Army upon Service. It is most
difficult to convict any prisoner before a Regimental Court-martial,
for I am sorry to say that Soldiers have little regard to the oath
administered to them; and the Officers who are sworn 'well and
truly to try and determine, *according to the evidence,* the matter before
them,' have too much regard to the strict letter of that administered
to them. This oath,[2] to the members of a Regimental Court-martial,
has altered the principle of the proceedings of that tribunal. It is
no longer a Court of honour, at the hands of which a Soldier was
certain of receiving punishment if he deserved it; but it is a Court

---

[1] 3 Gur Desp, p 302. 7 Castlereagh Desp, p 86

[2] It was imposed by the Mutiny Act of the previous year (45 Geo III, c If,
sec 17), and in 1836, the Duke of Wellington continued to attribute to it the same
evil consequences, see his evidence, p 331, before Committee on Military Punishment, 1836.

of Law, whose decisions are to be formed according to the evidence, principally of those on whose actions it is constituted as a restraint. But, admitting the regimental detachment Court-martial, as now constituted, to be a control upon the Soldiers equally efficient with that which existed under the old constitution of a Court-martial, which my experience tells me it is not, I should wish to know whether any British Army (this Army in particular, which is composed of 2nd Battalions, and therefore but ill provided with officers) can afford to leave with every hospital, or with every detachment, two Captains and four Subalterns, in order to be enabled to hold a detachment Court-martial. The law in this respect ought to be amended; and when the Army is on service in a foreign country, any one, two, or three Officers ought to have the power of trying criminals, and punishing them *instanter*; taking down all proceedings in writing, and reporting them for the information of the Commander-in-Chief on their joining the Army. Besides this improvement of the Law, there ought to be in the British Army a regular provost establishment, of which a proportion should be attached to every army sent abroad. All the foreign armies have such an establishment. the French *gendarmerie nationale*, to the amount of 30 or 40 with each of their corps, the Spaniards their *policia militar*, to a still larger amount, while we, who require such an aid more, I am sorry to say, than any of the other nations of Europe, have nothing of the kind, except a few serjeants, who are taken from the Line for the occasion, and who are probably not very fit for the duties which they are to perform.

"The authority and duties of the Provost ought, in some manner to be recognised by the Law. By the custom of British Armies, the Provost has been in the habit of punishing on the spot (even with death, under the orders of the Commander-in-Chief) Soldiers found in the act of disobedience of orders, of plunder, or of outrage. There is no authority for this practice except custom, which I conceive would hardly warrant it, and yet I declare that I do not know in what manner the Army is to be commanded at all, unless the practice is not only continued, but an additional number of Provosts appointed."

(2.) Lord Castlereagh to Sir Arthur Wellesley.[1]
(*Extracts*)

"*Downing Street*, 17th July, 1809.

"I have communicated your letter on the discipline of the Army to the Judge-Advocate, Attorney and Solicitor General. They feel

---

[1] 7 Castlereagh Desp., p. 96

all its importance, and have desired time to confer together upon it. I have also conversed upon it with Sir D. Dundas, who seems quite clear upon the practice, in all times past, of summary punishment for marauding, when armies have been in the field on actual service. He says it was done by the Duke of York, an instance of which I enclose, by Sir Ralph Abercromby, by many others, and, in the last campaign, by Moore—in short, he thinks, by all Commanders, who felt it necessary to the discipline of their Army; and he has no conception that any Army, more particularly a British one, can go on without it.

"You will observe, in the enclosed precedent, that the execution is ordered, not upon the view of the Commander-in Chief, or the Provost-Marshal, but upon the report of another General Officer, that such an offence had been committed. There is no doubt that such a practice always has existed, and has never been questioned when exercised to repress gross breaches of discipline in the progress of a campaign; but, as this extraordinary remedy is supposed to arise out of and to be alone justified by the necessity of the case, it does not appear that the mode and circumstances under which it is to be exercised have ever been defined with any precision. It is that extreme remedy which never can be made the subject of enactment, and will, therefore, probably always remain to be measured by the conscientious sense of its necessity operating at the moment on the judgment of the Officer who authorises it, and I know of no other protection he has for such exercise of authority than precedent, and the disposition all reasonable men would feel to support him, were it questioned.

"As far as I can recollect any principle, it seems to be most clearly justifiable, when inflicted instanter on the commission of the offence, and when the proofs are of a nature to place the guilt of the party beyond all doubt. Where time has intervened, and the offenders been committed to custody, where the guilt is to be collected from the evidence rather than from the view, there the intervention of a Court-martial seems the preferable course.

"I have not found any one who doubted that it would be clearly competent for the General commanding to punish with death, *upon his own view of the guilt*; but whether he can delegate such a power to his Provost-Marshal seems more questionable. The Commander-in-Chief thinks he can, according to the usages of War.

"As soon as Ryder returns to town, I propose having a meeting between the Military and the Legal Authorities, and shall send you the result. What I have stated in this letter you will consider as not more than what I have been able to collect in conversation. There seems much difficulty in treading back our steps on the mode of

constituting Courts-martial I much regretted the innovation in
the Mutiny Act at the moment; as it was obvious it was relinquishing to theory and reasoning what you could hardly ever hope to
resume by force of argument from an Assembly not composed of
professional men. On this part of the subject we are helpless till
Parliament reassembles, and, even then, I cannot look forward with
much confidence to the system being restored.

"This consideration does not alter the grounds materially on
which the summary exercise of punishment is to be justified. It
certainly, however, renders it the more indispensable, and in *so far*
it may fairly be considered as one feature more in the necessity that
warrants it The only additional part of the question, upon which
it may be necessary in this preliminary communication to say a
word, is that, whatever increase of the Provost Establishment you
may find requisite will be cheerfully sanctioned, and I conclude you
can be at no loss for proper instruments on the spot to employ."

---

(3) "EXTRACT[1] OF A GENERAL ORDER.
"*Head-Quarters, St Amand, 10th April,* 1794.
"Major-General Abercromby reported yesterday to His Royal
Highness the Commander-in-Chief that two men of the 14th Regiment had, during the preceding evening, attempted to rob the
house of a countryman, and, in the course of the attempt, they had
murdered the woman of the house, and that a child had been also
so much wounded that there was little prospect of its living.

'His Royal Highness feels himself called upon, by every tie of
justice, of humanity, and duty, to punish, by a signal act of severity,
the perpetrators of so horrid a fact Under this impression, he did
not hesitate a moment to order the Provost to proceed to the spot,
and, by the instant execution of the offenders, to put a stop to conduct, of which too many instances have occurred lately to leave His
Royal Highness any doubt of the necessity of an immediate and
vigorous interposition.

"The two men were executed this morning at the head of the
brigade "

(4.) SAME TO SAME[2]
(*Extract*)
"*12th August,* 1809.
"I have had my conference with the Attorney-General and
Ryder, on Martial Law They do not enable me to say much in

---

[1] 7 Castlereagh Desp, p 99   [2] Ib., p 103.

addition to my former letter. They seem fully impressed with the persuasion that the power of summary punishment, even to death, must reside in the Commanding Officer of an Army in the field, but in what precise mode, or under what particular circumstances to be exercised, they can give no opinion. They consider that the neces sity of the case can only be the rule, and that the power m' 'o regulated by the conscientious sense of the Commander, and, of course, upon his responsibility. They admit that this a painful duty, and of some hazard to an Officer to undertake, but they say, at the same time, that, to be effectual, it must be both *summary* and *arbitrary*, and that it is impossible, in this Constitution, that such a power should be entrusted, *a priori*, to any man. All they can say, with respect to the safety of having recourse to the exercise of such extraordinary means of repressing disorders is, that they have reason to believe that such powers have been in very general use in the field; and that they know of no instance in which the acts so done in the face of the Army, for the preservation of its discipline, have ever been subsequently questioned. The only practical suggestion they have enabled me to offer on your letter is, that the Mutiny Act allows three Officers to sit on detachment Court-martial, if more cannot be had."[1]

(CXIII.)

Chapter XVIII., *par* 49

CIRCULAR DESPATCH TO COLONIAL GOVERNORS, DATED 30TH JANUARY, 1867, ON THE SUBJECT OF MARTIAL LAW.

Presented to both Houses of Parliament by Command of Her Majesty, 24th June, 1867.

(CIRCULAR.)

" SIR,   " *Downing Street, January* 30, 1867.

"ALTHOUGH I do not know that there exists in the Colony under your government any law authorizing the proclamation of

---

[1] In the year 1806, three Mutiny Acts were passed (46 Geo III, cap 15, 48, and 66), and in the last of these its provisions were extended " to Gibraltar and His Majesty's other Dominions, or elsewhere beyond the Seas "

In the Mutiny Act of 1813 (53 Geo III, cap 17), its provisions were extended to " Spain and Portugal, and all other parts of Europe where His Majesty's Forces may be serving, and to all other Places," and the same words are found in the Mutiny Act of the present year, 1869

As to the necessity of having the power of summary punishment, see evidence of Lieutenant Blood, p 255, and of the late Duke of Wellington, p 326, before Commissioners on Military Punishment, 1836

Martial Law by the Governor, I think it advisable to communicate to you, for your information, and if necessary for your guidance, an extract of a Despatch addressed by me to the Governor of Antigua, in which I have stated the views of Her Majesty's Government on this subject.   "I have, &c.

(Signed)   "CARNARVON."

Extract of a Despatch from the Earl of Carnarvon to the Officer administering the Government of Antigua, dated Downing Street, 30th January, 1867, No. 40.

"An enactment which purports to invest the Executive Government with a permanent power of suspending the ordinary law of the Colony, of removing the known safeguards of life and property and of legalizing in advance such measures as may be deemed conducive to the establishment of order by the Military Officer charged with the suppression of disturbances, is, I need hardly say, entirely at variance with the spirit of English law. If its existence can in any case be justified, it can only be because there exists such a state of established insecurity as renders it necessary for the safety and confidence of the well disposed, that, in times of National Emergency, the Government should possess this extraordinary facility for the suppression of Armed Rebellion But whatever apprehensions or disturbances may exist in any of Her Majesty's Colonies, it is certain that no such chronic insecurity prevails in any of them, and in no Colony, therefore, should the power given by the present law to the Governor of Antigua be suffered to continue

"I think it, therefore, necessary to repeat the instructions given by my predecessor to Colonel Hill, and to request that you will cause to be submitted to the Legislature an Act repealing so much of the law as authorizes the proclamation of Martial Law.

"I have only to add, that in giving you these instructions, Her Majesty's Government must not be supposed to convey an absolute prohibition of all recourse to Martial Law under the stress of great emergencies, and in anticipation of an Act of Indemnity. The justification, however, of such a step must rest on the pressure of the moment, and the Governor cannot by any instructions be relieved from the obligation of deciding for himself, under that pressure, whether the responsibility of proclaiming Martial Law is or is not greater than that of refraining from doing so "

(CXIV.)

Chapter XIX., par. 2.

CONTROLLER OF ARMY ACCOUNTS.

THE office of Controller was originally created by Letters Patent in Queen Anne's reign. The original instructions, under the hand of Godolphin,[1] and dated 26th June, 1703, were in substance as follows —

" 1 The said Controllers are to take and keep an account of all the monies which shall be issued at the Exchequer, or otherwise to the respective Paymasters for the said forces, and to take care that they be duly charged therewith, for which purpose all orders for issuing monies to the said Paymasters are to be entered with the said Controllers.

" 2 The said Controllers are to take and keep an account of all arms, provisions, tents, and other things, which shall be delivered out of Her Majesty's stores to the use of any of the regiments, troops, or companies, and (in case where any deduction is to be made for them, or any of them) they are to take care that the value thereof be duly charged to the account of such regiment, troop, or company.

" 3. The General having approved and sealed the patterns for clothing, the Colonels are to contract for the said clothing, and then exhibit to the Controllers the said contracts, which are to specify the quantities, qualities, and prices of each particular The said Colonels, or their Agents, are likewise to exhibit to the Controllers the debt owing on the off-reckonings the 24th of February, 1703, from which day this rule shall commence. The Controllers are likewise to take care that the clothes for the Army in England be furnished according to the contracts and patterns (for which, as to the troops abroad, the certificate of the Captain-General, or of such person or persons as shall be appointed by him, is to suffice), and that the clothing do not exceed the off reckonings, and if any regiment is in debt, the debt is to be sunk annually as much as the service will bear, and the observations how the debt decreases are to be represented, from time to time by the Controllers, to the General and Lord High Treasurer, or Commissioners of the Treasury, for the time being The Controllers being satisfied that the contracts have been performed according to the patterns, shall certify the same respectively to the Paymasters, without which they are not to comply with any assignment for the payment thereof

---

[1] No. 49, Appendix to 10th Report of Commissioners on Public Accounts, 1783.

"4 They are, by themselves or their Agents, to inspect all the musters and muster-rolls to be taken of the said forces, or any of them, and the computations of pay made thereupon; and to settle methods in relation thereunto, as may best obviate all frauds and abuses concerning the musters, and on every muster to certify the respites and causes thereof to the General or Commander-in-Chief of our Forces and to our High Treasurer, or Commissioners of our Treasury, for the time being.

"5 They are to inspect the regimental accounts kept by the respective Paymasters of our Forces, and to take care that there be no error therein, either to the prejudice of us, or any of our officers or soldiers

"6. They are keep an exact account of all deductions from our Forces for poundage, and for one day's pay in the year, and of all other matters and things, which ought to compose the voluntary charge in the account of the said Paymaster, to be annually passed in the Exchequer, so that they may be able to attest the same before the said account be declared

"7. They are to take and keep an account of all payments which shall be made by the Paymasters to the Colonels, agents, clothiers, or others, and to examine the vouchers for the same, and also to inquire from time to time, whether the money received by the Colonels, or their agents, for subsistence and clearings, be justly and duly paid over to the Captains, for which the Colonels, or their agents, shall produce certificates or sufficient vouchers from the respective Captains to the Controllers once every year for the troops abroad

"8 They are likewise to inquire and satisfy themselves, from time time, concerning the performance of all matters and things required to be performed by the respective Paymasters and Muster-masters, or any other officers, by the late Act, intituled, 'An Act for punishing officers and soldiers who shall mutiny or desert Her Majesty's service in England or Ireland, and for punishing false musters, and for better payment of quarters in England,' and to take particular care that the muster rolls be immediately closed at the quarters or garrisons, and that the parchment roll be transmitted by the Deputy-Commissary directly to the Paymaster's office, to prevent any alteration after such closing

"9 They are, from time to time, to exhibit to us, and to our General and Commander-in-Chief of our Forces, and to our High Treasurer of England, or Commissioners of the Treasury, for the time being, all defaults which shall occur to them in relation to our said Forces, or any of them "

(CXV.)

Chapter XIX., *par*. 33

DUTIES OF THE CONTROLLERS OF ARMY ACCOUNTS, 1828

1. The Controllers, by their patent, are required to inquire into and report to the Lords of the Treasury all frauds, neglects and abuses which they shall observe in any branch of the Military expenditure, and to suggest such remedies as may occur to them

2. To examine and state for acquittance to the Treasury, the provision, store and implement accounts of the Commissariat Department on Foreign Stations, mentioned in the margin,[1] and of all persons entrusted with public stores, except those relating to the Ordnance.

3. To inspect the periodical cash accounts of all Commissaries on foreign stations as beforementioned, previous to their being forwarded to the Audit Office, in order to notice irregular and unauthorized expenditures, and prevent their recurrence or being established as precedents.

4 To report to the Lords of the Treasury on all papers referred to them, and which are generally connected with the following subjects —

> Abuses in the grant of any allowances, either pecuniary in kind, to the troops at all foreign stations.
>
> Claims for Military allowances
>
> Issues of provisions, forage and fuel, &c, to the troops at foreign stations
>
> Regulations for the mode of victualling the troops at different stations
>
> Contracts entered into by Commissaries for the supply of the troops, or other services.
>
> Grant of allowances for freight of specie.
>
> Expenditure relative to Military buildings abroad, &c

5 The Controllers have usually had referred to them, for examination and report, accounts for foreign subsidies, and where public money has been embezzled, or frauds committed, by persons connected with Military expenditure, the Controllers are often

---

[1] Bahamas, Bermuda, Cape of Good Hope, Canada, Gibraltar, Honduras, Jamaica, Ionian Islands, Mauritius, Malta, Nova Scotia and New Brunswick, Newfoundland, New South Wales, Van Diemen's Land, Portugal, and West Indies

required to investigate the transactions, which, on many occasions, have led to laborious inquiries, frequently rendering it necessary for them to exercise the powers entrusted to them of examining persons on oath, and requiring the production of books and papers of private individuals

6. The Controllers, *ex officio*, are Commissioners of Chelsea Hospital, in the view of controlling the expenditure of that establishment, and during the late war, one of them was detached on foreign service, to control and check the Military expenditure of the Army on the spot.

(CXVI.)

Chapter XX , par. 8.

Extract from the 12th Report of the "Commissioners on the Public Accounts of the Kingdom" upon the Ordnance Office.

Constitution of the Ordnance —"The Office of Ordnance is governed by a Master-General, and a Board under him, all appointed by separate Letters Patent

"The Board consists of five Principal Officers—the Lieutenant-General, the Surveyor-General, the Clerk of the Ordnance, the Storekeeper, and Clerk of the Deliveries, any three of whom form a Board.   The Master-General and Lieutenant-General are each, by virtue of his office, in two capacities, the one Military, the other Civil. In their Military capacity the Master General is Commander-in-Chief, and the Lieutenant-General second in command, over the Artillery and Engineers

Master-General —"In his *civil* capacity the Master-General is intrusted with the entire management of, and control over, the whole Ordnance Department, all Warrants from the King, Privy Council, or, in Sea Affairs, from the Board of Admiralty, and all letters from Secretaries of State conveying orders relative to the Ordnance, are directed not to the Board, but to the Master-General, and the Board carry them into execution under his authority, and in consequence of his direction, he can do alone any act which can otherwise, if he does not interpose, be done by the Board, he can order the issue of money; but that order *must* be executed

---

[1] 12th Report, 1784, p 152.

in the established mode . that is, by debenture. signed by *thee*
Board Officers.

Board.—"The Board are subordinate to the Master-General
they act under him, pursuant to his significations or directions   If
he does not interpose, they are competent of themselves to carry on
all the official business   they make contracts and agreements for
the purchase of Stores and performance of Services, and direct the
issue of Money and Stores, but if the Master-General chooses to
exert the power intrusted to him, he can control all their actions.

"During the absence of the Master-General, or the vacancy of
the office, the whole Executive Power devolves upon the Board   all
Warrants, Letters, and Orders are directed to the Lieutenant-
General and Principal Officers, they can order, sign, execute,
transact, and perform every service or matter incident to the Office
of the Ordnance.

"The other four Principal Officers have each of them, independent of his being a member of the Board, a separate and distinct
branch of business committed to his management

Surveyor-General.—"The Surveyor-General, or Master-Surveyor,
as he is styled in his Patent, is the second Board Officer, his
peculiar duty is, as his title imports, to survey all Stores received or
returned into the Storehouses of the Ordnance, he is interposed as
a check upon the quality and quantity of the Stores received into
the Magazines.

Clerk of Ordnance —"The Clerk of the Ordnance presides in that
Office, in which are recorded and preserved all the original authori-
ties, instruments, and vouchers, that warrant, describe, and authen-
ticate the proceedings of the Ordnance ; he is the Accountant of the
Ordnance, and as such keeps the Accounts of all the Cash and
Stores belonging to the whole department, he draws up the Annual
Estimate for Parliament, and the Monthly Estimate for the
Treasury

Storekeeper.—' The Storekeeper (or Principal Storekeeper, as he is
called, to distinguish him from other Storekeepers) has the custody
and keeps the Account, of the Ordnance and Stores received into,
and issued out of, the Tower.   The Storekeepers at the outports
and Garrisons keep the accounts of the like articles under their
charge   but their Accounts are subject to the examination both of
the Principal Storekeeper and of the Clerk of the Ordnance , and
for that purpose each Storekeeper, and every other person who
becomes accountable for Stores (except the Gunners of ships),
transmits an account of his receipts and issues, with the vouchers
and Orders, to the Board, who refer them to these two Officers for
their joint examination.

Clerk. of Deliveries.—" The Clerk of the Deliveries is the Officer who superintends and keeps the Account of the issues of the Stores and Ordnance, he prepares, pursuant to the direction of the Board, an instrument called a 'Proportion,' directed to a Storekeeper, authorising him to issue certain Stores, particularly specified, to a place therein named, this instrument, being signed by any three Board Officers, he delivers to the Storekeeper as his Warrant for the issue; he receives from him the articles specified, and delivers them to the person who is to receive or convey them, if the articles be arms or ammunition, he takes an indent, by which the person receiving engages to render an account of them."

(CXVII.)

Remain of Stores, &c, in 1599

Chapter XX, *par* 12

" The Remains of all Her Majesty's Ordnance, Powder, Shot, and other munition within the Tower of London, the Minories, and Woolwich Artillery Garden, and other places, as the same were taken by his Majesty's Auditors of the Prestes, the Officers of Her Majesty's said Ordnance, and other Commissioners, by virtue of the Warrant next following, the several days hereafter expressed, anno 1599.

" That is to saie, after our hearty commendations, forasmuch as Her Majesty's pleasure is to have a perfect and true Remain taken at this instant, of the whole quantity of Ordnance, Powder, Shot, Saltpetre, and all other several natures of principal Munition now remaining within the Tower of London, the Minories, and other places near adjoining thereunto, wherein any of Her Majesty's is kept and hath commanded us Her Highness's Commissioners for Ordnance causes[1] to appoint such her trusty servants and others whom we think most, to take the Remain and view thereof. We, therefore, according to Her Majesty's said direction, have made choice of you all, or any three of you at the least, whereof you John Comers, Her Majesty's Auditor, to be one to take the said Remain, and do heartily pray you and every of you for Her Majesty's better satisfaction, immediately and without delay to repair to the said Tower of London, and there to call unto you, for your better assistance, the Lieutenant of the Ordnance, the Surveyor, the Clerks of the Ordnance and Deliveries, and the Keeper of the Store, that you jointly together may proceed to the execution of Her Majesty's

---

[1] *Sic*

Service. And upon the end of the Remain taken within the said Tower, Minories, and other places adjoining thereurto, you do safely lock and make fast under your seals all and every the locks and doors wherein you shall from time to time find any provision, and the keys thereof to be delivered and kept by you, the Lieutenant of the Tower, until the other Remains at Woolwich, Rochester, and Her Majesty's ships be finished, and then the said keys to be by you redelivered unto the said keeper of the Store as before, whereof we pray you not to fail in anywise, and you do tender Her Majesty's pleasure in this behalf. And so we bid you very heartily farewell

"From the Court at Greenwich, this 4th of April, 1599.

> "NOTTINGHAM
> "THOS. BUCKHURST
> "J. FORTESCUE."

" *To Our very loving friends, viz., John Payton, Lieut. of the Tower, and Sir Robert German Knight, Thomas Fowler, Esq., Richard Carmarden, Esq., and John Coniers and Francis Gofton, Esqrs., Her Majesty's Auditors of the Prests.*"

[Then follows a Schedule of Stores, and a note on the several days on which the Remain was taken.]

(CXVIII.)

Chapter XX., par. 15.

ROYAL SIGN MANUAL ORDER[1] TO THE ORDNANCE BOARD FOR
THE ISSUE OF ARMS.

" GEORGE R

"WHEREAS it has been represented unto Us that the undermentioned Arms are wanting for the respective Regiments of Horse and Dragoons against each of their names set down to replace the like number broke and lost at the battle of Fontenoy, and at the skirmish at Clifton. Our Will and Pleasure therefore is that out of the Stores remaining within the Office of Our Ordnance under your charge, you forthwith cause the said Arms to be delivered to the respective Colonels or to their order, and you are to take the usual Indents for the same, and insert the charge thereof in your next

---

[1] Ordnance Regulations, p 309

Estimate to be laid before the Parliament   And for so doing this shall be as well to you as to all other Our Officers herein concerned a sufficient Warrant.

"Given at Our Court at Kensington, the 29th day of August, 1746, in the 20th year of Our reign,

"By His Majesty's command,

"HOLLES NEWCASTLE.

"*To our right trusty and right entirely beloved cousin and councillor, John Duke of Montagu, Master-General of Our Ordnance*

	Carbines.	Pairs of Pistols.	Bayonets.
Earl of Hartford's	84	80	.
General Honeywood's	29	21	.
Major-General Bland's .	33	16	43 "

(CXIX.)

Chapter XX , par 16

INDENTURE[1] FROM A COLONEL OF A REGIMENT FOR ARMS ISSUED TO HIM.

THIS Indenture, made between the Master-General and Principal Officers of His Majesty's Ordnance for and on behalf of His Majesty and A. B. witnesseth that the said A. B. doth acknowledge by these presents by virtue of the Board's order of [or other proper authority as the case may be] to have had and received the several sorts of good, well-fixed, and serviceable Arms and habiliments of war hereunder specified   For all which Arms and Habiliments of War the said A B doth hereby undertake to be accountable, and to maintain and continue the very same Arms in good repair, and to return and deliver the very same Arms into His Majesty's said Magazine, fixed and serviceable, when he shall be thereunto required (the hazard of the War only excepted).   And that in case any of the said Arms be lost, by negligence or by any other default, that then the said A B shall and will buy so many good Arms out of His Majesty's Magazine as shall re-supply the Arms so lost, at the rates usually paid by His Majesty for the like Arms.

---

[1] Ordnance Regulations, 1823, p 128, and Form L

(CXX.)

Chapter XX., par. 16

INDENTURE[1] FOR ARMAMENT AND STORES ISSUED TO A MASTER-GUNNER.

THIS Indenture, made the   day of   , 1823, between the Master-General of the Ordnance and the Principal Officers of the same, on behalf of the King's Most Excellent Majesty on the one part, and A. B., Master-Gunner of His Majesty's ship A, on the other part, Witnesseth that the said Master-Gunner hath received into his custody out of His Majesty's Stores within the Office of Ordnance, the Ordnance Stores and Habiliments of War undermentioned, well fixed and serviceable in every respect for fitting out the said A in His Majesty's Service. By order of the Board, dated the   . And the said Master-Gunner doth covenant with the said Officers, that at the end of the Service he shall or will deliver, or cause to be delivered back into His Majesty's Magazines every part or parcel of the said Stores which shall not be truly expended in the said Service, with a true and perfect account of the expenditure of the residue.   For   Service

---

(CXXI.)

Chapter XX., par. 17

NOTICE[2] FROM SECRETARY AT WAR TO BOARD OF ORDNANCE TO RECEIVE ARMS

" My LORD,   " *War Office, 9th September,* 1746

   " His Majesty having thought fit to order his Regiment of Horse commanded by His Grace the Duke of Kingston, to be disbanded at Nottingham on Monday next, the 15th inst., I have the honour to acquaint your Grace therewith, that you may please to order a proper Officer to repair to Nottingham, to collect and receive the Arms of the Non-Commissioned Officers and private men belonging to the said Regiment, and to give the necessary acquittance for the same.

                              " I am, &c.,

 " *His Grace the Duke of Montagu,*   " H FOX "
   ' *Master-General of the Ordnance.*"

---

[1] Ordnance Regulations, p 131, and Form S
[2] Ordnance Warrant Bk., p. 398

(CXXII.)

Chapter XX , par 43

WARRANT TO THE ORDNANCE, &c, FOR PRESERVING THE WORKS OF THE SEVERAL FORTS IN GREAT BRITAIN.

" GEORGE R

" WHEREAS our right, trusty and well-beloved Cousin and Councillor, GEORGE Viscount TOWNSHEND, Master General of Our Ordnance, hath represented unto Us, that great Damages are done to the Works at the several Forts and Castles, by grazing of Cattle on the Earth Works, and even letting them out for that Purpose by inclosing Our Ground near the Covered-Ways, and ploughing the same, and making Gardens in the Out-Works, &c   Also by destroying the Pallisadoes, Barriers, Guard-Houses, Barracks, &c.   To remedy which, We do hereby direct and command all Officers, and other Persons herein concerned, whether Governors, Lieutenant Governors, Majors or Adjutants of Our Places, or Officers commanding in Chief, for the time being, to give effectual Orders for preventing the same for the future , and that no Person whatsoever do presume to plough on our Ground or Covered-Ways, or in any of the Ditches or Out-works, or to permit any Beasts or Cattle to graze or feed on the same, or to plant or make any Gardens in the Bastions or Out-Works, or to make any Inclosures, or to erect any Sort of Building whatsoever, on or in any of the aforesaid Works or Lands thereunto belonging, without particular Leave in Writing, under the Hand and Seal of the Master-General of Our Ordnance, or Principal Officers of the same.   Nevertheless, WE think fit to permit cutting the Grass that may grow on the Side Works twice a year or oftener in the proper Seasons, provided they do not damage the said Works, and do use Ladders where they cannot reach it with the Scythes , and to prevent any further Damage to the Works, they are immediately to carry the Grass off the Works, and make it into Hay elsewhere.   It is Our further Will and Pleasure, that all Governors, Lieutenant-Governors, &c , or Officers Commanding in Chief in any of Our Garrisons, as also those belonging to Our Office of Ordnance, do duly represent when and wherein these Our Orders are not duly complied with, that then, upon Survey and Estimate made, upon Oath, of the Damages received, Defalcation, or Stoppages of so much Money as the said Estimates may amount to, shall be made out of the Pay of such Governors, &c , who ought to have prevented the same, by the Paymaster-General of Our Guards and Garrisons , who is hereby authorised to stop and pay the said Money to the Treasurer of Our Ordnance, or to such Person or Persons as shall be appointed by the Office of Ordnance to receive the same accordingly.

"Given at Our Court at St. James's, the first Day of September, 1778, in the Eighteenth Year of Our Reign.

"By His Majesty's Command,

"WEYMOUTH."

' *To our right, trusty and well-beloved Cousin and Councillor,* GEORGE *Viscount* TOWNSHEND, *Master-General of Our Ordnance, and to Our very loving Friends the Principal Officers of the same, and to the Paymaster of Our Guards and Garrisons, and to all Governors, Lieutenant Governors, &c. or Officers Commanding in Chief in any of Our Garrisons, or to any other Officers or Persons whom this does or may concern* "

(CXXIII.)

Chapter XX , par 52.

ORDER[1] FOR ESTABLISHING A CROWN MARK.

"THE King's Most Excellent Majestie, taking into his princely consideration the frequent abuses complained of by the Officers
A.D. 1627
of His Majestie's Armorie and Stores, as well in purloyning as in chopping and chaunging of Armes delivered out of his Stores for Land and Sea Service,

"And likewise being informed of an abuse no less frequent at musters and trainings in all the counties of these our Realms and Dominions, as well by borrowing Armes of the several Counties one from another, as also by borrowing Armes of the several Divisions in each County, one from another, by means whereof His Majestie's honour and service are much impaired, and the safety and defence of his Kingdom and people may be much endangered for want of necessary Armes and Munitions upon any sudden occurrence ·

"His Majestie therefore, for a timely remedy thereof, and for the preventing of the like in the future, hath, by the advice of his Privy

---

[1] 18 Rhym Fœd, p 978

Council, thought fit and appointed that all muskets, and other Armes, to be henceforth issued out of His Majestie's Stores for Land Service, shall be marked with the mark of C R, and for Sea Service with the mark of C R and an anchor.

"And His Majestie doth hereby strictly charge, prohibit and command that no person or persons whatsoever shall hereafter presume, attempt, or go about to sell or buy any of His Majestie's Armes or Munitions whatsoever, upon pain of incurring His Majestie's high displeasure, and the severest punishments that by the Laws and Statutes of this His Majestie's Realm of England, or by His Majestie's Prerogative Royal, can or may be inflicted upon the offenders for their contempt and disobedience in this behalf.

"And to the intent that the said abuse of borrowing Armes, either by several Counties, or by several Divisions in one and the same County, may likewise be prevented, His Majestie's express pleasure is, and he doth hereby straightly charge and command, that no person or persons whatsoever shall hereafter borrow any Armes or Munitions to be used or employed at any public musters. or any trainings in any County, or Division of County, of this His Majestie's Realm of England, or Dominion of Wales, but that every person and persons shall from time to time furnish him and themselves with such Armour, Weapons, and Munitions as is or shall be by the Lords-Lieutenant and Deputy-Lieutenants of each County respectively appointed and assessed

"And for the better effecting hereof, His Majesty doth hereby charge and command the said Lords-Lieutenant and Deputy-Lieutenants of each County respectively, to cause a separate distinct mark to be set and stamped upon all the Armes of each Company, whereby the same may be distinguished from the Armes of other Companies, and likewise to cause several distinct marks to be stampt upon the Armes of the several Divisions and Bands of each Company, whereby the Armes of one Division and Band may be known from another, that thereby all parts of these His Majestie's Realms and Dominions may be fitly and sufficiently stored with Armes and Munitions, both for offence and defence, as occasion shall require

"And His Majestie doth hereby charge and command as well all the Officers of His Majestie's Ordnance and Armoury for that which concerneth them, as all Lords-Lieutenant and Deputy-Lieutenants and all others to whom it shall or may appertain to take special care to see this His Majestie's pleasure put in due execution accordingly.

"Given at His Majestie's Court at Whitehall, this 9th day of March."

(CXXIV.)

Chapter XX, par 82.

THE SMALL ARMS FACTORY AT ENFIELD[1]

Enfield, 26th May, 1869.

A FACTORY was established at Lewisham in 1808, but was subsequently abandoned.

Between the years 1811 and 1816 another Factory was created at Enfield Lock, which became the nucleus of the present Royal Small Arms Factory at that station.

The primary object with which this Factory was established was the production of gun-barrels,—the water, the only motive power then existent, affording considerable facilities for the employment of such machinery as was used in their manufacture, but the close of the Continental War in 1815 had the effect of suspending the original intention For many years the operations at Enfield were on the most limited scale, and consisted chiefly in the repair of small arms generally, and the manufacture of cavalry swords, lances, &c.

On the introduction of percussion arms, a small number was made at this Factory, but not in their entirety, the rate of production commencing at about 1000 stand per annum, gradually increasing to 6000,—the greatest number ever produced in one year prior to 1857-8.

During the Session of 1854, a Parliamentary Committee was impannelled under the presidency of Sir William Molesworth, to enquire into the system under which small arms were obtained for the two Services

Of the various persons from whom evidence was taken many were gunmakers, and others machinists or engineers of eminence, amongst whom were Mr. Nasmyth, Mr. Whitworth, and Mr. Anderson, the chief engineer of the Royal Arsenal The last-named gentleman, in common with others, strongly advocated the establishment of a Government Factory for the manufacture of arms by machinery, pointing to the success which had attended the introduction of this system in the United States of America, and the illustration of its advantages as apparent in the Pistol Factory of Colonel Colt, which had been recently opened in this country. Field-Marshal Lord Raglan, then Master-General of the Ordnance, also expressed himself very strongly in favour of the project.

---

[1] I am indebted to the Superintendent, Colonel Dixon, R A , for this Note

Subsequently a Commission, consisting of Colonel Burn, R A , Captain Warlow, R.A., now Major Turberville, and Mr. Anderson, of the Royal Arsenal, visited the principal Government Factories in the United States where the fabrication of small arms was effected by machinery , and their report, together with the facts and opinions elicited by Sir W. Molesworth's Committee, resulted in the reorganization of the Enfield Establishment and its adaptation as a Factory for the manufacture of small arms by machinery on the interchangeable principle About this time also (February, 1855). Colonel Dixon, R A , the present Superintendent of the Royal Small Arms Factories, received his appointment, he being the first Military Officer entrusted with the entire control of this important section of the War Department The work of re-construction, commenced in the latter part of 1854, was completed by the end of the year 1857-8, at an outlay of 202,880*l*, including the value of such portions of the original Factory as were adapted to, or necessary for, the requirements of the new establishment.

The first machine-made rifles and bayonets were produced in 1857 8, the average rate of production being then about 850 per week, during the ordinary hours of labour.

This weekly production gradually increased, as the powers of the Factory were developed. until, in the later part of 1860-1, a maximum weekly production of 2100 rifles and bayonets was attained.

The productive capabilities of the Factory can be largely increased by an extension of the ordinary hours of labour, as in 1866 7, when, during a period scarcely exceeding six months, 100,177 muzzle-loading arms were converted to breech-loaders on the Snider principle, besides the fabrication, during that year, of 28,637 arms of various patterns.

The arms first and most largely manufactured were those known as Enfield Rifles, but, subsequently, arms of other patterns have been produced, including Short and Whitworth Rifles, the Richards breech loading Cavalry Carbine, and the Service patterns of Carbine both for the Cavalry and Artillery, with the implements (snap caps, nipple-wrenches, &c) adapted to each pattern. Smooth bore muskets, fusils, and cavalry carbines, for the native Troops in India, are also made.

The number of persons employed is in ratio with the production, both numerically and as regards variety of pattern

In 1860-1 the greatest number of arms (one pattern only) was manufactured, and the employés numbered 1838. In the succeeding year the total production was somewhat less, but three patterns were under construction, and the persons employed numbered 1860.

The amount voted in 1860-1 was 209,602*l*, and in 1861-2 270,149*l*

The Staff consists of one Superintendent, one Assistant-Superintendent, and one Chief Inspector of Small Arms, with a Manager, and the usual clerical officials.

(CXXV.)

Chapter XX , par. 87.

Claims of Inventors for Compensation.

"*War Office,* 23rd *February,* 1869.

"In consequence of the numerous claims for compensation for loss of time and for expenses incurred by private individuals in working out inventions of various kinds, as well as for rewards in consequence of such inventions, the Secretary of State considers it necessary to make known the following Regulations :—

"1st Persons who desire to submit any invention for consideration should do so by letter addressed to the Under-Secretary of State The letter should describe the invention, and state whether the person who offers it for consideration desires to make any claim to remuneration in connection with it. In the absence of such a statement it will be assumed that no such remuneration is expected.

"2. Expenses incurred before the submission of an invention will not be considered to give a claim for repayment. No liability on behalf of the public will be recognised on account of loss of time, or expenses incurred in connection with an invention after such submission, unless authority for such expenses has been previously given by letter signed by one of the Under-Secretaries of State, and the liability will be strictly confined to the limits of expenditure authorised in such letter.

"3 All claims for reward will be examined by a Council to be held at the War Office; and if any reward be recommended by the Council and approved by the Secretary of State, the sum will, with the concurrence of the Treasury, be included in the Estimates, together with the Report of the Council but it will not be regarded as due or be paid to the claimant until after the vote is passed by the House of Commons

"4 No claim for reward will be held to be established unless the invention has been adopted into the Service, or substantial benefit to the public has resulted from it   "Northbrook"

(CXXVI.)

Chapter XX., par 96

HISTORICAL NOTES ON THE ANCIENT AND PRESENT CONSTI-
TUTION OF THE ORDNANCE, HASTILY COLLECTED ON
READING MR BURKE'S BILL FOR SUPPRESSING THAT
BOARD.

IN all Wars before and after the Conquest of England, it was the
Custom to use various Sorts of Instruments, Engines, Machines,
Spears, Darts, Javelins, Bows and Arrows, Armour of Iron for
Horsemen, Footmen and Charioteers.

The Care and Provision of which, in general, was committed to
the Lieutenants of Counties —The Master Bowyer, Master Fletcher,
Master Carpenter, Master Smith, and other Mechanics had Patents
and Salaries from the Crown by Way of Retaining Fees, and were
famous for concealing their Craft. These People stiled themselves
Officers of Thaudinances The Monks appear in these ancient
Times to have been the Conductors of such Military Defences as
were then made use of in Earth or Masonry, and entrusted with
Money for paying the Expences.

Upon a Governor being appointed to a Garrison, Fort, or Castle,
a special Commission was issued under the Great Seal, appointing
Commissioners to take an Inventory or Remain of all the Imple
ments of War. The Governor then entered into Articles of Agreement with the State, covenanting that in Consideration of the
Armour, Ammunition, Victual, Provisions, Officers, Soldiers, Gunners
and Artificers, according to an Inventory annexed to the Indenture,
and in further Consideration of his being supplied with Money to
pay his Garrison, he covenanted to defend and keep the same for
His Highness and the State against all Traitors and Enemies whatsoever See two Trials in the reign of Richard II , quoted by
Seldon, in 'Privilege of Baronage of England,' fol 17, where John
Whiston and the Lord of Gomeniz were condemned to Death for
delivering up their Castles.

This Method continued to the End of the Reign of Henry the
Seventh, and great Part of Henry the Eighth , during which
Time few or no Accompts were kept or rendered of Money or
Ammunition

The Gunners in those Times frequently stiled themselves
Masters of the Ordnance

By the Journal of the Siege of Boulogne, at which King Henry was present, it appears that Sir Christopher Morrice served as Master of the Ordnance, and was hurt by a Hand Gun, having behaved very valiantly before, and killed all the Master-Gunners of Boulogne. (See 'Rymer's Fœdera,' vol. xv. fol. 55.)

In the Reign of Henry the Eighth, when the Use of Great Ordnance became General all over Europe, England was famous for all Sorts of Workmen in the Art of Manufacturing Military Weapons, from the Tower of London, the Minories, and adjacent Places for a Mile round was occupied as Founderies, Salt Petre Houses, Charcoal Houses, Sulphur Houses, and Shops for manufacturing all Manner of Warlike Implements, Fire Arrows, Fire Darts, Smoak Balls, Hand Guns, Harquebuses, which occasioned the employing a great Number of Mechanics in those abstruse branches, who continued the Custom of obtaining Patents with Salaries, by which they ingrossed the whole Trade to themselves They took their abode chiefly in and near the Tower, claimed great Merit in pretending to much Art and Mystery in all their Operations.

The same continued through the Reign of Queen Elizabeth, during which Time came into Use a very great Variety of Artillery and Warlike Machines and Engines of all Kinds. The Spanish Invasion gave Opportunities for Frauds and Impositions, the Officers and others taking Advantage of the Times to enrich themselves at the Expence of the State, insomuch that it became a Matter of Enquiry, and a solemn Commission issued, under which a minute Investigation took Place into the Whole of the Office of Ordnance, and an entire Reformation followed in the Year 1598, when the Outline of the Establishment of the Ordnance was first formed nearly upon the Plan of the Present Times, with an Officer at the Head to superintend the Whole by Land and Sea, under the Title of Great Master of the Ordnance

N B —Under this Commission an exact Inventory was made of all the Ordnance and Stores at every Place under the Charge of the Officers of the Ordnance, and on Board each Ship of the Navy, whether in Harbour or at Sea, and each Article valued

[Here it may not be amiss to give a description of that Office, as exercised in Europe, 1598, particularly in Spain, from which the idea of Establishment then took its first rise]

Upon the Report of the great Officers of State under the Commission of Queen Elizabeth the present Office of Ordnance was formed, a Master-General appointed to superintend the Whole by Sea and Land, with the Principal Officers nearly as at present, the

---

¹ 15 Rym Fœd, p 55.

Treasurer excepted, the Lieutenant-General executing that Office, and receiving 6d per pound out of all Monies paid

The Practice of the former Times was exploded as inconvenient and extravagant. The Ordnance Business was then committed, with great Powers, to the Master-General and Officers; such as pressing Ships, Hoys, Waggons, and Horses, and taking Timber by their Purveyors.

In the Reign of King James the First, another Commission of Enquiry took Place, little or no Alteration followed upon this except the removal of some Officers, and Punishment of others, for Corruption.

In Charles the First's[1] Reign Viscount Valentia, the Master-General of the Ordnance was joined in a Commission as Council to the Duke of Buckingham, when he commanded in chief the Fleet The Gunmakers' Company are, by the Charter granted them in the above Reign, conjoined to render an Account of all Small Arms made by them, and to whom sold, whenever the Master of the Ordnance calls for the same.

In the Civil War, Cromwell's Parliament voted[2] that the Keys of the Ordnance Storehouses be delivered to the Committee for Defence of the Kingdom The same Parliament, in 1643, appointed Sir David Walter Lieutenant-General

In 1648 the Parliament appointed Major-General Harrison, Lieutenant-General of the Ordnance. In 1650 they voted the Ordnance Stores and Storehouses to be disposed of as the Council of State should direct. In 1651, January 14, they voted the Naval Ordnance Stores to be provided by the Committee of the Navy The same Parliament, upon considering that the Poundage, during General Harrison being Lieutenant of the Ordnance, amounted to 3065l. upon the sum of 122,620l. 8s. 6d by Vote, dated 23 February, 1652, annihilated the Office of Lieutenant-General

Upon the Restoration, many Alterations took place from Time to Time Charles the Second, by Patent, gave the present Salaries to the Master-General, Lieutenant-General, and other Officers, and appointed a Treasurer, it being judged improper for the Lieutenant-General, as a Military Officer, to be Treasurer, and receive Poundage out of the large Sums that would then pass his Hands[3] Before this Time the Master-General and Principal Officers had the Power of selling the Places under them, and claimed the old Guns and Stores as their Perquisites

[1] See his Instructions, 18 Rym Fœd, p 182
[2] Com Journ., 20th August, 1642
[3] See General Instructions King Charles II, 1664

1677, *April* 26.—The King's Order in Council recites that the Governors of the Garrisons and Forts, as well as other Commissioners for Fortifications and Repairs, having received various Sums of Money, and also cut down the King's Timber, by Orders from the Exchequer, under Pretence of Repairs for Fortifications, without rendering any Account of either Money or Materials; the Council therefore committed the Care of all Fortifications and Repairs to the Ordnance, who are to present Estimates for the King's Approbation, and the Ordnance are empowered to call the Governors, Commissioners, and others to account for what they have done

27th May—King's Warrant puts the general Superintendence and Direction of all the Fortifications under the care of the Ordnance, and requires the Commissioners to render an Account to that Office.

1682—King Charles the Second, by Warrant (reciting that Abuses had crept into the Garrison), puts all the Master-Gunners and Gunners in Great Britain under the authority of the Master-General, authorising him to examine them, and turn out such as are unfit for Service, notwithstanding they might have been appointed by Patent from the Exchequer.

1683—General Regulations and Instructions were formed and established for the good Government of the Ordnance under the Master-General and Five Principal Officers, viz, Lieutenant-General, Surveyor-General, Clerk of the Ordnance, Storekeeper, Clerk of the Deliveries, which continue now in Force

James the Second, by Warrants, augments the Power of the Surveyor to sign the Books and Payments of Money while the Lieutenant-General is abroad.

N.B.—There was only one Foreign Garrison, viz, Tangier.

King William and Queen Anne—During the Wars of their Reigns, the Dutch found all the Artillery and Artillerymen for Sieges, by which Reason the Land Service Ordnance was not so extensive.

Upon the Union with Scotland, all the Garrisons, Forts, and Castles in Scotland, became an additional Charge upon the Ordnance. Upon the Peace of Utrecht, Gibraltar, Minorca, Annapolis, Placentia, became a further additional Charge upon the Ordnance.

These Garrisons requiring Engineers, Artillery Officers, and other Military Officers, the Ordnance began to form a Military Corps, by suffering all useless Places to sink, and by applying the Money arising from such Places as they became vacant (with His

Majesty's Approbation), towards two Companies of Artillery and a Corps of Engineers

The War of 1739 and 1743, together with the Rebellion, caused these two Companies to be augmented to ten Companies; and the War of 1756 caused the further augmentation of two Battalions, and the present War and Rebellion have caused more Augmentations of two Battalions, making in all five Battalions.

(CXXVII.)

Chapter XXI , par 3.

APPOINTMENT [1] OF THE SECRETARY AT WAR

" VICTORIA R.

"VICTORIA by the Grace of God, of the United Kingdom of Great Britain and Ireland Queen, Defender of the Faith, to Our right trusty and well-beloved Councellor, Fox Baron PANMURE, Knight of the most ancient and most noble Order of the Thistle, greeting We being well satisfied with your loyalty, integrity, and ability, do hereby constitute and appoint you Secretary at War to all Our Forces raised, or to be raised in Our United Kingdom of Great Britain and Ireland · You are therefore by virtue of this Our Commission to receive the said place into your charge, and you are diligently to intend the execution thereof, and faithfully and duly to execute and perform all things incident and belonging thereto. and you are to observe and follow such orders and directions as you shall from time to time receive from Us, or the General of Our Forces for the time being, according to the discipline of War, in pursuance of the trust reposed in you, and your duty to Us.

"Given at Our Court at Windsor, the 8th day of Februrary, 1855, in the 18th year of our Reign.

" By Her Majesty's Command.

"G GREY."

---

[1] 'Organization Report, 1860,' p 541.

(CXXVIII.)

Chapter XXI , par. 4.

MEMORANDUM [1] OF THE PRINCIPAL DUTIES OF THE SECRETARY AT WAR.

"The Secretary at War is responsible for the preparation of the Estimates of the ordinary services of the Army, and for the due application of the greatest part of the sums granted by Parliament on account of them, he directs the issues, regulates the expenditure, and settles the accounts; the Secretary at War receives and communicates to the Army the King's pleasure on financial matters, and exercises a direct control over all arrangements by which any charge is created, in addition to or different from those which have had the sanction of Parliament, the Secretary at War takes the King's pleasure for granting half-pay or pensions to Officers, their widows and children, or for depriving them of the same, he is the channel for publishing commissions in the Gazette, and recording military promotions; he prepares and introduces into Parliament Bills relating to the Army, and directs all law proceedings connected with the military service, he superintends, under the enactments of the Mutiny Act, all matters relating to the apprehension and escort of deserters, his authority is required for all movements of troops, he is the proper channel of reference on all questions between the civil and military part of the community, and is the constitutional check interposed for regulating their intercourse, and he is especially charged with the protection of the civil subject from all improper interference on the part of the military. Out of these duties arises a great variety of miscellaneous correspondence upon subjects connected with the discipline as well as the finance of the Army, and often embracing topics of great importance, which the Secretary at War is called upon to explain and discuss in the House of Commons, the principal part of the business connected with the examination and settlement of the public accounts rendered to the War Office is placed under the superintendence of the chief examiner of accounts, the remainder of the business of the office, after it has been registered, is disposed of under the superintendence of the first clerk. The Deputy Secretary at War is responsible for conducting, under the orders or authority of the Secretary at War, the whole business of the office, and when he is present it is his

---

[1] 'Army and Navy Promotion, 1833,' p 231.

duty to prepare the papers to be brought before the Secretary at War, and all the directions of the Secretary at War pass through his hands, when the deputy is absent, the Secretary at War communicates directly with the chief examiner of accounts, and with the first clerk, on the business of their respective departments."

(CXXIX.)

Chapter XXI, par. 4.

MEMORANDUM BY THE LATE LORD PALMERSTON, UPON THE OFFICE OF SECRETARY AT WAR WITH REFERENCE TO THE GENERAL COMMANDING-IN-CHIEF.

(Extract)

" *War Office,* 16 *August,* 1811

"SIR D. DUNDAS states that for a considerable time past the Secretary at War has assumed powers, and exercised an authority which is not of right belong to his office, derogatory to the dignity of the Commander-in-Chief, and subversive of the discipline of the Army. The immediate ground and foundation of this charge are three circumstances which have occurred since the appointment of Lord Palmerston as Secretary at War, and it might, therefore, perhaps appear sufficient for Lord Palmerston to give that explanation of these three cases, which he trusts would exculpate him from any blame on those points but as Sir D Dundas's Memorandum contains some general positions respecting the relations of the Commander-in-Chief and Secretary at War, it will be necessary, in the first instance, to give a short summary of the history and progress of the office of the Secretary at War, and a view of the nature and extent of the duties which that officer has heretofore discharged

"Sir D. Dundas seems to imagine that the Secretary at War[1] is, like the Adjutant and Quartermaster-General, subordinate to, and dependent upon, the Commander-in-Chief, and he founds this idea chiefly upon the wording of the Commission of the Secretary at War, which directs him 'to observe and follow such orders and instructions as you shall receive from Us or the General of Our forces according to the discipline of war.' It is, however, conceived

---

[1] See 6 & 7 Wm. & Mary, c 8 sec 5, which refers to "the Secretary of the Commander-in Chief of the Army"

that there will be no difficulty in proving, that, in the first place, 'the General of Our forces' does not mean a Commander-in-Chief, but a Captain-General; and that in point of practice, in matters of finance and as a civil servant of the Crown, the Secretary of War never has been in the habit of receiving orders and commands from any person but the King himself.

"Lord Palmerston has, with this object, examined with great care the records of the War Office from the earliest times,[1] particularly directing his attention to those periods when there existed Captains-General, or Commanders-in-Chief. the substance of the information which he has collected will be stated in this Memorandum; but he has added, as an appendix, more particular notes taken from the perusal of upwards of 50 folio volumes of records of the office.

" Although much stress cannot be laid upon precedents previous to the Revolution in 1688, yet it appears that, even as early as the reign of Charles II, the civil and financial business of the Army was understood to be distinguished from that which was purely military, and we find accordingly that warrants and orders connected with the former were countersigned and issued by one of the Secretaries of State. There are in the War Office numerous documents of this sort, signed by the King himself, and countersigned by Arlington, Clifford, Coventry, Williamson, and Sunderland, one of the most remarkable of which is a Warrant[2] ordering that ' no military establishment, or alterations thereof, shall be presented for Our signature without having been previously approved by Our Lord High Treasurer, and one of Our Secretaries of State, to whom We have referred the care and consideration thereof,' and this Warrant, which makes no mention either of the Captain-General or Commander-in-Chief, has been annually renewed down to the present time.

" The first Secretary at War, or, as he was at that time[3] indiscriminately called, Secretary to the Forces, was Mr. Locke, who is supposed to have been detached from the office of Secretary of State with a view of relieving that officer from a part of his labours. Mr. Locke's commission cannot be found, but it seems that he did not at first countersign the King's Warrants, which still for some time bore the signature of the Secretary of State.

" But by a Warrant addressed to the Duke of Monmouth, who was Commander-in-Chief at the time, the King directed that ' Whereas We continue to issue from Ourself some kinds of Warrants and Military Orders which did belong to the office of Our late

---

[1] 21 Jan., 1669　　[2] June, 1666　　[3] 27 Sept., 1576

General, and which he was wont to dispatch and sign, We being desirous to distinguish such Warrants and Orders from other affairs of Our Crown, passing Our Signet and Sign Manual, have thought fit, and it is Our will and pleasure, that all such kinds of Warrants and Orders as formerly issued from George Duke of Albemarle, Our late General deceased (in regard of that office, and which we continue to issue from Ourself), shall pass Our Sign Manual only, and shall be countersigned by the Secretary to Our forces, as by Our command '

"And accordingly, from that period downwards, there is no instance of any Warrant or Order, signed by the King, being countersigned by any military officer, but always by the Secretary at War, a Secretary of State, or the Lords of the Treasury.

"In 1679, the Duke of Monmouth, then Commander-in-Chief, was, by a Warrant addressed to the Attorney-General, appointed Captain General, with powers of a very ample and extraordinary nature, which have never been granted since   He was authorized to arm, muster, apportion, quarter, and pay the Army, to disperse and pardon rebels, and all officers, soldiers, and persons whatsoever were required to be obedient and assisting to him.

"On the 18th August, 1683, and, as it should seem, during the continuance of this commission, Mr Blathwayte was appointed to succeed Mr. Locke as Secretary at War   The entry of Mr. Blathwayte's commission has been found, and it is couched very nearly in the same words as that of the present Secretary at War, the only material difference being the statement in the beginning of Mr. Blathwayte's of the resignation of his predecessor, Mr. Locke. Mr. Blathwayte, therefore, as far as the wording of his commission went, was equally bound to obey the commands of the Captain-General.

"It appears, however, that Mr. Blathwayte communicated and transacted his business with the King before and after the Revolution, in the same manner as the Secretaries of State.   He took and signified the pleasure of James II upon all sorts of military subjects, and, as an instance of the manner in which he conceived himself attached to the person of the King, he deemed it necessary to ask specially his permission to go for a month into the country,[1] and in November, 1688, he attended him to Salisbury with his Army.

"Mr. Blathwayte seems indeed to have regulated almost all the affairs of the Army, as well with regard to discipline as finance, and down to the conclusion of the reign of James II. he issued orders

---

[1] 20 Jan, 1687

of almost every description, for paying, mustering, quartering, marching, raising, and disbanding troops, and also upon various points of discipline, such as the attendance duty, and comparative rank of officers and regiments

'Upon the accession of William III., Mr. Blathwayte was continued in office,[1] and transacted business with him in the same manner as with James II. In the year 1690, the Earl of Marlborough was made Commander-in-Chief, and was afterwards succeeded by the Dukes of Leinster and Schonberg, the latter of whom continued in office till the beginning of 1696. In 1690 we find the Treasury referring to Mr. Blathwayte for his opinion, and report all claims and applications made to them connected with military finance.

"In 1692, Mr. Blathwayte accompanied the King when he took the command of his Army in Flanders, and acted during that and the subsequent campaigns as Military Secretary to the King He issued in his name and by his command orders and regulations of every description to the Army, signed proclamations, safeguards and passes to persons, and protections to towns and villages, and gave orders even to the naval force forming part of the armament

"During the absence of Mr Blathwayte upon the Continent,[2] Mr. George Clarke, the Judge-Advocate-General, was appointed with a temporary commission and inferior powers to act as Secretary at War at home, and it is remarkable that by his commission he is required 'to follow such orders and instructions as you may receive from Us, the General of Our forces, or the Commander-in-Chief of Our said forces.' The insertion of these last words in this temporary commission marks in the strongest possible manner that the General mentioned in Mr Blathwayte's commission was not a Commander-in-Chief, and that the permanent Secretary at War was not liable to the authority of such an officer.

"Mr. Clarke, however, seems to have exercised very nearly the same powers, and to have used them in the same manner as Mr Blathwayte, and his commission does not appear to have rendered him in practice more dependent upon, and subordinate to, the Commander-in-Chief than Mr. Blathwayte himself had been to the Captain-General. Accordingly we find that Mr Clarke constantly signified the pleasure of the Queen Regent, and afterwards of the Lords Justices, and in some cases even that of the King, upon communication with him during his absence

---

[1] So little is the change of dynasty noticeable on the War Office books, that in one instance a pencil note by some official is the *only* indication that James II had lost and William III gained the Throne.	[2] 7 March, 1692

"The most remarkable instances of this sort are those in which he signed a Proclamation for pardoning deserters, granted leave of absence to officers, issued a Circular to the Army, by the King's command, about levy money, signed orders for apprehending deserters and enlisting debtors, and, what is very remarkable, an order from the Lords Justices to the Duke of Schonberg, the Commander-in-Chief, directing him to reprimand certain officers for neglecting to fill up their regiments, and to have them properly clothed and armed

"Mr. Clarke's Commission was only valid during the absence of the King, and when William used to return to England in the winter months, Mr. Blathwayte came with him and resumed the functions of his office, being again succeeded by Mr. Clarke whenever the King took the field in the summer. During these periods of temporary resumption, Mr Blathwayte continued to act nearly in the same manner as he had before done, and issued all kinds of orders to the Army. He called for states and returns of effectives, granted leaves of absence, and ordered officers to repair to their posts, pardoned deserters, disposed of prisoners of war, ordered colonels to account with their regiments, directed embarkations, and the raising and disbanding of regiments

"In 1695 an expedition was sent to the Straits of Gibraltar, and Mr Blathwayte issued its orders and instructions upon embarkation, the most remarkable points of these instructions are that the land officers were to command their men on shipboard, as well as on shore, that the Commanding Officer was empowered to hold Courte-martial, and that the Spaniards, with whom the expedition was destined to co-operate, were to have precedency in their own dominions.

'At the end of this year Mr Blathwayte issued, by order of the King, a general code of regulations for the dress and arming of the foot, and regulated in many instances the succession and promotion of officers

"In 1702, Mr. Blathwayte being still Secretary at War, the Duke of Marlborough was appointed Captain General, and continued to hold that commission till the end of the year 1711, when he was succeeded by the Duke of Ormond. This, therefore, is a period most particularly in point for the purposes of the present enquiry, as there existed the General, who is mentioned in the commission of the Secretary at War. But Mr. Blathwayte, from this period till his resignation in 1704, appears to have acted in the same independent manner as before, and to have constantly communicated with and signified the pleasure of the Queen. He gave numerous orders by the Queen's command for the embarkation of troops and horses for Portugal: for the disposal of recruits, for making detachments from some regiments, and for completing others for service; and among other things issued a circular to the Army directing patterns of the clothing of each regiment to be sent to General Churchill to be inspected.

"In April, 1704, Mr St. John was appointed Secretary at War, and one of his first acts was to send to the Transport Board a list which he had received from his predecessor of the forces to be transported to Holland, with orders from the Queen that they should be immediately embarked, and conveyed to their destination. During the four years he continued in office, he seems to have acted very much in the same manner as his predecessors, laying the matters of his office before the Queen, receiving her pleasure upon them, and communicating it to persons concerned He gave orders, by the Queen's command, relative to marching, quartering, mustering, pardoning, recruiting, embarking, and the hiring of transports; directed officers to join their corps, appointed escorts for treasure; ordered the Invalids to do duty at Kensington, in the absence of the Guards, superseded officers for absence without leave, called upon the Governor of Guernsey to explain his conduct in discharging, without authority, some prisoners of war, and signified to him the Queen's pleasure upon his explanation, transmitted to Mr. Secretary Hedges a list of the Staff for Lord Peterborough's expedition, as settled by the Committee of Lords; ordered the Commanding Officer at Lichfield to prohibit mass, and to confine the French prisoners to the distance of one mile from the town; called for a return of effectives of the several regiments under the immediate command of the Duke of Marlborough, Captain-General, as they stood before and after the battle of Blenheim, and for returns for all recruiting parties in England, corresponded with Mr. Secretary Hedges on proposals for raising regiments and relieving troops on foreign stations, signified the Queen's pleasure to the Ordnance for the delivery of stores; and countersigned a Warrant by the Queen, ordering all commissions to be entered in the office of the Secretary at War, and another strictly prohibiting their sale.

" The Duke of Ormond, who succeeded the Duke of Marlborough as Captain General, held that situation till December 1719, and was also Commander-in-Chief. Mr. William Pulteney was made Secretary at War in 1714, and we find we find that all matters of finance and claims of officers were referred to him by the Treasury and the King, and he reported, among other things, on various claims for half-pay and augmentations of allowances; on applications of officers to be restored after supercession, on a complaint of the inhabitants of Dunkirk of damage done to their town, and of the non-payment of supplies afforded by them; and upon a proposal for new regulating the general rate of subsistence for the Army.

"Mr. Craggs, who succeeded in 1717, seems to have had the same exclusive control over the finance of the Army, and to him all applications touching that subject, made either to the King or the Treasury, were constantly referred, he reported upon all sorts of claims for pay, allowances, clothing, &c; and in 1718 he summoned a Board of General Officers, and signified to them the Queen's pleasure that they should consider and report upon the state of military affairs in the island of Minorca. Mr. Pringle and Mr. Ireby, who succeeded to the office in 1718 and 1719, seem to have followed in all respects the practice of their predecessors

"From 1720 to 1744 it does not appear from the records of the War Office that there was any Captain-General or Commander-in-Chief, and during that period the whole management and government of the Army, both at home and abroad, seem to have devolved upon the Secretary at War

"In 1744, Lord Stair was appointed Commander-in-Chief, with very ample and extensive powers, the Warrant of his appointment being countersigned by Sir William Yonge, then Secretary at War. Lord Stair's commission continued in force till June, 1746; and in the mean time, in 1745, the King appointed another Commander-in-Chief, Marshal Wade, and a Captain-General, the Duke of Cumberland. The first ceased to hold his commission in December, 1745, but the latter continued Captain-General till October, 1757. There were thus at one time a Captain-General and two Commanders-in-Chief.

"This seems to be another period particularly deserving of attention, and the precedents of which bear strongly upon the point at issue between Sir D Dundas and Lord Palmerston, inasmuch as they prove that a Commander-in-Chief is an Officer not only inferior to, but co-existent with, a Captain-General, and the transactions which took place at that time show, that, in matters of finance at least, and as a civil servant of the Crown, the Secretary at War is independent even of the Captain-General.

"The Treasury appear to have referred to the Secretary at War at this time as much as before, all military financial matters, sometimes to him singly, and at others to him jointly with the Paymaster-General, or the Comptrollers of Army Accounts, but never to have thought that the Captain-General was in any degree entitled to interfere in such matters. Some very striking instances of this occurred at that time.

"In 1746, Lord Henry Beauclerk and General Huske memorialized the Duke of Cumberland, Captain-General, for compensation for accoutrements lost by their regiments at the battle of Fontenoy, praying that His Royal Highness would be pleased to move the King to grant the same   The Duke, however, transmitted these memorials to the Treasury, and that Board, instead of granting immediately the compensation asked for, referred the memorials to the Secretary at War, desiring him to consider the same, and report to them a state of the matter therein set forth, with his opinion what was fit to be done therein

"In the same year the Army in the North was in want of clothing, but the Captain-General, instead of giving orders himself to have a supply provided, stated the fact to the Secretary at War, and he signified to the Agents of the several regiments the King's pleasure that the clothing should immediately be supplied.

"In 1753 an estimate of the expense of making certain roads and bridges in the Highlands was laid before the Treasury; but though the Engineer told them that he had submitted his plan and estimate to the Captain General, who had given it his approbation, the Treasury did not choose to act upon it till they had referred it to the Secretary at War for his report.

"These three cases clearly prove that, according to the opinion and practice of Government at that time, the Secretary at War was the responsible adviser of the King on matters connected with the finance of the Army and military expenditures

"Sir William Yonge, who was appointed in 1735, and continued in office till 1746, exercised the same sort of powers as were vested in his predecessors.   He issued orders for marching, drafting, recruiting, completing, raising, augmenting, and disbanding regiments; discharged men, ordered officers to join their corps, and recruits to be forwarded to their regiments in Flanders, regulated the pay and allowances and forage of General and Staff Officers serving in Flanders, issued a general order, fixing the bounty to be given to recruits for the Guards; countersigned warrants of appointment to commands; signed a warrant empowering General St Clan to order money for his hospitals, and sent him instructions for their management, others relative to stoppages from soldiers, assignments of off reckonings, regulations for the full-pay and half-pay of corps and officers, and one in particular regulating the honours to be paid by His Majesty's Forces to the Master-General of the Ordnance He issued circular letters to the Army, calling for returns of effectives upon honour, he informed certain Colonels that His Majesty was not well pleased that so little progress had been made in recruiting their regiments, notwithstanding former orders, and desired that any officers who might have been negligent might be reported to him, that he might lay the matter before the King, he sent instructions to certain colonels that they might give them out in orders to their regiment, gave leave of absence to officers, signified the King's pleasure that an officer should be pardoned, but dismissed the service, and called for returns periodically of the progress made in recruiting, and in May, 1746, he signified to the Duke, the King's pleasure that certain regiments were to be reduced, in order that the Duke might send officers to re enlist such of the men as might choose to enter again into the service.

" Mr. Henry Fox succeeded Sir William Yonge in May, 1746, with undiminished powers and authority, and continued in office nine years, during the whole of which time, the Duke of Cumberland remaining Captain-General, the practice of the War Office seems to have been uniform and unchanged   All the matters relating to the financial and civil affairs of the Army, and many *more apparently connected with its discipline, being conducted by* the Secretary at War under the immediate orders of the King.

" Lord Barrington was appointed Secretary at War in 1755, and transacted the business of his office in the same manner as his predecessors ; was in every respect entirely independent of the Captain-General, and had a separate and complete control over every part of the Army.   In 1757, the Duke of Cumberland ceasing to be Captain General, Lord Ligonier was appointed Commander-in-Chief, and he continued so till the end of the year 1763, beyond which time he cannot be traced in the books of the War Office

" About this time a transaction took place which strongly illustrates the independent and authoritative manner in which, during the existence of a Commander-in-Chief, the Secretary at War was accustomed to act in matters connected with military finance

" In the summer of 1759, some great irregularities having prevailed respecting the delivery of forage to the troops encamped, the Secretary at War, by the King's command, summoned a board of General Officers to enquire into the circumstances, and he laid their report before the King   The result was that double charges to a great amount were discovered, and in June, 1760, Lord Barrington signified the King's pleasure upon the subject

" He informed certain Colonels ' that the King hoped that the circumstance had arisen from inadvertance in the officers, but as inadvertence in matters of duty is itself highly culpable, that it was His Majesty's pleasure that they should severely reprimand all the officers of their regiment who had been in any way concerned in the transaction, and caution them in the strongest manner against a negligence and inattention, which might subject them, as in the present instance to the severest censures of military law, and which would not a second time be passed over with the same lenity by His Majesty.' He added also that the money overcharged for forage was to be paid back to the contractor.

"He wrote at the same time letters to other Colonels, informing them of what had been done, and adding: 'though your regiment and many others were not in any way concerned in this transaction, His Majesty hath thought fit to order that the like caution should be given them, and accordingly I am to signify to you His Majesty's pleasure that you do take this opportunity of recommending to all your officers the strictest fidelity and exactness in their returns of kinds, and of reminding them that it is of the highest importance to His Majesty's Service that he should be able to depend as securely upon the care and fidelity, as upon the honour of his officers.'

"Many similar instances occurred in which the Secretary of War was the channel through which the King's pleasure was signified to the Army, and he seems to have been the regular and usual organ for such communications on all subjects in any way connected with finance or law. The Secretary at War, indeed, appears to have stood and acted formerly very much in the situation of the Secretary of State, and to have transacted some kinds of business which, since the finance of the Army has increased to its present extent, have been transferred to the Secretary of State for the War Department, and accordingly we find that everything relative to the exchange of prisoners passed through him; and in 1759 he conducted a long negociation upon that subject with the Court of France, and at all times corresponded with all the Governors and Commanders-in-Chief on foreign stations

"A very complete chain of documents appears in the books of the year 1758, showing the sort of business transacted at that time by the Secretary at War, during the existence of a Commander-in-Chief. Lieut.-General Bligh was selected to go on service in command of a body of cavalry. Lord Barrington first wrote to him, informing him, by the command of the King, that he was appointed to that service. He then wrote to the Treasury, to tell them that five regiments of cavalry were to go on foreign service, that their Lordships might give orders for a supply of bread and forage. He next sent orders to each regiment to hold themselves in readiness to embark. He then wrote to the Paymaster-General, signifying to him the King's pleasure, that he should issue subsistence to the men, and 12 months' off-reckonings to the Colonels; and, lastly, a letter to the Apothecary-General, desiring him to send immediately a supply of medicines for the expedition. Thus carrying through, by the immediate orders of the King, every detail connected with the financial arrangements of the expedition

"Lord Barrington, too, continued to issue many orders apparently much more connected with discipline than finance He communicated to corps distinctive appellations granted them by the King , he signified the King's pleasure upon points of rank and precedency, when disputes arose between officers , repremanded officers for improper conduct, granted or refused leave of absence to those whose regiments were abroad (the Commander-in-Chief at home having formerly no authority out of the kingdom), called for returns of effectives whenever he wanted them , and regulated, in many cases, the promotion of officers.

"In January, 1760, Lord Barrington wrote to Mr. Adair, the agent, expressing his surprise that the sale of an adjutancy should have been transacted without his having been consulted, ordered the arrangement to be stopped if the money had not been paid and if it had, the bargain to be annulled, and the money paid back again; and in another letter, a few days afterwards, he said it was the King's positive command that no commission of Staff Officers should for the future be sold.

"In 1760, also, Lord Barrington wrote to General Holdsworth, Governor of Dartmouth, in answer to a letter received from him, informing him that as Governor he certainly had a right to call for a return of all troops in his garrison, and to order such guards as he might think proper, but that the troops in town were not within his command. All matters connected with the increase or diminution of military establishments, and bearing therefore upon the public expenditure, seem to have been peculiarly under the direction of the Secretary at War, and accordingly he signified the King's pleasure upon all augmentations, reductions, and drafts, and on all proposals for raising new corps.

"In September, 1760, Lord Barrington issued a circular letter to several officers who were employed in raising independent companies, informing them that having reason to apprehend that His Majesty's confidence might be abused by the recommendation of persons not properly qualified as officers, it was the King's pleasure that they should make particular enquiry about those persons whom they might propose for commissions in their corps.

"In January, 1761, he desired Commandant Johnson to acquaint him whether he had any reasons to allege in excuse why His Majesty should not supersede him for having failed to raise the stipulated number of men for his independent company. In March of the same year, Lord Ligonier being still Commander-in-Chief, Lord Barrington wrote to Lord George Beauclerk, Commander-in-Chief in North Britain, to state to him, 'that he had laid before the King the trial of certain officers at Edinburgh, that the King was

highly displeased with their conduct, but as they had been punished
by law, he would not try them by Court-martial, but that it was
His Majesty's pleasure that Lord G. Beauclerk should reprimand
them as officers, in His Majesty's name, in the strongest terms for
their breach of military discipline as well as of civil duties'

"In March, 1761, Lord Ligonier being still Commander-in-
Chief, Mr. Charles Townshend succeeded Lord Barrington, and the
authority and independence of the office were kept unimpaired in
his hands. Some altercation, indeed, took place between Lord
Ligonier and Mr Townshend ; but as the latter continued in the full
exercise of all the authority of his predecessors, the points at issue
were effectually decided in favour of the Secretary at War whether
expressly so decided by His Majesty, or whether the opposition on
the part of Lord Ligonier was withdrawn, does not appear

"Mr. Welbore Ellis succeeded Mr Townshend in 1763, about
which time Lord Ligonier ceased to be Commander-in-Chief, and
Mr Ellis conducted, from that period till his resignation, the whole
business of the Army, including promotions of every description

"In 1766 the Marquis of Granby was appointed Commander-
in-Chief, and continued so till 1770, during which time Lord
Barrington was again Secretary at War The same observations
which have been made upon former periods apply equally to this,
the Secretary at War at all times acted under the immediate orders
of the King, to whom alone he was accountable, and from whom
only he received directions, and all matters in any way related to
the civil and financial concerns of the Army were under his exclusive control.

"It should be added that this applies to the Army at home,
because, with regard to the troops on foreign stations, the Secretary
at War transacted everything relative to them, as well discipline as
finance. He corresponded with all the Commanders-in-Chief and
Governors abroad, and conveyed to them the King's pleasure on all
points of promotion, exchanges, leaves of absence, financial arrangements and claims of all sorts; drafts, reductions, augmentations,
disbandments, and recruiting, the disputes of officers about rank
and precedency, and the arrangements and appointment of the
foreign staff

"An instance, unimportant in its subject, but tending, in proportion to its minuteness to illustrate the present enquiry, may be
found in a letter from Lord Barrington to Lord Lorne, in August,
1769, Lord Granby being at the time Commander-in-Chief Lord
Lorne applied for a piper to his regiment (the Royal), and Lord
Barrington refused it, pipers not being allowed to other regiments
But the language of the letter is worthy of attention, inasmuch as it

shows that Lord Barrington conceived that however he might, for his own satisfaction and information, advise with others, the responsibility of deciding upon a question involving an increase of establishment rested with him alone. He said · 'I have considered your application, and consulted with those whose opinions have most weight in my judgment. . . I should be sorry that at any time, but particularly when I was Secretary at War, the Royal should be deprived of any honorary distinction belonging to it, but no person whom I have consulted is of opinion that a Drum-Major or Piper can add to, or take away from, the honour of that most respectable corps.'

"In 1778, Lord Amherst was appointed General on the Staff, and his appointment was communicated to the Army by the Secretary at War   Lord Barrington, on the 25th March, wrote a circular letter, informing the Army that the King had been pleased to appoint General Lord Amherst to serve as a General on the Staff, and that it was His Majesty's pleasure that all matters respecting his military service which were to be transacted at home should pass through his hands, conveying also the King's commands that each Colonel should communicate the same to the regiment under his command, and direct his officers to govern themselves accordingly   It appears, however, that this appointment was confined to matters of discipline, and that Lord Barrington still gave orders relative to marching, embarking, recruiting, reductions, augmentations, raising of corps, leaves of absence, resignations, supercessions, and in some cases the promotion of Officers.

'In 1782, Marshal Conway was appointed Commander-in-Chief, and on the following day Mr. Townshend (afterwards Lord Sidney) succeeded Mr. Jenkinson as Secretary at War. Marshal Conway continued in his appointment till December, 1783   Mr Townshend, and Sir George Yonge, who succeeded him in July, 1782, seem, during the continuance of Marshal Conway as Commander-in-Chief, to have acted in the same manner as their predecessors, and to have been equally independent in all matters of law and finance, and to have communicated the pleasure of the King upon all subjects which came officially before them

"As an instance of the manner in which they acted, it appears that in May, 1782, certain pirates were condemned to be executed , and the Admiralty, being apprehensive that some tumult might take place, applied to the Secretary at War for military assistance to attend the execution and preserve order   Mr Townshend does not seem to have thought it necessary to have recourse, officially at least, to any authority but his own upon this occasion, but made the following reply to the Admiralty :—

"'There has not for many years been an instance of employing the Military on a duty of this kind, the objection to it must strike their Lordships in a general view, and I do not find that any particular and certain information has been laid before them which might convince them that such a measure is necessary on the present occasion. I hope, therefore, their Lordships will agree with me, that a proper exertion of the civil power will prevent any disturbances to-morrow.'

"In August, 1782, the Invalids petitioned the Commander-in-Chief to be placed on the same footing as the rest of the Army in point of pay and allowances. Marshal Conway, not considering himself authorised to decide upon the point, referred the petition to the Secretary at War, who returned it to him, stating at some length his reasons for not granting the prayer of the petition.

"In January, 1793, Lord Amherst was again placed upon the Staff as General, and his appointment was communicated to the Army by the Secretary at War in the same manner as in 1778, excepting that matters relative to the Foot Guards were ordered not to pass through Lord Amherst's hands, but were still to be transacted between the Secretary at War and the King.

"Sir George Yonge, who was at this time Secretary at War, did not however in any respect surrender his financial control over the whole of the Army, but exercised, in all matters involving expense, the same authority as before. In February, 1793, he issued a circular to the Colonels of regiments of Dragoons, by the King's command, stating that it being of the utmost importance that the late augmentations of men and horses should be completed, it was desirable, with that view, that the new commissions should be given to officers who would raise a certain number of men, and 'that in the execution of this arrangement, it was His Majesty's particular order that the Commanding Officers should render every requisite assistance for recruiting, &c.'

"As the complaint of Sir D. Dundas is that 'for a considerable time past,' the Secretary at War has assumed powers and used an authority that do not belong to him, it might perhaps appear to be sufficient for Lord Palmerston to have proved, by tracing the proceedings of the office in former times, that these powers and this authority have always heretofore been attached to it, and to allow the fact of their having continued to be exercised of late years, and before Lord Palmerston's appointment to rest upon the admission which the very charge itself contains. But it is, however, equally certain that, neither by Mr Wyndham nor by any of those persons who have succeeded him, has the authority or independence of the War Office been in any degree surrendered or compromised. To prove this it is only necessary to refer to the Book of Regulations,[1] which consists almost entirely of circular letters, orders, and instructions upon every subject connected with law or finance, issued at different times within the above-mentioned period to the Army by the Secretary at War, under the immediate orders of the King, and this book does not, as Sir D. Dundas seems to suppose, show merely the power of the Secretary at War to issue orders to the printer, but is the code by which the whole Army is governed in respect of the subjects to which it relates. Lord Palmerston, indeed, does not observe in Sir David Dundas' statement any answer to the references, which, in a letter to Mr. Perceval, he made to these regulations, excepting that the collection is imperfect, because some of them are altered or rescinded by others of a later date, but as the later regulations making these alterations were issued by the same authority as those which they amend, this circumstance, however it may affect the utility of the book, does not disprove the authority of the Secretary at War, and Lord Palmerston cannot but think that the pages referred to as instances are important to the question.

"In page 567[2] is an order from Mr. Wyndham to Generals Commanding on all foreign stations to transmit to him quarterly returns of the staff under their command. In page 563[3] is a circular from Mr. Yorke to the Commanding Officers of regiments in India, ordering the regular transmission of monthly Adjutant's rolls, and containing instructions as to the effects and credits of deceased soldiers. In page 577[4] is a circular from General Fitzpatrick, requiring a quarterly return of the name, age, and description of every soldier in the Army. In page 37[5] is a circular from General Fitzpatrick, communicating to the Army at large the increase of pay and of pension which was granted in 1806; and he concludes his letter by saying, 'I have great pleasure in being the channel of communicating to you these instances of His Majesty's gracious consideration for the Army.' The very first page,[6] indeed, contains a very important communication to the Army by Mr. Wyndham, in which he informs them that the part of the pay of the officers, previously withheld under the name of arrears, would in future be regularly issued with their subsistence.

"In 1802, on the formation of the Royal Garrison Battalions from the Invalids and Out-Pensioners of Chelsea, a difference of sentiment

---

[1] The work here referred to was published "by order of the Secretary at War" under date of the 25th April, 1807, and is one of the earliest collections of General Orders for the time   [2] 24th July, 1799   [3] 6th April, 1803
[4] 21st Feb, 1807.   [5] 15th July, 1806.   [6] 25th Jan, 1798.

arose between His Royal Highness the Commander in-Chief and Mr. Yorke, Secretary at War, upon the four principal points connected with the arrangement, namely —

"1st. As to the numbers of which the establishments were to consist

"2nd. As to the pay the men were to receive

"3rd As to the manner in which the clothing was to be furnished, whether Government were to provide it, or to allow off-reckonings to the Colonels.

"4th. As to the right to be given to the officers to retire upon full or half pay, in the event of reduction.

"Upon all these points His Majesty's confidential servants concurred in the opinion which was entertained by the Secretary at War; and the measure, as it was afterwards submitted by Mr Yorke to Parliament, was founded upon the principles he had recommended.

"Lord Palmerston trusts that the statement already given might of itself be sufficient to establish the independence of the Secretary at War, and his separate control over matters of law and finance, but fortunately the books of the War Office not only have enabled him to collect what has been the ancient and invariable practice of his predecessors, but also afford several records of the opinions which they entertained, and deliberately expressed, upon the nature and extent of the authority which they possessed, and he therefore considers it to be important to add a few extracts from those books, illustrating the view which Secretaries at War have heretofore taken of their situation and powers.

"Lord Barrington, who, from the length of time he held the office, may be considered as a valuable authority on this subject, wrote to the Treasury in 1759, remonstrating against subjecting the pay of General and Staff Officers to the pension tax, and added, 'It being equally the duty of my station to oppose any encroachments made on or by the officers of the Army.'

"In the same year, on a complaint to the Secretary at War by the Postmaster-General, of some irregularities which had taken place in the War Office in regard of franks, the Deputy Secretary at War stated that the business of the Adjutant-General is so closely connected with the Department of the Secretary at War, that it is almost always necessary that his Lordship's orders to the troops should be accompanied by others from the Adjutant-General, whose letters, therefore, upon His Majesty's service, are often forwarded from this office'

"In 1759, General Jeffreys having applied to Lord Barrington for leave of absence for an officer, Lord Barrington informed him in reply that he never himself gave leave of absence to any officer without the consent of the Commanding Officer of the regiment to which he belonged In the same year Lord Barrington informed the Treasury that the Judge-Advocate was, in respect of taxes, in the same situation with himself, and some other civil officers upon the Military Establishment, who are at present obliged to pay 5 per cent in their civil, and another 5 per cent in their military, capacity

"In 1761, Mr. Townshend informed Sir Henry Erskine that he found it was usual, when officers wanted leave to be absent from their corps, that the application should come to the Secretary at War from their Colonel, or at least with his approbation. Mr. Fane having in the same year applied respecting the quarters of a regiment, Mr. Townshend informed him that he had added several places to the Blandford quarters, but that he could not, by the practice of his office, extend them so far as Dorchester and Shaftesbury without the consent of the Commander-in Chief.

"It has already been stated that some discussion took place between Mr. Townshend and Lord Ligonier. Very soon after Mr. Townshend's appointment, a difference seems to have arisen between them upon the arrangements for quartering some regiments of Militia, and the following is an extract of a letter from Mr. Townshend to Lord Ligonier upon the subject.—

"'I am extremely sorry that anything should happen in which I have the misfortune to differ in my judgment from your Lordship, but I flatter myself I reason in support of my opinion on this point upon the principle of equality, the only rule that can preserve harmony in the Militia, or justify public office in any regulation relating to them.'

"In 1761, Lord Ligonier recommended to the King that a Captain Thompson should succeed to a commission that happened to be vacant, and it was settled that he should do so. Mr. Townshend, however, represented to the King in so strong a manner the superior claims of Major Appleton, of the regiment in which the vacancy arose, that the first arrangement was rescinded and Major Appleton obtained the commission

"Lord Ligonier was extremely offended at this change, and wrote in very strong terms to Mr. Townshend upon the subject, and a good deal of correspondence passed between them, of which the two following extracts are important

"Mr Townshend, in one letter, said 'that he had no further share in this alteration than as he represented to His Majesty the situation, service, and character of Major Appleton, a duty which he thinks annexed to his office, and which he shall never omit.'

"In another note he said —'Mr. Townshend shall always think it his duty, till he learns it is not from the King himself, to represent the situation and claims of any officers in the natural succession upon any vacancy, not by way of remonstrance against arrangements taken, as Lord Ligonier suggests, but merely by way of representation for His Majesty's information, and in discharge of what Mr. Townshend imagines to be a part of the duty of the Secretary at War.'

"In August of the same year, Mr. Townshend wrote a letter to Lord Strange, which is strongly expressive of his ideas of the authority of his office. 'Your Lordship having made your application to me upon the rank in question between your Lordship and Lord Denbigh, I consulted Lord Ligonier upon the point, but the War Office in no instance decides by any other authority than the directions of His Majesty, or the opinion of the Secretary at War, the latter of these I did myself the honour to transmit to your Lordship some time past, and hearing that opinion was not held decisive, I by the last post signify to your Lordship His Majesty's directions'

"In September following, Mr. Townshend wrote to his brother, Major-General Townshend   . . 'It were endless to enumerate the other officers whom I have without knowing them, sometimes saved, and at other times promoted, upon the single consideration of duty, a pleasing, though a thankless office. I wish to do more, I hope to succeed' This letter, written after the altercation with Lord Ligonier in the same year, seems to show that the King decided the point then at issue in favour of the Secretary at War

"In a letter to Lord Scarborough, Mr. Townshend says, 'Jealousy of me and a variety of motives prevent my having any weight in the department of the Commander-in-Chief. . . . . The constitution of rival offices often exposes me to a variety of mortifications and disappointments, whenever friendship leads me to express a wish, or any method of obviating a difficulty.'

"Mr. Townshend informed Lord Tyrawley, who was appointed Commander-in-Chief of the Forces in Portugal, that he was not a little surprised that he should think of taking out of the War Office the nomination of the Hospital Staff of his expedition

"To General Leighton, Lord Barrington wrote . . . 'But it is my duty to take what care I can of the half-pay. . . . I am of opinion that all vacancies at home shall go on in this way, but regiments like yours in the West Indies will meet with more indulgence.'

"In 1766, Lord Barrington wrote to a Board of General Officers, signifying to them the King's approbation of a report they had made, and adding some long observations about the sale of commissions. He concludes, "But the officer of the Crown who is entrusted with the important charge of the whole Army cannot be too vigilant. . But the poor, though deserving, officer should always find at the War Office a constant assertor of his rights and faithful guardian of his interests.' It is to be observed that there was not at that time any Commander-in-Chief, and this letter proves that when such an officer does not exist, the whole management and superintendence of the Army devolves upon the Secretary at War.

"In March, 1769, Lord Barrington wrote to a Mr. Lee a very striking and important letter, bearing as strongly upon the object of this Memorandum as that of Mr. Townshend, of August, 1761 'I have received your letter of the 21st instant, and the papers therein enclosed. Without entering into a detail of the business to which they relate, it is sufficient that I inform you that I never had the least idea of your being paid an annuity for life, as appears by my Warrants, that Mr Ellis never had, as appears by his, that the Commander-in-Chief has no business with, or authority in, trans-actions which relate to the public money, and that I do not think proper to advise the King to allow you anything further.'

"In March, 1782, Mr. Jenkinson (afterwards Lord Liverpool) gave the same strong and decided opinion in a letter to Lieutenant-Colonel Goldsworthy, in which he said, "I think it right at the same time to say that, in Articles of public expenditure, it is in my judgment the duty of the Secretary at War alone to decide.'

"In 1802, some correspondence took place between the Commander-in-Chief and Mr Yorke, then Secretary at War, with regard to the nature of the appointment of Regimental Pay-masters, in the course of which Mr. Yorke stated it to be his opinion 'that the War Office was perfectly warranted in considering the Paymaster as a public officer who was to look for the rule of his conduct to the existing Regulations, and to the instructions which he should receive from this Department, as having the exclusive control of the expenditures entrusted to his Administration'

"It has been shown by references already made from the books of the War Office that the Treasury have in all times past considered the Commander-in-Chief or Captain-General to have, according to Lord Barrington's expression, 'no business with, or authority in, translations which relate to the public money,' but even if that opinion could not be sufficiently collected from the history of the office, there is a recent decision of that Board which places the point beyond the possibility of a doubt

"On the 21st August, 1807, Mr. Huskisson transmitted to the Secretary at War a minute of the Treasury, dated the 19th of the same month, desiring him to take it into his serious and attentive consideration, and report his opinion thereupon to the Board. This minute recites that the Board of Treasury have read the first report of the Committee of Public Expenditure of the United Kingdom, and taken into their most serious consideration the several suggestions which it contains, and thereupon propose the adoption of certain regulations.

"The most important of these are, that large sums of money shall be placed in the hands of the Paymaster-General by Warrants from the Treasury, that the Power of applying any moneys placed in the hands of the Paymaster-General by these Warrants shall be vested in the Secretary at War and Lords of the Treasury, and in no other authority whatsoever. That the application of these sums for ordinary services shall be made by the Secretary at War alone, upon his sole authority and responsibility, and under his Warrant. That in all cases in which the Secretary at War shall think it requisite to recommend any increase of establishment or salary, or to alter or add to the regulations now in force with respect to the allowances to the Army or any part thereof, he shall communicate the same to the Treasury, and obtain their sanction before he submits the same to the King or to Parliament, as the nature of the case may be.

" It is difficult to conceive anything more strongly decisive on the point now under discussion than this deliberate opinion of the Treasury, pronounced in consequence of a report from a Select Committee of the House of Commons, specially appointed to enquire into and consider of the checks existing or necessary to be imposed upon the expenditure of the public money.

"It has been shown in the preceding pages that from the Revolution down to the beginning of the last war, by the course of office, by the recorded opinions of Secretaries at War, by the opinions and practice of the Treasury, and by the sanction given to all these by the several Sovereigns of the country, the independence of the Secretary at War, and his exclusive control and jurisdiction over all matters of law and finance, may be fully collected and proved, nothing, therefore, remains but to add the authority of the legislature, and that can also be adduced in support of those above-mentioned on this point

"Parliament has at various times passed Acts imposing distinct duties and responsibilities upon the Secretary at War, thereby incontrovertibly proving that in their opinion he is a civil servant of the Crown liable to no orders but from his Sovereign; because, to impose responsibility where there is not liberty of action is impossible, and it is obvious that no officer who is subordinate to, and dependent upon another, can by possibility be a free and independent agent.

"The Acts of Parliament in which the Secretary at War is mentioned, and in which duties and responsibilities are imposed upon him, or powers and authorities given him, are Mr. Burke's and other Pay Office Acts, by which he is required to lay before Parliament annual estimates of the expenses of the Army, and to examine and settle regimental accounts; the annual Mutiny Act, the Innkeepers' Act, the Pay and Clothing Acts of the Army and Militia, Militia Acts, Volunteer Acts, the Act regulating the Office of Agent-General, and, in short, almost all Acts relating to military matters require or authorise him to do or not to do certain things.

"In an Act of the 19th George III., cap. 10, directing men to be forthwith raised for the Army, the superintendence and direction of that service were placed in the hands of the Secretary at War, and it is remarkable that there is a special clause prohibiting any military officer from being one of the Commissioners who were in the several counties to carry the Act into execution. The operation of the Act was also to be superseded, whenever His Majesty thought fit, by notice from the Secretary at War

"But the most remarkable Act of this sort is that of the 8th of George II., regulating the quartering of soldiers during elections. The object of the Legislature was to secure the freedom of election from any interference on the part of the military, and for that purpose it was necessary to compel some responsible and ostensible officer, who had the power to do so, to remove all troops from places where elections were to be held Accordingly the Secretary at War was fixed upon for that purpose, and he is bound by this Act to move troops from such places one day previous to the election and to keep them away till one day after the election is over, under pain, should he omit or neglect to do so, of forfeiting his office, and of being incapable of ever again serving His Majesty in any capacity whatever, civil or military.

"If the Secretary at War were impeached at the bar of the House of Lords, for having violated the provisions of this law, would he be suffered to plead that he had been prevented from moving the troops by the order of the Commander-in-Chief, or Captain-General, or by his not being able to obtain their concurrence and consent? or would he not be told that such was precisely the case against which the Act intended to guard the liberty of the subject, that to him alone Parliament and the country looked for the execution of its law, and that even the Royal authority could not release him from an obligation which it had concurred with the other two branches of the Legislature to impose.

"The Secretary at War seems, indeed, to be the officer who stands peculiarly between the people and the Army, to protect the former from the latter, to prevent their public revenue from being drained by any unauthorised increase of military establishments, and their persons and property from being injured by any possible misconduct of the soldiery, and upon him will Parliament and the country justly fix the responsibility for any neglect of this part of his duty

"Everything, therefore which, relates not only to the finance of the Army, but also to those matters in which soldiers come in contact with the civil inhabitants of the country, such as the quartering, billeting, and marching of troops, requires the sanction and authority of the Secretary at War, and although, as these matters are also closely connected with those general arrangements of the military force, which must of necessity be requested by the Commander-in-Chief, or the Militia Officer in command of the Army, they are, therefore, in general settled and determined by him, yet this is only an arrangement and understanding which has been made for the convenience of office, and the more easily to carry on the public service, because orders of this sort are in fact issued by the Secretary at War, although the arrangement is made and communicated privately to him by the Commander-in-Chief. But if in any case the Secretary at war saw reason for objecting to any such arrangement, the Commander-in-Chief could not compel him to issue the orders, and without the orders of the Secretary at War, and of the Magistrates acting under the provisions of the Mutiny Act, although the troops might be bound by military discipline to march, in obedience to the commands of the Commander-in-Chief, they would not be entitled to quarters, or billets, or subsistence on their march, and would be liable to the severest punishments of criminal law, for any attempt to provide these things by force for themselves.

"The same reasoning holds good also in matters of finance. The Commander-in-Chief cannot by his own authority order the issue of money to any individual. His Warrant would not be noticed by the Paymaster-General, and no officer who should pay money by his order would be reimbursed, unless he obtained also the authority of the Secretary at War

"Independently, therefore, of its being inconsistent with the spirit of the constitution, and the undeviating practice of office from the revolution downwards, that the Commander-in-Chief should issue orders affecting the public expenditure, there is an inconsistency inherent in the thing itself, because his order is by itself of no authority, and if the arrangement which he proposes and orders, is afterwards approved by the Secretary at War, or through him by the Treasury, and the Secretary at War issues his order in support of that of the Commander-in-Chief, it is the order of the War Office, and not that of the Commander-in-Chief, that is the efficient authority, and in that case the latter is at least useless; but if the Secretary at War or Treasury should refuse to concur with the Commander-in-Chief, and should not sanction the arrangement which he had proposed or promulgated, then the order of the Commander-in-Chief is powerless, and would not indemnify the persons who might have acted under it, and it is obvious that nothing can tend more directly to lower the authority of any officer than his issuing orders which he has not legally the power to enforce.

" Lord Palmerston therefore submits that, according to the principles which regulate the British Constitution, power cannot be vested where there is no responsibility, or responsibility be imposed where authority does not exist. The Legislature have imposed a responsibility upon the Secretary at War, from which he cannot discharge himself, and it would be placing him in a situation perfectly anomalous and unknown to any one office in the Constitution, to deprive him of that independence, by which alone he can secure to himself the power of faithfully performing his duty.

" It is therefore submitted that to quote the wording of the Commission of the Secretary at War is not sufficient for the purpose of proving that he is subordinate to, and dependent upon, the Commander-in-Chief in any matter of Law or Finance connected with the Army; because, in the first place, setting aside every other consideration, it is quite clear from the Commission of Mr Clarke, that ' the General of our Forces ' mentioned in it is the Captain-General and not the Commander-in-Chief, and that the addition of the words ' according to the discipline of war ' (words which, it is to be observed, Sir David Dundas does not notice in his argument) prove that the orders he was so liable to receive from the Captain-General were in his Military capacity as a Staff Officer, and not in his Civil character as a political servant of the Crown, and as a Staff Officer he has now only a nominal existence. It must be remembered too that Mr Blathwayte's Commission, in which those words were first inserted, was made out before the Revolution, when Constitutional principles and ideas of civil liberty were not understood as they have been since those days, and when there existed a Captain-General, whom, not Military Officers alone, but all persons whomsoever, were ordered to obey, and possessed of powers unknown in later times. It is not, therefore, fair to infer from a form of words made out originally under such circumstances, and in such times, and copied, as was natural they should be, on each successive appointment, the situation and powers of the Officer at the present day, after all the changes and improvements that have since taken place in the Constitution and Government of the country. And because, in the second place, whatever might have been the intention of those who originally made out the Commission, it is quite certain that for more than a century it never has, in practice and in fact, borne the construction which Sir D. Dundas now attempts to put upon it.

"The Commission of Secretary at War is certainly in its nature, in some degree, a Military Commission, but it is also a Civil one. It enjoins him to take the place into his charge; and the appointment, even in the case of a General Officer, to whom it is not a first Commission, vacates a seat in the House of Commons.

"He is therefore a Civil servant of the Crown, and as such has of late years sat, at times, to advise His Majesty in the Cabinet. It seems, then, clear that the obedience which this Civil Officer is on any supposition to render to the Captain-General, according to the discipline of war, cannot relate to the administration of the public business which, in his political capacity, passes through his hands.

"Lord Palmerston trusts that the preceding detail and observations, and the Extracts in the Appendix from the books of the War Office (which have indeed run into a length much greater than he wished, but which the nature and importance of the subject rendered unavoidable), will satisfy the mind that the Secretary at War never could, by any construction of his Commission, be dependent upon or subordinate to the Commander-in-Chief, as distinguished from the Captain General, that he never has, in point of fact, been so, even to the Captain-General, in matters of Law and Finance, and that over these subjects he has always hitherto exercised an independent jurisdiction, under the immediate orders of his Sovereign, whose commands alone it is his duty to obey, and Lord Palmerston founds this position upon the ancient practice of his Office, upon the recorded opinions of Secretaries at War, and of the Treasury, upon the sanction of the successive Sovereigns who have sat upon the throne, and upon the Acts of the Legislature of the country.

"It may be necessary to say that in the preceding detail of the history of the War Office, Lord Palmerston has necessarily been led to state things as he found them recorded, that in some particulars, however, the arrangement of former times has been altered, that part of the business of a political nature which was formerly transacted in the War Office, has, since the separate establishment of a Secretary of State for the War Department, been conducted by him, while the Secretary at War has also of late years made it a point, while a Commander-in Chief exists, not to interfere in the patronage of the Army, or in matters purely connected with its discipline, and it is most foreign from Lord Palmerston's intention to wish in any degree to recall the practice of former times in those respects in which it has been altered for the convenience of the general arrangements of the Government, or by the sanction of competent authority deciding upon a full consideration of the subject.

"Nor would he think of contending that the independence which the Secretary at War has always enjoyed should be exercised by making innovations in the Service, or taking steps altering or affecting the interests of the Army, without previous communication with the Commander-in-Chief, because he is persuaded that without a good understanding and cordial co-operation and concert between the two Offices, the public service cannot be well and advantageously carried on. But, on the other hand, he must submit that it never has belonged to the Commander-in-Chief to issue by his authority Orders and Regulations affecting the expenditure of the public money, and that the Secretary at War is the accustomed, and, as he submits, the proper channel, for any signification of His Majesty's pleasure upon such subjects, and that if it should be decided to make the office of Secretary at War dependent upon that of Commander-in-Chief, it would in some important particulars require the authority of Parliament to alter those laws which have imposed special duties on the Secretary at War

"Sir David Dundas indeed imagines that the whole and absolute control over every part of the Military Service is vested in the Commander-in Chief. Lord Palmerston conceives himself to have proved that this never has hitherto been the case.

"If it should be thought necessary, for the better arrangement of the Army, to carry into effect the suggestions of Sir D Dundas, with regard to the relative situation of the two Offices of Commander-in-Chief and Secretary at War, Lord Palmerston will have the satisfaction of feeling that he has brought under view a true history of the real situation which the Constitution has, for above a century, placed these respective Offices, by which it will appear that the Office of Secretary at War has existed in point of fact, and has been considered in point of law, as a sort of barrier between the Military authority of the Officer in command of the Army and the Civil rights of the people, and that it has been considered also as a

Civil and Constitutional check on the expenditure of the money granted by Parliament for the maintenance of the Army, that such a state of dependence of the Secretary at War upon the Commander-in-Chief, as Sir D Dundas seems to think necessary, is wholly inconsistent with the efficiency of such a check; and especially with respect to some important duties of the Secretary at War, that they cannot be put under the control of the Commander-in-Chief in any other way than by an Act of Parliament repealing those duties which, by existing laws, have (with His Majesty's consent necessarily) been imposed upon the Office of Secretary at War. How far it should now be thought necessary that the Constitutional jealousy which created these checks, and which dictated those Parliamentary provisions, should be made to bend to the convenience or necessity of Military arrangement and control, and the checks themselves be done away, it is not for Lord Palmerston to determine, but he is persuaded that it would be felt that Lord Palmerston had greatly neglected his duty if he had not prepared this full statement of the history of his Office—if he had, by his silence and acquiescence in the plan of Sir D Dundas, left it to be concluded that the Crown was only restoring the two Offices to the relative situation in which they had heretofore existed, when in fact the Ministry was making a material alteration in those situations, and, above all, if he had not submitted that it could not be legally and constitutionally done without the interference of Parliament "

(CXXX.)

Chapter XXI, par 32

(1) OBSERVATIONS OF THE RIGHT HONOURABLE SPENCER PERCEVAL AND OF OTHER MEMBERS OF THE CABINET.

" SIR D DUNDAS required that such Regulations should be adopted as should completely define the relative authority of the respective Offices, so as to prevent any collision or misunderstanding in future, and such as should reduce the Office of Secretary at War to that state of subordination and control under the Commander in Chief, which he contended had, till of late, according to the original establishment of the Office, uniformly prevailed, and which it was essential to the dignity of the Office of the Commander-in-Chief, and to the well-being of the public service, should be restored.

" This representation of Sir D Dundas led to the observations of

Lord Palmerston, and Mr Perceval conceives that the important practical questions are two.—

1st What is the existing state of the relations between these two Officers at present?

2nd How far it is expedient to alter it?

' With this view of the subject, however natural it may have been for Lord Palmerston, for the purpose of repelling the supposition that the modern practice of his Office had been adopted on a spirit of encroachment, to have looked into the ancient history and practice of his Office for a century past, it appears to Mr Perceval that the subject may now be well disembarrassed of that research, as also of the distinction which Lord Palmerston contends for, between a Commander-in-Chief and a Captain-General of the Army.

"It may be disembarrassed of the first, because it is obvious that the modern practice, which Lord Palmerston admits should continue, is very different from the former as collected from the recorded transactions of the Office in former times, to which his Lordship refers, as well when there was a Captain-General as when there was not.

"If these transactions were to give the rule, the interference of the War Office in matters of promotion, and many other points of Military direction, would prevail to an extent which it is most foreign to Lord Palmerston's intention to contend for, and this as well under a Captain-General as under a Commander in-Chief It follows, therefore, that the reference to those early transactions from then proving too much, if they prove anything, can never decide upon the present question, and can establish nothing satisfactorily either as to what is the present law of these Offices, or as to what ought to be the practice between them So with regard to the distinction between the Commander-in-Chief and the Captain-General, Mr Perceval's impression is that if any such distinction ever was intended between the two, as should affect the questions now at issue between the Secretary at War and the Commander-in-Chief, that distinction is obsolete Unless the words 'the General of Our Forces' is to be understood as well to mean a Commander-in-Chief as a Captain-General, there are no words in the Commission of the Secretary at War which connect him even as to matters of discipline with the Commander-in-Chief, yet all usage shows that he is so connected, and Mr. Perceval conceives that that usage will afford the means of applying such a construction of the words 'General of Our Forces' in the Commission, as to consider them, for this purpose at least, synonymous with Commander-in-Chief

"It must be observed also that the words in the Commission are not Captain-General, but General of the Forces, and why the Commander-in-Chief, with the powers he now has, may not be understood by the words General of the Forces, Mr Perceval does not see, but even if this were not the true construction of those words, t would be immaterial, as there could be no possible objection in point of law, or expediency, against altering the words in the Secretary at War's Commission, by substituting the words Commander-in-Chief for General of the Forces. Mr. Perceval, therefore, in the first place, submits that the legal relationship between the Commander-in-Chief and the Secretary at War should be considered the same as if the words the Commission of the Secretary at War were Commander-in-Chief instead of General of Our Forces It is necessary then to see what these words are He is to observe and follow 'such Orders and Instructions as he shall receive from Us, or the General of Our Forces, according to the discipline of war' And the true construction of this instrument must, as Mr Perceval apprehends, afford the best interpretation of the duties of the Secretary at War in relation to the Commander-in-Chief At least the origin of their relations is to be traced up to this source, and they may be expected to be found continuing the same, except so far as any uniform practice may appear to affect them, as denoting His Majesty's pleasure, or except so far as any alteration in the duties of the Secretary at War may have been introduced by any Acts of Parliament giving either expressly or by necessary inference an independent authority to the Secretary at War.

" For there can be no question, as Mr Perceval supposes, but that an Act of Parliament (including necessarily the King's consent) may not only give to any Officer directly and expressly an authority which he would not have derived from his Commission, but also by imposing duties upon him for the execution of which he necessarily becomes responsible, give him indirectly, but by necessary implication, an independent authority in matters on which his Commission alone might have left him dependent upon the other office.

" Lord Palmerston seems to think that the words in his Commission, 'according to Military discipline,' may have been introduced for the purpose of confining the authority of the General of the Forces over the Secretary at War to matters of Military discipline, and of subtracting from that authority all financial and pecuniary matters Mr. Perceval is rather inclined to think that the jurisdiction of the Secretary at War over matters of Finance, supposing it to have existed before Mr. Burke's Act (the date assigned to it by the Commander-in-Chief), is rather to be referred to the other words of the Commission, directing him to obey such orders as he received from ' Us ' (the Sovereign). The practice under those words, which probably has been uniform, of the King's referring all matters of a pecuniary nature, from time to time as they arose, to the Secretary at War and consequently by such reference imposing upon him the duty of controlling such matters, may naturally have withdrawn them from the Commander-in-Chief But this again appears to Mr Perceval an unnecessary research into the ancient state of the Office for whatever the state of the Office was formerly, the question is, what it is now

"The Commander-in-Chief says, 'that the general official direction of financial arrangements rests with the Secretary at War, under the Warrant of His Majesty's authority countersigned by him, is fully acknowledged, nor was ever this point disputed in any of the discussions which have given rise to the present question,' but it must be recollected that the operation of Mr Burke's Bill, which was brought into Parliament and passed in 1783, has been the sole origin of the pecuniary detail, which since that period has placed the Secretary at War in communication with Corps on financial subjects closely connected with questions of discipline, which till then had been solely under the superintendence of the Commander-in-Chief

"Whatever, then, was the situation of the Office of Secretary at War, merely under his Commission, and the practice that had grown up under it, Mr. Burke's Bill, by imposing certain duties upon that Officer in the general official direction of financial arrangements, has given to him a correspondent authority, which, intended as a check upon Army Expenditure, cannot but be independent of Military authority. It is equally clear that all matters regarding the accounts of the Army are by that Act transferred to the Secretary at War. Parliament also has given one duty specifically to the Secretary at War, under the severest penalties of disability if he neglects it, namely, the removal of soldiers during the time of election These and whatever other duties there may be of the same kind, it is obvious imply an independence in the Office of Secretary at War, and therefore without reference to Parliament, it would be quite impossible to declare the complete dependence of the Office of Secretary at War on that of the Commander-in-Chief.

"The next question then is, whether it is advisable to introduce any Bill before Parliament for the purpose of removing the difficulties which these parliamentary regulations interpose, to prevent the Secretary at War from being made universally dependent upon the Commander-in Chief.

"Upon this question Mr. Perceval has no hesitation in stating it to be his most decided opinion that nothing could be more impolitic than an attempt to submit to Parliament any alteration of the kind An attempt to diminish any existing check upon Military expenditure would be misinterpreted and misunderstood, and would be worse received, and with more jealousy than almost any proposal which could be made

"The utmost, therefore, that Mr. Perceval conceives can with propriety be recommended, and that which he trusts will be satisfactory to both Offices, is that the Secretary at War should not issue any new Order or Regulation, however much connected with finance or accounts, or any other matter which may be peculiarly within the province of this Officer, without previously communicating his intention of issuing it to the Commander in-Chief; and in the event of the Commander-in Chief making any objection, if the Secretary at War should still persevere in thinking that it is his duty to issue it, he should be directed to suspend the issuing of such Order and Regulation, and forthwith to communicate both his own view and that of the Commander in-Chief, to the First Lord of the Treasury if on a matter of finance, and to the Secretary of State for the Colonies if relating to other duties in his Office, or to both, for them to obtain, as a measure of Government, the King's pleasure upon the propriety of its adoption.

"Such a Regulation, Mr. Perceval confidently trusts, would be found practically sufficient for all purposes.'

(2) *Of the Lord Chancellor*

"I AM unable, from any means of considering, or from the time which I have had to consider the subject of these papers, to offer any opinion upon the respective duties or powers of a Captain-General, or Commander-in-Chief, or a General of the Forces. I have some reason to believe that an opinion has been entertained by lawyers, that a thorough enquiry would tend to show that the legal powers of the Captain-General and Commander-in-Chief are different, but with reference to what is now prudent to be done, it does not seem necessary to establish how these points stand.

"I also think that, considering the terms of the Commission of the Secretary at War and the Commander-in-Chief, and attending to what usage, which I think would not be held to be inconsistent with some general words in the Commission, proves to have been done heretofore by the Secretary at War, it would be difficult in law to maintain that the Secretary at War has not powers, which I understand he is not now in the habit of exercising

"There are some points quite clear, viz. :—

"That it is undeniable that the Secretary at War has the powers, that Parliament has devolved upon him, whether he has them or not, by virtue of, and as inherent in his Office, and that he must by law have every power and every authority which is necessary to the execution of the duties which Parliament has imposed upon him, whether expressly given to him or not, and that he is bound to exercise those powers and authorities as long as he is bound to execute those duties, and that nothing can discharge him of the obligation but Parliament itself

"It is, I think, extremely probable that Parliament may have imposed upon the Secretary at War a great many duties, upon the supposition that there were already powers and authorities inherent in his Office, without taking the trouble to examine whether that supposition was well-founded, or without examining whether, if Parliament had been satisfied that he had not powers, which Parliament might imagine were inherent in his Office, they would have either charged him with those duties, or have given him those powers, but if they have charged him with the duties, the law will imply that they meant (whether they really meant it or not) to give him the powers

"As to any powers, therefore, which Parliament, either expressly or impliedly, has given the Secretary at War, as to Military finance or other Military matters impliedly, as necessary to the execution of duties which it has imposed upon him, however inconvenient the existence of such powers in him may be, Parliament alone can interpose effectually, in my opinion. As to the expediency of applying to Parliament to regulate as to points which have been or may become the subject of differences of opinion between the Offices. In the present temper of the times, which as to matters of finance of every kind, by leaving them almost entirely to the zeal and jealousy of House of Commons Committees, looks as if it aimed at excluding from the consideration of one of the two branches of the Legislature, entirely, and even of that branch of it from which those who are deputed to consider such subjects emanate, very materially, and with the disposition that seems to exist to increase, in every possible mode, checks upon expenditure, the wisdom of many of which seems very disputable, I cannot state that it seems to me to be at all expedient, and I doubt very much whether the result of such an application would not be an increase, possibly unnecessary and improvident, but an actual increase, of those checks upon Military expenditure. And I think that it is at least highly advisable to try, before any such application is made, whether the means suggested by Mr. Perceval may not in a sufficient degree render it unnecessary to risk what may be the result of such an application.

" ELDON."

(3) *Of the Earl of Liverpool.*

"I ENTIRELY agree with Mr. Perceval in the inexpediency of bringing the differences which have arisen between the Office of Commander-in-Chief and that of Secretary at War, before Parliament, if it can possibly be avoided.

"I am persuaded the result of such a reference to Parliament would be a review of our whole Military system as connected with the Civil administration of it, and there is no saying what innovation and pretended reforms might not grow out of such an enquiry such a discussion would at any time be inconvenient and dangerous, and ought to be avoided, if not absolutely necessary, but it would be particularly impolitic at the present moment when the Military Service is most deservedly popular, and when all those projects for reform, which were launched some years ago, appear to have been laid at rest I am convinced if such an enquiry were to take place, the House of Commons would adopt no propositions which would diminish the authority of any Officer (as a check upon the public expenditure) over whom they had a direct and immediate control

"Upon the subject of the dispute itself, I agree in the opinion given by Mr. Perceval. I have always considered the Office of Secretary at War as the legitimate check upon Army expenditure; but then it is upon the Army expenditure, according to the existing law and existing Regulations. It is impossible to say upon this principle that the Secretary at War, from the knowledge of existing abuses, may not be the most proper person to originate any new Regulations relative to Army accounts, but it appears to me to be quite clear that no new Regulation should be issued, and no new provision introduced into Parliament, without the approbation of the Commander-in-Chief or the determination of Government

"I think the proposition at the end of Mr. Perceval's paper will prevent all differences in future upon the respective jurisdictions of the two Offices There are no two Offices in the State connected with each other in any branch of Public Administration, in which it would be easy to define satisfactorily their separate authorities, or in which it would be possible for the public service to be carried on with advantage without previous communication upon all points of common interest.

"LIVERPOOL."

(4) *Of the Right Honourable Charles Yorke.*

"*Admiralty, December 8th,* 1811.

"MR. YORKE has looked over most of these papers (some of which he thinks he has seen before), and has perused with attention those which have passed between the War Office and Horse Guards since July last, as well as the observations of Mr Perceval, the Lord Chancellor, and Lord Liverpool upon them

"Mr Yorke can have no hesitation in concurring with Mr. Perceval's opinion on this subject. Mr. Yorke thinks that the Government would be very ill-advised to attempt an alteration of the present system of the War Office, which has been established by long practice, and by the authority of several Acts of Parliament; and whatever may have been its state in former times, it has for several years past (during which the King's son had been Commander-in-Chief, if not 'Captain-General of all the Forces') been found to be an efficient control over the ordinary and established expenditure of the Army, as well as a useful and satisfactory instrument of that branch of the Military Police which has reference to the Law of the land.

"Mr. Yorke thinks in particular that to bring the system of the two great Military Offices of the Horse Guards and War Office under review of Parliament (especially in a state of contest) at such a time as this, if it can by any means be avoided, would be a most imprudent and mischievous undertaking

"Mr Yorke cannot doubt that with due concert and co-operation between these Offices, the functions of each will proceed efficaciously and smoothly to the common end, *i. e.*, the good of His Majesty's Service   Differences of opinion upon particular points may and will occasionally arise, as they have frequently done heretofore, but they will be amicably and properly settled hereafter by means of due confidence and conciliation, as they have been formerly settled, without prejudice to the public business; and Mr. Yorke finds it impracticable to suggest any mode of terminating such differences (should they arise) more safely and conveniently than that suggested by Mr. Perceval and Lord Liverpool.

"There is one circumstance in the present situation of the War Office, which appears to deserve some attention. So late as during the whole period of Mr. Yorke's administration of that Office (though he was not in the Cabinet), and it is believed, during a part of Mr. Bathurst's time, the Secretary at War had 'the *entrée* of the Closet' on the business of his Department, and he was actually and personally the depositary of His Majesty upon it, which he afterwards communicated not only formally, but authentically, to the Army and its parts, by circular letter or otherwise.

"It is understood that for some years past the Secretary at War has not been in the habit of receiving His Majesty's personal commands on any of the business of his Office, but that these are now communicated either through the channel of the Commander-in-Chief or the Secretary of State, the latter, of course, very rarely. It follows, therefore, that the Secretary at War must of late have been much more in subordination to the Horse Guards, with reference at least to new and original communications of His Majesty's pleasure on Army business, not concerning the execution of Acts of Parliament, than heretofore."

(CXXXI.)

Chapter XXI, *par* 32.

MEMORANDUM SIGNED IN DUPLICATE BY HIS ROYAL HIGH-
NESS THE PRINCE REGENT, AND TRANSMITTED TO THE
COMMANDER-IN-CHIEF AND THE SECRETARY AT WAR

"GEORGE, P R

"His Royal Highness the Prince Regent, acting in the name and on the behalf of His Majesty, having had before him various representations from his Royal Highness the Commander-in-Chief, the late Commander-in-Chief, and the Secretary at War, respecting certain differences existing between the two Offices in regard to their respective duties, and desiring to put an end to all such differences for the future, is hereby pleased to command that the line of separation between the duties of the aforesaid Offices, which either usage or the provisions of any Acts of Parliament have introduced between the Financial and Account Departments on the one hand, and the military discipline of the Army on the other, should continue to be observed.

But as the financial measures of the War Office may, in their application, more or less affect the military discipline of the Army, His Royal Highness is further pleased to command that the Secretary at War should not issue any new Order or Regulation, however much connected with finance or account, or any other matter which may be peculiarly within the province of the War Office, without previously communicating his intention of issuing it to the Commander-in-Chief; and in the event of the Commander-in-Chief making any objection to such Order or Regulation, and the Secretary at War still continuing to think that it is his duty to issue it, the Secretary at War shall forthwith communicate a copy of his intended Order or Regulation, together with his own view of the expediency of the measure, and the objections stated by the Commander-in-Chief, to the First Lord of the Treasury or the Chancellor of the Exchequer, or to the Secretary of State for the Colonies, or

P of them for them to obtain the pleasure of His Majesty or of His Royal Highness the Regent, upon the propriety of carrying it into execution.

"And His Royal Highness further declares that, in requiring that His Majesty's or the Regent's pleasure should, in the case of such new and disputed Regulations, be obtained by the first Lord of the Treasury or Chancellor of the Exchequer, or by his Secretary of State, or by all of them, it is not his intention to abridge, or in any degree to alter the accustomed mode of direct communication on the part of the Secretary at War with His Majesty or His Royal Highness the Regent

"By command of His Royal Highness the Prince Regent, in the name and on the behalf of His Majesty, this 29th day of May, 1812 '

"LIVERPOOL."

Though countersigned by Lord Liverpool, this Warrant appears, from the following letter, to have been drawn by Mr. Perceval

---

"MY DEAR LORD,   "*War Office, June 2,* 1812

"I enclose a Memorandum relative to the discussions between the Commander-in-Chief and the Secretary at War for the signature of the Regent

"The substance of it was drawn up by Mr. Perceval a very short time before his death. I have since that period communicated upon the subject with His Royal Highness the Duke of York, and you will see by the copy of a note¹ from Colonel Torrens to me that the paper as it now stands contains an arrangement satisfactory to His Royal Highness as well as to myself. As it would hardly be fair by my successor to leave him an unsettled discussion of so long a standing, I should be very much obliged to you if, in the event of your seeing no objection to the paper, you would have the goodness to submit it to the Regent for his signature, and return it to me countersigned by yourself.

"My dear Lord, yours, &c,

"*The Earl of Liverpool,*   "PALMERSTON"
&c, &c, &c"

---

¹ "MY DEAR LORD,   "*Horse Guards, May* 39, 1812

'I return the Memorandum which you enclosed to me in your note of the 26th instant, and, having submitted it to the Duke, I am commanded to acquaint you that His Royal Highness considers it quite consistent with what has been already arranged, and that it has his entire concurrence and approval

"Yours, &c,

"*Lord Palmerston*"   "H. TORRENS"

(CXXXII.)

Chapter XXI, par 13

WARRANT[1] OF GEO. I. (29TH NOVEMBER 1741) APPOINTING
A BOARD OF GENERAL OFFICERS.

" WHEREAS it has been represented unto Us that many disputes and
inconveniences have and may arise touching the rank and precedency of the several Regiments which now do, and lately did, serve
in Our Army, and also in respect to the dates of all Commissions,
some of which have been very irregularly obtained, to the detriment
of many Officers in Our Service, to prevent which, and to put an
end to the great confusion and many disputes, disorders, and inconveniences that have arisen and may arise, for want of a just
economy and due regulation amongst Our Forces, and to do justice
to such Officers as have wrongfully suffered thereby: We have
thought fit hereby to direct that the said Board of General Officers
shall meet from time to time in the Great Room at the Ho
Guards, whose opinion We think necessary frequently to h
all affairs that may be referred to them, either by Us, Our Captain-
General of our Land Forces, or Our Secretary at War, relating to
Our Army, and whose care and inspection is absolutely necessary
for the good of Our service, five of which said General Officers We
do hereby appoint to be a quorum, and the eldest at any time
present to be the President, and to sit as often as Our service shall
require within the said three months, who are to redress all
manner of inconveniences and grievances whatsoever relating to
Our said Forces, and to determine and put an end to all matters
and complaints which shall be referred to them as aforesaid, which
determination of the said Board of General Officers shall be signed
by all present, as well negative as affirmative, and laid before Us
for Our Royal approbation, and when the same shall be confirmed
by Us, it shall be fixed and determined, and remain unalterable rule
and regulation, not only with respect to the rank and precedency of
the several corps of Our Army, but also the dates of all Commissions
in Our said Army, and shall be as a bar to all further proceedings
and complaints for the future To the intent, therefore, that Our
service, in reference to Our Forces, may be the better carried on
with the least disorder or pretence of complaint whatsoever Our
will and pleasure is, and We do accordingly authorise, command,
and require the said meetings of Our General Officers to be con-

---

[1] Court-martial Bk, pp 7-9

tinued and held in the Great Room at the Horse Guards as often as there shall be occasion, who are to hear, examine, and determine all such informations and complaints as shall be brought before them, or referred to them by Us, Our Captain-General of Our Forces, or Our Secretary at War, as well touching the ranks of all Regiments as the dates of all Commissions, and of the misbehaviour or misdemeanour of any Officer, Half-pay Officer, or Soldier or of any abuses which are or shall be committed in anywise relating to Our Forces, to redress grievances, irregularities, and other ill practices that have been or shall be committed amongst them, and to refer all such matters as they shall think proper to Courtsmartial, &c, and Our said General Officers are to make such observations as may be necessary in the course of their proceedings of any thing that may occur to them which will tend to the advantage of Our service, and that thereupon such Orders and Regulations may be made as shall be judged proper, and Our Judge-Advocate-General of Our Forces, or his Deputy, is from time to time to give notice to the General Officers when Our service requires their meeting together, and to give his attendance at all such meetings, as well as to receive and observe the directions of the said General Officers, according to the duty of his Office, and to keep a journal of all their proceedings, and particularly to make report unto Us from time to time, to Our Captain-General or Secretary at War, when any General Officer summoned shall fail to give his attendance, who, for such neglect, shall incur Our displeasure."

(CXXXIII.)

Chapter XXI, par. 24.

TREASURY AUTHORITY[1] FOR THE SECRETARY AT WAR TO PREPARE AND SIGN WARRANTS ON THE PAYMASTER-GENERAL.

"Sir,   "*Treasury Chambers 8th March,* 1715-6

"The Lords Commissioners of His Majesty's Treasury desire that when and as often as any money shall be imprested by their Lordships' Order to the late or present Paymasters of His Majesty's Forces, for any Services that require particular Warrants to be signed by the King, to authorise the making of such payments by

[1] *Letter Bk* 14C, p 21

such Paymaster or Paymasters, you do obtain the necessary Warrant to be signed by the King, authorising such payments to be made accordingly upon such Paymaster or Paymasters, certifying to you under their hands the receipt of such money, and the extraordinary uses and services to which it was particularly directed by their Lordships.

"I am, &c,

" To the Secretary at War."   "W. Lowndes."

(CXXXIV.)

Chapter XXI, par. 24

A List[1] of the Clerks in the Office of His Majesty's Secretary at War, with an Account of their respective Salaries

Whitehall, 30th Sept., 1720.

	Salary per Annum.
Mr. George Turnbill	£100
„ Aaron Tinell	90
„ Anthony Vezian	70
„ Peregrine Fury	66
, Edward Luckyn	60
„ Gilbert Eliott	50
„ Robert Haskey	50
„ John Woollcombe	50
„ Arthur Holdsworth	50
	£580

Geo. Treby

(CXXXV.)

Chapter XXI., par 25

Warrant[2] appointing Richard Arnold, Gentleman, to be Agent. By the Lords Justices, Parker, C. Townshend, P. Bolton, Berkeley, J. Craggs.

" Whereas we have thought it necessary for His Majesty's Service to give unto Brigadier-General Francis Nicholson the command of

---

[1] Mis Bk. 723, p 77.   [2] Mis Bk 593, p 85

an independent Company, to consist of 100 private men and non-commissioned Officers, for the defence of Carolina, according to an Establishment to be formed in that behalf We do therefore hereby constitute and appoint you to be Agent and Paymaster to the said Company You are therefore diligently to discharge the duty as such by taking care of the affairs, and keeping the accounts of the said Company from the commencement of the said Establishment, and the Paymaster-General of His Majesty's Guards and Garrisons, or any other Paymaster or Paymasters for the time being, are hereby authorised and desired to pay unto you all such sum or sums of money as shall from time to time be issued for payment of the said Company, according to the Establishment in that behalf And you are to pay, or cause the same to be paid, in the same manner as the other independent Companies are now paid, and to do all such other matters and things relating to the said Company as to His Majesty's Service shall appertain, this Our Warrant being first entered with the Auditors of His Majesty's Imprest, to the end you may duly account for all such sum or sums of money as shall come to your hands on account and for the use of the said independent Company. And for so doing this shall be your Warrant

"Given at the 'Cockpit' this 13th day of September, 1720, in the 7th year of His Majesty's reign.

"By their Excellencies' command,

"GEO TRLBY"

"*To Richard Arnold, Gentleman.*"

Memorandum [1]

Mr Eyre, of Chelsea Hospital, disputed this Warrant with Mr. Arnold, upon account of his having a Commission from the King to be agent to all the Invalids' Companies formed and to be formed, notwithstanding which the Lords Justices give it in favour of Mr Arnold, as being an independent Company of Foot (and not Invalids), upon which Mr Arnold told the Lords Justices that he did not dispute this Warrant for the value thereof, but purely to preserve the prerogatives of the Secretary at War, who granted the same, and in whose gift agencies of this nature are, and therefore begged of their Excellencies to allow him to resign to Mr. Eyre, which they agreed to, and signed a new Warrant for him on the 25th October, 1720.

---

[1] A MS note on this entry states that it is in the handwriting of Mr. Arnold.

(CXXXVI.)

Chapter XXV., par 3.

THE APPOINTMENT (BY PATENT) OF A SECRETARY OF STATE

" VICTORIA, &c., That We, very much confiding in the fidelity, industry, prudence, experience, and other shining virtues of our right trusty and well-beloved Counciller,

have nominated constituted, and appointed and by these presents Do nominate, constitute, and appoint him, the said

, one of Our Principal Secretaries of State, to have, hold, exercise and enjoy the said office of one of Our Principal Secretaries of State unto the said   with all salaries, commodities, pre-eminences, places, dignities, allowances, and emoluments whatsoever belonging or appertaining to the same office for and during Our pleasure.   In witness, &c.

"Given at Our Court at St. James's, this 8th day of March, 1858, and in the twenty-first year of Our reign

"By Her Majesty's Command,

"J. H WALPOLE"

(CXXXVII.)

Chapter XXV , par 6

EXTRACTS FROM RECORDS IN THE CUSTODY OF THE MASTER OF THE ROLLS, DEPOSITED IN THE STATE PAPER BRANCH RECORD OFFICE, PURSUANT TO THE ACT 1 & 2 VIC, c 94.

1. '*Domestic State Papers,*' *Chapter II, Vol 61, No 41, Notes (by Williamson)*[1] *on the Oath, Patent, Salary, Privileges, Functions, Allowances Duties, &c, of a Secretary of State.*

SECRETARY

Is sworne by ye Clerke of ye Councell in Waiting at ye Councell
Oath   Table, and is then sworne Privy Councellor, for which

---

[1] Probably Mr. Secretary Williamson, referred to Vol I., p 69, of this Work, and who gave 5000*l.* for his office.

onely single Fees are taken, as if he were onely sworne plaine Privy Councellor.

Then is expedited his Patent under y̕ Great Seale of England, y° Office of Principall Secretary is granted him onely (for pleasure); y° pencon or salary of 100ᵘ per annum, which was y° old salary, is for life   **Patent**

Next is assigned by Privy Seale dorm̕ y° quarterly summ of 462ᵘ10ˢ quarterly out of y° Post office during his being Secretary   **Salary**

Then in order to y° executeing of his office, y° Lord Chancellor is to be moved y̕ he may be made Justice of Peace (which he hath a right to be in all y̕ Countyes of England), and accordingly one or more commissions are drawne, directed to y° Lord Chancellor or some other Justices, for sweareing him to be Justice in those countyes whereof they are Justices of y° Peace, which may properly be done by y° Lord Chancellor at his own house (y° Clerke of y° Crowne being present with y° ¹Commissioners), y° Lord Chancellor being a General Justice of y° Peace in all Countyes (*q* whether y° Lord Chancellor can sweare a man Justice for a county where he is not himselfe sworne ?)   **Justice of Peace**

He is after y̕ Consecracon of a Bishop to bring him to doe his Homage to y̕° King (for y̕e Temporaltyes of his Bishoprike), which is to be done usually before or after prayers or divine service in or neare y° closett, y° Bishop, habited in Epalibus, kneeles on a cushcon before y° King who sitts, y° Bishop joining his hands and putting them in y° King's, between y° King's knees. The Secretary kneeling by, reads y° Oathe of Homage, which by y° Bishop's solicitacon is drawne up by y° Clerke of y° Signett and delivered to y° Secretary, y° Bishop repeats it after y° Secretary, and afterwards kisses y° Booke   **Functions**

Hee is allowed 30 ounces of Plate, though in Queen Elizabeth's time it is sayd y° Secreataiy's allowance was 60 ounces. 26 ounces of gilt plate as by a certificate from y° Master of Jewell-house.   **Plate at Newy. gift.**

Hee is allowed four tunnes of Wine, import free, for y° expence of his family (but other dues or customes he is to pay) This in money some few fees to officers deducted, comes to about   , and is procured upon a warrant from y° Lord Treasurer to y° Officers of y° Custome   **Allowance of Wine**

Vpon y° arrivall of a foreigne Minister, his letters of credence

---

¹ Q., Whether it be one or many Commissioners for each County ?

(or at least copyes of them) are to be brought to yᵉ Secretary of
State, who, having opened yᵉ Originals (in case they be
brought) and communicated them to His Majesty, is on
the audience day to returne them to yᵉ Publicke Minister,
to yᵉ end he may hymselfe present them to His Majesty at his
audience.

The first of yᵉ two Principall Secretaryes of State are allowed
1000 ounces of Plate by yᵉ King, to use in keeping his table, and it
is received out of yᵉ Jewell-house upon My Lord Chamberlain's
Warrant, upon Indenture entered into by yᵉ Secretary for safe delivering it.

2. '*Domestic State Papers,*' *Chapter II., Vol.* 61, *No.* 19. " *Oath of
Fidelity, Secrecy, &c., to be taken by a Secretary of State* "

The Oath of the Secretary [1]

You shall sweare to bee a true and faythfull servant vnto the
Kinge's Majestie as one of the Principall Secretaries of State to His
Majestie   You shall not knowe or vnderstand of any manner of
thinge to bee attempted, don, or spoken against His Majestie's person, honorable crowne, and dignitie Royall, but that you lett and
withstand the same to the vttmost of your power, and either cause
it to bee revealed to his Majestie himselfe, or his Privie Councell,
you shall keepe secrett all matters revealed and committed vnto
you, or that shall bee secrettly treated of in Counsell, and if any of
the said treatie or Councell shall touch any of the Counsellors, you
shall not reveale the same vnto him, but shall keepe the same vntil
such tyme as by the consent of His Majestie or the Councell, pub-
licacon shall be made thereof, you shall to your vttmost beare faith
and allegiance to the Kinge's Majestie, his heires, and lawfull successors, and shall assist and defend all Jurisdiccons, Pre-hemence,
and Authorities granted vnto His Majestie and annexed vnto his
Crowne against all forreyne princes, persons, prelates, and potentates,
&c., by Act of Parliament or otherwise.   And generally in all
thinges you shall doe as a faythfull and true Servant and Subject
ought to doe to His Majestie, soe helpe your God and the holy
contents of this Booke

---

[1] This form of oath continues to be administered, see ' Report on Oaths, 1867,'
p. 3

(CXXXVIII)

Chapter XXVI, par. 12.

PATENT[1] APPOINTING SIR D. DUNDAS COMMANDER-IN-CHIEF.

' His Majesty's Letters Patent under the Great Seal, 25th March 1809, after reciting and revoking the Patents which constituted His Royal Highness the Duke of York Captain-General and Commander-in-Chief, proceeds thus—

"And We, reposing special trust in your prudence, courage, and loyalty, do by these presents constitute and appoint you, the said Sir David Dundas, to be Commander-in-Chief during Our pleasure, of all and singular Our Land Forces employed, or to be employed, in Our service within our United Kingdom of Great Britain and Ireland. You are, therefore, carefully to discharge the said trust of Commander-in-Chief by doing and performing all and all manner of things thereunto belonging. And We do hereby command all Our officers and soldiers, who are or shall be employed in Our Land Service as aforesaid, to acknowledge and obey you as their Commander-in-Chief. And you are to observe and follow such instructions, orders, and directions, from time to time, as you shall receive from Us in pursuance of the trust reposed in you.

"In witness whereof We have caused these Our letters to be made Patent. Witness Ourself at Westminster, 25th March, forty-ninth year Our reign.

"By the King himself,

"BATHURST AND BATHURST."

(CXXXIX.)

Chapter XXVI, par. 13

LETTER OF SERVICE APPOINTING THE COMMANDER-IN-CHIEF.

"SIR,   "*War-Department, 15th July,* 1856.

"The Queen having been pleased to appoint your Royal Highness to serve as a General with four paid Aides-de-Camp, and one

---

[1] The late Duke of Wellington's Patent was in this form.

unpaid Aide-de-Camp, upon the Staff of the Army, I am commanded
to acquaint you it is Her Majesty's pleasure that your Royal
Highness do obey such orders as you shall receive from Her Majesty,
the Commander-in-Chief, or any other your Royal Highness' superior
Officer

" I remain, with the highest respect,

" Your Royal Highness' most obedient,

" Most humble and most devoted Servant,

(Signed)   " PANMURE."

" *General H R H the Duke of Cambridge, K G* '

(CXL.)

Chapter XXVI , par 23

DUTIES OF THE OFFICE OF THE COMMANDER-IN-CHIEF.[1]

" *Horse Guards, 29th August,* 1808

" THE Office of the Commander-in-Chief is divided, for the despatch
of business, into three principal Departments viz, (1) Promotional, (2) Civil and Miscellaneous, (3.) Confidential. The duties
of the two first Departments are detailed in the accompanying
Papers, the duty of the latter comprehends the whole correspondence upon every confidential matter with which the Commander-in-
Chief can in his public capacity be engaged The superintendence
and control of the whole business of this Office must necessarily
devolve upon the Military or Public Secretary

" The increase and extent of the Army, together with the circumstances of its situation, dispersed over all our Possessions in
separate but considerable bodies, has rendered the duties of this
Office infinitely more laborious than heretofore, nor can they, in
justice to the Public, or to the interest of the Army, be diminished
with regard to those who superintend them, as will clearly appear
by the following brief statement of the different subjects and departments upon and with which the Commander-in-Chief is necessarily
in immediate correspondence

" The first feature in the regular business of the Commander-in-

---

[1] 8th Report of Military Inquiry, p 210.

Chief's Office both in extent and importance is the correspondence with the General Officers on Foreign Stations

'Another extensive branch of correspondence exists under His Majesty's Regulations with each individual Corps, in addition to which all Officers in their own persons, or through their friends and Agents have a right to correspond with the Public Secretary on matters touching their individual interest and promotion, and which correspondence becomes a matter of duty on the part of the Commander-in-Chief, as connected with his administration of the Army, to superintend and direct, and when it is stated that the property of individuals to the annual amount of 420,000*l.*, arising from the purchase and sale of Commissions is concerned, it will be of itself be sufficiently convincing proof of the attention and accuracy required in this particular branch of the Promotional Department.

"These heads of the business of the Commander-in-Chief's Office passing through the Public Secretary, are merely mentioned to shew the outline of the general duties of this Office, but there are a variety of other very important points and very extensive detail, attending the business of the Army, which must be sufficiently obvious to any person in any manner acquainted with Military affairs, and of which one instance will be given in this place, this is, the duty of the Public Secretary to receive those Officers and others who may be desirous of conferring with him personally upon their Military Affairs, and which duty not only occupies from two to three hours of the best part of the day, but requires the greatest care to discharge with propriety and accuracy, and it is also a duty that could not, in justice to the Army, be in any manner dispensed with.

'Another most important and not less laborious duty has of late been assigned to the Commander-in-Chief's Office, which relates to the General Courts-martial of the Army. In the year 1805, upon consideration of the extensive powers at that time exercised by the Judge-Advocate-General, it was thought advisable by the Legislature to make a different arrangement with regard to the communication of the King's commands upon the proceedings of Courts-martial, and His Majesty therefore was pleased to order, that after the Judge-Advocate General had stated to him his opinion upon the regularity and legality of the proceedings, that they should be finally laid before His Majesty by the Commander-in-Chief, and who should then make known His Majesty's final commands to the Army, which duty had previously been performed by the Judge-Advocate-General. In consequence of this arrangement, it necessarily becomes an additional and necessary duty to prepare the Proceedings and Reports for His Majesty's consideration, and in like manner, to frame the Public Letters upon them for the guidance and information of those concerned. It must be obvious that this duty requires the greatest care and attention, and that it must occupy a very considerable portion of time

"As these affairs must necessarily increase with the augmentation of the Army, and with the additional business attendant upon the constant and active employment of our Military Force, it will in that event be absolutely necessary, at no very distant period, to require further aid in the execution of them, and consequently an augmentation would be then necessary to the present Establishment of the Office.

(Signed)　"J. W. Gordon"

Memoranda relative to the Promotional Department in the Commander-in-Chief's Office.

"*August 29th,* 1808

"All Promotions and Appointments in the Cavalry, Foot Guards, Infantry of the Line, and Fencibles, as likewise in all Foreign or Colonial Corps, pass through this Department, excepting the Commissions in the two Regiments of Life Guards, the Colonels of those Corps receiving the King's pleasure thereupon, without communicating with the Commander-in-Chief, unless in cases of exchange between Officers of the Life Guards and those of other Corps in which case the Exchanges must be sanctioned the Commander-in-Chief.

"The Officers of a few of the Volunteer Corps still continue to hold Commissions from His Majesty, and consequently their appointments pass also through the Commander-in-Chief's Office

"Under this head is included the examination of every recommendation, whether by or without purchase; as also the whole of the correspondence relative to promotions, whether with Colonels or other Officers of Regiments, or Regimental Agents of Corps at Home, or the Commander of the Forces in Ireland, or Generals commanding on Foreign Stations.

"Notifying every Appointment to the Commander of the Forces in Ireland, and to Generals commanding on Foreign Stations, as far as regards their respective commands, it includes also the noting all Candidates for Commissions, and the correspondence with those who recommend them

"In this, too, is comprehended all questions that arise relative to the rank of Officers, and innumerable references in regard to former questions brought before the Commander-in-Chief; as also various points respecting what may be called the *Unwritten Law* of the Army, or in other words, the Customs of the Service, Communications with other Officers on many of the points before-mentioned

"Though, at first sight, it might be supposed that no Money Transactions could pass through this Department, yet even it is not entirely free from these, as many Commissions originally vacant by purchase have been filled without, and consequently other Commissions are from time to time appropriated to repay the Individuals who had claims for these Commissions, the correspondence concerning which must necessarily pass through this Department, and also the late arrangement for paying off Half-pay Commissions, for which a correspondence must be entered into with every Regimental Agent, and an Account kept with them, a full explanation of which has been recently laid before the House of Commons, a copy of which is annexed

"The Promotions in Foreign Corps now on the Establishment, or be placed on it.

"Fencible Corps —The placing on the Establishment every new Corps that may be raised. The augmentation of every Regiment of the Line, or its Reduction

"This includes preparing the Papers to be laid before His Majesty, and, when approved, detailing the same to the War-Office, and notifying the Augmentation or Reduction to the proper Officers.

"If of Corps in Ireland, to the Commander of the Forces there, and to the Secretary of State for the Home Department, for the information of the Lord-Lieutenant.

'The whole of the correspondence relative to the Purchase and Sale of Commissions, and the Returns of the Names of all Purchasers, are kept in the Promotional Department, as is also a List of Officers noted for Promotion.

"A Statement is made out half-yearly of the number of Officers of different Ranks brought from the Half-pay to Full-pay Vacancies without Exchange, by which means the Half-pay is extinguished, and that being reckoned at a certain number of years purchase, these Statements shew the savings made to the Public by the Half-pay of these Officers ceasing.

(Signed)   "J W GORDON."

Memoranda relative to the Civil and Miscellaneous Department in the Commander-in-Chief's Office

"A DAILY communication exists between the Commander-in-Chief, through his Military or Public Secretary with the following Departments of Government, through the respective Under-Secretaries for the time being, viz.— —

　　'Lords Commissioners of His Majesty's Treasury.
　　"Secretary of State for the Home Department
　　"Secretary of State for the Colonial Department
　　"Secretary at War
　　"Board of Ordnance
　　"Directors of the East India Company.

"All application for pecuniary grants or favours, not provided for by special Regulations, are referred to the Treasury for consideration, such are, decisions of Board of Claims—indemnities for Losses by Shipwreck, and Pensions to any considerable amount to Officers' Widows, or remuneration for any special Service.

"All Military Correspondence, in any manner connected with the Civil Arrangements of the Kingdom, are addressed to this Department—All correspondence relative to Volunteer Corps, is referred to the Secretary of State for the Home Department

"All applications for the Pardon of Convicts for small offences, who are desirous of entering the African Corps, are made to him, and all correspondence necessary to be communicated to the Civil Government of Ireland, is addressed to him　No Troops are removed from, or sent to Ireland, without a communication to the Lord-Lieutenant through the Secretary of State.

"A very extensive and important correspondence is carried on with this Office, as the Secretary of State for the War and Colonial Department applies to the Commander-in-Chief for all information relative to the state of the Armies at Home and Abroad, and generally on all subjects connected with Military Affairs, and all application which relate to Extraordinary Military Expenditure in the Settlements Abroad are referred to him—Every authority under which the Commander-in-Chief acts, with respect to the Augmentation or Reduction of the Army, is derived from this Office.

"Every change in the Establishment of Regiments is communicated to the Secretary at War, the King's pleasure having been previously taken by the Commander-in-Chief.

"All applications for Camp Equipage when an expedition is

preparing, of the Supplies of Camp Equipage to Foreign Stations, and for all Medical Stores, are made to him.

" All Memorials for ordinary pecuniary Claims are referred to him The correspondence relative to Widows' Pensions is also sent to the Secretary at War

" All applications for relief from the Compassionate Fund, are recommended for his consideration, Widows and Orphans of Officers are entitled to relief from this Fund, at the discretion of the Secretary at War

" All correspondence with the Army Medical Board is addressed to the Secretary at War in the first instance. The Commander-in-Chief having no direct communication with the Board but for special Military purposes

" Officers transferred from 2nd to 1st Battalions of Regiments by seniority, and without promotion, are entitled to an allowance of 9d per mile, in aid of their travelling expenses, and application is made by the Military Secretary to the Secretary at War for that purpose

' All correspondence relating to Ordnance Service is sent to the Secretary, for the information of the Board, if the subject relates to the Civil Branch, and to the Adjutant-General of Artillery, if the subject relates to the Military Branch of that Department, but Papers of a demi-official nature are sent to the private Secretary, to be laid before the Master-General

" All Petitions from Chelsea Pensioners for Arrears of Pensions, or other matters of this description, are sent to the Chelsea Board

" A correspondence takes place with the Directors relative to the Passages of all Officers going out to the East Indies, and generally, upon all matters connected with the Embarkation of Troops and Recruits for India.

" The Judge-Advocate General transmits to the Commander-in-Chief, a copy of his Report to the King upon all cases which have been investigated by General Courts-martial, when the Commander-in-Chief takes His Majesty's pleasure upon the whole proceedings The King's commands are then signified to the General Officers of the Districts, or on the Stations where the Courts-martial were respectively held Copies of these letters are sent to the Judge-Advocate-General, and a notification made to the Secretary at War, in cases where a check upon the pay renders such communication necessary. The correspondence, in consequence, must necessarily pass through the Commander-in-Chief's Office.

' There is also a constant correspondence between the Commander-in-Chief's Office, the Treasury, and the War Office, on the subject of providing Passages for all Officers and their Families proceeding on Foreign Service, and upon all matters in any manner connected therewith

" There is a very extensive correspondence (though often of a trifling nature, yet it must be carefully attended to) from the Relations of Soldiers wishing to ascertain their existence, and a statement of their effects if dead; and to ascertain whether any Prize Money was due to them at their decease, if it appears that any such was due, the Prize Agent is called upon to account to the Relatives for the same.

(Signed)   " J. W. Gordon."

(CXLI.)

Chapter XXVI, par. 40.

Copy of any Documents now in Force upon the Subject of the respective Duties and Authority of the Secretary of State for War and the Commander-in-Chief.[1]

" Victoria R.

" Whereas, We deem it expedient, in order to prevent any doubts as to the powers and duties of the Commander-in-Chief with respect to the Government of our Army and the Administration of Military Affairs, to express Our Will and Pleasure thereon   Now our Will and Pleasure is, that the Military Command and Discipline of Our Army and Land Forces, as likewise the Appointments to and Promotions in the same, together with all powers relating to the Military Command and Discipline of Our Army, which, under and by any Patent or Commission from Us, shall have been, or shall from time to time be, committed to, vested in, or regulated by the Commander-in-Chief of Our Forces, or the General Commanding Our Forces in Chief for the time being, shall be excepted from the Department of the Secretary of State for War.

" And We are further pleased to declare Our Will and Pleasure to be, that all powers relating to the matters above enumerated shall be exercised, and all business relating thereto shall be transacted, by the Commander-in-Chief of Our Forces for the time being, and shall be deemed to belong to his Office, subject always

---

[1] Return to an Address of the Honourable the House of Commons dated 11th March, 1869

n Our General Control over the Government of the Army, and to the responsibility of the Secretary of State for the exercise of Our Royal Prerogative in that behalf, and subject to any powers formerly exercised by the Secretary at War.

"Given at Our Court at Balmoral, this 11th day of October, 1861, in the 25th Year of Our Reign.

"By Her Majesty's Command,

"G. C. LEWIS."

(CXLII.)

Chapter XXVI, par. 37

MEMORANDUM BY THE LATE LORD PALMERSTON AS TO THE DUTIES OF THE COMMANDER-IN-CHIEF'S OFFICE.

" *War Office, 9th June,* 1827.

"The following General Rules, founded upon the Principles observed by His late Royal Highness the Duke of York during his administration of the Army, are most humbly submitted by the Secretary at War for Your Majesty's most gracious consideration and approval, to be established henceforward for the guidance of those who may be entrusted by Your Majesty with the Superintendence of Your Majesty's Army —

"The Commander-in-Chief is bound to maintain Your Majesty's Regulations and orders, and not to allow them to be set aside or infringed by the Interposition of Favour and Influence. Upon this point, he should not consider himself at liberty to use any discretion *Maintenance of the General Regulations and Orders*

"In submitting the names of General Officers for the Command of Regiments, for Governments, and for Honorary Distinctions, he must be guided by a fair and impartial view of their *Military* Services and claims, these being the only considerations by which he ought on this matter to be swayed. *Regiments, Governments, and Honours.* The Interests of the Army, the credit of the Country, his own character, and, above all, the Honor of his Sovereign, are deeply concerned in his selecting those who are best entitled to favor and reward upon Military grounds The General Officer who has grown old in the meritorious discharge of useful Service in various Climates; the General Officer whose Service, though of life duration, has been particularly distinguished, and the individual who has suffered in limb and in health, all claim a share of his attention.

Their Services and Merits should be weighed with a just impartiality, and their names should be submitted on that principle for marks of Your Majesty's favour. A course of Service free from danger, hardship or labour, cannot be considered as constituting in any Class claims to that reward which is due to Meritorious exertion either in the Field at the head of Troops, or in important and laborious departments. The Army is a profession requiring active Exertion, and the Exposure of Life and Limb; and Reward and Distinction should follow that Exertion and Exposure.

" Where pretensions from Service are nearly equal, Seniority should be taken into account, but mere Seniority should not preponderate against Service of Extraordinary Merit Utility, or Distinction.

" The Selection of Officers for Employment on the Staff, whether Staff appointments on the General Staff or in the Departments of the Adjutant and Quartermaster-General, should be influenced by a regard to their Merit and Talents, and to their Qualifications for the peculiar duties which are to be assigned to them. In selecting those Officers whose names are to be submitted to Your Majesty for such appointments, recourse should be had to the Records which have been made at the Horse Guards under the Sanction of His late Royal Highness the Duke of York, of the Services, Claims, and Merits of the Officers of the Army.

" Civil duties being in many Instances combined with appointments upon the Staff abroad, the Selection of Officers for such stations must be made subservient to the views of Your Majesty's Government. But the Commander-in-Chief, or other responsible Military advisor of Your Majesty, must be careful that the *Military* Command be in all cases placed in Hands to which the Discipline and Honor of the Service may safely be confided.

" In recommending General Officers for employment on the Staff, the Commander in-Chief, or other Military Head, must bear in mind that the Duties of such Officers are highly important and that the Efficiency and Discipline of the Troops, their Character and credit, the strict attention of Regimental Officers to their Duty, and their correct and gentlemanlike conduct, depend in a great measure upon the superintending care of the General Officer under whose orders Regiments may be placed.

' It must also be recollected that sound judgment and good temper are not less requisite than a firm, steady, and strict enforcement of Discipline; and that local circumstances may often call for the exercise of great discretion, and for that Tact which is so necessary in an intercourse with individuals so various in character and in original condition. The selection should therefore not be guided by favour or Political Influence, but it should result from a knowledge and experience of the Merit and Qualifications of Officers. If an Officer selected for permanent employment on the Staff should be a Regimental Field Officer, he should be placed on the Half-pay of his Regimental Commission, and no Half-pay Officer should be brought upon full pay regimentally while employed in *any* situation on the Staff unless he gives up his Staff appointment. The only Staff appointments which confer the Brevet Rank of Colonel are those of Adjutant-General, Quartermaster-General [if the Officers be Lieutenant-Colonels when appointed], Field Officers of the Household Troops, Horse and Foot (in the Horse after Seven Years' Service in the Rank of Lieutenant-Colonel), and Aides de-Camp to the King. The appointment of Aides de-Camp to the King is a distinction which is naturally an object of ambition to every old Officer, independently of the advantage attached to it of obtaining the Rank of Colonel so much earlier than it could otherwise be attained. It will therefore be the duty of the Commander-in-Chief to submit for Your Majesty's consideration for such appointments the names of those Lieutenant-Colonels whose merit, and whose distinguished and useful Services may appear to him best to entitle them to that honour, due regard being had to Seniority, and care being taken that those included in the list submitted by himself are Lieutenant Colonels of the year succeeding that which comprehends those promoted by the last General Brevet, or that which may be in progress at the time.

"It will then be for Your Majesty to determine who shall be selected from that List of appointments with which is connected the honour of attendance upon Your Majesty's Person, or whether any Lieutenant Colonels shall be admitted to this mark of favour who are Junior to those whose claims may be submitted by the Commander-in-Chief.

"Garrison Staff situations should be reserved as a Reward, and retired Provision for Officers who from long service, from ~Garrison Appointments~ wounds, or from the effect of climate, have become unfit for Duties requiring much exertion, and the Records at the Horse Guards should be consulted for the Services and claims of those who may be candidates for such appointments.

"Regimental Promotions and Successions should be governed by strict Principle and Regulation, and should be unin- ~Regimental Promotions.~ fluenced by Favour and Interest. But, above all, in selecting Officers for the Command of Regiments, the utmost care must be taken to choose those who shall possess the necessary quali-

fications for the important Duties attached to those Commands.
For upon a proper and judicious performance of those Duties depend
the Character, Safety, and Health of Corps, the maintenance
Subordination and Discipline, and the general Character, Conduct,
and Habits of all the Ranks of the Army. A general observation
of the Service, the various Reports made, but especially the Half-
yearly Inspection Reports, are the sources which must furnish the
Commander-in-Chief with the information that is to guide him in
his recommendation of Officers for the command of Regiments, and
the selection should be directed by Experience and a conviction of
Merit, and not by Favour or Influence, as the charge of a Regiment
is too serious a responsibility to be placed in hands unknown or
untried, or to be confided to an Officer who has not shown himself
to be possessed of the necessary capacity and zeal.

"These observations apply in some, though in a less degree to
Officers of all Ranks, and it is the duty of the Commander-in-Chief
to endeavour to fill all Ranks of the Army properly and efficiently.
Your Majesty's Regulations provide for the Promotion and Succession of Officers by and without Purchase, and if they be strictly
observed, the Interests of the Service cannot be prejudiced, nor can
Injustice be done to Individuals. It is, therefore, the Duty of the
Commander-in-Chief to enforce a close adherence to those Regulations, and not to suffer Favour or Influence to occasion any departure
from them.

"The Established Rules, and those which must be invariably
observed, are, first, that no Officer, however deserving, shall be
promoted without Purchase over a Senior in Regimental or Army
Rank ; and, secondly, that no Officer shall be promoted by purchase
over a Senior in Regimental or Army Rank, who is prepared to
purchase, and has given in his name agreeably to Regulation.

"The Seniority of the deserving Officer depends upon the due
observance of these established principles, and he has a right to count
in this respect upon the Protection of the Commander-in-Chief and
the Justice of his Sovereign, so long as he does not forfeit his claim
to either by incorrect or irregular conduct, or by proof afforded of
Incapacity. The only exceptions to this general Principle are
when the Promotion of a Regiment is suspended on account of the
unsatisfactory state of its Discipline, Insubordination to the Commanding Officer, want of Harmony among the Officers, or general
Misconduct in Quarters or in the Field, &c., or when the vacancy
arises from the removal of an Officer, whether by sale or other
in consequence of a *Court-martial, or Court of Enquiry*, or on account
of conduct calling for the exercise of the Royal Prerogative. I

Long Important in the last mentioned Cases that the Officers of a Regiment should derive no advantage of promotion by such removal, in order that it may not be imputed to them that they fomented the difference, or encouraged the irregularities which led to the Removal, or were biassed in the Evidence which they may have given by any view to their own advancement.

"In these cases, Officers from the Half pay, or from other Corps, should be recommended for the vacant Commission; but care must be taken to select Officers who are Senior to those who are thus passed by.

"In recommending Officers for Appointments without Purchase, a reasonable proportion should be taken from the Half-pay List, both from consideration of Justice to the Officers on that List and with a view to reduce the charge of the Half-pay. But care must be taken to exclude from such selection those who may be objectionable from the Character they bore in their former Regiments, from Habits they may be known to have acquired while on Half-pay, from Physical Disqualifications, or from any other reasons which may be found in the Records of the Commander in-Chief's Office.

"When Exchanges from Full to Half pay take place, the Successor must be selected from the General List of Candidates, and the Officer retiring must not be allowed upon any account to find his own successor. This Rule applies equally to Exchanges where the difference is permitted to be given and received. The application of the retiring Officer must be unconditional, and the Successor must be selected from the General List of Candidates, without any communication between the Individuals In sanctioning Exchanges between two Officers on full pay, great care must taken not to admit of such as are suggested by the desire of one Corps to get rid of an obnoxious Individual by transferring him to another. The Individual who is considered unfit for one Corps must be deemed equally unfit for another, and in this respect no Corps can be entitled to a preference.

Exchanges

"In the recommendation of Officers for First Commissions by and without Purchase, care must be taken to select those who shall be most eligible in point of appearance, manner, and education, due regard being paid to priority of application, and, above all, with respect to Commissions without Purchase, to the claims or circumstances of the Parents, especially if the Candidates are the Sons of old Officers of the Army and Navy. The Orphan Son of an Officer who has fallen in the Service should more especially be the object of attention.

First Commissions

"The List of Candidates for First Commissions will probably

always continue to be as it was during the Administration of His, late Royal Highness the Duke of York, far greater than means can be found to provide for, especially when it is considered that the Cadets of the Royal Military College, who have passed a successful Examination, are entitled to Commissions without Purchase, and that a due proportion of First Commissions vacant without Purchase ought to be filled up by Cornets and Ensigns from the Half-pay   It is, therefore, just and reasonable that the applications of the oldest Candidates, if in all respects Eligible, should receive the earliest consideration, as it must be mortifying to Expectants of old date, to whom encouragement has from time to time been held out, to see themselves Superseded by Candidates of more recent date, but possibly of more Interest, and it seems proper, from the considerations above mentioned, that no Individual who has the means of purchasing a Commission should be recommended for one without Purchase, to the prejudice of those who are not so circumstanced

"In recommending Officers for the Purchase of Commissions, attention should be paid to select Individuals of good Family and Connexions and of sufficient means, and, above all, of good and liberal Education, with due regard to priority of application

"The Rule to be observed with respect to the Date of Regimental Promotions and appointments, is the following —
Dates of
Commissions   If the Individual is on the spot abroad where the vacancy occurs, his Commission bears the date of the recommendation from the Foreign Station, and if he is at home, that of the day on which his name is submitted to the King

"Antedates to Commissions are not to be given

"Relative alterations of date must be founded on proof of some previous mistake

"A step of Brevet Rank (though not higher than that of
Brevet Rank.   Lieutenant-Colonel) attaches to the appointment of Deputy Adjutant-General and Deputy Quartermaster-General at home and abroad.   To that of Military Secretary in Ireland after one Year's Service in that situation.   To the appointment of Inspecting Field Officer of Militia in North America, and to no other.   Promotion by Brevet is otherwise general, and to be conferred strictly according to Seniority in the several Ranks

"A Step of Brevet Rank may be conferred upon an Individual as an act of special favour, but such favour should be strictly limited so as to be the Reward of very distinguished Conduct in the Field for which an Individual may be particularly recommended by the General Officer under whose command he has served, and, even with this limitation, great discrimination should be observed as to the phase of the Service which may have produced the notice and recommendation. Officers above the Rank of Lieutenant-Colonel, or who are Companions of the Bath, may after retirement from the Service retain their Names in the Army List but without any other Military Privilege, or the Capacity of Command or Promotion, the Rank being merely nominal, but Local Rank on the Continent and elsewhere should not be given to Officers who have retired from the Service.

"The Permission to sell Commissions is allowed as an Indulgence to Officers who have purchased them, or who not having purchased have served with credit for a period of Twenty Years, but the permission cannot be claimed as a right in either case, and the Indulgence would in either be forfeited by misconduct. Death-bed applications for permission to sell for the Benefit of Heirs and Representatives are in no case to be admitted.

Permission to sell Commissions.

(Signed)   approved   "G. R."

(CXLIII.)

Chapter XXVII, par 3.

PATENT APPOINTING THE JUDGE-ADVOCATE-GENERAL
TO OFFICE

"VICTORIA, by the GRACE of GOD, of the United Kingdom of Great Britain and Ireland, Queen, Defender of the Faith, TO ALL TO WHOM *These Presents shall come, Greeting*· WHEREAS, &c., We of our especial grace, certain knowledge, and mere Motion, and for and in Consideration of the good and acceptable Services to Us done, and to be done, by Our trusty and well-beloved ———, as also for and in consideration of the Learning, Skill, and Ability of the said ———, HAVE given, and by these Presents DO give and grant unto the said ——— the said Office and Place of *Advocate General* or *Judge Martial* of all our Forces, both Horse and Foot, raised or to be raised for Our service within Our United Kingdom of Great Britain and Ireland, and in all other Our Dominions and Countries whatsoever (except Our Dominions where particular Advocates General or Judges-Martial are appointed), to HAVE, HOLD, *use, exercise, and enjoy* the said office and place unto him the said ——— by himself or his sufficient deputy or deputies for and during Our pleasure, the same to be exercised according to the power and authorities given and allowed in and by an Act of Parliament made in the first year of the reign of Our late Royal ancestor, King George the First entituled 'An Act for the better regulating the Forces to be continued in His Majesty's Service, and for the Payment of the said Forces and of their Quarters,' and according to such other Act or Acts of Parliament as shall from time to time be in force, allowing the executing Martial Law within the places aforesaid, together with all salaries, fees, pay, allowances, entertainments, profits, lodgings, and rooms for the office, rights, privileges, advantages, and emoluments whatsoever, to the office and place of Advocate-General or Judge-Martial of our said United Kingdom belonging or in anywise appertaining in as full and ample manner as the said ——— or any other person or persons hath or have held and enjoyed the same, And by these presents give and grant unto the said ———, and to his sufficient deputy or deputies, full power and authority at such time and times when Martial Law shall be allowed to be exercised as aforesaid, to administer an Oath to any Court-martial or to any person or persons that shall be examined as a witness or witnesses in any cause, trial, or hearing before a Court-martial or any commissioners or persons whatsoever appointed or to be appointed to examine, hear, or determine any matters or complaints touching or in anywise concerning any military affairs whatsoever.

(1.) [" And for the better advance of Our service in the execution of the said office, Our express will and pleasure is, that all officers and soldiers of Our said land forces obey him, the said ———, as Our Advocate-General or Judge-Martial, in that behalf constituted and appointed as aforesaid ·]

(2.) [" And We also will that the said ——— observe such orders as he shall from time to time receive from Us or any Commanders-in Chief for the time being of Our said land forces, now or hereafter to be by Us thereunto authorized and commissionated]

(3). [" AND WE DO *hereby* likewise grant unto the said ———, or to his deputy or deputies, full power and authority from time to time to administer an oath to any person or persons in order to the better discovering of the truth of any matter, cause, or thing which shall be at any time referred to or brought before him or them relating to any complaint or otherwise in any military matter whatsoever, at such time and times when Martial Law shall be allowed to be executed as aforesaid:]

'IN WITNESS whereof, We have caused these Our Letters to be made patent WITNESS Ourself at Our palace at Westminster, this ——— day of ———, in the ——— year of Our Reign

"BY WRIT OF PRIVY SEAL"

(CXLIV.)

Chapter XXVII. par 3

MEMORANDUM ON THE DUTIES OF THE JUDGE-ADVOCATE-GENERAL.[1]

These seem to be as follows —

I He is the responsible legal adviser to the Sovereign, as the Confirming Officer of the proceedings of all General Courts-martial in the United Kingdom, and the Channel Islands.

The Judge-Advocate-General exercises this function, not by virtue of any clause to that effect in the Letters Patent by which he is appointed, but of a provision in the Warrants issued by the Crown empowering Officers to convene General Courts-martial, in those places, which is as follows —

"We are further pleased to order that the proceedings of such General Courts-martial shall be transmitted to Our Judge-Advocate-General, in order that he may lay the same before Us for Our consideration, and afterwards send them to Our General Commanding-in-Chief, or in his absence, to the Adjutant-General of Our Forces, for Our decision thereupon And for so doing, this shall be, as well to you, as to all others whom it may concern, a sufficient Warrant and Authority."

II He is responsible legal adviser to the Sovereign as the Confirming Officer of the Proceedings of all General Courts-martial held out of the United Kingdom (except in India) for the trial of Commissioned Officers, in cases where such Officers are adjudged to suffer death, penal servitude as felons, or to be cashiered, dismissed, or discharged

---

[1] This Paper was (if I mistake not) prepared by Stephen Denison, Esq, when he held the office of Deputy Judge-Advocate General.

This function of the Judge-Advocate-General is also exercised by virtue of a proviso in the Warrant to Officers for convening General Courts-martial abroad, which is as follows —

" And We do hereby further authorize and empower you, when and as often as any sentence is given and passed by a General Court martial, legally constituted as aforesaid, to cause such sentence to be put in execution, or to suspend, mitigate, or remit the same, as you shall judge best, and most conducive to the good of Our Service, without waiting for Our further orders, except in the case of a *Commissioned Officer adjudged to suffer death, to be transported as a felon, or to be cashiered, dismissed, or discharged,* in which case, as in other instances wherein you shall think it proper to suspend the execution of any sentence, the Proceedings of the Court martial upon such trial, are to be transmitted to Our Judge-Advocate-General, in order that he may lay the same before Us and afterwards send them to Our General Commanding-in-Chief, or in his absence, to the Adjutant General of Our Forces for Our decision thereupon "

III He exercises the powers of a Supreme Court of Review, as regards the Proceedings of all District, Garrison, and General Courts-martial, whatsoever and wheresoever

(1) This power seems to attach to the Office, partly in virtue of a clause [No I] in the Letters Patent, partly in virtue of the 157th Article of War, which requires the proceedings of all District, Garrison, and General Courts-martial to be transmitted to the Judge-Advocate-General's Office for safe custody.

(2) Partly by virtue of the Articles of War, which from very early times appear not only to have invested the Judge-Advocate-General with all the rights of a public prosecutor in Military matters, but, prior to the year 1829, directed that he or his deputy should prosecute in the name of the Sovereign

See the following Articles —

Article 64, anno 1673.

Article 20, anno 1717.

" A General Court-martial shall not consist of less than thirteen Commission Officers, and the President not to be under the degree of a Field Officer, and the *Judge-Advocate-General,* or some person having a deputation to act for him, shall inform the Court, and prosecute in His Majesty's name, and in capital cases administer to the several members the following oath."

Article 75, anno 1829.

" In all trials by *General* or by *District* or *Garrison* Courts-mar tial, the Judge-Advocate, or person officiating as such, shall administer to each member the following oath, and in trials by *Regimental Courts-martial*, the same oath shall be administered by the President to the other members; and afterwards by any sworn member, to the President."

It is observable that this Article speaks of a Judge-Advocate or person officiating as such in all trials by General or District or Garrison Courts-martial, but this was corrected in the next year, see Article 90 anno 1830

In 1860 the 163rd Article of War provided that no officiating Judge Advocate should act as prosecutor

"(3) Partly by reason of there being no legal adviser to the Army, except the Judge Advocate-General. who has therefore become by usage the General Referee in all points of Military Law."

IV He is the supreme legal authority for the Army, by virtue of the last-mentioned clause in his Letters Patent.

V He is, however, to observe such orders as he shall receive, either directly from the Crown, or from any person holding the commission of Commander-in-Chief, as appears by the clause (2) in his Letters Patent

It seems difficult to determine the precise degree of obligation imposed by this clause.

VI He has by his Letters Patent the right of appointing a Deputy with full powers, "within Our United Kingdom of Great Britain and Ireland, and in all other Our Dominions and Countries whatsoever (except Our Dominions where particular Advocates-General or Judges-Martial are appointed)" At the present time this exception seems only to apply to India.

VII. He appears by another clause (3) in his Letters Patent to be invested with some sort of original jurisdiction in all matters which may form the subject of military enquiry, otherwise than by a Court-martial, but the nature and extent of this jurisdiction seem quite uncertain.

VIII He is the Conservator of the Proceedings of all District, Garrison, and General Courts martial (see Articles of War, section 157)

This duty was imposed upon him by Act of Parliament for the first time in the year 1750, and was confined by the Mutiny Act of that year to the proceedings of General Courts-martial only In the year 1830, the provision was extended to the proceedings of District and Garrison Courts-martial as well as General

In the year 1860 it was limited to twelve years from the date of deposit (Article 161). It may be observed that District and Garrison Courts-martial seem to have been instituted in the year 1829. Prior to that year the only Courts-martial in use were Regimental Regimental General, and General Courts-martial.

(CXLV.)

Chapter XXVII, par 11

Memorandum to be laid before the Presidents of all General or District Courts-martial

" Sir,   *Horse Guards, S.W., June* 24, 1865.

" I am desired by His Royal Highness the Field-Marshal Commanding-in-Chief to transmit for your information and guidance the enclosed Memorandum, in which the powers and duties of the newly-created Deputy Judge-Advocates are defined, a copy of which is to be laid before all presidents of General and District Courts-martial.

" I have, &c.

(Signed)   " J. Yorke Scarlett, A G "

" *The Officer Commanding at*   "

Memorandum.[1]

1. The Deputy Judge-Advocate at a General Court-martial should maintain an entirely impartial position and act as assessor to the Court

2 He should give his advice on all matters of law, evidence, or procedure, and, whether consulted or not, interfere to ensure the due formality and legality of the proceedings.

3. At the conclusion of the case he should sum up the evidence and give his opinion upon the law before the Court proceeds to deliberate upon its finding.

4 The officiating Judge-Advocate at a General Court-martial should represent the Judge-Advocate-General, should be deputed by

---

[1] On the 18th June, 1866, this Memorandum was recalled, and re-issued without paragraph 4

him and, if possible, be selected either from Officers who have passed an examination in military law or from barristers, it being understood that when counsel are employed, either for the defence or for the prosecution, the officiating Judge-Advocate should be a barrister.

5. The opinion of the Deputy Judge-Advocate ought to be conclusive upon any point of law or procedure which arises upon a trial at which he officially attends, whether he has or has not an opportunity of consulting the Judge-Advocate-General before a decision is made.

6. He should be responsible to the Judge-Advocate General for a proper record of the proceedings, but, in important cases, he should be assisted in the discharge of his duty by a sworn shorthand writer.

7. In all cases when a prisoner is undefended, he should take care that such prisoner should not lose any privilege that the law allows him in the conduct of the trial.

8. The seat and table of the Deputy Judge-Advocate should be at the right of the president of the court.

9. He should take no part in the conduct of the prosecution, but in other respects should fulfil the duties now cast upon Deputy Judge-Advocates.

10. With respect to District Court-martial, the Presidents are to be instructed to forward them as ordered by the Articles of War to the Judge-Advocate-General, but under cover to the Deputy Judge-Advocate of the district, who will read them, and draw the immediate attention of the Judge-Advocate-General to anything requiring notice in the proceedings.

(Signed)   "J. YORKE SCARLETT, A.G."

(CXLVI.)

Chapter XXVIII., *par.* 58

EXTRACT FROM THE JUDGMENT OF THE JUDGE OF THE PROVINCIAL COURT OF DUBLIN (DOCTOR BATTERSBY) IN MILLS *v.* CRAIG, 23RD DECEMBER, 1867, AS TO THE ECCLESIASTICAL STATUS OF ARMY CHAPLAINS.

THE position mainly relied on was that the statute 25 Vic, c. 4, which dispenses with the Royal Sign Manual to commissions in the Army, mentions, amongst them, the commissions of Military Chaplains, and, therefore, it is said that such is a legislative declaration, that Her Majesty may, by virtue of her Royal Prerogative, appoint Chaplains, and when once appointed, that *status* gives them a right to perform all divine offices *everywhere*, that any clergyman in holy orders can perform, the privilege being *personal*, and for this position 'Moleneaux *v.* Bagsbaw' (9 Jur., N. S., 553) is quoted. But it is not in point, for there a Chaplain appointed to a workhouse, under the statute 4 and 5 Wm IV, c 76, secs 46 and 109, with the licence of the Bishop, and thereby the workhouse was, by the Legislature, taken out of the parish, and out of the jurisdiction of the Perpetual Curate, just as St. Jude's was here taken out of the original parish of St James's The question is reduced to this narrow point, whether Her Majesty can lawfully enable as many clergymen as she pleases to perform all divine offices in the parishes of all other clergymen, against their will and if such power exists, whether it has been exercised by the commission now in evidence "It has been admitted in argument, and is undoubted law, that it is not competent for any clergyman of the Church of England to enter a parish without licence of the Incumbent, and to officiate in performing the duties of his vocation It is not competent for the Ordinary himself, without the leave of the Incumbent, to license any person to officiate within the limits of the parish of that Incumbent" (Per Dr. Lushington, "The office of the Judge promoted by Williams and Browne," 1 Curtis, 55. See also 'Trebec *v.* Keith,' 2 Atk 498, 'Farnworth *v.* the Bishop of Chester,' 4 B. & C 568, 'Moysey *v* Hilcoat,' 2 Hag 30, 'Blist *v* Woods,' 3 Hag 486; 'Dixon *v* Kershaw,' 2 Amb 528; 'Carr v. Marsh,' 2 Phil 198, 'Barnes *v* Shore,' 4 N. C. 593, 'Freeland v. Neill,' 6 N. C. 252, 'Hodson *v.* Dillon,' 3 Cur. 391). The King is said to have two jurisdictions: one temporal, the other ecclesiastical, the latter of which is derived from the common law though the form of the proceedings, and the coercive power exercised in the Ecclesiastical Courts, is often the form of the Civil and Canon Law, and this being indulged to them, the Judges of the common law will give credit to their proceedings, and determine in matters in which they have jurisdiction, and believe them consonant to the law of the Holy Church, although against the reason of the common law (Bacon's Ab Prerogative, D 419, 1 Bla. Com. by Christian, 14, Ayliffe Par Prof xxxiii, 'Marshal *v.* the Bishop of Exeter,' 29 L J. 354) If the King, as stated in Bacon, derived his ecclesiastical authority from the Common Law, the question will be, what was and is the Common Law on this subject? And, commencing from the earliest times, it will be found that the prerogative now claimed is at variance with the Common Law, which has always carefully preserved the parochial system, being one of the most useful arrangements ever made for the maintenance of discipline in the Church. It is said in Van Espin (tit. 16, c. 11, sec. 14), it is certain and without doubt that no priest or clerk, unless he have a benefice with cure of souls, can publicly preach without the approbation and express licence of the Ordinary of the place. The synods and decretals of the Bishops everywhere lay down that the pastors do permit no person to preach in their churches without the licence of the Ordinary in writing (1 C., secs 18, 19, 22). The King may erect a free chapel, and exempt it from ordinary jurisdiction, but Gibson (Codex 210, 211) doubts if he can license a subject to found and exempt it, and if the King of another country were to come into England, he could not have mass celebrated in such an oratory without the licence of the Bishop, because the priest celebrating it would incur punishment (Lynd 234 N. (d), Decret. Greg. Lit. 1, tit 22, c 3, p C8), and the Chaplains even of royal chapels are bound to keep the oath of canonical obedience to their superiors, that is to the "*Præsedente vel curato*" of the Mother Church (Lynd p 70, lib. 1, tit 15 (x), Ayliff, par. 166). It is argued that because the Respondent's commission here does not limit his duties, he may exercise his vocation everywhere; but the priest at his ordination "receives authority to preach the Word of God, and to administer the Holy Sacraments in the congregation where he shall be lawfully appointed thereunto," yet, notwithstanding this, he must have a licence for the particular place (17 & 18 Ch 2, c 6, sec 13) Mr Craig's commission does not purport to license him for any place. Lyndwood says in his Glossary (lit 3, tit 2, \ (h), Beneficenti, p 125) that "neither kings nor princes nor laymen, without the consent of the Bishop, can institute clerks in any church From whence, as it appears, either such an institution made by the King is a *usurpation* and contrary to law, or it is not an ecclesiastical benefice" This is speaking of the deanery of St. Martin's, and others of the gift of the King, in which there is neither institution nor induction, but the King grants by prescription, and no case has been quoted in which the King licenses a curate in the benefice of another clergyman, although he appoints to a chapel royal, in which the clerk has a privilege of exemption by reason of the place being frequented by the Sovereign in person, but not by reason of the ownership of the Sovereign. If the King intrude by his clerk into a benefice, the lands of His Majesty in that diocese are to be placed under an interdict. The words are—" *Si vero*

kujusmo li ... domus facta forma ex regia clestale, per totu Diaces moneatur. Domi s Rex, quod eas fecit infra tempus co petens revoce , alioqin terræ et loca, quæ Dominus Rex habet in illa Pious e qu facta fuerit collario, ecclesiastico supponentor interdicto cee u deo forma supe us annotatum.' (2nd Gibson's Codex, tit xx iii. cap 7. p 180 2nd ed Constitution of Boniface, a.d. 1261, 45 H 3) In short, th Sovereign is supreme ordinary, but bound to act according to ecclesiastical law in the Church, as he is according to the temporal law in other things In the case of a *Commenda* (Davies, Rep 206), which was a question whether the Bishop of Ossory, by virtue of a grant from the Crown *in commendam*, could, after a benefice, fill o the time of the grant, had become vac it, hold it as incumbent along with his bishopric. It was agreed on all hands, that although the King was supreme ordinary, yet neither he nor the Pope could deprive a beneficed clergyman of his rights or property, except for crime And it is there said, quoting "the Bishop of St David's Case" (11 Hen. IV) "*Non valet declaratio papæ vel regis i prejudicium tertii, robustus in pro ci b eficiorum titul, de non tollendo jus quæsitum*" And elsewhere he saith, "*Per clausulam, motu proprio, &c, papa non tollit jus tertii, talis presumitur mens papæ concede te, quali est juris, donatio principis intelligitur, sine prejudicio tertii*" By the Bill of Rights (1 Wm and Mary c. 2, sess 2) it is declared that the pretended power of suspending and dispensing with laws, or the execution of laws, is illegal; and that the Court of Commissioners for Ecclesiastical Causes, and all other Commissioners and Courts of like nature, are illegal and pernicious But the argument for the Respondent here insists that the law may still be set aside by royal prerogative The King can grant toll, a fair market, and the like but not toll travers, no through-toll, nor that the land shall be held in borough English, gavelkind, nor the like, for these are by custom, which cannot commence at this day by grant, and the King cannot make a law by his grant (Brook Tit Patent, sec 100) The King cannot license a man to sink a nuisance in a highway, so if one be bound in a recognizance to keep the peace to another, the King cannot release this duty to the prejudice of the third party (11 Hen VII, sec 35, p 12). The Queen cannot dispense with the Common Law (Bozoun's Case, 4 Co. 35 (n) F). In 2nd Inst. 186 it is said (Hussey, C. J., reported) that Sir John Markham said to the King, Edward IV, that the King could not arrest any man for suspicion of treason or felony, as any of his subjects might, because if the King did wrong the party could not have an action. If the King command me to arrest a man, and accordingly I do arrest him, he shall have his action for false imprisonment against me, albeit he ter in the King's presence Resolved by the whole Court in 16 Hen. VI., which authority might be a good variant for Markham to deliver his said opinion to Edward IV. If the Queen, therefore, being present, could not order an illegal act to be done by Major-General Conyngham, so that he could justify himself under that order, how could he authorize Mr. Craig to do it by any order received from her in her absence, if such there was, which does not appear. In the case of the 'Attorney-General v. Oldin and others' (2 L. R. Ex. 293), it was held that the execution of a *fi. fa.* in Hampton Court Palace was legal, notwithstanding the privilege of the Queen's servants from executions in royal palaces, because it had not been the actual residence of the Sovereign from the 10 Geo. II., A.D. 1737, and the privilege extended only to the actual residence of the Sovereign, and not to every palace owned by the Queen. The exemption there had been enjoyed for 342 years, and no execution had been executed before the one the subject of that case This decision establishes that the mere fact of property, even a palace belonging to the Crown, does not entitle it to the privileges attaching to a place where the Sovereign personally resides The statutes passed from time to time sustain the Common Law of the Church as above stated. Thus by the 2 Hen. IV., c. 15, A.D. 1400, it is provided that none presume to preach, openly or privately, without the licence of the diocesan of the same place first required and obtained. This Act contained provisions against sectarians, and was repealed by 2 Eliz. c. 1, sec. 4, A.D. 1560, but it was only declaratory of the Common Law, which continued as before (1 Court Arundel, A.D. 1408; 1 Bul. 381, Lynd. p. 67, No. 48, Case, Arund. 1) In 'God. Reports, Case 33, it is said "that by the statute of 25 Hen. VIII., c. 19, A.D. 1534, it being enacted that all former canons and constitutions, not contrary to the Word of God, the King's prerogative, or the laws and statutes of this realm, should remain in force until they were reviewed by thirty-two Commissioners appointed by the King, and that review being never made in that King's time, nor anything done therein by King Edward VI. (though he had also an Act of Parliament to the same effect), the said ancient canons and constitutions remained in force as before they were." And afterwards, in pursuance of that statute, the canons of 1603 were framed (which differ but little from the Irish canons of 1634), although the former are 141 in number, and the latter 100 Lord Hardwicke, in 'Colefatt v. Newcomb' (2 Atk. 668), says the only Act made *ex professo* upon the subject of the canons is that of 25 Henry VIII., c. 19, entitled "The Submission of the Clergy and Restraint of Appeals," whereby power was given

to that King, Henry VIII., to appoint thirty-two persons to review
and reform the Ecclesiastical Laws, which, however, was continued
by the several subsequent statute of 27 Hen. VIII, c 15, 35 Hen.
VIII, c. 16, 3 and 4 Ed VI, c 11, but was never completely
carried into execution　By the 28 Hen. VIII, c 5, s 1, Ire a.d.
1537, and 26 Hen. VIII, c 1, Eng a.d. 1535, it is enacted that the
King and his successor shall be the only supreme head on earth of
the whole Church of Ireland, and shall have full power and authority
to visit, repress, redress, reform, order, correct, restrain, and amend
all such errors, heresies, abuses, offences, contempts and enormities,
whatsoever they be, which by any manner, spiritual authority, or
jurisdiction, ought or may lawfully be reformed, &c　By the 2
Hen. VIII, c 31, s. 10, Ire., it is provided that all Archbishop
&c, shall and may use and exercise in the name of the King only,
all such canons, constitutions, ordinances, and provincials, being
already made, for the direction and order of spiritual and ecclesiastical causes, which be not controveant or repugnant to the King's
laws, statutes, and customs of this land, nor to the damage and hurt
of the King's Prerogative Royal, in such manner and form as *they
were used and executed before the making of this Act*, till such time as
the King's Highness shall order and determine according to his laws
of England, and the same to be certified either under the King's
Great Seal, or otherwise ordered by Parliament.　This statute
distinctly affirms the Common law of the Church as it then
was, and as afterwards adopted and continued by the Canons
The Canons of 1634, stated in the Patent affirming them and
annexed to the canons, as printed by the King's printer, to have
been agreed to in Convocation, and executed by the King according
to the form of a certain statute (28 Hen. VIII, c 13), or Act of
Parliament made in that behalf, and by his Prerogative Royal and
supreme authority in causes ecclesiastical, and ordered in all points
to be duly observed, not sparing to execute the penalties in them
severally mentioned upon any that shall wittingly or wilfully break
or neglect to observe the same, are binding, and being assented to
by the King, and in accordance with the Act of Parliament cannot
well be set aside by the Prerogative now (Middleton v Crofts,
2 Atk., Ap. 650)　By Canon "XXXVIII" no curate or minister
shall be permitted to serve in any place without examination and
trial first to be made of his sufficiency, sobriety, and fitness every
way for the ministration whereunto he is deputed, and being found
worthy, he shall be admitted by the Bishop of the diocese, in
writing under his hand and seal　And the said ministers and
curates, if they remove from one diocese to another, shall not be

any means, admitted to serve without testimony of the Bishop of the diocese, or ordinary of the place, as aforesaid whence they came, in writing, of their honesty, ability, and conformity to the Ecclesiastical Law of the Church of Ireland. Canon ' XXXIX." prohibits preaching without authority, and refers it to the Bishop to take such order thereon as he shall think convenient. The 13 and 14 Char. II., c. 6, s. 13, A.D. 1665, enacted that no person shall be received as a lecturer, or permitted or suffered, or allowed to preach as a lecturer, or to preach or read any sermon or lecture in any church, chapel, or other place of public worship within this realm of Ireland, unless he be first approved, and thereunto *licensed* by the Archbishop of the province, or Bishop or the diocese, &c. This Act expressly recognises the parochial system and government, and enforces it. In other cases, although the Crown or public officers are entitled by statute to appoint Chaplains, the licence of the Bishop is always received before such Chaplain can officiate. Under the English Prison Acts, although the Justices appoint the Chaplains, he cannot act without the licence of the Bishop (13 Geo. III., c. 58, s. 1, 55 Geo. III., c. 46, s. 5; 4 Geo. IV., c. 64, s. 28, 29, and 30, 5 Geo. IV., c. 85, and 2 and 3 Vic., c. 56, s. 15). So under the English Lunatic Asylum Statutes the visitors appoint Chaplains, but the Bishop must license them, and may revoke such licence (9 Geo. IV., c. 40, ss. 30 and 32, 'Regina v. Visitors of Middlesex,' 2nd Q. Bench, 446). So under the English Poor-law Acts the Commissioners may order the appointment of Chaplains, but no person can act as such without the consent of the Bishop (4 and 5 Vic., c. 76, ss. 9, 46, 48, 49, and 109; Art. 71, Arch. P. L. 97). In Ireland it has been held that, if the Lord-Lieutenant appoint a chaplain to a lunatic assylum, such Chaplain cannot officiate against the will of the Incumbent of the parish ('Nelligan v. Jones,' 7 I. J. N. S. 39). And although under the Irish Poor-law Acts the Guardians may appoint a Chaplain to the poor-house (1 and 2 Vic., c. 56, s. 48), giving a preference to some clergyman of the Established Church officiating within the parish in which such workhouse shall be situated, *if duly qualified*, Bushe, C. J., in the case of 'Reg. v. the Poor-law Commissioners' (2 J. and Sy. 725), when giving judgment, said that, notwithstanding the appointment of such Chaplains, the Rector is responsible for the due administration of spiritual duties towards the inmates of the poor-house. This was the case of a parochial chapel of ease, not a parish, and so the original Rector continued. And in a subsequent case 'Reg. v. the Belfast Lunatic Asylum,' 5 Ih. C. L. Rep. 375), where a question arose as to the power of the Lord-Lieutenant to appoint a Chaplain to a lunatic asylum, Lefroy C. J said "A serious question arises whether an office which the Legislature has not defined can be created by virtue of the Prerogative. There is no evidence of the origin of these commissions, or of the practice under them, and from anything that appears, Mr. Craig's may have been the first issued." Dr. Studdart, who is always very accurately informed on such subjects, states that, out of 41 Military Chaplains in Ireland, 37 are parochial clergy. In this form such commissions would be applicable to Chaplains serving in the colonies or in the field, to which there could be no objection, and the location of Chaplains in Ireland with chapels and congregations, may have been first adopted since the practice of collecting large bodies of troops in camp or garrison at home has been acted on, but however this may be, there is no trace in history, or in the law books, of such a case as the present, or of an officer with the privilege claimed by Mr. Craig, namely, the right of performing all divine offices for a congregation of all persons who will come to an unlicensed chapel, with open doors, within the parish of another Incumbent, and without the sanction of the diocesan. In the cases referred to, where such innovations have been made, Acts of Parliament have been passed to sanction them. If the decision now made be correct, the same course may be followed, but the Court cannot act upon the argument of inconvenience. It is to administer the law, not to make it, and no law has been quoted or found to support this claim, but, on the contrary, the whole tenor of the Canon Law, the Common Law, and the Statute Law are against it. The present case has also this peculiarity that, if the rights as claimed here exist, the body of persons called Military Chaplains are clergymen of the Church of England not subject to any ecclesiastical superior, nor to any ecclesiastical law, nor any restraint as to doctrines, principles, or preaching, unless such is to be administered by an individual called "Chaplain-General," or by a Court-martial, and if this be so, the Chaplain-General and Court-martial supersede, so far as Military Chaplains are concerned, all Church discipline heretofore existing It is contended the Respondent had the order of his superior officer to do what he is charged with, and is, therefore, justified, although he acted illegally ; but nothing has been quoted from the Mutiny Act or Articles of War to show that the superior officer could lawfully issue such an order, and if the act be an ecclesiastical offence, this suit is to restrain in future, not to punish for the past. If it were a temporal offence, and the Chaplain-General had no jurisdiction, the officer ought not to have obeyed, or if he did, he would not be protected by the order of his superior (1st Hale, P. C., 501)

(CXLVII.)

Chapter XXIX., *par* 4.

MEMORANDA OF THE LATE DUKE OF WELLINGTON, UPON
(1) THE REPORT OF THE COMMISSION OF 1837, AND (2)
THE DRAFT ORDER IN COUNCIL PROPOSED BY LORD MEL-
BOURNE'S MINISTRY FOR ESTABLISHING A CONSOLIDATED
WAR OFFICE.

(1.) *Addressed to Lord Fitzroy Somerset.*

"*Stratfieldsaye,* March 25, 1837.

'THE Report of the Commission is on the Table of the House of
Lords, and I have perused it.

"It has astonished me. I have always understood that it was
a principle of the Government of this country, that he who exercised the Military Command over the Army should have nothing
to say to its Payment, its Movement, its Equipment, or even the
Quartering thereof, excepting under the sanction of a Civil Officer,
who was himself a Subordinate in the Hierarchy of Civil Office,
and could not take the King's Pleasure, excepting upon matters
of account. The Secretaries of State were considered, and were,
responsible upon all the larger Political questions arising out of
the existence of the Army, while the Commander-in-Chief exercised
the Military Command, and, under their superintendence, administered the Patronage, as well for the benefit and encouragement
of the Army itself, as upon Constitutional grounds, in order to keep
this patronage out of the usual course of Parliamentary and Ministerial management.

'But it is the opinion of those who have framed this Report,
that all such precautions and checks are unnecessary, and that
an Office ought to be created which should have the whole and
sole Political and Civil control over the Army, excluding the
Secretaries of State, and that the Officer at the head of this Office
should alone take Her Majesty's Pleasure upon Army Questions,
provided only that he should be called the Secretary at War, and
be a Member of the Cabinet

"The power which would thus be vested in this Office would

be enormous. The Commander-in-Chief, charged with the Discipline, and still, I conclude, vested with the disposal of the Patronage, would be a mere instrument in his hands.

"We will suppose a discussion between them. How could the Commander-in-Chief maintain his ground against a Minister supported by the House of Commons and the Cabinet? Have we never seen a Secretary at War carry on the Discipline of the Army by an Adjutant- and a Quartermaster-General, himself administering its Patronage?

"But this is not all. the Ordnance has hitherto been an important feature in the Military affairs of the country. The Master-General—a great Officer of State, with very important duties to perform, and great Patronage—has in general been a Cabinet Minister, and the Military adviser of the Government. The Civil Officers under this Officer have, up to this moment. been considered the model of official efficiency and economy. But these Officers—hitherto quite separate from and independent of the Command of the Army, with all their Patronage—are to be brought under this new *Leviathan*—the Secretary at War, and the Treasury likewise are to be relieved from the duty of superintending the Commissariat and appointing its Officers.

"Thus, then, everything relating to the Political Command, the Pay, the Movement, the Equipment, the Stationing, the Barracks, the Stores, the Arms, the Forage and Provisions for the Army, is to be in the hands of one Cabinet Minister, a Member of the House of Commons—the Secretary at War.

"The Master-General is to continue in Command of the Artillery, and at the head of the Engineer Department, but he, as well as the Commander-in-Chief, must leap overboard upon the nod of the Leviathan.

"I confess that the most serious part of this affair is, that it takes *the Military power of the State totally and entirely out of the hands of the Person exercising the Royal Authority, and places it in the hands of one Member of the House of Commons and of the Cabinet.* This has not been; and is not the case at present. The change cannot be made in this form without injury to the power of the Crown.

"The King of France, the Emperor of Russia, the Emperor of Austria, the King of Prussia, command their Armies through the instrumentality of a *Ministre de la Guerre!* But these are despotic Sovereigns! The *Ministre de la Guerre* is responsible to the Sovereign!

"Here, the Secretary at War is, and will be, responsible likewise—not to the King—but to the House of Commons.

"In fact, this measure will transfer the *effective Command of the army from the King to the House of Commons*—of which body the Secretary at War will be the most powerful Member.

"WELLINGTON."

(2.) *Addressed to Lord Melbourne.*

(EXTRACT.)

"4th January, 1838.

"THE alteration proposed by this Order in Council ought next to be considered in its relation to the authority of the Crown, and to the Constitution of the Country.

"The Sovereign is the head of the Army. Voted by Parliament from year to year the Sovereign exercises Her power over the Army, as she does every other, by the advice of Her confidential servants They advise Her to select a Military Officer to exercise the command of the Army—to conduct its detail—and to recommend for Promotion and Commissions, in a view to the reward of merit and to the satisfaction of just claims, and upon the Constitutional ground of preventing the application of this Patronage to Parliamentary or party purposes.

"They consider of the amount of the Establishment of the Army to be proposed to Parliament in the annual Estimates, which, having been communicated to the Commander-in-Chief, he submits the same to the Sovereign for Her pleasure and approbation.

"In the use of the Army the Commander-in-Chief acts, as above stated, under the direction of one or other of the Secretaries of State, according to the locality and nature of the Service to be performed

"In modern times care has been taken that the Commander-in-Chief shall incur no expense whatever, and shall originate no measure or alterations which shall incur expense, without consulting the Department, whether Secretary at War, Secretary of State, Treasury, or Ordnance, which has the control over such expense.

"The Commander in-Chief cannot move a Corporal's Guard from one station to another, without a Route countersigned by the Secretary at War.

"This is the principle of the constitution of the British Army.

"The Sovereign commands through the instrumentality of a Military Officer, who cannot move a man excepting by the aid of the Officers of Account, the Secretary at War, or incur the expense of a shilling excepting by the consent of the responsible Department concerned

"How will it be hereafter?

"The Officer of Account, the Secretary at War, is to command Who is to control the expenditure? Not only has he the power over money, but he can issue his orders to the Ordnance for the issue of arms and equipments, without the intervention of the Secretary of State.

"The Army and its real and efficient Commander will stand in a very different relation towards Parliament, the Nation, and the Sovereign.

"The Officer of Account has the command. To whom does he account? The House of Commons?

"His deficiencies will be found in that assembly, and he must exercise the duties of the high office to which the Order in Council is about to call him, to the satisfaction of the House of Commons

"It has hitherto been understood that the Army once voted, Parliament ought not to interfere in its arrangements

"But this principle cannot be urged by an Officer himself at the head of the Army who is under the necessity of explaining and accounting for everything

"It is impossible that such a system should not occasion the greatest inconveniences and difficulties in the peaceable exercise of the authority of the Sovereign as the head of the Army.

"It is not uncommon to see the command of the Armies of other countries entrusted to the *Ministre de la Guerre.* But these countries are each governed by what is called a despotism. The *Ministre de la Guerre* is responsible for his acts, not to a House of Commons, but to the Sovereign himself.

"The concentration of all the authority in one hand is convenient, and gives strength and security to the Government of the Sovereign.

"But in our case the concentration of authority in the hands of the Officer of Account, responsible not to the Sovereign but to the House of Commons, creates a division of power, diminishes that of the Sovereign, to Her inconvenience and eventual injury.

"At the same time, as I have above shown, the arrangement will be in other respects inconvenient to the Service.

' I happen to know of more than one Sovereign in Europe who governs according to constitutional forms, and who, having found or having formed his administration of military affairs on the principle of concentration in the hands of a *Ministre de la Guerre,* has found it necessary to make an alteration, and to adopt the plan

CLVIII.] *Abolition of the Board of Ordnance.* 763

hitherto in use in this country, viz, to form two departments,—one for *la comptabilité de la guerre,* the other for *le commandement,*—the former only to be in relation with the Representative Body.

"The British Army, however necessary, is an anomaly in our system. It has worked with safety to the Constitution as at present constituted, and has promoted the honour and interests of the country.

"The variety of the checks and controls over the exercise of the Command are well understood, and have not been found to impede the successful working of the machine.

"Do not let us without reason make an alteration not necessary, which may render its working inconvenient and dangerous.

" WELLINGTON."

(CXLVIII.)

Chapter XXIX., *par* 4.

A FURTHER MEMORANDUM OF THE LATE DUKE OF WELLINGTON, ADDRESSED TO EARL RUSSELL, AGAINST THE ABOLITION OF THE BOARD OF ORDNANCE.

(EXTRACT.)

"*Horse Guards,* 30*th November,* 1849.

"I HAVE perused the proceedings of the Committee of the House of Commons in the last Session of Parliament on the Ordnance and Army Estimates, and the Reports and proceedings of Commissions appointed by His late Majesty King William the Fourth, to consider of a reformation of the Departments for the Administration of the affairs of the Army and Ordnance, and the exercise of the supreme Command over the Army and the Troops now serving under the Ordnance, which last had heretofore been communicated to me by the late Lord Melbourne, when they were laid before the Government, and upon which I gave him my opinion at the time.

"It appears to me to be quite practicable to give the Committee of the House of Commons, and to give to Parliament at all times, exact States of the Ordnance Stores at every station throughout the Empire

" To define the principle upon which the amount contained in each Magazine has been fixed, to alter the principle on which the amount of Store in each Magazine has been fixed, from time to time, as may be ordered by Government and to limit, to any sum that may be thought proper, the exercise of the power of the Master-General to incur expense, in order that he may immediately adopt remedial measures for any casual misfortune; such limited sum not to be exceeded, in any case, without the express sanction of the Lords Commissioners of the Treasury.

" But it is not necessary to put down the office of Master-General of the Ordnance, and to destroy the Ordnance, in order to attain these objects.

" The Officer filling the office of Commander-in-Chief of the Army has no power whatever of incurring expense, or of giving an order which can occasion expense.

" The Ordnance Department and the office of the Master-General is constituted for the service of the Navy, as well as for that of the Army.

" Even the exclusively Military Branch, the Corps of Artillery and Engineers, and Sappers and Miners, Surveyors, &c., respecting which it is recommended by the Reports of the Commissions above referred to, that they should be transferred to the Commander-in-Chief, have relation with the Navy as well as with the Army

" For instance, the Laboratory and all that relates to the making up and improvement in Ammunition and Armament, is an affair of the Navy, as well as of the Army. The Gun-Carriage Department is likewise essentially Naval as well as Military, and even the Ordnance Guns themselves are a Naval as well as a Military affair

" The defences of Ports and Dockyards are affairs jointly Naval and Military, to be arranged between the Ordnance and the Admiralty, over which the Commander-in-Chief of the Army can have no control

" All of which questions involve considerations of expense in which the Commander-in-Chief of the Army is, upon principle, prevented from interfering. Neither does it appear to me to be at all difficult for the Secretary at War to lay before Parliament exact Estimates of the cost to be incurred at each Station of the Army abroad on account of each Department of the Government, as well as the account of the general expense at home

" Looking at the casualties of the Service in recent years, it is obvious that such Estimates may be erroneous, however founded upon an accurate view of expenditure in the same length of period in former years.

"But it is obvious that excesses of expenditure over Estimate occasioned by such employment can and ought to be explained to Parliament by those whose duty it is to superintend the expenditure of the public money.

*   *   -   *   *   *   *

"It has been thought inconsistent with principle, to entrust with power a Military Officer holding a Commission from the Crown, but it will hereafter be quite safe to entrust with the Military Command of the Army, a Political Officer having power over the Movements of the Army, the Clothing, and Equipment of the Army, the Hospitals of the Army, with the additional power to be added over the Armament of the Army, and over the Barracks and Camp Equipage and other Stores, now administered by the Ordnance, but this Political Officer is in daily communication with, and, therefore, under the immediate influence of, the House of Commons.

"I consider it my duty to warn Her Majesty's servants of the change in the Constitution of the country, which will be involved in this alteration! A warning, which I shall consider it my duty to give to the Sovereign herself! But I go further; I warn the Government of the danger of this alteration in a Military view.

*   *   *   *   *   *   *

"The Ordnance Office is one of the most ancient of the Monarchy. Up to the period of the termination of the French Revolutionary War its duties were limited to the care and supply of the Armament, Arms, Ammunition, and Ordnance Stores, that is those for the service of the Army to the Fleets, Armies, and Fortresses of the country, the construction, preservation, and repair of these latter.

"The scientific corps of Officers and Troops in the Land Service of the Crown, Artillery, Engineers, Sappers and Miners, Surveyors, &c, were under the military command of the Master-General of the Ordnance, and the Civil Department of the Ordnance provided for the Barracks, Barrack supplies, clothing, and payment of this body of troops, then Camp supplies for field services, their pensions and allowances upon termination of their service and retirement.

"At the termination of the French Revolutionary War, the Administration of the day, desirous of diminishing expense, and the number of separate Departments existing, being satisfied with the conduct of the Ordnance Department, seeing that that Department already provided Barracks for the Troops serving under the Ordnance, desired that that Department might undertake the superintendence of the Barrack Department for the Troops in Great

Britain, which had been up to that period under the direction of the Barrackmaster-General, then the superintendence of the Barrack Department in Ireland, which had been under the superintendence of the Barrack Department in Ireland, and subsequently the superintendence of the Barrack Department in all parts of the world in which British Troops are employed, with the exception of the dominions under the Government of the East India Company.

"To these duties was subsequently added the superintendence of the Camp Equipage and Military Store Department, including Great Coats for the Infantry of the Army, Clothing for the Militia, and a certain portion of the Troops, principally Colonial and Local Corps, the Clothing of which was not supplied by contract with the Colonels of the several Regiments, which services had been theretofore performed by Mr. Trotter, under a contract, and afterwards in his capacity of Storekeeper-General.

"The duties of these several Departments, amalgamated with analogous duties for the service of the Troops serving under the immediate command of the Master-General of the Ordnance, were performed by the several Departments of the Ordnance to the advantage and satisfaction of the public, and most particularly of the Select Committee of the House of Commons of the year 1828, of which Sir Henry Parnell was chairman

"The business of the Ordnance Department was then considered as transacted in a manner so satisfactory, as that it was considered a pattern for others, and it is believed that when the Naval Department was revised and altered a short time subsequently, the mode of transacting business in the Ordnance Department was adopted as far as circumstances permitted

"Since that period, 1828-30, the Ordnance Department has undertaken the performance of other duties for the Army at large, which its Officers performed in the immediate service of the Troops, under the Master-General of the Ordnance. In 1834 the Department undertook the supply of Forage to the Horses of the Cavalry and Artillery in England. This service was performed so much to the satisfaction of the public and of the Government, that, in three years afterwards, the Ordnance was required to supply with Forage the Army serving in Ireland, which service has been conducted to the satisfaction of the Government.

"It does not appear that the Department has been overborne by the performance of all these duties, on the contrary, it has given general satisfaction. Its strength has been reduced since these additional duties have been required from it.

"I certainly thought, and still think, that the reduction of the office of the Lieutenant General of the Ordnance was injudicious.

'The Master General is a great Officer of State, and up to the year 1828 had been invariably a member of the Cabinet; and it is undoubted that the general business of the Government occupied much of his time and attention. It was his peculiar duty in the Cabinet to assist the Government with Reports and Opinions upon Military details connected with questions under their consideration. The want of such assistance must occur daily in time of war, but they must and do occur in time of general peace.

"The Lieutenant General of the Ordnance, by relieving the Master-General in the conduct of the details of the Military Service of the Troops under the Ordnance, and by his constant presence at the Meetings of the Board of Ordnance, relieves the Master-General from much duty requiring his personal superintendence and presence, and would give him more leisure for the performance of his duty as a member of the Cabinet.

"It appears, then, from this view of the subject, that there is no occasion for an alteration of the organization of the Ordnance Department, which is highly useful and necessary in the transaction of the Military affairs of the country.

*   *   *   *   *   *

"It appears to have been in the contemplation of the Members of the Commission, and the questions asked in the Committee manifest the existence of the same views in that body, that it would be expedient to place under the administration of the Secretary at War the Commissariat, as well as all other Departments having relation with the Army.

"The services of the Commissariat are not all required by the Army in some of the stations in which placed; and not at all times under all circumstances in any.

"The provisions of the Mutiny Act prescribe the mode in which means of land transport are to be provided; which are rarely necessary in some stations. Provisions can be found for the Troops without the interference of the Commissariat in many stations. The Medical Department has in its service Purveyors by whose services General Hospitals can be established without the assistance of a Commissariat. Such assistance is never required by Regimental Hospitals.

"The nature of the service required from the Commissariat, and of the Establishment to be formed to perform such services, must vary in every country, according to the natural state of cultivation,

population, and resources of the country in which the services of
the Troops are required; and with the nature of the service.

' I would earnestly recommend, therefore, that the Lords of the
Treasury should keep in their own hands and under their own
immediate control the Commissariat, and employ that department
only when required, in such proportions and in such manner as the
nature of the country, and of the services to be performed, should
require

"Some few years ago, when the Government was under the
necessity of considering of the means of protecting the people of
Ireland from the consequences of the march through different parts
of the country of large bodies in regular array, with bands and
banners under the lead of Priests or other Demagogues, to form
Monster Meetings, as they were at that time called, under pretence
of petitioning, it became necessary to organize the Troops in Ireland, with a view to their ready movement—to their being fed, and
supplied with fuel and ammunition, when collected in large bodies,
and when moved, and to the security of their Barracks and fortified
Posts, when they should be moved from them.

"The assistance of the Commissariat became necessary, and as
I happened to be well acquainted with the gentleman of the Ordnance Department[1] who superintended that branch of the Service in
Ireland, and supplied the horses of the Army with forage, and knew
that he had held a high situation in the Commissariat with the
Army in the field, I had full confidence in him, and concerted
with him the measures to be adopted. But the Treasury of that
day, 1841-2, considering that Establishments were to be formed,
and expense was to be incurred for which they would be responsible,
considered it necessary to send to Ireland a Gentleman selected for
that service, and he received his orders and directions from the
Treasury.

"This was quite proper, and as it should be, and I recommend
to the Government to keep this Department wholly and exclusively
under the direction of the Treasury.

"I have long formed an opinion upon the mode of the Commissary General accounting—which forms no part of the question
of the present day, but upon which I will give my opinion if
required.

"WELLINGTON. [2]

---

[1] The late Mr Booth

[2] It will be noticed that these communications are addressed to the Premier,
who, prior to the Crimean War, dealt with these Constitutional questions

(CXLIX.)

Chapter XXIX., par 21

MEMORANDUM SHOWING THE CHANGES WHICH HAVE TAKEN PLACE IN THE ORGANIZATION OF THE WAR OFFICE BETWEEN THE YEAR 1854 AND DECEMBER, 1869, WHEN SIR JOHN PAKINGTON QUITTED OFFICE

PRIOR to the year 1854, the different Departments connected with the Army, Militia, and Volunteer Forces, were as follow:—

(1) Two Secretaries of State for War and Colonies and for Horse.

(2) General Commanding-in-Chief

(3) Ordnance Office.
Master-General of the Ordnance
Clerk of the Ordnance
Surveyor-General of the Ordnance } Forming the Board of Ordnance
Principal Storekeeper
Inspector-General of Fortifications
Director-General of Artillery.

(4) Treasury (Commissariat)

(5) Secretary at War.

(6) Army Medical Department.

(7) Audit Office

(8) Commissioners of Chelsea Hospital

(9) Board of General Officers (for Inspection, &c , of Clothing).

(10) Paymaster-General.

On 12th June, 1854, a fourth Secretary of State was established for the Department of War, and on the 11th August, 1854, an Order in Council was passed providing the necessary Establishment for carrying on the duties of the Office

A D 1854
Duke of Newcastle

On the 14th November, 1854, another Order in Council was passed, adding a second permanent Under-Secretary of State for the War Department.

The other Military Departments still existed separately, but the Secretary of State for War assumed and exercised control over all of them

In December, 1854, the Commissariat was transferred from the Treasury to the War Department,[1] including the Banking business

---

[1] See Treasury Minute dated 22nd December, 1854

connected with the Treasury Chest, as well as the business hitherto performed by the Audit Office of the examination of the Commissariat Cash and Store Accounts.

In January, 1855, a Topographical Department was formed under a Director.

In February, 1855, the office of Secretary at War was combined with that of Secretary of State—the Secretary of State for War receiving, in addition to his Patent as Secretary of State, a Commission as Secretary at War.

A.D. 1855
Lord Panmure.

In March, 1855, the business connected with the Militia was transferred from the Home Office to the War Department

On the 18th May, 1855, a Patent was granted to the Secretary of State for War, vesting in him the administration of the Army and Ordnance, "except so far as relates to and concerns the Military Command and discipline of the Army, as likewise to the appointments to, and promotions in the same, so far as by Commission[1] the Military Command and discipline thereof shall have been committed to, vested in, or regulated by the Commander-in-Chief," and on the 25th May the Secretary of State transferred the Command and discipline of the Ordnance Corps to the General Commanding-in-Chief, who was thus placed in command of the whole Army. An Act (18 & 19 Vic., cap. 117) was also passed, vesting in the Secretary of State all the estates and powers formerly held and exercised by the Board of Ordnance.

On the 6th of June, 1855, an Order in Council was passed, settling the future constitution of the Civil Departments of the Army as follow:—

(1) Clerk of the Ordnance.
(2) Inspector-General of Fortifications
(3) Director-General of Artillery.
(4) Director-General of Naval Artillery.
(5) Director General of Stores.
(6) Director-General of Contracts.
(7) Director-General of Clothing.
(8) Accountant General, and
(9) Superintendents for each of the Manufacturing Departments

These Officers were in addition to those included in the Establishments of the War Department, War Office, &c.

In January, 1856, a Committee was appointed by the then Secretary of State (Lord Panmure) to consider and recommend a

A.D. 1856

---

[1] No such Commission was then in existence giving such plenary powers to the Commander-in-Chief Chap. XXVI, pars. 11-13

definite distribution of the duties of the Officers consolidated under the Secretary of State for War, and of the several classes of Clerks, so as by an uniform scale of remuneration to render them available for any branch of the War Department

The recommendations of the Committee, which reported on the 3rd January, 1856, were agreed to by the Treasury, and the consolidation of the several branches of the War Department was then completed

This consolidated Department thus included the duties of the Secretary of State's Office, the Militia business of the Home Office, the War Office, the Ordnance Office, Commissariat and Medical Departments, the examination of the Cash and Store Accounts of the Commissariat Department, the examination of the payments made by the Paymaster-General for non-effective Services, and the duties of the Board of General Officers relating to Clothing.

The Commissioners of Chelsea Hospital still retained the duty of placing soldiers on the Out-pension List, though the expenditure of both In and Out pensions was borne on the Army Estimates

On the 2nd February, 1857, another Order in Council was passed (revoking the Orders of the 11th August and 14th November, 1854, and 6th June, 1855), by which the following alterations were effected in the Superior appointments of the Office. A.D. 1857

(1) One Under-Secretary of State reduced.
(2) One Clerk of the Ordnance abolished
(3) One Director-General of Clothing[1] reduced.
(4) One Principal Clerk discontinued.

The Naval Director-General of Artillery was appointed Director of Stores, continuing to perform the duties of the former Office.

And the following Offices were created —

(1) One Assistant Under-Secretary of State.
(2) One Secretary for Military correspondence
(3) The Office of Deputy Secretary at War was merged into that of Under-Secretary of State

In July, the Topographical Department, the Military Depot of the Quartermaster-General's Office, and the Ordnance Survey, hitherto a branch of the Inspector-General of Fortifications' Office, were placed under an Officer of the Royal Engineers as a Director immediately responsible to the Secretary of State.

In September, the Banking business connected with the Treasury Chest was re transferred to the Treasury

---

[1] The duties of this office were subsequently performed by an Assistant-Director under the Director of Stores

In October, the Office of Examiner of Army Accounts was abolished, and a Senior Clerk, under the title of Assistant Accountant General, was appointed to perform the duties.

In 1857 the business connected with the Army Schools was taken from the Chaplain-General and entrusted to a Military Officer —Inspector-General of Schools. A Board of Military Officers, called the Council of Military Education, was also established on the 1st of June in this year for conducting the examination of Officers, and placed under the control of the General Commanding-in Chief.

In the same year, upon the gradual disembodiment of the Militia after the Russian War, a Military Officer, to act under the Secretary of State, was appointed as Inspector of Militia.

In April, 1858, the Treasury appointed a Committee to enquire into the duties of the Account Branch of the War Office. The main recommendation of this Committee was the transfer of the preparation of the Estimates to the Accountant-General. Owing to a change in the Government, nothing was done to carry out this recommendation.

A D 1858
General
Peel

In May, 1859, the following alterations in the organisation of the War Office were decided upon —

A.D. 1859

1. Transfer to the General Commanding-in-Chief of the purely Military duties of the Inspector-General of Fortifications and Director-General of Artillery, and the abolition of the latter office.

2. Formation of a permanent Defence Committee.

3. Reconstruction of the Ordnance Select Committee.

Consisting of Naval and Military Officers

4. Transfer of the management of Regimental Schools and Libraries to the Council of Military Education, and the abolition of the appointment of Inspector-General of Schools.

The Inspector-General of Fortifications still remained the Official Adviser to the Secretary of State on all questions relating to fortifications and other works, and was also charged with the execution of those works; he was also a member of the permanent Defence Committee, but he was wholly relieved of his Military duties as Commandant of the Corps of Royal Engineers.

The Ordnance Select Committee was re-constructed, and the President of the Committee took charge of that portion of the duties of the Director-General of Artillery which still remained in the War Office [1]

---

[1] See Circular, 490

In November, 1859, the Treasury appointed a new Committee to enquire into the duties of the Account Branch; and in June, 1860, the Committee made a first Report, repeating the recommendation of the Committee of 1858, in regard to the transfer of the Estimates to the Accountant-General, and further recommending the separation of the Account Branch from the General Office in respect of establishment and promotion.

A.D. 1859-60.
Lord Herbert.

The appointment of an additional Assistant Accountant-General was also recommended, who should be charged with the preparation of the Estimates and the Book-keeping Branch.

These recommendations were carried into effect in August, 1860.

The Volunteer Force having so largely increased in 1859, and a Military Officer being required to superintend the organization and discipline of the Force, an Inspector-General, with a Deputy, was appointed in January, 1860, and placed in charge of the Civil business of the Force.

In March, the transfer of the superintendence of Army Schools and Libraries to the Council of Military Education under the control of the General Commanding-in-Chief was carried out, and the appointment of Inspector-General of Schools abolished.

In November, a Librarian and Precis-writer was appointed.

In December, the Inspector of Militia was placed in charge of the Civil business of the Militia in the War Office, and the designation of the appointment was altered to that of Inspector-General.

In January, 1861 $(\frac{76+6}{16})$, a recommendation, founded on the report of the Select Committee on Military Organization, was referred to the Treasury for the appointment of a Director of Ordnance, who would relieve the President of the Ordnance Select Committee of that portion of his duties as Adviser to the Secretary of State on Artillery and Armaments, and also be placed in charge of the whole of the Manufacturing Departments.

A.D 1861

At the same time the Secretary of State expressed his intention of appointing at some future date a Director of Supplies, who would be charged with the supply and issue of all stores (not being munitions of War). In accordance with this proposal, a Director of Ordnance was appointed in July, 1861.

In May, the Secretary for Military Correspondence (Major-General Sir E. Lugard, G.C.B) was appointed Under-Secretary of State, the former appointment being abolished

About the same time a Military Officer, on half-pay and receiving Staff-pay, was appointed to assist the Under-Secretary of State.

In November, the Assistant Under-Secretary of State died, and his appointment was not filled up.

A.D 1861
Sir George
Lewis. In December, a Military Officer was appointed to assist the Director of Ordnance, and styled Assistant Director of Ordnance.

In February, 1862, a Committee, which had been appointed to inquire into the Establishments of the several branches of the War Office, fixed the number and classification of the Clerks to be in future borne on those Establishments, exclusive of the Account Department and Solicitors' Branch.

A.D. 1862

In May, the Office of Assistant Under-Secretary of State was revived, and Captain Galton, R.E., appointed thereto, the third Under-Secretary of State being at the same time abolished.

In June, the Barrack Department was transferred from the control of the Inspector-General of Fortifications, and was formed into a separate branch under an Engineer Officer as Superintendent.

In September, the designation of the Inspector-General of Fortifications was altered to Inspector-General of Engineers and Director of Works; in the former capacity he was reinstated in the command of the Corps of Royal Engineers and placed in immediate communication with the Commander-in-Chief, in the latter he was under the direct control of the Secretary of State for War. The Office of Deputy Inspector-General of Fortifications was abolished.

Two Deputy Directors of Works, one for Barracks and the other for Fortifications and Civil Buildings, were created. (These Officers of the Royal Engineers had previously held similar appointments under the Inspector-General of Fortifications.)

In June, the Clothing business was separated from the Store Department, and on 23rd February, 1863, was made into a distinct branch under a Director of Clothing.

A D. 1863.

In May, 1863, an Act (26 Vic., c. 12) was passed abolishing the Office of Secretary at War, and vesting in the Secretary of State the duties and powers of that office.

A.D 1863.
Earl de
Grey

In June, 1864, another Committee was proposed to the Treasury for the purpose of inquiring into the Establishment of the War Office. The reports of this Committee commenced in September, 1864, and continued from time to time until May, 1865.

A.D 1864.

Their recommendations resulted in the following important changes.—

A D. 1865

1. The separation of the department, which had been previously under the sole control of the Accountant-General, into two branches. One under the Accountant-General, the other under the Chief

Auditor of Army Accounts, an office for the first time created.[1] The latter Officer took over a portion of the duties hitherto performed by the Accountant-General and his two assistants; also the Audit of Barrack, Store, and Kit Accounts from the Barrack and Clothing branches, and eventually (1866) the audit of the Store Accounts from the Store Branch

2 Of the two Assistant Accountants General, one was abolished' on the appointment of the Chief Auditor, the other is to be abolished when a vacancy occurs.[2]

3. The abolition of the appointment of Librarian and Precis-writer.

4. The substitution of Out-Station Clerks of the Royal Engineer Department in place of War Office Clerks in the office of the Director of Works.

5. The substitution of Barrack Officers and Military Clerks in the place of War Office Clerks in the Barrack branch.

6. The separation of the Clerical Establishments of the Army Medical Department and Clothing Branch from the rest of the War Office on distinct and lower scales of pay

7 The withdrawal from the Commissariat of the Clerks on the Establishment of the War Office, and the substitution of Commissariat Officers and Staff.

8. The introduction into the Chief Auditor's Branch and Clothing Department of Military and pensioned Non-commissioned Officer Clerks.

9. The formation of a Regulation Branch, with a view to the codification of the regulations.

In August, 1866, it was decided, in consequence of the great and important changes in Naval Ordnance, to appoint an officer of the rank of Rear-Admiral, to be attached to the Admiralty and to Act as Director-General of Naval Ordnance. A.D. 1866
General Peel.

(The duties of this appointment had been previously discharged by the Director of Stores.)

In December, 1867, in consequence of the recommendation of a Committee, presided over by Lord Strathnairn, appointed in June, 1866, to consider the question of Army Transports, but subsequently directed by General Peel to extend its inquiries into the administration of the Supply Department of the Army, a Military Officer was appointed as Controller-in-Chief, to A.D. 1867.
Sir John Pakington.

[1] Date of Mr Whiffin's appointment as Chief Auditor, February 3rd, 1865.
[2] See 2nd Report of Committee, 25th November, 1864.

supervise and direct the various Departments of Transport, Commissariat, Store, Purveyor, and Barrack. Another Military Officer was appointed (temporarily) as his assistant.

In April, 1868, a Royal Warrant gave effect to this arrange-
A.D 1868   ment.

In consequence of this change, the appointments of Director of Stores and Superintendent of the Barrack Department were abolished in December, 1868.

In January, 1868, "with a view of increasing the efficiency of the local Military Forces, and also of securing unity of action in the event of their being at any time required for Service," an Inspector-General of Reserve Forces was appointed to supervise the Militia, Yeomanry, Volunteers, and Enrolled Pensioners,

In November, a Director-General of Ordnance was appointed in place of the Director of Ordnance. A Deputy was appointed at the same time

The Ordnance Select Committee was abolished, and a smaller Committee, styled the Artillery Committee, presided over by the Deputy Director-General of Ordnance, was appointed in its place.

The Director-General of Ordnance was also made Commandant of the Arsenal at Woolwich, and the heads of the various Manufacturing Departments were placed under his orders.

ABSTRACT SHOWING THE AMOUNTS VOTED IN 1853-4 AND 1868-9, ACCORDING TO THE CLASSIFICATION OF 1868-9, DIVIDED UNDER ARMY, ORDNANCE, COMMISSARIAT, AND MILITIA, FOR WHICH SEPARATE ESTIMATES WERE TAKEN IN 1853-4

VOTES.	1853-4				1868-9			
	Army	Ordnance	Commissariat and Militia.	Total.	Army	Ordnance	Commissariat and Militia.	Total.
1. Regimental Pay, &c	3,222,731	810,656		4,033,387	4,459,752	1,289,448	.	5,749,200
2 Commissariat	45,200	168,811	444,236	658,247	49,500	389,154	853,846	1,292,500
3 Clothing	279,147	78,300		357,747	397,900	99,000		496,900
4 Barrack		276,916	62,358	339,274		595,600	110,700	706,300
5. Divine Service	19,000	1,892		20,892	34,300	8,500	.	42,800
6 Martial Law	15,222			15,222	23,000		..	23,000
7 Medical and Purveyors	86,126	11,598		97,724	305,800	75,000		380,800
8 Disembodied Militia		.	476,738	476,738		..	986,800	986,800
9 Yeomanry Cavalry	88,000	..	..	88,000	88,000	.	..	88,000
10 Volunteer Corps		..			385,100	..	..	385,100
11 Enrolled Pensioners	48,042	.	.	48,042	64,600	.	.	64,600
12 & 13. Stores and Manufacturing Departments		600,261	.	600,261	..	1,491,400	.	1,491,400
14 Works	.	745,176	.	745,176	.	968,400	.	968,400
15 Educational	45,660	26,671		72,331	118,500	50,800		169,300
16 Surveys		96,000		96,000		118,600	.	118,600
17 Miscellaneous	42,654	3,798		46,452	79,849	62,851		142,700
18 Administration	{59,224	62,273	5,293	126,790}	[Cannot be distributed]			224,600
Now included in Civil Estimates	{52,748			52,748}				
TOTAL EFFECTIVE VOTES	£4,004,054	2,882,352	988,625	7,875,031	6,006,801	5,118,753	1,951,346	13,931,000
19 to 27. Non-Effective	2,020,962	171,215	47,241	2,239,418	1,679,536	410,000	34,864	2,124,400
TOTAL EFFECTIVE AND NON-EFFECTIVE VOTES	£6,025,016	3,053,567	1,035,866	10,114,449	7,685,837	5,558,753	1,986,210	15,455,400

(CLI.)

Chapter XXIX , par. 37.

DETAILED COMPARISON OF ARMY ESTIMATES 1853-4, AND 1868-9. NUMBER OF ALL RANKS AND OF HORSES.

	1853-4	1868-9
Horse Artillery	1,108	2,165
Life and Horse Guards . .	1,308	1,320
Cavalry	7,583	10,032
Artillery	11,007	16,651
Engineers	2,476	4,712
Military Train .. .		1,798
Foot Guards	5,260	5,960
Infantry . ..	78,581	71,357
Army Hospital Corps . . .		1,004
Commissariat Staff Corps .		601
West India Regiments .. .	3,417	3,468
Colonial Corps .	5,571	4,302
Military Store Staff Corps .. .		400
	119,314	126,770
Depôt of Forces in India	560	9,880
Total Force	119,874	136,650
HORSES.		
Horse Artillery	492	1,638
Life and Horse Guards	822	825
Cavalry . .	5,330	6,189
Artillery	2,093	2,596
Colonial Corps	900	450
Engineers		307
Military Train	..	996
Total Horses .	9,637	13,001

Vote		1853-4	1868-9
		£	£
1	General Staff, &c ..	88,216	101,815
	Regimental Pay and Allowances ..	3,783,801	5,363,180
	Native Indian Troops	4,500	30,000
	Recruiting Establishments, Levy Money, &c	85,731	103,248
	Purchase of horses, Veterinary expenses, &c	48,431	58,584
	Military Instruction .	6,053	42,380
	Savings Banks	2,050	2,000
	Allowances to discharged Soldiers	12,000	25,000
	Travelling expenses .	2,500	10,000
	Miscellaneous		9,989
		£4,033,387	5,749,170

Vote.		1853 4	1868-9
		£	£
2	Commissariat, Establishment Wages, &c	94,133	108,862
	Provisions	142,033	514,114
	Forage	285,883	443,388
	Transport, home and abroad	136,138	180,416
	Colonial Allowances	..	95,750
		£658,217	1,292,530
3	Clothing, &c.	£357,747	196,871
4	Barrack Establishments, Wages, &c	47,082	59,467
	Barrack Stores	47,829	116,000
	Washing, and repair of bedding, and paillasse straw	25,218	42,672
	Fuel and Light, and miscellaneous services	129,753	297,621
	Lodging money, Rents, &c.	89,392	190,500
		£339,274	706,260
5	Divine Service	£20,892	42,841
6	Judge-Advocate's Office, &c.	4,045	8,175
	Military Prisons, Subsistence, &c , including Clothing	41,177	80,538
		45,222	88,713
	Deduct Full-pay	30,000	65,713
		£15,222	23,000
7	Medical and Purveyors' Departments	59,138	256,511 [1]
	General Hospitals	2,047	4,150
	Hospital Expenses, including purchase of Medicine	9,539	73,636
	Hospital stores	10,000	6,000
	Washing and repair of Bedding	6,000	7,973
	Fuel and Light	8,000	19,330
	Miscellaneous, including Rent and Water supply	3,000	7,671
	Lunatics	.	5,200
		£97,724	380,771
8	Disembodied Militia, &c	£476,738	986,762

[1] Inclusive of Regimental Medical Officers.

Vote		1853-4	1868-9
		£	£
9	Yeomanry Cavalry	88,000	88,000
10	Volunteer Corps . .	.	385,150
11	Enrolled Pensioners, &c.	£48,042	64,000
12 & 13	Manufacturing and Military Store Establishments, &c. .	87,551	120,120
	Wages	141,013	656,798
	Materials, cost of manufactured and miscellaneous Stores	308,647	890,229
	Machinery . . .	6,600	44,242
	Freight, carriage of Stores, &c . .	15,074	23,981
	Accoutrements for the Militia	41,376	
		600,261	1,735,370
	Less Repayment Services ..		244,000
		£600,261	1,491,370
14	Engineer Establishment	49,489	100,544
	Works	695,687	867,903
		£745,176	968,447
15	Council of Military Education . .	1,100	8,205
	Royal Military Academy .	25,483	38,581
	Royal Military College . . .	16,888	44,686
	Regimental Schools, &c . .	10,371	39,015
	Royal Military Asylum ..	11,664	14,917
	Royal Hibernian Schools	6,355	11,378
	Instruction of Artillery Officers ..	220	2,942
	Medical School and Museum	250	9,600
		£72,331	169,324
16	Surveys	£96,000	118,000
17	Ordnance Select Committee, Experiments, &c.	.	58,013
	Jersey and Guernsey Militia .	2,588	12,432
	Telegraphic and signal stations . ..	944	2,267
	Grants in aid of Institutions	66	6,454
	Contagious Diseases Act	.	20,795
	Police	.	13,419
	Law charges . .	2,100	5,000
	Advertisements	1,754	5,000
	Miscellaneous ..		16,520
	Losses	3,000	1,800
	Field allowance .	36,000	1,000
		£46,452	142,700

Vote		1853-4	1868-9
18	Staff Civil Department of Secretary of State	£ 14,900	£ 30,042
	Clerks, &c ..	85,583	139,445
	Topographical Department		5,556
	Staff and Clerks, &c , Department of Commander-in-Chief	26,307	49,535
		£126,790	294,578[1]

	NON-EFFECTIVE.		
19	Rewards for Distinguished Service	21,974	26,700
20	Pay of General Officers	62,962	72,000
21	Full and Half-pay of reduced and retired Officers	545,670	470,800
22	Widows' Pensions, &c.	178,383	157,000
23	Pensions for wounds	52,343	23,800
24	Chelsea and Kilmainham	28,149	33,600
25	Out-pensions to Non-commissioned Officers and Men	1,191,150	1,184,600
26	Superannuation allowances	106,137	135,200
27	Militia, Yeomanry, and Volunteers	52,560	20,700
		£2,239,418	2,124,400

(CLII.)

Chap XXIX. par. 67

OBSERVATIONS BY PRINCIPAL BARRACKMASTER SMITH, ON THE EVIDENCE GIVEN BY COLONEL HERBERT, C B., ASSISTANT QUARTERMASTER-GENERAL, BEFORE THE COMMITTEE ON TRANSPORT, &C.

" SIR,   " *Barrack Office, Aldershot, 27th July,* 1867.

" 1. My attention has been drawn to the evidence given by Colonel Herbert, C.B , Assistant Quartermaster-General, before the Committee on the Transport and Supply Departments of the Army.

_____

[1] Voted in round numbers, 224,600*l.*

"2 That evidence not only reflects severely upon the Barrack Department but, also personally upon myself. I have, therefore, respectfully to beg that you will, in justice to one who has been in the public service fifty-nine years, of which forty-three years have been passed in the Barrack Department, lay before the Secretary of State for War the observations which I have to make upon Colonel Herbert's evidence, with my humble request that, if it be practicable, the same publicity may be given to them as has been given to Colonel Herbert's evidence.

"3. There are three reasons why no weight should be attached to that evidence, and I am sure, could the facts which I am now about to state have been laid before the Committee, they never would have attached that weight to Colonel Herbert's evidence which they have done.

"The first is the strong enmity which Colonel Herbert has openly expressed against the Barrack Department, and his determination to do all in his power to break it up.

"The second is contained in the enclosed letter from Colonel Herbert to myself,[1] dated 29th June last, by which it will be perceived that Colonel Herbert refuses to acknowledge the evidence published by the Committee as being his

"The third is the want of knowledge and correctness displayed in the evidence published as that of Colonel Herbert.

"The observations which I beg to submit are as follow:—

---

[1] "MY DEAR COLONEL,   "*Aldershot, June 29th*, 1867.

"I had written some replies to nearly all the questions you left with me relative to my statement to the Transport Committee, when I discovered these questions were founded upon evidence published, which I object to acknowledge as expressing my views. I was informed by the Secretary, shortly after the examination, that as Major Martindale objected to his evidence being published, mine would not be recorded, and that, therefore, it was useless to correct the proof-sheets, which had been sent to me for that purpose

"As the recorded evidence is most incoherent,—incorrect desultory conversation having been mixed up with answers to questions,—I felt it would have been most difficult to correct the sheets sent, and fully concurred it would not be advisable to publish evidence in the crude and incorrect state it was recorded. I therefore wrote a short memorandum containing an outline of my views, which I understood was to be published in lieu of the unmeaning evidence I am made to give by the reporter.

"To answer your questions founded upon this evidence would be to acknowledge it as mine; whereas, as recorded, I repudiate it as expressing my views, what I said, or what the Committee understood me to say.

"Believe me, &c.,

(Signed)   "ARTHUR HERBERT."

"4. All warrants sent to Barrackmasters are also sent to General Officers Commanding. The Warrant referred to as not having been sent [1] is not a Warrant, but a War Office Circular. All War Office Circulars however, are sent to General Officers Commanding, and if, as stated, Circular No. 845 was not sent to Aldershot,[2] it must either have been through inadvertence, or because it was considered as a reminder only to Barrackmasters of orders already existing. It is not the fact that the great thing which Barrackmasters have to do is the issue of coals and light.[3] Nor that there is a Warrant[4] or Circular authorizing a General Officer Commanding at home to order extra issues of coals and light, except of coals in case of unusual severity of weather, any order for which is immediately complied with in accordance with that Circular   It must be remembered that coals and light might be practically money, and that extra issues of them mean extra cost to the public.

"5. It is not the fact that I suggested that the troops should take coal for cooking purposes out of the coal allowed for warming their rooms.[5] The allowance for Deane's boilers is not ¾lb.[6] There is no difficulty in telegraphing[7] for authority to make extra issues. Indeed, Circular No 845, already referred to, absolutely directs this to be done in case of necessity, and such telegrams are often sent. The wants of the Service can thus be met, but, should the emergency be such as not to admit of even this delay, the practice of the Barrack Department is then to issue and apply for covering authority, should the Officer Commanding see fit to order the issue after the Barrackmaster has called his attention to the fact that the issue is contrary to the Regulations. No practical inconvenience can therefore result.

"6. It is absurd to intimate that it is beneath a General Officer to confer with a Barrackmaster, and still more so under the present system, which restricts such conference to Principal and District Barrackmasters[8]

"7. Previous to the year 1836, Barrack damages at home stations were repaired by contractors under the Engineer Department, as the evidence proposes should again be done,[9] but this was then put a stop to, owing to the delays and inconveniences that were found to arise, and the repairs were placed under Barrackmasters. I fear

[1] Reply 1771.

[2] I have since ascertained from the War Office that Circular 845 *was* circulated to General Officers Commanding, in the usual manner, and that a copy *was* addressed to the General Officer Commanding at Aldershot, on the 16th December, 1863.   [3] Reply 1771   [4] Ibid
[5] Ib. 1771.   [6] Ib. 1772   [7] Ib 1774   [8] Ib   [9] Ib 1778.

that, from their very nature, complaints must arise about Barrack damages, but it will be found that these damages are most materially less in regiments whose internal economy is strictly attended to by Commanding Officers than where this is less watched, and also that if the Queen's Regulations are strictly carried out by the troops—which in many instances they are not—no real ground of complaint on the part of the troops can arise for which efficient remedies have not been provided.

"8. A monthly examination of Barracks is not made by the Engineers,[1] and the Barrackmaster's inspection, and the Royal Engineer quarterly inspection, can, and should generally, be made to dovetail into each other[2] It is quite incorrect to say that a General Officer Commanding cannot put up a fence without the sanction of a Barrackmaster. The Barrackmaster can give no such sanction, but alterations cannot be made in or about Barracks without the sanction of the Commander-in-Chief and Secretary of State for War, and it is one of the duties of the Barrackmaster to see that no alterations are made without such sanction.[3]

"9. It is not the fact that any Barrack Serjeant complained to Colonel Herbert.[4] There is no reason why, when troops are quartered partly in Barracks and partly under canvas, as is at times the case at Aldershot and the Curragh, the Barrack Department should not issue fuel, light, and straw to the men under canvas, as well as to those in Barracks. It merely requires orders to do so, and could have been done at once, in the case instanced, had sanction been asked[5] It is not the fact, that under the proposed system, Barracks could be properly given over to a Regiment in about an hour, excepting the married men.[6] Coal is not bought by the Barrack Department,[7] it is obtained under contracts made in the War Office, and surveyed in accordance with the Queen's Regulations for the Army.

"10. I fear that unpleasant feelings must occasionally arise between the troops and the Barrack Department so long as the Regulations of the Service are not attended to For instance, it is no uncommon thing for Commanding Officers and Officers to request Barrackmasters to lend them articles of Barrack bedding, furniture, and utensils, contrary to regulations, and the refusal to do so almost invariably creates unpleasantness. I fear, too, that friction must sometimes arise, and especially under the system of five-year appointments, from Staff Officers ill acquainted with the Regulations

---

[1] Reply 1769.   [2] Ib 1780.   [3] Ib. 1778, 1826
[4] Ib 1780.   [5] Ib.   [6] Ib.   [7] Ib 1781.

of the Service, interfering with the duties of, or setting aside the regulations of, other Departments. But the fault does not rest with the Departments.

"11. It is a mistake to suppose that the sale of lands, so strongly objected to by Lord Strathnairn, was caused by the Barrack Department.

"12 The Memorandum at the end of Colonel Herbert's evidence is not that of a practical man, and its results would be not to introduce more simplicity, but increased friction, complexity, and expense.

"13. The Commissariat, and other branches named in it, are certainly required for the field, and have, as it is, more or less to do with the accommodation of troops in peace. The Quartermaster-General's Department furnishes the Route and sometimes indicates the particular Barracks to be occupied; the Royal Engineers provide and repair the Barracks, the Commissariat find food and forage, and fuel and light abroad; and the Military Store provide camp equipment, but any one conversant with the habits and wants of troops in Barracks knows that to try and provide for them through all these branches, instead of by the Barrack Department, could not result in more simplicity or in less delay and trouble. The plan of having one branch (the Quartermaster-General's) to allot the buildings, another branch (the Royal Engineers) to give over the buildings, another branch (the Store) to have charge of, and give over the stores required for the buildings, and this, too, on requisitions through another branch (the Quartermaster-General's) and another branch (the Commissariat) to issue fuel and light for the buildings, would not work. The quarterly inspection only, carrying with it the quarterly assessment of Barrack damages only when the Royal Engineers objected to fair wear, and the inspection of Barrack furniture only when a regiment left the station or returned articles into store, would not as efficiently protect the buildings, the stores, the troops, or the public, as the present system. The question of supply of fuel and light has already been discussed, and it certainly would not be more convenient for the troops or better for the Public Service to go to the Commissariat instead of to the Barrack Department. The employment of a Non-commissioned Officer to take general charge of stores and fuel and light at small stations is already in force, with the additional advantage that he now takes charge of the buildings also. Under the present system the Barrackmaster should, whenever practicable, employ the same contractor as the Royal Engineers; and there is no reason why, if the circumstances are similar, the Barrack Department should charge more than the Royal Engineers for putting in a pane of glass I cannot assume that this is often done, and I am certain that it would be put a stop to if properly represented

"14. In the nature of things my remaining period of service cannot be long, and it must be seen, therefore, that I have but little personal interest whether the Barrack Department is abolished or not   But I think it right to state my strong belief, after a service in it of *forty-three years*, that it is thoroughly qualified to perform the duties for which it is established, that it never was more efficient than at present, and that to substitute for it the cumbrous system proposed by the Committee, could only result in confusion, inefficiency, and vastly increased cost to the public.'

"I have, &c.,

(Signed)   " THOMAS SMITH,

" *Principal Barrackmas'er."*

' From 'Hart's List' it appears that Colonel Herbert's first Commission dates from 1839, and his experience of War is limited to the Eastern Campaign

INDEX TO VOLS. I. & II.

802

SEYMOUR]   *Index to Vols. I. and II.*   ['TOMMY ATKINS'

Ex. G. a. a.

THE END.

PRINTED BY WILLIAM CLOWES AND SONS, DUKE STREET, STAMFORD STREET, AND CHARING CROSS.

Lightning Source UK Ltd.
Milton Keynes UK
UKOW011843250412

191457UK00004B/4/P